ASIA'S JOURNEY
TO PROSPERITY
POLICY, MARKET, AND
TECHNOLOGY OVER 50 YEARS

ASIAN DEVELOPMENT BANK

CONTENTS

Foreword   xiv

Production Team   xx

Acknowledgments   xxii

Abbreviations   xxiv

Definitions   xxvii

ADB Regional Members   xxix

1   50 Years of Asian Development   1

1.1   Asia's rapid growth and poverty reduction over the past half century   1

1.2   What explains Asia's economic success?   6

1.3   Is there an Asian Consensus?   9

1.4   A half century of multifaceted development   11

1.5   Asia's remaining development agenda   25

2   The Role of Markets, the State, and Institutions   29

2.1   Introduction   29

2.2   The role of markets and the state   31

2.3   Evolving development thinking and policy on market versus state   35

2.4   Importance of good governance and strong institutions   39

2.5   Japan's postwar economic recovery and growth   42

2.6   Industrialization of Hong Kong, China; the Republic of Korea; Singapore; and Taipei,China   47

2.7   Economic liberalization and openness in Southeast Asia   52

2.8   Building a socialist market economy in the People's Republic of China   60

2.9   Toward market-led growth in India   67

2.10   Pursuing reforms in other South Asian countries   72

2.11   Transition in Central Asia and Mongolia   77

2.12   Seizing opportunities in the Pacific   81

2.13   Looking ahead   83

3   Dynamics of Structural Transformation   **85**
    3.1   Introduction   85
    3.2   Overview of Asia's structural transformation   86
    3.3   Critical contribution of agriculture   91
    3.4   Industrialization as the path to high income   94
    3.5   Large and growing imprint of services   100
    3.6   Urbanization as a geographic transformation   108
    3.7   Looking ahead   111

4   Modernizing Agriculture and Rural Development   **113**
    4.1   Introduction   113
    4.2   Asia's food problems in the 1950s   117
    4.3   Land reform: experiences and lessons   119
    4.4   Green Revolution and efforts to sustain its momentum   124
    4.5   Changing patterns of food consumption   134
           and product diversification
    4.6   Agricultural trade and food value chains   138
    4.7   Expanding the rural nonfarm economy   142
    4.8   Looking ahead   143

5   Technological Progress as Key Driver   **147**
    5.1   Introduction   147
    5.2   Measuring technology's contribution to growth   150
    5.3   Asia's technological progress   155
    5.4   Modalities of technological progress   161
    5.5   Country experiences on technology policies   171
    5.6   Recent technological trends and developments   178
    5.7   Looking ahead   182

6   Education, Health, and Demographic Change   **185**
    6.1   Introduction   185
    6.2   Rising educational attainment   187
    6.3   Healthier populations   196
    6.4   Changing demography   208
    6.5   Demographic dividend and other impacts   217
    6.6   Looking ahead   222

7   Investment, Savings, and Finance   **225**
    7.1   Introduction   225
    7.2   Asia's rapid capital accumulation   226

7.3 Domestic savings provided the bulk 228
of investment financing
7.4 External financing complements domestic savings 239
7.5 Asia's financial system 241
7.6 Looking ahead 251

8   Infrastructure Development **253**
8.1 Introduction 253
8.2 Energy 255
8.3 Transport 272
8.4 Urban water supply 280
8.5 Telecommunications and information 286
and communication technology
8.6 Looking ahead 293

9   Trade, Foreign Direct Investment, and Openness **295**
9.1 Introduction 295
9.2 Trends in Asia's trade and foreign direct investment 298
9.3 Evolution of trade and foreign direct investment 309
policies in Asia
9.4 Emergence of global value chains 315
9.5 Growing importance of services trade 319
9.6 Global and regional trade arrangements 321
9.7 Looking ahead 324

10 Pursuing Macroeconomic Stability **327**
10.1 Introduction 327
10.2 Macroeconomic performance in the past 5 decades 328
10.3 The evolution of fiscal, monetary, 332
and exchange rate policies
10.4 Avoiding debt crises in the 1980s 340
10.5 The Asian financial crisis and responses 341
10.6 The global financial crisis and responses 345
10.7 Looking ahead 349

11 Poverty Reduction and Income Distribution **351**
11.1 Introduction 351
11.2 Asia's approach to poverty and inequality 353
11.3 Asia's success in reducing poverty 358
11.4 Stable levels of inequality in the 1960s–1980s 364

11.5 Rising income inequality since the 1990s   368
11.6 Looking ahead   375

12 Gender and Development   **377**
12.1 Introduction   377
12.2 Improvements in women's education   379
12.3 Achievements in women's health   384
12.4 Women's labor force and market participation   388
12.5 Women's status in the household and in public life   398
12.6 Looking ahead   407

13 Environmental Sustainability and Climate Change   **411**
13.1 Introduction   411
13.2 Increased environmental pressure   413
13.3 Climate change   425
13.4 Asian efforts to address environmental and climate challenges   428
13.5 Engagement in international agreements and roles of development partners   436
13.6 Green industry contribution to environmental solutions   439
13.7 Looking ahead   440

14 The Role of Bilateral and Multilateral Development Finance   **443**
14.1 Introduction   443
14.2 Bilateral official development assistance flows   446
14.3 Multilateral development banks   447
14.4 Experiences of recipient countries   452
14.5 Experiences of Asian official development assistance providers   461
14.6 Looking ahead   466

15 Strengthening Regional Cooperation and Integration in Asia   **469**
15.1 Introduction   469
15.2 Why regional cooperation and integration?   470
15.3 Early movers of regional cooperation and integration in East Asia and Southeast Asia   472
15.4 Regional cooperation and integration in other subregions   476
15.5 ADB and its role in regional cooperation and integration   479
15.6 Looking ahead   479

Appendixes   **483**
1   Total Population (Midyear)   484
2   Gross Domestic Product   486
3   Gross Domestic Product Growth Rates   490
4   Gross Domestic Product Per Capita   492
5   Sector Shares in Output   494
6   Sector Shares in Employment   497
7   Exports of Goods and Services   500
8   Imports of Goods and Services   502
9   Current Account Balance   504
10   General Government Net Lending/Borrowing   506
11   Gross Domestic Savings   508
12   Gross Capital Formation   510
13   Public Spending on Education   512
14   Public Spending on Health   514
15   Poverty Rate   516
16   Net Enrollment Rate, Primary, Both Sexes   518
17   Gross Enrollment Ratio, Secondary, Both Sexes   520
18   Gross Enrollment Ratio, Tertiary, Both Sexes   522
19   Life Expectancy at Birth   524
20   Under-Five Mortality Rate (U5MR)   526

References   **529**

Index   **557**

TABLES, FIGURES, AND BOXES

Tables

1.1	Average Annual Per Capita GDP Growth	2
1.2	GDP Per Capita	3
1.3	Development Indicators	6
2.1	Shares of State-Owned Enterprises in the Industry Sector, People's Republic of China, 1995–2017	65
2.2	Delicensing and Trade Liberalization in India, 1980–1997	71
2.3	Average Annual Per Capita GDP Growth, Central Asia and Mongolia, 1991–2018	79
3.1	Output and Employment Shares by Sector, 1970–2018	89
4.1	Macroeconomic Indicators in Agriculture, Selected Economies, 1970–2018	115
5.1	Top 10 Patent Grantees in the United States	159
5.2	Industrial Robots	160
6.1	School Enrollment Rates, 1970–2018	189
6.2	Years of Compulsory Education, Developing Asia, 2018	193
6.3	Government Expenditures on Education, 1970–2018	195
6.4	Life Expectancy at Birth, 1960–2018	197
6.5	Under-Five and Maternal Mortality, 1960–2018	199
6.6	Prevalence of Wasting and Stunting	200
6.7	Immunization Coverage by Antigen, 1980, 2000, and 2017	202
6.8	Health Expenditures by Subregion, 2000, 2010, and 2016	206
6.9	Hospital Beds and Physicians by Region, 1960, 1970, 1990, and 2016	207
6.10	Population and Annual Population Growth Rate, 1960–2018	209
6.11	Fertility Rate, 1960–2018	211
6.12	Estimates of Demographic Dividends, 1960–2018	219
7.1	Stock and Growth of Physical Capital, 1960, 1990, and 2017	227
7.2	Gross Domestic Savings and Savings–Investment Gaps, 1960–2018	230

7.3   Measures of Financial Sector Development, 1990–2017   247
8.1   Primary Energy Consumption and CO$_2$ Emissions   258
      in Selected Economies, 1965 and 2018
8.2   Final Energy Consumption by Sector in   260
      Selected Economies, 1973 and 2017
8.3   Electricity Generation by Source in Selected Economies,   262
      1971 and 2018
9.1   Top Global Investors   307
9.2   Top Manufacturing Sectors of Foreign Affiliates   319
      Engaging in Trade in Asia, 2015
10.1 Currency Stabilization Support Programs   344
      during the Asian Financial Crisis
11.1 Poverty Reduction in Developing Asia,   361
      $1.90 per Day International Poverty Line, 1981–2015
11.2 Asia's Income Inequality in the Global Context, 2015   373
12.1 Mean Years of Completed Schooling,   380
      Population Aged 25–29, by Gender
12.2 Life Expectancy at Birth   385
13.1 Rural Population Residing on Degrading Agricultural   417
      Land by Region, 2010
13.2 Proportion of Wastewater Receiving Treatment,   419
      Selected Economies, Developing Asia, 2011
13.3 Water and Air Quality Standards, and Establishment   432
      of Environmental Ministries in Developing Asia

Figures
1.1   Global GDP Shares, 1960 and 2018   4
2.1   Government Effectiveness Score and Per Capita GDP   40
      in 2011, Developing Asia
3.1   Output and Employment Shares by Sector   88
      against Per Capita GDP, 1970–2018
3.2   Agricultural Land and Labor Productivity,   93
      Selected Asian Economies, 1980–2015
3.3   Manufacturing Output and Employment Shares,   96
      1970–2018
3.4   Value-Added of Skill- and Technology-Intensive   103
      Services and Other Services in Selected Asian
      and Advanced Economies
3.5   International Tourist Arrivals, 1995–2018   106

3.6   International Tourism Indicators for   107
       Selected Asian Economies
3.7   Urban Population, 1970–2020   109
3.8   Urbanization Rate and GDP, 2017   110
4.1   Impacts of Modern Variety Rice Adoption,   129
       Selected Asian Economies, 1961–2016
4.2   Food Consumption Patterns, Developing Asia,   134
       1961–2013
4.3   Changing Composition of Food Consumption   136
       in Calories, Developing Asia, 1983 and 2013
4.4   Shares of Agriculture Sector Gross Production Value,
       Developing Asia, 1971–1974 and 2010–2014   137
4.5   International Trade of Rice, Fruits, and Vegetables,   140
       Selected Economies, 1974–2016
5.1   Contribution of Factors of Production to   152
       GDP Growth, Asia
5.2   Contributions to Growth in the World, 1960–2014   155
5.3   The Flying Geese Pattern of Asian Exports   157
5.4   Research and Development Expenditure, 1981–2016   167
5.5   Adoption and Innovation of Technologies in Japan,   172
       1956–1988
5.6   Diffusion Speed of Technologies   179
6.1   Mean Years of Schooling, for Population   188
       Aged 20–24 Years, 1960 and 2010
6.2   Average Science and Mathematics Test Scores   191
6.3   Reduction in Communicable, Maternal,   201
       Neonatal, and Nutritional Deaths, 1990–2017
6.4   Access to Piped Water and Open Defecation Rates,   203
       2000 and Latest Year
6.5   Average Annual Population Growth,   210
       Developing Asia, 1950–2020
6.6   Total Population and Population by Age,   210
       Developing Asia, 1950–2018
6.7   Fertility and Life Expectancy in Asia   215
       and the Pacific, 2018
6.8   Stock of Asia and the Pacific's Outward Migration,   216
       1990–2017
7.1   Gross Domestic Savings and Components,   233
       Selected Asian Economies, 1990–2017

7.2 Net Capital Inflows by Nonresidents 240
to Developing Asia, 1970–2017
7.3 Net Capital Inflows by Nonresidents 242
to Developing Asia by Subregion, 1970s–2010s
7.4 Outstanding Domestic Debt Securities, 248
Selected Asian Economies, 1990–2017
7.5 Domestic Savings, Pensions, and Insurance Assets, 2017 249
8.1 Electricity Generation Per Capita 256
in Selected Economies, 1971 and 2018
8.2 Transport Infrastructure Stock, 1965 and 2014 273
8.3 Vehicle Registration, Selected Asian Economies 274
8.4 High-Speed Rail Activity in Key Regions, 2000–2016 277
8.5 Proportion of Population with Access to Safely Managed 281
Piped and Non-Piped Water in Selected Asian Economies
8.6 Fixed Telephone Subscriptions per 100 Inhabitants 288
8.7 Mobile Telephone Subscriptions per 100 Inhabitants 289
8.8 Internet Users 292
9.1 Exports of Goods and Services 299
9.2 Destination of Asia's Merchandise Exports 300
9.3 Asia's Top Merchandise Exports 301
9.4 Export Growth and Economic Growth, 1960–2017 302
9.5 Asia's Foreign Direct Investment Inflows and Outflows 304
9.6 Top 10 Asian Foreign Direct Investment Recipients 305
9.7 Top Global Investors into Asia 306
9.8 Share of Asia's Intermediate Goods Trade 316
9.9 Growth in Asia's Exports of Goods, Services, 320
and Travel, 2005–2017
9.10 Asia's World Trade Organization Accessions 322
9.11 Content of Free Trade Agreements in Asia, 1992–2015 323
10.1 Average Growth Rates and Unemployment by Decade, 329
1970–2018
10.2 Inflation by Decade, 1970–2018 330
10.3 Relative Frequency of Economic Crises, 1965–2014 331
10.4 Public Debt, 1970–2015 333
10.5 Fiscal Policy Cyclicality 334
10.6 World Commodity Prices, 1960–2019 335
10.7 Average Central Bank Independence, 1970–2010 338
10.8 Exchange Rate Flexibility in Developing Asia, 1990–2016 340
11.1 Economic Growth and Poverty Reduction, 1960s–1980s 359

11.2 Economic Growth and Poverty Reduction, 1981–2015   360

11.3 Changes in Gini Coefficients, Selected Economies   368
in East Asia, South Asia, and Southeast Asia, 1990s–2010s

11.4 Wealth Gini Coefficient, Selected Asian Economies, 2018   369

12.1 Literacy Rates by Gender   382

12.2 Sex Ratios at Birth in Asia   387

12.3 Labor Force Participation in Asia and the Pacific   390

12.4 U-Shaped Female Labor Force Participation with   391
Economic Development in the World, 1990 and 2017

12.5 Female Labor Force Participation Rate over the   393
Life Cycle by Pseudo-Cohort—Selected Asian Economies

12.6 Share of Vulnerable Employment of Women   395

12.7 Gender Wage Gap in the World by Income Level,   396
1995–2015

12.8 Possession of Appliances, Selected Asian Economies   399

12.9 Women's Time Spent on Unpaid Care   401
and Domestic Work, 2010–2017

12.10 Decisions on Major Household Purchases,   403
Selected Developing Asian Economies

12.11 Proportion of Seats Held by Women   404
in National Parliaments

12.12 Attitudes toward Women as Political Leaders,   405
2010–2014

13.1 Natural Forest Cover, Developing Asia, 1990–2015   414

13.2 Projected Mean Species Abundance, Developing Asia,   416
2000–2050

13.3 Capture Fisheries Production, Developing Asia,   420
1960–2017

13.4 Plastic Waste Disposal in Oceans, 2010   422

13.5 Waste Disposal and Recycling in   423
Selected Asian Economies

13.6 PM2.5 Emissions by Region, Developing Asia, 1970–2010   424

13.7 Greenhouse Gas Average Annual Emissions Growth   426
in World Regions, 1990–2014

13.8 Global Shares of Greenhouse Gas Annual Emissions,   427
1990 and 2014

13.9 Energy and Material Intensity in Developing Asia   435

14.1 Inflows of Bilateral Official Development Assistance,   446
Developing Asia

14.2 Inflows of Multilateral Development Finance, 449
Developing Asia

14.3 Evolution of ADB Loan and Grant Approvals, 1968–2016   450

14.4 Infrastructure Development of Thailand's 456
Eastern Seaboard

14.5 Bilateral and Multilateral Development Finance 457
Flows to Bangladesh

14.6 Bilateral and Multilateral Development Finance 459
Flows to Viet Nam

15.1 Intrasubregional Trade Share, 1992–2018 477

Boxes

4.1 Agrarian Reform in the People's Republic of China, 123
Viet Nam, and Central Asian Republics

4.2 ADB Support for Adopting 126
Green Revolution Technologies

5.1 Asia's Past Technological Advances 149
and How It Fell Behind

5.2 Technological Progress and Growth Accounting 153

5.3 ADB Support to Digital Technology 181

6.1 Family Planning and Declining Fertility 213
in the People's Republic of China

7.1 Asian Savings and Global Imbalances 231

7.2 Japan's Postal Savings System 236

7.3 Importance of Remittances for Developing Asia 243

8.1 The Lao People's Democratic Republic's 268
Hydroelectric Project

8.2 Reforming the Dhaka Water Supply 284
and Sewerage Authority

9.1 Asia's Experiment with Special Economic Zones 313

9.2 From Flying Geese to Global Value Chains 318

10.1 Tackling the "Resource Curse" 336

11.1 Japan's Economic Inequality Over the Past 50 Years 366

12.1 ADB's Role in Gender and Development 408

13.1 Benefits of International Cooperation 437
on Climate Change

15.1 The Successful Evolution of ASEAN 474
into the ASEAN Economic Community

15.2 ADB Subregional Cooperation Programs 480

FOREWORD

In 1966, when the Asian Development Bank (ADB) was established, the Asia and Pacific region was very poor. At that time, feeding a large and growing population was one of the most important challenges. Half a century later, Asia has emerged as a center of global dynamism.

Fifty years ago, there was pessimism about the prospects of industrialization and broad development for Asia. Japan, which began its modernization in the late 19th century, was in the midst of postwar high growth, but it was regarded by and large as an exception. The People's Republic of China was entering the turmoil of the Cultural Revolution. Growth in India was constrained by socialist ideas of central planning and "import substitution" policies. In Hong Kong, China; the Republic of Korea; Singapore; and Taipei,China—which later became known as the newly industrialized economies (NIEs)—growth started to pick up, but their future was still unclear. The Association of Southeast Asian Nations (ASEAN) was launched in 1967 by its original five members as a grouping for promoting regional peace. Yet, ASEAN economies had not initiated the strong growth based on reforms and the "flying geese" model. Central Asian countries were under the Soviet system. Many countries in the region suffered from conflicts and political instability.

The region's performance in its journey to prosperity over the past 50 years surpassed expectations by any measure—be it economic growth, structural transformation, poverty reduction, or improvement in health and education. In 1960, developing Asia's per capita gross domestic product (GDP) was $330 (in constant 2010 United States dollars). By 2018, it had risen to $4,903, a nearly 15-fold increase, while global per capita GDP tripled over the same period. As a result, the region's share of global GDP jumped from 4% to 24%; it increased from 13% to 34% when Japan, Australia, and New Zealand are included.

What were the reasons for the region's postwar economic success?

As discussed in Chapter 1, this book's position is that *there is no such thing as an "Asian Consensus."* The policies pursued in Asia can be explained by standard economic theories. And these policies are not so different from those prescribed by the so-called "Washington

Consensus." What made the difference was that many Asian countries took a pragmatic approach to implementing these policies.

Asian countries implemented import liberalization, opening up of foreign direct investment, financial sector deregulation, and capital account liberalization in a more gradual and sequential way. For instance, they learned that the liberalization of capital inflows should be preceded by adequate development of the domestic financial sector.

* * * * *

In the past half century, rapid population growth allowed many Asian countries to enjoy a "demographic dividend" due to the increasing share of the working-age population. During this period, Asia had a favorable external economic environment in terms of open trade and investment regimes of developed countries. Asian countries benefited enormously from rapid technological progress and globalization, particularly in recent decades. Moreover, the "convergence" process offered low-income economies an opportunity to grow fast.

However, even with favorable demographic and external conditions, the process of economic growth is not automatic. This book argues that Asia's postwar economic success owes much to creating effective policies and strong institutions. It was supported by governments' pragmatism in making policy choices, ability to learn lessons from their own and others' achievements and mistakes, and decisiveness in introducing reforms. In many countries, a clear vision for the future, which is often championed by forward-looking leaders and shared across a wide spectrum of social groups, made a difference—especially when backed by a competent bureaucracy.

While there were variations across countries on policy mix and timing, with occasional setbacks and reversals, successful Asian economies pursued policies needed for sustained growth. Over time, they adopted open trade and investment policies, facilitated agricultural modernization and industrial transformation, supported technological progress, invested in education and health, mobilized high level of domestic savings for productive investments, promoted infrastructure development, pursued sound macroeconomic policies, and implemented policies for poverty reduction and inclusiveness.

* * * * *

I have long felt that discussions about Asian economic success were often too simplistic. Many scholars, especially from outside Asia, tend to overemphasize the role of strong state intervention and guidance. But Asia's success essentially relied on markets and the private sector as engines of growth. Economies started to grow faster when policies shifted from state intervention to market orientation, while governments continued to play some proactive roles.

Market-oriented policies had the backing of a long tradition of commerce and technologies in many Asian countries. During Japan's Meiji modernization period (1868–1912), while the government created modern institutions following Western models and piloted industries, many railway lines were built by the local private sector. Electricity has always been provided by private companies in Japan. In China and India, in the early 20th century, industries led by domestic capitalists prospered in such sectors as textiles, paper, pharmaceuticals, steel, and shipbuilding.

Many Asian countries pursued "targeted industrial policy" to support industrialization, using tariffs, subsidies, preferential credit, and tax incentives. Some policies were successful, while others were not. Over time, industrial policies in Asia have evolved to become less intrusive, such as those promoting research and development. Targeted industrial policy, if used badly, can lead to "rent-seeking," unfair competition, and inefficiency. However, today, many agree that industrial policy can be effective if used wisely, especially at the early stages of development. This was the case for many of today's developed countries including France, Germany, and the United States. Industrial policy may more likely succeed when it promotes competition and if it is implemented transparently with clear policy targets and sunset clauses.

Export-oriented trade policies are also often overemphasized and misunderstood. Japan and the NIEs adopted export-oriented policies from early on. However, such policies should be rather called "outward-oriented," as they promoted exports to earn the foreign exchange needed for enabling more imports, including natural resources, capital goods, and technology. In fact, Japan incurred constant current account deficits until the mid-1960s and had to occasionally tighten macroeconomic policies. Many other Asian developing countries followed the NIEs, departing from import substitution. The import substitution strategy had been widely adopted by developing countries in the postwar period. It was influenced by socialist ideas and the desire for self-reliance after achieving independence from colonial powers. But under this strategy, trade protection, the lack of competition, and overvalued exchange rates led to serious inefficiencies and even triggered balance of payments crises at times, especially in Latin America.

*   *   *   *   *

I thought reflecting on the reasons for Asia's postwar success based on experiences of member economies would be a major task for ADB. When we started preparing the book of ADB's own history in 2015, *Banking on the Future of Asia and the Pacific*,[1] we already had an idea to write a companion volume about the development history of Asian economies.

Actual writing of this book, *Asia's Journey to Prosperity*, started in 2017 after ADB's own history book was published, and it has taken almost 3 years to finish the work. It depicts the 50 years of Asia's multifaceted development and transformation based on 14 themes. It emphasizes the importance of policy, market, and technology in achieving development. It covers the experiences of ADB's 46 developing member economies in the Asia and Pacific region, including the NIEs (which borrowed from ADB in the past). It discusses the experiences of Australia, Japan, and New Zealand, whenever necessary. Chapter 1 works as an executive summary for the following 14 chapters.

Compared with many other studies on Asian economic development, such as the well-known 1993 World Bank publication, *The East Asian Miracle*,[2] this book has several distinctive features.

First, it provides an overview of Asia's rapid transformation beyond the NIEs and several Southeast Asian countries (Indonesia, Malaysia, and Thailand), covering the time horizon from the immediate postwar period to the present. It captures the transition from centrally planned systems to market-oriented reforms, and the strong growth

---

[1]   McCawley, P. 2017. *Banking on the Future of Asia and the Pacific: 50 Years of the Asian Development Bank*. Manila: Asian Development Bank.
[2]   World Bank. 1993. *The East Asian Miracle: Economic Growth and Public Policy*. New York: Oxford University Press.

in the People's Republic of China, India, Cambodia, the Lao People's Democratic Republic, Viet Nam, and countries in Central Asia. Many Asian developing countries, including Bangladesh and the Philippines, have gathered growth momentum since the 2000s. Developing Asia, when excluding the NIEs, maintained about a 6% annual growth (meaning doubling income in 12 years) even after the 2008–2009 global financial crisis.

Second, this book reviews emerging issues and new trends for Asia and the world. It discusses challenges such as climate change, ocean health, and population aging, as well as responses to the Asian financial crisis and global financial crisis. It analyzes the impact of global value chains, new technologies such as artificial intelligence, and the increasing importance and variety of new services.

Third, many ADB staff from a wide range of member economies in Asia, North America, and Europe joined in writing this book and helped the deep understanding of countries' experiences and balanced views. In addition, staff engaged in operations contributed to the book's chapters related to health, education, gender, agriculture, energy, transport, water, environment and climate, and regional cooperation and integration.

In writing this book, we tried to make the narrative in each chapter as readable and interesting as possible, avoiding overly technical discussions while including various anecdotes, data, and country examples. The book also discusses the evolution of ideas on economic development that affected policymaking across Asia.

* * * * *

Many people argue that the 21st century is the "Asian century." But I have several reservations about this idea, while encouraged by Asia's success and its increasing economic stature. Asia has more than half of the world population, so we should not be surprised even if Asia's GDP surpasses half of the global GDP by 2050. Developing Asia still faces many challenges including persistent poverty; increasing income inequality; large gender gaps; environmental degradation; climate change (seriously affecting the Pacific island countries); and still inadequate access to health and education, electricity, and safe drinking water. There is no room for complacency.

In the past 50 years, the region was largely at peace except for periods of wars and conflicts in some countries. Peace and stability set the groundwork for Asia's economic success. Countries must continue to make utmost efforts to promote friendship and enhance cooperation in Asia and beyond.

Asia's experiences and innovations have been inspiring, but it will take some more time for Asia to become as influential as the West has been for the past five centuries. Asia must continue to make efforts to strengthen its institutions, contribute to the development of science and technology, assume more responsibilities in tackling global issues, and articulate its own ideas. I hope that a larger role played by Asia will lead to a more inclusive, integrated, and prosperous global community.

* * * * *

I appreciate the great contributions and hard work of the book's production team members, its management group, the secretariat, ADB staff across its departments, and consultants. I thank scholars from within and outside Asia for offering valuable comments.

Yasuyuki Sawada, Chief Economist and Director General of the Economic Research and Regional Cooperation Department (ERCD), and Juzhong Zhuang, Senior Economic Advisor at ERCD, led the production team and were main authors themselves. Niny Khor, Senior Advisor to the President, closely examined the substance and coordinated the process. Lea Sumulong of ERCD led the secretariat, which provided technical and research support. Relentless devotion by them and other contributors over the past 3 years made this book possible.

It is my wish that this work will serve the purpose of reviewing Asian development history over the past 50 years in a comprehensive manner, contributing to its greater understanding, and stimulating discussions to help address the remaining development challenges in Asia and the world.

Takehiko Nakao
President and Chair of the Board of Directors
Asian Development Bank
January 2020

PRODUCTION TEAM

Asia's Journey to Prosperity: Policy, Market, and Technology Over 50 Years was written by staff of the Asian Development Bank (ADB). The production was led by a management group comprising Yasuyuki Sawada, Chief Economist and Director General of the Economic Research and Regional Cooperation Department (ERCD); Juzhong Zhuang, Senior Economic Advisor at ERCD; Xianbin Yao, Special Senior Advisor to the President; Niny Khor, Senior Advisor to the President; and Lei Lei Song, Regional Economic Advisor, South Asia Department. They were supported by members of the ERCD management team Abdul Abiad, Edimon Ginting, Rana Hasan, Cyn-Young Park, and Joseph E. Zveglich, Jr.

President Takehiko Nakao provided leadership in conceptualizing the book, designing chapter structures, and providing inputs, based on his long-term experiences and insights in the areas of international finance and development. He spent a considerable amount of time as the "lead editor" in coordinating, editing, and finalizing this publication. Without his passion, this book would not have become a reality.

The following economists and experts from ERCD, other ADB departments, and ADB Institute contributed to writing the book chapters: Thomas Abell, Noritaka Akamatsu, Lilia Aleksanyan, Preety Bhandari, Giovanni Capannelli, Bruno Carrasco, David Dole, Bruce Dunn, Emma Xiaoqin Fan, Kathleen Farrin, Arjun Goswami, Robert Guild, Xuehui Han, Matthias Helble, Shikha Jha, Yi Jiang, Jong Woo Kang, Fahad Khan, Aiko Kikkawa-Takenaka, Jamie Leather, Minsoo Lee, Junkyu Lee, Steven Lewis-Workman, Jayant Menon, Peter Morgan, Keiko Nowacka, Patrick Osewe, Donghyun Park, Wilhelmina Paz, Daniele Ponzi, Madhavi Pundit, Rommel Rabanal, David Raitzer, Arief Ramayandi, Michael Rattinger, Lyaziza Sabyrova, Sonia Chand Sandhu, Manoj Sharma, Shigehiro Shinozaki, Yun Ji Suh, Sonomi Tanaka, Kiyoshi Taniguchi, Shu Tian, Duc Tran, Woochong Um, Paul Vandenberg, Emma Veve, James Villafuerte, Takashi Yamano, Naoyuki Yoshino, Yongping Zhai, and Bo Zhao.

Staff of ADB regional and other departments and resident missions reviewed the manuscript, validated facts, checked data, and provided comments.

Technical and research support were provided by a secretariat, led by Lea Sumulong and Jade Tolentino and comprising Roselle Dime, Reneli Gloria, Geraldine Guarin, and Flordeliza Huelgas. It was supported by Gemma Estrada, Eugenia Go, Iva Sebastian-Samaniego, and Mara Claire Tayag. Appendix tables were prepared by the Statistics and Data Innovation Unit led by Kaushal Joshi and Arturo Martinez, Jr., assisted by Raymond Adofina, Nalwino Billones, Joseph Bulan, Ephraim Cuya, Madeline Dumaua-Cabauatan, Patricia Georgina Gonzales, Melissa Pascua, Christian Flora Mae Soco, and Mic Ivan Sumilang. ADB loan disbursements data were provided by Setijo Boentaran, Nemia Silvestre, and Regina Sy. Sheila de Guzman, Mary Ann Magadia, Maria Melissa dela Paz, and Ma. Regina Sibal provided administrative and secretarial support throughout the book preparation.

The Department of Communications, headed by Vicky Tan, supported the overall production of the book. Layla Amar, Ma. Theresa Arago, Albert Atkinson, April Gallega, Cynthia Hidalgo, Alfredo de Jesus, Noren Jose, Rommel Marilla, Anna Sherwood, and Anima Slangen worked on the production. Anthony Victoria provided art direction for the cover. Infographics were created by Kevin Nellies and Ralph Romero. Map illustrations were prepared by Abraham Villanueva and Angel Villarez of the Office of Administrative Services. Guy Sacerdoti advised on English language and ADB style and usage.

Inputs from ADB consultants Sarah Daway-Ducanes, Margarita Debuque-Gonzales, Anil Deolalikar, Roselle Dime, Jonna Estudillo, Ruth Francisco, Jungsuk Kim, Naohiro Kitano, Joseph Lim, Epictetus Patalinghug, M. G. Quibria, Renato Reside, Jr., Dennis Trinidad, Marianne Vital, Robert Wihtol, and Josef Yap are gratefully acknowledged.

Yasuyuki Sawada
Chief Economist and
Director General, ERCD
Asian Development Bank

Juzhong Zhuang
Senior Economic Advisor, ERCD
Asian Development Bank

ACKNOWLEDGMENTS

The production team benefited significantly from substantive inputs by Professor Hal Hill (Australian National University) during the drafting of the book. Professor Jong-Wha Lee (Korea University), former Chief Economist of the Asian Development Bank (ADB), read the entire book manuscript carefully and provided invaluable comments.

The team received extensive comments from a group of external reviewers before and during a workshop at ADB headquarters in October 2019. The reviewers included Isher Judge Ahluwalia (Indian Council for Research on International Economic Relations), Muhamad Chatib Basri (University of Indonesia), Prasenjit K. Basu (REAL-Economics.com), Erik Berglof (London School of Economics and Political Science), John Gibson (University of Waikato), Cielito Habito (Ateneo de Manila University), Hal Hill, Stephen Howes (Australian National University), Yiping Huang (Peking University), Jong-Wha Lee, Tetsuji Okazaki (University of Tokyo), Rakhim Oshakbayev (TALAP Center for Applied Research, Kazakhstan), Nipon Poapongsakorn (Thailand Development Research Institute), Louis Putterman (Brown University), Binayak Sen (Bangladesh Institute of Development Studies), and Andrew Sheng (Asia Global Institute in Hong Kong, China).

The team was also helped by inputs from participants of a review workshop at ADB headquarters in February 2018, including Anil Deolalikar (University of California, Riverside), Jong-Wha Lee, Norma Mansor (University of Malaya), Keijiro Otsuka (Kobe University), Louis Putterman, Chalongphob Sussangkarn (Thailand Development Research Institute), and Jun Zhang (Fudan University).

The initial consideration of the publication was inspired by participants of a brainstorming workshop, chaired by then ADB Chief Economist Shang-Jin Wei, at ADB headquarters in June 2016. Participants were Isher Judge Ahluwalia, Ajay Chhibber (George Washington University), Suyono Dikun (University of Indonesia),

Huynh The Du (Fulbright School of Public Policy and Management in Viet Nam), Cielito Habito, Toh Mun Heng (National University of Singapore), Aigul Kosherbayeva (Economic Research Institute, Kazakhstan), Cassey Lee (Institute of Southeast Asian Studies), Rebecca Fatima Sta. Maria (Ministry of International Trade and Industry, Malaysia), Adoracion Navarro (Philippine Institute for Development Studies), Deepak Nayyar (Jawaharlal Nehru University), Tetsuji Okazaki, and Hyeon Park (University of Seoul).

ABBREVIATIONS

ABMI	Asian Bond Markets Initiative
ADB	Asian Development Bank
ADF	Asian Development Fund
AEC	ASEAN Economic Community
AFC	Asian financial crisis
AFTA	ASEAN Free Trade Area
AI	artificial intelligence
AIIB	Asian Infrastructure Investment Bank
APEC	Asia-Pacific Economic Cooperation
ASEAN	Association of Southeast Asian Nations
ASEAN+3	ASEAN plus the People's Republic of China, Japan, and the Republic of Korea
ASEAN+6	ASEAN+3 plus Australia, India, and New Zealand
BIMP-EAGA	Brunei Darussalam–Indonesia–Malaysia–Philippines East ASEAN Growth Area
BOT	build–operate–transfer
BPO	business process outsourcing
CAREC	Central Asia Regional Economic Cooperation
CCT	conditional cash transfer
CEDAW	Convention on the Elimination of All Forms of Discrimination against Women
CGIF	Credit Guarantee and Investment Facility
CLMV	Cambodia, the Lao People's Democratic Republic, Myanmar, and Viet Nam
CMIM	Chiang Mai Initiative Multilateralization
COP	Conference of the Parties
CPC	Communist Party of China
DAC	Development Assistance Committee
ECAFE	Economic Commission for Asia and the Far East
ESCAP	Economic and Social Commission for Asia and the Pacific
EU	European Union
FAO	Food and Agriculture Organization of the United Nations

FDI	foreign direct investment
FTA	free trade agreement
G20	Group of Twenty
G7	Group of Seven
GATT	General Agreement on Tariffs and Trade
GCF	Green Climate Fund
GDP	gross domestic product
GEF	Global Environment Fund
GFC	global financial crisis
GHG	greenhouse gas
GMS	Greater Mekong Subregion
GVC	global value chain
IBRD	International Bank for Reconstruction and Development
ICT	information and communication technology
IDA	International Development Association
IEA	International Energy Agency
IFAD	International Fund for Agricultural Development
IFI	international financial institution
IGES	Institute for Global Environmental Strategies
ILO	International Labour Organization
IMF	International Monetary Fund
IMT-GT	Indonesia–Malaysia–Thailand Growth Triangle
IRRI	International Rice Research Institute
Lao PDR	Lao People's Democratic Republic
MDB	multilateral development bank
MNC	multinational corporation
NDC	nationally determined contribution
NGO	nongovernment organization
NIEs	newly industrialized economies
ODA	official development assistance
OECD	Organisation for Economic Co-operation and Development
PACER	Pacific Agreement on Closer Economic Relations
PICTA	Pacific Island Countries Trade Agreement
PNG	Papua New Guinea
PPP	public–private partnership [Chapter 8]
PPP	purchasing power parity [Chapter 11 and Appendix 15]
PRC	People's Republic of China

R&D	research and development
RCEP	Regional Comprehensive Economic Partnership
RCI	regional cooperation and integration
ROK	Republic of Korea
SAARC	South Asian Association for Regional Cooperation
SASEC	South Asia Subregional Economic Cooperation
SDG	Sustainable Development Goal
SEZ	special economic zone
SMEs	small and medium-sized enterprises
SOE	state-owned enterprise
STEM	science, technology, engineering, and mathematics
TFP	total factor productivity
TVET	technical and vocational education and training
UHC	universal health coverage
UK	United Kingdom
UN	United Nations
UNCTAD	United Nations Conference on Trade and Development
UNDP	United Nations Development Programme
UNESCO	United Nations Educational, Scientific and Cultural Organization
UNFCCC	United Nations Framework Convention on Climate Change
UNFPA	United Nations Population Fund
UNICEF	United Nations Children's Fund
US	United States
WHO	World Health Organization
WTO	World Trade Organization

DEFINITIONS

The economies discussed in *Asia's Journey to Prosperity: Policy, Market, and Technology Over 50 Years* are classified by major analytic or geographic group as follows:

- **Developing Asia** comprises the 46 developing member economies of the Asian Development Bank (ADB), which are further grouped into Central Asia, East Asia, South Asia, Southeast Asia, and the Pacific. While today Hong Kong, China; the Republic of Korea; Singapore; and Taipei,China are all high-income economies, they borrowed from ADB in the past and have been classified as "developing member economies" at ADB.
- **Central Asia** comprises Armenia, Azerbaijan, Georgia, Kazakhstan, the Kyrgyz Republic, Tajikistan, Turkmenistan, and Uzbekistan (8 economies).
- **East Asia** comprises Hong Kong, China; Mongolia; the People's Republic of China; the Republic of Korea; and Taipei,China (5 economies).
- **South Asia** comprises Afghanistan, Bangladesh, Bhutan, India, Maldives, Nepal, Pakistan, and Sri Lanka (8 economies).
- **Southeast Asia** comprises Brunei Darussalam, Cambodia, Indonesia, the Lao People's Democratic Republic, Malaysia, Myanmar, the Philippines, Singapore, Thailand, and Viet Nam (10 economies).
- **The Pacific** comprises the Cook Islands, the Federated States of Micronesia, Fiji, Kiribati, the Marshall Islands, Nauru, Niue, Palau, Papua New Guinea, Samoa, Solomon Islands, Timor-Leste, Tonga, Tuvalu, and Vanuatu (15 economies).
- **Developed Asia** comprises Australia, Japan, and New Zealand.
- **Asia and the Pacific** comprises Developing Asia plus Developed Asia.
- **Association of Southeast Asian Nations** (ASEAN) comprises the same 10 countries grouped as Southeast Asia.
- **Newly industrialized economies** (NIEs) comprise Hong Kong, China; the Republic of Korea; Singapore; and Taipei,China.

- **Latin America and the Caribbean**, **Middle East and North Africa**, **Sub-Saharan Africa**, and **the Organisation for Economic Co-operation and Development** (OECD) follow the World Bank groupings.

Unless otherwise specified, the symbol "$" and the word "dollar" refer to United States dollars. *Asia's Journey to Prosperity: Policy, Market, and Technology Over 50 Years* is generally based on data available up to 15 October 2019.

ASIAN DEVELOPMENT BANK
REGIONAL MEMBERS

KAZAKHSTAN

UZBEKISTAN

GEORGIA

ARMENIA

AZERBAIJAN

TURKMENISTAN

KYRGYZ REPUBLIC

TAJIKISTAN

AFGHANISTAN

PAKISTAN

NEPAL

BHUTAN

INDIA

MALDIVES

BANGLADESH

SRI LANKA

MONGOLIA

PEOPLE'S REPUBLIC OF CHINA

JAPAN

MYANMAR

THAILAND

LAO PEOPLE'S
DEMOCRATIC
REPUBLIC

VIET NAM

REPUBLIC OF KOREA

TAIPEI,CHINA

HONG KONG, CHINA

PHILIPPINES

PALAU

CAMBODIA

BRUNEI
DARUSSALAM

MALAYSIA

SINGAPORE

INDONESIA

TIMOR-LESTE

PAPUA NEW GUINEA

FEDERATED STATES OF MICRONESIA

MARSHALL ISLANDS

KIRIBATI

NAURU

TUVALU

FIJI

SAMOA

NIUE

TONGA

COOK ISLANDS

SOLOMON
ISLANDS

VANUATU

NEW ZEALAND

AUSTRALIA

N

0   1000   2000
Kilometers

CHAPTER 1

50 YEARS OF ASIAN DEVELOPMENT

This book provides a historical overview of developing Asia's multifaceted journey to prosperity in the past half century. It highlights the region's impressive growth and transformation, and uncovers key contributing factors, while bringing out large variations across countries and over time. The book distills policy lessons and their implications for the future. It discusses mainly experiences of developing Asia—the 46 developing member economies of the Asian Development Bank (ADB) in the Asia and Pacific region, including Hong Kong, China; the Republic of Korea (ROK); Singapore; and Taipei,China.[1] Where relevant, the discussions also include the region's three developed countries—Australia, Japan, and New Zealand—and extend back to the 1950s or earlier.

1.1 Asia's rapid growth and poverty reduction over the past half century

The Asia and Pacific region achieved spectacular development over the past half century, surpassing expectations by any measure—be it economic growth, structural transformation, poverty reduction, or health and education. What was primarily an agrarian, rural, low-income region in the 1960s, with most economies struggling to

---

[1] While today Hong Kong, China; the ROK; Singapore; and Taipei,China are all high-income economies, they borrowed from ADB in the past and have been classified as "developing member economies" at ADB.

feed their growing populations, has today developed into a global manufacturing powerhouse, with diverse exports, growing innovation capacity, burgeoning cities, and an expanding skilled labor force and middle class.

Developing Asia's annual growth in per capita gross domestic product (GDP) averaged 4.7% between 1960 and 2018, the highest among regions worldwide (Table 1.1). Growth accelerated from 2.2% in the 1960s to 6.2% in the 2000s before moderating slightly to 5.5% during 2010–2018. In 1960, the region's per capita GDP was $330

Table 1.1: Average Annual Per Capita GDP Growth
(%)

	1960–1969	1970–1979	1980–1989	1990–1999	2000–2009	2010–2018	1960–2018
Developing Asia	2.2	4.0	5.0	4.9	6.2	5.5	4.7
Central Asia	...	...	...	(5.4)	7.8	3.1	2.0
East Asia	2.7	6.4	7.6	7.4	8.0	6.4	6.5
People's Republic of China	1.2	5.3	8.2	8.8	9.7	7.3	6.8
South Asia	1.9	0.6	3.1	3.3	4.3	5.3	3.1
India	1.8	0.6	3.3	3.7	4.6	5.8	3.3
Southeast Asia	2.2	4.5	3.0	3.2	3.7	4.1	3.5
The Pacific	3.7	2.0	(1.1)	1.6	1.5	1.9	1.5
NIEs	6.4	8.1	6.9	5.4	3.8	3.1	5.6
Developed Asia	8.1	2.8	3.4	1.3	0.7	1.5	2.9
Japan	9.1	3.1	3.7	1.2	0.4	1.5	3.1
Latin America and the Caribbean	2.7	3.6	0.0	1.0	1.7	1.1	1.7
Sub-Saharan Africa	1.6	1.6	(1.3)	(0.8)	2.5	0.9	0.7
OECD	4.3	2.5	2.2	1.8	1.0	1.4	2.2
World	3.5	2.1	1.2	1.1	1.6	1.8	1.9

... = data not available, ( ) = negative, 0.0 = magnitude is less than half of unit employed, GDP = gross domestic product, NIEs = newly industrialized economies, OECD = Organisation for Economic Co-operation and Development.

Sources: Asian Development Bank. Key Indicators Database. https://kidb.adb.org/kidb (accessed 2 August 2019); World Bank. World Development Indicators. https://data.worldbank.org (accessed 2 August 2019); and Asian Development Bank estimates.

(in constant 2010 United States [US] dollars). By 2018, it had risen to $4,903, a nearly 15-fold increase, while global per capita GDP almost tripled (Table 1.2). As a result, developing Asia's share of global GDP jumped from 4.1% to 24.0%; the region's share increased from 13.4% to 33.5% when Japan, Australia, and New Zealand are included (Figure 1.1).

Table 1.2: GDP Per Capita
(constant 2010 US dollars)

	1960	1990	2018
Developing Asia	**330**	**1,078**	**4,903**
Bangladesh	372	411	1,203
India	330	581	2,104
Indonesia	690	1,708	4,285
Kazakhstan	...	5,890	11,166
Malaysia	1,354	4,537	12,109
Papua New Guinea	1,012	1,393	2,400
People's Republic of China	192	729	7,755
Philippines	1,059	1,527	3,022
Republic of Korea	944	8,465	26,762
Singapore	3,503	22,572	58,248
Taipei,China	919	7,691	23,113
Thailand	571	2,504	6,362
Uzbekistan	...	1,003	2,027
Viet Nam	...	433	1,964
Developed Asia	**9,685**	**37,519**	**49,857**
Australia	19,378	35,913	56,919
Japan	8,608	38,074	48,920
OECD	**11,499**	**27,337**	**39,937**
United States	16,982	35,702	54,554
World	**3,758**	**7,186**	**10,882**

... = data not available, GDP = gross domestic product, OECD = Organisation for Economic Co-operation and Development, US = United States.

Sources: Asian Development Bank. Key Indicators Database. https://kidb.adb.org/kidb/ (accessed 2 August 2019); World Bank. World Development Indicators. https://data.worldbank.org (accessed 2 August 2019); United Nations, Department of Economic and Social Affairs, Population Division. 2019. *World Population Prospects 2019*. Online Edition. https://population.un.org/wpp/ (accessed 23 August 2019); Asian Development Bank estimates; and for Taipei,China: Directorate-General of Budget, Accounting and Statistics.

Figure 1.1: Global GDP Shares, 1960 and 2018

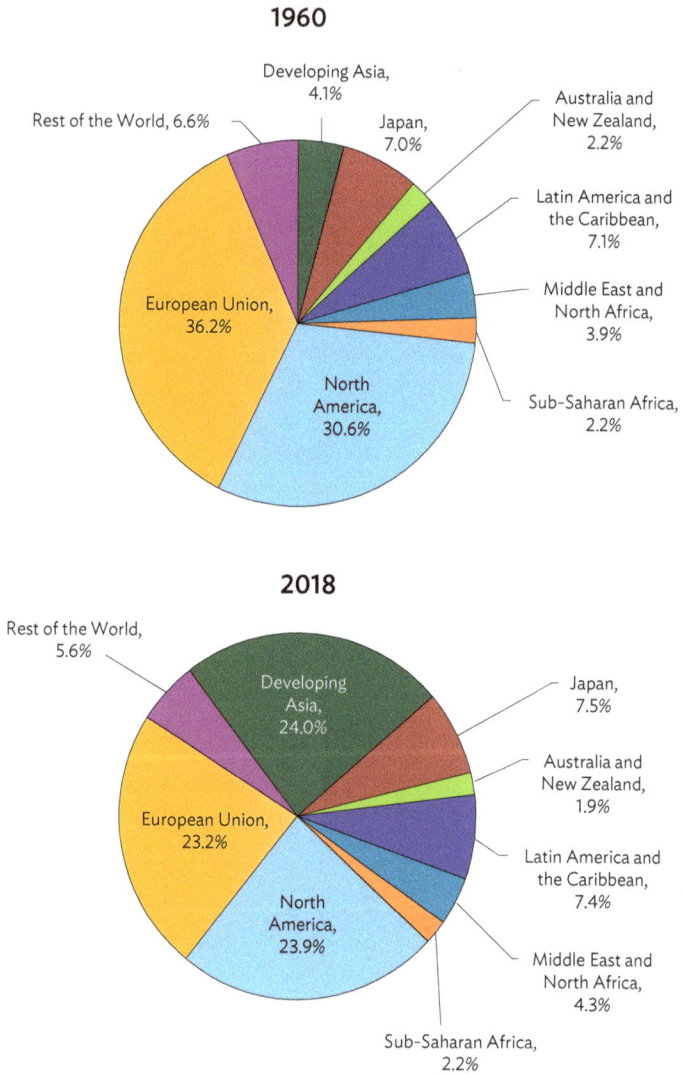

1960

Developing Asia, 4.1%
Rest of the World, 6.6%
Japan, 7.0%
Australia and New Zealand, 2.2%
Latin America and the Caribbean, 7.1%
Middle East and North Africa, 3.9%
European Union, 36.2%
North America, 30.6%
Sub-Saharan Africa, 2.2%

2018

Rest of the World, 5.6%
Developing Asia, 24.0%
Japan, 7.5%
Australia and New Zealand, 1.9%
Latin America and the Caribbean, 7.4%
European Union, 23.2%
North America, 23.9%
Middle East and North Africa, 4.3%
Sub-Saharan Africa, 2.2%

GDP = gross domestic product.

Notes: For 1960, data for the Middle East and North Africa refer to 1968 and data for New Zealand refer to 1970. Shares calculated using GDP in constant 2010 United States dollars.

Sources: Asian Development Bank. Key Indicators Database. https://kidb.adb.org/kidb (accessed 2 August 2019); and World Bank. World Development Indicators. https://data.worldbank.org (accessed 2 August 2019).

Developing Asia's phenomenal growth has been accompanied by a dramatic structural transformation. In the 1960s, more than two-thirds of the labor force was employed in subsistence agriculture. Today, more than 65% work in industry and services—and 85%–95% in some economies (such as Kazakhstan; Malaysia; the ROK; and Taipei,China). As one of the most open regions in the world, developing Asia accounted for 30.7% of global exports and 29.3% of global imports, and attracted 35.9% of global inward foreign direct investment (FDI) in 2018. In the 1960s, Asian exports were dominated by agricultural and primary commodities and light manufacturing products such as textiles and garments. Today, the region is known as "Factory Asia": it manufactures and exports a wide range of sophisticated and innovative goods—such as automobiles, computers, smartphones, machine tools, and robots.

Substantial investment in transport and energy has significantly improved its infrastructure. Developing Asia's electrification rate has reached 90%. The region now operates three-quarters of the global high-speed rail network. Technological progress, especially advances in information and communication technology (ICT), has fueled the growth of developing Asia's high value-added service industries in recent years. The region is now home to many global e-commerce and tech giants.

Developing Asia has also become more urbanized, with nearly half of its population in 2018 living in cities, up from 20% in 1960. Economic growth and urbanization have generated an expanding middle class, creating "Marketplace Asia." The strong domestic consumption from these new consumers now drives growth in developing Asian economies as well as that of the world.

Rapid economic growth and structural transformation significantly improved the region's broad development indicators—despite the remaining gaps with Organisation for Economic Co-operation and Development (OECD) countries (Table 1.3). For example, the rate of extreme poverty fell from 68.1% in 1981 to 6.9% in 2015 using the $1.90 per day international poverty line at 2011 purchasing power parity. Average life expectancy at birth increased from 45.0 years in 1960 to 71.8 years in 2018. The infant mortality rate fell from 137.8 to 26.2 deaths per 1,000 live births during the period. Mean years of schooling for those aged 20–24 years increased from 3.5 in 1960 to 8.9 in 2010.

Table 1.3: Development Indicators

	Developing Asia				OECD			
	1960	1980	2000	2018	1960	1980	2000	2018
Poverty (% of population)	...	68.1	33.1	6.9	...	1.3	1.2	0.9
Life expectancy (years)	45.0	59.3	65.8	71.8	67.8	72.6	77.2	80.5
Infant mortality rate (per 1,000)	137.8	80.1	48.1	26.2	49.1	25.1	9.4	5.9
Mean years of schooling (aged 20–24)	3.5	6.0	7.7	8.9	7.8	10.1	11.4	12.1

... = data not available, OECD = Organisation for Economic Co-operation and Development.

Notes: Poverty refers to the rate of extreme poverty using the $1.90 per day international poverty line at 2011 purchasing power parity for 1981, 2002, and 2015. Life expectancy refers to life expectancy at birth in years. Infant mortality rate refers to infant deaths per 1,000 live births. Mean years of schooling are for those aged 20–24; data for 2018 refer to 2010.

Sources: United Nations, Department of Economic and Social Affairs, Population Division. 2019. *World Population Prospects 2019*. Online Edition. https://population.un.org/wpp/ (accessed 23 August 2019); World Bank. PovcalNet Database. http://iresearch.worldbank.org/PovcalNet/home.aspx (accessed 28 September 2019); World Bank. World Development Indicators. https://data.worldbank.org (accessed 30 September 2019); and Barro, R., and J.-W. Lee. Database Version 2.2. http://www.barrolee.com (accessed 30 September 2019).

Despite the success, developing Asia still faces many challenges, as discussed in section 1.5. Priority areas that governments should tackle include persistent poverty; increasing income inequality; remaining large gender gaps; environmental degradation and climate change; and access to education, health services, electricity, and safe drinking water. There is no room for complacency.

1.2   What explains Asia's economic success?

According to Angus Maddison,[2] Asia produced roughly two-thirds of global GDP (in purchasing power parity terms) from the beginning of recorded history until the early 19th century, reflecting its large population and relatively high productivity. Following the Industrial Revolution that started in Great Britain, growth accelerated in Western Europe and North America. With the exception of Japan, which

---

[2]   Maddison, A. 2007. *Contours of the World Economy 1-2030 AD: Essays in Macro-Economic History*. New York: Oxford University Press.

pursued Western-style modernization from the late 19th century, Asian economies in general stagnated due to years of isolationism, colonization, weak institutions, outdated education systems, domestic conflict, and wars. They were unable to industrialize and modernize and, as a result, their importance to the global economy continued to decline.

In his classic 1968 book, *Asian Drama: An Inquiry into the Poverty of Nations*, Swedish economist Gunnar Myrdal portrayed a large part of developing Asia as a region in the "doldrums" constrained by rapid population growth and government inability to implement effective development policies.[3]

However, a half century on, Asia has transformed dramatically. What caused the change of Asia's fortune? How does one explain the region's postwar economic success?

Scholars and policy makers continue to debate these issues. After World War II, most of developing Asia ended colonial rule—often a source of domestic conflict—and gradually restored political stability. Asia was affected by the Cold War, but the region was largely at peace—except for periods of wars and conflicts in some countries. The region became more stable, especially after the Vietnam War was over in 1975 following the fall of Saigon (today's Ho Chi Minh City), Cambodia regained peace formally by the Paris Peace Agreements in 1991, and the domestic conflict in Sri Lanka ended in 2009. Yet Afghanistan still faces security challenges and needs special assistance from the international community. Peace and political stability set the groundwork for Asia's accelerated growth and development. They also provided conditions for rapid population growth and allowed many Asian countries to benefit from a "demographic dividend."

Moreover, compared with the previous 100 years, the past half century offered Asia a far more conducive external economic environment. Most advanced countries in the postwar period promoted and practiced free trade and investment. Asian countries benefited enormously from rapid technological progress and globalization, particularly in recent decades. In addition, there is little doubt that developing Asia's relatively low income in the 1950s and 1960s provided it with the potential to grow faster and catch up with advanced countries (known as "convergence").

---

[3] Myrdal, G. 1968. *Asian Drama: An Inquiry into the Poverty of Nations.* London: Alien Lane, The Penguin Press.

However, even with favorable external, political, and demographic conditions, the process of catch-up growth is not automatic. Bad policies and weak institutions can squander a country's economic potential. For example, insufficient investment in physical and human capital, macroeconomic instability, inward-oriented policies, and widespread corruption can all constrain a country's potential to catch up, innovate, and grow.

This book argues that Asia's postwar economic success owes much to creating better policies and institutions. These policies and institutions helped develop and nurture market economies and a vibrant private sector which, in turn, led to sustained technological adoption and innovation. This process benefited from governments' (i) pragmatism in making policy choices, including the practice of testing or piloting major policy changes before full-scale implementation; (ii) ability to learn lessons from its own and others' achievements and mistakes; and (iii) decisiveness in introducing (sometimes drastic) reforms when needed. In many countries, a clear vision for the future shared across a wide spectrum of society—often promoted by forward-looking leaders—made a difference, especially when backed by a competent bureaucracy and strong institutions.

There were variations on policy mix and timing across countries, with occasional setbacks and reversals. Some countries maintained stronger state control longer, and some resorted to more protectionist policies at times. However, over time, successful Asian economies, by and large, have pursued the policies listed below, as discussed in detail in the next 14 chapters of this book:

- rely on markets and the private sector as engines of growth, supported by governments' proactive promotion of development in areas where markets fail to work efficiently (Chapter 2);
- facilitate structural transformation from agriculture to industry and services including new services, and urbanization (Chapter 3);
- implement land reform, promote the Green Revolution, and facilitate agricultural modernization and rural transformation (Chapter 4);
- support technological progress by attracting FDI, investing in research and development (R&D), building necessary infrastructure, and protecting intellectual property rights (Chapter 5);

- invest in education and health—through compulsory basic education, technical and vocational education and training (TVET), tertiary education, targeted health interventions such as immunization, and the drive toward universal health coverage (Chapter 6);
- mobilize high-level of domestic savings for productive investment, mostly through banks, while seeking to deepen capital markets (Chapter 7);
- prioritize investment in infrastructure—energy, transport, water, and telecommunications—to support growth and raise living standards (Chapter 8);
- adopt open trade and investment regimes to ensure efficiency of resource allocation and enable access to global markets, foreign capital, and advanced technology (Chapter 9);
- pursue macroeconomic stability through sound fiscal, monetary, and financial sector policies, and appropriate exchange rate systems with increasing flexibility (Chapter 10);
- commit to poverty reduction and social inclusion by promoting inclusive economic growth and targeted social protection programs (Chapter 11);
- promote gender equality in education (such as more school years for girls), health (including declining maternal mortality), and labor market participation (Chapter 12);
- address environmental issues over time for land, water, and air, and, more recently, climate change including mitigation and adaptation (Chapter 13);
- engage with bilateral and multilateral development partners to benefit from both finance and knowledge (Chapter 14); and
- foster regional cooperation and integration (RCI) to promote trade and infrastructure connectivity, policy reforms, and good relationships among neighboring countries (Chapter 15).

1.3   Is there an Asian Consensus?

There have been much discussions whether there is an "Asian development model" that can explain Asia's success stories, or an "Asian Consensus" that is different from the so-called "Washington Consensus."

The term "Washington Consensus" was first used in 1989 by John Williamson,[4] a former staff member of both the International Monetary Fund (IMF) and the World Bank. It refers to a set of policy recommendations considered to constitute the standard reform package prescribed by the IMF and the World Bank to help crisis-affected countries, initially in the context of the Latin American debt crisis of the 1980s. According to Williamson, the Washington Consensus comprises 10 policy recommendations: (i) fiscal discipline, (ii) public expenditure reform, (iii) tax reform, (iv) financial liberalization toward market-determined interest rates, (v) competitive exchange rates, (vi) import liberalization, (vii) FDI liberalization, (viii) privatization of state-owned enterprises, (ix) deregulation, and (x) the protection of property rights.

The policies pursued in Asia that led to the region's rapid economic growth, poverty reduction, and broader development achievements are not so different from those prescribed by the Washington Consensus. They were also in line with standard economic theories. These include trade theory that predicts gains from trade when countries produce and export goods and services where they have comparative advantage; public economics that sees the need for governments to address externalities, provide public goods, and correct market distortions arising from imperfect competition including natural monopolies; theories related to information asymmetry, agglomeration and economies of scale, and coordination problems; and new institutional economics that highlights the importance of institutions and governance.

This book's position is that *there is no such thing as an "Asian Consensus."* What made the difference was that many Asian countries took a pragmatic approach to implementing these policies. They implemented import liberalization, opening up of FDI, financial sector deregulation, and capital account liberalization in a more gradual and sequential way. Asian economies also learned the lesson that liberalization of capital inflows should be preceded by adequate development of the domestic financial sector. They worked hard on (i) strengthening the necessary institutions that helped improve government effectiveness, (ii) supporting investment in education and

---

[4] Williamson, J. 1989. *What Washington Means by Policy Reform.* Washington, DC: Peterson Institute for International Economics.

health, (iii) fostering infrastructure development, and (iv) putting in place a conducive environment for private sector development.

The effectiveness of industrial policy has also been subject to heated debate. Many Asian countries adopted "targeted industrial policy" to support selected industries, using tariffs, subsidies, preferential credit, and tax incentives. Some policies were successful, while others were not. Over time, industrial policies in Asia have transformed to less intrusive ones such as those promoting R&D. As many argue, targeted industrial policy, if used badly, can lead to rent-seeking, unfair competition, and inefficiency over time. However, today, many also agree that industrial policy can be effective if used wisely, especially at the early stage of development (in protecting "infant industries"). Industrial policy can be useful even in more advanced stages, in particular where there are significant "positive externalities" such as innovation, or where there are "coordination problems" such as in developing new, nontraditional industries.[5] Industrial policy may more likely succeed when it is performance-based and promotes competition, and if it is implemented transparently—with clear policy targets, an effective implementation mechanism, and sunset clauses.[6]

1.4 A half century of multifaceted development

The role of markets, the state, and institutions

Development requires efficient markets, an effective state, and strong institutions. Markets, prices, and competition are critical for the efficient allocation of resources and creation of entrepreneurial incentives. The state is needed to establish strong institutions, intervene where markets fail to work efficiently, and promote social equity. Strong institutions ensure orderly functioning of markets and accountability of the state.

The role of markets and the state has been shaped by changes in development thinking. After World War II, state-led industrialization and "import substitution" strategies dominated development policy in developing countries. Nationalist and socialist ideologies had significant influence. The policy also had backing of development

---

[5] Cherif, R., and F. Hasanov. 2019. The Return of the Policy That Shall Not Be Named: Principles of Industrial Policy. *IMF Working Paper*. No. WP/19/74. Washington, DC: International Monetary Fund.

[6] Rodrik, D. 2004. Industrial Policy for the Twenty-First Century. *KSG Working Paper Series*. No. RWP04-047. Cambridge, MA: Kennedy School of Government, Harvard University.

thinking at that time, such as the "big push" and "dependency" (or "center–periphery") theories. According to the former, in the early stage of development, governments should promote industrialization through coordinated large investment.[7] According to the latter, rising prices of industrial products relative to primary commodities would cause "terms of trade" to deteriorate for developing countries and be a major cause of their economic woes.[8] Further, import substitution was considered necessary to protect infant industries and save the foreign exchange needed to import capital goods to support industrialization.

In Asia, the role of markets and the state has changed markedly over the past 50 years, reflecting countries' evolving economy and politics, as well as their histories. It has also been influenced by shifts in global development thinking.

Japan had a tradition of a strong private sector. This can be traced back to premodern merchants who had developed supply chains, banking, a futures market for rice, as well as irrigation and river transport under concessions from the shogunate and local governments. After the start of the Meiji Restoration in 1868, government policies focused on establishing modern institutions, piloting industry and education. Although the country resorted to "targeted industrial policy" after World War II, it was for addressing serious resource constraints during the recovery process from the devastation of the war. It was also in a way a continuation of the strong state intervention prevailing immediately before and during the war period. Since then, the policy has moved toward outward-orientation instead of import substitution, and reliance on market competition and private enterprises to drive growth, while the government played some proactive roles.

In the immediate years after World War II, many governments in developing Asia adopted import substitution industrialization policies with strong state control for nation-building and development. From the 1960s, however, Hong Kong, China; the ROK; Singapore; and Taipei,China shifted toward export-promotion and market-friendly policies. They grew into what later became known as the newly industrialized economies (NIEs). In the 1970s, Indonesia, Malaysia, and Thailand opened up to trade and FDI. They too became

[7] Rosenstein-Rodan, P. 1943. Problems of Industrialisation of Eastern and South-Eastern Europe. *Economic Journal.* 53 (210/211). pp. 202–211.
[8] Prebisch, R. 1962. The Economic Development of Latin America and Its Principal Problems. *Economic Bulletin for Latin America.* 7 (1). pp. 1–23.

"high-performing Asian economies"[9] in the following 2 decades. This pattern of development was referred to as the "flying geese" model.[10] Today, however, Asian economic relations are more in the form of networks as part of global value chains (GVCs) than the flying geese formation.

From the late 1970s, more Asian economies embarked on far-reaching market-oriented reforms and opened to the outside world. The People's Republic of China (PRC), after 3 decades of central planning that led to serious resource misallocation and widespread shortages, began its transition in 1978 toward a more market-oriented economy. The country piloted reforms starting with the adoption of the rural "household responsibility system," the introduction of dual-track prices, and the establishment of "special economic zones" in coastal provinces to attract FDI. It quickly adopted new technologies and learned macroeconomic management and business know-how from abroad, and subsequently launched comprehensive reforms nationwide, in the industry, trade, and financial sectors, leading to 40 years of rapid economic growth.

South Asia also joined the wave of economic reforms, after growth was constrained by decades of state-led industrialization. India started comprehensive reforms in 1991 to reduce government control, rely more on market forces, and liberalize trade and FDI, and the reforms were followed by growth acceleration. From the early 1990s, Central Asian countries started the transition toward market economies after the collapse of the Soviet Union. After initial shocks leading to recession, these countries have seen growth picking up since the early 2000s. And in recent years, many Pacific island countries also embraced market-oriented reforms.

Since the 1980s, there has been growing recognition in development thinking that the quality of governance and institutions matters. In recent years, developing Asia has intensified efforts to strengthen government effectiveness, regulatory quality, the rule of law, and anticorruption policy. These have been complemented by increased efforts to promote transparency and accountability, and widen citizen participation.

---

[9] World Bank. 1993. *The East Asian Miracle: Economic Growth and Public Policy*. New York: Oxford University Press.
[10] Akamatsu, K. 1962. A Historical Pattern of Economic Growth in Developing Countries. *The Developing Economies*. 1 (August). pp. 3–25.

Dynamics of structural transformation

Asia's rapid structural transformation was a key element to its postwar economic success. Most economies followed the experience of high-income countries: agriculture's share of output and employment declines as industry's share grows, followed by "deindustrialization" as services become dominant. All successful Asian economies worked hard on transforming agriculture and traditional rural economies. Urbanization proceeds together with changes in industrial structure—Asia added over 1.5 billion urban residents over the past 5 decades. Manufacturing and many services often benefit from "agglomeration economies" in cities, whereby increased interaction among more and different types of firms and workers in any given location contributes to boosting overall productivity.

Successful Asian economies promoted manufacturing, initially labor-intensive and over time shifting to capital- and skill-intensive industries. Developing manufacturing created opportunities for trade and innovation. Manufacturing exports generated the foreign exchange needed to finance imported capital goods. Also, manufacturing has high income elasticities of demand, which enabled Asian countries to benefit from rising incomes in both domestic and large global markets.

Services continue to gain in importance. In 2018, services accounted for 54% of developing Asia's total value added—although still much smaller than in developed countries. In general, the services sector expands as an economy becomes more developed. Because services are labor intensive, their expansion can help make growth more inclusive. Advances in ICT are transforming and upgrading the entire services sector, and high value-added services build synergies with manufacturing. Services trade is becoming increasingly important along with those embedded in GVCs. Tourism is expanding rapidly, as Asia is increasingly both a desirable destination and a source of travelers.

Modernizing agriculture and rural development

Agriculture plays an important role in any economy. It supplies food, provides labor and intermediate inputs to other sectors, and creates market demand for industrial goods and services. Asia's experience shows that productive agriculture and a dynamic rural economy are key to successful structural transformation and inclusive development.

Land reform—redistributing land to small farmers—was introduced in many countries in the 1950s or earlier, especially in East Asia. It increased production incentives and contributed to agricultural productivity growth. The Green Revolution began in the late 1960s with increased investment in irrigation, improved seed varieties, and the use of modern inputs such as chemical fertilizers and pesticides. It helped Asian farmers substantially increase yields of rice, wheat, and other crops, and allayed fears of widespread food insecurity. Following the Green Revolution, mechanization—such as the increased use of tractors and harvesters—also contributed to agriculture's modernization and structural transformation. In the past half century, developing Asia's per capita production of rice and wheat—the region's two most important staple crops—increased by 41% and 246%, respectively.

Asia's agriculture and rural economies have continued to transform. Food consumption has been changing with rising incomes and urbanization. The share of rice has declined, most notably in East Asia. And with greater dietary diversity, higher-value crop and livestock production now surpasses that of staple food. Agricultural value chains linking production, processing, marketing, and distribution have become more sophisticated, driven by market-oriented reforms and trade liberalization. Increasingly vibrant rural nonfarm economies have helped create rural jobs and raise rural incomes. These have, in turn, contributed to integrating rural and urban economies and narrowing the urban–rural income gaps.

Technological progress as key driver of growth

In its early stage of development, the region's success was primarily based on effective resource mobilization. Subsequently, it began to rely more on technological progress and efficiency gains—also known as "total factor productivity" growth. In the 1960s, Asia's industrial production was dominated by labor-intensive food processing, textiles, and garments. The region has since mastered more complex technologies to produce more sophisticated goods such as automobiles, smartphones, and robots. Asia's leading economies have transitioned from being users of foreign patents to becoming the world's top patent producers as well. In services, Asia is now at the global technological frontier in many areas, with ICT applications revolutionizing business and marketing processes.

Technological progress is not automatic. It requires deliberate effort by entrepreneurs, firms, and governments. Asian economies used a variety of channels and methods to secure, deploy, and innovate technologies. They adopted technologies by obtaining foreign licenses, importing machinery, learning through exporting, attracting FDI, conducting reverse engineering, and receiving technical cooperation aid. As countries mastered imported technologies to produce goods and services, they gravitated toward innovation by building capacity for R&D and fostering industrial clusters.

To support this process, Asian governments made significant efforts to (i) strengthen education and create a growing pool of engineers, scientists, and researchers; (ii) build national innovation systems that include research institutions, national laboratories, and science parks; (iii) introduce legal and institutional frameworks including an intellectual property regime; (iv) support private sector R&D including through tax incentives; (v) invest in ICT infrastructure such as high-speed broadband and mobile networks; and (vi) create a competitive market environment to stimulate innovation.

Education, health, and demographic change

Asia's success in building human capital has been a key contributor to rapid growth and transformation. It also led to better well-being of Asian people. Favorable demographic changes supported Asian growth.

Many Asian countries made education the legal right of every citizen. They used a variety of policy instruments to expand modern education, including public investment in schools, compulsory education, targeted programs to support low-income households, and broad educational reforms. By 2017, almost all countries in Asia and the Pacific had achieved universal or near-universal access to primary education, with many reaching the same for secondary education. Girls have also caught up with boys across many countries, contributing to closing the gender gaps. Tertiary education significantly expanded as well. The region's mean years of schooling for young adults aged 20–24 increased from 3.5 in 1960 to 8.9 in 2010.

The region also took great strides toward improving population health. During 1960–2018, life expectancy rose from 45.0 to 71.8 years and the under-five child mortality rate fell by a factor of six, thanks to improved living standards and investment in public health. Maternal mortality also declined substantially. Targeted health programs such as immunization, investment in safe drinking water and sanitation, and new medicines and medical technologies drove down death rates from preventable causes. Countries improved their overall health systems and have been working toward achieving universal health coverage.

Developing Asia's initially high fertility rates, decreasing mortality across all ages, and increased life expectancy led to rapid population growth and a rising share of the working-age population. The region's population increased from 1.5 billion in 1960 to 4.1 billion in 2018 (a 1.7% annual increase) and its working-age population increased from 855 million to 2.8 billion during the same period (a 2.1% annual increase). The increased share of the working-age population generated a demographic dividend. However, many Asian countries now face challenges from falling fertility rates and aging of population.

Investment, savings, and finance

Asian economies have made large investments in new factories and plants, as well as physical infrastructure such as roads, railways, and ports; and power plants and transmission lines. During 1960–2017, developing Asia's estimated physical capital stock increased from $3.9 trillion to $176.0 trillion (in constant 2011 US dollars). Investments increased productive capacity, supported technological innovation, and promoted industrial upgrading. They also contributed to improving living standards in the region.

Developing Asia's high investments were largely financed by domestic savings of households, corporations, and governments. The region's gross domestic savings as a percentage of GDP increased from 18.0% in the 1960s to 41.0% during 2010–2018. The key drivers of rising savings rates included rapid economic growth, favorable demographics, and policies such as savings promotion programs. Until the 1980s, net official inflows (including bilateral official development assistance [ODA] and multilateral development finance) were the largest source of developing Asia's external financing that complemented domestic savings. Since then, with many economies liberalizing trade and investment, inward FDI has become the largest source of external financing. For some countries, remittances from overseas workers have become a vital and stable source of financing household consumption and investment in micro and small enterprises.

Asia's bank-based financial system played a critical role in channeling domestic savings into domestic investment. In more recent decades, capital markets grew significantly, providing alternative sources of funding for domestic investment with longer maturities. After the 1997–1998 Asian financial crisis (AFC), the Association of Southeast Asian Nations (ASEAN) plus the PRC, Japan, and the ROK (ASEAN+3) worked together to promote local currency bond markets to minimize currency and maturity mismatches. Developing Asian economies have also taken measures to promote access to finance of small and medium-sized enterprises.

Infrastructure development

Large investment in infrastructure, financed by both public and private resources, has been one of the most important characteristics of fast-growing Asian economies. In addition to providing key inputs to growth, access to electricity, roads and railways, ports, safe drinking water, and quality communications are all essential parts of human well-being.

From 1971 to 2018, the region's electricity generation (including Australia, Japan, and New Zealand) increased 16.5 times, compared with a fivefold increase globally. Developing Asia now operates two-thirds of global high-speed rail networks. Access to improved water supply services reached over 90% in 2017, compared with less than 30% in the 1960s in many countries. Progress in telecommunications and ICT infrastructure enabled Asia to develop new services such as e-commerce, mobile payments, ride-sharing, and e-public services. It also increased opportunities for greater financial inclusion as well as better access to health and education.

Strong investment and policy reforms transformed Asia's infrastructure. The region's energy supply mix has diversified from mostly conventional sources such as coal, oil, natural gas, and hydropower, to include rapidly increasing renewables such as wind and solar. Transportation was marked by a shift from rails to roads initially, rapid motorization, and, more recently, more balanced development including new investment in railways and expansion of urban mass transit. In urban water supply, institutional reforms including public–private partnerships and corporatization improved governance, reduced water losses, and enhanced services of water utilities to serve rapidly urbanizing populations. Telecommunications and ICT developed rapidly as a source of economic development. Despite getting a late start, Asia quickly leapfrogged in many areas by adopting modern technologies in all infrastructure sectors.

Trade, foreign direct investment, and openness

In the 1950s and 1960s, many Asian economies adopted an import substitution strategy—but with limited success. From the 1960s, the four NIEs promoted exports as a growth strategy. From the 1970s onward, more countries followed similar strategies. By the 1990s, most Asian economies liberalized trade and investment, using FDI as a source of capital and new technology. To promote exports and FDI, many countries piloted special economic zones, provided tax and financial incentives, and launched reforms to improve the overall business environment.

Developing Asia's exports and imports both grew annually at 11% during 1960–2018, and the ratio of trade (exports plus imports) to GDP rose from 20% to 53%. There was also a significant shift in the composition of exports, from mostly raw materials to manufactured goods and from light to heavy industrial products along with high-technology exports. Inward FDI expanded rapidly from the second half of the 1980s, initially to Southeast Asia. Today, the region is one of the world's most popular FDI destinations. Asia is also becoming an important source of outward FDI.

Global and regional trade has entered a new phase since the early 2000s, as tariffs worldwide fell dramatically, free trade agreements proliferated, and the PRC and other countries joined the World Trade Organization (WTO). Outward-oriented trade reforms reinforced the increasing trend of FDI inflows to Asia and boosted the region's trade. Global and regional multinational firms increasingly outsourced production to Asia, integrating the region's economies more deeply into GVCs. More recently, services are increasingly traded as a part of GVCs.

Pursuing macroeconomic stability

Over the past half century, developing Asia had less growth volatility, lower average inflation, and fewer economic crises than other developing regions in the world. From the 1980s, monetary policy tools shifted from direct control over monetary aggregates toward using policy rates and open market operations, as financial markets deepened. Until the demise of the Bretton Woods system in the 1970s, countries controlled capital flows, adopted fixed exchange rate regimes, and conducted independent monetary policies. After the collapse of the Bretton Woods system, developing Asian economies started liberalizing capital markets, but continued to strongly manage exchange rates.

The 1997–1998 AFC served as a wake-up call for Asian policy makers. Financial liberalization, de facto currency pegs, and optimism over the region's continued high growth invited large capital inflows in the early 1990s. When the concern about the economic and financial sustainability emerged, sudden reversals of capital inflows led to currency and banking crises. Currency and maturity mismatches related to external borrowing and inefficient investment it financed were among the root causes of the crisis. Policy makers responded by adopting more flexible exchange rates, giving central banks greater independence, and increasing fiscal prudence. The crisis also underscored the importance of macroprudential measures to help curb excesses—such as foreign currency loan exposures or credit growth. The ASEAN+3 Chiang Mai Initiative emerged as a regional cooperative response to enhance financial resilience.

The reforms that followed the AFC provided a foundation for sustained high growth and cushioned the region from the impact of the 2008–2009 global financial crisis (GFC). The GFC was caused by excess borrowing and risky investment by many systemically important financial institutions in advanced countries. It also reflected widespread failure in financial regulation and supervision. In contrast to the severity of the impact on advanced economies and some other regions of the world, the GFC's damage to developing Asia was relatively moderate.

The GFC provided further impetus for strengthening macroeconomic management and financial regulation in developing Asia. Over the past decade, Asia has used macroprudential policies more extensively than any other region in the world. Regional financial safety nets were further strengthened under the Chiang Mai Initiative Multilateralization and with the establishment of the ASEAN+3 Macroeconomic Research Office in 2011 to provide macroeconomic surveillance.

Poverty reduction and income distribution

Developing Asia's rapid growth has led to a dramatic reduction in extreme poverty. At the $1.90 per day international poverty line, the poverty rate fell from 68% in 1981 to less than 7% in 2015. More than

1.3 billion Asians were lifted out of deprivation, making the region the largest contributor to global poverty reduction. Poverty reduction helped create an environment for maintaining political and social stability—a precondition for sound development—and led to the emergence of a middle-income class that, in turn, enabled domestic consumption-led growth.

Rapid economic growth has been the key driver of Asia's poverty reduction. The development of modern manufacturing and services created large amounts of better-paying jobs to absorb rural surplus labor. Policies that aimed to raise the income-earning capacity of poor and low-income households have also played a critical role. These policies included land reform; the introduction of Green Revolution technologies; education and health programs; and measures to broaden access to finance, infrastructure, and markets.

However, developing Asia's progress in improving income distribution has been mixed. During the 1960s–1980s, most developing Asian economies managed to keep income inequality stable, regardless of the initial level, despite large differences in the pace of economic growth. Many economies in East Asia and Southeast Asia grew rapidly with income inequality stable or declining somewhat—a pattern known as "growth with equity," benefiting from expanding labor-intensive manufacturing exports and inclusive policies. During the same period, income inequality in South Asia was generally stable, despite its slow growth.

Since the 1990s, rapid growth and poverty reduction have been accompanied by rising income inequality in many Asian countries. In developing Asia, technological progress and globalization led to rising wage differentials between skilled and less-skilled workers, even though they increased incomes for both. They also increased capital earnings more than labor income. Further, technological progress and globalization created opportunities for entrepreneurs to gain from the "first mover effect" and brought significant benefits for large landowners in newly favored locations. Widening urban–rural income gaps and increasing regional disparities, along with unequal access to opportunity, also contributed to rising income inequality. In response, many countries have adopted "inclusive growth" as a key goal of development strategies in recent years.

Gender and development

The Asia and Pacific region has made important progress in narrowing gender gaps and reducing inequalities in areas such as education, health, and employment. This is in recognition of gender equality as a means to achieving better development outcomes as well as an intrinsic right and a prerequisite for a just and inclusive society.

Access to education for women and girls has improved considerably. School enrollment rates for girls rose faster than those for boys, leading to gender parity in primary and secondary school enrollment in many countries. In 1960, women received fewer years of schooling in most Asian countries; in 2010, they completed more years in school than men in about half of the countries.

In the area of health, women's life expectancy also improved significantly. In 1960, women in developing Asia lived 1.8 years longer than men on average; by 2018, the gap increased to 3.8 years. There has also been a consistent decline in maternal mortality. In addition, female labor force participation increased substantially over the past half century—although gender gaps persist.

These advances have been driven by several factors. Rapid economic growth increased economic opportunities for women, particularly employment in wide-ranging areas. Government interventions in education and health have been effective. Legal and regulatory reforms, supported by strong policy commitments and complemented by shifts in social norms, have helped create an enabling institutional environment for gender equality in basic rights, voice, and decision-making power within households, firms, and societies.

Environmental sustainability and climate change

Asia's economic success during much of the past half century has come at the expense of the environment—under an approach of "growth first, cleanup later." Growth has been associated with increasing air and water pollution and land degradation. This led to millions of premature deaths each year, ecosystem fragility, and the declining productive potential of land and marine resources. Although the region has historically had per capita greenhouse gas emissions well below the world average, by the early 21st century, its emissions were growing fastest among the world's regions. Asia's ability to sustain economic progress in the future will be increasingly challenged by climate risk and resource depletion.

Facing these challenges, Asian countries have begun to take major steps to protect the environment, mitigate greenhouse gas emissions, and adapt to climate change. Key environmental policies have been adopted across the region in such areas as investment in renewable energy and public transport, framework legislation, safeguard policies, and air and water quality standards. Countries have also made greater use of market-based instruments such as tradable permits and payments for ecosystem services. The region is becoming a leading exporter of green products and services, which help improve environmental performance globally.

Developing Asia has been increasingly engaged in international efforts to solve global environmental challenges, most notably climate change. Such efforts are critically important, as the region can benefit substantially from coordinated approaches to global climate challenges. Nearly all countries in the region are party to the three major conventions and agreements on climate change—the 1992 United Nations Framework Convention on Climate Change, the 1997 Kyoto Protocol, and the 2015 Paris Agreement. ADB and other multilateral development banks (MDBs) are helping countries to achieve their nationally determined contributions under the Paris Agreement, through financing climate mitigation and adaptation and supporting capacity building.

The role of multilateral and bilateral development finance

Bilateral ODA and support from MDBs have made important contributions to the region's development. They contributed to resource mobilization, supported technological cooperation, and promoted knowledge sharing. Traditional bilateral donors, such as the US, Japan, Australia, New Zealand, the ROK, and European countries, have made large contributions. In recent years, the PRC, India, Thailand, and other emerging economies are becoming active donors.

In the early stage of development, developing Asia had to deal with capital shortages due to low domestic savings and high investment needs. Bilateral ODA and MDBs, including ADB and the World Bank, provided finance together with knowledge, initially for infrastructure development, and increasingly for health, education, and other social sectors. To enhance aid effectiveness, Asian countries built absorptive capacity and maintained ownership by aligning external support with national development strategies.

With the rising share of FDI and other sources of external finance, bilateral ODA and MDBs have reoriented their priorities, paying greater attention to policy reform and improved governance of countries. In recent years, development assistance is increasingly focused on supporting the global agenda such as the Sustainable Development Goals and the Paris Agreement on climate change.

Strengthening regional cooperation and integration in Asia

Regional cooperation and integration (RCI) in Asia and the Pacific has evolved during the postwar era. It was initially motivated by the need to secure peace and security after years of war and conflict across the region, and to move beyond former colonial links. The RCI scope has since expanded to promoting intraregional trade and investment and supporting regional public goods.

ASEAN is a successful example of RCI. It has worked toward an "ASEAN Economic Community" through cooperation in trade, investment, and harmonization of standards. It has also collectively promoted sound, market-oriented policies over time, engaging new members. Today, ASEAN plays an important role in providing a platform to draw in countries outside Southeast Asia for regional financial cooperation, wider trade agreements, and dialogue on broad regional and international issues.

In South Asia, the RCI priority is on high-quality connectivity through transport, energy, and trade facilitation. Central Asia is moving from cooperation on infrastructure connectivity to developing regional economic corridors and knowledge sharing in various areas. The Pacific island countries have prioritized trade, maritime and digital connectivity, the management of shared ocean resources, sustainable tourism, and capacity development for private sector investment.

The establishment of ADB in 1966 can be regarded as a prime example of RCI. It reflected the strong will and efforts of people in and outside Asia and the Pacific to work together for the development of the region. To support RCI, on its part, ADB has initiated several subregional programs such as the Greater Mekong Subregion (GMS), the Central Asia Regional Economic Cooperation (CAREC), and the South Asia Subregional Economic Cooperation (SASEC).

1.5 Asia's remaining development agenda

Despite its rapid economic growth and transformation, Asia's development gaps with advanced countries remain large. In 2018, developing Asia's average per capita GDP in US dollars (at market exchange rates) was just 14% of the OECD average. Asian countries need to tackle a wide range of remaining and emerging development challenges.

Make markets work better and strengthen governance and institutions. Asian countries should continue to reform their labor market, finance, and trade and investment regimes, to eliminate market rigidities and distortions. They can further promote development by supporting innovation and R&D, investing in higher education, maintaining an enabling environment for private sector investment, and combating anticompetitive practices. Depending on country needs, state-owned enterprises must continue to reform. Moreover, countries should improve regulatory quality, better control corruption, widen participation, and increase accountability.

Support the transition to higher income. Moving from middle to high income and overcoming the so-called "middle-income trap" require new and different drivers of growth, with a more innovative and knowledge-based economy. Upper-middle-income countries should also address rising income inequalities including gaps between advanced and lagging regions. Low-income countries should continue to focus on improving economic fundamentals, including investing in infrastructure, broadening access to education and health, and improving the investment climate.

Support the continuing agricultural and rural transformation. Countries should continue to promote agricultural productivity growth through the application of new technologies and further implementing land reform and consolidation. They should improve food value chains and agribusiness, while developing and enforcing food safety and nutrition standards. They must address remaining agricultural price distortions and respond to emerging environmental challenges, including climate change.

Invest in technological progress. To continuously adopt new technologies and promote innovation, Asian countries should develop a diverse cadre of educated and skilled labor force. They must invest in and manage the expansion of digital infrastructure, continue to support R&D, and foster links between the research community and business. They should also strengthen institutions that support innovation, including protecting intellectual property rights and promoting fair competition.

Narrow the gap in human capital and respond to demographic change. In education, future challenges include achieving universal access to secondary education, expanding tertiary education, and improving education quality. In health, governments must address the growing prevalence of noncommunicable diseases and expand universal health coverage. To reap the demographic dividend, countries with growing working-age population should ensure adequate investment in human capital and the creation of quality jobs. Countries should support the labor market participation of women through policies targeting the care economy, redistribution of unpaid care work within households, and family-friendly work policies such as provision of childcare facilities and paid parental leaves (e.g., maternity leave). For countries with aging populations, technology can help address the issue of shrinking working-age population and support caring for the aged. The large demographic diversity in Asia means both young- and older-aged countries can benefit from cross-border labor mobility.

Better balance savings and investment and strengthen the financial sector. Some Asian countries need to increase household consumption, while others should increase domestic savings and investment. To mobilize savings for productive investment, Asian countries must continue to diversify their financial systems, deepen capital markets with greater participation of institutional investors, promote financial inclusion, and strengthen financial regulations to mitigate risks. They must embrace financial innovation while maintaining stability. They can also benefit from greater regional financial cooperation.

Address infrastructure gaps. In 2017, over 400 million Asians remained without electricity, 300 million lacked access to safe drinking water, and 1.5 billion lacked access to sanitation facilities. Developing Asia needs more investment in transport, energy, urban water, and ICT. Continued capacity development and institutional reform can boost efficiency and deliver high-quality services. Private sector participation is essential to narrow the infrastructure gap. Also, regional cooperation has an important role to play in improving regional connectivity across Asia.

Maintain open trade and investment regimes. Developing Asia's economic success over the past half century owes much to trade and inward foreign investment. Asian governments should continue to promote open trade and investment by further reducing tariff and nontariff barriers, promote services trade including e-commerce and digital trade, and support small and medium-sized enterprises' access to international markets. They should work toward expanding regional and supra-regional arrangements and renew efforts to support the multilateral trading system.

Maintain macroeconomic stability. Asia has benefited from prudent macroeconomic and financial sector policies. However, policy makers should continue to be vigilant. Policy priorities for maintaining macroeconomic stability include strengthening public finance, making greater use of macroprudential policies, and maintaining exchange rate flexibility. Countries must closely monitor capital flows and, if necessary, manage market sentiment including using measures to smooth foreign exchange volatility caused by external shocks.

Eradicate poverty and reduce inequality. At the higher $3.20 per day poverty line typically used in lower-middle-income countries, 29% of Asians remain poor. To eradicate poverty and reduce inequality, governments must create more quality jobs, increase spending on education, expand universal health coverage, strengthen social safety nets, increase the role of taxes in income redistribution, reduce urban–rural income gaps and regional disparities, and continue governance reforms to promote equal opportunity.

Reduce gender gaps. Gender equality is an unfinished agenda. Policy priorities include continued investment in women's education, especially in science, technology, engineering, and mathematics (STEM), and broadening access to sexual and reproductive health. Governments must continue to invest in the basic infrastructure that meets the needs of women. They should bolster women's labor market participation and nurture female entrepreneurship and corporate leadership. Further legal and regulatory reforms must contribute to eliminating gender gaps in social, economic, and political representation.

Protect the environment and tackle climate change. Environmental degradation and climate change threaten the sustainability of Asian development. Asian countries must scale up efforts to protect the environment and act now for climate change mitigation and adaptation. They must (i) substantially invest in renewable energy, energy efficiency, sustainable public transport, and climate-resilient infrastructure; (ii) attract private sector investment for sustainable infrastructure; (iii) further strengthen framework legislation, safeguard policies, and air and water quality standards; (iv) ensure prices reflect environmental costs and climate change externalities; (v) build environmental governance capacity; and (vi) intensify regional cooperation on environmental issues.

Enhance bilateral and multilateral development partnerships. Developing Asia has benefited from development cooperation with both bilateral and multilateral partners in access to development finance, policy advice, knowledge exchange, and capacity building. Governments should continue to work with development partners and improve the effectiveness of development assistance.

Further strengthen regional cooperation and integration. Building on what has been achieved, greater cooperation is needed in conserving and managing shared natural resources—such as rivers, oceans, and forests, and in agriculture including policies and research. More focus on people is required. Promoting sustainable regional tourism is a priority. Countries should cooperate to amplify Asia's voice on global affairs, commensurate with its increased importance in the global economy. There is no question that governments and people must continue to make the utmost efforts to maintain peace and stability in the Asia and Pacific region.

CHAPTER 2

THE ROLE OF MARKETS,
THE STATE, AND INSTITUTIONS

2.1   Introduction

Development requires efficient markets, an effective state, and strong institutions. Markets, prices, and competition are critical for the efficient allocation of resources and creation of entrepreneurial incentives. The state is needed to establish strong institutions, intervene where markets fail to work efficiently, and promote social equity. Strong institutions ensure orderly functioning markets and state accountability. In practice, the state is usually responsible for regulating markets and maintaining the rule of law, providing education and health care, investing in infrastructure, redistributing income through taxes and social protection, managing the macro-economy, and protecting the environment. In many countries, the state is also involved in coordinating development and supporting industries.

In Asia, the role of markets and the state has evolved significantly over the past 50 years. Japan, recovering from the devastation of World War II, relied on market competition and private enterprises to drive growth, while the government proactively promoted investment, manufacturing exports, and technological innovation. These led to more than 20 years of rapid growth from the early 1950s. Many developing Asian economies adopted import substitution industrialization policies with strong state control for nation-building and development immediately after the war. From the 1960s, however, Hong Kong, China; the Republic of Korea (ROK); Singapore; and Taipei,China followed Japan's model and shifted toward export-promotion and market-friendly policies. They grew into what are now known as the newly industrialized economies (NIEs). In the 1970s, Indonesia, Malaysia, and Thailand opened up to trade and foreign direct investment (FDI). They too became high-performing Asian economies during the following 2–3 decades.

Inspired by these successes, more Asian economies from the late 1970s embarked on far-reaching market-oriented reforms and opened up to the outside world. After 3 decades of central planning that led to serious resource misallocation and widespread shortages, the People's Republic of China (PRC) began in 1978 its transition toward a more market-oriented economy. Over the next 40 years, it achieved remarkable development. In South Asia, after decades of state-led industrialization hampered growth, India also began economic reforms in 1991 to reduce government control, rely more on market forces, and open up trade and FDI. As these reforms progressed, development accelerated. From the early 1990s, Central Asian countries started the transition toward market economies after the collapse of the Soviet Union. And in recent years, many Pacific island countries also embraced market-oriented reforms.

Since the 1980s, there has been a growing recognition in development thinking that the quality of governance and institutions matters. Good governance and institutions make countries more likely to adopt the right policies, and once adopted, implement them more effectively. Strong state capacity—a major aspect of governance and institutions—was often considered a key contributing factor to Asia's postwar economic success. Some associate strong state capacity with the so-called "developmental state."[1] In some countries in the region, it has been argued that weak governance led to conflict, instability, and economic failure. In recent years, efforts intensified across Asia and the Pacific to strengthen government effectiveness, regulatory quality, the rule of law, and control of corruption, and to promote transparency, accountability, and wide citizen participation.

---

[1] World Bank. 1993. *The East Asian Miracle: Economic Growth and Public Policy*. New York: Oxford University Press.

This chapter reviews the evolving role of markets, the state, and institutions in Asian development over the past half century. Section 2.2 provides a conceptual discussion on the role of markets and the state. Section 2.3 examines the evolution of development thinking and policy. Section 2.4 discusses the rising importance of good governance and strong institutions in recent development thinking. Sections 2.5–2.12 look at country experiences of markets, the state, and policy reforms. Section 2.13 highlights future policy priorities.

2.2   The role of markets and the state

The role of markets and the state is one of the most important issues in development policy. There is now a consensus globally and in Asia that markets, prices, and competition should play the dominant role in resource allocation and in driving economic growth. But there are areas where market solutions fail to deliver socially optimal outcomes, and state intervention is needed to address these market failures. The state plays an important role in establishing strong institutions and promoting social equity.

Markets, prices, and competition have existed for several thousand years in human history. The idea they can act as an "invisible hand" to efficiently allocate resources was conceptualized by the British economist Adam Smith in his 1776 work, *An Inquiry into the Nature and Causes of the Wealth of Nations.*[2] Smith theorized that the unobservable market forces driven by profit motives of private actors could ensure optimal resource allocation, leading to the sustained creation of wealth. Since then, this free market doctrine has had a profound influence on economic thinking and policymaking across the world.

But relying on markets for resource allocation does not preclude the important role of the state. Even in ancient times, there were rules and laws introduced by the state to protect private property and support fair market transactions. In the PRC, for example, these can be traced back to the Qin dynasty (221–206 BC).[3] Historically, it was also common for the state to provide public infrastructure such as roads and irrigation. Dujiangyan, a massive water control and

---

[2]   Smith, A. 1776. *An Inquiry into the Nature and Causes of the Wealth of Nations.* London: William Strahan and Thomas Cadell.

[3]   Qian, M. 2013. *Chinese Economic History* [in Chinese]. Beijing: Beijing United Publishing House.

irrigation system built by the government in 256 BC in today's Sichuan Province, still plays an important role.

Modern economic theory highlights several important roles governments can play in a market economy.

The first is to establish institutions that help create markets and support their orderly functioning. This requires a government to introduce laws and regulations that maintain rule and order, protect property rights (including intellectual property), enforce contracts, ensure fair competition, maintain financial stability, and protect consumers. These are all essential institutions in a modern market economy that underpin trade, investment, and innovation. Currencies and central banking are parts of these institutions as well. Reforms that strengthen laws and regulations to foster open trade and investment regimes have been key elements of the region's economic success over the past half century (Chapter 9).

The second relates to what are known as "market failures" and "public goods" in economic theory. Government intervention is needed to address market failures that arise due to "externalities," "imperfect competition," and "information asymmetry," all making market solutions inefficient. Monopolies often arise due to high initial investment costs that deter potential competitors from entering markets. Regulation is needed to ensure they do not engage in unfair pricing and market practices. Banks need government regulation because they know more on their liquidity and solvency condition than their diverse deposit account holders. Externality can be either positive or negative—it exists when private costs or benefits deviate from the costs or benefits to society as a whole. One important example of negative externality is environmental pollution, where the social cost is not borne by polluters. Pollution must be addressed by governments through regulations and taxes (Chapter 13).

One important form of market failure relates to public goods— such as flood control, street lighting, police services, diplomacy, and national defense. Markets cannot provide these services efficiently because they are non-excludable (difficult to charge a fee) and non-rival in consumption (consumption by one person will not reduce consumption by others). Education and public health can be provided for specific consumers and paid for by charging fees—but they are considered "quasi-public goods" because of their large positive externality to the society (Chapters 6 and 8).

The third is to promote industries and support innovation. Governments in both developing and developed countries have used targeted "industrial policies" to support "infant industries" or, more generally, domestic industries, using a range of instruments such as tariffs and subsidies, especially at the early stage of development. Governments have also promoted research and development (R&D), for instance, by providing tax incentives and giving access to preferential credit through government-affiliated financial institutions. In the United States (US), government support to the National Aeronautics and Space Administration (NASA) and defense technology led to the development of new industries and later to commercial applications of new technologies (for example, the internet, the global positioning system, and advanced medicine). Governments can address "coordination problems" among multiple private players. For example, in many Asian countries, governments provide guidance for private investment through long-term plans, public investment, and financial incentives to promote industrial clusters and foster new, strategic sectors (Chapter 5).

The fourth is to maintain macroeconomic stability. In a modern market economy, the government plays an important role in managing business cycles and maintaining macroeconomic stability through monetary and fiscal policies. This idea gained wide acceptance after the Great Depression began in 1929, and underpinned the New Deal policies of the US and similar policies in Europe and Japan during the 1930s. British economist John Maynard Keynes' 1936 *The General Theory of Employment, Interest and Money* provided the theoretical argument for using active fiscal policies to cope with economic downturns when aggregate demand was deficient.[4] Monetarist theory in the 1960s highlighted the importance of stable and rule-based money supply to maintain economic stability and control inflation.

Over time, new theories and ideas of fiscal and monetary policies emerged, sometimes leading to contradicting policy prescriptions. Nevertheless, today there is a broad consensus that governments should use fiscal stimulus and monetary easing in times of economic downturns, and fiscal and monetary tightening in times of overheating. During the 2008–2009 global financial crisis, central banks in many developed countries injected large amounts of liquidity to support banks. After the crisis, they combined quantitative monetary easing

---

[4] Keynes, J. M. 1936. *The General Theory of Employment, Interest and Money*. London: Macmillan.

with countercyclical fiscal measures to support economic recovery. However, there is much less agreement on how to deal with prolonged slow growth with very low inflation in the developed world, a problem in recent years (Chapter 10).

The fifth is to promote equitable income distribution. Free markets do not automatically generate equitable income distribution because of differences in people's inherited wealth and access to opportunity such as land, finance, and education, for example. Excessive inequality in income and asset distribution is both unfair and detrimental to economic development and wealth creation. Government intervention is needed to address poverty and income inequality through taxation and spending on education, health, and social protection (Chapter 11). Promoting gender equality is also an important policy priority (Chapter 12).

Governments in Asia and the Pacific have done all these, although there were wide variations in policy priorities across countries and over time. And there are differences in views among countries and scholars on how proactive government should be.

The view in favor of a proactive government and government intervention has often been contested. One argument from the 1960s that became stronger in the 1980s was about "government failure."[5] The argument was that excessive government intervention can introduce new distortions leading to large deviations from optimal resource allocation. Government failure can arise when production subsidies protect inefficient firms; consumer subsidies (such as for energy and water) encourage inefficient and excessive consumption; price regulations cause shortages or overproduction; and excessive welfare payments lead to moral hazard, abuses, and fiscal imbalances.

Another argument relates to the effectiveness of industrial policy. Targeted industrial policy has often been criticized as it can lead to rent-seeking, unfair competition, and inefficiency over time. However, as discussed, it is widely accepted that industrial policy has a role to play, especially at the early stage of development. Many consider industrial policy useful even in more advanced development stages, especially where there are significant positive spillovers such as innovation, or when coordination is essential, such as in developing new, nontraditional industries. Many also believe that industrial policy will more likely succeed when it is performance-based and promotes

5   Krueger, A. 1990. Government Failures in Development. *Journal of Economic Perspectives*. 4 (3). pp. 9–23.

competition, and if it is implemented transparently with clear policy targets, sunset clauses, and an effective implementation mechanism.[6]

Finally, there is an argument that giving government too much power can potentially create problems of policy biases, "elite capture" (privileged elites abuse rules), and usurpation. This is the rationale for checks and balances, accountability and transparency, control of corruption, and wide citizen participation as key elements of good governance (section 2.4).

2.3 Evolving development thinking and policy on market versus state

In practice, the role of the state in an economy, especially in promoting industrialization and economic development, differs significantly across countries and over time. These variations reflect differences in country history, political system, policy experience, and stage of development. They are also influenced by changes in development thinking and shifts in policy paradigm.

State-led industrialization after World War II

After World War II, state-led industrialization dominated economic policy across the developing world. Many countries gained independence from colonial rule but were mired in widespread poverty. There was a strong desire to accelerate the pace of development and catch up with advanced countries through industrialization—which was also considered a matter of national pride and regaining economic independence from foreign powers. Because industrialization required large-scale investment, it had to be led by the state—as only the state had the power to mobilize the needed resources. Moreover, socialism was gaining wide acceptance across a large part of the developing world given the Soviet system's ostensible success. Socialist countries such as the PRC pursued centrally planned industrialization.

State-led industrialization strategies of the 1950s–1970s, accompanied by "import substitution" trade policies, had intellectual backing. New economic ideas, such as the "big push" (through coordinated large investment),[7] "unbalanced growth" (emphasizing

---

[6]   Rodrik, D. 2004. Industrial Policy for the Twenty-First Century. *KSG Working Paper Series.* No. RWP04-047. Cambridge, MA: Kennedy School of Government, Harvard University.

[7]   Rosenstein-Rodan, P. 1943. Problems of Industrialisation of Eastern and South-Eastern Europe. *Economic Journal.* 53 (210/211). pp. 202–211.

targeted industries and concentrated investment in specific industries),[8] the "dual economy" (considering the transfer of surplus labor from rural subsistence to urban capitalism as a key source of growth),[9] and "stages of growth" (traditional society, precondition for takeoff, the stage of takeoff, drive to maturity, and age of mass consumption),[10] attracted a great deal of attention among both academics and policy makers. A common belief of these ideas was that poor countries, which failed to generate sufficient investment for economic growth and were stuck in a low-level equilibrium trap, needed state interventions such as coordinated investment programs in order to break out of the trap.

State-led industrialization needed state-owned enterprises (SOEs) to implement large investment in key sectors, especially capital-intensive heavy industries. And it was often supported by import substitution. High tariffs would protect domestic infant industries. Also, as industrialization required importing capital goods and developing countries uniformly faced foreign exchange constraints, import substitution was also considered a way to save on foreign exchange.

The import substitution policy was also influenced by the then popular "dependency" or "center–periphery" theory that sees increases in the wealth of advanced nations as coming at the expense of developing countries. According to this theory, rising prices of industrial products relative to primary commodities caused terms of trade to deteriorate for developing countries and were a major cause of their economic problems. These ideas advocated an inward-looking approach to industrial development.[11]

The state's active role in the economy and public ownership of key industries was widely accepted by developed countries as well after World War II, especially in Europe, as many governments already had large-scale control of the economy when the war ended. Furthermore, socialist ideology and concerns over market failure strongly influenced government policy. In the United Kingdom (UK) and France, for example, many industries were nationalized after the war.

---

[8] Hirschman, A. 1958. *The Strategy of Economic Development*. New Haven: Yale University Press.
[9] See Lewis, W. A. 1954. Economic Development with Unlimited Supplies of Labor. *The Manchester School*. 22 (2). pp. 139–191.
[10] See Rostow, W. 1959. The Stages of Economic Growth. *Economic History Review*. 12 (1). pp. 1–16.
[11] Prebisch, R. 1962. The Economic Development of Latin America and Its Principal Problems. *Economic Bulletin for Latin America*. 7 (1). pp. 1–23.

While these ideas and development theories significantly affected economic policy in the developing world for a considerable time, their influence was limited in some Asian economies, including Japan, the NIEs, Malaysia, and Thailand. From early on, these economies moved away from import substitution toward outward-oriented and market-friendly policies.

Shifting to market-led growth since the 1980s

From the late 1970s, economic policy shifted in some developed countries away from strong state intervention toward greater reliance on free markets, and it influenced the policies in developing countries.

One reason was the poor performance of nationalized industries and the observed inefficiencies of the economy more generally in many developed countries. Around that time, there was a rise of "neoliberal" economic philosophy in the West. Rooted in the classical liberalism of the 19th century, neoliberal economic thinking advocated free markets, private enterprise, and minimum government intervention. This ideology was embraced by the Margaret Thatcher government in the UK (1979–1990) and the Ronald Reagan administration in the US (1981–1989). In the UK, many nationalized industries were privatized in the 1980s. In Asia, Japan also privatized several public corporations during the period, including the Japanese National Railways and the Nippon Telegraph and Telephone Corporation, and, more recently, Japan Post (including postal savings).

The neoliberal economic thinking also had a significant impact on economic policy in the developing world, especially in Latin America, which experienced a "lost decade" in the 1980s due to a region-wide debt crisis. The crisis had external causes—including the two oil price shocks in the 1970s—but also had roots in domestic policy. It was believed that excessive state intervention and trade protection made Latin American economies inefficient and uncompetitive.[12] This led to policy discussions that focused on government failure and the belief that it could be worse than market failure. In response to the debt crisis, multilateral financial institutions and bilateral lenders provided financial assistance based on "structural adjustment programs"—that came with policy conditions following neoliberal economic thinking. The policy advice, later known as the

---

[12] Ferguson, R. W. 1999. *Latin America: Lessons Learned from the Last Twenty Years.* Speech given to the Florida International Bankers Association, Inc. Miami. 11 February.

"Washington Consensus," called for growth led by free markets and for liberalization, deregulation, and privatization.

In the 1980s, there was a wave of market-oriented reforms in other parts of the developing world as well as socialist countries. The former Soviet Union and Central and Eastern European countries started economic reforms from the mid-1980s in an attempt to revive their stagnant economies (before the Soviet system collapsed in 1991). In Asia, economic difficulties in the PRC due to the Cultural Revolution, the fiscal crisis in Indonesia at the end of the oil boom in the mid-1980s, and the weak economic performance and balance of payments crises in South Asia triggered a review of policies in many countries. The PRC launched market-oriented reforms in 1978, Viet Nam in 1986, India in 1991, and Central Asian countries in the 1990s after independence. These reforms were also inspired by the impressive economic achievements in Japan, the NIEs, and several Southeast Asian economies.

Over the past 20 years, however, there have been growing criticisms over neoliberal policy and the Washington Consensus.[13] Radical reforms mechanically following the Washington Consensus without due consideration of countries' circumstances did not lead to better economic performance, especially in Latin America and Africa. The "shock therapy" of rapid liberalization and mass privatization plunged the Russian economy into years of deep recession. On the other hand, many believed that the PRC's economic success was the result of gradual reforms combining market forces with state intervention.[14] The 2008–2009 global financial crisis also highlighted the problem of overreliance on unfettered market forces.

The discussion on the role of market and state will continue. This book's position is that the PRC's success is essentially due to market-oriented reforms after 1978. More broadly, the policies pursued in Asia can be explained by standard economic theories and may not be so different from those prescribed by the Washington Consensus. What made the difference was that many Asian countries took a pragmatic approach to implementing these policies.

---

[13] Stiglitz, J. 2016. The State, the Market, and Development. *WIDER Working Paper.* No. 2016/1. Helsinki: United Nations University World Institute for Development Economics Research.

[14] Lin, J. Y. 2012. *New Structural Economics: A Framework for Rethinking Development and Policy.* Washington, DC: World Bank.

2.4   Importance of good governance and strong institutions

Since the 1980s, there has been growing recognition of the importance of good governance for sustained economic growth and wealth creation in development thinking. This followed the growing influence of "new institutional economics" in the 1980s.[15] Empirical observations show that country economic performance depends not only on the nature of policies pursued by government, but also the quality of governance and institutions.[16] The same government interventions can lead to different outcomes depending on the quality of governance and institutions.

It is now widely agreed that governance is about how the government exercises its power in managing a country's economic and social resources. Good governance requires transparency, accountability, and wide citizen participation; rule of law and political stability; and control of corruption. Good governance also requires strong state capacity to design and implement good policies. Asia's development experience thus far suggests that strong state capacity must be supported by competent bureaucracy, and success is also often associated with forward-looking and visionary political leaders.[17] There have been efforts to promote good governance in Asia and worldwide in the past 20–30 years.

Good governance and strong institutions are preconditions for market forces to efficiently allocate resources, for maintaining fairness within society, and for achieving sustained and inclusive growth. Institutions are either formal or informal. Formal institutions refer to constitutions, statutes, and explicit rules and regulations enforced most importantly by the state with its coercive power. Informal institutions, on the other hand, include the unwritten rules such as traditions, norms and codes of behavior, taboos, and other social mechanisms based on and enforced through interpersonal ties and relationships.

Development practitioners have devised various measures to assess the quality of governance and institutions, but they are mostly focused on six dimensions: (i) voice and accountability, (ii) political stability and the absence of violence, (iii) government effectiveness,

---

[15]   North, D. 1990. *Institutions, Institutional Change and Economic Performance.* Cambridge: Cambridge University Press.

[16]   Acemoglu, D., and J. A. Robinson. 2012. *Why Nations Fail: The Origins of Power, Prosperity, and Poverty.* New York: Crown Publishing Group.

[17]   World Bank. 1993. *The East Asian Miracle: Economic Growth and Public Policy.* New York: Oxford University Press.

(iv) regulatory quality, (v) the rule of law, and (vi) control of corruption.[18] A global cross-country study by the Asian Development Bank (ADB) finds a positive association between the quality of governance and pace of economic development.[19] This relationship varies across different dimensions of governance, depends on a country's stage of development, and differs among individual indicators of development (such as the growth rate, poverty reduction, education, and health).

In Asia, the same ADB study found that government effectiveness has the highest correlation with per capita gross domestic product (GDP) (Figure 2.1), followed by regulatory quality. The study also found that government effectiveness and regulatory quality have a much stronger correlation with the pace of economic growth in Asia than other regions of the world.

Figure 2.1: Government Effectiveness Score and Per Capita GDP in 2011, Developing Asia

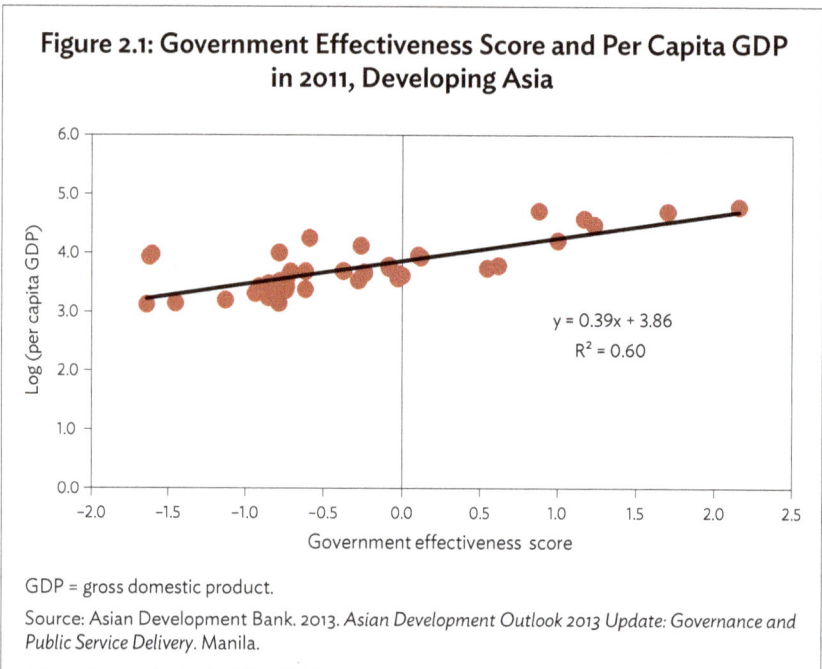

$y = 0.39x + 3.86$
$R^2 = 0.60$

GDP = gross domestic product.
Source: Asian Development Bank. 2013. *Asian Development Outlook 2013 Update: Governance and Public Service Delivery.* Manila.

---

[18] Kaufmann, D., A. Kraay, and M. Mastruzzi. 2007. The Worldwide Governance Indicators: Answering the Critics. *Policy Research Working Paper.* No. 4149. Washington, DC: World Bank.
[19] ADB. 2013. *Asian Development Outlook 2013 Update: Governance and Public Service Delivery.* Manila.

Countries at different stages of development may face different constraints.[20] At the low-income stage, igniting growth is a priority, and government effectiveness (that ensures adequate investment in education and infrastructure) and regulatory quality (that promotes private investment) are important. At a higher income level, the development priority will likely be sustaining growth, and transparency, accountability, and wide citizen participation could become more important.

These findings appear to support the argument that strong state capacity played a critical role in producing Asia's economic "miracle." Visionary political leaders, such as President Park Chung-hee in the ROK, Prime Minister Lee Kuan Yew in Singapore, Prime Minister Mahathir Mohamad in Malaysia, and reformist leader Deng Xiaoping in the PRC, provided long-term visions and guidance for economic and social development. Competent and politically neutral bureaucracies based on meritocracy played an important role in achieving these visions, through development planning, industrial policies, and effective implementation.

Some have argued that the workings of informal institutions also contributed to Asia's postwar economic success.[21] Examples include a diligent work ethic, prioritizing education, and a strong sense of trust and cooperation in society. For instance, according to the World Values Survey, trust among people in Asian countries measured higher on average than the rest of the world.[22] Grameen Bank, a microfinance institution and community-based development organization founded in Bangladesh, is another example of how formal and informal forces can work together to support development.

A related concept is "social capital," which is a subset of informal institutions and focuses on social relationships, networks, and associations that create shared knowledge, mutual trust, social norms, and unwritten rules. Some argue that social capital can bridge

---

[20] Rodrik, D. 2008. Thinking about Governance. In North, D., D. Acemoglu, F. Fukuyama, and D. Rodrik, eds. *Governance, Growth, and Development Decision-Making*. Washington, DC: World Bank.

[21] Berger, P. L., and H. H. M. Hsiao, eds. 1988. *In Search for an East Asian Development Model*. New Brunswick, NJ: Transaction Books.

[22] Zhuang, J., E. de Dios, and A. Lagman-Martin. 2010. Governance and Institutional Quality and the Links with Growth and Inequality: How Asia Fares. In Zhuang, J., ed. *Poverty, Inequality, and Inclusive Growth in Asia*. London: Asian Development Bank / Anthem Press.

gaps created by market and government failures, supporting efficient resource allocation and facilitating growth.[23]

2.5 Japan's postwar economic recovery and growth

Modernization and industrialization during the Meiji period

Japan started modern economic growth shortly after the 1868 Meiji Restoration, which returned the governing power from the Tokugawa Shogunate to the emperor. The country encountered modern Western powers in the 1850s and opened up to the outside world at their request after more than 200 years of isolationist foreign policy. Several treaties were signed, beginning with the US in 1854. Influenced by the Opium War between China and the UK, Japan realized it needed to modernize and strengthen its economic and military power.

Thus, the Meiji period (1868–1912) ended feudal privileges based on class and established key economic and political institutions of modern capitalism following the Western models. These included (i) markets for land, labor, and capital; (ii) a modern tax system, banks, a stock exchange, a central bank, and commercial and company laws; (iii) compulsory primary education (from 1886) and universities (the University of Tokyo was founded in 1877 with departments of medicine, science, law, and literature initially, and engineering, agriculture, and economics added later); and (iv) a political system based on constitutional rule, a parliament (which was established in 1890 and achieved male suffrage in 1925), and a governing cabinet. As Japan initiated its drive toward large-scale industrialization, authorities emphasized the importance of learning from advanced Western countries and promoting trade. Many of Japan's early technological and knowledge achievements came through imported foreign machinery and hired foreign experts, and by sending students abroad.

Since the Meiji modernization, Japan's industrialization—except for the militarist period from the 1930s to the years immediately after World War II—was primarily driven by the private sector, modeled after the UK and the US. In its early years, the government established publicly owned pilot companies to transfer western

---

[23] Hayami, Y. 2008. Social Capital, Human Capital and the Community Mechanism: Toward a Conceptual Framework for Economists. *The Journal of Development Studies*. 45 (10). pp. 96–123.

technology (such as textiles, coal, and steel) that were later privatized. Even important infrastructure services were provided by private firms. For instance, electricity has always been provided by region-based private companies (except from 1939 to 1951). Many railway lines were built by Japanese merchants who had accumulated capital, even from the pre-Meiji period, to transport silk from inland to coastal areas, before being nationalized by the Railway Nationalization Act of 1906. Electric railway networks in urban suburbs were developed from the 1910s to the mid-1930s by many private companies, together with new residential and commercial areas with leisure facilities.

By the early 1900s, Japan had already become a major global industrial power. However, its economic success was interrupted by imperial and expansionist ambitions and subsequently military disaster, with the economy devastated by its defeat in World War II.

Postwar restoration

Immediately after the war, the priority was to restore the economy under state planning and control. The country had to address serious resource constraints including finance and foreign exchange during the recovery from the devastation of the war. This was also in a way a continuation of strong state intervention prevailing immediately before and during the war period. The government controlled prices, introduced rationing, and managed trade and foreign exchange. It implemented a Priority Production Plan, focusing on several key industries (coal, steel, and fertilizers), supported through price controls and subsidies, low-interest loans, and allocation of restricted material imports. Three major economic reforms were introduced: (i) land reform to redistribute land from landowners to tenant farmers at nominal prices, (ii) dissolution of big business (zaibatsu) to break up monopolies and promote market competition, and (iii) labor reform to grant workers the right to organize labor unions.

After the initial reconstruction, Japan saw rapid, sustained economic growth from 1950 to 1973—more than 8% annual growth in per capita GDP—known as the postwar economic miracle. During this period, government direct control over the economy was gradually relaxed or removed, partly under pressure from the allied occupation authorities, and markets increasingly determined resource allocation. Japan did not have a large SOE sector before the war, and those that did exist were dissolved or privatized after the war. There were no SOEs in manufacturing.

While growth was driven by private firms and market forces, the government played an important role in proactively promoting investment, manufacturing exports, and technological innovation, especially during the early years of the postwar period. It designed medium-term economic plans at the macro level beginning in 1955 and implemented targeted industrial policy at the micro level. The macro plans set targets for growth and various sector, social, and economic indicators, but the targets were more indicative than directive. The 1960 Income Doubling Plan aimed to double Japan's per capita income in 10 years—the target was achieved in 7 years.[24]

Evolution of targeted industrial policy

The focus and tools of Japan's targeted industrial policy evolved over time. It began with direct controls and price subsidies to implement its Priority Production Plan immediately after the war. In 1949, the government established the Ministry of International Trade and Industry (MITI) to implement industrial policy, succeeding the Ministry of Commerce and Industry. In the 1950s and 1960s, the policy focus shifted to industrial "rationalization" (for instance, by supporting firms to exit from coal mining) and "support for advanced knowledge and technologies." Over time, Japan's targeted industrial policy priorities shifted from raw materials and light industries to heavy and chemical industries and to high-technology products. Japan was thus able to constantly upgrade its manufacturing capability and move up value chains.

In the 1950s–1960s, the targeted industrial policy tools were mainly (i) the preferential allocation of scarce foreign exchange to priority industries and firms; (ii) high import tariffs and quotas, and regulating FDI to protect infant industries; (iii) preferential credit, largely channeled through public financial institutions such as the Development Bank of Japan and Export–Import Bank of Japan; and (iv) tax incentives (e.g., accelerated depreciation) for investment. There were well-defined eligibility criteria. MITI also used a system of consultative arrangements—"deliberation councils" comprising sector leaders, company executives, academia, and civil society—and "Administrative Guidance" to share information and reconcile diverse interests over policies.

---

[24] Ito, T. 1996. *The Japanese Economy*. Cambridge, MA and London: The MIT Press.

In the 1960s, Japan increasingly integrated its economy globally. It liberalized trade and foreign investment, while preferred foreign exchange allocation, import quotas, high tariffs, and FDI regulations were gradually phased out. Japan joined the Organisation for Economic Co-operation and Development (OECD) and became an Article 8 member of the International Monetary Fund (IMF) in 1964. The liberalization of trade, inward FDI, and foreign exchange was part of its obligations as member of these international organizations. It was also influenced by the pressure from trading partners.

By 1973, Japan's per capita GDP (in 2010 US dollars) reached $22,138, surpassing that of the UK and approaching nearly 90% that of the US—from about 50% in 1960. It reemerged as a major industrial power globally. Industry's share of GDP was 43% and services 52%. It began leading world manufacturing production and led exports in many sectors, particularly consumer electronics, automobiles, shipbuilding, machine tools and equipment, and semiconductors.

How to explain Japan's postwar economic miracle

Numerous studies ask what explains Japan's postwar economic miracle. It is likely a variety of factors were at play. Some were external, such as US financial assistance, which provided needed capital during the initial stage of recovery, and the Korean War, which created external demand for Japan's industries in the early 1950s. The prewar legacy of industry and technology—including shipbuilding, airplanes, and precision machinery for the military—was also important. While much of its industrial capacity was damaged or destroyed, Japan already had the basic human capital needed for restoring and expanding industries after 1945. Other important aspects of Japan's prewar legacy were the solid institutions of a modern market economy.

Japan also benefited from favorable demographic change. In the 1950s and 1960s, the growth of Japan's working-age population exceeded total population growth—generating a demographic dividend of nearly 1 percentage point annually, on average, in per capita GDP growth (Chapter 6). The rising share of the working-age population also contributed to a large increase in the savings rate, along with other factors such as rapid economic growth and government policy that encouraged savings—such as the Postal Savings Program. Japan's gross domestic savings rate increased from about 24% of GDP in 1955 to 42% in 1970. This provided needed financing for high domestic investment, which rose from 24% of GDP to 41% during the same period. High investment led to rapid capital accumulation, industrial upgrading, and labor productivity growth.

While Japan's postwar growth was largely driven by the private sector, the government also played important roles.

First, major reforms introduced immediately after the war—including land reform, labor reform, and the breakup of big business; broad access to education; job creation supported by rapid growth in manufacturing; and job security (life employment)—significantly improved wealth and income distribution, widely sharing the benefits of growth. This helped maintain social stability, foster vigorous consumption, and sustain the economic expansion. Indeed, from the 1950s to the 1970s, Japan's rapid growth was accompanied by equity in income distribution, as shown by the Gini coefficient of per capita disposable income (Chapter 11).

Second, large public investment in infrastructure and education enabled growth to accelerate without hitting bottlenecks. During 1960–1980, Japan's paved roads increased from 23,800 to 511,000 kilometers. From 1960 to 1970, annual electricity generating capacity increased from 23.7 million to 68.3 million kilowatts. After the war, compulsory education was extended from 6 to 9 years. During 1950–1970, Japan's mean years of schooling of its working-age population increased from 7.6 to 9.8.[25] It also introduced universal health coverage in 1961. These contributed to improving the country's overall human capital.

Third, the government's targeted industrial policy succeeded in promoting industry—although not in every targeted industry. In the beginning, the country resorted to targeted industrial policy in order to address serious resource constraints. Over time, the policy has moved to outward-oriented instead of import substitution, and has relied on market competition and private enterprises to drive growth, while the government took some proactive roles. Various support for manufacturing exports enabled Japanese firms to compete in international markets and benefit from economies of scale. In the early stage, Japan restricted car imports and inward FDI in the automobile industry, but it promoted competition among domestic firms. When more developed, car markets were opened to foreign competition.

---

[25] Godo, Y. 2011. Estimation of Average Years of Schooling for Japan, Korea and the United States. *PRIMCED Discussion Paper Series*. No. 9. Tokyo: Hitotsubashi University.

After 1973, Japan's pace of growth slowed due to several factors, including the 1973–1974 and 1979 oil shocks, and convergence forces as Japan reemerged as a major industrialized nation. Nevertheless, it continued to grow substantially faster than other industrialized countries during the 1970s and 1980s. From the 1990s onward, after the burst of the asset bubble and population aging turned the demographic dividend into a tax, Japan's growth slowed further. As the economy matured, the role of industrial policy shifted toward promotion of collaborative research in high-tech industries such as semiconductors, computers, biotechnology, and robotics. Since the late 1990s, Japan initiated a series of structural reforms, including deregulation in services, to stimulate growth and respond to the aging population.

Japan's postwar economic miracle inspired many other countries as they pursued industrialization and modernization. Japan offered both a workable growth model and technology transfer and FDI. In the early 1960s, scholars used the so-called "flying geese" model[26] to describe Asia's sequential postwar development process (Chapter 9). According to this model, economies in earlier development stages align behind industrial nations, such as Japan in Asia, in a "wild geese formation." Economies behind the leaders are engaged in low-wage production, but as costs rise, they, in turn, pass on this type of production to countries further behind. Today, Asia's economic landscape has changed significantly, with more leaders in different sectors. Asian economies are now linked more as a network than as a wild geese formation.

2.6 Industrialization of Hong Kong, China; the Republic of Korea; Singapore; and Taipei,China

The four NIEs were among the low-income economies in the world in 1960, with per capita GDP (in 1960 US dollars) ranging from $160 for the ROK and Taipei,China (5% of the US) to around $430 for Hong Kong, China and Singapore (14% of the US). Over the subsequent 3 decades, the per capita GDP of the NIEs, as a group, grew by an average 7.2% per year. The NIEs are now all high-income economies, with 2018 per capita GDP (in 2018 US dollars) ranging from $25,000 for Taipei,China to $64,600 for Singapore (US per capita GDP was $62,600). The NIEs' remarkable success in stimulating growth, accelerating structural

---

[26] Akamatsu, K. 1962. A Historical Pattern of Economic Growth in Developing Countries. *The Developing Economies.* 1 (August). pp. 3–25.

transformation, and building strong technological innovation capabilities has inspired many countries. They have become a model for the developing world.

With the exception of Hong Kong, China, which was a British colony until 1997 and maintained a free market economy, the NIEs largely followed Japan's postwar economic model, with growth driven by market forces and a proactive government promoting manufacturing exports. While there were similarities, there were also differences among the NIEs.

Their initial conditions were quite similar in many respects. They all experienced years of war and conflict before their economic takeoff. Taipei,China was under the rule of the Kuomintang government after 1945; the ROK gained independence in 1948 and battled the north from 1950 to 1953; Singapore separated from Malaysia in 1965; and Hong Kong, China was under British rule until 1997. Like other developing economies at the time, they had limited modern industry and lacked capital, skills, and other resources. In 1960, agricultural employment accounted for 66% in the ROK and 56% in Taipei,China. Manufacturing employment was higher in the two city economies of Hong Kong, China (35%) and Singapore (22%).[27] From the 1950s, all had begun industrializing.

The ROK; Singapore; and Taipei,China all began with import substitution in the 1950s. But they moved quickly to adopt export-promotion strategies in the 1960s. The NIEs' industrialization began by promoting labor-intensive light industries such as textiles and footwear. As income and labor costs rose, they gradually moved to more capital-, skill-, and technology-intensive industries.

For example, the ROK invested significantly in heavy and chemical industries in the 1970s, under the strong leadership of President Park Chung-hee (1963–1979); from the late 1980s–1990s, its focus shifted to information and communication technology. Singapore, under Prime Minister Lee Kuan Yew (1959–1990), promoted petrochemicals and pharmaceuticals along with finance and regional headquarters services in the 1980s and 1990s. Taipei,China also began to develop high-tech industries in the late 1980s–1990s, such as semiconductors and high precision machinery.

---

[27] Chowdhury, A., and I. Islam. 1993. *The Newly Industrializing Economies of East Asia.* London: Routledge.

To promote exports, the NIEs used a variety of instruments: export targeting; export credit, preferential foreign exchange allocations, and duty-free imports for exporters; tax incentives; low-interest loans; and export processing zones (EPZs). Support was often linked with export performance to create competition and strengthen incentives. They also established mechanisms such as "councils" to enhance communications between businesses and government and to help address coordination issues. In the ROK, for example, the council held monthly export-promotion meetings in the 1960s and 1970s—often presided by the President and joined by top bureaucrats and business leaders. Over time, export promotion became more nondiscriminatory, for example, through investments in R&D.

Apart from providing export incentives, the ROK and Taipei,China also used import tariffs and nontariff barriers to protect domestic infant industries at the initial stage of economic takeoff. However, compared with other developing economies, their level of protection was lower and, from the 1970s, they began liberalizing trade by reducing tariffs and nontariff barriers.[28] Hong Kong, China and Singapore adopted much freer trade policies early on. Import liberalization gave the NIEs access to essential intermediate inputs for producing final goods for export.

The NIEs also benefited significantly from foreign ideas and technology. They acquired these in a variety of ways, such as importing capital goods, promoting exports, purchasing licenses, and attracting FDI (through providing incentives, reducing restrictions, or both). From the mid-1980s, after the yen appreciated following the Plaza Accord, large amounts of Japanese FDI went to the NIEs, starting the process of creating a regional production network.

The NIEs did differ on FDI policy. Early on, the ROK emphasized national technological capacity in domestic firms and restricted inward FDI, so inward FDI was relatively small. In 1965–1984, for example, FDI accounted for only 2% of its domestic capital formation.[29] By contrast, Singapore offered incentives to attract FDI, especially by multinationals. In 1965–1984, inward FDI accounted for 10% of domestic capital formation. Singapore is considered a success story of FDI-led industrialization. Hong Kong, China also adopted

---

[28] World Bank. 1993. *The East Asian Miracle: Economic Growth and Public Policy.* New York: Oxford University Press.

[29] World Bank. 1993. *The East Asian Miracle: Economic Growth and Public Policy.* New York: Oxford University Press.

an open FDI policy, although it did not provide many incentives. In Singapore and Hong Kong, China, a large proportion of exports were produced by foreign-invested firms. Taipei,China also welcomed FDI, for example, by creating EPZs, but these had certain conditions such as local content requirements and export performance.

The NIEs were all market economies with the private sector playing a major role in driving growth. However, compared with Japan, SOEs were also important in the NIEs—with the exception of Hong Kong, China, which was close to being a laissez-faire free market economy. In the ROK, growth was mainly driven by private firms, some of which later developed into chaebols—family-based business conglomerates. But the government also established many SOEs to support its economic takeoff from the 1960s. One example was state-owned Pohang Iron and Steel Company (POSCO), which later grew into one of the world's top steel manufacturers. From the 1980s, the government started a privatization program. In 1985, SOEs accounted for only 2.7% of the ROK's total nonagriculture employment.[30] POSCO was privatized in the early 1990s.

Compared with the ROK, the SOE sector was much larger in Taipei,China. In addition to public utilities, SOEs were involved with manufacturing such as petroleum refining, petrochemicals, steel, shipbuilding, heavy machinery, transport equipment, and fertilizer; and they were usually large. While SOEs were important, the private sector, comprising numerous small and medium-sized firms, was critical in driving growth. In the 1960s and 1970s, SOEs accounted for 13%–14% of GDP and 28%–35% of gross fixed capital formation.[31] In the late 1980s, the government began a privatization program. By the early 2000s, SOE importance had declined, accounting for 11% of gross domestic capital formation.

In Singapore, the government established many government-linked corporations (GLCs) after independence to lead in establishing new industries and attract private investment. GLCs covered seaports, shipbuilding, airports, airlines, shipping, steel, banking, housing, and other manufacturing. In 1974, GLCs were estimated to account for 14%–16% of manufacturing output. The government established Temasek Holdings Private Limited in 1974 to hold and manage GLC

[30] Savada, A. M., and W. Shaw, eds. 1990. *South Korea: A Country Study*. Washington, DC: GPO for the Library of Congress.
[31] Wade, R. 1990. *Governing the Market: Economic Theory and the Role of Government in East Asian Industrialization*. Princeton: Princeton University Press.

investment and assets owned by the government to ensure they would be run commercially. As a shareholder on behalf of the government, Temasek's policy was not to direct business operations of the companies in its portfolio. Instead, it left business decisions to their respective boards and management. During 2008–2013, GLCs, with the government as the controlling shareholder, accounted for 37% of Singapore's stock market capitalization.[32]

The NIEs' policy of outward-orientation and combining market forces with proactive government support succeeded in promoting exports and technological advancement. In 1970–1985, annual manufacturing export growth was 28% in the ROK; 24% in Singapore; 26.4% in Taipei,China; and 15% in Hong Kong, China.[33] Similar to Japan, rapidly rising exports enabled firms to benefit from economies of scale and compete globally. Exports also brought in much-needed foreign exchange that was used to import foreign technology and raw materials. Over time, the NIEs' exports became more diversified and technologically sophisticated. During 1965–1994, the share of electrical machinery in total non-oil exports increased from just 0.3% to 20.8% in the ROK; from 1.4% to 15.1% in Taipei,China; from 1.8% to 23.4% in Singapore; and from 3.1% to 13.1% in Hong Kong, China. Outward-oriented trade and industrial policies allowed these economies to become an integral part of global value chains in manufacturing.

The NIEs also benefited from large investments in infrastructure and human capital. Fiscal prudence put them in a strong position for governments to invest in education, transport and power, and water and sanitation, while maintaining fiscal sustainability and macroeconomic stability. From 1960 to 2000, mean years of schooling of the working-age population increased from 4–5 to 10–12. They also benefited from high domestic savings and demographic dividends. In the ROK, the gross domestic savings rate increased from 9% in the 1960s to 38% in the 1990s. In Singapore, the savings rate increased from 10% to 49% over the same period. In the ROK, the rising share of the working-age population generated a demographic dividend equivalent to 1.4 percentage points in annual per capita GDP growth during the 1970s–1990s (Chapter 6).

[32] Tan, C., W. Puchniak, and U. Varottil. 2015. State-Owned Enterprises in Singapore: Historical Insights into a Potential Model for Reform. *NUS Law Working Paper*. No. 2015/003. Singapore: National University of Singapore.

[33] Chowdhury, A., and I. Islam. 1993. *The Newly Industrializing Economies of East Asia*. London: Routledge. p. 17.

Also, compared with many other economies in Asia, the NIEs had strong state capacity for designing and implementing development policies. Their technical bureaucrats were more insulated than many other Asian economies from political pressures and changes in the government. This allowed them to pursue more consistent policies for promoting economic growth. They also benefited from forward-looking political leaders with a clear vision of their economic future, and were enthusiastic about learning from advanced economies and absorbing advanced technologies.

2.7 Economic liberalization and openness in Southeast Asia

Most countries in Southeast Asia were under colonial rule before World War II. After the war, one by one, they gained independence. Over the following 20–30 years, the region was buffeted by instability. Cambodia, the Lao People's Democratic Republic (Lao PDR), and Viet Nam suffered from prolonged wars. There were conflicts between countries as well. In some countries, there were fears over the perceived threat from the growing influence of communism, leading to domestic conflicts, such as in Indonesia. In others, domestic power struggles led to military coups, such as in Thailand, or the imposition of martial law, such as in the Philippines.

To promote peace and security in the region, Indonesia, Malaysia, the Philippines, Singapore, and Thailand took a historical step in 1967 to establish the Association of Southeast Asian Nations (ASEAN). As conflicts subsided and wars ended, more countries joined ASEAN: Brunei Darussalam in 1984; and Viet Nam, the Lao PDR, Cambodia, and Myanmar in the 1990s. Over time, ASEAN was transformed from primarily a security arrangement to a regional grouping to foster economic cooperation and market-oriented policy reforms (Chapter 15).

When Southeast Asian countries gained independence, their economies were dominated by subsistence agriculture and primary commodity exports. Governments were proactive in pursuing development. Like the NIEs, development policies were initially dominated by an import substitution industrialization strategy with state control to various degrees. But it failed to deliver good economic outcomes. The decline in commodity prices in the 1980s after the 1970s boom created macroeconomic difficulties, prompting many governments to shift toward export orientation, economic liberalization, promotion of inward FDI—from Japan;

the ROK; Taipei,China; and elsewhere, along with market-led growth. Governments were also influenced by policy advice from developed countries and multilateral financial institutions such as ADB, the IMF, and the World Bank at the time market-oriented policies were gaining acceptance. While this broad pattern applies to most Southeast Asian countries, there were differences among them.

Indonesia, Malaysia, the Philippines, Thailand, and Brunei Darussalam

In Indonesia, in the first 2 decades after independence was declared in 1945, development policy was inward-looking and involved heavy state intervention. A licensing system was used to control imports and investment. Newly established SOEs took over large portions of the economy. Economic mismanagement and political instability led to economic deterioration and brought down the Sukarno government in 1967.

From 1968, the new Suharto government took a more favorable view of domestic and foreign private investment as a part of his New Order policies. The Ministry of National Development Planning (BAPPENAS) played an important role in designing and planning policies—while its role evolved as the country's policy shifted from state control toward greater market orientation. The government introduced a Foreign Investment Law providing a 30-year guarantee of non-nationalization and abolished import licensing.

From 1974 to 1981, Indonesia benefited from the oil and commodity boom, enabling the government to invest heavily in capital- and resource-intensive industries, and in infrastructure, education, and health. Annual per capita GDP growth accelerated from less than 1.0% in the 1960s to 4.5% in the 1970s. As the state's role in the economy grew with the increased revenue from commodities, the government changed its policy and gradually tightened regulations on foreign and domestic private investment. It also tightened control over imports to protect domestic industry.

In the first half of the 1980s, the end of the oil and commodity boom led to macroeconomic imbalances and problems for SOEs. The government responded with a combination of fiscal, monetary, and exchange rate policy adjustments, including an early attempt at SOE reform. In 1986, the government launched a program of broad trade and regulatory reforms, signaling a major policy shift to promote exports. A package of financial incentives, currency devaluation, and reforms of export and import procedures was introduced to promote non-oil exports. Major exporters were given unrestricted, duty-free access to imports. Domestic and foreign private investment and the financial sector were also deregulated. Following these reforms, growth in manufacturing production, exports, investments, and GDP all accelerated. In 1986–1990, Indonesia's per capita GDP grew 4.3% annually, compared with 3.2% in 1980–1985. To further boost investment and liberalize trade, the second wave of policy adjustments was implemented in the early 1990s.

In Malaysia, the first decade after independence in 1957 saw the government largely continuing colonial-era open-door and market-oriented policies on trade and industry. The government also attempted to redress ethnic and regional economic disparities through rural development as well as social and physical infrastructure. To reduce rural poverty, the government established the Federal Land Development Authority in 1956 to facilitate and implement settlements of rubber and palm oil smallholders. During this period, while some import-competing industries were protected, the government did not target individual sectors and protection was lower than in many other developing countries. Inward FDI was welcomed—although its impact on the economy was limited.

In 1971, the government adopted its New Economic Policy (NEP) following racial riots in 1969. The NEP contained many elements intended to promote the economic participation of *bumiputeras*, mainly ethnic Malays. While commodities (such as rubber, timber, palm oil, and petroleum) continued to account for the majority of the country's exports throughout the 1970s, the government began more actively promoting labor-intensive manufacturing exports such as textiles, footwear, garments, and electronics. This came after it recognized the limitation of import substitution given the country's small domestic market. Incentives offered to export-oriented ventures included tax concessions and low-interest rate credit. The government also established special economic zones (SEZs) to attract foreign investors (from Japan and elsewhere) to assemble or process duty-free imported materials for export. By 1980, an estimated 70% of manufacturing exports originated from SEZs, mostly from foreign-owned firms.[34] In the 1970s, per capita GDP grew 5%–6% annually, compared with 3.5% in the 1960s.

---

[34] World Bank. 1993. *The East Asian Miracle: Economic Growth and Public Policy.* New York: Oxford University Press. p. 135.

In the early 1980s, the government started a heavy industrialization program using earnings from resource exports. The objective was to develop industries such as steel, cement, automobiles, and chemicals through public investment, import protection, and other incentives for domestic firms with "pioneer" status. However, the attempt was short-lived. From the mid-1980s, the decline in commodity prices and fiscal imbalances prompted the government to shift away from state-led industrialization. Under Prime Minister Mahathir Mohamad, the country promoted exports, liberalized trade and FDI, and developed the private sector. Private investment was encouraged across a broad range of manufacturing exports. The government also divested many SOEs. Malaysia's manufacturing exports, as a share of total merchandise exports, increased from 20% during 1975–1985 to 54% during 1985–1995. Inward FDI as a share of gross domestic capital formation increased from 10.8% in 1981–1985 to 14.7% in 1986–1991.[35] By the 1990s, Malaysia had become the world's leading exporter of semiconductor chips.

Like its neighbors in Southeast Asia, the Philippines' development policy also shifted from import substitution to trade liberalization and export promotion over time. However, its shift took much longer than many of its ASEAN neighbors. After gaining independence in 1946, the government pursued industrialization. In 1949, it introduced import and foreign exchange controls in response to a balance of payments crisis. They evolved into an import substitution policy aimed at building a national industrial base. Some priority industries were identified but oriented toward supplying the domestic market instead of exports. The policy, however, did not succeed in promoting either manufacturing or economic growth. Per capita GDP grew at just 1.8% annually in the 1960s, compared with 4.6% in Thailand and 3.5% in Malaysia. The policy also made the Philippines vulnerable to external shocks and balance of payments crises.

From 1972 to 1981, President Ferdinand Marcos placed the Philippines under martial law with the stated reason of tackling communism and Muslim insurgencies. Growth was higher but driven in large part by debt, particularly foreign currency borrowing. The introduction of export incentives in the early 1970s after a balance of payments crisis provided some relief to export-oriented activities,

---

[35] Jomo, K. S., ed. 2001. *Southeast Asia's Industrialization: Industrial Policy, Capabilities, and Sustainability*. New York: Palgrave.

but its overall impact on trade was limited due to the widespread use of quantitative restrictions.[36] An overvalued Philippine peso, a raft of large-scale government projects, and persistent twin (current account and fiscal) deficits led to ballooning debt, placing the economy under severe stress. In 1983, the country fell into political and economic crises in the aftermath of the assassination of opposition leader and former Senator Benigno Aquino. The gradually escalating crisis brought down the Marcos government in 1986 after the "People Power" revolt.

Successive Philippine governments since 1986 have introduced various reforms to restore economic stability, stimulate growth, and reduce poverty. But episodes of political instability continued, making growth volatile until the early 2000s. The economy contracted in the mid-1980s. Per capita income grew a mere 0.55% annually in the 1990s and only recovered to its 1982 peak in 2004. Philippine per capita income was among the highest in developing Asia in the early 1960s. But unlike its neighbors, it was unable to develop a robust manufacturing sector, benefit from manufacturing exports, and attract FDI. Steady growth returned after 2000 as political stability was restored and governments introduced more reforms to improve fiscal conditions and macroeconomic management, strengthen financial regulation, liberalize trade, promote exports, attract FDI, address infrastructure bottlenecks, and tackle governance issues.

Thailand was the only country not colonized in Southeast Asia. Historically, the Thai economy was relatively open and market-oriented, with growth largely driven by the private sector. However, throughout the 1960s and 1970s, the government also adopted an import substitution industrialization strategy. In the 1970s, import protection increased, particularly favoring textiles, pharmaceuticals, and automobile assembly. The oil shocks of the 1970s exposed weaknesses in the economy, and as a result, the industrialization strategy from the 1980s shifted away from import substitution toward export orientation. The government reduced export taxes, devalued the Thai baht, and reduced tariffs. The Board of Investment (BOI), established in 1960 with the mandate of attracting FDI, was given a new role of promoting exports, especially labor-intensive manufacturing goods, by using export incentives, promoting trading companies, and establishing EPZs. From the second half of the 1980s, Thailand introduced broader-based import liberalization.

---

[36] Hill, H. 2013. The Political Economy of Policy Reform: Insights from Southeast Asia. *Asian Development Review*. 30 (1). pp. 108–130.

The BOI's special promotion privileges made the country attractive to foreign investors. Most FDI in the 1960s and 1970s was concentrated in production for the protected domestic market. With the policy shift toward promoting exports, those produced by foreign-invested firms increased over time. In 1983, the government revised the criteria on foreign ownership of businesses to allow majority foreign ownership of firms in EPZs. This contributed significantly to Thailand's boom in FDI and manufacturing exports— including assembled cars—in the 1980s and early 1990s. Between 1980 and 1988, Thailand's inward FDI increased by more than five times. In the early 1990s, more than half of Thailand's exports were manufactures, including electrical appliances, machinery, transport parts and assembled cars, and chemicals. Most of these exports were produced by foreign investors, mostly Japanese, or joint ventures.

By the late 1980s and early 1990s, the major economies in Southeast Asia had substantially liberalized trade. Rising imports, with de facto pegged exchange rates, led to large current account deficits, especially in Thailand and Indonesia. At the same time, 2 decades of robust growth and an increasingly market-friendly business climate made these economies attractive destinations for foreign investors—including short-term portfolio investors. The Philippines was an exception, as it just emerged from economic and political crises and continued to suffer lingering political instability. To attract more foreign investment, these countries quickened financial market and capital account liberalization, partly influenced by the prevalent policy thinking at the time, including that of international financial institutions such as the IMF. Capital inflows surged, but due to weak financial regulation and poor risk management, a large part of the inflows were short-term bank loans denominated in foreign currencies, with much of these going to long-term investments in non-tradable sectors such as real estate. This led to currency and maturity mismatches.

With vulnerability building, investor speculation and the ensuing panic triggered sudden capital flow reversals, causing the collapse of de facto fixed exchange rate systems across the region. The currency crisis began in Thailand in July 1997 and spread to Malaysia, the Philippines, and Indonesia, and later to the ROK. It quickly developed into domestic banking crises. The "twin crises" plunged these countries into deep recession in 1998. Thailand, Indonesia, and the ROK requested emergency balance of payments support from the IMF, together with large-scale borrowing from the World Bank, ADB, and bilateral partners (Chapter 10).

After the 1997–1998 Asian financial crisis, economic recovery in affected countries was swift. Governments launched major reforms to strengthen financial and banking regulations, reform corporate governance, and improve macroeconomic management, along with corporate and financial restructuring. Central banks were given greater independence. Public debt management was strengthened. Exchange rates became more flexible. Measures were introduced to monitor capital flows more closely. They also continued to deepen market-oriented structural reforms. As a result, these countries weathered the 2008–2009 global financial crisis well.

Brunei Darussalam is one of the two high-income countries in Southeast Asia. It gained independence from British rule in 1984 and joined ASEAN the same year. Based on its rich oil and natural gas resources, it has a small, yet wealthy, economy and has maintained high living standards, with per capita GDP at $31,628 (in current US dollars) in 2018. For many decades, Brunei Darussalam has been a major producer and exporter of oil and natural gas in the region. It will continue to be an important player in the oil industry in the near future. For many years, the primary goal of the government has been to diversify the economy away from hydrocarbon production and encourage private sector investment and employment. This remains a key challenge.

Cambodia, the Lao People's Democratic Republic, Myanmar, and Viet Nam

Cambodia, the Lao PDR, Myanmar, and Viet Nam (CLMV) were latecomers to developing Asia's rapid economic takeoff because of the many years of wars, conflicts, political instability, and economic mismanagement. Since the mid-1980s, one after another they have started the transition from central planning to market economies and from inward-looking to outward-oriented development strategies, all at differing speeds.

Viet Nam was the first to embark on market-oriented economic transition among the CLMV. Before the end of the Vietnam War and unification in 1975, Viet Nam was divided—a North under socialist central planning and a South under a market system. The first decade after unification saw the government extend central planning across the entire country. But in December 1986, the Sixth National Congress of the Communist Party of Viet Nam decided to adopt a socialist-oriented market economy.

The change in direction was triggered by three factors: the failure of agricultural collectivization following reunification; the looming cessation of Soviet aid, which was equivalent to about 10% of GDP at that time; and the evident success of the PRC's 1978 reforms, against which Viet Nam traditionally benchmarked itself.

Known as *Doi Moi*, the market-oriented reforms were sweeping and comprehensive. Prices were liberalized. Farmers were allowed to own land and sell crops on the open market. The government initially granted increased decision-making authority to SOEs, and later privatized many of them. It allowed private firms to be established and grow. It also opened up trade by replacing import licensing with tariffs, attracted FDI by lowering the cost of doing business and establishing SEZs, and promoted manufacturing exports.

Viet Nam joined ASEAN in 1995, the Asia-Pacific Economic Cooperation (APEC) group in 1998, the World Trade Organization (WTO) in 2007, and the Comprehensive and Progressive Agreement for Trans-Pacific Partnership (CPTPP) in 2018. Along the way, it signed the US–Viet Nam Bilateral Trade Agreement in 2001, which normalized relations with its former adversary and facilitated access to US markets. The government also invested heavily in infrastructure and human capital.

Viet Nam's market-oriented reform transformed the country from one of the poorest in the world into a middle-income economy and one of the most dynamic emerging markets in Asia. It has become a hub for FDI in Southeast Asia, with many multinational companies setting up ventures. Its manufacturing exports as a share of GDP increased from 16.2% in 1997–1999 to 58.2% in the 2010s. In 2017, Viet Nam was the largest exporter of clothing and the second-largest exporter of electronics (after Singapore) in Southeast Asia. Viet Nam's economic reform has continued. Its Five-Year Socio-Economic Development Plan of 2016–2020 emphasized the importance of continued efforts to reform SOEs, develop the private sector, improve the investment climate, and deepen integration with the global economy.

The Lao PDR introduced central planning after the civil war (which was affected by the Vietnam War) ended in 1975. It introduced agricultural collectivization in the countryside and nationalization of industry and commerce in towns and cities. From 1986, it began pro-market reforms by launching a "new economic mechanism," to introduce market incentives, abandon rural collectivization in favor of family-based farming, reform SOEs, develop the private sector, and open up the economy to trade and foreign investment.

Cambodia suffered the most tragic conflicts for many years, finally ending in 1979. International support strengthened over time, marked by the signing of the Paris Peace Agreements in 1991. Since then, Cambodia has also pursued market-oriented reforms. The country has become a major exporter of garments, supported by accession to the WTO in 2004 and the Multifibre Arrangement in 2005.

Myanmar was under military rule until 2011. Since then, the country has started comprehensive reforms. It introduced an electoral democracy, worked toward reconciling ethnic groups, strengthened macroeconomic policy (including unifying exchange rates), and implemented various market-oriented structural reforms. It enacted a commercial law and FDI legislation, and strengthened bank regulation and supervision. It also scaled up investment in transportation, energy, and communications. Myanmar's growth rate has been one of the highest among Asian countries in recent years, with a rapidly expanding domestic market and increasing FDI.

Support from bilateral and multilateral institutions in both finance and policy advice contributed much to the CLMV transition. ADB financed many infrastructure projects and provided reform recommendations. Viet Nam resumed borrowing from ADB and the World Bank in the early 1990s after repaying arrears with the support of donors. Similarly, bilateral official development assistance and new lending from multilateral development banks returned to Myanmar quickly after military rule ended (ADB restarted lending to Myanmar in 2013 after the settlement of arrears). In 1992, ADB started the Greater Mekong Subregion (GMS) program of regional cooperation, which today includes the CLMV countries plus Thailand and the PRC. The initiative aims to maintain and strengthen economic linkages between these countries as their transition advances.

2.8 Building a socialist market economy in the People's Republic of China

Pre-1949 efforts to develop national industries

Pre-1949 efforts to develop modern industries can be traced back to the 1860s. After being defeated by Western powers in the Opium Wars in 1842 and 1860, the Qing government attempted to introduce western advanced technologies and establish state-owned modern industries, known as the "Westernization Movement," initiated by pro-West bureaucrats. The reform was implemented but was not as comprehensive as Japan's modernization program because of opposition from the Empress Dowager Cixi and conservative bureaucrats. The Qing government's focus initially was on developing industries for defense purposes—such as steel, weapon manufacturing, and shipbuilding. This was later extended to include light industries such as textiles, paper and printing, pharmaceuticals, and glassware manufacturing for civilian consumption. Over time, more enterprises were set up by indigenous merchants and entrepreneurs, and overseas Chinese.

The Westernization Movement, however, failed to stop the downfall of the Qing dynasty. The Xinhai Revolution in 1911 led to the establishment of a new republic. During that period, domestic industries continued to grow, despite persistent political turmoil and civil war. Early industrialization peaked during World War I, when rising foreign demand for the country's goods and falling imports provided a golden opportunity for national industries to expand. The government of the newly established republic supported national industries through measures such as the introduction of a patent system and preferential taxation.

From the early 1930s, however, domestic industries were badly hit by several major events: the Great Depression, the war of resistance, and the war of liberation. By 1949, when the Communist Party of China (CPC) established the PRC, the economy was precarious, dominated by subsistence agriculture. Domestic industries were small, accounting for 12.5% of national income,[37] with some mining and heavy industries scattered in the northeast and light industries in coastal cities such as Shanghai and Tianjin.

The experience of postwar central planning

PRC leaders set the ambitious goal of modernizing through socialist industrialization, by pursuing a Soviet-type command economy with public ownership of the means of production. Land was redistributed from rich landowners to poor farmers. The State Planning Commission took charge of economic planning. Under the first five-year plan of 1953–1957, the PRC implemented close to 1,000 large-scale investment

---

[37] China State Statistical Bureau. 1990. *China National and Provincial Historical Statistics Collection.* Beijing.

projects to develop heavy industry, many supported by technical and financial assistance from the Soviet Union. The socialist transformation brought most industrial and commercial firms under state ownership and organized more than 90% of handicraft firms and household farms into cooperatives under collective ownership.

During 1958–1962, the PRC suffered severe economic difficulties. The Great Leap Forward led to huge waste and large economic disruption. The people's commune movement weakened farmers' production incentives, which, together with severe floods, led to a significant drop in agricultural output, causing large-scale food shortages. At the same time, the withdrawal of the Soviet Union assistance and continued blockages imposed by Western countries cut off the PRC from the world. In response, the government began focusing in 1961 on readjustment and recovery, giving greater priority to agriculture and light industry and decentralizing decision-making. In some provinces, local governments piloted what later would be called the "household responsibility system" to give farmers incentives to increase crop production. The initiative was short-lived and stopped. The readjustment and recovery took 3 years until 1965 and was followed by the Cultural Revolution from 1966 to 1976.

The Cultural Revolution was primarily a political upheaval and did not involve major changes to the basic economic model, except that economic policy shifted further left. Its impact was felt throughout the economy. Government economic agencies were paralyzed, with planning and coordination curtailed. Factory management was taken over by revolutionary committees with limited technical or managerial expertise. The role of markets was dismissed, and private production stopped in both rural and urban areas. The economy was largely cut off from world markets and foreign technology.

Despite all of this, the PRC still made progress in economic and social development between 1949 and 1977. Industry expanded, especially heavy industry. In the first half of the 20th century, the economy expanded just 0.23% annually. PRC per capita income grew 2.7% annually during 1961–1970 and 4.3% from 1971 to 1980, although official national accounts statistics before 1978 covered only material production and were based on administrative prices. Human development indicators improved markedly, for example, in education and health. However, until 1978, rigid central planning; the absence of a private sector, market, and competition; isolation from the rest of the world; and frequent political upheavals made the PRC economy inefficient and lacking dynamism, with widespread shortages of consumption goods.

Market-oriented reforms and opening up after 1978

Following the downfall of the "Gang of Four" in 1976, new leaders, led by the long-time reformist Deng Xiaoping, launched a far-reaching program of market-oriented reform and the "opening-up" policy. The historic CPC meeting in December 1978 accepted that "practice is the sole criterion for testing the truth" and declared that the country will put ideology aside and focus instead on economic development. In 1977–1978, top leaders made more than a dozen trips to Japan, the US, and Europe to see personally the economic achievements of advanced countries. They realized how the PRC lagged behind after decades of isolation and that the only way out was reform. For instance, when Deng Xiaoping visited Japan in October 1978, he was very much impressed by the bullet train system—shinkansen—and Panasonic's color TV production lines. He remarked that the PRC "really needs to run" to catch up.[38]

Notably, the reforms since 1978 have been gradual and pragmatic; in Deng Xiaoping's words, they were carried out like "crossing the river by feeling the stones." This is in contrast to the "shock therapy" adopted by the former Soviet Union and Eastern European countries years later.

The reform began in rural areas by piloting and later introducing nationwide household responsibility systems, dismantling the commune system to restore production incentives for farmers. Initially, these were not policy choices of the top leadership, but a response to many spontaneous and self-driven initiatives from local governments and village leaders in several provinces—including Anhui, Sichuan, and Tianjin. At the same time, reforms in the procurement system allowed agricultural products to be sold at market prices. These rural reforms became a great success, leading to significant increases in agricultural productivity, farm production, and rural incomes, and a reduction in rural poverty.

---

[38] China Daily. 2014. *What Did Deng Xiaoping Learn during His Visit to Japan in 1978?* [in Chinese]. 15 August. https://world.chinadaily.com.cn/dxpdc110znjn/2014-08/15/content_18323338.htm.

From 1984, the reform focus shifted to the urban economy, industry, and SOEs. The government introduced a dual-track system to minimize shocks: production within state plans continued to be subject to controlled prices, while production outside the state plan could be traded at market prices. The dual-track price system allowed enterprises to react to demand and supply and allowed private enterprises to grow, simultaneously keeping the planning system running. The approach was considered fit for the PRC and adopted by top leaders after extensive discussions among academics, government officials, and foreign experts including Nobel laureates, with two symposiums playing an influential role: the Moganshan Conference (in a mountain resort in Zhejiang province) in 1984 and Bashanlun Conference (during a cruise on the Yangtze River) in 1985. The dual-track system lasted until the early 1990s, when it was gradually phased out and most prices decontrolled, partly due to concerns over growing rent-seeking and associated corruption. By the early 2000s, prices covering 90% of PRC products had been liberalized.[39]

The enterprise reform initially involved granting more autonomy to SOEs. Contract responsibility systems and performance-based bonuses were introduced to incentivize enterprise management and workers that were employed under a fixed-wage and permanent employment system. At the same time, private enterprises and rural village- and township-enterprises were allowed to grow, often supported by local governments. The Shanghai Stock Exchange was reestablished in 1990 after being closed for more than 40 years and the Shenzhen Stock Exchange opened in 1991. After years of political and ideological debate on the role of planning and markets involving senior-level officials, in 1992, the 14th Congress of CPC declared a "socialist market economy" was the ultimate goal of reform. In 1993, the Constitution was amended to remove the term "planned economy."

PRC reforms accelerated after Deng Xiaoping's "Tour of the South" in 1992. The government embarked on comprehensive macroeconomic policy reforms including of the fiscal system, monetary policy, banking sector, and foreign exchange regime. It began privatizing small and medium-sized SOEs as part of a new enterprise reform strategy focusing on restructuring major SOEs and relaxing

---

[39] Huang, Y. 2015. From Economic Miracle to Normal Development. In Zhuang, J., P. Vandenberg, and Y. Huang, eds. *Managing the Middle-Income Transition: Challenges Facing the People's Republic of China*. London: Asian Development Bank / Edward Elgar.

control over small ones. As a result, the number of SOEs fell to 4% of all enterprises by 2010. In 2017, SOEs produced 25% of industrial value added, owned 48% of industrial capital assets, and employed 18% of the industrial labor force (Table 2.1). Remaining SOEs are mostly large companies listed on stock exchanges but majority-owned by the government. They are mostly in resources, public utilities (power and transport), finance, and telecommunications. SOE reform remains an important challenge for the PRC.

Table 2.1: Shares of State-Owned Enterprises in the Industry Sector, People's Republic of China, 1995–2017
(%)

	1995	2000	2005	2010	2017
Value added	53.8	54.3	37.6	31.3	25.3
Employment	65.2	53.9	27.2	19.2	17.9
Fixed assets	73.7	72.6	56.1	49.3	47.5

Note: The share of employment in 1995 refers to 1996 data, and the share of total fixed assets in 1995 refers to 1998 data.

Sources: CEIC Data Company Ltd. CEIC Database. https://www.ceicdata.com/en (accessed 3 June 2019); and National Bureau of Statistics of China. *China Statistical Yearbook 2018*. http://www.stats.gov.cn/english/Statisticaldata/AnnualData/ (accessed 3 June 2019).

The opening-up policy since 1978 has mainly involved trade, foreign investment, and knowledge exchange. The government initially replaced administrative restrictions on exports and imports with tariffs, quotas, and licensing; gradually phased out the use of quotas and licensing; and over time reduced tariffs. It also established many SEZs and designated several coastal cities as open cities to promote exports and attract FDI. To reform the foreign exchange system, the government eased administrative control initially, introduced a dual exchange rate system from the mid-1980s, unified the dual rates in 1994, and moved toward a managed floating exchange rate system. The government also promoted academic and technical knowledge exchanges between PRC scientists, scholars, and students with their foreign counterparts. Since 1978, tens of thousands of PRC students have been sent abroad for university studies, mostly to the US, Japan, the UK, Australia, and Canada. In 2001, the PRC joined the WTO.

The introduction of market-oriented reforms and the opening-up policy was followed by accelerating economic growth. The PRC's annual per capita GDP growth rose to 8.2% in the 1980s, 9.2% in the 1990s–2000s, and 6.9% in 2011–2018. The PRC is now the world's second-largest economy and largest merchandise exporter. Rapid growth of manufacturing exports and inward FDI has made the PRC the world's factory. Increasingly, the country's growth is supported by indigenous innovation. Rapid growth has reduced poverty and improved living standards. When reforms started, more than 80% of the population lived in extreme poverty (at the $1.90 per day international poverty line). By 2017, it had declined to less than 1%.

Explaining the People's Republic of China's 4 decades of rapid development

What can explain the PRC's success? Introducing market-oriented reforms and the opening-up policy was key—as these unleashed the society's entrepreneurship and creativity potential. It led to more efficient resource allocation and integrated the economy globally. In addition, two other factors played critical roles: (i) a pragmatic approach to reform, and (ii) the government's proactive role in promoting development.

The pragmatic approach to reform involved several institutional innovations that helped gradually develop market institutions, minimizing disruption. One was the responsibility system, first used in rural reform and later applied to SOE reforms and central-local government fiscal relations. Another was the dual-track system on prices, SOEs, and foreign exchange reform. A further innovation was piloting policy reforms before nationwide implementation, increasing the chance of success.

While the PRC economy became increasingly market-oriented and private sector-driven, the government has remained proactive in supporting development, more than most other Asian countries. Local governments played an important role in developing local economies. They provided cheap land and tax incentives to foreign investors and helped local private firms access finance. They also invested heavily in infrastructure, often financed by monetizing land— promoting urbanization and boosting growth. In recent years, the government has stepped up support for innovation and new industries.

The PRC is well on its way to becoming a high-income country. However, sustaining rapid growth has become increasingly harder as rural surplus labor disappears and the demographic dividend ends. Growth must increasingly come from gains in productivity. Attaining high-income status requires continued and deeper reforms.

The Decision on Major Issues Concerning Comprehensively Deepening Reforms by the Third Plenum of the 18th Congress of the CPC in November 2013 highlighted goals of future economic reform. The PRC will continue to develop a socialist market system where both public and private ownerships are important; all types of enterprises (private and public, and domestic and foreign) have equal access to markets; and "market forces play a decisive role in resource allocation." SOE reforms will deepen by separating ownership from management and strengthening corporate governance. At the same time, the government will continue to promote, support, and direct development of the non-state sector and proactively develop a mixed economy with cross-ownership shareholdings. The 19th Congress of the CPC in October 2017 reaffirmed these goals while stressing the central role of the party.

2.9 Toward market-led growth in India

In South Asia, two centuries of British colonial rule ended with newly independent nations (except Nepal and Bhutan, which were never colonized) in precarious conditions in the late 1940s. The top priority of the new governments was to accelerate growth through industrialization. Socialist ideology had a strong influence in South Asia since the early 20th century, and it was often closely associated with independence movements and a desire to avoid foreign influences. But instead of adopting a Soviet-type socialist model, South Asian countries allowed private firms to coexist with the public sector and opted for a mixed-economy model. Heavy state control over the economy, however, led to dismal growth and slow development. From the 1980s, South Asian countries began liberalizing markets, and as a result, growth accelerated. This section focuses on India.

Pre-independence industrial development

India had well-developed traditional industries during the Mughal Empire (1526–1858). Economic historians estimate it produced about 25% of world industrial output in 1750 and was a major contributor to global textile exports.[40] However, a long-run decline began around 1750 due to (i) political instability and battles between competing groups as the Mughal empire began to weaken, and (ii) massive imports of cheap factory-based textiles and other manufacturing goods from Europe, particularly the UK, in the 1800s.

The development of modern industries was slow under British rule (first through the East India Company from 1764 to 1857 and later through direct British government control from 1858 to 1947). An important reason was that British policy focused on using Indian resources to meet British needs rather than supporting indigenous industrial development—for example, by keeping tariffs low compared with other countries and discouraging Indian suppliers of manufacturing inputs.

Nevertheless, there was some success in India's industrial development, led by a small group of merchants and traders. Jamsetji Tata (1839–1904) was able to use capital generated from trade with Japan, the PRC, and other parts of East Asia and Southeast Asia, to establish modern cotton textile factories. He later diversified into steel production, in 1907 establishing Tata Iron and Steel Company (TISCO). Many other Indian merchants and traders followed his example, investing profits generated from World War I and the economic boom following the war to set up industrial enterprises. Industries included textiles, sugar, paper, cement, steel, shipbuilding, and even some automobile production by the 1940s. Thus, in 1946, the share of modern manufacturing in national income was 8.7%, compared with 1.9% in 1900.

Post-independence state-led industrialization

After independence in 1947, India used state-led industrialization to accelerate economic growth, address widespread poverty, and modernize the economy. The government chose key sectors to become state monopolies (for example, railways), and established exclusive rights to new investment in industries such as iron and steel, shipbuilding, mineral oils, coal, aircraft production, and telecommunications, where new private investment was not allowed. While private firms were allowed in many other sectors, they faced regulatory requirements such as licensing (to guide the sector, location,

---

[40] The 25% covers the entire Indian subcontinent. See Bairoch, P. 1982. International Industrialization Levels from 1750 to 1980. *Journal of European Economic History.* 11 (2). pp. 269-333.

and quantity of private investment) and import, foreign exchange, credit, and price controls. The government established a planning agency to devise and implement five-year plans. Import controls included high tariffs, quotas, and licensing. These were deemed necessary to develop a diversified industrial base and ensure scarce foreign exchange was used to import capital goods.

Although the economy was under heavy state control with an inward-looking import substitution industrialization strategy from the 1950s to the 1970s, state control changed in intensity over time.[41] Policies in 1951–1965 were considered more liberal than afterward. Investment licensing and import controls were less stringent until foreign exchange shortages grew serious. Some also considered the FDI regime relatively open during this period, as Prime Minister Jawaharlal Nehru saw the need for both foreign capital and technology.

But state control tightened from 1965 in response to a series of shocks and resulting economic problems. They included 2 years of serious drought, three wars with neighbors, a 1966 currency devaluation that largely failed, and losses in some state elections by the dominant Congress Party. Prime Minister Indira Gandhi assumed office in 1966 and drove economic policy further toward state control with a greater focus on income redistribution. Measures included more stringent import licensing; nationalization of banks, oil companies, and coal mines; restrictions on foreign companies and on the use of foreign exchange; restrictions on investment by large firms in sectors "reserved" for small enterprises; and barriers to laying off workers by firms with 300 or more employees (the 1976 threshold of 300 was further tightened to 100 in 1983).

India's state-led import substitution industrialization strategy had mixed results. The economy expanded 4% annually in the 1960s and 3.1% in the 1970s. This was much better than the less than 1% annual growth in the first half of the 20th century. However, in per capita terms, annual growth was just 1.8% in the 1960s and 0.6% in the 1970s, well below those in East Asia and Southeast Asia.

Market-oriented reforms

The weak economic performance in the 1960s and 1970s led some officials to begin advocating for relaxing state controls. Subsequently, in the second half of the 1970s and 1980s, successive governments

---

[41] Panagariya, A. 2008. *India: The Emerging Giant*. Oxford: Oxford University Press.

attempted to introduce economic liberalization, with each more significant than the preceding one. In industry, reforms mainly involved adjusting the existing industrial licensing system by reducing the number of industries covered. Similarly, in trade, measures were introduced to modify import licensing by reducing the number of import items banned or restricted. In the 1980s, several export incentives were introduced. Yet, despite these reforms, the essential economic management framework through licensing and controls remained until 1991, when India was hit by a balance of payments crisis.

Throughout the 1980s, India ran current account deficits. They grew particularly large during the second half of the decade, especially over the 3 years leading to the 1991 crisis. This was partly due to steady growth of private investment and merchandise imports in response to liberalization. At the same time, there was a rapid rise in central government spending, leading to a massive buildup of fiscal deficits—nearly 10% of GDP, on average, during 1985–1990. External debt increased rapidly and foreign exchange reserves dropped to just 1 month of imports in 1990–1991. As a result, India entered an IMF stand-by program in January 1991 with large financial support.

Yet the situations continued to deteriorate. The Gulf War in 1990 resulted in an oil price hike and drop in remittances from the Middle East—worsening the balance of payments. Prime Minister Rajiv Gandhi was assassinated in May. In mid-1991, India's credit rating was downgraded, limiting the country's access to world financial markets. The government had to ask the IMF and the World Bank for further emergency assistance in July 1991.

The IMF stand-by programs and World Bank structural adjustment loan came with policy conditions. ADB financial sector policy-based loan and bilateral assistance followed. Many of the proposed policy reforms were in line with the emerging consensus among Indian policy makers at the time. Most significantly, the 1991 reform program under Prime Minister P. V. Narasimha Rao and Finance Minister Manmohan Singh (who later became Prime Minister) was a departure from the old licensing and control framework. India abolished industrial licensing subject to a negative list (Table 2.2); ended public sector monopolies in many industries; initiated a policy of automatic approval of FDI up to 51% ownership; and significantly reduced import licensing. Over time, India also reduced tariffs on nonagricultural goods.

Table 2.2: Delicensing and Trade Liberalization in India, 1980–1997

	1980	1985	1990	1997
Cumulative share of three-digit industries delicensed	Nil	36.6	39.3	91.1
Cumulative share of real output delicensed	Nil	47.7	56.9	92.6
Cumulative share of employment delicensed	Nil	43.1	47.8	88.1
Tariff rate	119.2	142.3	132.5	47.6

Note: The dataset covers 64 three-digit registered industries in 16 Indian states.
Source: Aghion, P., R. Burgess, S. Redding, and F. Zilibotti. 2008. The Unequal Effects of Liberalization: Evidence from Dismantling the License Raj in India. *American Economic Review*. 94 (4). Table 1, p. 1400.

Since 1991, India has introduced more sweeping reforms, ranging from taxation to finance, telecommunications, electricity, and transport. Competition was enhanced in finance through, for example, the entry of new private and foreign banks, interest rate deregulation, and listing of almost all public sector banks. Monetizing fiscal deficits ended in the late 1990s. The 2003 Fiscal Responsibility and Budget Management (FRBM) Act strengthened fiscal discipline. One of the most prominent recent reforms was the introduction of a Goods and Services Tax in 2017 under the administration of Prime Minister Narendra Modi, replacing fragmented state taxes. India also streamlined business regulations—including those for starting a business, obtaining construction permits, and electricity connections. In 2016, it passed an Insolvency Bankruptcy Code, unifying laws for insolvency and bankruptcy.

These systematic reforms helped improve India's economic performance significantly. Annual per capita GDP growth rose to 4.7% in 1991–2017 from about 2% during the 1960s–1980s. Annual trade growth (including both exports and imports of goods and services) reached more than 11% in 1991–2017, compared with 5%–6% in the 1960s–1980s. Average annual FDI inflows increased by 14 times between the 1990s and the 2010s. Accelerating economic growth also led to more rapid poverty reduction. From 1990 to 2015, India's extreme poverty rate at the $1.90 per day international poverty line declined from 47.4% to 13.4%. India still needs deeper integration with the global economy and further reforms in labor and land markets, national railways, and the banking system to sustain high growth.

2.10 Pursuing reforms in other South Asian countries

Pakistan

During the first 3 decades after independence in 1947 with the partition of British India, Pakistan pursued a state-led import substitution industrialization policy. In the 1950s and 1960s, the government supported specific sectors (mainly sugar, jute, and chemicals) through import licensing, export subsidies, and multiple exchange rates; but the interventions were considered relatively benign and the country had a thriving private sector.

The 1960s saw an acceleration of growth, driven by expanding manufacturing production, the Green Revolution that boosted the agriculture sector, and inflows of foreign aid and investment due to geopolitical factors related to the Cold War. However, growth came with rising inequality, especially between East Pakistan and West Pakistan, culminating in civil conflict, which led to war with India and the separation of East Pakistan in 1971 as an independent Bangladesh. Subsequently, Pakistan pursued socialist-inspired nationalization by taking over large-scale manufacturing enterprises and establishing many SOEs.

Toward the end of the 1970s, economic and political instability led to the second military takeover in 20 years. The new government reversed many of the early 1970s socialist policies and privatized much of the industry the previous government took over. High private investment, inflows of foreign aid, and increased remittances from the Middle East contributed to solid growth. While Pakistan returned to electoral democracy at the end of the 1980s, twin trade and fiscal deficits resulted in a balance of payments crisis, leading to a structural adjustment program with the IMF. The program included policy conditions on privatizing banks and SOEs, introducing a managed floating exchange rate, and liberalizing trade and investment.

Implementing these structural reforms proved difficult. Pakistan continued to suffer from rising public debt and frequent balance of payments difficulties in the 1990s. There was another military takeover in 1999. The country enjoyed a period of high growth from 2001 to 2006, partly due to large foreign aid associated with the war against terrorism. But the oil price shocks of 2007–2008 hit Pakistan hard, and it had to enter into multiple IMF programs in the following 10 years to stabilize the economy. After 2010, the pace of growth gradually picked up, partly supported by increasing FDI, especially as economic cooperation with the PRC strengthened. Economic growth, however, slowed sharply from mid-2018, following fiscal and monetary policy tightening to rein in high and unsustainable twin deficits.

Pakistan's economic growth has been volatile over the past half century, affected by frequent political instability, geopolitical factors, and balance of payments crises. With electoral democracy now taking root, the new government under Prime Minister Imran Khan is taking on a wide range of structural reforms with the help of an IMF program in 2019 complemented by financing from ADB, the World Bank, and some bilateral partners. These reforms cover consolidating fiscal conditions, strengthening corporate governance of SOEs, and improving the investment climate. It is hoped that these reforms will address the chronic balance of payments problems and build more sustained and stable growth.

Bangladesh

As one of the world's most impoverished and least developed countries at the time of independence in 1971, Bangladesh initially pursued a state-led development strategy. The government nationalized banks, shipping companies, and major industries (including textiles, jute, and sugar mills). The country was under military rule from 1975 to 1990. During this period, some nationalized industrial companies were handed back to their former owners and private sector development and export-oriented growth were encouraged. Foreign aid started to pour into the country in the early 1980s, and international donors encouraged the government to privatize SOEs and liberalize the economy.

From the 1980s, a series of market-oriented reforms allowed the private sector a greater role in procuring, distributing, and importing agricultural inputs, while reducing subsidies. The government also removed urban and rural food rationing and subsidies in favor of targeted, in-kind assistance such as "food for work" programs.[42] A successful population control program helped keep population growth in check. Public investment and the Green Revolution helped increase agricultural productivity and made Bangladesh self-sufficient in food.

---

[42] Ahmed, R., S. Haggblade, and T. Chowdhury, eds. 2000. *Out of the Shadow of Famine: Evolving Food Markets and Food Policy in Bangladesh*. Baltimore: Johns Hopkins University Press.

Industry has been dominated by ready-made garments (RMG), which accounted for 6% of employment and 84% of total exports in 2018. The RMG success was largely the result of market forces. A 1979 joint venture with a company from the ROK catalyzed and fostered the RMG industry, with most early entrepreneurs learning skills and obtaining technology from the joint venture (Chapter 5). The state helped the RMG industry by setting up bonded warehouses and allowing exporters to use export orders as collateral to borrow.

Unique to Bangladesh is the contribution of nongovernment organizations (NGOs) to development. NGOs emerged soon after the independence in 1971 as a civil society response to assist those affected and address social issues in this war- and disaster-ravaged country. With the increased foreign aid, NGOs proliferated and became a prime channel for implementing many social development projects supported by international donors. NGOs provided microcredit services, health care, sanitation, and education. They also partnered with government in providing other services such as safety net programs, agricultural extension, social forestry, disaster management, and skills training.[43] Microfinance has played a critical role in agriculture and rural transformation.[44]

Bangladesh has emerged as one of the fastest-growing countries in Asia (and globally) in recent years, driven by strong domestic demand, robust RMG exports, improving infrastructure, higher agricultural growth, and surging remittance inflows. To sustain this momentum in the medium to long term, the government under Prime Minister Sheikh Hasina now focuses on mobilizing domestic resources by creating a broader tax base and better revenue collection; upgrading education including science, technology, engineering, and mathematics (STEM), including for girls; diversifying its industrial base (including generic pharmaceuticals); and improving the business climate.

Sri Lanka

Sri Lanka also pursued an inward-oriented policy of import substitution and state-led industrialization during the first 30 years after independence in 1948. The state nationalized basic and strategic industries and introduced import licensing and high tariffs to control

---

[43] World Bank. 2006. *Economics and Governance of Nongovernmental Organizations in Bangladesh.* Washington, DC.

[44] Sawada, Y., M. Mahmud, and N. Kitano, eds. 2018. *Economic and Social Development of Bangladesh: Miracle and Challenges.* London: Palgrave.

imports.[45] In agriculture, most plantations—including tea and rubber—came under state ownership through the Land Reform Act of 1972. These policies, coupled with a 1971 oil shock, resulted in reduced economic growth and a deterioration of macroeconomic conditions.

A change in government in 1977 paved the way for the extensive liberalization and market-oriented reforms in the 1980s. Trade liberalization was forcefully pursued. Tax incentives and export processing zones (EPZs) were introduced to encourage FDI. Most price controls and multiple exchange rates were removed. However, the ethnic conflict from the early 1980s stalled promising benefits from trade liberalization, hampered foreign investment, and hurt tourism.

Despite setbacks brought about by civil war, the government continued with a "second wave" of liberalization in the 1990s. These reforms included privatizing SOEs in telecommunications and reverting large plantations to private management under a 100-year leasing arrangement. The tariff structure was simplified, import duties reduced, and in 2001, a floating exchange rate was introduced.

Sri Lanka was able to weather the 1997–1998 Asian financial crisis, but suffered a series of natural disasters and external shocks during the following 10 years, including prolonged droughts, terrorism, the 2004 Asian tsunami, and the 2008–2009 global financial crisis. These forced the government to repeatedly seek IMF assistance. The prolonged civil war that started in July 1983 finally ended in May 2009. The country began reconstruction and reconciliation, especially in the northern provinces. From 2010 to 2012, Sri Lanka saw growth pick up, benefiting from a peace dividend and continued market-oriented reforms. Yet growth slowed during 2015–2019 due to balance of payments difficulties.

Compared with other South Asian countries, Sri Lanka has had relatively better social indicators such as high literacy and low infant mortality rates over the decades. However, because of domestic conflict, political instability, and frequent shifts in economic policies, it has been difficult to sustain high growth. To reach its growth potential—including agribusiness and tourism, for example—Sri Lanka needs to continually work toward effectively managing its external debt, maintain macroeconomic stability, and implement structural reforms. It should attract more FDI to integrate more deeply with the regional and global trading system.

---

[45] Athukorala, P., et al., eds. 2017. *The Sri Lankan Economy: Charting a New Course.* Manila: Asian Development Bank.

Afghanistan, Nepal, Bhutan, and Maldives

Since the late 1970s, Afghanistan had been ravaged by external aggression, then a civil war, and now continued conflicts and security threats. As a result, many people died, much of the country's infrastructure was destroyed, trade and investment disrupted, large amounts of capital lost, and GDP contracted substantially. In 2001, after the fall of Taliban rule and the signing of the Bonn Agreement, an interim administration was established and the process of reconstruction and reform started.

Afghanistan has the natural advantage of being a geographical hub to connect Central Asia with South Asia and holds potential in agribusiness and specific manufactured products. Since 2001, the country has harnessed international support to rebuild its political system, institutions, infrastructure, and economy, and shown improvement on various economic and social indicators. However, security threats and conflicts continue to be major challenges to the economy and foreign investment. The country's development needs remain huge and sustained international assistance is critical in helping the country achieve sustained and inclusive growth. Since 2002, ADB has provided a total of $5.6 billion in assistance to support sectors such as transport, energy, agriculture, natural resources, and rural development.

Nepal was never colonized, and the 1951 revolution ended the rule by the elite Rana family, restoring direct rule by the King with a cabinet led by the Nepali Congress, the largest political party at that time. Since then, Nepal had seen continued domestic conflict until the mid-2000s. It has gone through absolute monarchy, constitutional monarchy, and a federal republic. The first five-year plan for 1956–1961 and subsequent plans followed an import substitution policy focusing on industrialization through price controls and public corporations. Land reform in 1964 gave land entitlement to many landless people.

Nepal has promising potential in hydropower, a variety of agricultural products given the different elevations of arable land, and tourism based on its historical heritage and the Himalayas. The successful political transition from a constitutional monarchy to a federal republic in 2008, the declaration of a new Constitution in 2015, and successful elections under the new Constitution for all three tiers of governments in 2017 paved the way for future development based on market-oriented reforms, strong investment supported by the international community, and regional cooperation.

Bhutan was never colonized either. It remained almost entirely closed off to the outside world until the 1960s—when it had no roads usable by motor vehicles, the economy depended on subsistence agriculture, and life expectancy and per capita income were among the lowest in the world. Its first five-year plan began in 1961 with large-scale development programs supported by India. Over the years, the focus of planning shifted from basic infrastructure to hydroelectricity and services. The construction and generation of hydroelectricity have driven Bhutan's economic growth.

Since the 1960s, the economy has undergone extensive transformation and reforms toward more open policies resulting in large development gains. "Gross National Happiness" was instituted as the government's primary goal and enacted in its 2008 Constitution. In the 2010s, the government adopted reforms to improve the investment climate, identify high potential sectors, renew focus on small and cottage industries, and promote public–private partnerships.

Maldives gained independence from the UK in 1965 and became a republic in 1968. It was one of the poorest countries in Asia at that time. Since then, it has developed many resorts across its dispersed islands and transformed the country into a major tourist destination. In 2018, tourism accounted for more than a quarter of GDP. The public sector, including SOEs, dominates the economy, accounting for 40% of total employment.

Challenges to Maldives include the impact of global warming and its scattered geography. The country has more than 1,000 islands, of which 187 are inhabited. Eighty percent of its territory is less than 1 meter above sea level. The government is now taking measures to strengthen environmental protection, promote sustainable tourism, and diversify the economy.

2.11 Transition in Central Asia and Mongolia

After the dissolution of the Soviet Union and gaining independence in 1991, the five Central Asian countries (Kazakhstan, the Kyrgyz Republic, Tajikistan, Turkmenistan, and Uzbekistan) and the three South Caucasus countries (Armenia, Azerbaijan, and Georgia)—collectively the Central Asian subregion—embarked on transition to a market economy. Unlike countries in Central and Eastern Europe and the Russian Federation—which adopted a "big bang" approach of rapid liberalization and mass privatization—most Central Asian countries adopted a more gradual approach, though with large variations. The transition has proven complex and has often been marked by multiple economic crises, reform reversals, and instability along the way. While the transition is far from complete, significant progress has been made, especially in price and trade liberalization, privatization of small-scale SOEs, the development of the private sector, and macroeconomic stabilization.

Independence created shock waves across these economies. It led to an immediate collapse of demand and supply networks among tightly integrated former republics under central planning. They were hit hard partly because their economic role in the Soviet system was primarily as suppliers of raw materials to more industrialized areas, with most lacking an independent industrial base. Production slowed dramatically with per capita GDP declining at double-digit rates for several years in many countries (Table 2.3).

Those rich in natural resources—such as Kazakhstan (oil), Azerbaijan (oil and gas), and Turkmenistan (gas)—fared better. But even they could not escape sharp economic downturns. Accompanying the production collapse was skyrocketing inflation (three- to four-digit levels) due to declining output, a widespread shortage of consumer goods, large fiscal deficits, and rapid expansion of money supply by several central banks—in the early transition years, Central Asian countries continued to use the Russian ruble as currency.

Faced with these challenges, macroeconomic stabilization became a key part of reform. To bring inflation under control, they all introduced national currencies: Azerbaijan in August 1992; the Kyrgyz Republic in May 1993; Armenia, Kazakhstan, Turkmenistan, and Uzbekistan in November 1993; Tajikistan in May 1995; and Georgia in October 1995. Over time, their central banks gained more independence. Governments also worked to reduce fiscal deficits through tax reforms, including the introduction of a value-added tax, and personal and corporate income taxes, and by reducing government expenditures, in particular, direct subsidies to SOEs. These stabilization measures, together with other structural reforms, were effective in bringing inflation under control: declining to double-digit levels in the late 1990s and single digits by the early 2000s for most countries. The fiscal situation also improved, with deficits falling in oil-importing countries and turning to surpluses in oil-exporting ones.

Table 2.3: Average Annual Per Capita GDP Growth, Central Asia and Mongolia, 1991–2018
(%)

	1991–1995	1996–2000	2001–2005	2006–2010	2011–2015	2016–2018
Central Asia	(11.4)	3.1	8.4	6.7	3.6	1.8
Armenia	(8.2)	6.1	12.9	5.1	4.1	4.0
Azerbaijan	(16.8)	6.1	12.4	15.2	0.8	(1.6)
Georgia	(19.9)	8.8	8.3	6.0	5.2	4.1
Kazakhstan	(8.7)	3.8	10.0	4.7	3.2	1.7
Kyrgyz Republic	(13.2)	4.1	2.8	3.4	3.1	2.2
Tajikistan	(18.7)	(1.0)	7.8	4.4	4.5	4.7
Turkmenistan	(10.9)	3.4	4.1	8.9	8.6	4.5
Uzbekistan	(6.0)	2.2	4.1	6.6	5.9	3.4
Mongolia	(3.5)	1.9	5.4	5.0	8.2	2.6

( ) = negative, GDP = gross domestic product.
Sources: Asian Development Bank (ADB). Key Indicators Database. https://kidb.adb.org/kidb (accessed 16 September 2019); World Bank. World Development Indicators. https://databank.worldbank.org/reports.aspx?source=world-development-indicators (accessed 2 August 2019); and ADB estimates.

GDP growth returned in the second half of the 1990s, despite the impact of the 1998 Russian financial crisis. The early 2000s saw strong per capita GDP growth across the entire Central Asian subregion—8.8% annually on average—supported by strong commodity exports, rapid credit expansion, and high remittances. Growth in resource-rich countries was particularly high, due to the commodity boom. But these countries, together with remittance-dependent economies, especially the Kyrgyz Republic and Tajikistan, were hit by the 2008–2009 global financial crisis and the 2014 downward oil price shocks.

Centrally administered prices were a key feature of the Soviet economic system, and it led to severe resource misallocation and widespread shortages. While price liberalization initially triggered inflation, it contributed subsequently to economic stabilization as markets responded to price signals. In 1992, the Kyrgyz Republic became the first Central Asian country to fully liberalize prices and abolish state production orders. Other countries adopted a more gradual approach. For instance, Kazakhstan liberalized most prices in 1994; Tajikistan, affected by civil war, did so in 1996. By 1998, all countries were well advanced in price liberalization, except Turkmenistan and Uzbekistan.

Accompanying price liberalization was trade liberalization. The Kyrgyz Republic was again the front-runner, introducing full current account convertibility in 1995. In 1998, it became the first Central Asian country to join the WTO. As trade reform progressed, more countries joined the WTO—Georgia in 2000, Armenia in 2003, Tajikistan in 2013, and Kazakhstan in 2015. Uzbekistan recently renewed its WTO accession process. Regional cooperation has also progressed, especially in trade and connectivity, through frameworks such as the Eurasian Economic Union (Armenia, Belarus, Kazakhstan, the Kyrgyz Republic, and the Russian Federation) and the 11-member Central Asia Regional Economic Cooperation (CAREC) Program, supported by ADB since it was formally established in 2001.

Privatization of SOEs was another key step of the transition toward a market economy, but it proved to be complex and difficult. Again, the privatization approach adopted by Central Asian countries was much more gradual than those in Central and Eastern Europe and the Russian Federation. Small-scale privatization advanced rapidly in most countries. There were greater variations for large SOEs. Armenia, Azerbaijan, Georgia, the Kyrgyz Republic, and Tajikistan used voucher schemes, while Turkmenistan and Uzbekistan opted for manager- and employee-buyouts. While SOEs remain an important part of their economies, the private sector expanded rapidly. In 2010, by some estimates, the private sector contributed 45%–75% of GDP in most Central Asian countries.

Mongolia was also seriously affected by the demise of the former Soviet Union because of their close ties. Under the Soviet system, the country's economy and living standards were sustained by large Soviet aid flows, including energy, food supplies, raw materials, capital equipment, and market access. These disappeared virtually overnight following the Soviet collapse. Together with the "big bang" approach to transition adopted by Mongolia—involving rapid liberalization and mass privatization—the economy plunged into deep recession during the first half of the 1990s.

Mongolia is a resource-rich economy with large reserves of copper, coal, and gold. Relatively stable growth returned from 1995, and the country joined the WTO in 1997. While the economy was briefly disrupted by a debt crisis in 2000–2001, per capita GDP recovered to its pre-transition level by 2003. Mongolia had a sharp, but short-lived, growth slowdown in 2009 due to the global financial crisis, but enjoyed a period of rapid growth in 2010–2014, when it was briefly one of the world's fastest-growing economies, fueled mainly by a mining boom. Mongolia has been and remains vulnerable to external shocks coming from fluctuations in commodity prices.

Given their land-locked geography, resource-based economies, and the need to diversify industry to sustain growth, Central Asian countries and Mongolia can draw on deeper regional cooperation and greater investment in connectivity and human resources. They will gain from continued reforms—such as privatizing larger SOEs, strengthening financial institutions, introducing competition policy, and reforming governance in firms and state institutions.[46]

2.12 Seizing opportunities in the Pacific

Pacific island countries share a unique set of challenges and opportunities. Most are small (except Papua New Guinea [PNG], which has a relatively large population of 8 million);[47] have limited natural resources (except PNG and Timor-Leste, which have large natural gas reserves) and narrowly based economies; and are remote from major markets, vulnerable to external shocks, and highly dependent on external assistance. The lack of sufficient human and institutional capacities constrain development. They also face climate-related challenges such as rising sea levels and more frequent extreme weather events.

Compared with other subregions, economic growth in the Pacific has been slow and unstable. These countries were former colonies and gained independence mostly from the 1970s onward. Like many other newly independent economies, the state plays an important role in the economy. SOEs dominate core infrastructure services such as transport, power, telecommunications, and water and sanitation, in addition to education, health care, and other essential

---

[46] The European Bank for Reconstruction and Development provides assessments of transition progress for all the formerly socialist countries in Central and Eastern Europe, the Russian Federation, and Central Asian countries in their annual Transition Report.

[47] Pacific island countries in this chapter refer to ADB's 15 Pacific members: the Cook Islands, the Federated States of Micronesia, Fiji, Kiribati, the Marshall Islands, Nauru, Niue, Palau, Papua New Guinea, Samoa, Solomon Islands, Timor-Leste, Tonga, Tuvalu, and Vanuatu.

social services. And with opportunities for profitable business ventures limited by geography, SOEs also often provide services and products that the private sector would normally run, such as hotels, shipping services, and manufacturing.

Pacific governments have worked to reform their economies toward greater reliance on markets and the private sector, and to strengthen institutional capacity to seize opportunities from globalization, technological progress (such as digital technologies), and Asia's rapid economic growth.

One notable area is SOE reform. The poor performance of SOEs has long been a constraint on growth. Fiji began SOE reform in the early 1990s. In recent years, many more countries have initiated SOE reform through partial privatization and public–private partnerships; and by strengthening legal, regulatory, and governance frameworks. For instance, Fiji privatized 51% of Ports Terminal Limited and entered into a management contract for Suva and Lautoka ports in 2013. Kiribati adopted an SOE Act in 2012 and privatized Kiribati Supply Company Limited, a hardware company in business for over 30 years, in 2013. Samoa privatized SamoaTel in 2010 and adopted an SOE divestment and ownership policy in 2015. These reforms improved SOE performance.[48]

Supported by development partners such as ADB and the World Bank, Pacific island countries are working on broad public sector governance reforms and strengthening institutional capacity. The public sector, including SOEs, represents over a third of GDP on average. Recent reforms aim to strengthen budgetary management, accounting frameworks, internal auditing and financial reporting, debt management, and capacity development and training.

Another structural reform is trade liberalization, which can be traced back to the late 1980s.[49] In recent years, Pacific island countries pursued trade liberalization mainly through regional and multilateral agreements. In August 2001, they signed the Pacific Agreement on Closer Economic Relations (PACER), providing an umbrella agreement between 16 members of the Pacific Islands Forum (which also includes

---

[48] ADB. 2016. *Finding Balance 2016: Benchmarking the Performance of State-Owned Enterprises in Island Countries.* Manila.

[49] Narayan, P., and B. C. Prasad. 2006. Trade Liberalization and Economic Growth: Empirical Evidence for Fiji from the Computable General Equilibrium Model. *Discussion Paper Series.* No. 07/06, Vol. 1. Queensland: Faculty of Business and Economics, Griffith University.

Australia and New Zealand) on the trade liberalization process. In 2001, they signed the Pacific Island Countries Trade Agreement (PICTA), a free trade agreement on trade in goods among 14 members of the Pacific Islands Forum (excluding Australia and New Zealand), which entered into force in 2003. PICTA members are required to gradually lower tariffs on goods traded among island states over a 10-year period and remove nontariff barriers. More recently, negotiations were concluded for PACER Plus—a regional development-centered trade agreement covering goods, services, and investment.

At the multilateral level, six Pacific countries are WTO members— Fiji, PNG, Samoa, Solomon Islands, Tonga, and Vanuatu.

Pacific island countries can promote sustainable tourism by preserving their cultural traditions and the environment. Expanding communications and internet access, supported by ADB and others, have provided greater connectivity to global markets. International support for structural reforms, building institutional and human capacities, climate adaptation, disaster risk management, and financial inclusion remain important for the subregion.

2.13 Looking ahead

Fifty years of Asian development show that sustained growth, poverty reduction, and economic catch-up require efficient markets, an effective state, and strong institutions. Market-oriented reforms, open trade and investment regimes, effective government support, and strong state capacity together have transformed developing Asia into one of the world's most dynamic regions.

Going forward, developing Asia should continue efforts in the following areas.

First, make markets work better and more efficiently. Depending on individual country circumstances, governments should continue to implement structural reforms in the labor market, the financial sector, and trade and investment regimes to reduce and eliminate market rigidities, distortions, and barriers. Also, most countries have room to strengthen competition policy, intellectual property protection, contract enforcement, and corporate governance.

Second, as a country becomes more developed and the private sector matures, government support for growth should gradually move toward measures that have large spillovers to the wider economy and do not constrain competition—such as supporting innovation and R&D, investing in higher education, and maintaining an enabling environment for private enterprises. Continuing SOE reform is another priority, by making SOEs compete on an equal footing with the private sector, and by privatizing them when appropriate.

Third, governments should continue to improve capacity in providing quality public goods, addressing market failure, and responding to emerging challenges. They must build and maintain good physical infrastructure; make adequate investment in education and health; and respond to challenges such as environmental degradation, climate change, urbanization, and population aging. They should also effectively pursue macroeconomic stability.

Fourth, governments should pay more attention to income redistribution, social equity, and equalizing opportunity through progressive taxation and public transfers. Good quality public education and health services also contribute to inclusiveness. While the region's extreme poverty has declined dramatically, income inequality has widened in many countries and remains stubbornly high in others. If the benefits of growth are not equally shared and many are left behind, there will be less incentive for people to participate in national development, and social tensions and instability can rise and may undermine growth and its sustainability.

Fifth, countries should continue to reform public sector governance. Maintaining the rule of law, improving regulatory quality, and scaling up anticorruption efforts offer large gains. Greater participation and accountability are increasingly important as citizens demand a greater say in national affairs with rising incomes and increasing access to advanced technology.

CHAPTER 3

DYNAMICS OF STRUCTURAL TRANSFORMATION

3.1 Introduction

For the last 5 decades, structural transformation in Asia has been the primary driver behind the region's rising income and geographic movement of capital and labor. It goes beyond shifting resources across broad industry sectors—from agriculture to manufacturing and services. Structural transformation involves diversifying and deepening production, linking processes to global value chains, and moving resources from rural areas to cities. The process increases labor productivity for the overall economy, as resources shift toward more productive sectors, and more investment and increased efficiency lift productivity within sectors. Historically, most successful high-income countries followed similar patterns of economic development, but Asia's transition has been particularly rapid. Structural transformation also facilitates urbanization, which, in turn, supports the changing industrial composition.

This chapter examines developing Asia's structural transformation process over the past half century, looking at both aggregate performance as well as cross-country differences. Section 3.2 looks at the region's shifts in economic structure among agriculture, industry, and services, and the contribution these shifts made to productivity growth. Sections 3.3–3.5 examine progress in diversifying and upgrading economic activities within each of these three broad sectors and their contributions to productivity growth. In particular, section 3.5 discusses the growing importance and diversity of services. Section 3.6 reviews the region's urbanization process and its importance in raising living standards and the quality of life. Finally, section 3.7 explores the challenges that today's policy makers in developing Asia need to confront, depending on the stage of development of their economy.

3.2 Overview of Asia's structural transformation

Economic literature has long viewed development as a process of transforming the productive structure of an economy and accumulating the physical and human capacities needed to drive this change.[1] Development and growth occur as new economic activities emerge, old ones are replaced, and resources are reallocated from less productive firms and activities to more productive ones. During structural transformation, resources are reallocated across and within the three broad sectors of economic activity: agriculture, industry,[2] and services. The process involves upgrading technology, upskilling labor, and shifting resources from rural to urban areas.

The most striking feature of development when viewed over a long time span is the secular decline in the share of agriculture and corresponding increase in the combined share of industry and services, whether measured in terms of output or employment.[3] Industry's share increases to a certain point and then starts to decline, as the economy shifts from the industrialization stage to a "deindustrialization" stage, while services' share continues to increase.

Over the past half century, developing Asia has followed a similar pattern of structural transformation as today's high-income countries, though at a much faster pace (Figure 3.1, Table 3.1, and Appendixes 5 and 6). From 1970 to 2018, the share of agricultural output in total gross domestic product (GDP) and employment in developing Asia declined

---

[1] For a review of the literature, see Asian Development Bank (ADB). 2013. *Key Indicators for Asia and the Pacific 2013: Asia's Economic Transformation: Where to, How, and How Fast?* Manila.

[2] According to the United Nations (UN) International Standard Industrial Classification of All Economic Activities, revision 4, the industry sector comprises economic activities categorized as (i) mining and quarrying; (ii) manufacturing; (iii) electricity, gas, steam, and air-conditioning supply; (iv) water supply, sewerage, waste management, and remediation activities; and (v) construction.

[3] ADB. 2013. *Key Indicators for Asia and the Pacific 2013: Asia's Economic Transformation: Where to, How, and How Fast?* Manila.

as countries grew richer. A pattern of structural change in industry is clear, especially its employment share. Industry's shares of GDP and employment expanded in most Asian countries, but in high-income economies including the newly industrialized economies (NIEs), these two shares began to decline (deindustrialization), suggesting an inverted-U shape relationship. Services was already the largest sector by output and employment for most countries in 1970, rising steadily with income, although its composition changed substantially over time.

The decline in agriculture's share of GDP was especially prominent in the People's Republic of China (PRC) and India: from 31.9% in the 1970s to 7.2% in 2018 in the PRC and from 39.6% to 16.0% in India. The region's two city economies—Hong Kong, China and Singapore—always had low shares of agricultural output (including fishing) and employment. In developing Asia as a whole, the share of agriculture in GDP dropped from 31.9% in the 1970s to a low of 8.5% in 2018, while the share of employment decreased from 71.0% to only 33.5%, reflecting a slower pace of labor productivity growth in the agriculture sector.

While industry's share of GDP remained about the same in the PRC and increased by a small margin in India between 1970 and 2018, it increased significantly in countries such as Bangladesh and Thailand. Economies reliant on mining—such as Azerbaijan, Mongolia, and Papua New Guinea—tend to have relatively high industry-to-GDP shares.

Industry's share of employment in developing Asia increased from 14.1% in the 1970s to 25.5% in 2018, which was comparable to the Middle East and North Africa (26.7%), but higher than other regions such as Sub-Saharan Africa (11.4%) and Organisation for Economic Co-operation and Development (OECD) members (22.7%). In 2018, developing Asia's industry share of GDP (37.5%) was lower than the Middle East and North Africa (42.4%). In natural resource-rich countries, industry's employment share is small even though its GDP share is large (because mining is particularly capital-intensive).

Services has always been an important contributor to both production and employment. In the 1970s, it already accounted for the largest share of GDP in most countries, and its share has grown in parallel with the decline in agriculture's. The growing role of services is evident in all subregions and country income groups both for GDP and employment. For example, in the Republic of Korea (ROK), which grew rapidly through export-oriented industrialization, industry's dominance is giving way to services. A similar pattern is happening in

Figure 3.1: Output and Employment Shares by Sector against Per Capita GDP, 1970–2018

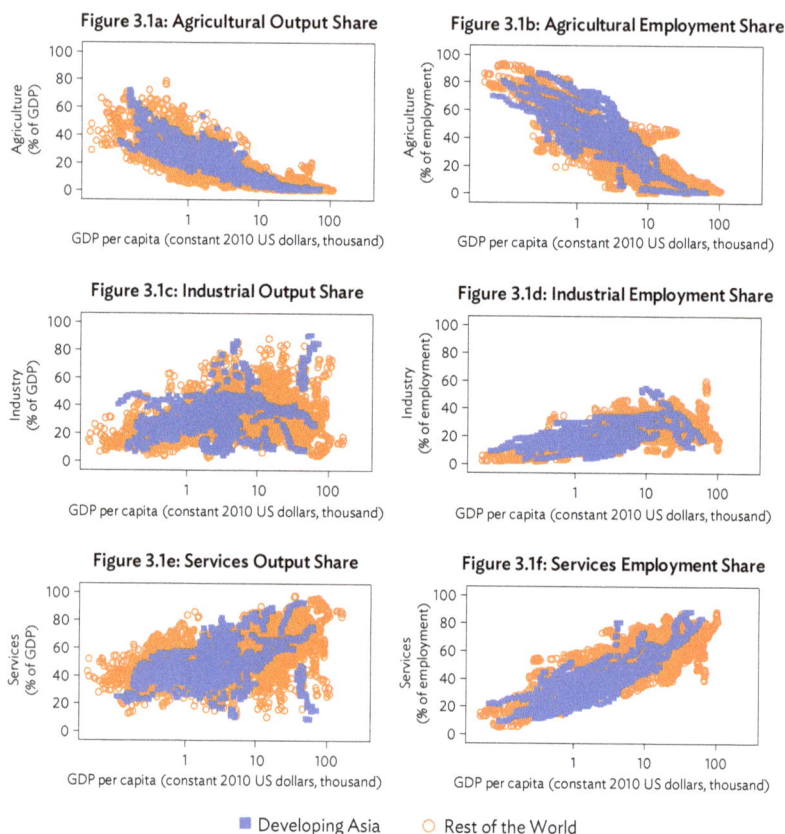

Figure 3.1a: Agricultural Output Share

Figure 3.1b: Agricultural Employment Share

Figure 3.1c: Industrial Output Share

Figure 3.1d: Industrial Employment Share

Figure 3.1e: Services Output Share

Figure 3.1f: Services Employment Share

■ Developing Asia   ○ Rest of the World

GDP = gross domestic product, US = United States.

Notes: The years of data for each economy vary depending on availability, with 1970 as the earliest year and 2018 as the latest. Sector shares are rescaled to sum to 100.

Sources: For output shares: World Bank. World Development Indicators. https://data.worldbank .org/indicator (accessed 2 August 2019); United Nations (UN). UN Statistics Division Database. https://unstats.un.org (accessed 28 August 2019); national sources; and Asian Development Bank estimates. For employment shares: International Labour Organization (ILO). ILOSTAT Database. https://www.ilo.org/ilostat (accessed 28 August 2019); Organisation for Economic Co-Operation and Development (OECD). OECD Employment and Labour Market Statistics. https://www.oecd-ilibrary.org/employment/data/oecd-employment-and-labour-market -statistics_lfs-data-en (accessed 28 August 2019); Timmer, M. P., G.J. de Vries, and K. de Vries. 2015. Patterns of Structural Change in Developing Countries. In Weiss, J., and M. Tribe, eds. *Routledge Handbook of Industry and Development*. Abingdon: Routledge. pp. 65–83 (for the Groningen Growth and Development Center 10-Sector Database) (accessed 28 August 2019); and Asian Development Bank estimates.

Table 3.1: Output and Employment Shares by Sector, 1970–2018

Table 3.1a: Sector Shares in Output (gross value added as a % of GDP)

	Agriculture			Industry			Services		
	1970–1979	1990–1999	2018	1970–1979	1990–1999	2018	1970–1979	1990–1999	2018
Developing Asia	**31.9**	**14.9**	**8.5**	**33.8**	**36.5**	**37.5**	**34.3**	**48.6**	**54.0**
Central Asia	...	23.3	10.3	...	32.7	39.9	...	43.9	49.8
East Asia	28.0	11.2	6.3	41.3	39.1	39.5	30.7	49.7	54.1
People's Republic of China	31.9	20.1	7.2	44.2	45.0	40.7	23.9	34.9	52.2
South Asia	40.5	27.8	16.5	24.0	28.5	28.7	35.6	43.6	54.8
India	39.6	28.1	16.0	25.6	30.0	29.8	34.8	41.9	54.2
Southeast Asia	27.1	12.6	10.4	31.2	36.9	36.4	41.8	50.4	53.2
The Pacific	30.2	26.8	16.6	26.2	29.5	31.2	43.6	43.7	52.3
Developed Asia	**5.3**	**2.0**	**1.7**	**41.8**	**35.0**	**27.2**	**52.9**	**62.9**	**71.2**
Australia	6.6	3.4	2.7	37.4	28.4	24.7	56.0	68.2	72.6
Japan	4.9	1.9	1.1	42.8	35.7	28.1	52.3	62.5	70.8
Latin America and the Caribbean	**12.3**	**7.2**	**5.3**	**36.9**	**32.5**	**27.9**	**50.7**	**60.3**	**66.8**
Middle East and North Africa	**10.1**	**9.0**	**4.2**	**52.1**	**40.7**	**42.4**	**37.8**	**50.4**	**53.4**
Sub-Saharan Africa	**21.3**	**17.9**	**18.2**	**29.8**	**30.4**	**27.8**	**48.9**	**51.7**	**54.0**
OECD	**4.5**	**2.3**	**1.5**	**34.7**	**30.2**	**23.7**	**60.8**	**67.5**	**74.8**
World	**8.1**	**4.2**	**4.1**	**35.4**	**31.3**	**28.5**	**56.5**	**64.5**	**67.4**

... = data not available, GDP = gross domestic product, OECD = Organisation for Economic Co-operation and Development.

Notes: Sector shares are rescaled so that the sum of shares in value added is equal to 100. Latest data refer to 2015 for Turkmenistan, Tuvalu, and Vanuatu, and 2016 for the Federated States of Micronesia, New Zealand, Papua New Guinea, and Tonga. Data for Australia; Hong Kong, China; Indonesia; and Japan are from 2017.

Sources: World Bank. World Development Indicators. https://data.worldbank.org/indicator (accessed 2 August 2019); United Nations (UN). UN Statistics Division Database. https://unstats.un.org (28 August 2019); national sources; and Asian Development Bank estimates.

Table 3.1b: Sector Shares in Employment (% of total employment)

	Agriculture			Industry			Services		
	1970–1979	1990–1999	2018	1970–1979	1990–1999	2018	1970–1979	1990–1999	2018
Developing Asia	**71.0**	**54.7**	**33.5**	**14.1**	**20.1**	**25.5**	**14.9**	**25.2**	**41.0**
Central Asia	...	40.2	29.8	...	20.0	23.9	...	39.8	46.3
East Asia	74.5	52.2	25.6	14.4	24.0	28.5	11.2	23.8	45.9
People's Republic of China	76.4	54.1	26.8	13.7	23.6	28.6	9.9	22.2	44.6
South Asia	67.4	60.9	43.6	14.4	15.6	23.8	18.1	23.6	32.6
India	68.6	61.8	43.9	14.0	15.7	24.7	17.4	22.5	31.5
Southeast Asia	61.1	52.0	32.1	12.2	16.1	22.1	26.7	31.9	45.8
The Pacific	...	66.4	61.7	...	6.3	6.9	...	27.3	31.4
Developed Asia	**12.8**	**5.9**	**3.4**	**35.9**	**32.3**	**23.6**	**51.3**	**61.8**	**73.0**
Australia	7.2	5.2	2.6	34.6	23.0	19.4	58.2	71.8	78.1
Japan	13.4	5.9	3.4	36.1	33.7	24.5	50.5	60.4	72.1
Latin America and the Caribbean	32.6	22.0	13.9	24.4	22.3	21.0	43.0	55.6	65.0
Middle East and North Africa	50.6	27.7	16.9	18.7	24.6	26.7	30.8	47.7	56.3
Sub-Saharan Africa	61.9	61.3	53.5	13.2	10.1	11.4	24.9	28.5	35.2
OECD	11.4	8.3	4.6	35.9	28.6	22.7	52.7	63.1	72.7
World	51.1	42.0	28.2	21.0	21.7	23.0	28.0	36.3	48.8

... = data not available, OECD = Organisation for Economic Co-operation and Development.

Sources: International Labour Organization (ILO). ILOSTAT Database. https://www.ilo.org/ilostat (accessed 28 August 2019); OECD. OECD Employment and Labour Market Statistics. https://www.oecd-ilibrary.org/employment/data/oecd-employment-and-labour-market-statistics_lfs-data-en (accessed 28 August 2019); Timmer, M. P., G.J. de Vries, and K. de Vries. 2015. Patterns of Structural Change in Developing Countries. In Weiss, J., and M. Tribe, eds. *Routledge Handbook of Industry and Development*. Abingdon: Routledge. pp. 65–83 (for the Groningen Growth and Development Center 10-Sector Database) (accessed 28 August 2019); and Asian Development Bank estimates.

the PRC, which also leveraged manufacturing to propel rapid growth. The relative importance of services also grew in countries such as India and the Philippines. As a result, the pattern of structural change in services is clearer and more uniform than that in industry.

3.3 Critical contribution of agriculture

Structural transformation in developing Asia began with the growth in agricultural productivity (Chapter 4). The food problem was the foremost concern 50 years ago. At that point, agriculture in much of Asia was predominantly subsistence farming of food crops (such as rice and wheat), where farmers cultivated small plots of owned or leased land, using manual labor and applying age-old technologies, while being at the mercy of the vagaries of weather. In countries going through socialist transformation, such as the PRC, the Central Asian republics, and Viet Nam, agriculture was structured under state or collective systems. Consequently, farm productivity was low, unstable, and unable to meet growing food demand. Many countries had to rely on imports or food aid to fill the gap. Regionally, the priority was to transform traditional agriculture and improve food productivity.

Since the late 1960s, the "Green Revolution" has brought major changes to traditional agriculture. This technology-led transformation involved developing and disseminating a series of high-yielding modern varieties of crops, primarily rice and wheat, together with improved production practices.

More than a technological fix, the Green Revolution encompassed policy and institutional changes along with increased investment. In 1972, Asian countries, on average, directed 15% of public spending to agriculture. As investments in support of the Green Revolution picked up, the value of agriculture spending had doubled in real terms by 1985.[4] Critical investments included rehabilitating irrigation systems, improving farm-to-market roads, and establishing networks of agricultural research and extension services.

Governments also directly intervened in markets—establishing rural credit systems; subsidizing key inputs such as fertilizers, power, and water; and providing price support—to ensure farmers could profit from adopting these new technologies, especially in small farms. Although many countries started land reform prior to the

---

[4] Rosegrant, M., and P. B. R. Hazell. 2000. *Transforming the Rural Asian Economy: The Unfinished Revolution*. New York: Oxford University Press.

Green Revolution, implementing these reforms varied greatly, and consequently, performance was mixed. Where implemented well, tenure reforms corrected exploitative leasing terms, and redistribution schemes helped improve land ownership structures.

These changes led to remarkable growth in agricultural productivity. Expanded irrigation and cultivation of higher-yielding, faster-growing varieties generated strong growth in yields per hectare. Cereal production in Asia more than doubled between 1970 and 1995, from 313 million tons annually to 650 million tons. Despite a 60% jump in population during the period, calories available per capita increased by nearly 30%. Higher food production came with a decline in food prices—for example, the real price of rice in 2000 was roughly one-third of the 1970 cost.[5]

Changes in dietary demands in Asia due to rising incomes and more open foreign trade enabled production diversification into higher-value crops and livestock, which contributed to increased land and labor productivity (Figure 3.2). Increased land productivity came mostly from more intensive land use with modern varieties, modern inputs, and a shift from single to multiple cropping per year. Adopting high-value crops also helped raise land productivity. For instance, between 1970 and 2015, Viet Nam more than doubled land productivity (from $600 per hectare to $1,600 per hectare) and labor productivity (from less than $400 per worker to over $1,000 per worker). Similar patterns occurred in the Philippines, Indonesia, and other Southeast Asian countries. South Asian countries, such as India and Pakistan, also increased land productivity by adopting modern agricultural technology, though they remain at a comparatively lower level.

As the potential gains from Green Revolution technology were exhausted, rice and wheat land productivity nearly reached its technical limits. Meanwhile, rising wages of agricultural labor under this economic transformation induced farmers to substitute machines for labor. Japan's agricultural land productivity, for example, remained at the same level over the past 3 decades, while its labor productivity increased by more than 20% (Figure 3.2). Malaysia's experience appears similar.

---

[5] Otsuka, K. 2012. Economic Transformation of Agriculture in Asia: Past Performance and Future Prospects. *Asian Journal of Agriculture and Development*. 9 (1). pp. 1–19.

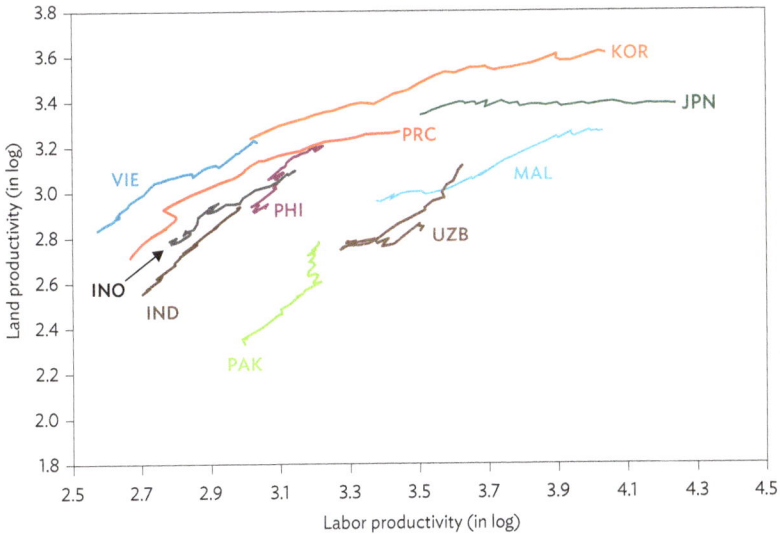

Figure 3.2: Agricultural Land and Labor Productivity, Selected Asian Economies, 1980–2015

IND = India, INO = Indonesia, JPN = Japan, KOR = Republic of Korea, MAL = Malaysia, PAK = Pakistan, PHI = Philippines, PRC = People's Republic of China, UZB = Uzbekistan, VIE = Viet Nam.

Note: Values are in constant 2004–2006 international dollars, in base-10 logarithmic scale.

Source: United States Department of Agriculture Economic Research Service. 2019. *International Agricultural Productivity*. https://www.ers.usda.gov/data-products/international -agricultural-productivity.

Agricultural growth contributed to the development of other sectors. In the early stages of development, surplus labor in subsistence agriculture can shift to the industry sector without reducing agricultural output until the excess labor is exhausted (the so-called "Lewis turning point").[6] This helps keep wages in industry stable during the early stage of industrialization. Further, the increased food surplus helped prevent the rise of living costs for urban workers. Low food prices enabled urban households to spend more on education and health, in the long run contributing to the increased supply of productive labor.

---

[6] Lewis, W. A. 1954. Economic Development with Unlimited Supplies of Labor. *The Manchester School*. 22 (2). pp. 139–191; and Ranis, G., and J. C. H. Fei. 1961. A Theory of Economic Development. *American Economic Review*. 51 (4). pp. 533–565.

Agricultural development also helped industry by increasing demand for agricultural inputs (fertilizers, pesticides, and tractors) while increasing supplies of agricultural raw materials to manufacturing (such as cotton for textile and wheat for instant noodles). The rural population's improved living standards increased domestic demand for nonagricultural goods and services, providing a nascent and expanding market to nurture the growth of firms outside agriculture in the early stage of development. Finally, rural savings were channeled to finance urban and industrial development. Overall, the continued dynamism in agriculture and the rural economy is an integral part of the economy-wide structural transformation.

3.4 Industrialization as the path to high income

Industrialization has been indispensable on the road to high per capita income. East Asia's rapid structural transformation toward industry, manufacturing in particular, is a key part of its success.[7] Workers moved out of agriculture and into manufacturing, and the manufacturing sector itself transformed as it diversified and upgraded. In postwar Japan, for example, shifts in labor between sectors helped boost overall economic productivity—and therefore the growth rate—but most of the gains came from productivity growth in the nonagriculture sectors.[8] Many manufactured goods have high income elasticities of demand, which generate strong demand as incomes rise, and they exhibit economies of scale in production. The shift in employment to industry also enhances incentives for workers to acquire skills adapted to new tasks, which, in turn, strengthens the foundation for future growth.

When accompanied with greater trade openness, manufacturing geared toward export markets can generate the foreign exchange needed to finance capital goods imports. Openness helped further boost manufacturing productivity by attracting foreign direct investment that introduced new technologies and forged links to global value chains. The rise of cross-border production networks in the 1990s further enhanced industry's role, especially in East Asia and Southeast Asia (Chapter 9).

---

[7] See Felipe, J. 2018. Asia's Industrial Transformation: The Role of Manufacturing and Global Value Chains (Parts 1 and 2). *ADB Economics Working Paper Series*. Nos. 549 and 550. Manila: ADB.

[8] Aoki, S., et al. 2011. The Role of the Government in Facilitating TFP Growth during Japan's Rapid-Growth Era. In Otsuka, K., and K. Kalirajan, eds. *Community, Market, and State in Development*. London: Palgrave Macmillan.

Why manufacturing is an engine of growth

A significant part of the reason Asian economies grew so fast is that policy makers recognized the important role manufacturing plays in (i) diversifying and upgrading an economy, (ii) earning sufficient foreign exchange for imports, and (iii) ultimately raising living standards.

Manufacturing matters for growth for several reasons. A structural shift toward manufacturing spurs greater capital accumulation. More than agriculture, where constraints on arable land tend to create decreasing returns to scale, manufacturing exhibits economies of scale. Technological advances can spill over to other firms and generate cost-reducing innovations in production. This can lead to situations where a doubling of capital and labor can more than double output. A significant portion of technical progress occurs in manufacturing. In particular, the manufacture of capital goods (such as machinery and equipment) and consumer durables (such as automobiles) has been the "learning center" of capitalism in technological terms as well as process and organizational innovation.

Historically, the share of PRC manufacturing in total output has been very high. It still accounts for about 30% now (Figure 3.3). Even as the PRC lost millions of manufacturing jobs due to the intensified restructuring of state-owned enterprises that began in the mid-1990s, new private sector manufacturing jobs emerged, especially in labor-intensive light industries. As a result, the share of manufacturing employment increased from about 15% in the 1980s to around 22% in 2018. Manufacturing in several Asian economies (especially Malaysia; the ROK; Singapore; and Taipei,China) have undergone important transformations, shifting output and employment to more technology- and scale-intensive subsectors (Chapter 5). In contrast, the share of India's manufacturing sector has changed little since the 1970s, with the share of output (16%) and employment (11%) relatively stable.

Manufacturing particularly links to other productive sectors and has positive spillover effects. Linkage effects refer to intersectoral purchases and sales, while spillover effects refer to knowledge flows between sectors. Both linkage and spillovers are strong within manufacturing as well as between manufacturing and services and agriculture. For example, the main customers of high-productivity service activities are manufacturing firms.

Figure 3.3: Manufacturing Output (gross value added as a % of GDP) **and Employment** (% of total) **Shares, 1970–2018**

Figure 3.3a: Percentage of GDP

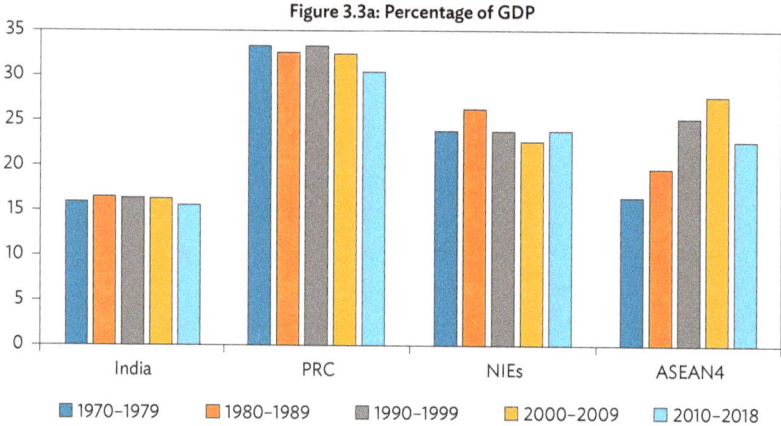

India   PRC   NIEs   ASEAN4

■ 1970–1979 ■ 1980–1989 ■ 1990–1999 ■ 2000–2009 ■ 2010–2018

Figure 3.3b: Percentage of Total Employment

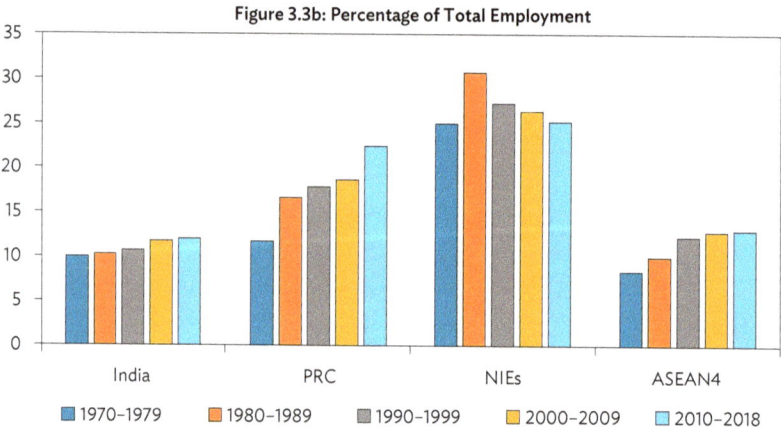

India   PRC   NIEs   ASEAN4

■ 1970–1979 ■ 1980–1989 ■ 1990–1999 ■ 2000–2009 ■ 2010–2018

ASEAN = Association of Southeast Asian Nations, GDP = gross domestic product, NIEs = newly industrialized economies, PRC = People's Republic of China.

Notes: ASEAN4 includes Indonesia, Malaysia, the Philippines, and Thailand. NIEs include Hong Kong, China; the Republic of Korea; Singapore; and Taipei,China.

Sources: For output shares: World Bank. World Development Indicators. https://data.worldbank .org/indicator (accessed 2 August 2019); United Nations (UN). UN Statistics Division Database. https://unstats.un.org (accessed 28 August 2019); national sources; and Asian Development Bank estimates. For employment shares: International Labour Organization (ILO). ILOSTAT Database. https://www.ilo.org/ilostat (accessed 28 August 2019); Timmer, M. P., G.J. de Vries, and K. de Vries. 2015. Patterns of Structural Change in Developing Countries. In Weiss, J., and M. Tribe, eds. *Routledge Handbook of Industry and Development*. Abingdon: Routledge. pp. 65–83 (for the Groningen Growth and Development Center 10-Sector Database) (accessed 28 August 2019); and Asian Development Bank estimates.

Interaction between manufacturing and openness

As the producer of physical and nonperishable products, manufacturing has higher tradability than agriculture or services. A development strategy based on manufacturing allows a country to become increasingly engaged in international trade and, in particular, exporting. This remains true, although improvements in transportation (such as containerization, refrigeration, port efficiency, and other aspects of the timely movement of goods) broadened the range of international trade in agricultural goods, and progress in information and communication technology (ICT) opened possibilities for international trade in some services.

A country's growth becomes constrained by its balance of payments if it cannot generate sufficient foreign exchange to import the necessary capital goods to spur future development. The core of the problem lies in the differences between the income elasticities of goods a country exports and those that it imports. Agricultural products tend to have low income elasticity of demand, such that consumer spending on these goods rises more slowly than growth in income (known as Engel's Law). In contrast, most industrial products, largely produced by advanced economies, have high income elasticity, with demand for these goods growing even faster than income. If a developing country does not have a strong manufacturing sector, it will end up running a deficit in merchandise trade. This is one assertion of the "center–periphery" model (Chapter 2).

Critically, Asia's industrialization since the 1960s has gone hand in hand with increasing openness. Fast export and industrial output growth relaxed the balance of payments constraint, which allowed successful Asian economies to sustain higher rates of GDP expansion. Rapid expansion of exports and industrial output also boosted productivity, setting the stage for higher future growth. In contrast, countries that persisted in pursuing import substitution development strategies—such as many Latin American and South Asian economies in the past—were unable to kick-start this virtuous cycle and had more modest growth as a consequence (Chapter 9).

While market forces and openness are critical conditions for developing manufacturing, evidence shows that some type of proactive industrial policy helped industrialization and upgrading. Virtually no country in the world has industrialized and moved up the development ladder without an appropriate balance between government engagement and market forces (Chapter 2).

In general, exports raised firm efficiency as exposure to larger world markets enabled firms to benefit from economies of scale and forced them to enhance competitiveness and technological development. Exporting is associated with increased rates of technological learning, as firms adjust to the different demands of trade partners and as they develop producer–user relationships. Foreign buyers of electronics provided East Asian producers with information and advice on product designs, quality, production processes, and procurement of capital goods and inputs. When some countries adopted targeted industrial policies, competing on world markets provided a means for governments to test and benchmark manufacturing firms, allowing them to examine whether their efforts in developing a manufacturing base were successful.

The economic transformation of successful Asian economies included a shift toward goods whose demand increases when consumers grow richer (high income elasticity). These types of goods compete on non-price factors—such as branding, quality, reliability, speed of delivery, and extent and efficacy of the distribution network—which play a bigger role in consumer choices at higher income levels. Recent work on complexity, an idea that encompasses diversification at the country level and sophistication at the product level, shows that the export structure of many Asian countries shifted significantly during the last few decades, from products like simple footwear and basic textiles to precision machinery and high-end branded consumer durables (Chapter 5).[9]

Deindustrialization and scope for services-led development

The share of agriculture in output and employment falls and the shares of manufacturing and services correspondingly rise during the early stage of industrialization. However, as industrialization proceeds, labor productivity growth in manufacturing reduces the need for more workers and thus, the employment share of manufacturing begins to decline. As a result, the share of employment in industry tends to peak and then begins to decline—the stage of structural transformation known as "deindustrialization."

---

[9] See Hidalgo, C., and R. Hausmann. 2009. The Building Blocks of Economic Complexity. *Proceedings of the National Academy of Sciences*. 106 (26). pp. 10570–10575; and Felipe, J., et al. 2012. Product Complexity and Economic Development. *Structural Change and Economic Dynamics*. 23 (1). pp. 36–68.

The newly industrialized economies (NIEs) (other than Taipei,China) have clearly begun to deindustrialize. This is particularly evident in Hong Kong, China, where industry's share of employment decreased by nearly 40 percentage points over 5 decades. Deindustrialization is the natural consequence of the NIEs' economic dynamism as they transition to service-led economies. This process was similar to that of the OECD countries.[10]

Unlike the historical pattern of moving from agriculture to industry and then to services, some countries are making a direct transition from agriculture to services. In India and the Philippines, a vibrant services sector—epitomized by business process outsourcing enabled by advances in ICT—contributed much to their rapid growth. Whether countries can bypass industrialization and leapfrog directly from agriculture-led growth to services-led growth remains a contentious issue. In modern history, countries that moved up from middle income to high income typically developed strong manufacturing sectors. Traditionally, there are several characteristics of manufacturing that boost economic development as discussed earlier: tradability of products, more rapid creation of jobs for unskilled labor, the need for scientific and technological expertise (which have large spillover impacts), and division of labor and scale economies.[11] On the other hand, it is possible that advances in ICT may dramatically change this pattern by fostering these characteristics within services.

While the "leapfrogging" debate continues, what is far more certain is that economic dynamism requires both a productive manufacturing sector and a productive services sector. In fact, there is a great deal of synergy between manufacturing and services. Better transportation services, for example, improve the ability of factories to deliver their products to markets at home and abroad. Spillover effects also flow from manufacturing to services. Better ICT hardware, for example, facilitates and enhances online education and remote medical care.

---

[10] Rowthorn, R., and R. Ramaswamy. 1997. Deindustrialization: Causes and Implications. *IMF Working Paper Series.* No. WP/97/4. Washington, DC: International Monetary Fund; and Rowthorn, R., and R. Ramaswamy. 1999. Growth, Trade, and Deindustrialization. *IMF Staff Papers.* 46 (1). pp. 18–41.

[11] See Yang, X., and S. Ng. 1998. Specialization and Division of Labour: A Survey. In Arrow, K. J., Y. K. Ng, and X. Yang, eds. *Increasing Returns and Economic Analysis.* London: Palgrave Macmillan.

3.5 Large and growing imprint of services

Definition of services and their diversity

The services sector has been growing both in terms of GDP and employment, and this will most likely continue in most countries. But services is perhaps the most diverse of the three broad sectors of an economy. It covers activities as diverse as bespoke tailoring, haircuts, convenience store sales, legal advice, architectural design, computer engineering, and business process outsourcing.

According to the United Nations International Standard Industrial Classification of All Economic Activities, revision 4, the services sector comprises economic activities categorized as (i) wholesale and retail trade; repair of motor vehicles and motorcycles; (ii) transportation and storage; (iii) accommodation and food service activities; (iv) information and communication; (v) financial and insurance activities; (vi) real estate activities; (vii) professional, scientific, and technical activities; (viii) administrative and support service activities; (ix) public administration and defense; compulsory social security; (x) education; (xi) human health and social work activities; (xii) arts, entertainment, and recreation; (xiii) other service activities; (xiv) activities of households as employers; undifferentiated goods- and services-producing activities of households for own use; and (xv) activities of extraterritorial organizations and bodies.

To complicate things further, there is often a great deal of diversity within service subsectors. Because of the enormous range of quality within each subsector, broadly defined service subsectors cannot be strictly categorized as "high value added" or "low value added." For example, the quality of education can vary greatly—which explains why parents all over the world compete to get their children into good schools. In traditional services such as haircutting and restaurants, there is plenty of scope to add value. This explains why highly skilled celebrity hair designers or stylists command hundreds, if not thousands, of dollars for one haircut. The restaurant industry also ranges from street hawker food stalls to Michelin 3-star restaurants.

Besides being more diverse, the intrinsic value of services is also more difficult to measure than agriculture or manufacturing. The importance of productivity gains from services may be understated due to the difficulty of measuring their output, and hence productivity. Unlike rice, apples, and beef (agriculture), or cars, laptops, and mobile phones (manufacturing), services output is intangible—such as expert advice from a lawyer or the auditory experience of a concert—and the quality (reflected in value added) is difficult to capture.

Accurate measurement of the value of services is further hindered by the "servicification" of manufacturing.[12] This refers to manufacturing firms increasingly outsourcing services such as marketing, designing, and data processing, which increases the scale of the services sector. On the other hand, those services that are not outsourced tend to be an increasingly important part of the value of a manufacturing firm's output, which leads to undercounting services.

The boundary between services and manufacturing is becoming more and more blurred. In a typical global value chain, activities at the beginning of the value chain (such as research and development, and industrial design) and those at the end (such as distribution and marketing) are services. Activities traditionally thought of as manufacturing (such as fabrication and assembly) generally occur in the middle of the chain.[13]

Growing importance of services

Notwithstanding these measurement issues, the economic importance of services in Asian economies is clearly on the rise. Services already loom large in the region's economic landscape, accounting for 54% of regional output in 2018. However, the share of services to GDP in developing Asia remains well below that of the OECD (Table 3.1). As noted, the deindustrialization process in economies approaching high income means that the process of structural transformation will tilt further toward services in the future. Services will become a growing share of household consumption.[14] When incomes rise, people spend more for health, entertainment, and other recreation. As technologies advance, people tend to want more real experiences through tourism and concerts. Entertainment and game industries are growing across national borders, benefiting from digital and other technologies. K-pop is one good example of success in marketing internationally.

---

[12] Mercer-Blackman, V., and C. Ablaza. 2019. The Servicification of Manufacturing in Asia: A Conceptual Framework. In Helble, M., and B. Shepherd, eds. *Leveraging Services for Development: Prospects and Policies*. Tokyo: Asian Development Bank Institute.

[13] Miroudot, S. 2019. Services and Manufacturing in Global Value Chains—Is the Distinction Obsolete? In Helble, M., and B. Shepherd, eds. *Leveraging Services for Development: Prospects and Policies*. Tokyo: Asian Development Bank Institute.

[14] ADB. 2012. *Asian Development Outlook 2012 Update: Services and Asia's Future Growth*. Manila.

Job creation is critical for inclusive growth, and services are labor-intensive by their very nature. Moreover, manufacturing is poised to become less labor-intensive, with some modern firms now using robots rather than people along the assembly line.

The services sector has already made a huge contribution to employment and thus inclusive growth in Asia (Table 3.1). Importantly, many traditional service jobs remain in the informal sector, shifting to the formal services sector as economies develop. Hence, services will continue to create more jobs in developing Asia, including the shift from the informal to formal sector. Vibrant, high-productivity services will create high-quality, high-wage jobs.

The development of services may also support inclusive growth by fostering greater gender equality. Since service jobs tend to be less physically demanding than manufacturing, they are often more conducive to providing employment for women. A World Bank analysis shows that across 77 countries, services accounts for a higher proportion of female employment than male employment, with the reverse true for manufacturing.[15]

Shift toward high value-added services

Technological progress is fueling the growth of high value-added service industries and activities across Asia, with advances in ICT transforming and upgrading the entire services sector. The PRC has seen the rise of e-commerce giants Alibaba and JD.com. India has its own tech giants such as Infosys and Wipro. Besides technological progress, rapidly rising disposable incomes and the fast-growing middle class across the region are boosting demand for more personalized services tailored to individual preferences. For example, the number of gourmet restaurants and luxury hotels has risen sharply in Asian cities in recent years.

One type of high value-added service is skill- and technology-intensive services (STIS), serving both businesses and consumers. STIS tend to be more sophisticated, add more value, and offer better wages compared to other services. The increased importance of STIS can be proxied by the GDP share of information and communication, finance and insurance, and professional and business services. By this measure, developing Asia still has relatively small STIS sectors (Figure 3.4).

---

[15] World Bank. 2012. *World Development Report 2012: Gender Equality and Development.* Washington, DC.

Figure 3.4: Value-Added of Skill- and Technology-Intensive Services and Other Services in Selected Asian and Advanced Economies (% of GDP)

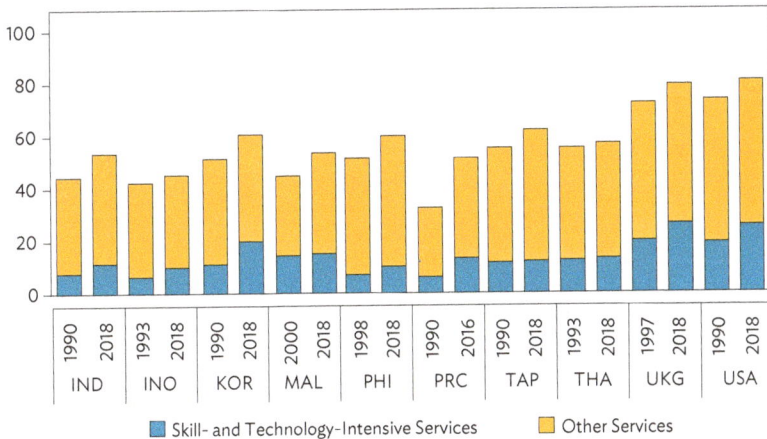

GDP = gross domestic product; IND = India; INO = Indonesia; KOR = Republic of Korea; MAL = Malaysia; PHI = Philippines; PRC = People's Republic of China; TAP = Taipei,China; THA = Thailand; UKG = United Kingdom; USA = United States.

Note: Skill- and technology-intensive services include information and communication, finance and insurance, and professional and business services.

Source: Asian Development Bank estimates based on data from CEIC Data Company. https://www.ceicdata.com/en (accessed 6 July 2019).

The expansion of high value-added services raises growth directly and also indirectly through manufacturing synergies. Business services have particularly large spillovers for manufacturing.[16] For example, more and better industrial design, ICT, and marketing services can improve productivity and the international competitiveness of manufacturing firms. Spillovers can also flow from manufacturing to services, as discussed in the previous section.

Similar to the blurring of the boundary between manufacturing and services, technological progress is making the distinction between STIS and traditional services less clear. One prominent example is the merging of ICT with services such as retail and transportation. For example, Alibaba is an e-commerce retail giant, offering a wide range of

---

[16] Shepherd, B. 2019. Services Policies and Manufacturing Exports. In Helble, M., and B. Shepherd, eds. *Leveraging Services for Development: Prospects and Policies*. Tokyo: Asian Development Bank Institute.

services including its own innovative e-payment system and delivery. Other well-known examples are the ride-sharing start-ups Grab and Gojek in Southeast Asia, which use ICT to add value to traditional taxi services.

Asian countries can benefit from further deregulation to foster greater competition in service industries and develop STIS. Historically, regulatory reforms covering service industries have delivered significant economic benefits, such as higher labor productivity and lower prices. For example, telecommunication charges—such as those for international calls—fell drastically as a result of telecommunication market deregulation in many countries.

Increasing tradability of services

A key consequence of technological progress, especially ICT, is the growing tradability of many services. A generation ago, services were regarded as typical non-tradables in economics textbooks. The advent of ICT made it possible for India and the Philippines to become global leaders in business process outsourcing. This industry has become a major source of foreign exchange earnings (through service exports), growth, and employment in the two countries. Many multinational companies transferred their call centers and customer service units—as well as internal business functions such as human resources or finance and accounting—to these two countries. Advanced research activities are being relocated to developing countries as well, including India and the PRC.

Globally, cross-border services trade, as a share of world income, has grown steadily over the past quarter century. And this has occurred despite rigorous domestic regulations covering financial, medical, and legal services, among others, which hinder their cross-border trade.[17] In almost all countries, services trade liberalization has lagged far behind goods trade. Services trade became an important part of the multilateral trading system only after the World Trade Organization was established in 1995. Now, bilateral and regional trade agreements increasingly incorporate services trade liberalization.[18]

---

[17] Fiorini, M., and B. Hoekman. 2019. Restrictiveness of Services Trade Policy and the Sustainable Development Goals. In Helble, M., and B. Shepherd, eds. *Leveraging Services for Development: Prospects and Policies*. Tokyo: Asian Development Bank Institute; and Jensen, J. 2013. Tradable Business Services, Developing Asia, and Economic Growth. In Park, D., and M. Noland, eds. *Developing the Service Sector as an Engine of Growth for Asia*. Manila: ADB.

[18] OECD. 2018. OECD Services Trade Restrictiveness Index. *Trade Policy Note*. March. Paris.

In Asia, services trade has grown rapidly in recent years. Exports of commercial services rose sharply from $515 billion in 2005 to $1,325 billion in 2017, growing faster than merchandise exports.[19] The growing role of regional and global value chains in the production of manufactured goods—along with the synergy and blurring distinction between manufacturing and services in those value chains—is fueling trade in services. And there remains substantial scope for further growth.

Further reducing barriers to services trade will encourage Asian providers to level up their game in the face of greater competition. Empirical analysis reveals a trend toward higher productivity for some service industries in Asia, comparable to that of the region's globally competitive manufacturing industries.[20] The region's manufacturing firms in global value chains can become more competitive from a more efficient regional services sector and vice versa. Services trade liberalization enables manufacturers to access service inputs at more competitive prices in global markets, thereby boosting productivity.

In the future, services trade will play an even more important role in global trade. For example, ICT enables millions of students to attend online courses from foreign universities and doctors to remotely treat patients in other countries.

Rise of tourism

Tourism is growing rapidly worldwide and, as a result, becoming a crucial industry for many economies. Fifty years ago, international travel was largely confined to a small rich elite. Today, tourism is open to many more people.[21]

Since 2011, international tourist arrivals have grown at an average annual rate of 4.8% globally, adding about 55 million new travelers annually. By 2018, the figure had reached 1.4 billion, of which 348 million (25%) were destined to Asia (Figure 3.5). Over the same period, international tourist receipts grew by 4.9% per year, reaching $1.45 trillion in 2018, of which $436 billion went to Asia (30%). The importance of international tourism increased significantly

---

[19] Helble, M., and B. Shepherd, eds. 2019. *Leveraging Services for Development: Prospects and Policies*. Tokyo: Asian Development Bank Institute.

[20] Shepherd, B. 2019. Productivity and Trade Growth in Services: How Services Helped Power Factory Asia. In Helble, M., and B. Shepherd, eds. *Leveraging Services for Development: Prospects and Policies*. Tokyo: Asian Development Bank Institute.

[21] For an overview, see Park, D., and S. Wayne. 2019. *Role of Tourism for Sustainable Development*. Background note prepared for the ADB Annual Meeting 2019. Fiji. 1–5 May.

Figure 3.5: International Tourist Arrivals, 1995–2018
(million)

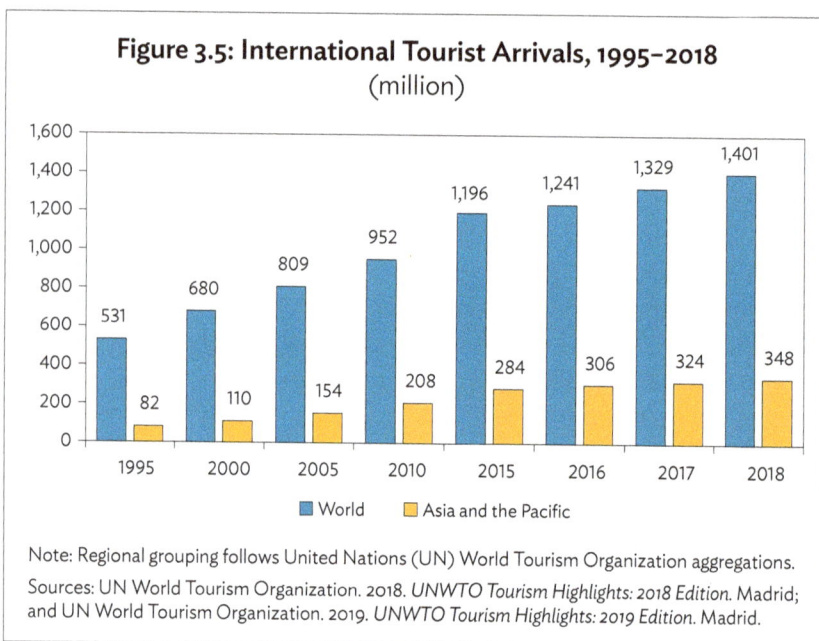

Note: Regional grouping follows United Nations (UN) World Tourism Organization aggregations.
Sources: UN World Tourism Organization. 2018. *UNWTO Tourism Highlights: 2018 Edition.* Madrid; and UN World Tourism Organization. 2019. *UNWTO Tourism Highlights: 2019 Edition.* Madrid.

in Asia, with some variation among countries (Figure 3.6). Domestic tourism has also grown dramatically.

Asia is not just receiving more tourists. People from Asia's emerging economies have been traveling far more in recent years domestically, regionally, and globally. Whereas emerging markets were once primarily destinations for tourists from advanced countries, they have become a major source of global travelers. In 2018, 359 million Asian tourists traveled abroad, accounting for 26% of all international tourists.

Tourism contributes to inclusive growth by generating many new jobs. It is inherently a labor-intensive industry, like other services, but with a focus on visitor satisfaction. Its economic contribution can be measured narrowly by considering only direct effects (such as spending on hotels and airline tickets) or more broadly by adding indirect effects (such as tourism-related investments in new airplanes or hotel construction).

In Asia (including Australia, Japan, and New Zealand), direct economic effects (contribution to GDP) of international and domestic tourism amounted to $0.9 trillion (3.2% of GDP) in 2017, with indirect effects adding $2.7 trillion (9.8% of GDP). Tourism is important especially for small countries with unique cultural traits, historical artifacts, or natural beauty. For example, in Fiji, total international tourism receipts were 34% of GDP in 2018. But not all receipts are counted as a contribution to GDP (value added in a country), because the tourist industry also requires many inputs from abroad—including food and beverages, global hotel chain services, and foreign workers, among others. Tourism receipts, after accounting for imported inputs, were 17% of GDP, but the impact was estimated to reach about 40% of GDP when indirect effects were added.

Figure 3.6: International Tourism Indicators for Selected Asian Economies

Figure 3.6a: Tourism Receipts (% of GDP)

Figure 3.6b: Tourist Arrivals (2018, million)

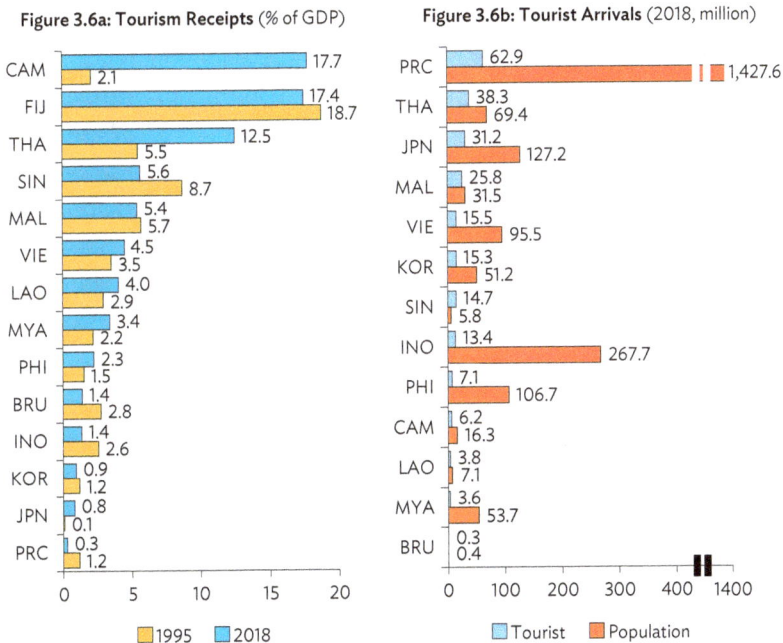

GDP = gross domestic product, BRU = Brunei Darussalam, CAM = Cambodia, FIJ = Fiji INO = Indonesia, JPN = Japan, KOR = Republic of Korea, LAO = Lao People's Democratic Republic, MAL = Malaysia, MYA = Myanmar, PHI = Philippines, PRC = People's Republic of China, SIN = Singapore, THA = Thailand, VIE = Viet Nam.

Notes: The initial years for Brunei Darussalam, Myanmar, and Viet Nam in Figure 3.6a are 2001, 2000, and 2003, respectively. Data for 2018 for Myanmar refer to 2017.

Source: UN World Tourism Organization. 2019. *UNWTO Tourism Highlights: 2019 Edition.* Madrid; and World Bank. World Development Indicators. https://data.worldbank.irg/indicator (accessed 10 October 2019).

In addition to the rapid expansion of disposable income and the dramatic increase of the middle class, especially in emerging economies, conducive policies (such as open sky agreements), the widespread use of social media that facilitates travel planning and reservations, and low-cost air travel (including regional budget airlines such as AirAsia) contributed significantly to the rise in tourism. Although the industry is not generally viewed as an STIS, it holds much potential to add value by including higher-end services, leveraging technology, and utilizing branding. There are also new tourism subsectors such as medical tourism, wellness tourism, and ecotourism.

Despite its many benefits, there is growing recognition of potential negative side effects to further increases in tourism. For example, a sudden surge of tourist traffic can seriously damage environmentally fragile attractions such as beaches or coral reefs. It also can create inconvenience and hardship for local residents, who must deal with increased traffic congestion or a sharp escalation of real estate prices and cost of living. If the environment is damaged and the community disrupted—a negative outcome in itself—it makes the tourism business unsustainable.

Thus, the concept of "sustainable tourism" is attracting more attention. There are several measures that can promote sustainable tourism: (i) ensure guidelines and regulations protect local communities and protect local heritage, (ii) invest in tourism infrastructure such as airports and broadband networks, (iii) build capacity of tourism professionals, and (iv) improve travel facilitation such as visa-free entry for short-term visitors. Bhutan, for example, has started restricting the number of tourists and aims at higher-end travel to enhance tourism's economic impact and sustainability. Also, tourist services can have positive spillovers to manufacturing and inclusive growth. In Bali, Indonesia, for example, tourism has led to an expansion of garment and art exports, which draw on tradition and culture.

3.6 Urbanization as a geographic transformation

Urbanization is central to structural transformation. The shift of resources away from agriculture to industry and services is intertwined with the shift of people from rural to urban areas and the consequent growth of cities. Moreover, manufacturing and many services often benefit from "agglomeration economies," whereby increased interactions among more and different types of firms and workers in any given location boost productivity. The benefits accrue as there are greater opportunities for workers to find suitable jobs, stronger networks of interdependent experts interacting in larger and denser locations, and more scope for spillover of ideas and knowledge between firms and workers. These reinforce traditional advantages of cities, such as port access or proximity to navigable rivers.

The urbanization process is closely associated with stages of economic development. Middle-income countries tend to have at least 50% urbanization rates, with the proportion in high-income countries above 70%. Given Asia's dramatic structural transformation over the past 50 years, it is not surprising that the share of population residing in urban areas in developing Asia rose from 20% to 46% from 1970 to 2018, an increase from about 375 million to almost 1.9 billion urban dwellers (Figure 3.7). If these trends continue, the UN projects some 3 billion people—or two-thirds of developing Asia's population—will be living in cities by 2050.

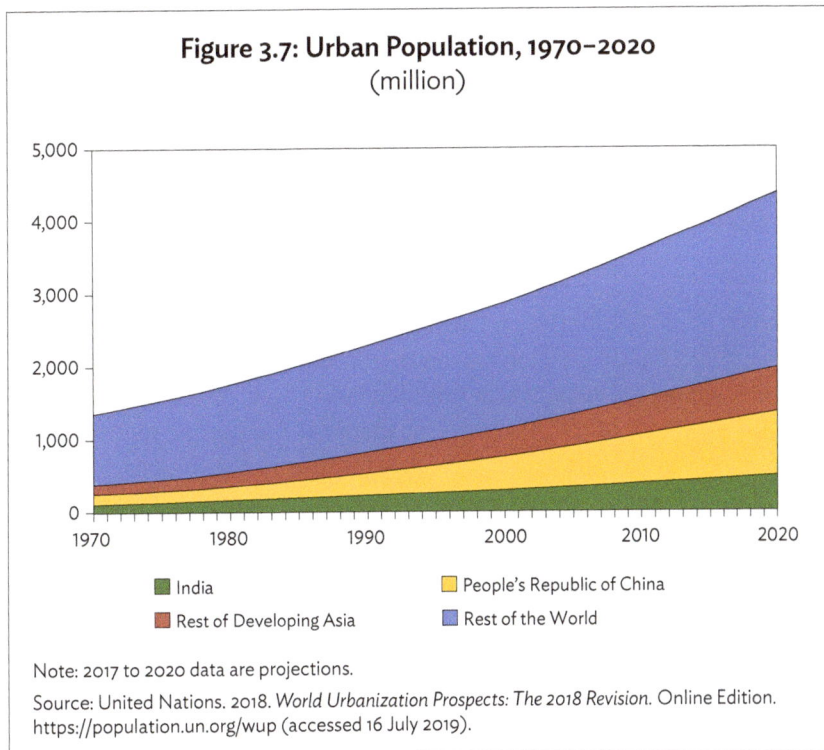

Figure 3.7: Urban Population, 1970–2020
(million)

Note: 2017 to 2020 data are projections.

Source: United Nations. 2018. *World Urbanization Prospects: The 2018 Revision*. Online Edition. https://population.un.org/wup (accessed 16 July 2019).

Figure 3.8: Urbanization Rate and GDP, 2017

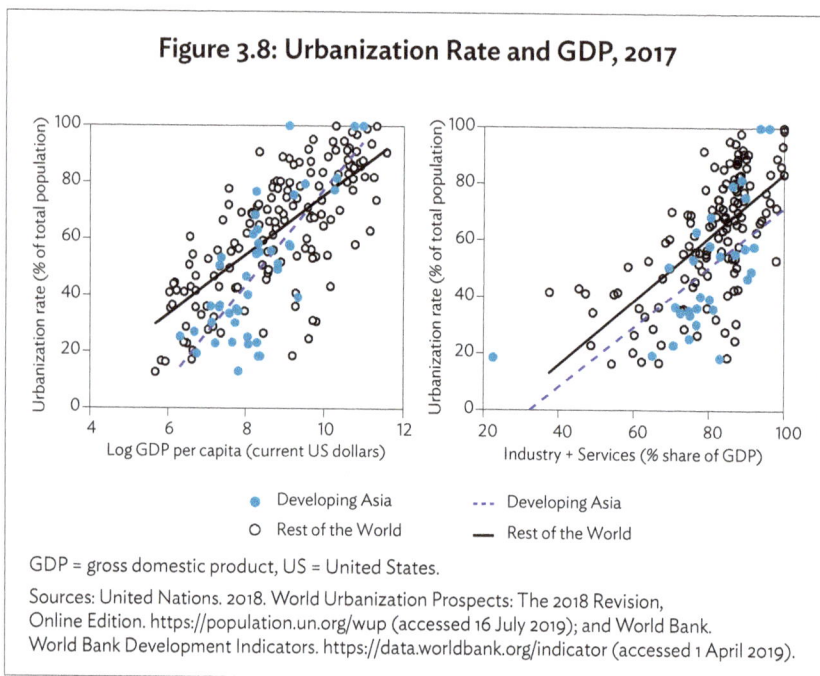

GDP = gross domestic product, US = United States.

Sources: United Nations. 2018. World Urbanization Prospects: The 2018 Revision, Online Edition. https://population.un.org/wup (accessed 16 July 2019); and World Bank. World Bank Development Indicators. https://data.worldbank.org/indicator (accessed 1 April 2019).

Thus, urbanization rates are positively correlated with income per capita (Figure 3.8). At the same time, the rate of urbanization is increasing with the share of industry and services to GDP. Not surprisingly, cities generate a large portion of GDP.[22] While the growth of industry's and services' share of GDP goes hand in hand with urban growth, cities cannot prosper without the support of the rural economy. This link between rural and urban economies underscores the need for balanced development—among cities, secondary cities, and rural areas—which includes modernizing agriculture.

Although other countries in the world achieved high rates of urbanization earlier, the process is unfolding faster in Asia. Because of its faster pace of economic development, Asia achieved a level of urbanization in 95 years that took 100–200 years in other regions.[23] In many respects, Asia's urbanization process has been compressed.

Urbanization is often a natural process associated with changing job opportunities as part of structural transformation, and the

---

[22] ADB. 2008. *Managing Asian Cities*. Manila.

[23] ADB. 2012. *Asian Development Outlook 2012 Update: Services and Asia's Future Growth*. Manila.

attraction of cities such as better access to education and health. Some countries have tried to control migration from rural areas to cities. In the PRC, the *hukou* registration system manages migration from rural to urban areas. More recently, the government has taken steps to relax the system to encourage migration from rural areas to secondary cities. Some governments, such as those of Indonesia, Japan, and the ROK, have tried to deconcentrate populations for more balanced regional development.

Asia is expected to continue high-speed urbanization, resulting in rising numbers of densely populated, increasingly large cities. Worldwide, the number of megacities (cities with more than 10 million inhabitants) is expected to grow from 29 in 2015 to 37 in 2025. Most of them are expected to be in Asia, and 6 out of the world's 10 largest ones are already in Asia (including two from Japan). Asian megacities will increase from 15 to 20 (from 17 to 22 if Tokyo and Osaka are included).[24]

While Asia reaps many benefits from urbanization, its speed has meant that accumulation of physical and institutional infrastructure has often lagged behind growth of the urban population. This can have negative consequences for urban dwellers such as traffic congestion, environmental degradation, health problems, and even rising crime. A key challenge for governments is to harness the agglomeration economies of cities while minimizing urbanization's negative effects.

3.7 Looking ahead

The shift from agriculture to manufacturing and services, and rapid urbanization propelled much of the region from low- to middle-income status. Sustained rapid growth brought the share of developing Asia's population living in middle- or high-income countries from less than 10% in 1991 to more than 95% by 2015. Moving from middle to high income will require further structural changes.

Policies needed to do this—to continue sustainable and inclusive growth for developing Asia—have common elements, many of which are discussed in this book. These common elements include the promotion of efficient markets, strong governance, technological advancement, human capital development, infrastructure investment, open trade and investment regimes, prudent macroeconomic policies, measures to address inclusiveness and gender equality, and support

---

[24] UN. 2018. *World Urbanization Prospects: The 2018 Revision.* Online Edition. https://population.un.org/wup (accessed 16 July 2019).

for the environment. At the same time, overcoming the challenges of further structural transformation hinges on an economy's development status and other specific conditions.

Low-income countries, or those that recently graduated to lower-middle-income status, must undertake policy reforms and investments to raise agricultural productivity, invest more in basic infrastructure (both rural and urban), improve secondary education and technical and vocational education and training, and further improve the business environment to attract more foreign direct investment. They would benefit from applying the lessons of their successful regional peers.

For economies at or near upper-middle-income status, such as the PRC and Malaysia, transitioning to high income and avoiding the "middle-income trap" will require new and different drivers of growth. They must focus more on investing in higher education and research, increasing ICT networks and other high-quality infrastructure, and deepening and broadening financial markets.[25] They should address rising income inequalities between advanced and lagging regions, including the reform of residential registration systems. They should further strengthen economic institutions and policies, such as intellectual property protection and stronger competition laws, to create an environment conducive for attracting new players, new products, and new services.

For high-income economies like the NIEs, the innovation challenge is even more acute as they are at (or near) the global technology frontier. These economies will also need to strengthen policies that avoid widening the income gap between high- and low-skilled labor to maintain social cohesion. At the same time, they must address challenges coming from a declining working-age population and rapid aging.

Given rapid urbanization, appropriate investments in urban infrastructure are needed—especially network infrastructure such as transport, water supply, sanitation, and waste management—as well as education and health services. To mitigate the concentration of populations in big cities, connectivity between cities and between urban and rural areas must be strengthened. It is important to have strong governance and civil participation for planning and regulations regarding city development, land use, and environmental protection.

---

[25] ADB. 2017. *Asian Development Outlook 2017: Transcending the Middle-Income Challenge.* Manila.

CHAPTER 4

MODERNIZING AGRICULTURE AND RURAL DEVELOPMENT

4.1   Introduction

Economic growth is typically accompanied by declining shares of agriculture in total value added and employment. This pattern of structural change aptly depicts Asia's development over the past 50 years (Table 4.1). Yet the decreasing share of agriculture in gross domestic product (GDP) masks its importance.[1] As the region's economies transformed, agriculture played an important role in supplying food and surplus labor, providing inputs to other sectors, and creating new market demand for industrial goods and services. Asia's experience shows that a productive agriculture and dynamic rural economy is a key factor for countries that have undergone successful structural change and inclusive development.

This chapter presents a historical overview of how agriculture and rural economies have transformed as an integral part of Asia's overall economic transformation. Over 50 years ago, Asia's agrarian economies elicited pessimism. Many believed Asian nations would suffer from food shortages (and famines in the worst cases) because of explosive population growth, stagnant grain yields, and the

---

[1]   Timmer, C. P. 2014. *Managing Structural Transformation: A Political Economy Approach.* UNU-WIDER Annual Lecture No. 18. Helsinki: United Nations University World Institute for Development Economics Research.

near-exhaustion of farmland. In addition, agriculture was seen as an inferior partner in overall development—a sector deemed unprofitable for investment but from which resources had to be extracted for financing industrialization.

Land reform (introduced in many countries, especially in East Asia) distributed land to small farmers, increased incentives, and contributed to increased productivity. The Green Revolution began in the late 1960s with increased investment in irrigation, improved seed varieties, and modern inputs such as chemical fertilizers and pesticides. It fundamentally altered the perception of agriculture. It helped Asia's farmers substantially increase yields of rice, wheat, and other cereal crops, and allayed fears of widespread food insecurity.

Following the Green Revolution, mechanization, such as the increased use of tractors and harvesters, contributed to agriculture's structural change. As economies continued to grow, other changes occurred in rural Asia. First, farm production diversified beyond food grains, responding to rising incomes and changing consumption patterns. Livestock, fruit, and vegetable production outpaced that of cereals. The diversity of diets has been most notable since the 1990s as consumption of rice—Asia's traditional food staple—started to fall among middle-income and increasingly urban populations. Second, market reforms and trade openness since the 1980s have increasingly commercialized agriculture with greater private sector involvement. Supported by new infrastructure and communications, food systems that linked production, processing, marketing, and distribution became more integrated. Third, rural nonfarm economies expanded beyond agriculture or small-scale industry and commerce. In particular, the rapid growth of small towns and secondary cities forged closer ties between rural and urban economies. The expanding nonfarm economy helped absorb labor released from farming and improved labor productivity.

The story of agricultural and rural transformation policy centers on food, employment, and income. This chapter discusses how institutional and policy changes—including land reform, market liberalization, and public investment—have facilitated the process. As the scope and speed of change differ across Asia, the chapter will highlight country experience in transforming traditional agriculture, which grew to become Asia's region-wide strategic imperative. Indeed, one of the initial priorities of the Asian Development Bank (ADB) was agriculture—symbolized by the grain husks in its logo.

Table 4.1: Macroeconomic Indicators in Agriculture, Selected Economies, 1970–2018

Subregion/ Economies	Agriculture Share to GDP (3-Year Average) (%)			Agriculture Share to Employment (3-Year Average) (%)			Annual Growth Rate of Agricultural GDP (%)		Annual Growth Rate of GDP (%)		Annual Growth Rate, Agriculture Value Added per Worker (%)
	1975– 1977	1995– 1997	2015– 2018	1975– 1977	1995– 1997	2015– 2018	1970– 1989	1990– 2018	1970– 1989	1990– 2018	1992– 2018
Central Asia											
Georgia	...	31.5	8.3	...	49.0	45.2	...	(0.2)	4.3	0.4	1.7
Kazakhstan	...	12.5	4.7	...	36.7	16.1	...	0.9	...	3.0	4.9
Uzbekistan	...	30.2	33.6	...	38.3	33.6	3.2	4.0	...	4.3	2.0
East Asia											
Mongolia	...	36.7	12.7	...	47.2	29.1	2.9	3.3	6.0	4.4	2.9
PRC	31.1	18.9	7.8	...	50.9	27.5	3.9	4.0	8.6	9.4	6.4
Republic of Korea	25.5	5.5	2.2	...	11.2	4.9	3.5	1.2	9.6	5.1	4.9
Taipei,China	11.9	2.9	1.8	7.9	4.1	4.3	...	...	9.7	4.7	0.8
South Asia											
Afghanistan	...	...	21.6	...	64.5	38.7	...	2.6	...	6.8	2.0
Bangladesh	54.3	25.8	14.6	...	65.2	41.7	0.9	3.8	2.5	5.6	3.2
India	37.8	27.1	17.2	...	61.4	44.8	2.8	3.1	4.3	6.3	2.9
Nepal	68.3	41.6	30.1	...	79.5	70.7	2.3	3.0	3.3	4.5	1.6
Pakistan	32.0	26.1	24.5	...	43.1	41.7	3.5	3.2	5.9	4.2	0.3
Sri Lanka	30.3	22.5	8.5	...	38.3	26.7	2.4	2.7	4.2	5.3	3.4

continued on next page

Table 4.1 continued

Subregion/ Economies	Agriculture Share to GDP (3-Year Average) (%)			Agriculture Share to Employment (3-Year Average) (%)			Annual Growth Rate of Agricultural GDP (%)		Annual Growth Rate of GDP (%)		Annual Growth Rate, Agriculture Value Added per Worker (%)
	1975–1977	1995–1997	2015–2018	1975–1977	1995–1997	2015–2018	1970–1989	1990–2018	1970–1989	1990–2018	1992–2018
Southeast Asia											
Cambodia	...	47.5	25.7	...	75.2	31.0	...	3.8	...	6.0	4.7
Indonesia	27.6	13.7	13.8	59.1	43.1	31.5	3.6	3.1	6.5	4.9	3.5
Lao PDR	...	40.6	18.8	...	84.5	68.5	...	3.2	4.1	6.9	1.7
Malaysia	29.4	11.6	8.5	...	18.9	11.5	4.3	1.9	7.0	5.8	1.9
Philippines	29.4	20.4	9.7	...	42.1	26.6	2.6	2.1	3.9	4.5	2.1
Thailand	26.1	9.1	8.4	...	50.8	31.3	4.4	1.8	7.4	4.5	3.4
Viet Nam	...	26.9	17.6	...	65.6	41.5	3.1	3.5	4.5	6.8	3.8
The Pacific											
Fiji	24.9	19.1	12.2	...	46.8	39.8	3.6	0.5	3.6	2.7	0.5
Papua New Guinea	31.5	33.5	17.8	...	71.6	67.9	...	2.3	2.6	4.1	3.0

... = data not available, ( ) = negative, GDP = gross domestic product, Lao PDR = Lao People's Democratic Republic, PRC = People's Republic of China.

Sources: Asian Development Bank estimates; World Bank. World Development Indicators. https://data.worldbank.org/indicator (accessed 2 August 2019); United Nations Statistics Division. https://unstats.un.org (accessed 28 August 2019); International Labour Organization. ILOSTAT Database. https://www.ilo.org/ilostat (accessed 28 August 2019); and for Taipei,China: Directorate-General of Budget, Accounting and Statistics.

This chapter has the following sections. Section 4.2 reviews Asia's food problems in the 1950s, giving the historical context for transformation forces that unfolded subsequently. It is followed by section 4.3 with an overview of land reform experience across Asia. Section 4.4 describes how the Green Revolution started and highlights the impacts of the technology-led transformation on solving Asia's food problem. Key policy and institutional changes needed to sustain the Green Revolution momentum are discussed in section 4.5. Section 4.6 presents continuing transformations of food systems including changes in consumption patterns, production diversification, agricultural trade, and agribusinesses and supply chains. Section 4.7 discusses how transformations are extended to rural nonfarm economies, to foster rural–urban integration. Finally, section 4.8 discusses, among other things, key priorities for advancing agricultural modernization and rural development including food security, food safety, and well-functioning agricultural markets.

4.2   Asia's food problems in the 1950s

In the immediate years after World War II, many developing countries won independence. Leaders saw an opportunity to establish a more stable, more productive, and economically independent modern state. Developing large-scale industry was one way to express economic independence. Many countries initially tried to promote industry—especially heavy industry—and quickly recognized they had to pay greater attention to agriculture.[2]

Indeed, the prevailing reality of Asia's predominantly agrarian economies was stark. When assessing the progress of developing Asia's postwar industrial development in 1958, the United Nations (UN) Economic Commission for Asia and the Far East (ECAFE) said "agricultural expansion in a number of the countries in the region has hardly materialized to the extent anticipated ... Per capita food production in the region is not yet restored even to prewar levels ..."[3] In many Asian countries, agriculture continued to be weak and

---

[2]   During the colonial era, the production of export-oriented tropical commodities, such as tea, rubber, and palm oil, came from large plantations. By the 1950s, most became smallholder production systems. Since then, there has been a resurgence of investment in plantation agriculture in some Southeast Asian countries such as Cambodia, the Lao People's Democratic Republic, and Myanmar (Byerlee, D. 2014. The Fall and Rise Again of Plantations in Tropical Asia: History Repeated? *Land.* 3 (3). pp. 574–597).

[3]   UN ECAFE. 1964. *Annual Economic Survey*. Bangkok. p. 1.

vulnerable. Many had to rely on food aid and imports to meet growing demand. Five years later, in its 1964 annual survey, ECAFE said "the net import into the developing ECAFE region increased by 41% from 4.2 million tons in 1951/52–1953/54 to 5.9 million tons in 1960/61–1962/63."[4] Without an increase in production, ECAFE estimated net import of cereals in 1970 might have to triple from the early 1960s level. During 1963 and 1964, cyclical food shortages and speculation precipitated food crises in a few countries. This again drew government attention to the severe problem of food supply.

"Getting Agriculture Moving"[5] became a new strategic priority in Asia. There were just a few examples of how to do so. In the late 19th century, Japan showed how productive agriculture could power economic growth by introducing new technology, extension services, and better education, and developing transportation networks and logistics services.[6] Taipei,China's experience since the early 1950s was a more recent example of how active support for agriculture facilitated overall economic development.[7] Difficult policies such as land reform were swiftly implemented, large investments were made to rehabilitate irrigation systems and develop rural infrastructure, and rural cooperatives were established to assist smallholders by supporting agricultural marketing and input supply. Combined, these measures led to a surge in domestic agricultural production in Taipei,China, which grew by 4.4% annually between 1954 and 1967—the fastest in Asia.[8]

The experience of Japan and Taipei,China showed that Asia's sluggish agriculture in the 1950s and early 1960s was due to a failure to invest in rural development.[9] There were also deep-seated misconceptions about peasant behavior: individual farmers were often regarded as tradition-bound and unresponsive to markets. T. W. Schultz countered these in *Transforming Traditional Agriculture* (1964).[10]

---

[4]   UN ECAFE. 1964. *Annual Economic Survey*. Bangkok. p. 1.
[5]   Mosher, A. 1966. *Getting Agriculture Moving: Essentials for Development and Modernization*. New York: Agricultural Development Council.
[6]   Ohkawa, K., and H. Rosovsky. 1960. The Role of Agriculture in Modern Japanese Economic Development. *Economic Development and Cultural Change*. 9 (1). pp. 43–67.
[7]   Fu, T., and S. Shei. 1999. Agriculture as the Foundation for Development. In Thorbecke, E., and H. Wan, eds. *Lessons on the Roles of Government and Market*. New York: Springer Science+Business Media LLC.
[8]   Wade, R. 2003. *Governing the Markets: Economic Theory and the Role of Government in East Asian Industrialization*. Revised edition. Princeton: Princeton University Press.
[9]   James, W. E., S. Naya, and G. M. Meier. 1987. *Asian Development: Economic Success and Policy Lessons*. San Francisco: International Center for Economic Growth.
[10] Schultz, T. W. 1964. *Transforming Traditional Agriculture*. New Haven and London: Yale University Press.

He observed that the "rational peasant" was poor but efficient, operating at minimum cost within the limits of existing technology. The basic challenge of rural development was to open new opportunities through research and technological advances. At the same time, education could increase the capacity of farmers to skillfully adopt innovation. Economic incentives would speed the process by making increased production more profitable and offsetting the high risks associated with new methods.

Therefore, transforming traditional agriculture was foremost about changing Asian policy makers' mind-set about agriculture. This point was forcefully made in the 1969 *Asian Agricultural Survey*,[11] ADB's first regional study after it was established in 1966, with professors T. W. Schultz and Kazushi Ohkawa co-chairing the Survey Advisory Committee.

The survey had a clear optimistic vision. Transforming traditional agriculture required modern farming technology and removing the institutional and infrastructural constraints to farmers adopting new technology. When modern technology was effectively introduced, the survey envisioned "large parts of agriculture in this region will become profitable, the supply price of farm food products will begin to recede, producing for consumers generally a real consumer surplus, and it will shift the comparative advantage back in favor of this region."[12]

4.3   Land reform: experiences and lessons

Among development alternatives, rural institutional reform became the dominant theme in agriculture and in supporting overall development. Land reform was an important element. Many economies in Asia had begun land reform programs as early as the late 1940s; "land to tillers" was a popular agenda. Since then, land reform has had two distinct phases: the first was from the late 1940s to 1970s; the second during the 1980s and 1990s. The first wave was in Japan; the Republic of Korea (ROK); Taipei,China; and newly independent economies. The second occurred in transitional economies that were decollectivizing agriculture. While distinct, both had similar economic justification—farmers without permanent title in the land they farmed or oppressed by heavy rents would not have any incentive to invest

---

[11]   ADB. 1969. *Asian Agricultural Survey*. Manila.
[12]   ADB. 1969. *Asian Agricultural Survey*. Manila. pp. 7–8.

labor and capital for expanding farm output. Land reform had multiple goals on top of economic goals.[13] It had a redistributive focus to address asset inequality. And politically, redistributing land from landowners to tenants and landless laborers helped establish more egalitarian societies, which promoted social and political stability for development and prepared better educated workers for industry.

After World War II, land reform in Japan; the ROK; and Taipei,China was carried out over the short span of 5 to 10 years. Special circumstances made land reform in the three economies swift.[14] Japan's reforms were directed by United States (US) occupation forces, although even before the war, its Ministry of Agriculture drafted a comprehensive land reform plan—used as the basis for the reform program under US occupation.[15] The Democratic People's Republic of Korea began land reform immediately after independence from Japan, and the ROK introduced its farming land reform law in 1949 to compete against communist influence. In Taipei,China, reform was enforced by the Nationalist government which had just left the mainland. It was implemented more thoroughly because there was limited interference from indigenous landed interests.

The three northeast Asian economies (Japan; the ROK; and Taipei,China) initially implemented reforms to improve rental terms for tenant farmers. But the emphasis soon shifted to redistribute lands from large landowners to tenants and laborers, with redistribution done below market prices. Also, in all three economies, there was a 3-hectare limit for farms. A critical implementation mechanism was the creation of land committees with tenants and owner–farmers outnumbering landowners. In Japan, 33% of arable land was redistributed to some 61% of rural households. In the ROK, 27% of arable land was redistributed to 46% of rural households. Similarly, 27% of arable land was redistributed to 63% of rural households in Taipei,China.[16] Studies found that land reform in the three economies improved welfare and increased agricultural productivity.

---

[13] Lipton, M. 2009. *Land Reform in Developing Countries*. London: Routledge.
[14] Hayami, Y., and Y. Godo. 2005. *Development Economics: From the Poverty to the Wealth of Nations*. 3rd edition. New York: Oxford University Press; and Studwell, J. 2013. *How Asia Works: Success and Failure in the World's Most Dynamic Region*. New York: Grove Press.
[15] Kaiji, I. 1991. Japan's Postwar Rural Land Reform: Its Merits and Demerits. In Committee for the Japanese Agriculture Session, XXI IAAE Conference, ed. *Agriculture and Agricultural Policy in Japan*. Tokyo: University of Tokyo Press.
[16] Deininger, K. 2003. *Land Policies for Growth and Poverty Reduction*. Washington, DC: World Bank.

Elsewhere in Asia, land reform progressed slowly with mixed outcomes. In the Philippines, land reform programs started in the 1940s. But they were ineffective until 1972, when the 1963 Agricultural Land Reform Code was vigorously implemented under a newly created Department of Agrarian Reform. The individual landholding ceiling was 7 hectares and applied only to farms producing rice and maize. It exempted sugarcane and other plantations, and applied only to tenanted areas. To evade the law, landowners registered land under family member names and evicted tenants, preventing their access to land and forcing them to work as agricultural laborers.[17] Even after 4 decades of land reform legislation, just 10.8% of arable land had been transferred to former tenants by 1985.[18] Over the years, land reform codes have become more complicated and implementation arrangements more complex. Still, officially, land reform continues to be part of an important unfinished agenda for inclusive development.

In South Asia, land reform had limited success. In the 1950s, India abolished the long-standing zamindari or "permanent settlement" system, ending one of the most iniquitous landownership systems in north India.[19] Under the zamindari system, introduced at the end of the 18th century, feudal lords were declared proprietors of the land, peasants became tenant farmers, and rents were collected by a series of intermediaries who squeezed the farmers. In the 1950s, Pakistan also worked to reform systems similar to the zamindari.

The subsequent reforms in India to redistribute land rights and improve terms of tenancy were implemented unevenly across states and remain incomplete. Surplus land was distributed to landless and near-landless poor farmers, while there was widespread evasion and avoidance of ceilings legislation. During the 1970s and 1980s, "5.7 million households received an average of 0.4 hectare each from direct ceilings effects alone, benefiting some 27 million people; further, tenurial rights to almost 10 million hectares of land were transferred."[20] Although there were large absolute numbers of beneficiaries and affected land areas, nationwide implementation remained limited as reforms were

[17] Studwell, J. 2013. *How Asia Works: Success and Failure in the World's Most Dynamic Region.* New York: Grove Press.
[18] Deininger, K. 2003. *Land Policies for Growth and Poverty Reduction.* Washington, DC: World Bank.
[19] Rosegrant, M. W., and P. B. R. Hazell. 2000. *Transforming the Rural Asian Economy: The Unfinished Revolution.* New York: Oxford University Press.
[20] Lipton, M. 2009. *Land Reform in Developing Countries: Property Rights and Property Wrongs.* London: Routledge. p. 287.

concentrated in just a few Indian states. In two Indian states—Kerala and West Bengal—political activism helped enforce tenancy contracts, benefiting many poor tenants.

The Government of India has a clear stance on continuing land reform and improving land administration, outlined in recent planning documents. Implementation continues to be a major challenge for several reasons. India's land tenure governance is complex both in terms of legislation and organizational framework. Rural land markets are inefficient due to poor land records, tenancy restrictions, and land ceiling laws that lead to concealed ownership and transaction barriers.[21] These institutional constraints continually fragment operational landholdings. And the ever smaller farm size limits the potential for growth in agricultural productivity.

Socialist countries took rather different paths to address landownership. For example, the People's Republic of China (PRC) in the early 1950s took drastic measures to confiscate holdings from landowners and distributed them to the landless. Several years later, the government began collectivization and peasants returned the land they had received. The collective agriculture system continued until the late 1970s, when the government started comprehensive economic reforms, initially in rural areas (Box 4.1).

There were other approaches in dealing with land distribution. After World War II, Thailand initiated land settlement programs to encourage rural people to settle on previously forested land. Malaysia introduced a land allocation program to encourage the expansion of rubber plantations.[22] In the Pacific, customary land rights continue to be respected when addressing land distribution.

Land policies (including land reform) remain important. In India, for example, 40% of farmers were landless in early 2000. More than half of rural households were landless in the early 2010s. In the Philippines, the share of landless farmers rose from 58% in the 1970s to 70% in 2010. Past assessments of land reform remain relevant.[23]

---

[21] Organisation for Economic Co-operation and Development (OECD)—Food and Agriculture Organization of the United Nations (FAO). 2018. *Agricultural Outlook 2018–2027*. Rome.

[22] Poapongsakorn, N., and Y. S. Tey. 2016. Institutions, Governance, and Transformation in Southeast Asian Agriculture. In Habito, C. F., D. Capistrano, and G. Saguiguit, Jr., eds. *Farms, Food, and Futures: Toward Inclusive and Sustainable Agricultural and Rural Development in Southeast Asia*. Los Baños, Philippines: Southeast Asian Regional Center for Graduate Study and Research in Agriculture.

[23] International Fund for Agricultural Development. 2016. *Rural Development Report: Fostering Inclusive Rural Transformation*. Rome.

ADB's 2nd Asian Agriculture Survey in 1978 cited key lessons to strengthen land reform in Asia: (i) the need for serious commitment at the top, (ii) simple and clear technical design of enactments, (iii) effective organization among beneficiaries, and (iv) the provision of necessary support services to beneficiaries.[24] Further measures are needed to modernize, simplify, and strengthen land administration. In some countries, land title records are neglected or not updated. Land titling systems need to be upgraded and digitized if possible. This is to address the growing concern of land fragmentation. It also enables land markets to function efficiently and to use land as collateral for credit.

Box 4.1: Agrarian Reform in the People's Republic of China, Viet Nam, and Central Asian Republics

People's Republic of China: Rural reform began in 1978 with the introduction of the household responsibility system; agricultural land was distributed to individual farmers through land use rights, with the state remaining as the formal owner. This land reform, together with the increased procurement prices for agricultural products, unleashed farmers' production incentives and led to significant increases in output. The success of these reforms gave the government confidence to pursue further change. A series of land laws since 1979 have extended contract periods. The standard contract term for agricultural land was extended to 30 years, according to the Land Administration Law of 1998. The 2007 Property Law established that farmers' land use rights were private property rights.

Viet Nam's *Doi Moi*: After the war with the United States ended in 1975, socialist transformation in Viet Nam forced farmers to join agricultural cooperatives—although collectivization in the south was not particularly successful.[a] During 1987–1989, Viet Nam implemented a package of measures under its *Doi Moi* policy, which fundamentally changed the nature of the economy from a centrally planned to market-oriented system. One of the measures (Resolution 10) started de-collectivization. Resolution 10 obliged agricultural cooperatives to contract land to peasant households for 15 years for annual crops and 40 years for perennial crops. The 1993 Land Law extended these to 20 years and 50 years, respectively. Throughout the reform period, agricultural production grew steady.

continued on next page

---

[24] ADB. 1978. *Rural Asia: Challenge and Opportunity*. Manila.

Box 4.1 *continued*

Central Asian Republics: Immediately after the collapse of the Soviet Union, the Central Asian republics saw a severe decline in agricultural output. Comprehensive reforms were introduced covering land privatization, trade liberalization, and the liberalization of input and output markets. Farmers obtained land and could decide on what to produce. Their immediate response was to produce for food self-sufficiency—because the dissolution of the Soviet Union disrupted existing supply chains. In southern countries, the production of cereal and root crops, such as potatoes, increased significantly as they could no longer rely on imports from Kazakhstan and other former Soviet Union countries. Gross production of cereal and root crops almost doubled in the Kyrgyz Republic and tripled in Uzbekistan. Gradually, new trade relationships developed across the subregion and with other countries—contributing to the growth of nonfood crops where there was comparative advantage.

[a] Kirk, M., and N. D. A. Tuan. 2010. Land Tenure Policy Reforms: Decollectivization and the Doi Moi System in Vietnam. In Spielman, D. J., and R. Pandya-Lorch, eds. *Proven Successes in Agricultural Development: A Technical Compendium to Millions Fed.* Washington, DC: International Food Policy Research Institute.

Sources: Deininger, K. 2003. *Land Policies for Growth and Poverty Reduction.* Washington, DC: World Bank; Food and Agriculture Organization of the United Nations. FAOSTAT 2019. http://www.fao.org/faostat/en/#data/QC (accessed 1 May 2019); Kirk, M., and N. D. A. Tuan. 2010. Swinnen, J. F. M., and L. Vranken. 2010. Reforms and Agricultural Productivity in Central and Eastern Europe and the Former Soviet Republics: 1989-2005. *Journal of Productivity Analysis.* 33 (3). pp. 241–258.

4.4   Green Revolution and efforts to sustain its momentum

Start of the Green Revolution

The Green Revolution, which began in Southeast Asia during the late 1960s, was a major technological advancement—instrumental in transforming traditional agriculture. It boosted grain productivity, successfully solved the food problem during economic transformation, and moved Asia into a new stage of agricultural development.

The Green Revolution is a package of modern farming practices that includes using high-yielding varieties of primarily rice and wheat, applying modern inputs (especially fertilizer), and improving irrigation. There are two salient points. First, developing high-yielding varieties is not a one-shot phenomenon. It is best understood as a process of crop breeding and steady productivity gains, as varieties need to continuously improve to adapt to evolving crop disease and production conditions. Second, the effect of improved technologies on production can occur only when sufficient fertilizer and irrigation are available.

For irrigation, governments, with the support of external financiers such as ADB, made significant investments (Box 4.2). On average, Asian countries spent 15.4% of public expenditure on agriculture in 1972. They doubled agricultural spending in real values by 1985.[25]

Modern wheat and rice strains were developed by crossing varieties that were fertilizer responsive, short-statured, and suitable for moderate climate and tropical weather.[26] Modern wheat varieties were developed by the Maize and Wheat Breeding Program of the Rockefeller Foundation in Mexico. Later, the program was renamed the International Maize and Wheat Improvement Center (CIMMYT). Modern wheat varieties quickly spread across India and other wheat-producing countries.

In 1966, the International Rice Research Institute (IRRI) in the Philippines developed an improved rice variety by crossing a tall tropical Indonesian rice strain and a short variety from Taipei,China. The new variety was named IR8, later commonly known as "miracle rice." Because IR8 was short, it could remain standing with heavy grains at its head and had strong resistance against tropical disease and conditions because of genes inherited from its Indonesian parent.

Previously, any increase in rice production came only from expanding cultivated land. With the necessary inputs, modern varieties significantly increased yields. In addition, with improved irrigation, modern varieties could grow during any season and had medium growth duration. This allowed farmers to grow rice two to three times a year.

The successful development of modern varieties led to subsequent improvements that enhanced resistance to crop disease. The results were staggering. Rice yields increased from 2 tons per hectare in the early 1960s to about 7 tons per hectare in East Asia and 4 tons per hectare in South Asia and Southeast Asia in the mid-2010s. Wheat yields also increased from 1 ton per hectare in the early 1960s to over 5 tons per hectare in East Asia and 3 tons per hectare in South Asia in the mid-2010s.[27]

---

[25] Rosegrant, M. W., and P. B. R. Hazell. 2000. *Transforming the Rural Asian Economy: The Unfinished Revolution*. New York: Oxford University Press.

[26] The idea of developing short modern varieties of rice and wheat can be found in prewar Japan, and a short wheat variety called Norin 10 became one of the parental varieties for Green Revolution wheat. This was developed by Norman Borlaug who won a Nobel Prize in 1976 for his contribution to global food security.

[27] Evenson, R. E., and D. Gollin. 2003. *Crop Variety Improvement and Its Effect on Productivity: The Impact of International Agricultural Research*. Wallingford: CABI Publishing; and FAO. 2019. *FAO Statistics (FAOSTAT)*. http://www.fao.org/faostat (accessed 1 May 2019).

Box 4.2: ADB Support for Adopting Green Revolution Technologies

The Asian Development Bank (ADB) assisted its developing member economies in adopting Green Revolution technologies, mostly by financing investments to develop and rehabilitate irrigation systems. In 1969, ADB approved the Tajum Irrigation Project, covering 3,200 hectares in Central Java, Indonesia.[a] This was ADB's first loan to Indonesia and the first agriculture project supporting the Green Revolution in Asia. Before the project, Tajum farmers were only able to cultivate one crop of rice *padi* (wet rice growing) during the wet season. With the project, a three-crop sequence was possible with much higher yields.

Starting with this project, ADB expanded agricultural financing. In 1968–1976, agricultural loans amounted to 19% of total ADB lending. In 1977–1986, agriculture accounted for 31% of ADB financing, making it the largest operational sector. In subsequent years, ADB support for agriculture declined as lending priorities shifted toward broad-based infrastructure and social development, governance and public management, and regional cooperation.

Following the 2008 food price crisis, ADB reignited its support for food security. Strategy 2030 explicitly emphasizes agriculture and rural development given the sector's role in addressing the development priorities of climate change, nutrition and health, poverty reduction, and gender equality (responding to the feminization of agriculture).

[a] ADB. 2016. *ADB Through the Decades: ADB's First Decade (1966–1976)*. Manila.

Sources: ADB Annual Reports; and ADB. 2018. *ADB Strategy 2030: Achieving a Prosperous, Inclusive, Resilient, and Sustainable Asia and the Pacific*. Manila.

India, Indonesia, and the Philippines

India had to deal with the 1942–1944 Bengal famine during the last few years of British rule. At least 1.5 million people perished due to food shortages largely caused by food supply mismanagement.[28] After independence in 1947, India was unable to feed its population and had to depend on imports and food aid from the US. Indonesia and the Philippines also relied on large volumes of food-grain imports. In the Philippines, imports peaked at 18% of consumption in 1965.

---

[28] Sen, A. 1981. *Poverty and Famines: An Essay on Entitlement and Deprivation*. Oxford: Clarendon Press.

In Indonesia, rice imports tripled in the second half of the 1950s, and despite large imports, prices doubled in 1957–1958. Fluctuating international prices of staple crops and rapid population growth raised fears among consumers and politicians of food shortages and potential famine.[29]

In the mid-1960s, the governments of the Philippines, Indonesia, and India introduced agricultural policies that offered a package of modern variety seeds, investments in irrigation systems, subsidized farm inputs, and extension services.[30] The Philippines created the Rice and Corn Production Council under President Ferdinand Marcos to coordinate government agencies and the private sector to increase rice and maize production. Farmers quickly adopted the modern varieties released from IRRI and began using chemical fertilizers. As a result, by the mid-1970s, more than 60% of land devoted to rice used modern varieties, and fertilizer use increased to more than 50 kilograms per hectare (Figures 4.1a and 4.1b).

In Indonesia, the fall of the Sukarno government in late 1965 marked a drastic policy change. In 1967, the new Suharto government introduced several programs to increase rice production and stabilize food supply. He created the *Badan Urusan Logistik*, a food logistics agency directly under the President. It set a high floor price for rice to encourage production and a ceiling price for consumers. By the mid-1980s, with investment and input subsidies, 60% of the rice area cultivated used modern varieties and fertilizer application, with yields reaching 3.9 tons per hectare (Figures 4.1a and 4.1b).

India's Prime Minister Jawaharlal Nehru strongly supported agricultural development. The real progress, however, started only after his death in 1964. Improved varieties of wheat and rice began spreading across fertile and irrigated areas in Punjab and Haryana. Modern varieties of wheat had instant success, while rice varieties needed further improvement to fit India's heterogeneous agroecological conditions, especially in the south and east. Areas using modern varieties of wheat and rice and fertilizers gradually increased throughout the 1970s and 1980s.

---

[29] Djurfeldt, G., and M. Jirstrom. 2005. The Puzzle of the Policy Shift – The Early Green Revolution in India, Indonesia, and the Philippines. In Djurfeldt, G., H. Holmen, M. Jirstrom, and R. Larsson, eds. 2005. *The African Food Crisis: Lessons from the Asian Green Revolution.* Wallingford: CABI Publishing.

[30] Djurfeldt, G., et al. 2005. African Food Crisis–The Relevance of Asian Experiences. In Djurfeldt, G., H. Holmen, M. Jirstrom, and R. Larsson, eds. 2005. *The African Food Crisis: Lessons from the Asian Green Revolution.* Wallingford: CABI Publishing.

Because of modern agricultural technology and strong policy support, the three countries increased rice and wheat production and reduced cereal imports. The Philippines achieved rice self-sufficiency periodically in the late 1960s and early 1980s (Figure 4.1d). Indonesia briefly achieved self-sufficiency in the mid-1980s. India's rice production more than doubled from the late 1970s to the 2000s, helping the country achieve self-sufficiency in the 1980s. And this was during the period when India's population doubled. In 2016, India became the world's largest rice exporter, surpassing Thailand.

Bangladesh, the People's Republic of China, and Viet Nam

In 1979, the Government of Bangladesh liberalized agricultural inputs, privatizing imports and marketing irrigation equipment and chemical fertilizers. Low-cost shallow well (or groundwater) irrigation pumps helped farmers cultivate rice during the dry season (called *Boro*). Over time, *Boro* rice production accounted for 60% of the country's rice production. New rice varieties more suitable for rainy and dry seasons contributed to the expansion of fields using modern varieties.[31] Still, chronic flooding during monsoon seasons, worsening salinity near bay areas, and overexploitation of underground water supply due to the increased use of tube wells remain challenges.

The PRC's Green Revolution was marked by two periods— before and after the 1978 economic reforms. As early as the late 1950s, PRC agronomists successfully cross-bred short, high-yielding rice varieties, introducing them on a limited scale in the south.[32] By 1975, the PRC established a national high-yielding variety rice seed system over a much wider region. After the 1979 reforms, the Green Revolution had a substantial impact on the country's agriculture. This was due to several factors. First, the PRC's opening up facilitated active research exchange with other countries including agriculture that contributed to further improving farm technology. Second, the high-yielding rice variety was rapidly adopted nationwide due to much-improved producer incentives under the household responsibility system and increased rice prices. Adding to the momentum was a renewed

---

[31] Hossain, M. 2009. The Impact of Shallow Tubewells and Boro Rice on Food Security in Bangladesh. *IFPRI Discussion Paper Series*. No. 00917. Washington, DC: International Food Policy Research Institute.

[32] Yuan Longping of Hunan Agricultural College, PRC, made pioneering contributions to developing hybrid rice varieties in the 1970s. Yuan is called the "Father of Hybrid Rice" in the PRC.

Figure 4.1: Impacts of Modern Variety Rice Adoption, Selected Asian Economies, 1961–2016

Areas under Modern Varieties, Fertilizer Use, Paddy Yields, and Self-Sufficiency

Figure 4.1a: Share of Sown Area of Modern Rice Variety (% of total area)

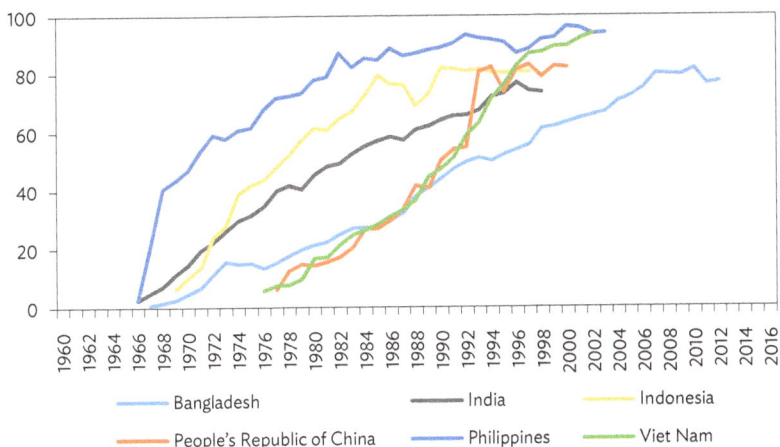

Legend:
- Bangladesh
- India
- Indonesia
- People's Republic of China
- Philippines
- Viet Nam

Figure 4.1b: Fertilizer Use (kg/ha)

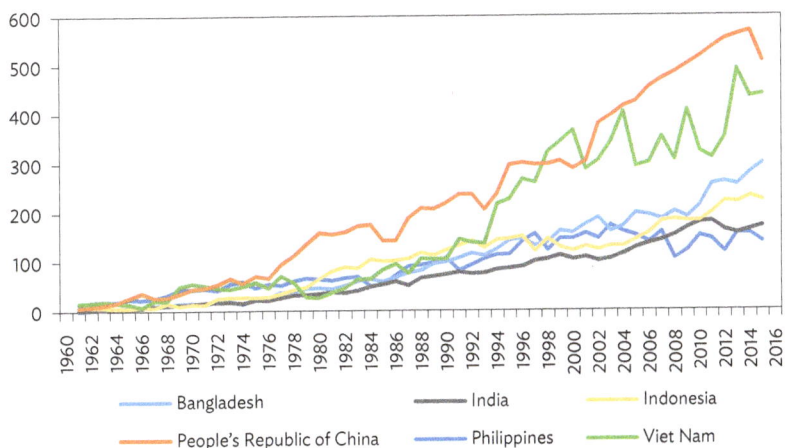

Legend:
- Bangladesh
- India
- Indonesia
- People's Republic of China
- Philippines
- Viet Nam

continued on next page

Figure 4.1 *continued*

Figure 4.1c: Rice Yield (ton/ha)

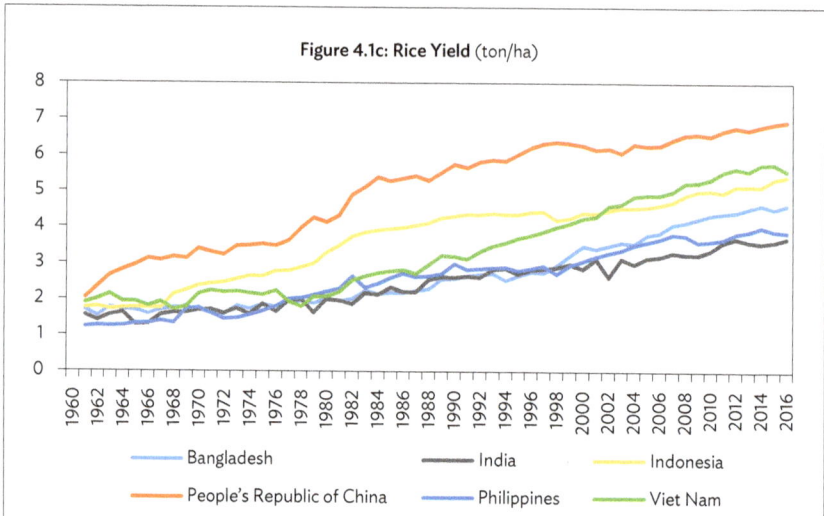

Bangladesh — India — Indonesia
People's Republic of China — Philippines — Viet Nam

Figure 4.1d: Rice Self-Sufficiency: Net Import as % of Domestic Availability (3-year average)

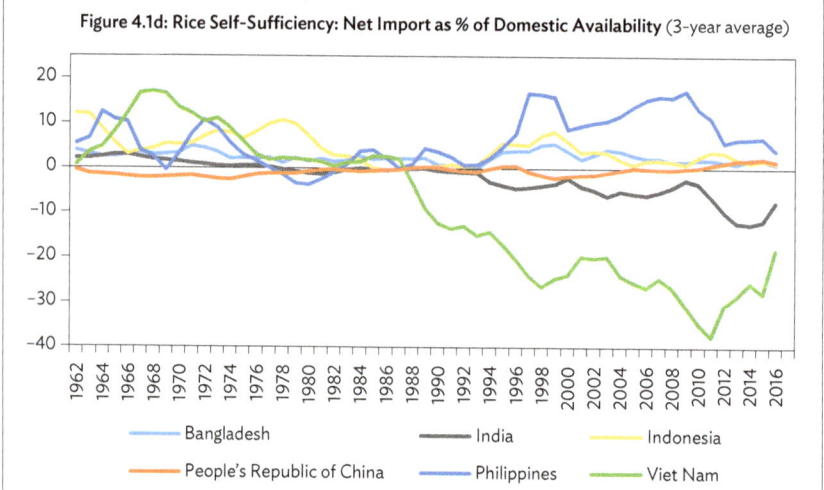

Bangladesh — India — Indonesia
People's Republic of China — Philippines — Viet Nam

ha = hectare, kg = kilogram.

Sources: International Rice Research Institute. *World Rice Statistics.* http://ricestat.irri.org:8080/wrsv3/entrypoint.htm (accessed 1 May 2019); and Food and Agriculture Organization of the United Nations. 2019. *FAO Statistics* (FAOSTAT). http://www.fao.org/faostat (accessed 1 May 2019).

emphasis on public investment in rural infrastructure and strengthening farming support services. Areas using improved rice varieties increased over 100 times from 135,000 hectares in 1976 to 15.3 million hectares in 1990, and rice yields increased by over 40%.[33] Third, the Green Revolution extended from rice and wheat to maize and other food crops.

In Viet Nam, the number of modern varieties rose rapidly in 1981–1990 after the *Doi Moi* liberalization in 1986. Agricultural reform made Viet Nam a major rice exporter. Rice production growth came from continuous improvement in seed varieties. Hybrid and improved varieties imported from the PRC contributed to the Green Revolution in north Viet Nam while those developed by IRRI were cultivated in south Viet Nam. National agricultural research systems successfully developed location-specific varieties.[34]

Sustaining Green Revolution momentum

The widespread adoption of Green Revolution technologies contributed to solving the region's food problems. Sustaining this transformative momentum has continued to be a strategic priority for Asian agriculture. Two issues are particularly important. One is the role that public policies play to allow markets to function better. The second is the need to sustain farm productivity by continuing research support, agricultural mechanization, and sustained public infrastructure investment.

First, the Green Revolution presumed a strong and proactive public sector to help farmers adopt modern farming technology. Over time, it was realized that the outcome depended on the effectiveness and appropriateness of public engagement. As early as 1972, Hla Myint, a prominent economist from Myanmar, said "the fundamental question raised by the Green Revolution is ... what policies ... to turn it from a technological innovation into a genuine dynamic force for economic development ... *without appropriate policies*, the Green Revolution might be cut short before its full benefits are realized."[35]

---

[33] Jiang, J., and D. Wang. 1990. China's "Green Revolution" and Sustainable Development of Agriculture. *Science and Technology Review* [in Chinese]. October.

[34] Ut, T. T., and K. Kajisa. 2006. The Impact of Green Revolution on Rice Production in Vietnam. *The Developing Economies*. 44 (2). pp. 167–189.

[35] Myint, H. 1972. *Southeast Asia's Economy: Development Policies in the 1970s*. New York: Praeger Publishers.

Myint said that appropriate policies refer to how to organize the delivery of agricultural support services such as input supply, product processing and marketing, and rural credit systems. A critical issue is the involvement of private entrepreneurs. Appropriate policies also refer to the pricing principles supporting food production and stimulating broad-based rural development. He questioned the wisdom of raising the price of rice paid to farmers and subsidizing the use of modern inputs. While these pricing policies succeeded in inducing farmers to expand production scale rapidly, the question was whether economic incentives given to farmers were able to efficiently allocate resources between rice production and other crops—and more generally between agriculture and the rest of the economy.

The issues Myint raised in the 1970s continued to occupy policy makers' attention. In many countries, agricultural reforms started in the 1980s. With trade liberalization, agricultural price distortions declined over time when measured against border prices, although trade restrictions remained for some politically important tradable agricultural products.[36] Rice was the main example, with importing countries maintaining explicit import quotas and exporting countries restricting the types and amounts of rice for exports. Rice trade policy reforms continue in Asia. In 2018, the Government of the Philippines introduced the Rice Tariffication Act to replace quantitative restrictions to rice import with tariffs.

Asian developing countries also gradually restructured input supply and output marketing systems. State involvement was reduced and policy environments improved to enable private sector participation in support services. Domestic food prices became more realistic by phasing out input subsidies for farmers and general food subsidies for consumers. Countries identified and introduced direct and transparent methods to support low-income consumers and needy farmers to improve productivity.[37]

The second concern is about the sustainability of agricultural productivity. The international technology transfer underlying the Green Revolution had first taken place in favorable agricultural

---

[36] Anderson, K., G. Rausser, and J. Swinnen. 2013. Political Economy of Public Policies: Insights from Distortions to Agricultural and Food Markets. *Journal of Economic Literature*. 51 (2). pp. 423–477.

[37] Hayami, Y., and Y. Godo. 2004. The Three Agricultural Problems in the Disequilibrium of World Agriculture. *Asian Journal of Agriculture and Development*. 1 (1). pp. 3–14; and OECD–FAO. 2017. *Agricultural Policy Monitoring and Evaluation 2017*. Rome.

areas and later extended to unfavorable agricultural areas. Because of this sequence, rice yield in Asia continued to increase. Since the 1990s, national budget support and international donor assistance have declined. The apparent complacency over current and future food supplies remains worrying.[38] Research support must push technological frontiers—introducing new varieties is critical, given climate change and soil salinity. Also, more investment is needed to develop, diffuse, and adopt new technologies.

Asian countries have taken multipronged approaches to raise farm productivity while focusing on reducing production costs for both rice and agriculture as a whole. Mechanization came to East Asia, and also to areas in South Asia and Southeast Asia, where labor shortages developed out of rapid economic transformation. Tractors, harvesters, and rice planters replaced manual labor. Unlike large machines developed and used in Europe and North America, small-scale machines were developed to suit the small plots in developing Asia. With rising labor costs, mechanization became increasingly important. There remain concerns, however, that small and fragmented land plots and insecure land rights could slow the land consolidation needed for mechanization to enjoy scale economies.

Declining investment and research support for agriculture became a global phenomenon. The full impact of the neglect became evident much later, in 2008, when a food price crisis, coupled with the global financial crisis, hurt developing countries, particularly in Africa. It awakened the international community to refocus more on agriculture.[39] Comprehensive measures to enhance land, labor, and water efficiencies are needed. Expanding the scope and scale of agricultural research and extension services is also needed. Countries and international organizations are repackaging agricultural interventions to address challenges such as macro- and micro-nutritional deficiencies, gender inequality, and climate change.[40]

---

[38] Pingali, P. L., M. Hossain, and R. V. Gerpacio. 1997. *Asian Rice Bowls: The Returning Crisis.* Los Baños, Philippines: International Rice Research Institute and Centre for Agriculture and Bioscience International.

[39] World Bank. 2007. *World Development Report 2008: Agriculture for Development.* Washington, DC.

[40] Chapter 12 discusses gender in detail. Chapter 13 also discusses agriculture-related environmental and resource depletion challenges.

4.5   Changing patterns of food consumption and product diversification

Changes in consumption patterns

Asia's food consumption patterns in terms of calorie intake changed substantially over the past few decades, as several recent studies point out.[41] There is (i) a decline in consumption of rice and wheat, and (ii) an increase in consumption of animal-sourced foods and fruits and vegetables. A staple is the most important source of calories. Rice is traditionally the staple for most people; wheat is a staple in some areas. Though not shown in Figure 4.2, traditional staples in the Pacific are mostly root crops such as sweet potatoes and taro. Per capita consumption of staple foods, especially rice, has started to level off or decline after a long period of increase. This is most notable in East Asia and Southeast Asia (Figure 4.3).

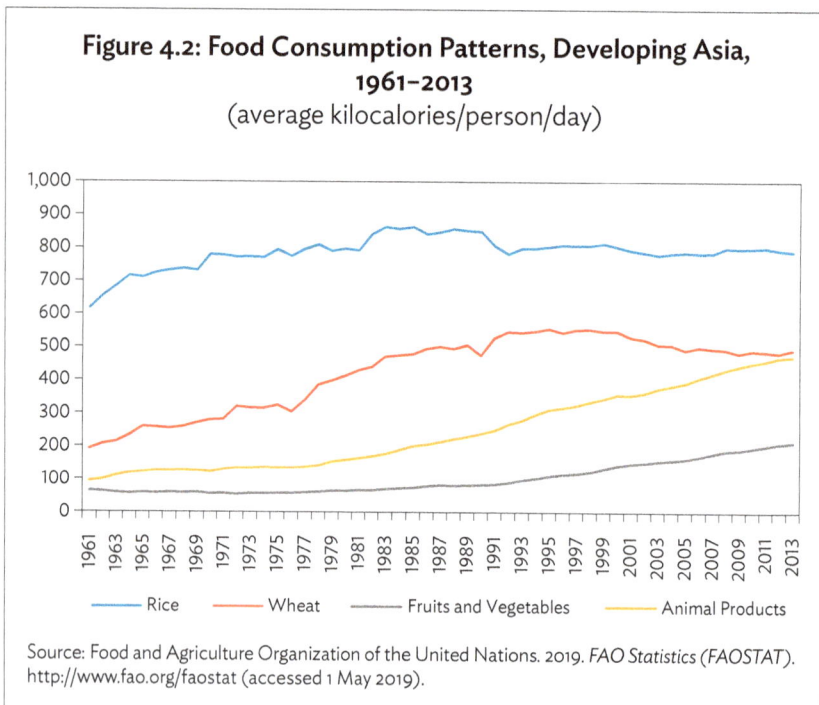

Figure 4.2: Food Consumption Patterns, Developing Asia, 1961–2013
(average kilocalories/person/day)

Source: Food and Agriculture Organization of the United Nations. 2019. *FAO Statistics (FAOSTAT)*. http://www.fao.org/faostat (accessed 1 May 2019).

---

[41] Timmer, C. P. 2012. Structural Transformation, the Changing Role of Rice, and Food Security in Asia: Small Farmers and Modern Supply Chains. *Asian Journal of Agriculture and Development*. 9 (1). pp. 21–35; and FAO. 2018. Diets Are Diversifying with Implications for Farmers and Nutrition. In FAO. *Dynamic Development, Shifting Demographics, and Changing Diets*. Bangkok. p. 172.

Dietary diversity is important for a balanced intake of different nutrients. The main food groups beyond staples are animal-sourced foods (including meat, fish, eggs, and dairy products), fruits, vegetables, and beans. Consumption of animal-sourced foods and fruits and vegetables has been rising in the region. For animal-sourced foods, the increases were most rapid in East Asia and Southeast Asia. Available refrigeration at home and within value chains may be partially behind the increased consumption of perishable foods such as meat, fish, fruits, and vegetables.

Changing consumption patterns are mainly due to rising incomes. As incomes increase, starchy staples account for a smaller share of dietary energy, reflecting a desire for dietary diversity. This leads to decreased consumption of these staples on a per capita basis given the limits of an individual's energy intake. Declines in rice consumption have been greater in urban than rural areas, and declines have been greater for those at the upper end of the income distribution than the poor.[42]

A Food and Agriculture Organization of the United Nations (FAO) study[43] found diversification within starchy staples, again reflecting the desire for variety, especially for urban residents and young people. Urban residents in southern PRC, where rice is the traditional staple, tend to increase wheat consumption (up to a point) and reduce rice consumption as incomes rise. The reverse is true in urban areas in northern PRC, where traditional wheat consumers tend to increase rice consumption (again up to a point) as incomes increase. Data from household surveys show that income is a key driver for consumption of several different types of nutritious foods.

Prices of fruits and vegetables rose more rapidly than the overall price of food in nearly all countries. This occurred over 10 to 15 years. These sustained price increases reflect reinforcing demand and supply. First, consumers want to diversify their diets as their incomes grow (demand). Second, fruit and vegetable cultivation (supply) is relatively labor intensive, implying that farmers need to find ways to use labor more efficiently.

---

[42]   Timmer, C. P. 2014. Food Security in Asia and the Pacific: The Rapidly Changing Role of Rice. *Asia & the Pacific Policy Studies.* 1 (1). pp. 73–90.

[43]   FAO. 2018. Diets Are Diversifying with Implications for Farmers and Nutrition. In FAO. *Dynamic Development, Shifting Demographics, and Changing Diets.* Bangkok. p. 172.

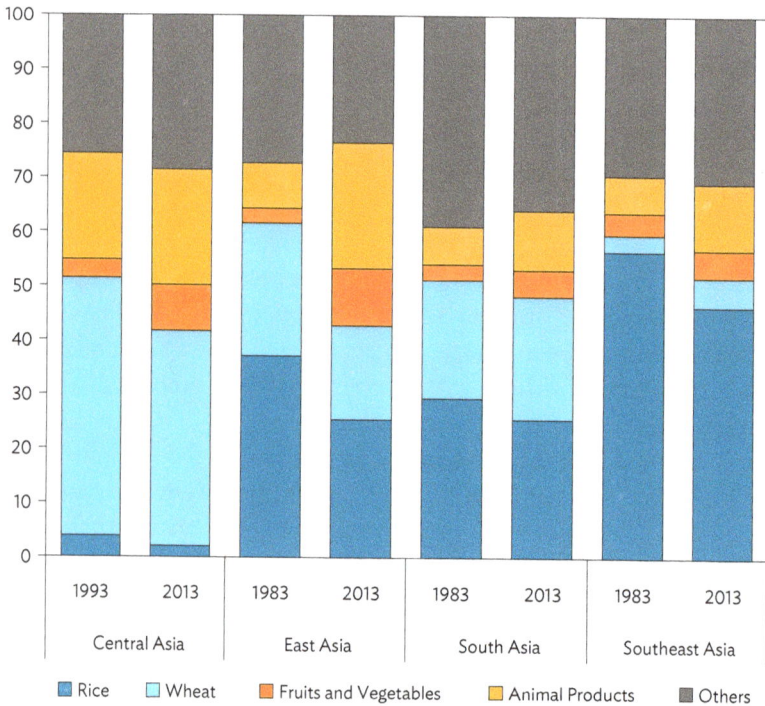

Figure 4.3: Changing Composition of Food Consumption in Calories, Developing Asia, 1983 and 2013 (% of total)

Notes: "Others" include starch and other cereals, sugar crops and sweeteners, and vegetable oils and oil crops. Pacific economies are excluded due to data unavailability of Papua New Guinea.

Source: Food and Agriculture Organization of the United Nations. 2019. *FAO Statistics (FAOSTAT)*. http://www.fao.org/faostat (accessed 1 May 2019).

Production diversification

As consumption patterns change, Asian agriculture has gradually transformed, moving from largely cereal- or grain-based production to higher-value production—such as high-value crops, livestock, and fisheries. The value of agricultural production (in 2010–2014 constant prices) increased over six times in 50 years. In the 1960s, cereal production dominated, accounting for 40% of total agricultural production. In the 1990s, livestock, and vegetable and fruit production significantly increased, now exceeding the value of cereal production.

These changes, however, occurred unevenly across Asia (Figure 4.4). In East Asia, mostly in the PRC, the change has been drastic. The production share of cereals declined from 50% in 1971–1974 to 20% in 2010–2014. During the same period, the production value of fruits and vegetables increased from 15% to 40%, and the production value of livestock increased from 20% to 35%. Although less drastic, the share of cereal production value declined by 10 percentage points from about 50% in 1971–1974 in Southeast Asia, while the share of other crops, including oil crops, sugarcane, and other industrial crops, expanded.

Figure 4.4: Shares of Agriculture Sector Gross Production Value, Developing Asia, 1971–1974 and 2010–2014
(% of total)

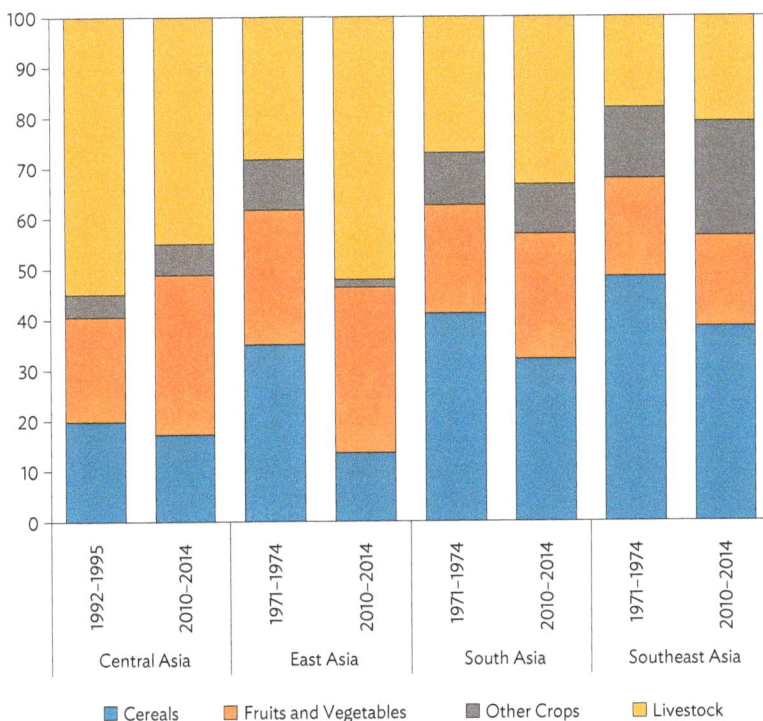

Notes: "Other crops" include oil crops, roots and tubers, and sugar. Pacific economies are excluded due to data unavailability of Papua New Guinea.

Source: Food and Agriculture Organization of the United Nations. 2019. *FAO Statistics (FAOSTAT)*. http://www.fao.org/faostat (accessed 1 May 2019).

Meat production in Asia grew significantly over the past 5 decades. A large share of increased meat production occurred in the PRC. The country is the world's largest producer of pork, accounting for about 45% of global production. Outside the PRC, India is the largest meat producer—with beef and poultry as the main products. Indonesia, Myanmar, Pakistan, the Philippines, Thailand, and Viet Nam follow. In Central Asia, the share of livestock production decreased as diets diversified, though total meat production continues to grow.

Production diversification goes hand in hand with farm specialization, with different farms specializing in different crops. In Thailand, the PRC, and elsewhere, farmers have increasingly specialized in a smaller number of crops, particularly over the past 10 to 15 years. Today, livestock farms are often specialized in particular livestock (such as poultry, pig, beef cattle, or dairy). This trend is important, as more Asian farmers are moving out of subsistence agriculture and producing for markets. Farmers are becoming commercially oriented, connected to markets through improved logistics and transport, and respond quickly to changing market conditions, often assisted by information technology.

4.6 Agricultural trade and food value chains

Shifting patterns of agricultural trade

Aside from domestic product diversification, international trade allows countries to specialize in production based on comparative advantage and economic opportunity. Trade liberalization in agriculture (as discussed earlier) contributed to increased external engagement. Because a country's agricultural production depends on agroecological conditions, those with less diverse conditions benefit from international trade. Indeed, agricultural trade benefits from comparative advantage. Trade in processed food, such as vegetables and meat, has grown significantly due to the high income elasticities of demand and where there are fewer trade barriers or quarantine-related restrictions.

One example that took advantage of trade liberalization is the expansion of oil-crop (palm oil) production in Malaysia, targeted for the lucrative export market. Oil-crop production is suitable for Malaysia, with its narrow range of latitude. As this occurred, rice and maize cultivation areas declined—with Malaysia relying more on imports. In contrast, countries with comparative advantage in cereal production have become net exporters.

Thailand became a major rice exporter in Asia in the 1970s and remained the world's largest rice exporter until 2016, when India became the top exporter (Figure 4.5a). India exports high-value basmati rice to Europe and other high-income countries as well as non-basmati rice to Africa, the Middle East, and other Asian countries. Following India, Pakistan has become a major basmati rice exporter and is now the fourth-largest rice exporter globally. The third-largest rice exporter is Viet Nam. The combined share of these four rice exporters is around two-thirds of global exports. Cambodia and Myanmar are expected to become major rice exporters in the future.[44] One caveat is that if the production expansion is based on subsidies or distorted prices for water, fertilizer, and other inputs, these could misallocate resources and create unsustainable patterns of agricultural production.

Rising production of fresh vegetables and fruits resulted in increased trade of these higher-value crops (Figures 4.5b and 4.5c). Before the 1970s, the number and volume of traded fruits and vegetables were limited. Since then, however, the traded number and volume of these products have grown significantly partly due to the development of value chain technology. Major traded vegetables include tomatoes, onions, cucumbers, and cabbage. They are exported as fresh, frozen, preserved, or processed. As value chains grow, their value expands both ways. The PRC is the largest exporter of both vegetables and fruits (Figures 4.5b and 4.5c). It also imports large volumes, although India imports more vegetables than the PRC. Thailand and Viet Nam also export and import vegetables and fruits.

Meat production and trade have increased markedly, requiring massive imports of animal feed from outside Asia. The import volume of maize, soybeans, and sorghum increased dramatically among major Asian livestock producers (Figure 4.5d). Viet Nam is the largest maize importer, followed by the PRC.

Growth of food value chains and agribusinesses

Significant changes in consumption patterns, product diversification, and international trade have helped transform Asia's "agri-food" economy, especially with the rapid expansion of food value chains and agribusiness—various businesses connected with producing,

[44] FAO. 2018. Diets Are Diversifying with Implications for Farmers and Nutrition. In FAO. *Dynamic Development, Shifting Demographics, and Changing Diets*. Bangkok. p. 172.

Figure 4.5: International Trade of Rice, Fruits, and Vegetables, Selected Economies, 1974–2016
(average annual, $ billion)

Figure 4.5a: Rice Trade

Figure 4.5b: Vegetables Trade

Figure 4.5c: Fruits Trade

Figure 4.5d: Maize Trade

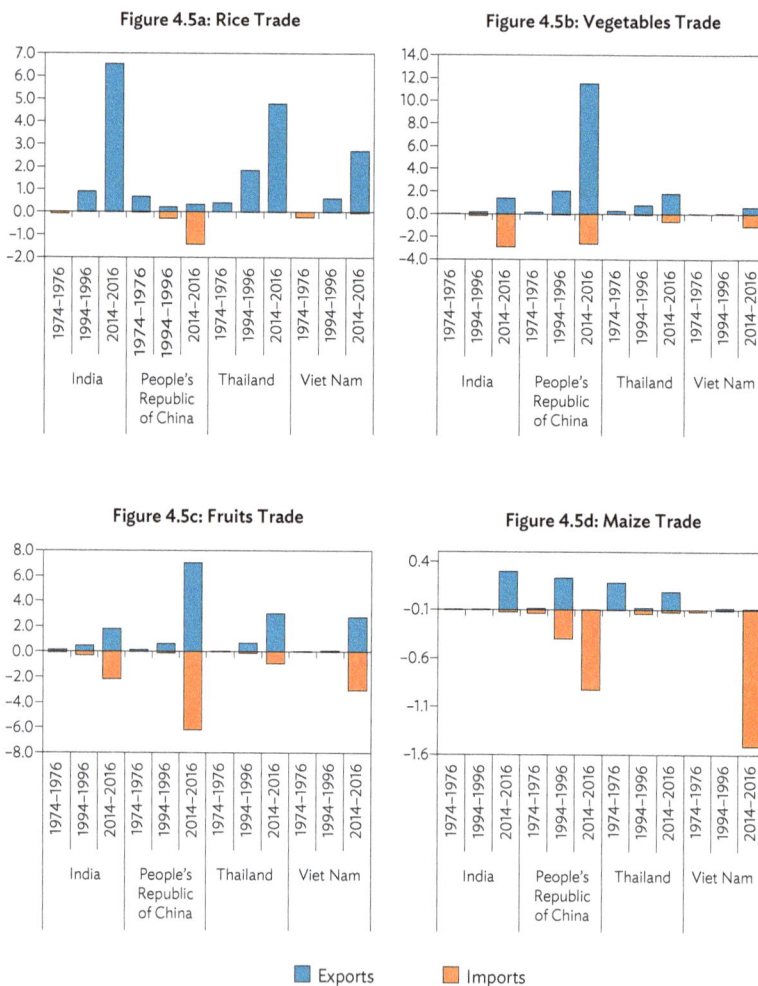

■ Exports　　　■ Imports

Source: Food and Agriculture Organization of the United Nations. 2019. *FAO Statistics (FAOSTAT)*. http://www.fao.org/faostat (accessed 1 May 2019).

processing, and distributing farm products such as food and beverage manufacturing.[45] Food supply chains have shifted from locally fragmented chains to geographically integrated ones. Some segments have declined—the influence of traditional village traders giving way to urban wholesale markets and specialized wholesale and logistics stores. The steady growth of physical infrastructure such as roads and storage over the past decades greatly improved transportation, communications, and knowledge sharing for the agriculture sector.

Market-led value chains continue to change as well. The private sector's role is critical, as the scale of investment and knowledge required are far beyond the capacity of governments to provide. New information technology has been adopted for more efficient processing and distribution of food products, to ensure quality and safety, and for contract enforcement. Food traceability system is also introduced in food supply chains and agricultural trade. These changes form an integrated feedback loop from table to farm, with contracts giving farmers production instructions.

Contract farming is a special production–procurement system designed to address logistics challenges. It is commonly used in vegetable and fruit production. Due to their perishable nature, coordination is critical to ensure timely delivery from producers to retail stores using proper equipment such as cold storage. Contract farming helps ensure product quality to meet market demand in high-end urban and export markets, often by providing farmers the technical assistance to meet food safety requirements. In contract farming, farmers and buyers make advance agreements on volume, quality, time of delivery, use of inputs, and pricing. In Asia, vegetables and fruits are increasingly produced and marketed through contract farming.[46]

Major changes have occurred almost unnoticed, even in staple food value chains. A recent three-country study (Bangladesh, India, and the PRC)[47] by ADB and the International Food Policy Research Institute documents the transformation of value chains of rice and potatoes. The changes included the rapid rise of supermarkets, modern cold storage facilities, large rice mills, and commercialized

[45] Reardon, T., and P. Timmer. 2014. Five Inter-Linked Transformations in the Asian Agrifood Economy: Food Security Implications. *Global Food Security*. 3 (2). pp. 108–117.

[46] Otsuka, K., Y. Nakano, and K. Takahashi, 2016. Contract Farming in Developed and Developing Countries. *Annual Review of Resource Economics*. 8 (1). pp. 353–376.

[47] Reardon, T., et al. 2012. *The Quiet Revolution in Staple Food Value Chains: Enter the Dragon, the Elephant, and the Tiger*. Manila: Asian Development Bank.

small farmers using input-intensive, mechanized technology. In recent years, the spread of information and communication technology into rural areas has been an important driver of change within the rural economy.

Although the GDP share of direct "agricultural value added" has declined, "agribusiness value added" (which includes manufacturing, processing, and food value chains, such as transport, logistics, and distribution services) has grown significantly over the past 2–3 decades. In Indonesia, for example, agribusiness value added in 2014 was equivalent to 70% of agricultural value added. Expanding agribusiness not only increases value added but also absorbs surplus rural labor.

Urbanization and increasing women's participation in the labor market have also been important in expanding agribusiness. Studies find that, due to urban traffic congestion, longer work hours, and more women working outside the home, urban residents tend to place high value on the convenience of food preparation, leading to increased expenditures on processed foods.

4.7 Expanding the rural nonfarm economy

Traditionally, rural nonfarm economic activities have been important in Asia. Diversification into nonfarm income helps households diversify income risk from different sources. According to Asian household studies over the years, income diversification contributed significantly to risk coping for rural households. This is especially true for households in low-potential agricultural areas without irrigation. Farming is inevitably a risky business. Weather shocks, crop disease, insect and animal damage, postproduction losses, and price fluctuations can ravage output and revenues. Current prevention or mitigation is insufficient.

As Asia continues to transform, the rural nonfarm economy has become a critical driving force. It helps integrate rural and urban economies. Agriculture is land-intensive, so farming is naturally located in rural areas. High value-added industry and services tend to be in urban or peripheral areas. Income gaps between rural residents (farmers) and urban residents (factory and office workers) tend to increase. The rural nonfarm sector helps narrow these gaps.

Historically, the rural nonfarm sector played a significant role in industrial development.[48] As economies made the industrial transition from light to heavy industry, many saw vibrant rural nonfarm economic development initially fostering light industry, then widening to a variety of other industries. In Japan, for example, important industries during the prewar period—especially silk production, reeling, and weaving for silk export—operated from cottage-type factories in rural areas. Local traders played a major role in transmitting market information and technology. Taipei,China (with its development of small and medium-sized enterprises) and the PRC (with rural township and village enterprises) showed how rural-based industries could successfully integrate into urban economies. In South Asia, the cotton industry was an important part of the rural economy until the 19th century. Today, it is reviving.

Nonfarm sector development is needed because they help create employment opportunities for rural labor, slow rural–urban migration, promote more equitable income distribution, and reduce rural poverty. In the Philippines, for example, rural nonfarm employment, as a share of rural employment, increased from 35% in 1983 to 41% in 2003. The rural labor force has been moving out of farming, as nonfarm work has become more profitable.

Agriculture and farming are decreasing in importance as a share of rural household income—there are fewer Asian households specializing exclusively in agriculture. A recent review of field survey findings shows that from 1992 to 2004, the percentage of rural households specializing in farming decreased from 44% to 25% in Viet Nam, 35% to 16% in Indonesia, and 27% to 19% in Nepal.[49] Nonfarm incomes are a growing share of rural household incomes. Most rural households earn income off the farm from a variety of sources.

4.8 Looking ahead

There have been significant changes to Asia's agriculture and rural economies over the past 50 years, but the progress has been uneven across the region. Asia's agriculture and rural sectors continue to

---

[48] Estudillo, J. P., T. Sonobe, and K. Otsuka. 2007. Development of the Rural Non-Farm Sector in the Philippines and Lessons from the East Asian Experience. In Balisacan, A. M., and H. Hill, eds. *The Dynamics of Regional Development: The Philippines in East Asia.* Cheltenham: Edward Elgar.

[49] Davis, B., et al. 2010. A Cross-Country Comparison of Rural Income Generating Activities. *World Development.* 38 (1). pp. 48-63.

face major challenges, both old and new. Food security, nutrition and food safety, diversification, rural employment, land consolidation, strengthening of agricultural markets and food supply chains, and rural–urban integration all remain important priorities for many developing Asian countries.

Going forward, policy makers will also need to take into account new opportunities, emerging concerns, and changing circumstances. For example, there is an opportunity for greater adoption and application of information technology and other new technologies in agriculture and rural areas. The changing demographics, especially the aging of rural populations, must be a part of rural revitalization strategies. Looming impacts of climate change, environmental stress, and natural resources depletion add to the urgency and complexity of agricultural policymaking and implementation.

Specifically, the following key priorities are critical to continue agricultural transformation and rural development. These are among salient features of ADB's new operational priority on promoting rural development and food security under ADB's Strategy 2030.

First, technology remains a key driver of productivity growth. Research and the application of technology will occur both in agricultural production systems and across the entire food chain. This enables connecting smallholder farmers to markets, while measures are introduced to mitigate risks in adopting new smart technologies. Climate-smart technologies (such as drip irrigation and drought-tolerant crop varieties) have been developed with more coming. Smart technologies are also increasingly being applied—ranging from satellite images, the internet of things, artificial intelligence, and big data analytics.

Second, land reform and land administration remain part of the ongoing agenda for many Asian countries. The lack of clear land rights impedes effective land and credit markets, and discourages land consolidation for mechanization and agricultural productivity growth. Farmland consolidation can be an important solution for countries with rural labor shortages and aging farmers.

Third, improving food value chains and agribusiness supports the promotion of agricultural trade. This requires more investment to improve transport infrastructure and logistics services. Continuing efforts are also needed to reduce trade barriers and improve customs and quarantine services for agricultural trade.

Fourth, food safety and nutrition standards must be developed and enforced across the entire food system. Public policy and investment need to accord greater attention to the issue of safety and nutrition. Malnutrition is a development concern of multiple dimensions with impacts lasting through generations. Addressing this concern will require active engagement and support of many stakeholders including government ministries, communities, the private sector, and families.

Fifth, remaining agricultural price distortions should be addressed. This helps improve transparency of government expenditures and resource allocation efficiency. More Asian countries are moving in this direction, including a shift from food price subsidies to targeted income transfers to poor households.

Sixth, emerging challenges must be addressed—including ecosystem protection for forest, land, and water resources; environmental management for air, soil, and water pollution; and climate resilience to drought, floods, and salinization. Agriculture can also contribute to climate change mitigation by better managing forests and land, and adopting low-carbon farming practices.

Finally, agricultural and rural development policy design and implementation must be better integrated into national development strategies for more balanced, inclusive, and sustainable growth.

CHAPTER 5

TECHNOLOGICAL PROGRESS AS KEY DRIVER

5.1 Introduction

Asia's growth and development over the past 50 years was built on significant advances in technology. Japan and the newly industrialized economies (NIEs), i.e., Hong Kong, China; the Republic of Korea (ROK); Singapore; and Taipei,China, used technology to improve productivity and raise living standards to advanced economy levels. Other countries are following. Evidence of the region's transformation and its move to the global technological frontier can be seen in the goods and services it produces. Asia pioneered the use of high-speed trains and currently operates three-quarters of the global high-speed rail network. Asia also manufactures more than 50% of the world's automobiles, produces 75% of its robots, and provides 50% of global high-technology exports.

Historically, Asia created a variety of technologies indigenously—such as papermaking, printing, gunpowder, and the compass. However, it began to fall behind the West in the 15th century, and the gap widened further with Europe's industrial revolution (Box 5.1). As a result, Asia needed to catch up technologically. During Japan's modernization in the late 19th century, the most important way to adopt technology was to invite experts from Europe and the

United States (US) in science, medicine, agriculture, and engineering. They brought expertise in minting, printing, railways, textiles, and other areas. Japan educated its own scientists and engineers, and developed the capacity to make trains, high-quality steel, and armaments by the end of the 19th century.

For the most part, technological progress is not automatic. Instead, it requires deliberate effort from firms, researchers, and governments. Asian economies used a variety of channels and methods to secure, deploy, and innovate technology: inviting experts, sending missions and students abroad, obtaining foreign licenses, importing machinery, engaging in trade, conducting reverse engineering, attracting foreign direct investment (FDI), and receiving technical cooperation aid. As these countries mastered imported technologies to produce goods and services, they built the capacity to move from adoption to innovation using research and development (R&D).

To support this process, Asian governments built a human capital base of engineers, scientists, and other researchers; and gave them opportunities and incentives to learn and apply their knowledge. Governments also spurred technology by (i) building national systems of innovation that include universities, research institutions, national laboratories, and science parks; (ii) setting the legal and institutional framework, including an intellectual property regime; (iii) supporting private sector R&D and other related investments through tax incentives, subsidies, and credit; (iv) building information and communication technology (ICT) infrastructure, including high-speed broadband and mobile networks; and (v) creating a competitive market environment that sparks innovation.

This chapter discusses the role of technological progress in Asia's growth and transformation. Section 5.2 sets out the theoretical and conceptual links between technology and economic growth. Section 5.3 summarizes key achievements in technological progress in the region. Section 5.4 then describes the main drivers and channels that fueled both technological adoption and innovation in Asia. Section 5.5 describes country experiences. Section 5.6 presents recent technological trends and developments. Section 5.7 concludes with suggestions for further progress, particularly on how to help middle-income countries transition to the innovation stage.

Box 5.1: Asia's Past Technological Advances and How It Fell Behind

Asia created a variety of technologies that predate its interaction with the West. These indigenous technologies contributed to its economic advance during the first and well into the second millennium. However, Asia subsequently fell behind the West in science and technology starting from the Renaissance and then, more critically, from the Industrial Revolution in Great Britain in the late 18th century.

The most well-known and oft-cited Asian inventions were China's four breakthrough technologies: papermaking, from about 100 AD; movable-type printing; gunpowder; and the compass from around 1000 AD. These were not only breakthroughs for Asia but were also global innovations.

In Asia, indigenous agricultural technologies developed over time as societies sought to develop a stable food supply for an expanding population. Cultivation techniques, large-scale water management and irrigation systems, and seed varieties were advanced over time, notably for rice production. Asia also progressively improved construction technologies in stone, concrete, marble, and other materials—as can be seen today in the palaces, mosques, temples, and tombs that remain from past centuries.

In textiles, Asia pioneered the production and weaving of silk that lent its name to the Central Asian trade route—the Silk Road—connecting the region with eastern Europe. Silk required mastery of sericulture and techniques for spinning thread and weaving cloth. Asia also created muslin, a simple-weave cotton textile, with techniques that originated in Bengal and spread to other parts of Asia. The textile traded widely across the region and into Europe, but production declined after being undermined by British colonial policy that promoted textiles made in England.

Europe's industrial revolution was ignited by the application of science to industrial production to make steel, generate steam power, create machinery, and evolve improved materials from chemical processes. Technology, together with commercial activity—both supported by institutions such as patent laws, limited liability corporations, and accounting systems—allowed for steady, significant increases in production and standards of living in the West. That region opened up a significant gap with other areas of the world. Asia accounted for close to 60% of global output at the onset of the Industrial Revolution, but its share declined as the West surged ahead. By 1960, developing and developed Asia's share had fallen to less than 13% (Chapter 1).

Source: Asian Development Bank.

5.2 Measuring technology's contribution to growth

Asia's technological progress over the past 50 years has been significant. Compared with the 1960s, the range and quality of goods and services produced has grown phenomenally. Vehicles, computers, smartphones, and other manufacturing goods are now produced in Asia. Their production is made possible by the use of technology embodied in digitally controlled machine tools, mechanized production lines, and robots. In services, ICT revolutionized how customers express demand and how it is satisfied by suppliers. In agriculture, Asia benefited from the new technologies of the Green Revolution, including the shift to high-yielding seed varieties, chemical inputs, improved irrigation, and the use of mechanized cultivation—all of which greatly increased farm productivity (Chapter 4).

Fully capturing Asia's technological progress is not straightforward. There is no single, accurate measure of a country's level of technology. One way to measure technology's contribution to growth is based on what is called "total factor productivity."

Total factor productivity

The aggregate production function models economic output—gross domestic product (GDP)—based on four inputs. Two tangible inputs of capital (machines and equipment) and labor (the number of workers) are combined with two intangible inputs of improvements in human capital (skills and knowledge of workers—measured by years of schooling as a proxy) and elements of technology and innovation (Box 5.2). Contributions of technology and innovation to GDP growth are measured as a "residual" after accounting for the contributions of the other three factors.

This residual is called total factor productivity (TFP). It mainly captures advances in product and process technologies, as well as greater efficiency associated with managerial, institutional, and policy reforms. TFP also includes any other contributions to GDP not accounted for by the increase (or decrease) in capital, labor, and human capital. For example, as human capital is proxied by years of schooling, it does not consider the quality of education and training, so these are quantified as part of TFP. Likewise, some elements of technological progress can be included in TFP, while others appear as the increased value of capital (such as more expensive and sophisticated capital goods).

One widely cited controversy highlighted by Krugman's 1994 paper "The Myth of Asia's Miracle"[1] is about the nature of high growth in Asia's high-performing economies.[2] Based on the findings of two papers by other scholars,[3] Krugman argued that Asia's efficiency (or TFP) growth was small, with development driven mostly by mobilizing resources—capital and labor. He suggested that Asia's growth model resembled the Soviet economy and, hence, could not be sustained.

The analogy with the Soviet system was misplaced. Based on market functions, Asian economies successfully mobilized resources in the early stages of development by investing in capital—actively supported by high savings and absorbing excess rural labor, along with better education. This, in itself, was a significant achievement compared with the experience of other regions globally. Because it is market based, for many economies, growth driven by mobilizing resources can evolve into innovation-based growth—beyond the process of convergence, or catching up. This is what happened in Asia, as an Asian Development Bank analysis clearly shows (Figure 5.1).

Increasing role of technology in Asia

Over the past half century, growth in Asia has relied increasingly on TFP. Figure 5.1 shows the contribution of the four input factors to growth for three periods. The calculation includes 21 Asian economies. In the first period, 1970–1985, growth was driven by capital accumulation and increased labor inputs, whereas the rate of growth attributable to TFP was slightly negative. The contribution of TFP may be negative because of the difficulty of capturing, in this variable, the technology embodied in machinery, which instead is captured in the capital stock variable (as discussed earlier). This was also a period of considerable global economic turbulence (inflation, oil and debt crises, along with other factors) that reduced growth rates, leading to lower or negative TFP growth.

---

[1] Krugman, P. 1994. The Myth of Asia's Miracle. *Foreign Affairs.* 1 (November/December). pp. 62–78.

[2] World Bank. 1993. *The East Asian Miracle: Economic Growth and Public Policy.* New York: Oxford University Press.

[3] Young, A. 1995. The Tyranny of Numbers: Confronting the Statistical Realities of the East Asian Growth Experience. *Quarterly Journal of Economics.* 110 (3). pp. 641–680; and Kim, J.-I., and L. J. Lau. 1994. The Sources of Economic Growth of the East Asian Newly Industrialized Countries. *Journal of the Japanese and International Economies.* 8 (3). pp. 235–271.

**Figure 5.1: Contribution of Factors of Production
to GDP Growth, Asia**
(% of total contribution)

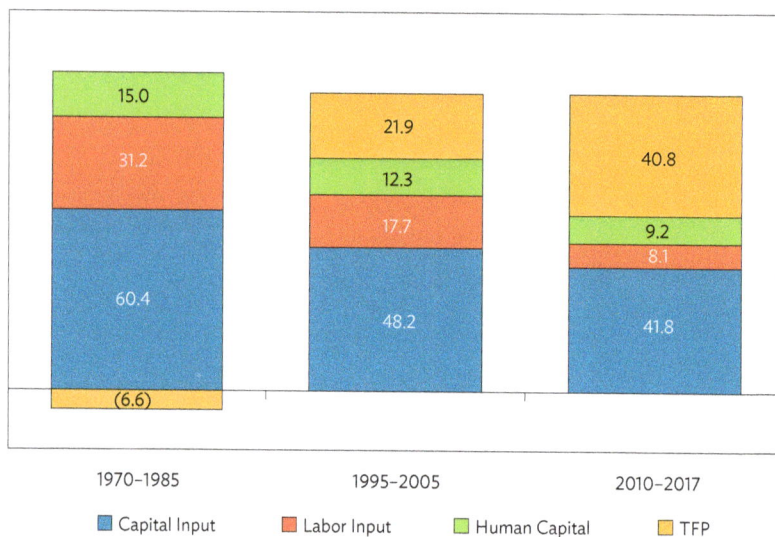

( ) = negative, GDP = gross domestic product, TFP = total factor productivity.

Notes: Central Asia is excluded for 1970–1985. The 21 economies for the first period include Bangladesh; Brunei Darussalam; Cambodia; Hong Kong, China; India; Indonesia; Japan; the Lao People's Democratic Republic; Malaysia; Mongolia; Myanmar; Nepal; Pakistan; the People's Republic of China; the Philippines; the Republic of Korea; Singapore; Sri Lanka; Taipei,China; Thailand; and Viet Nam. The latter two periods also include Armenia, Kazakhstan, the Kyrgyz Republic, and Tajikistan. In 2017, the 25 economies accounted for 99% of the total GDP of the Asian Development Bank's developing member economies plus Japan.

Sources: Estimates based on data from Feenstra, R. C., R. Inklaar, and M. P. Timmer. 2015. The Next Generation of the Penn World Table. *American Economic Review*. 105 (10). pp. 3150–3182. http://www.ggdc.net/pwt (accessed 1 July 2019); and Asian Productivity Organization (APO). APO Database. https://www.apo-tokyo.org/wedo/measurement (accessed 1 July 2019).

In the second period, from 1995 to 2005, TFP makes a positive contribution to growth across a slightly expanded group of 25 economies that now includes Central Asia. The positive contribution of TFP complements the role of the three other factors, with capital remaining the single most important source of growth. In the latest period, 2010–2017, the TFP contribution increases further, accounting for about 40% of growth. Throughout the three periods, improvements in human capital make a positive contribution.

Box 5.2: Technological Progress and Growth Accounting

The importance of technological progress in propelling economic growth is well understood in economic literature. Modern growth theories are founded on the aggregate production function framework, in which technological progress is one of the critical production inputs. The framework shows that an economy's gross domestic product (GDP) (Y) is determined by four elements: technology (A), capital (K), labor (L), and human capital (H).

For example, the Cobb–Douglas form of the production function, which has been empirically validated, assumes constant returns to scale in capital, labor, and human capital (growth of each of these inputs at the same rate will increase the production at that rate), and diminishing marginal productivity of capital, labor, and human capital (assumes imperfect substitution among these three factors):

(1) $Y = A K^a L^b H^{1-a-b}$

where $0 < a < 1, 0 < b < 1$, and $a+b < 1$.

Based on this aggregate production function, using total differentiation, one can derive a "growth accounting" formula, which explains GDP growth based on the growth of technology, capital, labor, and human capital:

(2) $\Delta Y/Y = \Delta A/A + a \Delta K/K + b \Delta L/L + (1-a-b) \Delta H/H$

where Δ denotes the change in a variable. With this equation, the rate of technological progress ($\Delta A/A$) can be computed as a "residual" because the growth of GDP, capital, labor, and human capital, as well as share parameters, a and b, are given by data.

(3) $\Delta A/A = \Delta Y/Y - a \Delta K/K - b \Delta L/L - (1-a-b) \Delta H/H$

Human capital, which represents the skills and knowledge of the workforce, is often quantified by average schooling years of the working-age population. Figures 5.1 and 5.2, for example, are based on the growth accounting formula shown by Equation (2).

As we can see from Equation (2), GDP growth ($\Delta Y/Y$) can be strengthened by technological progress ($\Delta A/A$) through technological adoption and innovation through, for example, investment in research and development. Countries can also increase GDP growth by supporting growth of human capital ($\Delta H/H$) by investing in education and improving

continued on next page

Box 5.2 *continued*

its quality. In addition, according to the "endogenous growth" models that appeared between the mid-1980s and 1990, technological progress ($\Delta A/A$) is a function of human capital (H). Therefore, based on this idea, investment in human capital contributes to both higher GDP growth directly and technological progress ($\Delta A/A$), which, in turn, leads to further GDP growth.[a] For developing countries, technological progress ($\Delta A/A$) stemmed from adopting foreign technology in addition to investments in local innovation.[b]

In the long run, however, the population growth rate ($\Delta L/L$) will slow and even become zero or negative due to demographic change (Chapter 6), which will lead to slower growth according to Equation (2). In the absence of population growth, i.e., $\Delta L/L=0$, the contribution from a capital increase to GDP growth will also diminish as the growth of capital ($\Delta K/K$) will be smaller. This is because $\Delta K/K$ is a product of a (fixed) savings rate ($\Delta K/Y$) and average capital productivity (Y/K) where capital per worker increases due to capital accumulation, leading to a decline in marginal capital productivity ($\Delta Y/\Delta K$) as well as average capital productivity (Y/K). Even in this case, growth can be sustained and strengthened by technological progress ($\Delta A/A$) and growth of human capital ($\Delta H/H$).

[a] Lucas, R. E., Jr. 1988. On the Mechanics of Economic Development. *Journal of Monetary Economics*. 22 (1). pp. 3–42; Romer, P. 1990. Endogenous Technological Change. *Journal of Political Economy*. 98 (5). pp. S71–S102; Grossman, G. M., and E. Helpman. 1991. *Innovation and Growth in the Global Economy*. Cambridge, MA and London: The MIT Press; and Aghion, P., and P. Howitt. 1997. *Endogenous Growth Theory*. Cambridge, MA: The MIT Press.

[b] Comin, D., and B. Hobijn. 2010. An Exploration of Technology Diffusion. *American Economic Review*. 100 (5). pp. 2031–2059.

Source: Asian Development Bank.

Figure 5.2 decomposes the growth of two groups of economies in the world in the decades from the 1960s onward. The contribution of TFP was 28% for economies that reached a high-income level from initial middle-income status, whereas the contribution was just under 10% for economies that remained middle-income. The results suggest that significant technological improvement and greater efficiency may be needed to progress from a middle- to a high-income level, overcoming the middle-income challenge (or the so-called middle-income trap).

Figure 5.2: Contributions to Growth in the World, 1960–2014
(% of total contribution)

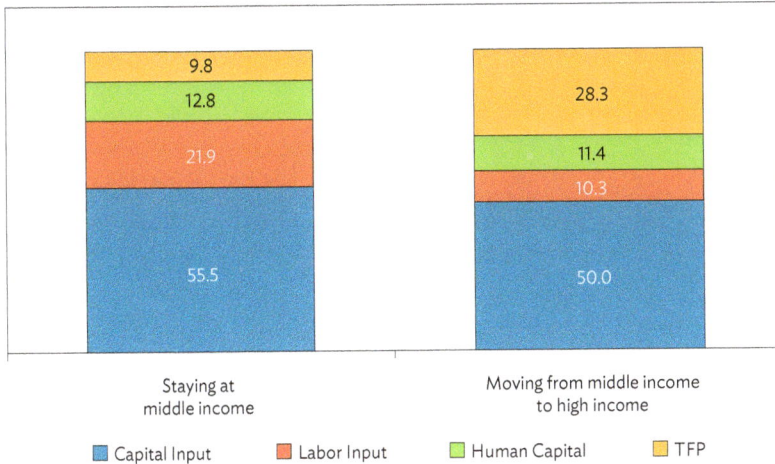

Staying at middle income	Moving from middle income to high income
TFP 9.8	TFP 28.3
Human Capital 12.8	Human Capital 11.4
Labor Input 21.9	Labor Input 10.3
Capital Input 55.5	Capital Input 50.0

■ Capital Input   ■ Labor Input   ■ Human Capital   ■ TFP

TFP = total factor productivity.

Notes: The calculations include both Asian and non-Asian economies and are the sum of a decade-by-decade analysis. Those that stayed middle income did so through the decade, while those that moved to higher income started the decade at middle income and moved to high income by the end of the decade. The number of economies included varies by decade. For the "staying at middle income" group, about 40 economies were used for each decade. For the "moving from middle income to high income" group, the number ranges from 14 in the 1970s to four in the 1980s.

Source: Asian Development Bank. 2017. *Asian Development Outlook 2017: Transcending the Middle-Income Challenge.* Manila.

5.3   Asia's technological progress

Three proxy measures can be used to capture the evolution of technology in the region: (i) the complexity of a country's exports, (ii) the number of patents awarded, and (iii) the number of robots manufactured and sold for use in production.

Product sophistication

In tangible terms, Asia's technological progress can be seen in the goods it produces and, by extension, those it is able to export to competitive global markets. In the 1960s, a sizable share of Asia's production and exports were in agricultural and primary commodities, as well as light manufacturing products such as textiles and garments. These have low technological and skill intensity, but nonetheless offer a first step on the industrialization ladder. The region has since mastered more complex technologies to produce more sophisticated goods—such as electric appliances, vehicles, computers, smartphones, and machine tools. For example, some 56% of automobile production worldwide takes place in Asia recently.[4] Currently, the top two smartphone companies globally, by sales, are based in the People's Republic of China (PRC) and the ROK, and Asian firms account for eight of the top 10.

Technological differences between a shirt and a computer are obvious, but more detailed measures are needed to gauge systematically the overall sophistication of a country's production capabilities and, hence, its technology. This can be done using the concept of product complexity. An index of the complexity of products is calculated and then applied on a weighted basis to a country's export basket.[5] The calculations are based on the value added of exports, not gross export value. This means that a country does not receive a high score and/or share for products it is merely assembling using highly complex, but imported, components. Figure 5.3 shows the distribution of exports based on product complexity for several Asian economies. The vertical axis indicates each economy's share by product groups out of total Asian exports on a value-added basis. The horizontal axis depicts 13 product groups ranging from low complexity (on the left) to high complexity (on the right).

A high point near the right side of the graph shows that a greater share of an economy's exports is complex. For example, Japan has a high share of the most complex goods (transport equipment or vehicles) at the rightmost vertical line (Figure 5.3a). Many economies export considerable quantities of electrical and electronic goods,

---

[4] Organisation Internationale des Constructeurs d'Automobiles (OICA). 2018. Production Statistics. http://www.oica.net/category/production-statistics/2018-statistics/.

[5] The calculation for Figure 5.3 has four steps. First, product complexity is calculated. The complexity for product "A" is based on two criteria: (i) ubiquity, which is the number of economies that export A; if there are fewer exporting economies, it is considered more complex; and (ii) diversity, for an economy that exports A, it is the range of other products (non-A) that the economy exports. If the economy exporting A exports a broad range of other products, then A is considered more complex. Combining (i) and (ii) creates a product complexity index score for all goods traded globally. Second, the index is applied to the exports of each of the 10 economies shown in Figure 5.3. Total Asian exports (from 24 economies) are also calculated for the products. Third, exports are assigned to 13 product groups (vertical lines). And fourth, each economy's share of total Asian exports is calculated. Throughout, export value added is used, not export value, and for manufactured products only.

Figure 5.3: The Flying Geese Pattern of Asian Exports
(average for 2013–2017)

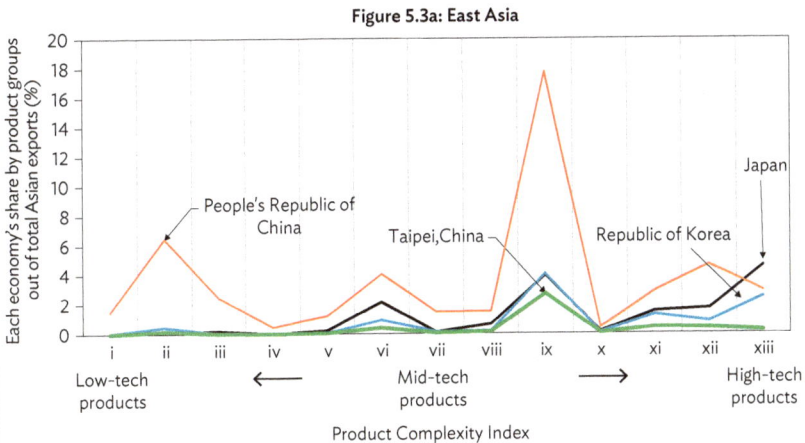

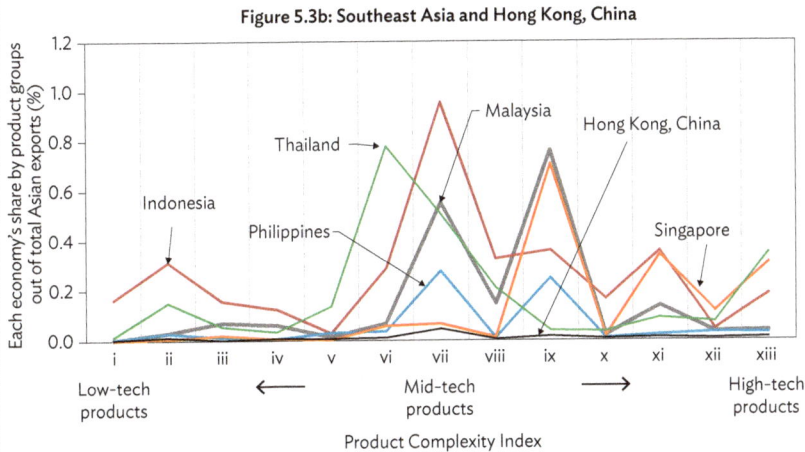

Figure 5.3a: East Asia

Figure 5.3b: Southeast Asia and Hong Kong, China

Notes: Data are for manufactured exports on a value-added basis, averaged for 2013–2017. Input–output data are used to calculate value added. The y axis depicts each economy's exports of a product group as a share of total Asian exports of all product groups. Total Asian exports is based on 24 economies. The x axis represents the following product groups, arranged by increasing complexity: (i) leather and footwear; (ii) textiles and textile products; (iii) manufacturing not elsewhere classified (nec) and recycling; (iv) wood and products of wood and cork; (v) other nonmetallic minerals; (vi) basic metal and fabricated metal; (vii) food, beverages and tobacco; (viii) rubber and plastics; (ix) electrical and optical equipment; (x) pulp, paper, printing, and publishing; (xi) chemicals and chemical products; (xii) machinery, nec; and (xiii) transport equipment.

Sources: Estimates based on data from United Nations. UN Comtrade Database. https://comtrade.un.org/data (accessed 1 July 2019); and Asian Development Bank. Multi-Regional Input–Output Database (accessed 1 July 2019).

notably the PRC, as depicted by the spike at the products of high mid-tech complexity (product group ix). Another spike occurs for food and beverages at the seventh vertical line, especially among middle-income economies included in Figure 5.3b.

Generally, the graph shows that high-income economies have a larger share of more complex goods in their export basket, whereas middle-income economies have a larger share of mid-complexity goods. This reinforces the "flying geese" model often used to signify the pattern of industrialization in the region, which generalizes dynamic patterns of industrial catch-up. In this process, industries relocate from advanced to developing economies sequentially, starting in light industries requiring lower technology, such as footwear and garments. But, at the same time, we can observe the emergence of intra-industry trade in addition to interindustry trade: Figure 5.3 shows overlapping export patterns in each product sophistication level. This indicates that the inter-economy and interindustry "flying geese" development model evolved over time into a more complex and dynamic structure of intra-industry regional and global value chains (Chapter 9).

Number of patents

The creator of a new technology captures the commercial gains by registering a patent. Thus, the annual registration of new patents offers one way of gauging innovation activity. Over the past 50 years, Asia's leading economies have transitioned from being users of foreign patents to producers of domestic ones.

The trend is seen clearly in the number of patents granted in the US (Table 5.1). In 1965–1969, only one of the top 10 foreign economies that were awarded patents in the US was from Asia (Japan), with all others from Europe and Canada. However, by 2015, there were four Asian economies among the top five (Japan; the ROK; Taipei,China; and the PRC), with India ranked 10th. Moreover, if each economy's total patents granted (domestically and in other countries under the Patent Cooperation Treaty) is considered, the PRC ranked first in the world in 2018.

Over 5 decades, Asia transformed itself from primarily adopting technology from others to creating new technology. Asian companies and research institutions are increasingly protecting their intellectual property in overseas markets, illustrating the region's expanding globalization of its homegrown R&D and business activities.

Table 5.1: Top 10 Patent Grantees in the United States
(annual averages)

Rank	1965–1969	Number of Patents	1975–1979	Number of Patents	1985–1989	Number of Patents	1995–1999	Number of Patents	2005–2009	Number of Patents	2015	Number of Patents
1	Germany	3,810	Japan	6,255	Japan	15,768	Japan	25,988	Japan	33,937	Japan	52,409
2	UK	2,739	Germany	5,650	Germany	7,432	Germany	7,772	Germany	9,196	ROK	17,924
3	France	1,524	UK	2,663	France	2,689	France	3,212	ROK	6,573	Germany	16,549
4	Japan	1,416	France	2,121	UK	2,668	UK	2,925	Taipei;China	6,118	Taipei;China	11,690
5	Canada	935	Switzerland	1,327	Canada	1,540	Canada	2,583	Canada	3,366	PRC	8,116
6	Switzerland	935	Canada	1,161	Switzerland	1,285	Taipei;China	2,473	UK	3,254	Canada	6,802
7	Sweden	583	Sweden	835	Italy	1,094	ROK	2,273	France	3,146	France	6,565
8	Netherlands	508	Italy	713	Sweden	860	Italy	1,319	Italy	1,356	UK	6,417
9	Italy	469	Netherlands	651	Netherlands	855	Switzerland	1,163	Netherlands	1,237	Israel	3,628
10	Belgium	187	Soviet Union	401	Australia	404	Sweden	1,031	Australia	1,202	India	3,355

PRC = People's Republic of China, ROK = Republic of Korea, UK = United Kingdom.

Notes: These refer to patents for inventions covering the creation of a new or improved—and useful—product, process, or machine. The origin of a patent is determined by the residence of the first-named inventor. Periods refer to years when patents were granted.

Source: United States Patent and Trademark Office (USPTO). Various years. USPTO Annual Reports. Alexandria.

Robots

Robots, along with computers, were an innovation of the Third Industrial Revolution but their increased sophistication, auto-adjustment, and cyber-linkages are at the heart of the Fourth Industrial Revolution (4th IR).[6] They enhance productivity and generate a high level of standardized quality. Asia is the global leader in both producing and using robots. Japan is the single largest manufacturer, accounting for over half of global robot production. The PRC and the ROK are also leading producers. The three countries accounted for about 75% of all robots made globally in 2015 (Table 5.2a).

The PRC is by far the largest user of new robots worldwide (Table 5.2b). Nearly 138,000 units were shipped (sold) to the PRC in 2017. Indeed, nearly as many robots were sold in the PRC than in the next four buyers combined (Japan, the ROK, the US, and Germany). Among the top 15 purchasers worldwide are five other Asian economies: Taipei,China; Viet Nam; Singapore; India; and Thailand.

Table 5.2: Industrial Robots

Table 5.2a: Production of Industrial Robots, World and Selected Economies, 2010–2015

	2010	2011	2012	2013	2014	2015
	Number of units ('000)					
World	120.6	166.0	159.3	178.1	220.6	253.7
	(Percentage shares)					
Japan	61.3	59.1	59.8	53.6	54.8	54.4
Republic of Korea	14.2	12.8	10.0	8.9	12.2	12.6
PRC	...	...	...	5.3	7.2	8.0
Germany	9.8	11.4	11.6	11.1	9.4	7.8
Other economies	14.7	16.7	18.6	21.0	16.4	17.1

... = data not available, PRC = People's Republic of China.

Source: United Nations Conference on Trade and Development (UNCTAD). 2017. Box 3.1 in *Trade and Development Report 2017. Beyond Austerity: Towards a Global New Deal*. Geneva.

continued on next page

---

[6]   There are four industrial revolutions: the First Industrial Revolution was based on the introduction of steam power, steel, and the use of machines from the late 1700s; the Second Industrial Revolution was based on electricity and mass production from the early 1900s; the Third Industrial Revolution was based on computers and robots from the 1960s; and the Fourth Industrial Revolution is based on cyber-physical systems, sensors, artificial intelligence, and the Internet of Things, and began in the late 2000s.

Table 5.2 *continued*

Table 5.2b: Estimated Annual Shipments (Buyers) of Multipurpose Industrial Robots, World and Selected Economies, 2016–2021

	2016	2017	2018[a]	2019[a]	2020[a]	2021[a]
	Number of units ('000)					
World	294.3	381.3	421.0	484.0	553. 0	630. 0
	(Percentage shares)					
PRC	29.6	36.2	39.2	43.4	45.2	46.0
Japan	13.1	11.9	12.8	11.6	10.7	10.2
Republic of Korea	14.1	10.4	9.7	8.7	8.0	7.3
United States	10.7	8.7	8.3	7.7	7.4	7.3
Germany	6.8	5.6	5.3	4.9	4.5	4.1
Taipei,China	2.6	2.9	3.1	2.9	3.1	3.2
Viet Nam	0.5	2.2	0.6	0.6	0.8	1.1
India	0.9	0.9	1.1	1.0	1.1	1.2
Thailand	0.9	0.9	1.0	1.0	1.1	1.1

PRC = People's Republic of China.

Note: Shipments are sales/purchases that occur within the economy; the source of those purchases may be domestic producers or imports.

[a] Forecast.

Source: International Federation of Robotics. 2018. *Executive Summary: World Robotics 2018 Industrial Robots*. Frankfurt am Main.

5.4   Modalities of technological progress

Asia's technological advancement over the past 50 years is the result of a mix of market forces, structural transformation, seized opportunities, and government support. In general, a country's development is likely to undergo an initial phase of adoption-based technological progress and growth, and a later phase of own innovation-based growth.

In the adoption phase, a country exploits the latecomer's advantage by using technologies already developed by advanced economies. Adoption is a cost-effective method of technical progress, as it does not involve "reinventing the wheel." There are a variety of channels or modes through which adoption takes place. Licensing, reverse engineering, machine imports and trade in general, FDI, and technical cooperation aid are important channels of learning and technological transfer. Trade enhances the productivity of capital and also transfers information about the market. FDI complements domestic savings and investment, facilitating capital accumulation and the transfer of technologies and management skills.[7] Technical cooperation aid is composed of a set of activities that augment the level of knowledge and technical skills.[8]

Over time, as countries develop and their technological level begins to converge with advanced countries, they must move on to innovation. Innovations can take the form of introducing new products, new services, or new processes. Innovating countries focus more on R&D, the upskilling of human capital—including through higher education and lifelong learning—and the protection of intellectual property rights. Rewards from being the first mover dilute as new entrants join and compete more effectively. Innovation must be done on a rolling basis, and market competition will generate strong incentives for continuous innovation.

In many countries, including advanced economies and Asian emerging economies, the process of adoption and innovation occur simultaneously. Innovation becomes more important at the later stage of development to remain at the global technological frontier.

Licensing

New technologies can be acquired by obtaining licenses for patents, industrial designs, and other intellectual property from abroad. Using licenses effectively requires human capability. Asia's now high-income economies used licensing extensively during development and they, along with other economies, continue to do so. For example, Taipei,China began its electrical and electronics sector in the late 1950s with licenses for key designs from Japan. It began by producing electrical meters and later used licensed technology for television production.

Many companies in Taipei,China began adopting the original equipment manufacturer (OEM) business model based on licensed technology, producing parts and products marketed by other manufacturers. Foxconn, established in 1974, has become the largest OEM company in the world, currently manufacturing more than a

[7]   Borensztein, E., J. De Gregorio, and J.-W. Lee. 1998. How Does Foreign Direct Investment Affect Economic Growth. *Journal of International Economics.* 45 (1). pp. 115–135.

[8]   Comin, D., and B. Hobijn. 2011. Technology Diffusion and Postwar Growth. In Acemoglu, D., and M. Woodford. *NBER Macroeconomics Annual 2010, Volume 25.* Chicago: Chicago University Press; and Sawada, Y., A. Matsuda, and H. Kimura. 2012. On the Role of Technical Cooperation in International Technology Transfers. *Journal of International Development.* 24 (3). pp. 316–340.

third of global consumer electronics, including for companies such as Apple and Nintendo. Many manufacturers in Taipei,China shifted away from OEM to developing their own designs and marketing their own brands, such as Acer and Asus, an example of the shift from adoption to innovation.

Today's middle-income countries use licenses extensively to gain access to technologies. For example, Thailand spent $5 billion for intellectual property imports in 2018 and the PRC $35 billion. As an economy develops its own technology, it starts to sell technology licenses to firms abroad and becomes a licenser (exporter/seller of licenses). In 2003, Japan moved from being a net importer of intellectual property (patents, copyrights, and others) to a net exporter, currently exporting twice as much as it imports. While other Asian countries remain net importers, the ROK may soon become a net exporter.[9]

Engaging in trade

International trade has been an important driver of technological adoption and innovation. In general, trade facilitates technological progress directly by transferring information contained in imported capital goods and intermediate inputs.[10] In fact, Asia acquired technologies for efficient production of manufactured goods, initially by importing machines and instruments in addition to obtaining foreign licenses from abroad. With a large gap in technology between the West and Asia in the early phase of the region's development, these imported capital goods and intermediate inputs were important for rapid technological catch-up and technological deepening.

Exports can also contribute to technological progress because exporting firms can learn about foreign technologies through the export process, and about competing products in global markets—often called "learning-by-exporting." Moreover, exports generate foreign exchange that can be funneled into innovation for further exports by, for example, enabling the purchase of licenses and machinery. This iterative process can also enhance overall productivity through learning-by-doing.

---

[9]   Intellectual property imports to the ROK were valued at $9.9 billion against exports of $7.8 billion in 2018. Data are from World Bank. World Development Indicators. https://data.worldbank.org (accessed 24 June 2019).

[10] Grossman, G. M., and E. Helpman. 1991. Trade, Knowledge Spillovers, and Growth. *European Economic Review*. 35 (2–3). pp. 517–526; and Romer, P. 2010. What Parts of Globalization Matter for Catch-Up Growth? *American Economic Review: Papers and Proceedings*. 100 (2). pp. 94–98.

Trade incentivizes a country to promote R&D and skills development where it holds comparative advantage, enabling technological upgrading. This dynamic mechanism has occurred in Asia. As time progressed, Asia's leading economies have produced their own capital goods, such as construction equipment and precision machinery, for both domestic and international markets. Some countries are becoming major global providers of capital goods.

Higher growth in many Asian countries after liberalizing trade policies is a clear example of the dynamic technological gains arising from outward-oriented trade regimes. A key drawback of a trade strategy that focuses on import substitution without sufficient export promotion is that it fails to generate technological and knowledge spillovers and the foreign exchange needed to import capital goods and acquire technology (Chapter 9).

Foreign direct investment

FDI can be a key conduit for technology transfer, as multinational corporations (MNCs) carry with them the latest technologies as well as new business models and management know-how. Countries differed in their approaches to FDI. While Japan and the ROK relied more on licensing, machine imports, and their own research than on FDI, other high-growth Asian economies made extensive and substantial use of FDI to drive growth, especially in the early stage of development. Singapore offered an environment conducive for MNCs in manufacturing, finance, and logistics. Taipei,China took a hybrid approach, leveraging MNCs for key technologies but also building capacity in domestic enterprises. In both cases, technological spin-offs occurred, with human capital important for gaining the benefits of FDI.[11]

Some countries took a more active approach. Malaysia, Thailand, and the PRC built their manufacturing base on large amounts of FDI and used an active strategy that included special economic zones. Joint ventures were another important tool for technological transfer. From the 1960s to the 1980s, many countries also attempted to leverage FDI to build the capacity of local enterprises using local content requirements (LCRs). Foreign companies required to source locally could help build the technological capacity of domestic suppliers. However, foreign companies often found these policies constraining,

---

[11] Borensztein, E., J. De Gregorio, and J.-W. Lee. 1998. How Does Foreign Direct Investment Affect Economic Growth. *Journal of International Economics.* 45 (1). pp. 115–135.

notably when the technological capacity of domestic firms was below the required standards. The use of LCRs has fallen as it contradicts international trade rules.

Technology transfer through FDI may occur in unintended ways. The establishment of the ready-made garment sector in Bangladesh is an intriguing example. In the early 1970s, the ROK faced barriers to garment exports due to quota restrictions under the Multifibre Arrangement. To "jump the quota," one of the ROK's main producers, Daewoo, established a local joint venture with Desh Garments Ltd. to produce and export clothing from Bangladesh. To ensure its new venture would be efficient and profitable, Daewoo invited 130 Desh supervisors for training at its modern facility in the ROK. The obvious intention was that the trainees would return and apply their newly acquired expertise to the joint venture. An unintended consequence was that 115 of the trainees soon left Desh and either established their own companies or joined other new firms in Bangladesh. Partly as the result of this infusion of expertise, the ready-made garment sector grew rapidly, dominated by domestically owned firms. They are mostly producing for foreign clothing brands, but some have developed their own designs and brands. Bangladesh is currently the second-largest exporter of garments globally, after the PRC.

Technical cooperation aid

Asia has benefited from technical cooperation aid provided from advanced to less-developed countries. This aid can facilitate adoption of new technologies and raise an economy's absorptive capacity, thereby increasing the pace other foreign technologies are adopted.

Following World War II, US technical cooperation to the ROK; Taipei,China; and several Southeast Asian countries came in a variety of forms, including sending experts to the region and inviting students and trainees to the US.

Over time, Japan, Europe, and Australia played an increasingly important role in facilitating technological transfer to other Asian economies through aid programs. The ROK and some other Asian countries are also now becoming donors of technical assistance. Technical cooperation aid has been one of the main pillars of bilateral and multilateral official development assistance to Asia (Chapter 14).

A recent study found a positive and significant correlation of technical cooperation aid with aggregate technological progress.[12] Among the different channels of international technological transfer, international trade was the largest contributor, followed by technical cooperation aid and FDI.

Reverse engineering

Historically, reverse engineering has been a common technique for acquiring technology. Reverse engineering disassembles a product to learn how it was produced.[13] While certainly a form of adoption, the process requires a high level of engineering know-how. Machines and products are easy to take apart, but understanding and then replicating the engineering is the hard part. Also, some chemical products and materials are very difficult to reverse engineer.

For example, the founder of Toyota Motors, Kiichiro Toyoda (the son of textile machine innovator and maker, Sakichi Toyoda) imported a US car in 1933 and reverse engineered it to make the first Model A1 car in 1935. LG Electronics produced the ROK's first transistor radios in 1958 through reverse engineering US and Japanese products. Samsung reverse engineered semiconductors starting with basic dynamic RAM chips at the research laboratory it set up in 1982. The company subsequently moved up to higher-capacity chips and became a world leader. In the 1970s, Taipei,China start-ups used reverse engineering to learn how to produce computers. Acer, Mitac, and other local firms initially sold the products of global computer companies, notably minicomputers and microprocessors. Through constant interaction with pioneers in the computer business and sponsored training, Acer became a global brand of computer equipment.

While reverse engineering is considered an adoption technique, it can be an important step in the transition to innovation through learning. When a firm has the capability to reverse engineer a product and produce its own version, it can then move on to improve the basic design and produce new products.

---

[12] Sawada, Y., A. Matsuda, and H. Kimura. 2012. On the Role of Technical Cooperation in International Technology Transfers. *Journal of International Development*. 24 (3). pp. 316–340.

[13] Nabeshima, K. 2004. Technology Transfer in East Asia: A Survey. In Yusuf, S., M. Anjum Altaf, and K. Nabeshima, eds. *Global Production Networking and Technological Change in East Asia*. Washington, DC: World Bank.

Research and development

As economies develop and move closer to the global technological frontier, they focus more on indigenous innovation. In Asia, more human resources and funding have been channeled into corporate laboratories and public research institutes. Japan and the ROK are among the top countries globally in R&D as a share of GDP, with both investing more than 3% (Figure 5.4). The ROK doubled its share over the past 2 decades as it became a global leader in electronics. The PRC raised its R&D considerably in the 2 decades to 2016—from 0.5% to 2.0% of GDP. Its share is now similar to Singapore and is above Hong Kong, China.

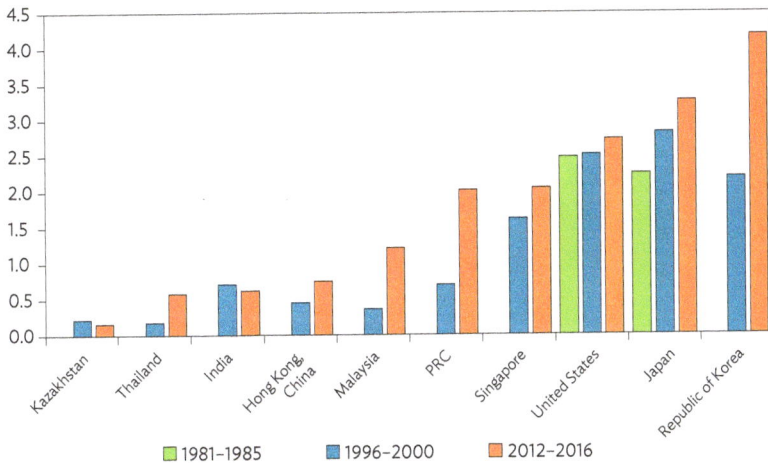

Figure 5.4: Research and Development Expenditure, 1981–2016
(% of GDP)

GDP = gross domestic product, PRC = People's Republic of China.

Notes: Data refer to average for the period indicated. Data for the period 1981–1985 are only available for Japan and the United States. For the period 1996–2000: for Kazakhstan, data refer to 1997–2000; for Thailand, data for 1998 are missing; for Hong Kong, China, data refer to 1998–2000; and for Malaysia, data for 1997 and 1998 are missing. For the period 2012–2016: for Thailand, data refer to 2013–2016; for India, data refer to 2015; for Malaysia, data refer to 2014–2015; and for Singapore, data refer to 2012–2014.

Sources: For 1981–1995: Organisation for Economic Co-operation and Development (OECD). OECD Data. https://data.oecd.org (accessed 3 July 2019); and for 1996–2016: World Bank. World Development Indicators. https://databank.worldbank.org/source/world-development -indicators (accessed 24 June 2019).

Other middle-income economies in Asia have also recently increased spending on R&D as part of broader national strategies to promote innovation. In Thailand and Malaysia, research spending as a share of GDP has more than tripled since the late 1990s (Figure 5.4). In these economies, research has focused in part on domestically prominent industries. For example, a large portion of research in Thailand is in its important food processing sector, the medical sector (given the rapid expansion in medical tourism), and the automotive sector. In India, information technology (IT) software accounts for a large share of overall R&D spending. In fact, many foreign firms have set up R&D centers with a heavy IT concentration.[14]

Part of the support for R&D comes through government research and educational institutions. The last half century saw the development of high-quality universities in Asia. Of the top 100 global universities in physical sciences and mathematics, 15 are from the region.[15]

Industrial clusters and agglomeration

Technological learning occurs when enterprises locate near each other in clusters and as part of industrial estates and technology parks. This proximity generates technological (Marshallian) externalities, i.e., knowledge spillovers between firms through general interaction, the sourcing of parts and components, the movement of workers, and competitive pressures. Many clusters develop naturally, based either on access to a key raw material or the establishment of one or more lead firms that induce related firms to locate nearby. Modern technology clusters are often located near universities and research institutes. Broadly, the concentration of industries in or adjacent to cities provides agglomeration effects where firms can rely on suppliers and workers and get access to markets. The result can be increasing returns to scale.[16]

Asia is home to a great variety of traditional clusters and, more recently, ones that have been induced by government coordination.

---

[14] Expenditures by foreign R&D centers in India are not generally included in the country's R&D expenditure data. Basant, R., and S. Mani. 2012. Foreign R&D Centers in India: An Analysis of Their Size, Structure and Implications. *Indian Institute of Management Working Paper Series*. No. 2012-01-06. Ahmedabad.

[15] Figures are from Times Higher Education, World University Rankings 2019.

[16] Asian Development Bank. 2019. *Asian Development Outlook 2019 Update: Fostering Growth and Inclusion in Asia's Cities*. Manila.

In Japan, Ota Ward in Tokyo[17] and Higashi-Osaka City are well-known clusters for small and medium-sized enterprises from the prewar period, producing precision parts and plastic and metal molds. Toyota City in Japan[18] and Ulsan in the ROK are examples of large auto industry clusters (Toyota and Hyundai) involving many subsidiary and contracting companies. Well-known traditional clusters in South Asia include the world's largest concentration of producers of hand-stitched footballs and surgical instruments, both located in Sialkot, Pakistan. India has a large variety of clusters including brassware in Moradabad and knitwear in Tirupur. Bengaluru is well known for its clusters of software and business process outsourcing (BPO) industries. Thailand hosts production clusters for automobiles and hard disk drives, while Bangladesh and Cambodia are known for garments. Hsinchu Science Park in Taipei,China is famous for the development of electronics. The site was selected for its proximity to the science and engineering facilities of two major universities. The Industrial Technology Research Institute is also nearby and has spun off two of the three largest semiconductor fabrication facilities in the world.

Shenzhen in southern PRC is an urban and high-tech metropolis that is home to some of the country's largest and more progressive companies. It was the first special economic zone established and is often called the PRC's Silicon Valley. The city is home to Huawei, the electronics firm; Tencent, the internet giant; and ZTE, a leader in telecommunications equipment. Tsinghua University and Peking University in the capital are major institutes of teaching and research in engineering and technology and have supported the development of firms in electronics and technology, especially in Zhongguancun, Beijing.

Market competition

International and domestic market competition has been a major force in promoting Asia's technological progress, as discussed in the trade subsection. Where there is competition, firms maintain or increase their market position by adopting new processes and products. They can engage in various types of technology acquisition and innovation.

---

[17] Whittaker, D. 1997. *Small Firms in the Japanese Economy*. Cambridge, United Kingdom: Cambridge University Press.

[18] Fujita, K., and R. C. Hill. 1993. Toyota City: Industrial Organization and the Local State in Japan. In Fujita, K., and R. C. Hill, eds. *Japanese Cities in the World Economy*. Philadelphia: Temple University Press. pp. 175–202.

At low levels of competition—when only one or a few firms dominate a market—there is little incentive to innovate as the market is already secured. This has been a problem in some countries where governments have monopolized ownership and prevented the entry of private competition. For instance, India nationalized key strategic industries and controlled private sector entry through a licensing system before 1990.

For market competition to facilitate innovation, proper policies are critical—including laws on fair competition, bankruptcy, consumer protection, and intellectual property. Competition policies aim to enhance a consumer's freedom of choice and a firm's freedom to trade and access markets. They balance short-term efficiency with long-term, dynamic efficiency and societal benefits. To promote fair competition in the marketplace, countries have also been paying greater attention to the quality of government institutions and regulatory capacity, including open and transparent government procurement, anticorruption measures, and corporate governance.

Competition is important, but excessive competition may reduce margins and inhibit the accumulation of funds needed to finance innovation. A multitude of micro and small firms engaged in fierce competition leaves thin margins and little opportunity to invest in R&D. It also inhibits the creation of large firms that can reap economies of scale. Some existing research therefore suggests an inverted U-shaped relationship between competition and innovation with very low and very high levels of competition slowing technology development.[19]

Selecting capable companies and concentrating on a smaller number of firms can occur naturally through moderate competition, mergers and acquisitions, and the exit of inefficient enterprises. For example, in Japan's postwar motorcycle sector, the number of manufacturers grew from five at the end of the war to 127 by 1953. Technology levels were initially very low (most firms were small workshops), which allowed for easy entry by the burgeoning number of entrepreneurs. In the 1950s, some leading firms invested in advanced production machinery imported from the US and Europe to produce innovative designs. By the 1960s, the market became dominated by just four firms—Honda, Yamaha, Suzuki, and Kawasaki—which later

---

[19] Aghion, P., et al. 2005. Competition and Innovation: An Inverted-U Relationship. *Quarterly Journal of Economics*. 120 (2). pp. 701–728.

became the most innovative motorcycle manufacturers globally.[20] In this way, market competition fostered innovation.

Structural transformation and technological advance

Asia's experience also shows that technological progress is part of a process of structural transformation (shifts in production and employment) from agriculture to industry (especially manufacturing) and services.

The initial transformation process was linked to improved agricultural productivity through adaptive research and technological transfers across different ecological environments. An important example was the Green Revolution, the diffusion of modern rice and wheat varieties in Asia beginning in the 1960s (Chapter 4). Chemical fertilizers, pesticides, and mechanization also increased agricultural productivity.

Technological development in agriculture and manufacturing are mutually reinforcing. As technological advances in manufacturing generated sustainable productivity growth and expanded employment opportunities,[21] the resulting labor movement from agriculture to nonagriculture sectors raised agricultural wages, "inducing" the use of labor-saving technology. Agricultural productivity improved with the use of modern inputs such as machinery, chemical fertilizers, and pesticides produced by the nonfarm sector.[22] It is almost impossible for agricultural modernization to occur in heavily populated Asian countries unless industrialization proceeds in tandem with agricultural development.[23]

5.5   Country experiences on technology policies

Asia exhibits a diversity of experiences and strategies for technological upgrading. As discussed earlier, some countries relied more on FDI. Other countries also adopted targeted industrial policies (Chapter 2). In any case, adoption and innovation require deliberate efforts with

---

[20]   Yamamura, E., T. Sonobe, and K. Otsuka. 2005. Time Path in Innovation, Imitation, and Growth: The Case of the Motorcycle Industry in Postwar Japan. *Journal of Evolutionary Economics*. 15 (2). pp. 169–186.

[21]   Hayashi, F., and E. C. Prescott. 2008. The Depressing Effect of Agricultural Institutions on the Prewar Japanese Economy. *Journal of Political Economy*. 116 (4). pp. 573–632.

[22]   Hayami, Y., and V. W. Ruttan. 1985. *Agricultural Development: An International Perspective*. Baltimore and London: Johns Hopkins University Press.

[23]   Watanabe, T. 1992. *Asia: Its Growth and Agony*. Hawaii: University of Hawaii Press.

supporting social capability and absorptive capacity, to make them work. Human capital is a key requirement for technology adoption. Moving to new processes and products requires supportive government policies regarding physical infrastructure, institutions of learning and research, and patents to protect innovation. Two of the most important drivers of technological progress are an open trade and investment regime and market competition. All these are part of a broad national strategy of technology and innovation.

Japan

While Japan had a tradition of developing technologies in many areas in the prewar period, the country relied more on imported foreign technology through licensing and other modalities during the postwar recovery and catching-up process, and later increasingly moved on to innovation. This sequence is depicted in Figure 5.5 and was observed in other countries as well. During the initial phase of technological adoption by private companies, the Japanese government played a critical role in importing technologies and establishing a stringent framework for adoption (given serious foreign exchange constraints).

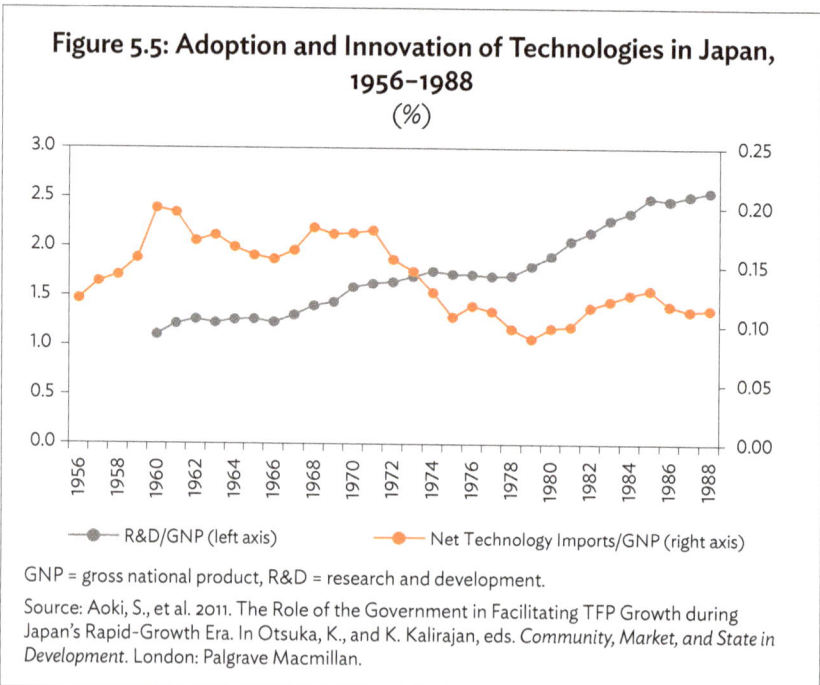

Figure 5.5: Adoption and Innovation of Technologies in Japan, 1956–1988
(%)

GNP = gross national product, R&D = research and development.

Source: Aoki, S., et al. 2011. The Role of the Government in Facilitating TFP Growth during Japan's Rapid-Growth Era. In Otsuka, K., and K. Kalirajan, eds. *Community, Market, and State in Development*. London: Palgrave Macmillan.

This policy framework, initiated in 1950 through the Foreign Investment Law, was used to selectively adopt what were thought to be key technologies. Regulations associated with the Foreign Investment Law were relaxed gradually and mostly disappeared by 1968, as demand for imported technologies by domestic industries increased sharply and foreign exchange was no longer scarce.

Over time, firms engaged more intensively in R&D to further increase their technology level. While the government's share of R&D was smaller than other developed countries, it was highly involved in the establishment of R&D consortiums in addition to supporting broader science and technological research.

Republic of Korea

The ROK grew from a poor country with low technological development in the early 1960s to a leading center of innovation in electronics, chemicals, automobiles, and other industries. This transformation relied on intensive use of technological adoption from abroad that over time became the basis for the shift to indigenous innovation. A key aspect of the country's transition was active state intervention to promote development based on technology. The government played a decisive role in providing the human capital and creating incentives for firm-level upgrading. Instead of relying on FDI, the government fostered the development of large conglomerates, known as chaebols, which invested heavily in physical capital and innovation. The deliberate use of an export-oriented trade strategy allowed some protection to infant industries, but also pushed firms to compete in foreign markets. Government support—especially access to low-cost finance and foreign exchange—was tied to export performance. With those resources, firms were incentivized to upgrade process and product technology.

From the 1980s, the government shifted its focus to innovation. It set up a national R&D program in 1982 and offered tax credits to encourage firm-level research and worker training. The private sector responded. The ratio of business R&D to technology imports increased from 2.5 in 1981 to 10 in the early 1990s, and total R&D rose from less than 1% of GDP in 1981 to nearly 3% by 2005.[24] During this period, the share of research financed by government declined relative to the private sector as the government became more of a facilitator.

---

[24]   Chung, S. C. 2007. Excelsior: The Korean Innovation Story. *Issues in Science and Technology.* 24 (1). pp. 1–11.

Singapore

Over the past 5 decades, Singapore's national innovation system has shifted from technology use to technology creation. The shift had four successive phases: (i) learning to use technology transferred to Singapore from MNCs; (ii) adapting to and improving externally acquired technology by domestic firms; (iii) innovating both products and processes by investing in R&D; and (iv) pioneering new technological innovations.

The government played a major role in shaping Singapore's rapid technological progress more recently. In the 1970s and 1980s, the economy relied mainly on technology provided by MNCs. This changed in the 1990s with the establishment of a National Science and Technology Board and the launching of two five-year National Technology Plans. Along with investing in public R&D, efforts in the 2000s focused on building research infrastructure and attracting private R&D. The government developed its Third National Science and Technology Plan 2001–2005, placing greater emphasis on high-technology entrepreneurship and advanced basic research in the life sciences and ICT.[25]

People's Republic of China

The PRC's efforts to gain access to technology has also gone through several distinct phases as it moved from adopter to innovator. After its founding in 1949, the PRC relied on a variety of foreign sources for technological advancement. The Soviet Union initially played a key role until it withdrew its advisers in 1960. Western countries and Japan stepped in to become the main suppliers after the late 1970s reform and opening up. Technology was acquired by purchasing turnkey plants and advanced machinery, as well as through licensing, technical consulting, and technical cooperation. Five advanced countries—the US, Japan, Germany, France, and the United Kingdom—provided most of the technology.[26]

---

[25] Wong, P. K., and A. Singh. 2008. From Technology Adopter to Innovation: Singapore. In Edquist, C., and L. Hommen, eds. *Small Country Innovations System: Globalization, Change and Policy in Asia and Europe*. Cheltenham, United Kingdom and Northampton, MA: Edward Elgar.

[26] Fu, X., W. T. Woo, and J. Hou. 2016. Technological Innovation Policy in China: The Lessons, and the Necessary Changes Ahead. *Economic Change and Restructuring*. 49 (2–3). pp. 139–157.

Technology transfer through FDI and markets became a new focus from 1985 onward. That year, the government initiated science and technology policy reforms, including promoting interaction between universities and industries. The government mandated joint ventures between foreign and domestic firms to facilitate technological transfer to the domestic economy. From 1995, it strengthened promotion of domestic science and technology by providing tax incentives for firms to set up R&D units. In 2006, it introduced "indigenous innovation" as a strategic priority. A series of R&D strategies were emphasized in subsequent five-year plans.[27] A broader national technology development plan, "Made in China 2025", was adopted in 2015 to increase domestic content in the high-technology sectors—such as automotive, electronics, robotics, aeronautics, and others—that are dominated by foreign companies.

These policies boosted PRC investment in R&D—the annual growth rate averaged 18.7% during 2000–2018. The PRC has become among the world's major spenders on R&D and has built one of the largest national R&D teams. It had a workforce of about 4.2 million full-time equivalent researchers in 2018.[28]

India

India evolved from a labor-intensive economy to one with strong competitiveness in IT, generic medicines, and others. India became a global hub in exportable software services and IT-enabled services.[29] The software and IT-enabled service industry today supplies about 8% of India's output and accounts for $137 billion in exports.[30]

After independence, India embarked on an inward-oriented industrial strategy, focusing on import substitution and championing domestic (often state-owned) firms. Technological learning, except from the Soviet Union, was very limited. From the mid-1980s, the country began to pursue a market-oriented and globally open policy. This occurred at a time when IT was growing rapidly worldwide, with

---

[27] Wu, Y. 2012. Trends and Prospects in China's Research and Development Sector. *Australian Economic Review*. 45 (4). pp. 467–474.

[28] National Bureau of Statistics of China. Various years. *China Statistical Yearbook*. http://www.stats.gov.cn/english/Statisticaldata/AnnualData/ (accessed 4 September 2019).

[29] Software services are customized assistance to firms, whereas software products, such as Microsoft Word or Stata, are generic packages sold to customers.

[30] India Brand Equity Foundation (IBEF). *IT and ITeS*. https://www.ibef.org/download/it-ites-feb-2019.pdf; and IBEF. https://www.ibef.org.

a significant increase in computer usage within firms and a transition from mainframe to personal computers. India's top IT firms, such as Infosys, were established during this period and rapidly expanded operations.[31] At the same time, India had been expanding training of engineers and applied scientists, notably through Indian Institutes of Technology. By the late 1980s, nearly 150,000 English-speaking engineers were graduating annually. In 1985, Texas Instruments became the first foreign firm to set up an IT software research center, based in Bengaluru.

The government established software technology parks and liberalized the use of firm-level satellite connections that facilitated frequent and low-cost data transfer. Hardware imports were liberalized and made duty-free for software exporters. These infrastructure and trade policy changes—combined with a gaping wage differential between engineers in India and the US—induced a massive flow of software outsourcing to India in the 1990s. The 12-hour time difference facilitated this shift, allowing for a combined 24-hour workday.

Along with software services, India developed a substantial industry in IT-enabled services, also known as BPO or business process management (BPM). The internet allowed the offshoring of back-office activities (such as managing customer accounts and medical transcriptions) and direct customer support (such as call centers and online chat support). These activities first started when American Express (the credit card firm) moved back-office activities to India in the late 1980s. It developed further when General Electric made a similar move in the late 1990s.[32]

Thailand

In the 1970s, Thailand began building a manufacturing sector based on FDI, which brought in the technology it needed. One priority was the automobile sector, where the government set technological upgrading targets and LCRs to develop a domestic supplier base. The Board of Investment provided a range of fiscal incentives for investment and, later, also for innovation.[33]

---

[31] Infosys was created in 1981 and Tech Mahindra in 1986. HCL Technologies moved into software in 1991. TCS was established much earlier in 1968. Wipro began as a vegetable company in 1945 and moved into IT from the late 1970s.

[32] Athreye, S. 2005. The Indian Software Industry and Its Evolving Service Capability. *Industrial and Corporate Change.* 14 (3). pp. 393–418.

[33] Organisation for Economic Co-operation and Development (OECD). 2013. *Innovation in Southeast Asia.* OECD Reviews of Innovation Policy. Paris.

In the 1980s, the government began building public research infrastructure. The National Center for Genetic Engineering and Biotechnology was established in 1983, followed 3 years later by both the National Metal and Materials Technology Center, and the National Electronics and Computer Technology Center. A fourth center, the National Nanotechnology Center, was added in 2003. The four centers employed over 2,000 researchers by the early 2010s. The National Innovation Agency (NIA), established in 2003, provides grants and concessional loans for innovative projects.

In 2014, the government unveiled Thailand 4.0, a vision to lead the country into the Fourth Industrial Revolution (4th IR). The strategy is closely tied to a massive infrastructure program southeast of Bangkok known as the Eastern Economic Corridor. The government aims to upgrade industries in next-generation automotive production, affluent medical and wellness tourism, agriculture and biotechnology, food innovation, robotics, aerospace, and logistics and aviation.

Malaysia

Malaysia has focused attention on science and technology in economic planning since 1986 under the First National Science and Technology Policy, which was part of the Fifth Malaysia Plan, 1986–1990. This was followed in 1991 with the creation of Vision 2020, which established a framework for a future knowledge-based economy.

The Tenth Malaysia Plan, 2011–2015 provided a more focused framework for governing science and technology and included the *Unit Inovasi Khas* (UNIK), a special innovation unit under the Prime Minister's Office, to integrate innovation policy. The unit helps commercialize research by universities and public research institutions. UNIK also prepares the National Innovation Policy. It works in parallel with the Malaysian Innovation Agency, which was set up in 2011 to spearhead the country's innovation agenda. Malaysia introduced a range of fiscal and non-fiscal measures to promote research and innovative activities by foreign and domestic firms.[34]

---

[34] OECD. 2013. *Innovation in Southeast Asia*. OECD Reviews of Innovation Policy. Paris.

Kazakhstan

From the early 2000s, Kazakhstan introduced policies and programs to develop a national system of technology and innovation. Public financing was added in 2003 to promote development of high-tech and knowledge-based industries. The first domestic venture capital fund was launched 2 years later and, in 2006, a major infrastructure initiative began with the establishment of a special economic zone information technology park.[35] The country's innovative ecosystem includes an independent cluster fund, industrial zones, technoparks, technology commercialization centers, international centers of technology transfer, and venture capital funds.

5.6 Recent technological trends and developments

While many Asian countries have made significant progress in adopting and innovating technology, various new technologies have emerged more recently, both globally and in the region. The speed of innovation and advent of new technologies has increased due to the increased number of people doing R&D (most released from other activities indicating productivity gains), and greater interaction between researchers and entrepreneurs worldwide (given the dramatic progress in communications and transport). A large part of innovation today occurs in services. Asian countries are part of these new trends and, in fact, lead innovation in some areas.

A few examples of the new technologies include ICT-enabled BPO, online payments, e-commerce, 5G cellular networks, artificial intelligence, sophisticated robots, new logistics technologies using drones and satellite-based technology, social media, and shared economies such as Airbnb and Uber. Platform companies—such as Amazon, Google, Facebook, and Apple from the US, as well as Alibaba, Tencent, and Baidu from the PRC—are changing the way of life, altering the existing industrial structure, amassing huge financial and human resources, and influencing the global economy and society.

---

[35] Satpayeva, Z. T. 2017. State and Prospects of Development of Kazakhstan Innovative Infrastructure. *European Research Studies Journal.* 20 (2). pp. 123–148.

In fact, rather than slowing down, the speed of global technological innovation appears to be accelerating.[36] For example, while it took about 45 years for the penetration rate of landline telephones in the US to rise from 5% to 50%, it took only 9 years for the entire world to reach the same rate for mobile phones (Figure 5.6).

This current technological change is driven by the 4th IR, which builds on the ICT revolution and is fueled by the convergence of digital, physical, and biological innovation. Under the 4th IR, industrial processes are programmed, self-monitored, and self-adapted

Figure 5.6: Diffusion Speed of Technologies

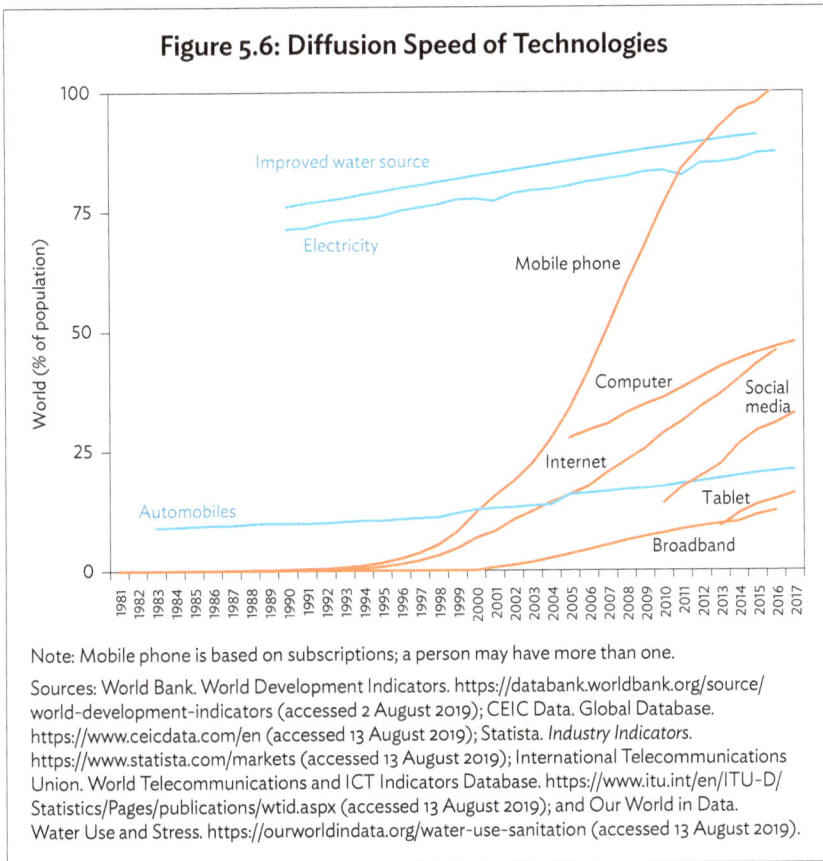

Note: Mobile phone is based on subscriptions; a person may have more than one.

Sources: World Bank. World Development Indicators. https://databank.worldbank.org/source/world-development-indicators (accessed 2 August 2019); CEIC Data. Global Database. https://www.ceicdata.com/en (accessed 13 August 2019); Statista. *Industry Indicators.* https://www.statista.com/markets (accessed 13 August 2019); International Telecommunications Union. World Telecommunications and ICT Indicators Database. https://www.itu.int/en/ITU-D/Statistics/Pages/publications/wtid.aspx (accessed 13 August 2019); and Our World in Data. Water Use and Stress. https://ourworldindata.org/water-use-sanitation (accessed 13 August 2019).

---

[36] Paradoxically, some recent research suggests that productivity growth has been declining, although there are counter arguments. See Gordon, R. 2018. Why Has Economic Growth Slowed When Innovation Appears to Be Accelerating? *NBER Working Paper Series.* No. w24554. Cambridge, MA: National Bureau of Economic Research.

by electronics to connect with machinery on the factory floor. More sophisticated robots and computing capacity, artificial intelligence, and machine learning underpin these changes. New advances in nanotechnology, materials, and biogenetics are also affecting the process. Beyond the factory, the 4th IR has transformed the link between producers and consumers, both in how demand is assessed (for example, through big data), how demand is made (through smart devices), and how goods and services are delivered (through the internet and with drones).

Some Asian countries are already leading innovation in several areas. Japan leads in robotics, partly induced by the declining workforce. The ROK is now the largest producer of semiconductors. The PRC has become a global leader in areas such as 5G cellular networks, e-commerce, and artificial intelligence. India is a major global player in the software industry.

The region is also home to many creative, practical, and indigenous innovations that improve everyday lives. For example, Indonesia's Gojek began as a motorcycle taxi company but has grown into a leading on-demand mobile app service company—offering a wide range of services including transportation, logistics, payments, and food delivery. Another well-known innovator is Grab, which was founded in Malaysia and has become the dominant ride-sharing app across Southeast Asia.

India and the Philippines leveraged the ICT revolution and the English fluency of its workforce to become a major provider of BPO services. In the Philippines, the BPO sector currently accounts for 6% of GDP and 4.2% of formal employment. Low-skilled BPO services are evolving into high-end services such as cybersecurity, sophisticated credit negotiations, legal and accounting services, data analysis, and new IT applications. Many Central Asian countries today have national strategies to develop fintech industries, sophisticated logistics hubs, and technology-based agribusiness.

Asian technological development based on the "flying geese" model has been changing. Countries now have a chance to leapfrog from lower stages of technological development to the frontier. Technologies connect countries via trade, FDI, global value chains, and the mobility of people (Chapter 9). The core challenge for developing Asia is to keep up with the accelerated speed of global technological progress and take advantage of the opportunities provided (Box 5.3).

Box 5.3: ADB Support to Digital Technology

A key element of Strategy 2030 of the Asian Development Bank (ADB) is to incorporate advanced technology and new ideas into operations. The Digital Technology and Development Unit is supporting seven sector groups (education, energy, finance, health, transport, urban, and water) and eight thematic groups (climate change and disaster risk management, gender equity, governance and public management, social development, the environment, rural development and food security, regional cooperation and integration, and public–private partnerships) in sharing of ideas and knowledge across operations.

Box Figure: ADB's Digital Technology Projects (Loans and Grants) by Sector, 2010–2018

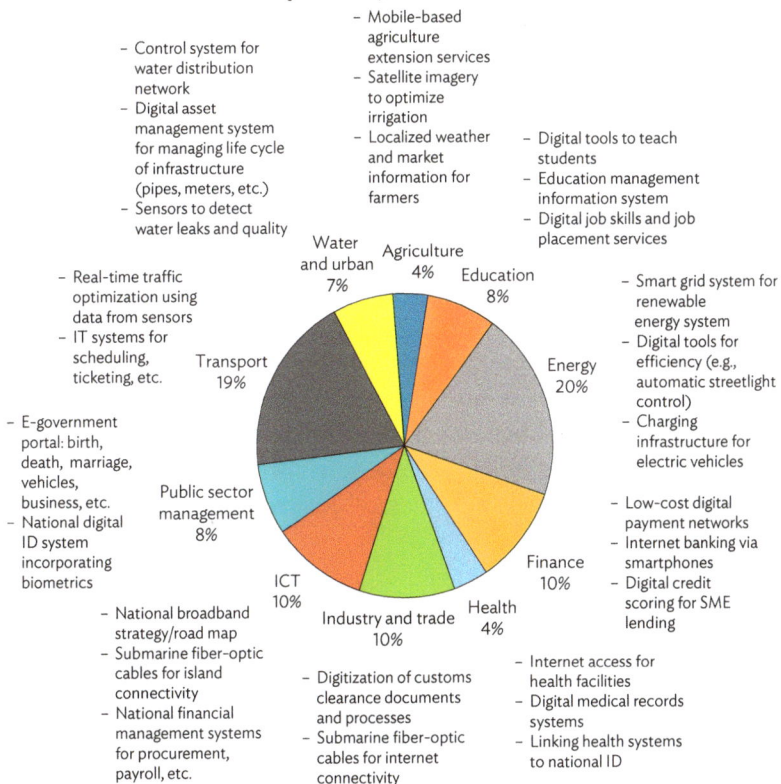

– Control system for water distribution network
– Digital asset management system for managing life cycle of infrastructure (pipes, meters, etc.)
– Sensors to detect water leaks and quality

– Mobile-based agriculture extension services
– Satellite imagery to optimize irrigation
– Localized weather and market information for farmers

– Digital tools to teach students
– Education management information system
– Digital job skills and job placement services

– Real-time traffic optimization using data from sensors
– IT systems for scheduling, ticketing, etc.

– Smart grid system for renewable energy system
– Digital tools for efficiency (e.g., automatic streetlight control)
– Charging infrastructure for electric vehicles

– E-government portal: birth, death, marriage, vehicles, business, etc.
– National digital ID system incorporating biometrics

– Low-cost digital payment networks
– Internet banking via smartphones
– Digital credit scoring for SME lending

– National broadband strategy/road map
– Submarine fiber-optic cables for island connectivity
– National financial management systems for procurement, payroll, etc.

– Digitization of customs clearance documents and processes
– Submarine fiber-optic cables for internet connectivity

– Internet access for health facilities
– Digital medical records systems
– Linking health systems to national ID

Water and urban 7%, Agriculture 4%, Education 8%, Energy 20%, Transport 19%, Public sector management 8%, ICT 10%, Industry and trade 10%, Health 4%, Finance 10%

ICT = information and communication technology, ID = identification, IT = information technology, SME = small and medium-sized enterprise.

Note: There were 105 loans and grants during 2010–2018 for digital technology projects. Percentages refer to sector shares of this number.

continued on next page

Box 5.3 *continued*

> The Digital Technology for Development Unit was established in 2018 to promote the use of digital technologies in sectors and across themes. ADB supported 105 digital technology projects and 210 technical assistance projects in 2010–2018, and these numbers are increasing, with the shares across sectors becoming increasingly diverse.
>
> Source: Asian Development Bank.

5.7 Looking ahead

There is no question that new technologies drive productivity increases and create the foundation for better-paying jobs and economic growth in Asia. To continue innovating and adopting new technologies to achieve sustainable and inclusive growth, policy makers in the region can focus on five priorities.

First, governments can develop a diverse cadre of educated and skilled people in science and technology. Strong science and mathematics programs in secondary schools provide a platform for quality science and engineering education and vocational training at the tertiary level. Governments can further promote human capital development by enhancing the mobility of people between countries. It is also important to train and retrain workers and promote lifelong learning.

Second, countries can invest in and manage the expansion of digital infrastructure. The internet and cloud computing can be used to develop, share, and create new ideas and expand economic activity. Governments can also help increase low-cost broadband access and set effective cybersecurity policies to ensure consumer and privacy protection.

Third, governments should continue to promote R&D. This can be done through public research institutes, higher education, and financial and tax incentives for private sector R&D and for technology start-ups. Fostering links between the research community and business is essential. Governments can provide a vision for future technological development that leverages a country's comparative advantage and encourages the private sector to take a more focused and coordinated approach.

Fourth, countries can foster good institutions for innovation. Governments should protect intellectual property rights and promote fair competition. They can promote new technologies by using them to improve public service delivery in education, health, social protection programs, administrative services, and other areas.

Fifth, countries have to consider the impact of new technologies on jobs, inequality, privacy, and other social consequences such as data-driven discrimination and crimes. In particular, there are concerns that new technologies, such as artificial intelligence and robotics, can cause widespread job loss and deepen inequality.

Regarding the impact on jobs, there are several reasons for optimism. First, new technologies often automate specific tasks, not an entire job. ATMs, for example, have not replaced bank tellers but broadened their role in managing customer relations. Second, automation proceeds only where it is both technically and economically feasible. Many sophisticated technologies can replace what humans have been doing, but they are too expensive. Third, rising demand offsets job displacement driven by automation. Jobs created by rising demand based on higher productivity and income can more than compensate for job losses due to technological advances. This is clear when comparing jobs lost from the invention of steam locomotives and automobiles to the new jobs these innovations created. Fourth, technological change and economic growth create new occupations and industries. Many new job titles have come out of digitization, and new types of jobs are arising in health care, education, finance, and other services. New technologies are also being developed and used to minimize environmental degradation and help achieve climate change mitigation and adaptation. In the process, they are contributing to the creation of green jobs.

Nevertheless, new technologies alter skill requirements and may cause unemployment as some firms downsize their workforce or close. In addition, less-skilled workers are more likely to experience low wage growth, thereby exacerbating income inequality (Chapter 11). Governments can respond to these challenges by ensuring workers are protected from the downside of new technologies and are able to harness the new opportunities they provide. This requires coordinated action on skills development, labor regulation, social protection, and income redistribution.

CHAPTER 6

EDUCATION, HEALTH, AND DEMOGRAPHIC CHANGE

6.1   Introduction

Human capital and demographics are critical drivers of economic development. Demographic change affects the size of a country's total population, working-age population, and labor force. Human capital development, the result of investment in education and health, is itself a goal for the welfare and empowerment of the people, and a key component of the Sustainable Development Goals. It is also an important determinant of economic growth, as investment in human capital raises labor productivity and contributes to technological progress, along with investment in physical capital (Chapter 7), innovation (Chapter 5), and the increased efficiency associated with policy and institutional reforms (Chapter 2). Numerous studies have shown that investing in human capital, measured by various indicators, is positively associated with the pace of growth.[1]

Developing Asia has gone far in expanding education over the past 50 years—driven by public investment, policies that broaden access, and education reforms. Almost all Asian countries achieved

---

[1]   Barro, R., and J.-W. Lee. 2013. A New Data Set of Educational Attainment in the World, 1950–2010. *Journal of Development Economics*. 104 (September). pp. 184–198; and Barro, R. 1996. Determinants of Economic Growth: A Cross-Country Empirical Study. *The NBER Working Paper Series*. No. w5698. Cambridge, MA: National Bureau of Economic Research.

universal or near-universal access to primary education. Many also achieved universal or near-universal access to secondary education, significantly expanded technical and vocational education and training, and tertiary education.

The region has also made great strides in improving the health of its population. Life expectancy increased from 45 to 72 years and the under-five mortality rate declined sixfold during 1960–2018. These gains were largely due to improved living standards and investment in public health, through both targeted health programs and strengthening of health systems.

Economic development is also impacted by demographic changes through its effects on the population size, labor force, and dependency ratio—defined as the number of children aged below 15 years and elderly (aged 65 years and above) per working-age population (aged 15–64 years). When the working-age population grows faster than the nonworking-age population, a country can reap a "demographic dividend" if it can create sufficient jobs to employ those of working age. On the other hand, population aging and declining working-age population can create a "demographic tax" and negatively impact on savings, investment, and consumption, thus constraining growth.

Developing Asia's initially high fertility rates, decreasing mortality across all ages, and increased life expectancy led to rapid population growth and a rising share of the working-age population. From 1960 to 2018, the region's population increased from 1.5 billion to 4.1 billion (a 1.7% annual increase) and its working-age population increased from 855 million to 2.8 billion (a 2.1% annual increase). The higher share of the working-age population generated a demographic dividend. However, many countries now face falling fertility rates—associated with rising incomes, urbanization, and increasing gender equality—and the challenge of population aging.

This chapter looks at developing Asia's achievements in expanding human capital and its changing demographic profile, their key drivers, and how they contributed to the region's growth and transformation. Section 6.2 examines developing Asia's improved education outcomes and key driving factors. Section 6.3 focuses on health. Section 6.4 examines changing demographics. Section 6.5 estimates Asia's demographic dividend. Finally, section 6.6 highlights the challenges in narrowing the still large gaps in human capital and responding to rapid demographic transition occurring over a large part of the region.

6.2 Rising educational attainment

Increasing mean years of schooling

The past half century saw an impressive increase in educational attainment across developing Asia. The region's average mean years of schooling for young adults aged 20–24 increased from 3.5 in 1960 to 8.9 in 2010 (Figure 6.1). The increase was most pronounced (7–10 years) in the four newly industrialized economies (Hong Kong, China; the Republic of Korea [ROK]; Singapore; and Taipei,China), Bangladesh, India, Indonesia, Malaysia, Sri Lanka, and Thailand. In 1960, young adults in 22 of the 29 Asian economies with available data had only 6 years or less of education on average. By 2010, there were only three countries with mean years of schooling at 6 or less. Developing Asia also made impressive progress in narrowing gender gaps in schooling (Chapter 12).

Rising school enrollment at all levels

Rising school enrollment rates, especially in primary and secondary schools, were the main reason for the increase in mean years of schooling. At all levels of education, developing Asia's average enrollment ratios have always been much higher than those of Sub-Saharan Africa, but lower than Latin America and the Caribbean—although variations are large among Asian countries (Table 6.1).[2]

In 1970, only 59.3% of school-age children attended primary school in South Asia and 71.2% in Southeast Asia. By 2018, most had achieved universal or near-universal access to primary education. The progress in secondary education was equally impressive, although gaps remain significant in South Asia and the Pacific. Among the three most populous countries in Asia, the secondary gross enrollment rate of the People's Republic of China (PRC) increased from 27.5% to 95.0%, India's increased from 23.8% to 73.5%, and Indonesia's from 18.2% to 88.9%.

Tertiary enrollment has also expanded, especially in newly industrialized economies. The ROK and Singapore achieved universal or near-universal access to tertiary education in 2017—94.3% and 84.8%, respectively—higher than most developed countries. But developing

---

2   The net enrollment rate is the share of a country's total school-age population attending school. The gross enrollment rate is the ratio of all students, including those attending adult education and foreign students, to a country's total school-age population (including foreign students). Accordingly, the gross enrollment rate can be greater than 100%.

Figure 6.1: Mean Years of Schooling, for Population Aged 20–24 Years, 1960 and 2010

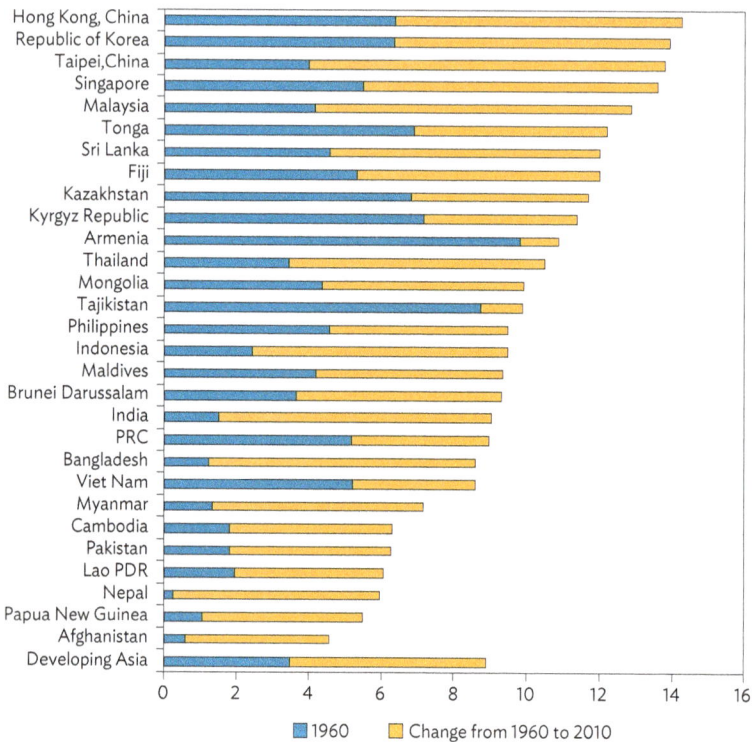

Lao PDR = Lao People's Democratic Republic, PRC = People's Republic of China.

Note: In this chart, mean years of schooling is the average number of completed years of education of an economy's population aged 20–24.

Source: Barro, R., and J.-W. Lee. 2013. A New Data Set of Educational Attainment in the World, 1950–2010. *Journal of Development Economics.* 104 (September). pp. 184–198. For the Barro and Lee Database version 2.0. http://www.barrolee.com (accessed 17 April 2019).

Asia, as a whole, still has large gaps in tertiary education enrollment. In many developed economies, the high tertiary enrollment ratio partly reflects the rising importance of adult education and, in some, the increase in international students, especially from Asia.

Technical and vocational education and training (TVET) in Asia has received growing attention in recent years. Studies attribute rapid economic growth in some countries partly to the efforts to align

Table 6.1: School Enrollment Rates, 1970–2018
(% of school-age population)

	Primary (net)			Secondary (gross)			Tertiary (gross)		
	1970	1990	2018	1970	1990	2018	1970	1990	2018
Developing Asia	**77.3**	**87.0**	**93.3**	**25.0**	**39.0**	**78.9**	**2.4**	**6.5**	**34.3**
Central Asia	...	...	92.9	...	99.9	95.9	...	25.7	26.4
East Asia	94.1	97.9	99.8	28.3	39.7	95.2	0.4	5.4	53.0
People's Republic of China	94.0	97.8	99.9	27.5	36.7	95.0	0.1	3.0	50.6
Republic of Korea	95.9	99.8	97.3	39.0	92.9	100.3	6.8	36.5	94.3
South Asia	59.3	76.1	88.5	23.2	34.4	69.3	4.3	5.4	24.2
India	61.0	77.1	92.3	23.8	37.2	73.5	4.9	5.9	28.1
Southeast Asia	71.2	92.4	94.6	22.9	41.8	87.5	5.5	10.2	34.1
The Pacific	...	64.9	77.7	19.8	22.7	54.4	1.7	3.1	...
Developed Asia	**99.0**	**99.6**	**97.8**	**84.3**	**99.1**	**112.4**	**17.2**	**30.2**	**73.2**
Japan	99.3	99.8	98.2	85.0	94.7	102.4	17.3	29.4	63.6
Latin America and the Caribbean	**83.2**	**90.3**	**93.7**	**27.7**	**76.9**	**95.9**	**6.9**	**17.0**	**51.8**
Sub-Saharan Africa	**39.3**	**53.1**	...	**11.4**	**22.6**	**43.3**	**0.9**	**3.0**	**9.1**
OECD	**88.0**	**98.1**	**95.6**	**68.8**	**86.2**	**106.6**	**22.1**	**38.2**	**73.5**
World	**71.7**	**82.0**	**89.4**	**40.1**	**51.3**	**75.6**	**9.7**	**13.6**	**38.0**

... = data not available, OECD = Organisation for Economic Co-operation and Development.

Notes: Weighted averages use official school-age population as weights. Some figures are not for the exact year indicated in the table. Rates can be more than 100% because of the enrollment of overage students.

Sources: World Bank. World Development Indicators. https://databank.worldbank.org/reports.aspx?source=world-development-indicators (accessed 2 August 2019); United Nations Educational, Scientific and Cultural Organization (UNESCO). UIS Stat Database. http://data.uis.unesco.org/ (accessed 2 August 2019); and Asian Development Bank estimates. For the People's Republic of China's net enrollment rates: National Bureau of Statistics of China. Various years. *China Statistical Yearbook.* http://www.stats.gov.cn/english/Statisticaldata/AnnualData/ (accessed 2 August 2019); for Singapore: Government of Singapore, Ministry of Education. 2018. *Education Statistics Digest 2018.* https://www.moe.gov.sg/docs/default-source/document/publications/education-statistics-digest/esd_2018.pdf; and for Taipei,China: Ministry of Education. 2018 Education Statistical Indicators.

TVET systems with their economic development strategies.[3] Available data suggest that many Asian countries have done well in expanding TVET, but there are large variations.[4] Both demand- and supply-side factors likely contributed to cross-country variations. In the PRC, for example, its large manufacturing sector likely generated strong demand for TVET skills.

Large variations in education quality across the region

While developing Asia made impressive progress in expanding the quantity of education, performance is mixed when it comes to education quality. A large body of empirical evidence suggests education quality has a significant causal impact on an individual's potential to earn and on an economy's growth and competitiveness.[5]

The Programme for International Student Assessment (PISA) and Trends in International Mathematics and Science Study (TIMMS), two of the most recognized international standardized tests, assess cognitive skills of 14–15-year-old students randomly selected from participating economies, and thus offer some measure of education quality. Figure 6.2 shows the percentages of student participants in these tests who scored 400+ (basic skill level) and 600+ (advanced skill level) in science and mathematics for participating Asian economies,[6] mostly in 2015 but with some 2003, 2007, and 2009 results. For comparison, it also shows results for the United States (US) and Organisation for Economic Co-operation and Development (OECD) countries as a group.

There are large variations across Asian economies in education quality as measured by these test results. Some Asian economies performed better than the OECD average for both 400+ and 600+ marks. Of these, Singapore and Kazakhstan were among

---

[3] Cheon, B. Y. 2014. Skills Development Strategies and the High Road to Development in the Republic of Korea. pp. 213–238. In Salazar-Xirinachs, J. M., I. Nübler, and R. Kozul-Wright, eds. *Transforming Economies: Making Industrial Policy Work for Growth, Jobs and Development*. Geneva: International Labour Organization–United Nations Conference on Trade and Development.

[4] TVET can be provided by the formal education system through schools, polytechnic institutions, or universities; it can also be offered at workplaces through a variety of channels, including on-the-job training, internships, and apprenticeships.

[5] Asian Development Bank (ADB). 2013. *Key Indicators for Asia and the Pacific: Asia's Economic Transformation: Where to, How, and How Fast?*. Manila.

[6] Only two states in India participated in the 2009 PISA test for mathematics, science, and reading, but both subsequently withdrew from the test. In the PRC, the PISA test was administered in only four more-developed provinces and is, therefore, not representative of the country as a whole.

Figure 6.2: Average Science and Mathematics Test Scores
(% of student participants scoring 400+ and 600+)

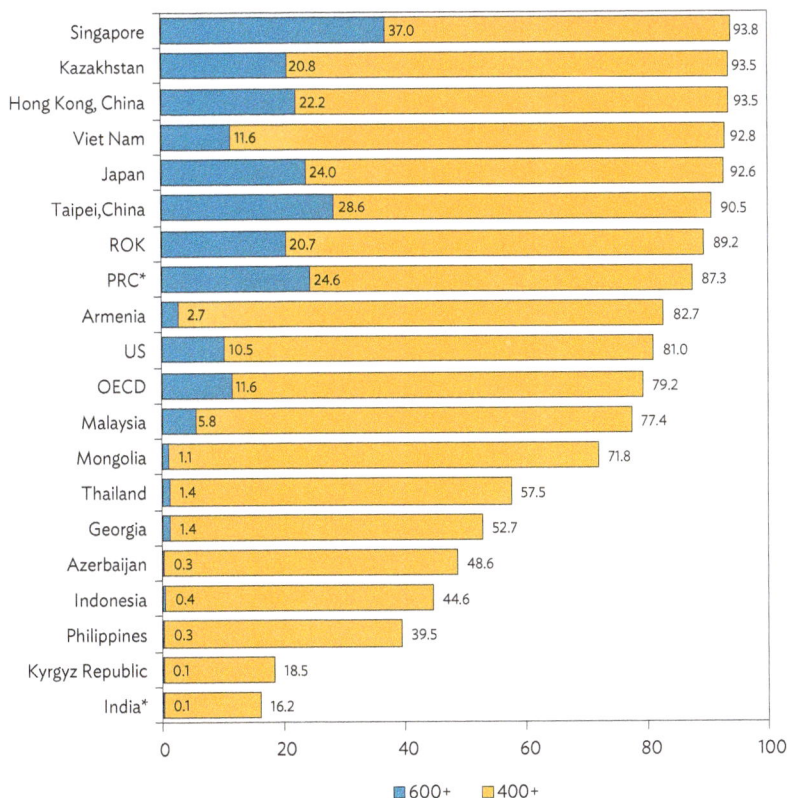

Country	600+	400+
Singapore	37.0	93.8
Kazakhstan	20.8	93.5
Hong Kong, China	22.2	93.5
Viet Nam	11.6	92.8
Japan	24.0	92.6
Taipei,China	28.6	90.5
ROK	20.7	89.2
PRC*	24.6	87.3
Armenia	2.7	82.7
US	10.5	81.0
OECD	11.6	79.2
Malaysia	5.8	77.4
Mongolia	1.1	71.8
Thailand	1.4	57.5
Georgia	1.4	52.7
Azerbaijan	0.3	48.6
Indonesia	0.4	44.6
Philippines	0.3	39.5
Kyrgyz Republic	0.1	18.5
India*	0.1	16.2

■ 600+   ■ 400+

OECD = Organisation for Economic Co-operation and Development, PRC = People's Republic of China, ROK = Republic of Korea, US = United States.

Notes: PRC* includes only Beijing, Shanghai, Jiangsu, and Guangdong. India* includes only Himachal Pradesh and Tamil Nadu. The test scores are standardized to range from 0 to 1,000. Data are for 2015 Programme for International Student Assessment (PISA) / Trends in International Mathematics and Science Study (TIMSS) scores except for Armenia and the Philippines (TIMSS 2003); Mongolia (TIMSS 2007); Azerbaijan, India, and the Kyrgyz Republic (PISA 2009).

Sources: Organisation for Economic Co-operation and Development (OECD). 2016. *PISA 2015 Results in Focus*. Paris; OECD. 2010. *PISA 2009 Results: Learning Trends*. Paris; International Association for the Evaluation of Educational Achievement (IEA). 2016. *Trends in International Mathematics and Science Study 2015*. Chestnut Hill, MA: TIMSS & PIRLS International Study Center, Boston College; IEA. 2008. *Trends in International Mathematics and Science Study 2007*. Chestnut Hill, MA: TIMSS & PIRLS International Study Center, Boston College.; and IEA. 2004. *Trends in International Mathematics and Science Study 2003*. Chestnut Hill, MA: TIMSS & PIRLS International Study Center, Boston College.

the top performers on both measures. On the other hand, in some countries, less than 50% of student participants hit the 400+ mark and less than 1% scored 600+. Despite the limitations, these results show that many Asian economies still have a long way to go to improve education quality.

Public policy and investment in education

Public policy played a critical role in expanding education. Historically, while education has always held particular importance in society in many parts of Asia, it was accessible only to the elite in most countries. With the exception of Japan, which introduced compulsory primary education in 1886 during the Meiji modernization, it was mainly after World War II that leaders of newly independent Asian nations stressed the need to spread education across the population and emphasized its importance for economic takeoff and industrialization. There were several dimensions of public policy in expanding education during the past half century.

The first was to establish access to education as a basic right, and it became a key element of national development strategies. Many Asian countries inherited education systems from their colonial period that were often fragmented, with limited facilities for technical or higher education. After independence, policy makers launched national plans and programs to expand and reform education systems, initially as part of nation-building and later as a key component of development strategies. Early efforts focused on recognizing education as part of citizen rights (in constitutions or education laws), reforming curricula, training teachers, and increasing the number of schools at all levels.

In the ROK, for instance, a year after the Korean War, the government introduced a six-year plan (1954–1959) for compulsory primary education. In the PRC, the government launched a mass campaign to eliminate illiteracy, including the introduction of simplified Chinese characters. In Southeast Asia, Indonesia's 1945 Constitution declared that "every citizen has the right for education," and Malaysia's Education Act 1961 introduced compulsory and free primary education for all school-age children. In South Asia, India began reforming its elitist education system in the 1950s by targeting free and compulsory primary education for all. In Sri Lanka, the Free Education Policy introduced in 1945 entitled every child aged 5–16 years to free education.

The second dimension was to implement programs to broaden access to education. Many countries started by offering free primary schooling, and later, as income levels rose, expanded programs to include lower secondary and higher secondary levels. As of 2018, most developing Asian economies provided at least 9 years of compulsory education, most offering 9–12 years (Table 6.2).

Legal rights to schooling notwithstanding, demand-side factors—such as high out-of-pocket expenses and opportunity costs in lost income from attending schools—still discourage low-income or disadvantaged households in some countries from sending children to school. Thus, many countries offer educational assistance to these households to encourage school attendance. Such social assistance includes cash transfers, feeding programs, scholarships, or school vouchers. One successful example is the Bangladesh Female Secondary School Stipend Program launched in the early 1990s, which has helped increase female enrollment and their continuation into secondary education.

Table 6.2: Years of Compulsory Education, Developing Asia, 2018

	Years of Compulsory Education
Tonga	15
Nauru	14
Marshall Islands, Philippines	13
Armenia, Mongolia, Pakistan, Palau, Turkmenistan, Uzbekistan	12
Sri Lanka	11
Azerbaijan, Kyrgyz Republic, Viet Nam	10
Afghanistan; Brunei Darussalam; Georgia; Hong Kong, China; Indonesia; Kazakhstan; Kiribati; Lao People's Democratic Republic; People's Republic of China; Republic of Korea; Tajikistan; Thailand; Timor-Leste	9
India, Samoa, Tuvalu	8
Malaysia, Singapore	6
Bangladesh, Myanmar	5

Source: World Bank. World Development Indicators. https://databank.worldbank.org/reports .aspx?source=world-development-indicators (accessed 15 November 2019).

In recent years, several Asian countries have expanded their social protection systems and have begun implementing conditional cash transfer programs to increase school attendance by children from poor families. The Philippine "4Ps"—*Pantawid Pamilyang Pilipino Program*—supported by the World Bank and the Asian Development Bank (ADB), is now the world's fourth-largest conditional cash transfer program, benefiting more than 10 million children (20% in high school) from the poorest households. The program offers social assistance grants to households on the condition that children stay in school and get regular health checkups; if mothers receive prenatal care; and if parents regularly attend community sessions on positive child discipline, disaster preparedness, and women's rights.[7]

The third dimension was education reform. One key element is to align education development with the changing needs of the economy and society over time. The newly industrialized economies are often cited as success stories. In the ROK, for example, primary education first provided workers with skills suitable for 1960s labor-intensive industries. In the 1970s and 1980s, the development of the secondary education system contributed to the growth of capital-intensive industries. And in the 1990s, the expansion of tertiary education laid the basis for its growing knowledge-based economy. In Singapore, the focus of education policy from the 1980s shifted from increasing quantity to improving quality. The government strengthened secondary education, developed TVET, and expanded tertiary education to meet growing demand for the higher skills associated with the economy's higher-income status.

Many other countries launched similar efforts. The PRC started expanding secondary education and strengthening tertiary education as early as the 1950s when it adopted the Soviet model to develop science- and technology-based curricula. The Cultural Revolution in 1966–1976 disrupted the entire education system, especially tertiary education. In 1977, the PRC restored the university entrance examinations. Subsequently, it took a wide range of reforms to modernize the system, leading to a rapid expansion of university enrollment, especially since 1999.

---

[7] World Bank. 2017. *FAQs about the Pantawid Pamilyang Pilipino Program (4Ps)*. https://www.worldbank.org/en/country/philippines/brief/faqs-about-the-pantawid -pamilyang-pilipino-program.

Table 6.3: Government Expenditures on Education, 1970–2018
(% of GDP)

	1970–1979	1980–1989	1990–1999	2000–2009	2010–2018
Developing Asia	2.1	2.5	2.7	3.3	3.6
Central Asia	...	...	...	...	4.0
East Asia	1.8	2.3	2.4	3.2	3.6
People's Republic of China	1.8	2.0	1.8	3.0	3.6
South Asia	...	...	3.6	3.3	3.7
India	...	...	3.8	3.5	4.0
Southeast Asia	2.9	1.6	2.7	3.7	3.6
The Pacific	6.3	...	...	4.6	...
Developed Asia	4.5	5.1	4.8	4.3	3.9
Australia	6.0	5.2	5.0	5.0	5.3
Japan	4.5	5.2	3.5	2.7	3.2
Latin America and the Caribbean	...	...	3.5	4.2	4.9
Sub-Saharan Africa	...	...	3.3	3.6	4.1
OECD	5.0	4.9	4.8	5.1	5.2
World	...	...	4.2	4.2	4.6

... = data not available, GDP = gross domestic product, OECD = Organisation for Economic Co-operation and Development.

Sources: Asian Development Bank. Key Indicators Database. http://kidb.adb.org (accessed 1 September 2019); World Bank. World Development Indicators. https://databank.worldbank.org/reports.aspx?source=world-development-indicators (accessed 2 August 2019); and Asian Development Bank estimates. For Taipei,China: Directorate-General of Budget, Accounting and Statistics.

India inherited a relatively well-developed university system from the colonial era. After independence, the government established the highly regarded Indian Institutes of Technology in 1958 and Indian Institutes of Management in 1961. In response to concerns that investment in tertiary education may have come at the expense of basic education, the government passed the Right to Education under its Constitution and launched the *Sarva Shiksha Abhiyan* program from the early 2000s, to reaffirm their commitment to education for all.

Central Asia has a strong mathematics and science curriculum inherited from the Soviet era. The newly independent nations suffered from severe economic recession in the early 1990s, forcing them to cut fiscal expenditures, particularly in education, with the quantity and quality of services deteriorating as a result. From the mid-1990s, governments instituted various reforms—including curricula modernization, local language as the medium of instruction, decentralization of education management to local governments, development of student assessment systems, raising teacher salaries, and increasing access to higher education.

The fourth dimension was increased public spending and investment in education. In the 1970s, developing Asia's public spending on education was among the lowest in the world—at 2.1% of gross domestic product (GDP) (Table 6.3). But over the next 4 decades, the region caught up with other regions globally, by nearly doubling public spending on education as a ratio to GDP. Some countries still have scope to increasing public spending on education. For instance, it was less than 2% of GDP in Cambodia and Myanmar in the 2010s.

6.3 Healthier populations

In the 1950s and 1960s, people in developing Asia had short life expectancy, suffered widespread undernutrition, high child and maternal mortality, and poor access to modern health care. Over the following 50 years, the region significantly improved people's health, especially in extending life spans and reducing preventable deaths from infectious disease and pregnancy complications. Apart from improving living standards, public policies have been a key contributor to these gains. The policies ranged from targeted programs against specific, high-burden diseases (rapidly reducing mortality rates) to investments in more inclusive health-care systems. To maintain this momentum, universal health coverage (UHC) has become a major priority in many Asian countries.[8]

---

[8] Universal health coverage means that "all people and communities can use the promotive, preventive, curative, rehabilitative and palliative health services they need, of sufficient quality to be effective, while also ensuring that the use of these services does not expose the user to financial hardship." World Health Organization (WHO). Universal Coverage and Health Financing. https://www.who.int/health_financing/data-statistics/en/ (accessed 8 September 2019).

Rising life expectancy and falling mortality rates

Life expectancy at birth in Asia across all subregions has increased dramatically over the past 50 years.[9] In 1960, developing Asia's average life expectancy at birth was just 45 years (Table 6.4); by 2018, it was 71.8 years—meaning Asians are living, on average, a quarter century longer than in 1960. In 2018, life expectancy in Japan and Australia reached 84.5 and 83.3 years, respectively. Notably, Japan introduced UHC in 1961 and Australia in 1975.

A major contributing factor to the rapid rise in life expectancy was the decline in child and maternal mortality. Developing Asia's under-five mortality rate in 2018 had fallen to about a sixth of its 1960 level, while maternal mortality ratios in 2015 had fallen to a third of its

Table 6.4: Life Expectancy at Birth, 1960–2018
(years)

	1960	1980	2000	2018	Increase 1960–2018
Developing Asia	**45.0**	**59.3**	**65.8**	**71.8**	**26.7**
Central Asia	58.7	64.2	65.7	71.8	13.0
East Asia	44.6	66.9	65.7	76.9	32.3
People's Republic of China	43.7	66.8	71.4	76.7	33.0
South Asia	42.3	53.9	62.7	69.2	26.9
India	41.4	53.8	62.5	69.4	28.0
Southeast Asia	51.3	59.9	67.1	72.1	20.8
The Pacific	42.5	53.1	60.6	65.9	23.4
Developed Asia	**68.3**	**75.9**	**80.8**	**84.1**	**15.8**
Australia	70.7	74.4	79.6	83.3	12.5
Japan	67.9	76.3	81.2	84.5	16.6
Latin America and the Caribbean	**56.2**	**64.7**	**71.7**	**75.5**	**19.3**
Sub-Saharan Africa	**40.2**	**48.3**	**50.4**	**61.3**	**21.1**
OECD	**67.8**	**72.6**	**77.2**	**80.5**	**12.7**
World	**50.1**	**61.2**	**66.3**	**72.4**	**22.2**

OECD = Organisation for Economic Co-operation and Development.

Source: United Nations. 2019. *World Population Prospects 2019*. Online Edition. https://population.un.org/wpp (accessed 1 September 2019).

[9] Life expectancy at birth is defined as the average number of years that a newborn could expect to live if he or she were to pass through life subject to the age-specific mortality rates of a given period.

1990 level (Table 6.5).[10] These deaths were avoided by better nutrition and sanitary conditions, and through targeted interventions that made the first 1,000 days of life (from conception to 2 years) safer for children and mothers. Despite the large declines in mortality rates overall, there remain significant variations across countries and subregions.

Declining child undernutrition

In addition to reducing child mortality, the region also made progress in improving the nutrition of children, although with large variations across subregions. Child undernutrition was significantly reduced in East Asia and Central Asia in terms of stunting (height-for-age is more than 2 standard deviations below the World Health Organization [WHO] child growth standards median) and wasting (weight-for-height is more than 2 standard deviations below the WHO child growth standards median) (Table 6.6). In the PRC, stunting among children below 5 years old declined from 32.3% in 1990 to 8.1% in 2016. In Central Asia, it declined from 26% to 11.4% during 2000–2016. However, in South Asia, Southeast Asia, and the Pacific, reductions were less impressive. In 2016, the under-five child stunting prevalence remained at 38% in South Asia, 46.8% in the Pacific, and 31% in Southeast Asia, despite the significant drop in child mortality.

Without exception, all subregions in Asia and the Pacific have significantly reduced death rates from communicable, maternal, neonatal, and nutritional causes since 1990 (Figure 6.3). The largest reductions were in South Asia and Southeast Asia. Often referred to as preventable deaths, their reductions helped extend the lives of all segments of the population.

These impressive gains in health across developing Asia would not have happened without the concerted effort of governments, civil society, and other stakeholders.

Targeted health programs

Many factors contributed to the significant improvement in health (notably, rising life expectancy and falling mortality rates) in the region over the past 50 years. One was the steep rise in incomes and improved living standards. Rising incomes allowed Asian households to consume more and better food, live in better housing, access better

---

[10] Data on maternal mortality ratio are not widely available for earlier periods.

Table 6.5: Under-Five and Maternal Mortality, 1960–2018

	Under-Five Mortality (deaths under age 5 per 1,000 live births)				Maternal Mortality (maternal deaths per 100,000 live births)			
	1960	1980	2000	2018	1990	2000	2010	2015
Developing Asia	**215.0**	**121.9**	**69.8**	**31.7**	**368.8**	**268.3**	**156.1**	**121.3**
Central Asia	136.5	97.9	64.1	23.6	68.8	50.5	37.6	32.7
East Asia	205.0	61.7	36.8	11.0	94.2	56.2	34.3	26.2
People's Republic of China	212.0	63.3	38.3	11.2	96.8	58.0	35.1	26.7
South Asia	244.4	169.0	92.3	44.6	558.5	390.0	230.9	183.4
India	240.1	165.5	89.8	38.5	555.9	374.3	214.8	174.3
Southeast Asia	178.0	104.5	48.2	24.9	321.9	200.2	134.8	108.6
The Pacific	197.9	118.4	72.2	46.3	484.2	349.9	221.1	188.9
Developed Asia	**37.2**	**10.4**	**4.9**	**2.8**	**12.9**	**9.5**	**6.1**	**5.8**
Australia	24.7	13.2	6.3	3.6	8.2	8.6	6.5	5.9
Japan	39.3	9.8	4.5	2.4	13.5	9.6	5.6	5.4
Latin America and the Caribbean	**155.3**	**83.9**	**34.4**	**18.8**	**138.6**	**102.2**	**81.8**	**67.7**
Sub-Saharan Africa	**271.8**	**199.6**	**153.3**	**76.0**	**994.6**	**857.4**	**632.1**	**553.0**
OECD	**68.9**	**34.5**	**12.9**	**7.1**	**30.6**	**24.8**	**15.3**	**13.3**
World	**188.0**	**116.3**	**76.3**	**39.3**	**385.3**	**340.5**	**246.1**	**216.2**

OECD = Organisation for Economic Co-operation and Development.

Sources: For under-five mortality rate: United Nations, Department of Economic and Social Affairs, Population Division. 2019. *World Population Prospects 2019. Online Edition.* https://population.un.org/wpp (accessed 18 June 2019); and for maternal mortality ratio: World Health Organization (WHO). 2015. *Trends in Maternal Mortality: 1990 to 2015: Estimates by WHO, United Nations Children's Fund (UNICEF), United Nations Population Fund (UNFPA), World Bank Group, and the United Nations Population Division.* Geneva.

Table 6.6: Prevalence of Wasting and Stunting

	Wasting Prevalence			Stunting Prevalence		
	% of children below 5 years old					
	1990	2000	2016	1990	2000	2016
Developing Asia	12.0	10.8	12.2	47.7	39.6	27.3
Central Asia	...	7.0	3.3	...	26.0	11.4
East Asia	4.2	2.5	1.9	32.3	17.3	8.1
People's Republic of China	4.2	2.5	1.9	32.3	17.8	8.1
South Asia	19.1	16.2	19.6	60.8	52.0	38.0
India	20.3	17.1	21.0	61.9	54.2	38.4
Southeast Asia	11.7	7.7	9.9	47.4	40.4	31.0
The Pacific	...	...	12.9	...	...	46.8
Latin America and the Caribbean	...	...	1.3	22.9	16.9	9.9
Sub-Saharan Africa	...	...	7.5	48.7	43.2	34.6
United States	0.7	0.4	0.5	3.2	3.3	2.1
World	...	...	7.5	39.3	32.6	22.7

... = data not available.

Note: Where no data are available for the specific year headings, available data for the earliest and/or nearest years are used.

Source: United Nations Children's Fund (UNICEF), World Health Organization, and World Bank. Joint Child Malnutrition Estimates. https://www.who.int/nutgrowthdb/estimates/en/ (accessed 2 August 2019).

quality drinking water and improved sanitation, and importantly, afford higher-quality health services. At the same time, proactive public policy and programs also contributed to better health overall.

Targeted health programs, such as immunization, school-feeding, investment in clean drinking water and sanitation, skilled birth delivery, and investment in new medical technologies, rapidly drove down death rates from preventable causes. By WHO estimates, six conditions account for about 89% of all under-five child deaths in low-income countries: (i) pneumonia and other acute respiratory infections (19%); (ii) diarrhea (18%); (iii) malaria (8%); (iv) measles (4%); (v) HIV/AIDS (3%); and (vi) neonatal conditions—mainly preterm birth, birth asphyxia,

Figure 6.3: Reduction in Communicable, Maternal, Neonatal, and Nutritional Deaths, 1990–2017
(number of deaths per 100,000 population)

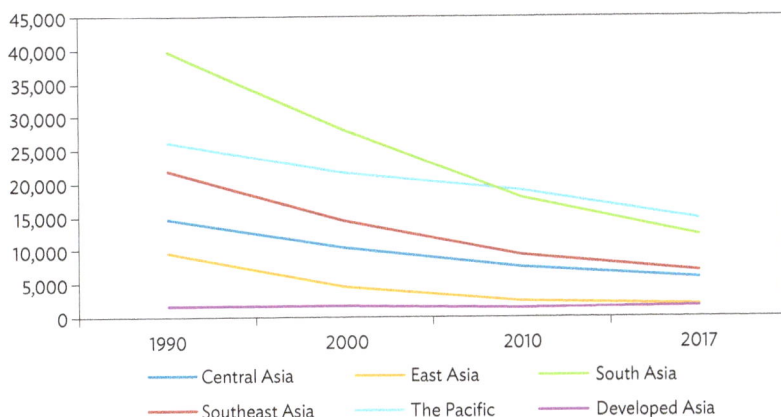

Source: University of Washington Institute for Health Metrics and Evaluation. *Global Health Data Exchange 2017.* http://ghdx.healthdata.org/ (accessed 22 November 2019).

and infections (37%).[11] These were all significantly reduced by using new medicines such as antibiotics, and targeted programs such as immunization and sanitary campaigns, reproductive health programs (midwife training and family planning), and controlling mosquito-borne diseases (malaria and dengue), in addition to better living conditions.

In many Asian countries, national immunization programs began as early as the 1950s and 1960s. The PRC, for example, started mass immunization against smallpox in the 1950s and started introducing vaccines against tuberculosis (BCG); oral poliovirus vaccine (OPV); diphtheria, tetanus, and pertussis (DTP); and measles (MCV) in the 1960s. India started its BCG campaign in 1951 and launched a National Smallpox Eradication Program in 1962. The WHO's Expanded Programme on Immunization was established in 1976 to make vaccines available to all children in the world, and was introduced across large parts of Asia in the late 1970s (Table 6.7). These programs eliminated smallpox globally and wild polio across Asia (with the exception

---

[11] World Health Organization (WHO). 2011. *The Partnership for Maternal, Newborn and Child Health, updated September.* Geneva.

Table 6.7: Immunization Coverage by Antigen, 1980, 2000, and 2017
(% of live births receiving vaccine)

	East Asia and the Pacific	South Asia	East Asia and the Pacific	South Asia	East Asia and the Pacific	South Asia
	1980		2000		2017	
BCG	16	2	85	75	94	91
DTP1	13	23	92	75	97	90
DTP3	9	6	83	60	94	86
MCV1	4	0	84	58	93	86
POL3	5	2	84	60	94	86

Notes: BCG = vaccine against tuberculosis; DTP1 = first dose of vaccine against diphtheria, tetanus toxoid, and pertussis (whooping cough); DTP3 = third dose of vaccine against diphtheria, tetanus toxoid, and pertussis; MCV1 = first dose of measles containing vaccine; POL3 = third dose of polio vaccine. Country coverage of East Asia and the Pacific, and South Asia follows World Health Organization definitions. East Asia and the Pacific in this table includes Australia, Japan, and New Zealand.

Source: United Nations Children's Fund (UNICEF). UNICEF Immunization Database. https://data.unicef.org/topic/child-health/immunization/ (accessed 31 August 2018).

of Afghanistan and Pakistan). More recently, Thailand's HIV/AIDS prevention program was another notable success.

In addition to immunization, medical advances and the availability of new drugs allowed better treatment of many infectious diseases. For example, powerful antibiotics such as penicillin changed health care dramatically worldwide, including developing Asia. Diseases such as pneumonia, tuberculosis, malaria, and diarrhea that had once killed hundreds of thousands, and even millions, of people globally became treatable. The impact of these medicines on child survival was particularly large—infectious diseases were a prime cause of death at birth and during childhood. Their effect on maternal health was also significant, as effective antibiotics cut the very high maternal deaths.[12]

Targeted programs that improved access to safe drinking water and sanitation also had a major impact in low-income, high-mortality environments. Many countries in Asia increased their share of the population with access to piped drinking water (Figure 6.4a). Many reduced the share of population using open defecation (Figure 6.4b). Improving drinking water sources and sanitation directly

---

[12]   ADB. 1997. *Emerging Asia: Changes and Challenges.* Manila.

Figure 6.4: Access to Piped Water and Open Defecation Rates, 2000 and Latest Year

Figure 6.4a: % of Population with Access to Improved Sources of Piped Water

Figure 6.4b: % of Population Using Open Defecation for Sanitation

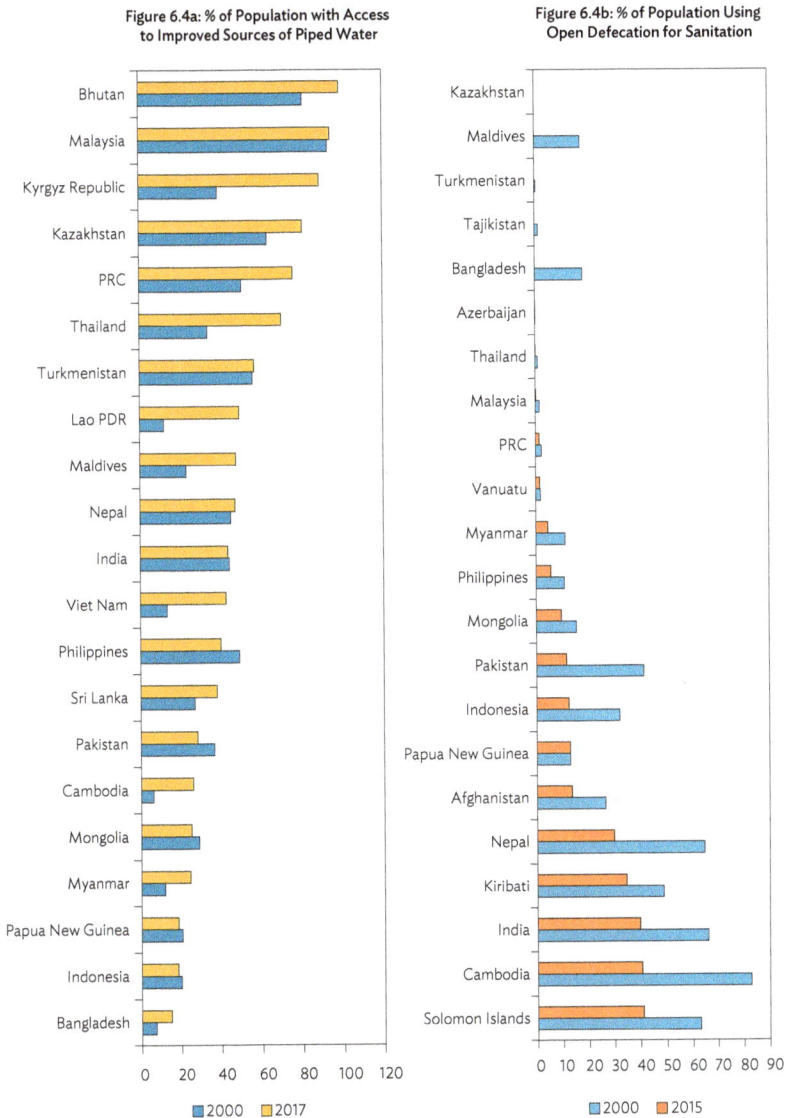

Lao PDR = Lao People's Democratic Republic, PRC = People's Republic of China.

Source: World Health Organization/United Nations Children's Fund Joint Monitoring Programme for Water Supply and Sanitation. Global Data for Water Supply, Sanitation, and Hygiene. https://washdata.org/data (accessed 2 August 2019).

benefit health, as the vast majority of deaths due to diarrhea are due to unsafe water and poor hygiene.

Despite this progress, large gaps remain in accessing safe drinking water and sanitation in much of developing Asia. More than half the population in many South Asian and Southeast Asian countries lacked access to piped water in 2017. In Cambodia, India, and Nepal, about 30% of the population was practicing open defecation in 2015. They are making access to safe water and sanitation a priority.

Investment in health-care systems

Asian economies improved their overall health-care systems by (i) raising government spending on health; (ii) implementing reforms to health service delivery, institutions, and financing; and (iii) encouraging private health sector participation.

Health financing reforms play a critical role in improving health systems. Economies that implemented comprehensive UHC systems have reaped major benefits. Hong Kong, China; Japan; the ROK; Singapore; and Taipei,China put in place strong UHC systems over the past 50 years, contributing to sustained positive health outcomes and avoiding high health-care costs.

Many countries in the region are currently reforming health finance to work toward achieving UHC. In Thailand, the adoption of the UHC "30 Baht" scheme in 2001 reduced the share of out-of-pocket spending to total health expenditure from 34% in 2000 to 12% in 2016.[13] The PRC is very close to achieving UHC, with over 95% of the population now covered by state-sponsored health insurance. The government plans to cover those still uninsured through social health insurance reforms and deepening health insurance coverage. In 2018, India launched a major government health program to insure its poorest 500 million citizens. Indonesia expanded social health insurance coverage from 133 million in 2014 to 203 million people in 2018.[14]

Regionally, increased budget allocations to health systems underscore government commitment. In 2016, East Asia had the highest public spending on health as a percentage of GDP (3.1%), followed by Central Asia (2.1%), the Pacific (2.0%), Southeast Asia (1.9%), and South Asia (0.9%) (Table 6.8). Nonetheless, the region's

---

[13] World Bank. World Development Indicators. https://databank.worldbank.org/reports .aspx?source=world-development-indicators (accessed 2 August 2019).

[14] Agustina, R., et al. 2019. Universal Health Coverage in Indonesia: Concept, Progress, and Challenges. *The Lancet*. 393 (10,166). pp. 75–102.

average public spending on health (2.5% of GDP) in 2016 remained much lower than developed countries. There is clearly room for developing Asia to expand health budgets.

Also, developing Asia's combined public and private health spending as a percentage of GDP (4.8% in 2016) was about half the global average. WHO recommends total health expenditure to be around 5% of GDP, with out-of-pocket health spending accounting for no more than 30%–40% of the total. Many Asian countries need more public finance to progress toward UHC.[15]

The number of hospital beds and the number of physicians per 1,000 people are important measures of the availability of health services. Table 6.9 shows that developing Asia's health service delivery expanded significantly with the number of hospital beds per 1,000 people more than doubling from 1 in 1960 to 2.3 in 2015. The region also saw the number of physicians per 1,000 people double between 1960 and 2016, from 0.6 to 1.2. However, gaps with developed countries remain large. In some subregions, the number of physicians per 1,000 people declined partly due to low wages and emigration to other countries. Hospital beds per capita declined in many countries (including advanced economies) due to public sector budget constraints and policies that promote outpatient services and primary health care.

Service delivery reform played an important role in improving health-care systems, especially by expanding primary health care. Primary health care—which covers prevention, treatment, and general care (such as regular blood pressure measurement)—has been heralded as a high-impact, efficient, and comprehensive solution to society's rapidly changing needs, including aging. Asia's significant health gains were realized by investing in primary health care. One early example was the PRC in the 1960s, which introduced a nationwide network of primary health-care facilities staffed by "barefoot doctors" (trained village health workers). Viet Nam's comprehensive and well-functioning countrywide network of communal health centers supported by district hospitals also contributed.

Engaging the private sector is another way to spread health-care coverage and efficiency. In Japan and the ROK, private hospitals have been contracted as part of national health insurance schemes. Incentives for private companies to produce generic drugs transformed the pharmaceutical industry in South Asia, resulting in

---

[15] WHO. 2009. *Health Financing Strategy for the Asia Pacific Region (2010–2015)*. Geneva.

Table 6.8: Health Expenditures by Subregion, 2000, 2010, and 2016

	Total Current Health Expenditure (% of GDP)			Of Which Government Health Expenditures (% of GDP)			Out-of-Pocket Current Expenditure (% of total current health expenditure)		
	2000	2010	2016	2000	2010	2016	2000	2010	2016
Developing Asia	**3.9**	**4.1**	**4.8**	**1.2**	**2.0**	**2.5**	**55.9**	**43.9**	**39.5**
Central Asia	5.0	4.1	5.5	2.0	1.8	2.1	57.5	52.2	57.1
East Asia	4.3	4.5	5.2	1.3	2.4	3.1	55.3	39.5	35.5
People's Republic of China	4.5	4.2	5.0	1.0	2.2	2.9	60.1	40.8	35.9
South Asia	4.3	4.5	5.2	0.9	0.8	0.9	69.1	65.3	64.4
India	4.0	3.3	3.7	0.8	0.9	0.9	71.7	65.2	64.6
Southeast Asia	2.8	3.4	3.9	1.2	1.4	1.9	41.6	42.9	37.1
The Pacific	3.6	2.9	3.1	2.7	1.7	2.0	8.9	12.4	10.0
Developed Asia	**7.2**	**9.0**	**10.6**	**5.7**	**7.2**	**8.5**	**16.3**	**15.3**	**14.4**
Australia	7.6	8.4	9.3	5.2	5.8	6.3	21.0	19.7	18.9
Japan	7.2	9.2	10.9	5.8	7.5	9.1	15.9	14.6	13.5
Latin America and the Caribbean	**5.9**	**7.9**	**8.6**	**2.5**	**3.5**	**4.1**	**41.9**	**39.2**	**36.7**
Sub-Saharan Africa	**5.1**	**5.3**	**5.2**	**1.7**	**1.9**	**1.8**	**32.4**	**33.5**	**36.7**
OECD	**9.3**	**11.6**	**12.6**	**5.6**	**7.4**	**10.1**	**16.3**	**14.6**	**13.9**
World	**8.6**	**9.6**	**10.0**	**4.9**	**5.8**	**7.4**	**19.1**	**18.9**	**18.6**

GDP = gross domestic product, OECD = Organisation for Economic Co-operation and Development.

Note: Private enterprises and other nongovernment organizations account for the difference between total current health expenditure and the sum of government and out-of-pocket current health expenditure.

Source: World Bank. World Development Indicators. https://databank.worldbank.org/reports.aspx?source=world-development-indicators (accessed 2 August 2019).

Table 6.9: Hospital Beds and Physicians by Region, 1960, 1970, 1990, and 2016

	Hospital Beds (per 1,000 people)				Physicians (per 1,000 people)			
	1960	1970	1990	2015	1960	1970	1990	2016
Developing Asia	1.0	1.1	1.9	2.3	0.6	0.5	1.0	1.2
Central Asia	...	...	11.9	4.9	...	...	3.7	2.7
East Asia	1.5	1.6	2.6	4.5	1.1	0.9	1.1	1.8
People's Republic of China	1.4	1.5	2.6	4.2	1.1	0.9	1.1	1.8
South Asia	0.5	0.6	0.7	0.7	0.2	0.2	1.0	0.7
India	0.5	0.6	0.8	0.7	0.2	0.2	1.2	0.8
Southeast Asia	0.9	1.0	1.5	1.3	0.1	0.1	0.2	0.6
The Pacific	4.8	6.1	3.7	...	0.2	0.2	0.1	0.1
Developed Asia	9.3	12.4	14.7	11.6	1.0	1.1	1.8	2.6
Australia	11.2	11.7	9.2	3.8	1.1	1.2	2.2	3.5
Japan	9.0	12.5	15.6	13.4	1.0	1.1	1.7	2.4
Latin America and the Caribbean	3.4	3.5	2.5	2.2	...	...	1.2	2.0
Sub-Saharan Africa	1.4	1.4	1.2	...	...	...	0.1	0.2
OECD	8.7	8.9	5.7	3.8	...	...	1.8	2.6
World	...	3.1	3.6	2.7	...	...	1.3	1.5

... = data not available, OECD = Organisation for Economic Co-operation and Development.

Source: World Bank. World Development Indicators. https://databank.worldbank.org/reports.aspx?source=world-development-indicators (accessed 2 August 2019).

drastic cost reductions. Countries should continue to promote public–private partnerships in areas such as elderly care to address emerging challenges in the region.

6.4 Changing demography

Rapid population growth

Between 1960 and 2018, developing Asia's population increased from 1.5 billion to 4.1 billion,[16] growing on average 1.7% annually (Table 6.10). This was driven by rising life expectancies and a high, while declining, fertility rate. Average annual population growth since 1960 has been highest in the Pacific (2.2%), followed by South Asia (2.0%), Southeast Asia (1.9%), Central Asia (1.7%), and East Asia (1.3%). East Asia's lower population growth was partly due to the PRC's family planning program since the early 1970s, including the one-child policy between the early 1980s and 2016. The region's population growth rose from an annual average of 1.98% in the 1950s to 2.36% in the 1960s. Since then, due to falling fertility rates, it has been on the decline—to an annual average 0.96% during 2010–2017 (Figure 6.5).

Changing age structure and declining fertility rates

Asia's rapid population growth has been accompanied by a significant change in its age structure, also driven by rising life expectancies and declining fertility rates (Figure 6.6). In 1960, 36.4% of developing Asia's population was aged 14 years or below, 59.7% aged 15–64 years—the working-age population—and only 4% aged 65 years or above. In 2018, those aged 14 years or below declined to 24%, the working-age population increased to 68.1%, and those aged 65 years or above increased to 7.9%. In fact, for most of the period since the 1960s, developing Asia's working-age population grew faster than its total population, creating favorable demographic conditions. However, Asia's aging population (aged 65 years or above) also doubled, presenting a major future challenge.

The fertility rate in developing Asia declined rapidly over the past half century. In 1960, the total fertility rate—the average number of children expected to be born during a woman's childbearing years—was 6.1 (Table 6.11). In 2018, it fell to the 2.1 replacement level.

---

[16] Including Australia, Japan, and New Zealand, Asia's population increased from 1.6 billion to 4.2 billion between 1960 and 2017.

Table 6.10: Population and Annual Population Growth Rate, 1960–2018

	Average Annual Growth Rate, 1960–2018		Number (billion)	
	Total Population	Working-Age Population (15–64)	Total Population, 2018	Working-Age Population (15–64), 2018
Developing Asia	**1.7**	**2.1**	**4.082**	**2.779**
Central Asia	1.7	1.9	0.089	0.058
East Asia	1.3	1.7	1.513	1.078
People's Republic of China	1.3	1.7	1.428	1.016
South Asia	2.0	2.3	1.814	1.193
India	1.9	2.2	1.353	0.903
Southeast Asia	1.9	2.3	0.654	0.443
The Pacific	2.2	2.3	0.012	0.007
Developed Asia	**0.7**	**0.6**	**0.157**	**0.095**
Australia	1.5	1.7	0.025	0.016
Japan	0.5	0.4	0.127	0.076
Latin America and the Caribbean	**1.9**	**2.2**	**0.641**	**0.429**
Sub-Saharan Africa	**2.7**	**2.7**	**1.078**	**0.587**
OECD	**0.8**	**0.9**	**1.298**	**0.845**
World	**1.6**	**1.8**	**7.631**	**4.988**

OECD = Organisation for Economic Co-operation and Development.

Source: United Nations, Department of Economic and Social Affairs, Population Division. 2019. *World Population Prospects 2019*. Online Edition. https://population.un.org/wpp (accessed 18 June 2019).

The fertility rate dropped below 2.1 in several economies such as the PRC (1.7); Thailand (1.5); Singapore and Taipei,China (1.2); and the ROK (1.1).

Several factors can explain the plummeting fertility rates since the late 1960s in Asia. These include rising incomes, industrialization, urbanization, improved education and increased employment opportunities for women, declining child mortality rates, high cost of educating children, and the erosion of traditional values. These have influenced a couple's choice to have fewer children, either because of high opportunity costs for working women, or reduced value of having more children, especially compared with a time when they relied on traditional farming.

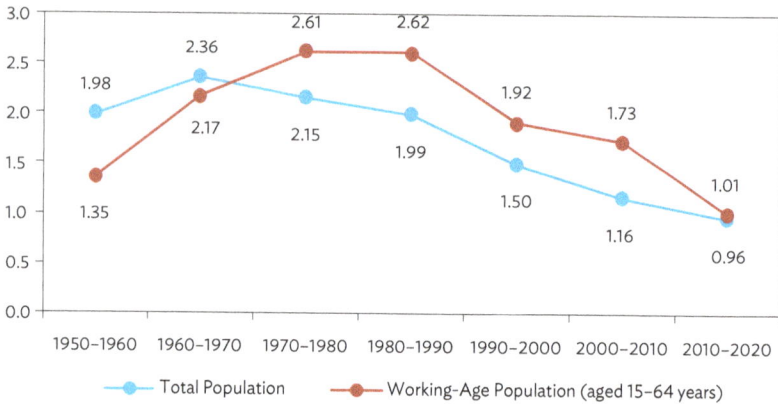

Figure 6.5: Average Annual Population Growth, Developing Asia, 1950–2020 (%)

Source: United Nations, Department of Economic and Social Affairs, Population Division. 2019. *World Population Prospects 2019*. Online Edition. https://population.un.org/wpp (accessed 18 June 2019).

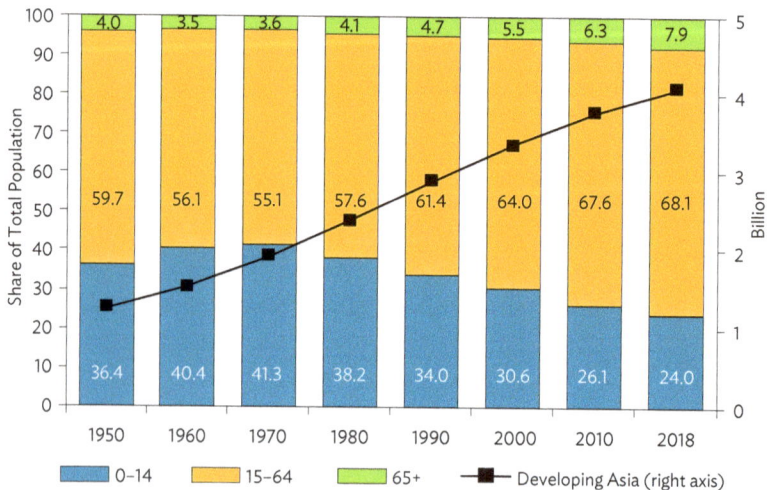

Figure 6.6: Total Population (billion) **and Population by Age** (% of total), **Developing Asia, 1950–2018**

Source: United Nations, Department of Economic and Social Affairs, Population Division. 2019. *World Population Prospects 2019*. Online Edition. https://population.un.org/wpp (accessed 18 June 2019).

Table 6.11: Fertility Rate, 1960–2018
(live births per woman)

	1960	1980	2000	2018	Change in 1960–2018
Developing Asia	**6.1**	**3.7**	**2.5**	**2.1**	**(3.9)**
Central Asia	5.2	3.8	2.4	2.6	(2.6)
East Asia	6.1	2.5	1.6	1.7	(4.4)
People's Republic of China	6.2	2.5	1.6	1.7	(4.5)
South Asia	6.0	5.0	3.3	2.4	(3.6)
India	5.9	4.7	3.1	2.2	(3.6)
Southeast Asia	6.1	4.2	2.5	2.2	(3.9)
The Pacific	6.3	5.3	4.4	3.6	(2.7)
Developed Asia	**2.2**	**1.8**	**1.4**	**1.5**	**(0.7)**
Australia	3.3	1.9	1.8	1.8	(1.4)
Japan	2.0	1.8	1.3	1.4	(0.7)
Latin America and the Caribbean	**5.8**	**3.9**	**2.5**	**2.0**	**(3.8)**
Sub-Saharan Africa	**6.6**	**6.7**	**5.6**	**4.7**	**(1.9)**
OECD	**3.1**	**2.1**	**1.8**	**1.7**	**(1.4)**
World	**5.0**	**3.6**	**2.7**	**2.5**	**(2.5)**

( ) = negative, OECD = Organisation for Economic Co-operation and Development.

Source: United Nations, Department of Economic and Social Affairs, Population Division. 2019. *World Population Prospects 2019*. Online Edition. https://population.un.org/wpp (accessed 18 June 2019).

These factors also led to late marriage and childbearing. In 1965, for example, the average woman in countries such as Bangladesh, India, Pakistan, and the PRC married before she turned 20, and in areas where arranged marriages were part of the culture, girls, on average, became brides before the age of 18. By 2005, the average age of the first marriage for women increased by 3.5 years or more in Bangladesh, Pakistan, and the PRC, and 2.5 years in India. Late marriage led to delayed childbearing. For instance, in the ROK, the maternal age at first birth increased from 26.2 in 1993 to 31.4 in 2016.[17]

---

[17] OECD. OECD Family Database. http://www.oecd.org/els/family/database.htm (accessed 9 September 2018).

National family planning programs also significantly contributed to the decline in the fertility rate in many Asian countries.[18] Most Asian countries introduced family planning as part of their development strategies. The most salient example was the PRC and its one-child policy (Box 6.1).

Rapid demographic shifts and cross-country diversity

A key feature of Asia's demographic shift is its rapid pace. Demographic changes that occurred in Asia over the past 5–6 decades took more than 200 years in Western Europe.[19] One important reason is that Asia had much faster economic and social development over the past half century than advanced economies did historically. This came with rapid improvements in basic sanitation, availability of safe drinking water, and nutrition. There were also substantial medical advances and wider availability of vaccines, new drugs, and treatment that made many diseases preventable or treatable.

While the pace of demographic change has been rapid for Asia as a whole, there are significant variations across countries, leading to large demographic diversity. A significant part of Asia is seeing population aging. But other countries still have relatively high fertility rates and young populations.

A stylized fact about demographic transition is that a country goes through four phases: (i) pre-industrialization with high mortality and high fertility, (ii) still high fertility with declining mortality leading to increasing population, (iii) both declining fertility and further declining mortality leading to aging populations, and (iv) low fertility and low mortality leading to stable population (if the fertility rate is at the 2.1 replacement level) or declining population (if the fertility rate is well below 2.1). Thus, Asian economies can be divided broadly into four groups (Figure 6.7).

The first group consists of several low-middle-income and low-income economies, such as Afghanistan, Pakistan, Papua New Guinea, and Tajikistan.[20] These countries are in the second phase of

---

[18] Gubhaju, B. 2007. Fertility Decline in Asia: Opportunities and Challenges. *The Japanese Journal of Population*. 5 (1). pp. 19–42.

[19] Bourgeois-Pichat, J. 1981. Recent Demographic Change in Western Europe: An Assessment. *Population and Development Review*. 7 (1). pp. 19-42.

[20] World Bank defines low-income economies as those with a gross national income (GNI) per capita of $1,025 or less in 2018, calculated using the World Bank Atlas method. Lower middle-income economies are defined as those with a GNI per capita between $1,026 and $3,995.

Box 6.1: Family Planning and Declining Fertility in the People's Republic of China

The fertility rate of the People's Republic of China was 6.2 in 1960 and increased slightly to 6.3 in 1965 (Box Figure). In the early 1970s, the government began its family planning campaign, calling for "later marriage" (at 23 years for women and 25 years for men), longer interval between births (more than 3 years), and fewer children (two at most).[a] Subsequently, the total fertility rate declined rapidly to 2.5 in 1980.

In 1980, the universal one-child policy was introduced as a temporary measure, calling for couples to have only one child to curb the surging population and alleviate social, economic, and environmental pressure. After a brief rebound in the mid-1980s due to a "cohort effect" (an increase in the number of women of childbearing age), the fertility rate began declining again from 1986, to 1.6 in 2000. Although the total fertility rate has been on the rise since 2000, increasing to 1.7 in 2018—reflecting a more lenient one-child policy implementation—it remains below the replacement level. In 2016, the government ended its one-child policy and introduced a universal two-child policy.

Some empirical studies estimate the People's Republic of China's family planning policies averted well over 500 million births between 1970 and 2015.[b] But others have argued that economic development may have played a more fundamental role, citing many other Asian countries that also experienced rapid declines in fertility rates in recent decades.

Box Figure: People's Republic of China's Fertility Rate, 1960–2018
(live births per woman)

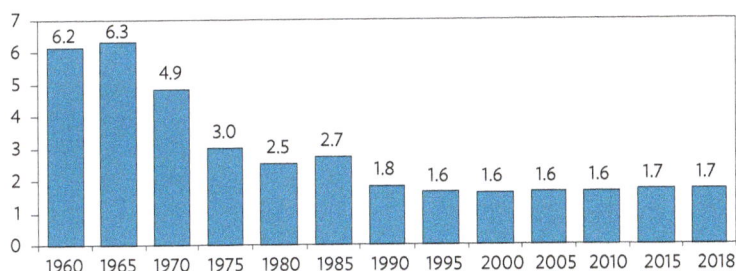

[a] Zhang, J. 2017. The Evolution of China's One-Child Policy and Its Effects on Family Outcomes. *Journal of Economic Perspectives*. 31 (1). pp. 141–159.

[b] Goodkind, D. 2011. Child Underreporting, Fertility, and Sex Ratio Imbalance in China. *Demography*. 48 (1). pp. 291–316.

Source: United Nations, Department of Economic and Social Affairs, Population Division. 2019. *World Population Prospects 2019*. Online Edition. https://population.un.org/wpp (accessed 18 June 2019).

demographic transition. Their fertility rates have declined somewhat, but remain much higher than the replacement level, and life expectancy is below 70 years. Rapid population growth will lead to a high young dependency ratio and strong employment demand—placing great pressure on socioeconomic development. Investment in health and education would help reap a demographic dividend in the coming decades.

The second group consists of economies such as Bangladesh, Georgia, India, Indonesia, the Philippines, Uzbekistan, and Viet Nam. These countries are in the early or middle part of the third phase. Most are lower-middle-income economies, with the rest at upper-middle-income status. Their recent and current fertility levels are in the range of 2–3, with life expectancy at birth in the range of 67–77 years. Most see working-age populations grow and can enjoy a demographic dividend for many years. Creating enough jobs is their major challenge over the next 20–30 years.

The third group consists of several upper-middle-income countries such as Armenia, Malaysia, Maldives, the PRC, and Thailand. Their populations are in the latter part of the third phase of demographic transition. Their recent and current fertility levels are in the range of 1.5–2.0, with life expectancy at birth mostly in the range of 70–79. Their working-age population has started to decline, and population aging has kicked in and will accelerate in the coming years—turning the demographic dividend into a demographic tax. For these economies, sustaining growth with a declining working-age population poses a major challenge.

The fourth group consists of all high-income Asian economies, including Hong Kong, China; Japan; the ROK; Singapore; and Taipei,China. These economies have gone through the first three phases and are now in the fourth phase. Their recent and current fertility levels are in the range of 1.1–1.4, much lower than the 2.1 replacement level, with an 80+ year life expectancy at birth. These economies have seen, and will continue to witness, rapid aging. Many experienced a decline in the working-age population for many years and even started seeing a decline in total population. Responding to aging, declining labor force, and shrinking population is a major challenge for these economies.

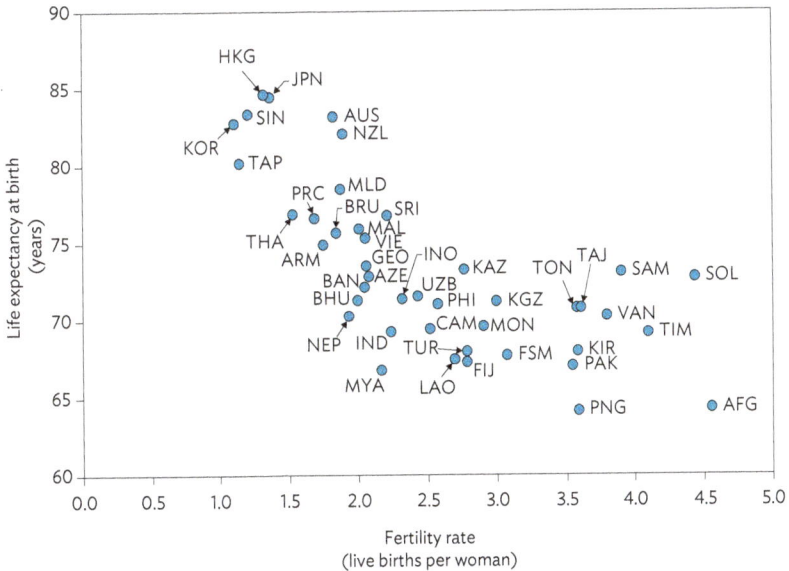

Figure 6.7: Fertility and Life Expectancy in Asia and the Pacific, 2018

AFG = Afghanistan; ARM = Armenia; AUS = Australia; AZE = Azerbaijan; BAN = Bangladesh; BHU = Bhutan; BRU = Brunei Darussalam; CAM = Cambodia; FIJ = Fiji; FSM = Federated States of Micronesia; GEO = Georgia; HKG = Hong Kong, China; IND = India; INO = Indonesia; JPN = Japan; KAZ = Kazakhstan; KGZ = Kyrgyz Republic; KIR = Kiribati; KOR = Republic of Korea; LAO = Lao People's Democratic Republic; MAL = Malaysia; MLD = Maldives; MON = Mongolia; MYA = Myanmar; NEP = Nepal; NZL = New Zealand; PAK = Pakistan; PHI = Philippines; PNG = Papua New Guinea; PRC = People's Republic of China; SAM = Samoa; SIN = Singapore; SOL = Solomon Islands; SRI = Sri Lanka; TAJ = Tajikistan; TAP = Taipei,China; THA = Thailand; TIM = Timor-Leste; TKM = Turkmenistan; TON = Tonga; UZB = Uzbekistan; VAN = Vanuatu; VIE = Viet Nam.

Source: United Nations, Department of Economic and Social Affairs, Population Division. 2019. *World Population Prospects 2019.* Online Edition. https://population.un.org/wpp (accessed 18 June 2019).

Cross-border labor mobility

Asia can leverage its demographic diversity to benefit both younger- and older-aged economies. Cross-border labor mobility holds great potential. High-income Asian economies, such as Japan and the ROK, are facing a shortage of workers due to a sharp decline in fertility and population aging. On the other hand, the size of the working-age population will continue to expand in younger-aged Asian countries

Figure 6.8: Stock of Asia and the Pacific's Outward Migration, 1990–2017
(million)

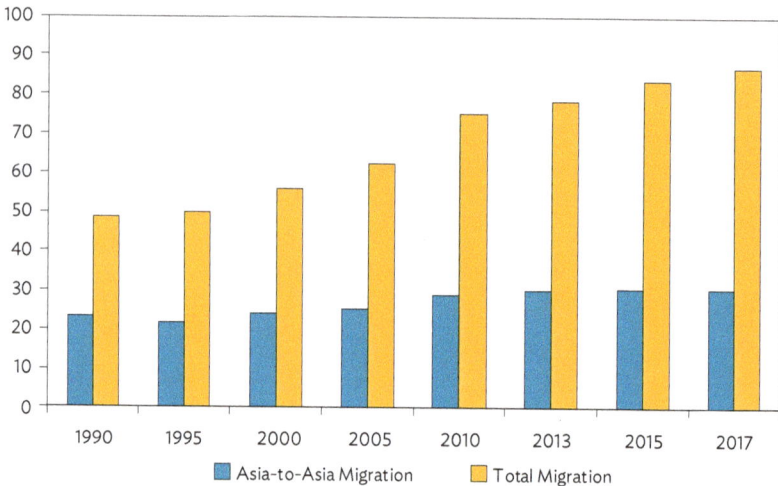

Source: Asian Development Bank calculations using data from United Nations, Department of Economic and Social Affairs, Population Division. *International Migrant Stock: The 2017 Revision.* https://www.un.org/en/development/desa/population/migration/data/estimates2/estimates17.asp (accessed 1 May 2018).

such as India and the Philippines. In principle, both groups stand to gain from cross-border labor mobility. Source countries can increase foreign exchange earnings; destination economies can alleviate labor shortages; and both can benefit from skills and knowledge transfers.

In recent decades, outward international migration from Asia and the Pacific has grown significantly. The stock of outward migrants (working abroad for at least 1 year)[21] from the region (including

---

[21] United Nations (UN) recommendations on international migration statistics define the "stock of international migrants present in a country" as "the set of persons who have ever changed their country of usual residence, that is, persons who have spent at least one year of their lives in a country at the time the data are gathered other than the country in which they usually live" (United Nations, Department of Economic and Social Affairs, Statistics Division. 1998. *Recommendations on Statistics of International Migration, Revision 1.* New York. para. 185). International migrant stock consists of persons crossing borders for various reasons—for employment, family reunification, study, and fleeing from conflict and violence. Some events involve the creation of new borders, generating large numbers of international migrants—as during the 1991 dissolution of the Soviet Union.

Australia, Japan, and New Zealand) increased from 48.3 million in 1990 to 86.9 million in 2017 (Figure 6.8). In 2017, the largest source of outward migrants in Asia and the Pacific was India (accounting for 19.6% of the total), followed by the PRC (11.5%), Bangladesh (8.6%), Pakistan (6.9%), the Philippines (6.6%), Afghanistan (5.5%), and Indonesia (4.8%). The growth in outward migration was mainly from Asia to non-Asian countries. The stock of Asian outward migrants residing or working in Asian countries increased from 22.9 million to 30.2 million.

While cross-border labor mobility benefits both source and destination countries, it should be managed well to maximize benefits while minimizing associated costs. For source countries, governments should set policies and programs that promote safe and legal migration, such as predeparture orientation, consular support, monitoring recruitment agencies, and collaborating with destination countries. They should promote the productive use of remittances by channeling them into domestic investment in education, health, and infrastructure that help create quality job opportunities in their own countries. Governments should also assist returning workers for smooth reintegration. Destination countries should implement well-designed immigration policies and foreign worker programs that respond to labor market conditions. They should also support migrant workers to develop skills, protect them from unfair treatment and abuses, and help integrate long-term migrants.

Regional cooperation can play an important role in facilitating cross-border labor mobility. The efforts of the Association of Southeast Asian Nations (ASEAN) countries to put in place a system of the mutual recognition of skills in the ASEAN Economic Community are a good example.

6.5 Demographic dividend and other impacts

Measuring demographic dividend

A major channel through which demographic change affects economic growth is the changing share of the working-age population (aged 15–64 years). As discussed, when the working-age population grows faster than the total population and the share of the working-age population rises, a country can enjoy a demographic dividend. This is because every worker will have fewer dependents to support, making per capita income grow faster than if the working-age population increases at the same rate as the total population. Conversely, when the working-age population grows slower than the total population, or the share of the working-age population declines, a country's per capita income will grow slower than if the share of the working-age population remains unchanged—a demographic tax. The difference between working-age population growth and total population growth can give a crude measure of the demographic dividend (when positive) or tax (when negative).

The working-age population in different age groups will likely have different labor market participation rates, unemployment rates, working hours, labor productivity, and consumption patterns. A recent United Nations (UN) study provides estimates of the demographic dividend for individual countries worldwide from 1955, incorporating these factors (Table 6.12).[22]

During 1960–2018, the demographic dividend contributed 0.32 percentage points out of developing Asia's average annual per capita GDP growth of 4.7%, compared with 0.37 percentage points for Latin America and the Caribbean, less than 0.1 percentage points for developed Asia and the OECD, and 0.23 percentage points globally. The size of the demographic dividend for developing Asia varied over time. There was a demographic tax of 0.41 percentage points in the 1960s due to the growing number of dependent children; and a demographic dividend of 0.57–0.63 percentage points in the 1980s, 1990s, and 2000s. The dividend declined to 0.35 percentage points in the 2010s. The demographic dividend is not realized unless the working-age population is employed and productive.

There are large cross-country differences. The ROK benefited significantly from demographic dividends in the 1970s–1990s, ranging from 1.01 to 1.83 percentage points of per capita GDP growth. But today, it is experiencing a demographic tax. The PRC's demographic dividend reached its peak at 1.40 percentage points in the 1980s; it still enjoyed a sizable 1.13 percentage points dividend in

---

[22] The demographic dividend arising from a change in the share of the working-age population is also called the "first" demographic dividend. The UN study estimates the first demographic dividend as the difference between the growth rate in the number of effective workers and the growth rate in the number of effective consumers. The number of effective workers is the sum of workers in each age group weighted by an index that considers differences in labor participation, unemployment, working hours, and labor productivity across age groups. The number of effective consumers is the sum of the population in each age group weighted by an index that considers differences in consumption patterns across different age groups. The indexes were derived from data from about 60 countries worldwide (including many from Asia). The indexes were assumed to be the same across countries and over time.

Table 6.12: Estimates of Demographic Dividends, 1960–2018
(percentage points of annual per capita GDP growth)

	1960–1970	1970–1980	1980–1990	1990–2000	2000–2010	2010–2018	1960–2018
Developing Asia	(0.41)	0.23	0.62	0.57	0.63	0.35	0.32
Central Asia	(0.73)	0.24	0.53	0.31	0.78	0.35	0.23
East Asia	(0.60)	0.58	1.38	1.21	0.67	(0.01)	0.54
People's Republic of China	(0.86)	0.74	1.40	1.13	0.26	(0.09)	0.43
Republic of Korea	(0.09)	1.01	1.83	1.50	0.65	(0.01)	0.83
South Asia	(0.18)	(0.21)	(0.06)	0.37	0.80	0.85	0.24
India	(0.31)	0.07	0.26	0.37	0.51	0.46	0.22
Southeast Asia	(0.44)	0.37	0.82	0.71	0.61	0.35	0.39
Indonesia	(0.46)	(0.05)	0.61	0.95	0.75	0.30	0.35
Philippines	(0.25)	0.49	0.64	0.42	0.44	0.35	0.34
Singapore	(0.31)	1.82	1.88	0.85	0.05	(0.19)	0.68
Thailand	(0.28)	0.46	1.48	1.23	0.52	(0.29)	0.54
Viet Nam	(1.37)	0.27	1.00	0.86	0.86	0.17	0.28
The Pacific	(0.07)	0.15	0.42	0.26	0.31	0.21	0.21
Developed Asia	0.16	0.39	0.39	0.17	(0.32)	(0.44)	0.07
Australia	(0.20)	0.30	0.44	0.20	(0.12)	(0.32)	0.05
Japan	1.07	0.54	0.01	(0.13)	(0.67)	(0.58)	0.07
Latin America and the Caribbean	(0.23)	0.25	0.59	0.67	0.58	0.40	0.37
Sub-Saharan Africa	(0.38)	(0.30)	(0.12)	0.10	0.37	0.42	0.002
OECD	(0.26)	0.26	0.45	0.38	0.06	(0.28)	0.10
United States	(0.43)	0.26	0.57	0.29	(0.04)	(0.30)	0.06
World	(0.43)	0.24	0.56	0.56	0.35	0.14	0.23

( ) = negative, GDP = gross domestic product, OECD = Organisation for Economic Co-operation and Development.

Note: The Pacific includes the Federated States of Micronesia, Fiji, Papua New Guinea, Samoa, Solomon Islands, Timor-Leste, Tonga, and Vanuatu.

Source: Mason, A., et al. 2017. Support Ratios and Demographic Dividends: Estimates for the World. *UN Population Division Technical Paper*. No. 2017/1. New York: United Nations.

the 1990s. Today, the PRC also faces a demographic tax. Singapore and Thailand, after benefiting significantly from demographic dividends in the 1970s–1990s, now face a demographic tax as well. On the other hand, Indonesia, India, and the Philippines continue to enjoy sizable demographic dividends.

Growth in total real GDP (apart from per capita GDP) is also affected by a change in the size of the total population. For instance, during Japan's 1960–1970 period of high growth, total GDP grew 10.4% annually, of which 2.2 percentage points were due to a demographic change: 1.1 from total population growth and 1.1 from a demographic dividend (associated with the rising share of the working-age population). In 2010–2018, Japan's total GDP grew just 1.0% annually. Demographic change had an impact of –0.8 percentage points: –0.2 from total population decline and –0.6 from a demographic tax. For the US in 2010–2018, while it suffered a demographic tax of –0.3 percentage points, total population growth contributed 0.7 percentage points to its more solid 2.2% average annual GDP growth during the period. These comparisons show that while demographics affect growth, other factors, such as capital accumulation and improvements in human capital and in total factor productivity, were more important. In Japan during 1960–1970, the contribution to GDP growth from these other factors was 8.2 percentage points, while in 2010–2018, it was 1.8 percentage points. In the case of the US, the other factors also contributed 1.8 percentage points to GDP growth in 2010–2018.

Other impacts of demographic change

Aside from generating a demographic dividend or tax associated with changes in the share of the working-age population as discussed, demographic changes can affect economic growth in other ways.

One channel is through affecting the savings rate. Economic growth can be promoted through a higher household savings rate associated with a rising share of the working-age population. In the early stages of development, high dependent ratios and lower share of the working-age population are often associated with low household savings, as families with young children face large expenses for childcare. When children grow older and enter the labor force, and the share of the working-age population increases, aggregate household savings rates would increase. This promotes growth in countries where there is a shortage of savings relative to large investment needs. It has been suggested that close to 5 percentage points of the rise in Asia's savings rate over the past half century was attributable to the region's demographic transition.[23]

Recent studies highlight the possibility of a so-called "second demographic dividend," meaning an increase in adult longevity causes individuals to save more in preparation for old age, contributing to capital accumulation and economic growth.[24]

On the other hand, an aging society is generally thought to have negative impacts on economic growth through several channels— in addition to reducing the share of the working-age population and, in some cases, declining total population size.

First, higher savings due to population aging can weaken domestic consumption and can be considered a tax instead of dividend in countries where there are excessive savings. For instance, in Japan, the processes of aging and longer life expectancy prompt almost all population age groups to save for the future, which have led to weak consumption and dampened growth.

Second, a declining population, which often comes with an aging society, can weaken total consumption (hence, loss of scale economies) and, accordingly, investment for productive capacity.

Third, an aging society is often associated with a reduced demand for new products and services, leading to a less vigorous, more stagnant domestic market, and less innovation to respond to emerging needs of the younger population, along with more risk aversion and less entrepreneurship on the supply side.

Fourth, aging can have a negative impact on public finance due to the rising need for health services, pensions, and care for the aged. This will move resources away from other public expenditures such as higher education, and infrastructure investment and maintenance.

At the same time, an aging society can create new industries and lead to innovations to complement the shrinking workforce and help provide elderly care services. It may also induce infrastructure

---

[23] Collins, S. 1991. Saving Behavior in Ten Developing Countries. In Shoven, J. B., and B. D. Bernheim, eds. *National Saving and Economic Performance.* Chicago: National Bureau of Economic Research and the University of Chicago Press; Kelley, A., and R. Schmidt. 1996. Saving, Dependency, and Development. *Journal of Population Economics.* 9 (4). pp. 365– 386; and Lee, R., A. Mason, and T. Miller. 1997. Saving, Wealth, and the Demographic Transition in East Asia. *East-West Center Working Papers: Population Series.* No. 88-7. Honolulu: East-West Center.

[24] Lee, R., and A. Mason. 2006. What Is the Demographic Dividend? *Finance and Development.* 43 (3). p. 5.

investment such as elevators for subways and other barrier-free facilities. Expanding quality health care also provides opportunities for growth and employment. Tourism and other wellness services can grow to serve the aging population.

6.6 Looking ahead

Developing Asia has achieved much in human capital investment, thanks to large public spending, targeted interventions, and policy and institutional reforms. However, there remain significant gaps in educational attainment and health outcomes when compared with advanced countries.

In education, the challenges include (i) achieving universal access to secondary education in low-income and lower-middle-income countries where gaps remain large, (ii) improving education quality, and (iii) expanding tertiary education and TVET. All these require greater public investment in education and continued reforms in education systems to broaden the access and improve their effectiveness and efficiency.

The quality of education matters. Many Asian countries need to invest more in reading, mathematics, and science to keep abreast of rapid technological progress, including robotics and artificial intelligence, which may change the nature of work and the future tasks workers must do. In a technology-driven economy, it will be more important than ever that workers have the capacity and skills to learn and relearn.

In health, Asian countries should continue to (i) invest in health-care systems to address the growing burden of noncommunicable diseases (NCDs), due in part to population aging and changing diets; (ii) build systems that prevent, detect, and respond to future outbreaks, as the region is prone to pandemics; and (iii) increase public spending on health care and work toward achieving UHC.

In 2017, the top four NCDs—cardiovascular disease, cancer, chronic respiratory disease, and diabetes—caused over 75% of the deaths in developing Asia (up from 54% in 1990). This can be seen as a success in the context of the epidemiological transition, where the proportion of preventable deaths is greatly reduced by initial targeted programs. However, the vast majority of premature deaths due to NCDs occur in low- and middle-income countries, many of which are in Asia.

Demographic change matters to economic development. Many countries in Southeast Asia, South Asia, Central Asia, and the Pacific still have young populations. And they can benefit from a demographic dividend for many years to come. The challenge is to ensure adequate human capital investment and the creation of sufficient quality jobs.

As demographic change continues, more and more Asian countries will begin experiencing declining working-age populations and aging. As a result, the demographic dividend will become a demographic tax. This will have significant implications for a country's potential economic growth, public finance, and health-care system. For these countries, growth will have to rely more on improving labor productivity. They will also need to develop affordable, adequate, and sustainable health systems, pensions, and care for the aged.

In more advanced countries, which have already aged, public policies should support the participation of women and seniors in the workforce to reap a "gender dividend" and "silver dividend." By doing so, governments can help provide better childcare facilities and maternity and paternity benefits, promote better use of technology to complement the shrinking working-age population and care for the aged, and enhance the sustainability of the health-care and pension systems.

The large demographic diversity in Asia means both young- and older-aged countries can benefit from cross-border labor mobility. Source countries should make productive use of remittances and promote the welfare of migrant workers. Destination countries should implement well-designed immigration policy and foreign worker programs, along with developing skills of migrant workers and protecting their rights. Regional cooperation can play an important role in facilitating cross-border labor mobility.

CHAPTER 7

INVESTMENT, SAVINGS, AND FINANCE

7.1 Introduction

Rapid and sustained economic growth requires adequate investment. The economic history of Asia over the past 50 years bears testimony to this inexorable fact. All fast-growing economies made large investments in new factories and plants, as well as physical infrastructure such as roads, railways, ports, power plants and transmission lines, urban water supply, and telecommunications, often provided or supported by the government (Chapter 8). These investments increased productive capacity, raised labor productivity, facilitated technical progress, accelerated economic growth, and improved living standards.

Asia's high investments were financed largely by domestic savings—by households, corporations, and governments. In many countries, external financing also played an important role. Bilateral official development assistance and multilateral development bank funding were essential especially in the early stages of development (Chapter 14). Foreign direct investment (FDI) became the largest source of external finance after countries began liberalizing inward investment (Chapter 9). Remittances from overseas workers have also provided a stable source of financing in some countries.

Asia's bank-based financial system played a critical role in channeling domestic savings to domestic investment. More recently, capital markets have grown significantly to provide long-term financing, especially since the 1997–1998 Asian financial crisis.

This chapter examines the patterns of investment, savings, and finance in developing Asia during the past 50 years of rapid growth and transformation. Section 7.2 describes Asia's rapid capital accumulation, including investment in productive capacity and infrastructure. Section 7.3 looks at savings by households, corporations, and governments as sources of domestic investment financing, and their corresponding policy and institutional drivers. Section 7.4 focuses on sources of external financing. Section 7.5 examines the role of Asia's financial system in channeling savings to investment, including the roles of banks, capital markets, and small and medium-sized enterprise (SME) finance. Section 7.6 briefly discusses the future challenges of investment, savings, and finance in Asia.

7.2 Asia's rapid capital accumulation

In the 1960s, most Asian economies had low investment rates— investment as a share of gross domestic product (GDP). The average gross investment rate for the region was 20.3%, comparable to Latin America and the Caribbean (Appendix 12). Only a few economies had gross investment rates exceeding 20%, including Hong Kong, China; the People's Republic of China (PRC); the Philippines; and Taipei,China.

Over the following several decades, however, there was a significant increase in investment rates across Asia. By the 2010s, developing Asia's average gross investment rate was 38.9%, almost double the levels of Latin America and the Caribbean, and the Organisation for Economic Co-operation and Development (OECD). The rate was highest for East Asia (42.9%), driven by the PRC, followed by South Asia (32.2%), Southeast Asia (28.6%), and Central Asia (26.9%).[1]

These rapidly rising investment rates led to a significant expansion of developing Asia's capital stock, from $3.9 trillion in 1960 to $176 trillion in 2017 (in constant 2011 United States [US] dollars), growing by 6.9% annually (Table 7.1). While all developing Asian subregions (except the Pacific where data are not available) had significant increases, it was most pronounced in East Asia, where it

---

[1] World Bank. World Development Indicators. https://data.worldbank.org (accessed 2 August 2019).

surged from \$1.3 trillion in 1960 to \$108.2 trillion in 2017. This increase came mainly from the PRC, where capital stock increased from \$1 trillion to \$94.9 trillion. During the same period, capital stock also grew considerably in South Asia and Southeast Asia.

Developing Asia directed a substantial proportion of investment toward improving infrastructure (Chapter 8). The region's total primary energy consumption increased 13.5 times during 1965–2018, while the global primary energy consumption increased 3.7 times. The PRC's electricity generation increased 50 times, from 139 terawatt-hours (TWh) in 1971 to 7,146 TWh in 2018. The same figures for India increased 25 times, from 66 TWh to 1,643 TWh. Road kilometers per million people in the PRC increased 4.5 times, from 730 in 1965 to 3,260 in 2014. In India, it increased 2.9 times, from 1,461 to 4,224. But there were also large variations across countries in infrastructure development.

Rapid investment growth contributed to rapid economic growth which, in turn, supported a further increase in investment. Developing Asia's rapid capital accumulation was driven by several

Table 7.1: Stock and Growth of Physical Capital, 1960, 1990, and 2017
(constant 2011 US dollars, trillion)

	1960	1990	2017	Annual Growth (%) 1960–1990	1990–2017	1960–2017
Developing Asia	3.9	25.6	176.0	6.5	7.4	6.9
Central Asia	...	1.3	2.4	...	2.4	...
East Asia	1.3	9.9	108.2	7.0	9.2	8.1
People's Republic of China	1.0	6.6	94.9	6.5	10.4	8.3
South Asia	1.4	6.9	34.8	5.4	6.2	5.7
India	1.2	5.6	29.9	5.3	6.4	5.9
Southeast Asia	1.1	7.4	30.5	6.5	5.4	6.0

... = data not available, US = United States.

Notes: Data are not available for the Pacific island countries. Data for 1960 are not available for Central Asia and Bhutan, Brunei Darussalam, Cambodia, Maldives, Mongolia, and Myanmar.

Sources: Feenstra, R., R. Inklaar, and M. P. Timmer. 2015. The Next Generation of the Penn World Table Version 9.1. *American Economic Review*. 105 (10). pp. 3150–3182 (accessed 4 May 2019); and Asian Development Bank estimates.

factors. In many countries, investment was propelled by a strong push for industrialization. In the 1960s and 1970s, industrialization was often led or promoted by governments. They emphasized heavy industries that were capital-intensive and required large outlays of capital investment. State-owned enterprises often played a critical role in these investments, although private sector investment was also important, especially in the newly industrialized economies (NIEs) of Hong Kong, China; the Republic of Korea (ROK); Singapore; and Taipei,China.

Since the 1980s and especially the 1990s, most Asian economies have implemented market-oriented reforms that led to a surge in investment by the private sector. The PRC began market-oriented reforms and introduced an open-door policy from the late 1970s, followed by an upsurge in private investment—from 12.2% of total fixed asset investment value in 1995 to 14% in 2000 and 61% in 2018.[2] India started economic liberalization from 1991 and experienced a similar rise in gross capital formation by the private sector—from 10% of GDP in 1980 to 15% in 1990, 17% in 2000, and 21% in 2017.

Foreign investors also played an important role in driving investment in many Asian economies, especially over the past 2 to 3 decades. From the 1980s, many foreign companies came to Asia to produce goods for developed markets, later focusing on local markets as well. Since the mid-1980s, developing Asia has seen inward FDI grow rapidly, following the introduction of market reforms that allowed easier FDI entry, initially from Japan and other developed economies, and increasingly from the NIEs and the PRC. These FDI inflows were not disrupted by the Asian financial crisis. In 2017, the region continued to be the world's top recipient of FDI, accounting for 35% of the global total, with the PRC as the top destination (Chapter 9).

7.3 Domestic savings provided the bulk of investment financing

Asia's high investment was financed mainly through domestic savings by households, corporations, and governments, although external financing was an important supplement.

In theory, with perfect capital mobility and information, domestic investment may not depend on domestic savings because it can be financed by external capital. But country experiences in and

---

[2] National Bureau of Statistics of China. 1995, 2000, and 2018. *Statistical Communiqué on the National Economic and Social Development*. Beijing.

outside Asia show that countries with high savings, tend to have high investment, which, in turn, leads to high growth.[3]

Aggregate savings

In the 1960s, developing Asia's gross domestic savings rate averaged 18.0% of GDP, the lowest among regions globally (Table 7.2). The savings rate was also lower than the investment rate (resulting in a current account deficit) by 2.4 percentage points, meaning a portion of domestic investment was funded by external financing. Over time, developing Asia's savings rate increased significantly. From the 1990s, domestic savings exceeded domestic investment, and developing Asia as a whole became a net saver (current account surplus). In the 2010s, the region's average gross domestic savings rate reached 41%, primarily driven by a rapidly rising rate in the PRC (48.3%). The excess of gross domestic savings over investment reached 3.3% of the region's GDP in the 2000s, before moderating to 2.1% in the 2010s after the global financial crisis.

During the past half century, East Asia was mostly a net saver, except for several years in the early 1960s, late 1970s, and early 1980s. However, South Asia has consistently been a net borrower, with its savings–investment gap at 6.7% of GDP in the 1960s; it has declined in recent years, but remained at more than 4% of GDP, on average, in the 2000s and 2010s. Southeast Asia was primarily a net borrower before the 1997–1998 Asian financial crisis; it became a consistent net saver afterward. The Pacific was also a net borrower in most years, except the 1990s, when it posted net savings mainly due to resource-rich Papua New Guinea. Most Pacific island countries still struggle to mobilize sufficient domestic resources to finance substantial infrastructure needs (section 7.4). Central Asia was a net borrower after independence in the 1990s, but has become a net saver since 2002 (except in 2016), also driven by resource-rich countries such as Azerbaijan, Kazakhstan, and Turkmenistan. Since the late 1990s, developing Asia's high net savings was reflected in large current account surpluses (Box 7.1).

There are three principal sources of domestic savings: households, corporations, and the government. Household savings are part of the disposable income that is not consumed. Gross corporate savings mainly comprise retained earnings (after corporate tax and

---

[3] Feldstein, M., and C. Horioka. 1980. Domestic Saving and International Capital Flows. *The Economic Journal*. 90 (June). pp. 314–329.

Table 7.2: Gross Domestic Savings and Savings–Investment Gaps, 1960–2018
(% of GDP)

	1960–1969	1970–1979	1980–1989	1990–1999	2000–2009	2010–2018
Developing Asia	**18.0**	**24.9**	**27.4**	**32.9**	**36.6**	**41.0**
	(-2.4)	(-1.4)	(-1.3)	(0.6)	(3.3)	(2.1)
Central Asia	...	...	...	12.8	32.7	35.5
	...	...	...	(-7.2)	(5.2)	(8.7)
East Asia	25.7	34.4	34.6	36.9	40.4	45.6
	(0.9)	(1.6)	(1.0)	(1.8)	(4.1)	(2.7)
People's Republic of China	27.0	36.6	35.0	39.7	44.5	48.3
	(1.8)	(2.5)	(-1.4)	(1.6)	(4.0)	(2.0)
South Asia	8.4	11.2	14.7	21.9	26.8	28.1
	(-6.7)	(-6.2)	(-6.4)	(-2.6)	(-4.4)	(-4.1)
India	8.4	12.6	15.8	23.9	29.9	31.5
	(-7.3)	(-6.1)	(-6.0)	(-2.1)	(-3.9)	(-3.0)
Southeast Asia	16.1	23.6	28.7	32.9	32.2	33.6
	(-2.7)	(-1.0)	(0.6)	(0.9)	(7.7)	(5.0)
The Pacific	1.2	16.5	11.1	23.5	20.4	...
	(-18.6)	(-8.4)	(-14.4)	(2.3)	(1.1)	...
Developed Asia	**30.5**	**35.6**	**32.4**	**31.5**	**25.9**	**23.4**
	(-1.6)	(0.5)	(1.3)	(1.3)	(0.9)	(-0.4)
Australia	30.5	28.8	25.5	24.3	25.1	25.7
	(-1.6)	(-0.1)	(-2.4)	(-0.8)	(-1.5)	(-0.5)
Japan	...	37.0	33.3	32.2	26.0	22.6
	...	(0.7)	(1.7)	(1.5)	(1.3)	(-0.5)
Latin America and the Caribbean	**20.0**	**21.2**	**23.4**	**20.1**	**21.3**	**19.8**
	(-0.5)	(-2.5)	(2.5)	(-0.3)	(1.4)	(-0.7)
Sub-Saharan Africa	...	...	**30.7**	**23.1**	**23.5**	**20.2**
	...	...	(1.4)	(0.1)	(1.7)	(-1.6)
OECD	...	**25.2**	**23.7**	**23.4**	**22.1**	**21.4**
	...	(-1.3)	(-0.9)	(-0.1)	(-0.6)	(0.1)
World	...	**26.0**	**24.8**	**25.1**	**25.5**	**25.1**
	...	(-1.1)	(-1.0)	(0.2)	(0.9)	(0.8)

... = data not available, GDP = gross domestic product, OECD = Organisation for Economic Co-operation and Development.

Notes: Data on savings–investment gaps are in parentheses. Data for Taipei,China refer to gross national savings.

Sources: World Bank. World Development Indicators. https://data.worldbank.org (accessed 2 August 2019). For Taipei,China: Directorate-General of Budget, Accounting and Statistics.

Box 7.1: Asian Savings and Global Imbalances

The world witnessed a buildup of large global imbalances, or more precisely, global current account imbalances, in the run-up to the 2008–2009 global financial crisis. A set of countries, mostly East Asian and Southeast Asian economies, several industrialized countries in Europe, and oil exporters, had persistently high current account surpluses (excess savings over investment); while the United States (US) had persistently high current account deficits (excess investment over savings) (Box Figure).

Box Figure: World Current Account Balance, 1997–2018
(% of world GDP)

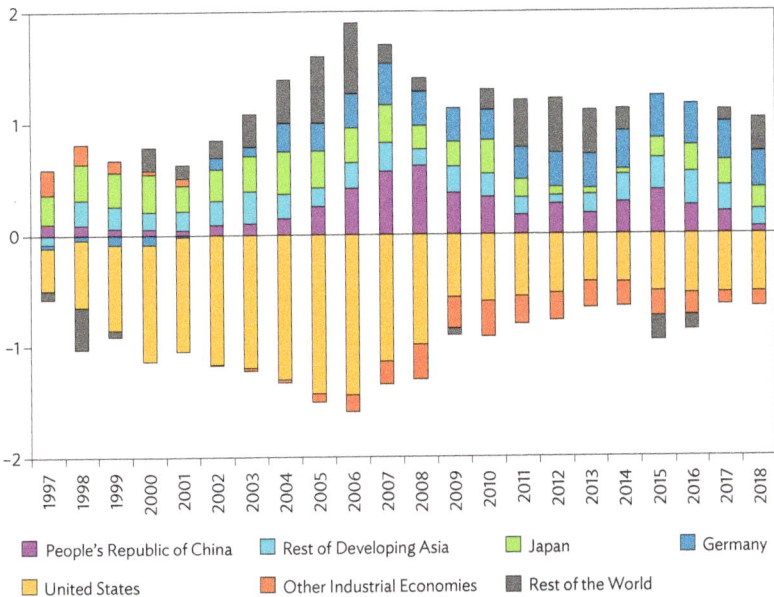

GDP = gross domestic product.

Sources: Asian Development Bank. 2019. Asian Development Outlook 2019. Manila; and International Monetary Fund. 2019. World Economic Outlook Databases. https://www.imf .org/en/Publications/SPROLLs/world-economic-outlook-databases#sort=%40imfdate%20 descending (accessed 22 July 2019).

Some observers considered this as one of the sources of financial vulnerability that led to the global financial crisis. They argued that emerging markets (especially economies in Asia) and oil exporters saved too much with excess savings largely invested in US assets, keeping

continued on next page

Box 7.1 continued

US interest rates low and leading to excessive risk-taking by financial institutions in US markets. This view was popularly dubbed the "global savings glut."[a] Others, however, disputed that global imbalances arose more from low household savings and high fiscal deficits in the US, and the excessive risk-taking by its financial institutions. They also argued that the excessive risk-taking was mainly due to the lack of adequate regulation and supervision over complex securitization products.

While savings rates remain high in emerging markets in Asia (especially the People's Republic of China), their external imbalances have declined after the global financial crisis. Developing Asia has expanded domestic consumption significantly, supported by a growing middle class, a more developed financial sector and expanding consumer credit, and improving social safety nets. For instance, the People's Republic of China's current account surplus was 10% of its own gross domestic product in 2007. It has been declining since and was 0.4% of gross domestic product in 2018.[b]

[a] Bernanke, B. 2005. *The Global Saving Glut and the U.S. Current Account Deficit.* Speech at the Sandridge Lecture. Virginia Association of Economics. 10 March. Richmond, Virginia.

[b] Asian Development Bank. 2019. *Asian Development Outlook 2019 Update.* Manila.

Source: Asian Development Bank.

dividend payments, but before investment). Government savings is the excess of government revenues over current expenditures of central and local governments (before capital investment). The relative importance of different sources of domestic savings differed across economies as well as over time (Figure 7.1).

Household savings

In the PRC, the household savings rate increased from about 20% of GDP before 2005 to 23% after 2005. In India, it increased from 17%–18% of GDP in the 1990s to 23% in the 2010s. In the ROK and Taipei,China, the household savings rate declined over the past 3 decades and is now about 7% of GDP. The household savings rate has also been in the range of 6%–7% of GDP in Indonesia and Thailand in recent years, but much lower in the Philippines.

Numerous studies have tried to explain high and/or rising household savings rates in some developing Asian countries, although the reasons likely differ from country to country. One is rapid economic growth, which can lead to higher savings rates. This can be explained by either the so-called "habit persistence" or "permanent income"

Figure 7.1: Gross Domestic Savings and Components, Selected Asian Economies, 1990–2017 (% of GDP)

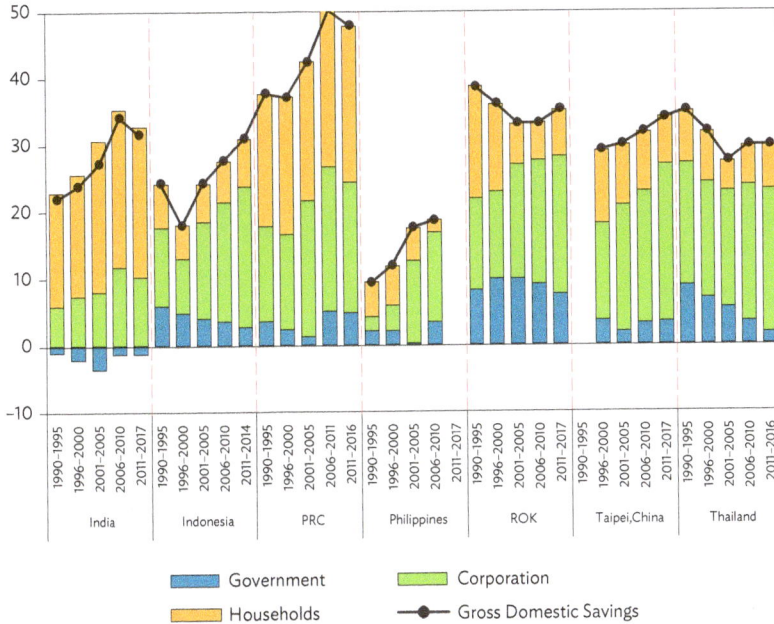

GDP = gross domestic product, PRC = People's Republic of China, ROK = Republic of Korea.

Notes: Sector and gross domestic savings are period averages based on available official estimates. Economies may follow different approaches in classifying savings by sector. For the Philippines, sector data are based on 1968/1993 System of National Accounts framework. Data for the PRC and Thailand are from flow of funds accounts. For India, for 2012 onward, data correspond to new base year 2011/12; before 2012, data correspond to old base year 2004/05.

Sources: CEIC Data. Global Database. https://www.ceicdata.com/en (accessed 24 March 2019); and Haver Analytics. Haver Analytics Database. http://www.haver.com/datalink.html (accessed 24 March 2019). For Taipei,China: Directorate-General of Budget, Accounting and Statistics.

hypothesis. The former posits that consumers form habits over time based on their past behavior and this produces an inertia or "hysteresis"; as a result, current consumption does not change as much as income.[4] According to the "permanent income" hypothesis, consumers base current consumption decisions on permanent income rather than

---

[4]   Brown, T. M. 1952. Habit Persistence and Lags in Consumer Behaviour. *Econometrica*. 20 (3). pp. 355–371.

current income; they might be reluctant to increase consumption if they are uncertain whether the income increase will be permanent or temporary.[5]

The second set of explanations relates to demographic factors based on the so-called "life-cycle hypothesis." According to this theory, individuals want to smooth consumption over their lifetime— they take on debt (or save less) when they are young, anticipating that future income streams will allow them to pay off debt; save (or save more) during middle age to maintain their consumption level when they retire; and after retirement, draw down on previous savings. The past 50 years have seen a rapid rise in the share of the working-age population in many Asian countries, likely contributing to rising household savings rates.

Recent empirical studies support this hypothesis, finding that young and old households save less than middle-aged ones in the Philippines; the PRC; the ROK; Taipei,China; and Thailand.[6] Empirical studies have also shown negative correlation between dependency ratios (both young and old) and savings rates, based on data from economies in East Asia, Southeast Asia, and South Asia.[7] As dependency ratios declined in many economies over the past 50 years, associated with rising shares of the working-age population, savings rates increased as a result, consistent with global cross-country studies.[8] Apart from age-related factors, in the PRC, the sex ratio imbalance in favor of boys has also been suggested as one motive for savings because families save to prepare houses and consumer durables for their sons' future marriage.[9]

---

[5]   Friedman, M. 1957. *A Theory of the Consumption Function*. Princeton: Princeton University Press.

[6]   See, for example, Deaton, A., and C. Paxson. 2000. Growth and Savings among Individuals and Households. *Review of Economics and Statistics*. 82 (2). pp. 212–225; and Chamon, M., and E. S. Prasad. 2008. Why Are Saving Rates of Urban Households in China Rising? *NBER Working Paper*. No. w14546. Cambridge, MA: National Bureau of Economic Research.

[7]   Kim, S., and J.-W. Lee. 2007. Demographic Changes, Saving, and Current Account in East Asia. *Asian Economic Papers*. 6 (2). pp. 22–53; and Horioka, C., and A. Terada-Hagiwara. 2012. The Determinants and Long-Term Projections of Saving Rates in Developing Asia. *Japan and the World Economy*. 24 (2). pp. 128–137.

[8]   See, for example, Chinn, M. D., and E. S. Prasad 2003. Medium-Term Determinants of Current Accounts in Industrial and Developing Countries: An Empirical Exploration. *Journal of International Economics*. 59 (1). pp. 47–76; and Bosworth, B., and G. Chodorow-Reich. 2007. Saving and Demographic Change: The Global Dimension. *Center for Retirement Research at Boston College Working Paper*. No. 2007-2. Boston: Boston College.

[9]   Wei, S.-J., and X. Zhang. 2011. The Competitive Saving Motive: Evidence from Rising Sex Ratios and Savings Rates in China. *Journal of Political Economy*. 119 (3). pp. 511–564.

The third set of explanations relates to financial sector development, including access to savings facilities and household borrowing constraints.

A stable bank-based financial system in many Asian countries enabled access to financial services by small and rural savers at low transaction costs, encouraging household savings. This occurred even though many countries kept nominal interest rates below equilibrium levels, a phenomenon known as "financial repression" common in developing countries. It has been suggested that, while there was financial repression in many developing Asian countries, the level of repression was often mild because of low inflation and tax incentives for saving (such as tax exemption for interest earnings), so real interest rates remained positive to attract household savings.[10]

Many Asian economies have well-established voluntary household savings mobilization programs. One example is postal savings, inspired by Japan's success (Box 7.2). Bangladesh; India; Kazakhstan; Malaysia; the Philippines; the PRC; the ROK; Singapore; Taipei,China; and Viet Nam all developed extensive postal savings systems. In some economies, agricultural and fisheries cooperatives also provided savings deposit services to rural households.

The ROK established its postal savings system as early as the 1960s. In Taipei,China, about 40% of household savings in the formal financial sector were in postal savings during the mid-1980s. In the PRC, postal savings became increasingly popular among households more recently, with the number of branches mushrooming from less than 2,500 in 1986 to 37,000 in 2009.[11] In India, the Post Office Savings Bank (POSB) had over 154,000 branches by the late 1990s.[12]

Less-developed consumer credit markets may have contributed to high household savings as well. In many Asian economies, mortgages, credit card facilities, and other consumer credit services were not well developed until very recently. When households cannot borrow from formal financial institutions, they either use informal financial arrangements or save more to finance durable purchases such as cars and electronic appliances, or large family events such as weddings or

---

[10] World Bank. 1993. *The East Asian Miracle: Economic Growth and Public Policy.* New York: Oxford University Press.
[11] Garon, S. 2012. Why the Chinese Save? *Foreign Policy.* 19 January. https://foreignpolicy .com/2012/01/19/why-the-chinese-save/.
[12] World Bank. 2002. *The Reform of India Post: Transforming a Postal Infrastructure to Deliver Modern Information and Financial Services.* Washington, DC.

Box 7.2: Japan's Postal Savings System

Japan's postal savings system (popularly known as Yu-cho) is the world's largest postal savings system in terms of deposits. It was established in 1871, following the example of Great Britain, which started the post office savings system in 1861. With its extensive postal network, Yu-cho was able to reach "small" rural household savers. The tax-exempt nature of these deposits, as well as the minimum costs of making deposits and withdrawals, led to tremendous growth; for instance, from 1905 to 1914, they grew almost fourfold compared with a far more modest increase of ordinary bank deposits.

From the postwar period until 2001, postal savings, together with the national pension system, were the main sources of funding for the government's Fiscal Incentive Loan Program (FILP). This program funded industries such as synthetic fiber, oil refining, machinery, and electronics industries during the postwar recovery. At the height of high-speed economic development, FILP financed public infrastructure investment such as highways and railways, as well as small and medium-sized enterprises, housing, and regional development through government-affiliated financial institutions such as the Development Bank of Japan, Export–Import Bank of Japan, and Housing Finance Corporation.

Japan's postal system—including postal savings—was privatized in the 2000s. Many government-affiliated institutions are consolidated and started issuing their own bonds without government guarantees.

Source: Asian Development Bank.

---

education. When formal consumer credit markets were liberalized in Taipei,China in 1987, for example, the average propensity to save by households declined from 29% in the early-1990s to 26% in 1996, and declined further to about 20% in the 2010s.

In recent years, credit to households increased in many Asian countries. In 2018, household credit as a percentage of GDP was 68% in Malaysia and Thailand, and 53% in the PRC, compared with 62% in the European Union and 78% in North America. More recently, in Indonesia and the Philippines, consumer loans have grown rapidly, including for cars and motorbikes.

The fourth set of explanations for high household savings relates to precautionary savings, largely due to underdeveloped social security systems, such as the lack of universal health coverage and inadequate pension provisions. These precautionary saving motives played an important role in high household savings in many Asian countries, particularly the PRC.

This is consistent with recent empirical studies. In Taipei,China, there was a 9%–14% decline in average savings after the National Health Insurance system was introduced in 1995.[13] There was a similar decline in the private household savings rate in Thailand, beginning in the early 1990s, when a three-pillar social security system was introduced, consisting of social assistance, social insurance, and social service.[14] A similar decline in savings also occurred in the Philippines between 1994 and 2006 due to expanding social security coverage in the early 1990s.[15]

Gross corporate savings

From the 1990s to the 2010s, the gross corporate savings rate increased in the PRC; the ROK; Taipei,China; and Indonesia from below 15% of GDP to about 20% or higher (Figure 7.1). Over the same period, the corporate savings rate increased from 18% of GDP to 21% in Thailand, from 2% to 13% in the Philippines, and from 6% to 10% in India. During 2010–2017, gross corporate savings accounted for 60%–70% of total domestic savings in Indonesia; the Philippines; the ROK; Taipei,China; and Thailand; about 40% in the PRC; and 30% in India. Growing gross corporate savings rates are a global phenomenon, and many developed countries have also seen them increase significantly over the past 3 to 4 decades.

Several factors have been suggested for rising gross corporate savings rates globally: (i) declining labor income shares associated with technological progress, globalization, and the diminished bargaining power of trade unions; (ii) falling prices of investment goods possibly associated with technological progress; (iii) lower dividend payouts in some countries to retain greater income for investment; (iv) reductions in corporate income tax rates; (v) low interest rates which increased

[13] Chou, S., J. Liu, and J. Hammit. 2003. National Health Insurance and Precautionary Saving. *Journal of Public Economics*. 87 (9–10). pp. 1873–1894.
[14] Pootrakool, K., K. Ariyapruchya, and T. Sodsrichai. 2005. Long-Term Saving in Thailand: Are We Saving Enough and What Are the Risks? *Monetary Policy Group Working Papers*. No. 2005-03. Bangkok: Bank of Thailand.
[15] Terada-Hagiwara, A. 2009. Explaining Filipino Households' Declining Saving Rate. *ADB Economics Working Paper Series*. No. 178. Manila: Asian Development Bank.

corporate profits; and (vi) the emergence of highly profitable platform companies that do not need to make huge investments in physical or tangible capital.

Many of these factors also apply to Asia. In the PRC, for example, labor's income share in industrial value added declined from 48% in the early 1990s to 42% in the mid-2000s, and in India, it decreased from 50% to 22% (for the formal industry sector).[16] Many listed companies in developing Asia have limited dividend payments. In the PRC, for instance, about 50% of listed firms did not pay dividends until recently.[17]

Government savings

Government savings is important to gross domestic savings in Indonesia; the PRC;[18] the ROK; Taipei,China; and Thailand. India's government savings rate, however, continued to be negative, meaning government revenues fell short of current expenditures, with capital investment financed by bond issuance and borrowing. Philippine government savings also were small, which, until recently, led to insufficient government infrastructure investment.

High government savings rates often go hand in hand with fiscal prudence (Chapter 10). Asian Development Bank (ADB) studies have documented the role fiscal prudence played in Southeast Asian economies—such as Indonesia, Malaysia, and Singapore—in augmenting government savings.[19] A strong commitment to fiscal prudence and sustainability both boosted public savings and created a stable economic environment conducive to higher private savings. In recent years, fiscal reforms to increase tax revenues or cut subsidies in several Asian economies—such as India, Indonesia, and the Philippines—increased government savings and enabled larger public infrastructure spending.

[16] Asian Development Bank (ADB). 2012. *Asian Development Outlook 2012: Confronting Rising Inequality in Asia.* Manila.
[17] Tyers, R., and F. Lu. 2008. Competition Policy, Corporate Saving and China's Current Account Surplus. *ANU Working Papers in Economics and Econometrics.* No. 2008-496. Canberra: Australian National University College of Business and Economics.
[18] Zhang, L., et al. 2018. China's High Savings: Drivers, Prospects, and Policies. *IMF Working Paper.* No. WP/18/277. Washington, DC: International Monetary Fund.
[19] ADB. 1997. *Emerging Asia: Changes and Challenges.* Manila; and Harrigan, F. 1996. Saving Transitions in Southeast Asia. *EDRC Report Series.* No. 64. Manila: Asian Development Bank.

7.4 External financing complements domestic savings

Developing Asia's gross domestic investment rate was higher than its gross domestic savings rate during the 1960s, 1970s, and 1980s (Table 7.2). This excess investment was financed by foreign savings from nonresident capital inflows such as official flows, FDI, private debt (bank lending and bonds), and portfolio equity investment. Since the 1990s, savings rates have exceeded investment rates.

The domestic savings–investment gap equals the current account balance. A positive gap indicates a surplus, while a negative gap shows a deficit. The deficit requires external financing. However, even if a country runs a current account surplus, there can still be net capital inflows by nonresidents. In such a case, the current account surplus and net capital inflows by nonresidents will offset investment by residents abroad (including FDI) and increasing foreign exchange reserves.

Before 1990, net official flows (bilateral official development assistance, multilateral development financing, and other official flows) were the largest source of external financing for developing Asia (Figure 7.2) (Chapter 14). It was close to 60% (or about 6% of gross domestic investment) in the early 1970s. But it declined over time to less than 40% (or 4% of gross domestic investment) in 1990.

Inward FDI was the second-largest source during the 1970s and 1980s. However, it has become the largest source of external financing since the 1990s, when Asian economies started liberalizing trade and investment (Chapter 9), reaching 13.3% of gross domestic investment in 2000 and hovering around 5.7%–7.0% in recent years.

In developing Asia, external private debt—including borrowing from foreign commercial banks and bond purchases by foreign investors—was the third-largest source of external financing in the 1970s, 1980s, and 1990s. Bank lending saw net outflows in 1998–2002 following the Asian financial crisis, and only recovered after 2004. Bond financing increased in the years leading to the crisis, and again in the years leading to and after the global financial crisis. Inward portfolio equity investment increased significantly after the Asian financial crisis, but has been more volatile.

In the years leading to the Asian financial crisis, many banks in Indonesia, Malaysia, the ROK, and Thailand borrowed extensively from foreign sources. These were primarily short-term bank loans or bonds largely denominated in US dollars and unhedged. The banks

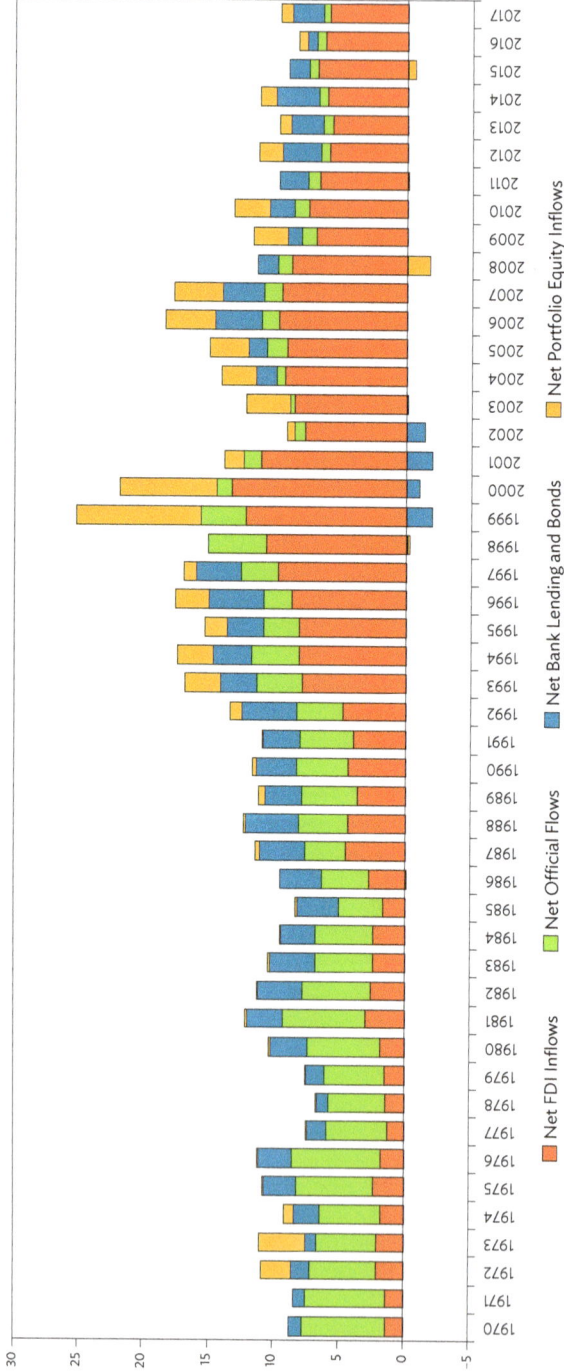

Figure 7.2: Net Capital Inflows by Nonresidents to Developing Asia, 1970–2017
(% of gross domestic investment)

Net FDI Inflows   Net Official Flows   Net Bank Lending and Bonds   Net Portfolio Equity Inflows

FDI = foreign direct investment.

Notes: Bonds are securities issued with a fixed rate of interest for a period of more than 1 year. They include net flows through cross-border public and publicly guaranteed and private nonguaranteed bond issues. Data are in current United States dollars.

Sources: Asian Development Bank estimates; World Bank. World Development Indicators. https://data.worldbank.org (accessed 2 August 2019); United Nations Conference on Trade and Development (UNCTAD). UNCTADStat. https://unctadstat.unctad.org (accessed 28 August 2019); and Organisation for Economic Co-operation and Development (OECD). OECD Statistics. https://stats.oecd.org (accessed 26 August 2019).

then provided long-term loans denominated in local currency to domestic firms. This created currency and maturity mismatches that rendered the financial system vulnerable to currency speculation. Since the Asian financial crisis, Asian countries have taken significant steps to strengthen banking regulations and develop local currency bond markets to provide long-term financing (Chapter 10).

The importance and composition of external financing differ from subregion to subregion (Figure 7.3). The Pacific had the largest external financing as a ratio to gross domestic investment. Their largest source of external financing has been net official flows since the 1970s (when data became available), followed by net FDI. In Southeast Asia, the largest source was net official flows during the 1970s and 1980s, but this has shifted to net FDI since the 1990s. The same happened in South Asia, although external financing as a ratio to gross domestic investment was much lower, given less open capital accounts and the larger size of South Asian economies. In East Asia, the largest source of external financing was net official flows in the 1970s and net FDI since the 1980s. In Central Asia, net official flows were the largest source of external financing in the 1990s. Since then, net FDI has become the largest source.

In developing Asia, remittances (which are a part of current account transactions and not a part of capital flows) have also become a vital and stable source of external financing in recent years (Box 7.3). Global remittance flows to developing Asia were estimated at $297 billion in 2018, equivalent to more than half of net inward FDI inflows to the region. In developing Asia, remittances were 1.3% of GDP on average in 2018, with the ratio reaching as high as 19.1% for low-income and 3.7% for lower-middle-income Asian countries.

7.5 Asia's financial system

Bank-based versus market-based financial systems

A well-functioning financial system helps support economic growth by mobilizing and pooling savings; facilitating payments, and financing trade of goods and services; and promoting efficient financial resource allocation. It also helps find new entrepreneurs, diversify and manage risks, monitor investments, and apply corporate governance. A large number of empirical studies have found that financial sector development leads to greater capital accumulation, faster productivity

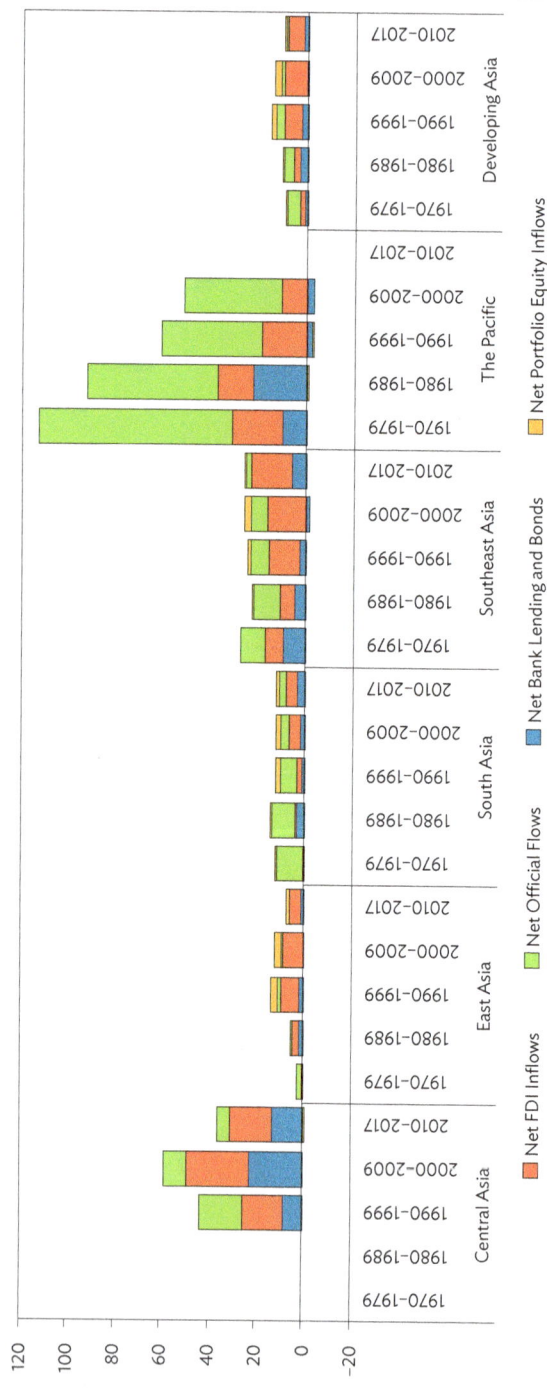

Figure 7.3: Net Capital Inflows by Nonresidents to Developing Asia by Subregion, 1970s–2010s
(% of gross domestic investment)

FDI = foreign direct investment.

Sources: Asian Development Bank estimates; World Bank. World Development Indicators. https://data.worldbank.org (accessed 2 August 2019); United Nations Conference on Trade and Development (UNCTAD). UNCTADStat. https://unctadstat.unctad.org (accessed 28 August 2019); and Organisation for Economic Co-operation and Development (OECD). OECD Statistics. https://stats.oecd.org (accessed 26 August 2019).

Box 7.3: Importance of Remittances for Developing Asia

Remittances to developing Asia have increased steadily since 1990 and have become an important source of foreign exchange earnings for many countries (Box Figure). They are visibly more stable compared with other types of financial flows.

Box Figure: Financial Flows to Developing Asia by Type, 1990–2018
($ billion)

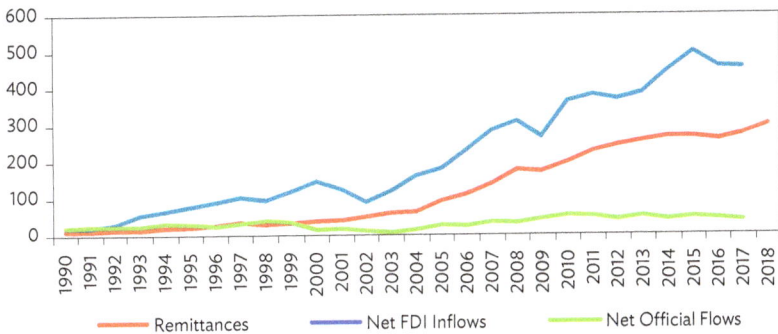

FDI = foreign direct investment.

Sources: Asian Development Bank estimates; Knomad Database. https://www.knomad.org (accessed 26 November 2019); World Bank. World Development Indicators. https://data .worldbank.org (accessed 15 October 2019); United Nations Conference on Trade and Development (UNCTAD). UNCTADStat. https://unctadstat.unctad.org (accessed 28 August 2019); and Organisation for Economic Co-operation and Development (OECD). OECD Statistics. https://stats.oecd.org (accessed 26 August 2019).

Among the top 10 remittance-recipient economies globally in 2018, five are in Asia—India ($78.6 billion), the People's Republic of China ($67.4 billion), the Philippines ($33.8 billion), Pakistan ($21.0 billion), and Viet Nam ($15.9 billion). Together, they received $216.8 billion in remittances in 2018, or 31.4% of the global total. For many economies in Central Asia and the Pacific, remittances are large as a ratio to gross domestic product—over 30% in Tonga; at least 10% in Kiribati, the Marshall Islands, and Samoa; and around 30% in the Kyrgyz Republic and Tajikistan.

The fact that remittances target specific economic needs of their beneficiaries underscores their importance in both supporting consumption and financing investment. Remittances are important sources of financing for micro and small enterprises that are critical for job creation and poverty reduction.

Source: Asian Development Bank.

growth, and better economic performance.[20] Furthermore, the positive impact of financial development on growth is more pronounced in emerging economies than in advanced economies as financial constraints are more binding in the former.[21]

While the initial structure of a country's financial system is often determined by historical, institutional, economic, legal, and political factors, there is now a consensus that an effective financial system requires both banks and capital markets.[22] Some argue that banks have an advantage, particularly during the early stage of development. This is because banks can mobilize large sums of savings from small savers into medium- to long-term corporate investment. Banks can also monitor these investments on behalf of a large number of savers because they can extract critical information through their long-term relationships with borrowers. For example, until the 1980s, the largest provider of bank loans for corporate borrowers in Japan was often called the "main bank," and it could influence corporate governance by monitoring company activities and having executives participate in board meetings when needed.

On the other hand, bonds and equity markets have the advantage of better spreading risk across a large number of investors with diverse risk profiles. Market-based financial systems are usually better at financing riskier investments—such as technological innovations—and providing long-term finance. Also, a market-based system can promote strong market discipline and better corporate governance through disclosure requirements, price signals, and the functions of boards representing equity holders. Capital markets offer investment opportunities for institutional investors—such as pension funds and life insurance companies.

The market-based system is also considered better able to prevent financial crises, as losses incurred during financial distress can be absorbed by bond and equity holders instead of impairing bank balance sheets—thus avoiding bank runs and protecting payment systems. However, as the global financial crisis in 2008–2009 made

---

[20] Zhuang, J., et al. 2009. Financial Sector Development, Economic Growth, and Poverty Reduction: A Literature Review. *ADB Economics Working Paper Series*. No. 173. Manila: Asian Development Bank.

[21] Estrada, G., D. Park, and A. Ramayandi. 2015. Financial Development, Financial Openness, and Economic Growth. *ADB Economics Working Paper Series*. No. 442. Manila: Asian Development Bank.

[22] Levine, R. 2002. Bank-Based or Market-Based Financial Systems: Which Is Better? *Journal of Financial Intermediation*. 11 (4). pp. 398–428.

clear, financial crises can occur regardless of financial structure—the crisis started in the US, where capital markets were considered most developed.

There have been a lot of discussions about the causes of the global financial crisis. Since the 1990s, with the rapid development of structured finance, banks have invested heavily in market-linked products such as mortgage- and asset-backed securities through special purpose vehicles. Banks were also increasingly involved in derivatives markets (such as currency and credit-default swaps) and exposed to broader market risk. This created a channel through which distress in mortgage-backed securities (reinforced by more sophisticated securitization such as collateralized debt obligations) could quickly spill over to the banking system and impact the entire financial system. This is what happened during the global financial crisis.

After the global financial crisis, there have been serious efforts to reduce systemic risk, including through addressing the "too-big-to-fail" problems—and strengthening firewalls between banking and other investment services. But the boundary remains less clear-cut than what regulations intended. In many ways, the banking sector and capital markets are complements rather than substitutes in providing financial services, and risks can spill over between them.[23] Regulators and the financial industry should remain vigilant and respond to any sign of possible irregularities.

Bank-based financing in Asia

Before the 1997–1998 Asian financial crisis, finance across most of developing Asia was bank-based (many state-owned). Banks played a dominant role in mobilizing domestic savings into investment. While some economies developed capital markets, investment through equities and bonds was small. In the ROK, for example, during 1970–1979, bank loans accounted for 82% of financing of nonfinancial corporations, with equity 4% and bonds 14%.[24] In Malaysia, from 1986 to 1991, bank loans accounted for 95% of financing of nonfinancial corporations, despite government efforts to develop stock and corporate bond markets.

---

[23] Eichengreen, B. 2015. *Financial Development in Asia: The Role of Policy and Institutions, with Special Reference to China.* Prepared for the Second Annual Asian Monetary Policy Forum. 29 May. Singapore.

[24] World Bank. 1993. *The East Asian Miracle: Economic Growth and Public Policy.* New York: Oxford University Press.

Fast-growing Asian economies—especially the ROK; Singapore; and Taipei,China—were quite successful in channeling domestic savings into investment using the banking system, partly due to several selective policy interventions. These included establishing public development banks; guiding banks to provide loans to targeted firms and sectors, and providing credit guarantees (for SMEs); moderate interest rate repression; and regulations covering outward foreign investment. Public development banks were substantial lenders of long-term financing in Indonesia; the ROK; and Taipei,China.[25]

According to measures of financial sector development (Table 7.3), Asia's financial deepening is an ongoing process and less than the OECD average in terms of outstanding debt securities and stock market capitalization as a ratio to GDP. Despite the rapid growth of capital markets after the Asian financial crisis, bank credit remains the most important source of private sector financing in most Asian economies. In 2010–2017, in 10 selected major developing Asian economies (Hong Kong, China; India; Indonesia; Malaysia; the Philippines; the PRC; the ROK; Singapore; Thailand; and Viet Nam), outstanding bank credit was, on average, 111.5% of GDP; stock market capitalization was 83.7% of GDP; and outstanding corporate bonds was 39.7% of GDP (albeit a threefold increase over 1990–1994).

Increasing importance of capital markets

Capital markets existed in Asia as early as the late 19th century and early 20th century. India's Bombay Stock Exchange was established in 1875 under British rule. The Tokyo Stock Exchange was established in 1878. The "Shanghai Sharebrokers' Association" was founded by foreign entrepreneurs in 1891 and renamed the "Shanghai Stock Exchange" in 1904. Indonesia's first stock exchange opened in 1912 under Dutch rule. Hong Kong, China's securities market can be traced back to 1866, but the stock market was formally established in 1891, and renamed the "Hong Kong Stock Exchange" in 1914.

Despite these early developments, for the region as a whole, stock markets played a limited role in providing financing for corporate investment before the 1990s. The same was true for Asia's bond markets.

---

[25] In Japan, banks in special relationships with big businesses through cross shareholdings (typically being part of the same corporate group—the bank-centered "financial *keiretsu*") played a major role in corporate finance during industrialization. While ROK chaebols did not own banks, which were nationalized during the 1960s, they nevertheless received guaranteed loans from the banking sector because of their close connections.

Table 7.3: Measures of Financial Sector Development, 1990–2017
(amount outstanding as % of GDP)

		Developing Asia	Developed Asia	OECD	Latin America and the Caribbean	Sub-Saharan Africa	PRC	India
Private credit by deposit money banks	1990–1994	60.8	161.1	107.5	23.7	40.7	77.2	22.4
	1995–1999	76.9	171.5	120.2	28.8	51.3	89.2	21.7
	2000–2004	84.9	172.9	132.9	23.0	46.6	108.6	28.6
	2005–2009	84.0	159.6	141.3	30.7	49.4	101.8	40.7
	2010–2017	111.5	155.2	138.6	46.4	46.3	131.0	48.3
Domestic private debt securities	1990–1994	11.1	40.1	45.9	1.4	18.6	2.9	0.8
	1995–1999	12.7	49.3	53.4	6.8	12.8	4.1	0.8
	2000–2004	18.4	59.8	63.0	9.9	13.4	10.7	0.4
	2005–2009	27.9	71.8	66.7	14.9	17.9	29.7	2.4
	2010–2017	39.7	60.5	51.0	21.0	18.7	40.7	5.0
Stock market capitalization	1990–1994	43.3	76.7	53.8	15.2	87.4	5.7	20.5
	1995–1999	49.7	64.7	79.2	22.6	94.8	15.9	29.9
	2000–2004	56.8	67.1	92.8	24.3	76.0	33.7	35.1
	2005–2009	85.4	89.0	92.0	44.5	103.4	50.4	81.5
	2010–2017	83.7	83.7	95.3	40.2	107.1	55.2	69.9

GDP = gross domestic product, OECD = Organisation for Economic Co-operation and Development, PRC = People's Republic of China.

Notes: Regional averages are weighted by GDP. Economic regions follow the composition provided by the Asian Development Bank. Developing Asia includes Hong Kong, China; India; Indonesia; Malaysia; the Philippines; the PRC; the Republic of Korea; Singapore; Thailand; and Viet Nam. Sub-Saharan Africa domestic private debt securities figures refer to South Africa only.

Source: World Bank. Global Financial Development Database. https://www.worldbank.org/en/publication/gfdr/data/global-financial-development-database (accessed 5 November 2019).

In Japan, capital markets played an important role in prewar financing, while the economy became more dependent on bank financing in postwar high growth era.

The 1997–1998 Asian financial crisis severely affected Indonesia, Malaysia, the Philippines, the ROK, and Thailand (Chapter 9). After the crisis, policy makers prioritized capital market development—especially local currency bond markets and nonbank financial institutions—as a more diverse long-term financing alternative to banks.

Although banks remain dominant, more recently, capital markets in Asia increased their size and importance in channeling domestic financial resources for domestic investment. For instance, between the 1990s and 2010–2017, outstanding corporate bonds as a percentage of GDP increased from 9% to 22% for the four members of the Association of Southeast Asian Nations (ASEAN)—Indonesia, Malaysia, the Philippines, and Thailand (ASEAN4), from 28% to 51% for the NIEs, from 4% to 41% in the PRC, and from 1% to 5% in India (Figure 7.4). During the same period, outstanding government bonds as

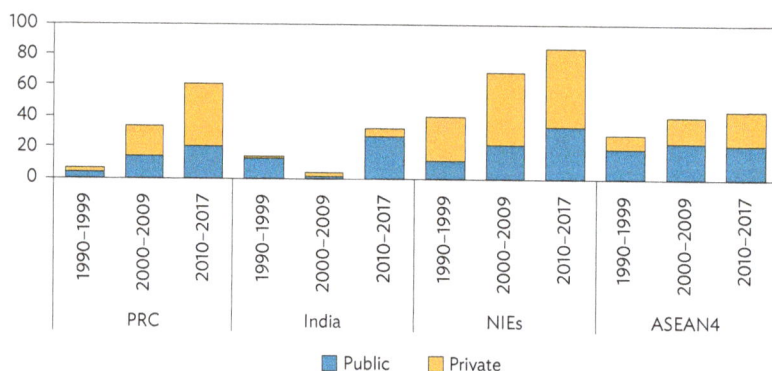

Figure 7.4: Outstanding Domestic Debt Securities, Selected Asian Economies, 1990–2017
(% of GDP)

ASEAN = Association of Southeast Asian Nations, GDP = gross domestic product, NIEs = newly industrialized economies, PRC = People's Republic of China.

Notes: ASEAN4 includes Indonesia, Malaysia, the Philippines, and Thailand. For India, 2010–2017 average refers to 2010–2011 data.

Source: World Bank. Global Financial Development Database. https://www.worldbank.org/en/publication/gfdr/data/global-financial-development-database (accessed 5 November 2019).

a percentage of GDP increased from 20% to 22% for the ASEAN4, 12% to 34% for the NIEs, 4% to 21% in the PRC, and 14% to 28% in India.

While capital market size has grown, much more needs to be done to make them deeper and more liquid. One priority is to expand the institutional investor base, such as pension funds and insurance companies, as long-term investors. Compared with advanced countries, institutional investor participation in capital markets in developing Asia remains limited (Figure 7.5).

Developing Asian economies have also strengthened regional cooperation to develop capital markets. For example, the Asian Bond Markets Initiative (ABMI), launched in December 2002 by ASEAN plus the PRC, Japan, and the ROK—collectively known as ASEAN+3— aims to develop local currency bond markets, supported by ADB. ABMI seeks to develop local currency bond markets to minimize the currency and maturity mismatches that made the region vulnerable to the sudden capital inflow reversals during the Asian financial crisis.

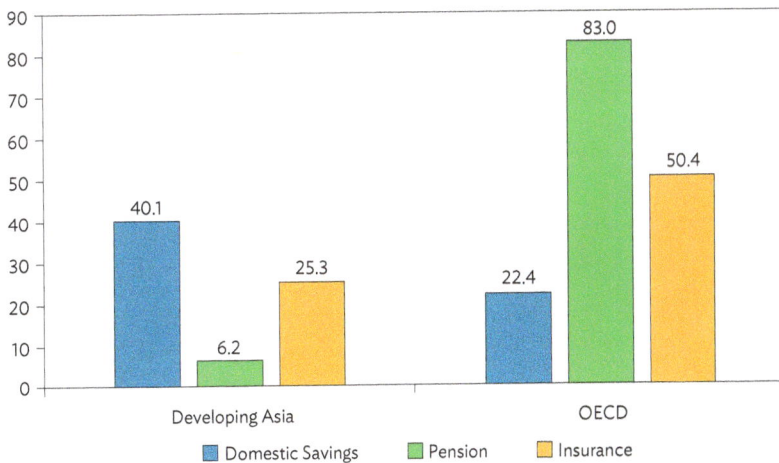

Figure 7.5: Domestic Savings, Pensions, and Insurance Assets, 2017
(% of GDP)

GDP = gross domestic product, OECD = Organisation for Economic Co-operation and Development.

Source: World Bank. Global Financial Development Database. https://www.worldbank.org/en/publication/gfdr/data/global-financial-development-database (accessed 15 November 2019).

Since its launch, ABMI has (i) supported governments to strengthen regulations for bond markets, (ii) established the Credit Guarantee and Investment Facility (CGIF) in 2010 to provide credit enhancement to regional corporate bond issuers, (iii) launched the *AsianBondsOnline* website to disseminate data and information on ASEAN+3 bond markets, and (iv) facilitated the development of cross-border bond market infrastructure by establishing the ASEAN+3 Bond Market Forum and Cross-Border Settlement Infrastructure Forum.

Promoting small and medium-sized enterprise access to finance

Broadening access to finance by SMEs is key to boosting inclusive economic growth. SMEs are the backbone of most Asian economies. They create jobs, promote competition, and stimulate domestic demand. However, poor access to finance is often a critical constraint to their growth in developing Asia. A recent ADB report on SME finance (covering 20 developing Asian economies) states that, while SMEs made up an average 96% of registered firms, employed 62% of the labor force, and contributed 42% of economic output, they only received 19% of total bank loans in 2014.

Limited access to bank credit is a structural problem for SMEs, mainly because of the asymmetric information between banks and borrowers. This leads to high collateral and guarantee requirements and adds to transaction costs. Developing Asian countries have taken various measures in recent years to promote SME access to finance. For example, Papua New Guinea and Solomon Islands made it easier for companies to borrow using movable assets as collateral. Thailand expanded the guarantee of SME loans by the state-owned Thai Credit Guarantee Corporation. Indonesia and the Philippines introduced mandatory bank lending quotas for SMEs. An increasing number of countries are supporting SME finance through fintech and digital solutions as part of national strategies for financial inclusion. Extension of credit to micro and small enterprises managed by women is also a priority in many countries. ADB has been supporting this area including through legal reform to provide land titles to women in some countries.

7.6 Looking ahead

Future policy challenges regarding investment and savings for Asian economies are multifaceted and depend on country situations—such as demographics, resource endowment, policies, and institutions.

For example, countries with high investment and savings rates, such as the PRC, need to increase domestic consumption. Policy measures may include promoting consumer credit and strengthening social protection. For countries with low savings rates, low investment rates, and persistent current account deficits—often with low per capita income—governments should introduce policies to increase domestic savings, including government savings through raising tax revenues. They can also more effectively use external financing from FDI, remittances, and bilateral and multilateral development finance.

Regarding financial systems, future priorities include (i) developing and deepening capital markets and supporting greater participation by institutional investors; (ii) increasing the financial sector efficiency, by allowing greater competition; (iii) promoting financial inclusion by improving access to underserved groups such as SMEs, women, and low-income households; (iv) strengthening financial regulation to safeguard the financial system, protecting consumers, and addressing money laundering; and (v) embracing financial innovation.

CHAPTER 8

INFRASTRUCTURE DEVELOPMENT

8.1 Introduction

This chapter offers a historical perspective on the role infrastructure plays in the development of Asia and the Pacific. It describes the evolution of infrastructure across the region from basic facilities after World War II to modern systems in the new millennium. This history takes national, regional, and global perspectives on complex infrastructure developments.

Infrastructure is a precondition for economic development, and essential for sustainable and inclusive growth. It facilitates participation in the workforce, the production of goods and services, and distribution of products to markets, and promotes technological progress (Chapter 5).

The quantity and quality of infrastructure investment are also key determinants for improving the lives of people. Access to electricity, roads and railways to support the movement of people, safe drinking water, and quality communications are all essential parts of people's welfare. Infrastructure helps children to go to school, women to work outside their homes, and people to stay healthy, and promotes more social interaction.

In many Asian countries, infrastructure investment accelerated from the 1950s to the 1970s, together with the efforts of industrialization. Both the public and private sectors contributed significantly to Asia's infrastructure development over the past 50 years. As a region, developing Asia has consistently invested a much higher share of gross domestic product (GDP) in infrastructure than other regions in the world (Chapter 7).[1]

While there has been much progress in infrastructure development in Asia, there remain large infrastructure deficits and differences among countries. In 2017, about 350 million people in the region were still without electricity, 300 million lacked improved sources of drinking water, 1.5 billion lacked improved sanitation facilities, and 1 billion lived more than 2 kilometers from an all-season road.[2] Asia's contributions to emissions and climate change remain a concern (Chapter 13).

As public spending on overall infrastructure investment in Asia and the Pacific is insufficient, the private sector must increasingly participate to mobilize knowledge, efficiency, and additional funds for high-quality, bankable projects.

More infrastructure packages are being structured as public–private partnerships (PPPs). A typical infrastructure PPP is structured as build–operate–transfer (BOT), where private firms finance and build the infrastructure, then operate it over a fixed period to generate returns before transferring ownership to the government. They are not a panacea to build infrastructure without taxpayer money, but when PPPs are designed and implemented well, they do open new growth channels by mobilizing more resources and enabling reforms for infrastructure development. By drawing on private sector expertise and skills, PPPs can deliver high-quality construction, operational performance, and risk-sharing, in addition to financing.

There is now greater international consensus among governments, the private sector, and development partners on the need to promote high-quality infrastructure projects that are sustainable, economically efficient for life-cycle costs, socially and environmentally

---

[1] Abiad, A., et al. 2020. The Past and Future Role of Infrastructure in Asia's Development. In Susantono, B., D. Park, and S. Tian, eds. *Infrastructure Financing in Asia*. Singapore: World Scientific.

[2] Asian Development Bank (ADB). 2017. *Meeting Asia's Infrastructure Needs*. Manila; and World Bank. 2019. *Rural Access Index*. https://datacatalog.worldbank.org/dataset/rural-access-index-rai.

sound, resilient against natural disasters and climate change, and well governed to avoid unproductive investments and unsustainable debt.

The focus in this chapter is on the history of infrastructure development, covering energy in section 8.2, transport in section 8.3, urban water supply in section 8.4, and telecommunications and information and communication technology (ICT) in section 8.5. Section 8.5 also discusses technological evolution in detail as new digital technologies offer opportunities for enhancing economic development and people's lives in the coming years. The chapter covers policy issues, the roles of the state and the private sector, infrastructure for Asian connectivity, and meeting Asia's infrastructure needs.

8.2 Energy

In 1831, electricity became viable for use in technology when Michael Faraday, an English scientist, demonstrated that mechanical energy can be converted into electricity through an experiment moving a magnet in and out of a coil which induced a current. He opened the door for the Belgian engineer, Floris Nollet, to design a coal-fired generator in 1850. These engines helped bring electricity to Asia on 25 March 1878, when an arc lamp was switched on and a telegraph launched at the Imperial College of Engineering in Toranomon, Tokyo. In 1882, the first Chinese power plant in Shanghai started providing electricity for business and residential lighting and later for industrial manufacturing. In 1905, the first electric streetlight came on in the Krishna Rajendra Market in Bangalore (now Bengaluru), India, which thus became the first Asian city with electric streetlights.

Primary energy sources—coal, oil, natural gas, nuclear, hydropower, wind, solar, geothermal, ocean (tidal, wave, and thermal), and biomass—can be consumed for electricity and other purposes such as transport (cars, railways) and heat (space heating or steam for industries) as final energy consumption. Electricity generation per capita from 1971 to 2018 grew dramatically (Figure 8.1).

The conversion efficiency and losses during transmission and distribution determines how much "primary energy consumption" is available for "final energy consumption" (primary energy consumption net of conversion efficiency and losses). In the case of electricity, the conversion efficiency is generally low, only about 35%, on average, for coal-fired plants. Therefore, improving energy efficiency is an effective way to meet the growing energy demand.

Figure 8.1: Electricity Generation Per Capita in Selected Economies, 1971 and 2018 (kWh/capita)

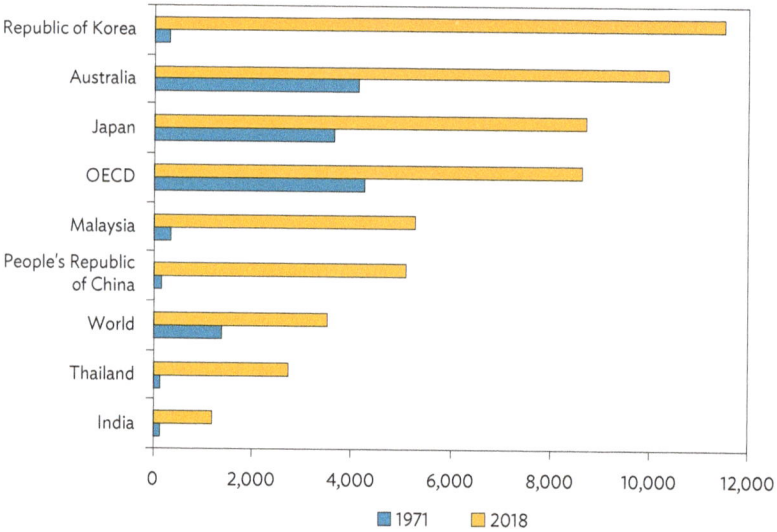

kWh = kilowatt-hour, OECD = Organisation for Economic Co-operation and Development.

Note: Per capita electricity generation estimated with Enerdata's electricity generation data and World Bank's population data.

Sources: Enerdata. 2019. *Global Energy Statistical Yearbook*. https://www.enerdata.net/publications/world-energy-statistics-supply-and-demand.html; and World Bank. World Development Indicators. https://data.worldbank.org/ (accessed 29 October 2019).

Asia's primary and final energy consumption

In the Asia and Pacific region (including Australia, Japan, and New Zealand), total primary energy consumption increased by 13.5 times during 1965–2018, while the global primary energy consumption increased by 3.7 times and that of Organisation for Economic Co-operation and Development (OECD) members doubled. Today, fossil fuels (coal, oil, and natural gas) remain the dominant primary source of energy in the world, including in Germany and the United States (US) (Table 8.1). In Asia and the Pacific, coal is the primary energy source, followed by oil and natural gas, although the region's dependency on fossil fuels decreased somewhat as nuclear and renewable energy grew. Hydropower had a relatively small, but stable, share. Emerging renewable energy sources (solar, wind, and geothermal) remain comparatively small but are growing fast, propelled by the rapid expansion of wind and solar power. Nuclear energy still has a smaller share compared with OECD countries.

Along with rapidly growing energy consumption, carbon dioxide (CO_2) emissions have also grown. From 1965 to 2018, worldwide CO_2 emissions tripled, while emissions in Asia and the Pacific grew by a factor of 12 and the region's share of worldwide emissions grew from 13% to almost half. Therefore, low-carbon transition through large-scale deployment of energy efficiency and renewable energy in Asia and the Pacific will be crucial to mitigate the global climate change threat (Chapter 13).

As for final energy consumption by end users, the industry and residential sectors are the two largest energy consumers in developing Asia, followed by transport (Table 8.2). Among Asian countries, the People's Republic of China (PRC) has an industry dominant energy consumption pattern. By comparison, transport has a higher share of final consumption in OECD countries, particularly in the US and Australia, while the share of industry remains relatively strong in Germany. In Table 8.2, energy is also used in commercial and public buildings, agriculture, fisheries, and forestry. "Non-energy use" refers to oil, coal, and natural gas used primarily for chemical products such as plastics and fertilizer.

Electricity generation and use

From 1971 to 2018, electricity generation increased 16.5 times in Asia and the Pacific compared to a threefold increase in OECD countries and a fivefold increase globally. In 2018, the electricity generation mix in Asia and the Pacific remained dominated by coal, followed by hydropower and gas. Electricity generation from emerging renewable energy is still small, but the growth rate is high. Solar power generation grew at 66.6% and wind power at 25.1% per year between 2010 and 2018. Coal and natural gas also remain the major fuel for power generation in OECD countries such as Australia, Germany, Japan, and the US (Table 8.3).

Over the past 5 decades, Asia and the Pacific made steady progress in providing residential electricity. In 2017, the electrification rate in developing Asia reached 91% overall, compared with 67% in 2000, and less than 15% in 1970 in rural areas. Progress in electrification

Table 8.1: Primary Energy Consumption and CO$_2$ Emissions in Selected Economies, 1965 and 2018

Table 8.1a: Values for 1965

%, Share	World	OECD	A&P[a]	USA	GER	FRA	AUS	JPN	KOR	PRC	IND
Oil	42.0	44.6	37.0	45.3	34.4	49.2	44.8	56.9	20.3	8.4	24.0
Natural gas	14.6	15.5	1.1	28.6	1.0	3.9	–	1.0	–	0.7	0.4
Coal	37.5	33.4	54.1	22.2	63.1	37.2	50.0	31.8	77.2	87.0	67.4
Nuclear	0.2	0.2	–	0.1	–	0.2	–	–	–	–	–
Hydropower	5.6	6.1	7.7	3.6	1.4	9.5	5.0	10.3	2.5	3.8	8.2
Renewables[b]	0.1	0.2	0.1	0.2	–	–	0.2	–	–	–	–
Total primary energy consumption (Mtoe)	3,703	2,610	442	1,250	255	111	35	153	6	131	53
Total primary energy consumption per capita (toe/capita)	1.11	3.08	...	6.43	3.36	2.23	3.05	1.55	0.22	0.18	0.11
Total CO$_2$ emissions (Mt)	11,194	7,701	1,426	3,480	910	328	114	447	25	489	168
CO$_2$ emissions per capita (tons/capita)	3.44	8.36	...	17.45	...	7.06	10.62	3.91	0.87	0.67	0.33

continued on next page

Table 8.1 continued

Table 8.1b: Values for 2018

%, Share	World	OECD	A&P[a]	USA	GER	FRA	AUS	JPN	KOR	PRC	IND
Oil	33.6	38.9	28.3	40.0	34.9	32.5	37.0	40.2	42.8	19.6	29.5
Natural gas	23.9	26.6	11.9	30.5	23.4	15.1	24.7	21.9	16.0	7.4	6.2
Coal	27.2	15.2	47.5	13.8	20.5	3.5	30.7	25.9	29.3	58.2	55.9
Nuclear	4.4	7.9	2.1	8.4	5.3	38.5	–	2.4	10.0	2.0	1.1
Hydropower	6.8	5.7	6.5	2.8	1.2	6.0	2.7	4.0	0.2	8.3	3.9
Renewables[b]	4.0	5.8	3.8	4.5	14.6	4.4	5.0	5.6	1.6	4.4	3.4
Total primary energy consumption (Mtoe)	13,865	5,669	5,986	2,301	324	243	144	454	301	3,273	809
Total primary energy consumption per capita (toe/capita)	1.83	4.35	...	7.03	3.91	3.62	5.77	3.59	5.83	2.35	0.60
Total CO_2 emissions (Mt)	33,891	12,405	16,744	5,145	726	312	417	1,148	698	9,429	2,479
CO_2 emissions per capita (tons/capita, 2014)	4.98	9.55	...	16.50	8.89	4.57	15.39	9.54	11.57	7.54	1.73

– = zero, ... = data not available, CO_2 = carbon dioxide, Mtoe = million ton of oil equivalent, toe = ton of oil equivalent, A&P = Asia and the Pacific, AUS = Australia, FRA = France, GER = Germany, IND = India, JPN = Japan, KOR = Republic of Korea, OECD = Organisation for Economic Co-operation and Development, PRC = People's Republic of China, USA = United States.

[a] Asia and the Pacific includes Developing Asia, Australia, Japan, and New Zealand.

[b] Renewable energy includes solar, wind, geothermal, and biomass.

Note: Per capita CO_2 emissions is from World Bank's database.

Sources: BP. 2019. BP Statistical Review of World Energy 2019. https://www.bp.com/en/global/corporate/energy-economics/statistical-review-of-world-energy.html; and World Bank. World Development Indicators. https://data.worldbank.org/ (accessed 29 October 2019).

Table 8.2: Final Energy Consumption by Sector in Selected Economies, 1973 and 2017

Table 8.2a: Values for 1973

%, Share	World	OECD	Asia[a]	USA	GER	FRA	AUS	JPN	KOR	PRC	IND
Industry	33.0	34.0	23.7	30.0	36.5	29.4	38.6	44.8	37.1	32.1	23.7
Transport	23.2	24.7	10.0	31.5	14.9	17.4	32.7	17.4	14.3	4.4	8.7
Residential	23.4	19.5	55.7	18.1	25.2	15.0	12.8	9.0	35.4	56.3	58.1
Commercial and public service	7.9	10.2	2.7	11.3	11.3	25.7	2.8	8.6	5.1	1.4	4.3
Agriculture, forestry, fisheries, and others	6.4	3.8	5.5	2.4	4.9	2.2	6.7	4.4	1.7	4.9	2.2
Non-energy use	6.1	7.8	2.4	6.8	7.1	10.3	6.4	15.8	6.3	0.8	3.1
Total final consumption (Mtoe)	**4,658**	**2,817**	**291**	**1,315**	**242**	**142**	**40**	**234**	**18**	**364**	**143**
Total final consumption per capita (toe/capita)	**1.19**	**3.04**	...	**6.21**	**3.06**	**2.67**	**2.96**	**2.16**	**0.51**	**0.41**	**0.24**

continued on next page

Table 8.2 continued

Table 8.2b: Values for 2017

%, Share	World	OECD	Asia[a]	USA	GER	FRA	AUS	JPN	KOR	PRC	IND
Industry	29.0	22.0	32.1	17.3	24.8	18.1	27.5	29.5	26.4	49.5	34.7
Transport	28.9	33.7	20.8	41.2	25.4	29.4	40.8	24.2	19.4	15.6	16.6
Residential	21.3	18.5	28.0	16.1	24.4	25.0	12.9	15.7	11.7	16.7	29.4
Commercial and public service	8.1	13.1	4.4	13.5	15.2	15.4	9.8	16.9	11.6	4.3	4.1
Agriculture, forestry, fisheries, and others	3.7	2.7	4.7	2.4	–	3.0	3.2	1.9	2.1	5.9	7.4
Non-energy use	9.1	10.1	9.9	9.6	10.1	9.2	5.9	11.8	28.7	8.1	7.8
Total final consumption (Mtoe)	9,721	3,711	1,310	1,518	227	154	82	293	183	1,993	591
Total final consumption per capita (toe/capita)	1.29	2.86	...	4.67	2.75	2.31	3.32	2.31	3.56	1.44	0.44

– = zero, ... = data not available, Mtoe = million ton of oil equivalent, toe = ton of oil equivalent, AUS = Australia, FRA = France, GER = Germany, IND = India, JPN = Japan, KOR = Republic of Korea, OECD = Organisation for Economic Co-operation and Development, PRC = People's Republic of China, USA = United States.

[a] Asia refers to developing Asian economies excluding the PRC.

Note: Total final consumption per capita estimated with the total final consumption data from the International Energy Agency (IEA) and World Bank's population data.

Sources: IEA. Statistics. https://www.iea.org/statistics/; and World Bank. World Development Indicators. https://data.worldbank.org (accessed 29 October 2019).

Table 8.3: Electricity Generation by Source in Selected Economies, 1971 and 2018

Table 8.3a: Values for 1971

%, Share	World	OECD	A&P[a]	USA	GER	FRA	AUS	JPN	KOR	PRC	IND
Oil	20.8	21.6	40.7	13.8	11.6	28.1	3.4	62.2	80.6	8.3	6.3
Natural gas	13.3	12.9	1.6	23.5	6.5	4.8	3.3	1.4	–	–	0.6
Coal	40.0	39.4	30.2	44.8	74.6	29.4	70.7	11.8	6.9	70.1	49.1
Nuclear	2.1	2.7	1.3	2.4	1.9	6.0	–	2.1	–	–	1.8
Hydropower	23.1	23.1	26.1	15.5	4.6	31.3	22.2	22.5	12.5	21.6	42.2
Solar	...	–	–	–	–	–	–	–	–	–	–
Wind	...	–	–	–	–	–	–	–	–	–	–
Geothermal	...	0.1	0.2	–	–	–	–	–	–	–	–
Tidal	–	–	–	–	–	0.3	–	–	–	–	...
Biomass, waste, etc.	0.6	0.2	–	–	0.8	0.1	0.5	–	–	–	–
Total electricity generation (TWh)	**5,253**	**3,848**	**743**	**1,703**	**329**	**156**	**53**	**386**	**11**	**139**	**66**
Electricity generation per capita (kWh/capita)	1,397	4,247	...	8,201	4,201	2,979	4,097	3,652	335	165	116

continued on next page

Table 8.3 *continued*

Table 8.3b: Values for 2018

%, Share	World	OECD	A&P^a	USA	GER	FRA	AUS	JPN	KOR	PRC	IND
Oil	3.1	2.0	1.9	0.8	0.8	0.4	2.2	5.0	2.3	0.1	1.6
Natural gas	22.9	27.8	11.6	34.2	12.9	4.9	17.7	34.3	26.3	2.8	4.7
Coal	37.8	25.8	59.0	28.3	37.0	2.0	60.5	32.9	44.0	66.8	72.9
Nuclear	10.1	17.5	4.5	18.9	11.7	72.3	–	6.2	22.5	4.1	2.3
Hydropower	16.3	13.3	14.4	7.1	3.3	12.1	8.0	8.6	1.2	17.2	9.2
Solar	2.2	3.0	2.7	2.0	7.2	1.7	4.2	6.4	1.4	2.8	2.5
Wind	4.8	6.6	3.7	6.3	17.4	5.0	5.9	0.7	0.4	5.0	3.9
Geothermal	0.3	0.5	0.3	0.4	–	–	–	0.2	–	–	–
Tidal	–	–	–	–	–	0.1	–	–	0.1	–	...
Biomass, waste, etc.	2.4	3.5	1.9	1.9	9.6	1.6	1.5	5.7	1.6	1.2	2.9
Total electricity generation (TWh)	**26,582**	**11,226**	**12,317**	**4,439**	**647**	**571**	**259**	**1,051**	**593**	**7,146**	**1,643**
Electricity generation per capita (kWh/capita)	**3,500**	**8,612**	...	**13,568**	**7,802**	**8,524**	**10,363**	**8,306**	**11,484**	**5,131**	**1,215**

– = zero, ... = data not available, kWh = kilowatt-hour, TWh = terawatt-hour, A&P = Asia and the Pacific, AUS = Australia, FRA = France, GER = Germany, IND = India, JPN = Japan, KOR = Republic of Korea, OECD = Organisation for Economic Co-operation and Development, PRC = People's Republic of China, USA = United States.

^a Asia and the Pacific includes Developing Asia, Australia, Japan, and New Zealand.

Note: Electricity generation per capita estimated with Enerdata's electricity generation data and World Bank's population data.

Sources: Enerdata. 2019. *Global Energy Statistical Yearbook*. https://www.enerdata.net/publications/world-energy-statistics-supply-and-demand.html; and World Bank. World Development Indicators. https://data.worldbank.org (accessed 29 October 2019).

significantly improved the quality of life, facilitated community services such as health and education, and enabled productive use of electricity for rural populations.

Overall, electricity in Asia and the Pacific saw the evolution of a different mix of sources; from coal, oil, and hydropower, to natural gas and nuclear, to emerging renewable energy including wind and solar. Electricity development in the region can be categorized into three distinct periods of evolution. First, during the 1950s through the 1980s, there were large investments starting with hydropower to an increasing dominance of fossil fuels such as oil and coal. Second, from the 1990s to the 2000s, energy supply was diversified to large hydropower plants, natural gas, and nuclear in some countries. Electricity and other energy consumption increased dramatically. And third, from the 2010s onward, renewable energy, particularly solar and wind, was increasingly mainstreamed for electricity generation, together with improving energy efficiency.

1950s–1980s: From hydropower to the increasing dominance of coal in electricity generation

Hydropower was among the first utility-scale power plants in Asia. In Japan, the Keage Hydroelectric Power Station near Kyoto began operations in 1891, based on a US hydropower project design. Other Asian economies soon followed, building hydropower plants in India (1897); Taipei,China (1905); and Nepal (1911). Initially, hydropower plants were small (about 100 kilowatts [kW] to 1,000 kW) and built near towns, mainly due to technical limitations in long-distance transmission. Along with the evolution of electricity transmission technology, the capacity of hydropower stations grew. Hydropower maintained a relatively stable share in Asia and the Pacific's primary energy mix, with the proportion declining slightly only as other fuel sources grew faster.

Between the 1950s and 1980s, low-cost, coal-fired power was considered one of the most economical options to serve baseload generation capacity. In addition, it needed shorter construction time compared with hydropower or nuclear plants.

Also, Asia and the Pacific gravitated from oil toward coal because the region has many coal resources—42% of the world's proven reserves. The region's oil reserves account for just 2.8% of the global total—most economies import supplies from the Middle East.

The share of oil for electricity generation peaked at 49% in 1973 as two rounds of oil crises in the 1970s created an upward spiral of oil prices. Subsequently, oil use for electricity generation declined as coal became more competitive and readily available. In 1976, the Asian Development Bank (ADB) approved its first coal project, a $12 million loan to the Republic of Korea (ROK) for the rehabilitation and expansion of existing coal mines. In 1987, the first ADB energy sector loan of $33 million to the PRC was for the conversion of an oil-fired power plant of 200 megawatts into a coal-fired power plant. The last ADB-supported coal project was in 2013 for a supercritical coal-fired power plant in Jamshoro, Pakistan, as ADB energy operations shifted toward renewables and energy efficiency.

As Japan was heavily dependent on imported oil for primary energy and electricity generation, the government responded to the twin 1970s oil crises by adopting regulations and financial incentives to encourage energy conservation, particularly in industry, in addition to a shift to other energy sources. From 1975 to 1985, Japan's energy intensity (measured as energy consumption per unit of real GDP on a purchasing power parity basis) fell by 24%.

During this period, the growth rate of hydropower was slower, while solar and wind began to be implemented as small pilots—planting the seeds for future growth. In 1983, the PRC imported 10 kW of solar photovoltaic (PV) modules from Japan to provide electricity to rural households in western Gansu Province, one of its earliest solar PV plants.

Nuclear energy was considered by several countries with limited local energy resources as a way toward energy self-sufficiency. The first nuclear power plant in Japan, the Tokai Nuclear Power Plant, was commissioned in 1966 using British technology, followed by several light water reactor plants built in cooperation with US companies. India's first nuclear power plant, the Tarapur Atomic Power Station in Maharashtra, was built by US firms and started commercial operation in 1969. The ROK, now a world leader in nuclear power generation, commissioned its first plant using US technology in 1978 (by the 1980s, there were eight more nuclear power reactors under construction).

Developing large-scale power generation and transmission networks required strong public sector intervention. Electricity generation and transmission were generally operated by state-owned enterprises (SOEs) (except in Japan, where there were 10 regional private power companies). However, while public institutions were able to efficiently make large-scale power investments, SOE monopolies and vertically integrated power utilities had limited capacity to operate these assets efficiently. Financial and technical performance suffered. In many developing economies in the region, electricity tariffs were frequently distorted. In the PRC, the national average tariff was $0.02 in 1986, well below the long-run marginal cost of supply, estimated in the range of $0.03–$0.04 per kilowatt-hour. Institutional reforms were needed to commercialize SOE utilities to improve efficiency, reduce costs, and ensure tariffs covered production costs.

1990s–2000s: Promoting energy diversification with large hydropower and natural gas

By 1995, the region's share in global primary energy consumption reached about 27%. Coal consumption accounted for 44% of total energy consumption in the region, much higher than the 26% world average. During this period, Asian countries started promoting diversification for electricity generation, including the use of large hydropower and natural gas.

Technological progress made construction of large-scale dams technically and economically feasible with multiple functions including irrigation and flood control. Between 1995 and 2005, hydropower generation in the region increased by 50%. In the PRC, which faced severe electricity shortages in the early 1990s, the government decided to proceed with the Three Gorges Dam Project, the world's largest hydropower plant with a capacity of 22.5 gigawatts (GW), including flood control. The first generating unit began operations in 2003. However, further hydropower expansion in the region using large dams and reservoirs was constrained by increasing concerns over potentially negative social and environmental impact, including resettlement of the people and the effects on biodiversity. Strict social and environmental safeguards led to higher costs, which reduced the financial viability of large hydropower projects.

As power systems became bigger in many countries in the region, natural gas-fired power plants were needed to meet both baseload and peaking demand. Natural gas consumption through gas turbines and combined-cycle gas turbines (CCGTs) is more efficient than other fossil fuel systems. The generation efficiency of CCGTs can reach 60% compared with 45% for ultra-supercritical coal power plants. CO_2 emissions from natural gas is about 55% lower than burning coal, with much lower emissions of other air pollutants (sulfur dioxide, nitrogen oxides, and particulates). Natural gas has also been used increasingly in industries and households as cleaner fuels. From 1995 to 2005, natural gas consumption in the region increased by 92%. During this time, solar and wind energy began to grow rapidly, though from a very low base.

As electricity generation capacity grew substantially, the power grid system was also enhanced. Technological progress—such as higher voltage and aluminum cables—helped expand transformers' power by a factor of 500, while transmission voltages grew 100-fold compared with early years. These advances led to lower transmission and distribution losses.[3] Rural electrical grids were enhanced and expanded. The region's electrification rate reached 74.7% in 1995 and 82.7% in 2005. Since the 1990s, building efficient transmission and distribution lines has been a priority of ADB support in the energy sector.

During this time, many countries followed Japan's example of improving energy efficiency through regulation and financial incentives. In the PRC, energy intensity fell by 28% during 1995–2005 as more efficient technologies were adopted, mostly on the supply side.

Energy sector reforms in the region accelerated during the 1990s and 2000s, with the objective of finding a balance between the public and private sector roles—with support from international financial institutions. From 1990 to 1999, private sector investment in power occurred in many Asian developing countries, with the PRC, the Philippines, and Indonesia included in the top five countries attracting private investment.[4]

In the Philippines, independent power producers were established through BOT arrangements in the early 1990s. They helped the country resolve electricity shortages, but also led to unsustainable government debt due to guarantees provided to private investors on a "take-or-pay" basis (the government must pay even if it does not take the electricity due to low demand). With support from ADB and other development partners, the Philippines adopted the Electric Power Industry Reform Act in 2001 to restructure the power sector. It unbundled generation and transmission companies, introduced performance-based regulations for transmission and distribution, and created a wholesale electricity spot market to encourage

---

[3]   Smil, V. 2017. *Energy and Civilization: A History*. Cambridge, MA: The MIT Press.
[4]   World Bank. 2018. *Contribution of Institutional Investors: Private Investment in Infrastructure 2011–H1 2017*. Washington, DC.

Box 8.1: The Lao People's Democratic Republic's Hydroelectric Project

The Lao People's Democratic Republic (Lao PDR) has huge hydropower potential from its river networks and an ambition to become the "battery" of the Greater Mekong Subregion. To tap its resources, 27 public and private parties, including the Asian Development Bank and the World Bank, financed the construction of Nam Theun 2, a 1,070-megawatt hydroelectric project in 2005. It is the largest cross-border power project financing so far in the Lao PDR. The project was developed and operated by the Nam Theun 2 Power Company, which is jointly owned by the Government of the Lao PDR and electricity companies from Thailand and France.

The project exemplifies how collaboration among international financial institutions (IFIs) can attract significant commercial investment. Of the total $1.3 billion financing, a joint IFI finance package of $217 million catalyzed about $740 million from international and Thai commercial banks (the remaining amount of approximately $560 million was financed by export credit agencies, project sponsor, and partner companies).

The project had benefits on multiple fronts. By developing hydroelectric resources, the project facilitated electricity exports (to Thailand), earned foreign exchange, and promoted regional economic development. As a public–private partnership, it meets economic growth objectives using private resources and expertise. It also has a regional development impact by helping Thailand meet its power demand and diversify power supply to lessen its heavy reliance on natural gas. The loan agreement includes a provision for using project revenue for poverty reduction initiatives.

The project included a social development plan for resettling households affected by land acquisition and managing all social impacts, including those downstream of the project and affecting ethnic minorities. The project relocated 1,310 households satisfactorily. All affected households have restored their livelihoods to pre-project levels, and those resettled have benefited from new housing, infrastructure, better educational facilities, and health services. By 2011, resettler incomes had grown beyond the national rural poverty line on a sustainable basis.

Source: Asian Development Bank. Lao PDR: Nam Theun 2 Hydroelectric Project. https://www.adb.org/projects/37910-014/main.

competition from power generation plants. By the end of the 2000s, financial viability had been restored and the Philippine power sector had become one of the most extensively privatized in Asia and the Pacific. In the PRC, the Ministry of Electric Power Industry was dissolved in 1998, with five competing power generation companies and two electricity grid companies created in 2002.

2010s to present: Mainstreaming renewables and energy efficiency

In 2018, the Asia and Pacific region became both the largest consumer of primary energy worldwide (43% of the global total) and the largest CO_2 emitter (49%). Coal remains a significant component of the region's primary energy mix. However, the growth of coal consumption in the region slowed significantly, to 1.9% annually, on average, from 2010 to 2018 after decades of sustained high growth. For example, in the PRC, the world's largest coal producer and consumer, coal consumption peaked in 2013. Hopefully, this marked a clear transition toward more renewable energy sources and greater energy efficiency.

Japan's Fukushima nuclear power plant accident (following the 2011 tsunami) led to the immediate shutdown of all operating nuclear power plants in the country (though several have now restarted). It led to a drive for greater energy efficiency. The meltdown also considerably slowed construction of new nuclear plants in the PRC, India, and other Asian countries.

Due to technological progress and larger markets, solar and wind electricity generation continues to see massive cost reductions worldwide. The global weighted average cost for solar PV power installation fell 74% (from \$4,621/kW in 2010 to \$1,210/kW in 2018), and the installation cost for onshore wind power declined nearly 22% (from \$1,913/kW in 2010 to \$1,497/kW in 2018).[5] As a result, solar and wind power installation has accelerated across the region.

The adoption of the Sustainable Development Goals and the 2015 Paris Agreement have become key driving forces for Asia and the Pacific to move toward a new low-carbon energy paradigm. Public concern over heavy air pollution in Asia's megacities is also behind the low-carbon transition. Many countries in the region have explicit targets for the share of renewables and energy efficiency in their nationally determined contributions under the United Nations (UN)

---

[5] International Renewable Energy (IRENA). 2019. *Renewable Power Generation Costs in 2018*. Abu Dhabi. https://www.irena.org/Statistics/View-Data-by-Topic/Costs/Global-Trends.

Framework Convention on Climate Change—seven countries in the Pacific have committed to achieving 100% renewable electricity generation.[6]

Renewable energy received policy support from, for example, feed-in tariffs (a guarantee of fixed electricity prices for renewable energy producers paid by governments) and a renewable energy purchase obligation, known as Renewable Portfolio Standard, along with capital subsidies. In 2018, the region had 56% of global solar installed capacity, 42% hydropower, and 40% wind.[7]

Along with progress in renewable energy, energy efficiency in the region is increasingly considered the "first fuel"—limiting demand growth instead of increasing energy supply. In 2012, India launched a "Perform, Achieve, Trade" (PAT) scheme—a market-based trading scheme to improve industrial energy efficiency by trading energy efficiency certificates in India's most energy-intensive sectors. In the PRC, its Energy Conservation Law mandated energy efficiency labels for electric appliances, with five stars for the most energy-efficient appliances. Estimates show that sales of these saved 10 terawatt-hours of electricity in 2017 (equivalent to 3 million households' annual consumption). Energy intensity has also been significantly reduced.

ADB supports renewable energy, whether solar, wind, hydropower, or geothermal. In May 2010, it launched its Asia Solar Energy Initiative (ASEI) to assist in identifying, developing, and implementing 3.0 GW of solar power within 3 years across the region. ASEI reached 3.8 GW by 2014. Between 2011 and 2018, ADB supported 11.6 GW of renewable energy installation.

Over the past decade, Asia has made further progress in rural electrification, with Central Asia and South Asia increasing access rates from 75% in 2010 to 91% in 2017. India has done particularly well. Between 2010 and 2016, India expanded electricity access to an additional 210 million people—by 2017, 87% of the population had access to electricity.[8] ADB has been supporting the "Energy for All initiative," which includes off-grid solar power systems in remote Pacific island countries.

---

[6] The Cook Islands, Fiji, Niue, Papua New Guinea, Samoa, Tuvalu, and Vanuatu.
[7] IRENA. 2019. *Renewable Power Generation Costs in 2018*. Abu Dhabi. https://www.irena .org/Statistics/View-Data-by-Topic/Costs/Global-Trends.
[8] International Energy Agency. 2018. *World Energy Outlook 2018*. Paris.

From the initial phase of public sector reforms, the power sector increasingly turned to markets and private investment and ownership, helped by the creation of new regulatory frameworks. Competition was introduced at each segment of the electricity market, and subsidies were gradually removed to ensure efficiency and sustainability. For example, by 2010, all of India's state power monopolies were unbundled into generation, transmission, and distribution companies, regulated by independent state energy regulatory commissions. In Japan, the retail electricity market was fully liberalized in 2015. All electricity consumers, including households, are now able to choose the electricity supplier they prefer based on price and power source.

Future trends: Technology innovations for sustainability

Achieving universal energy access and expanding renewable energy remain the region's energy priorities. In Asia and the Pacific in 2017, 350 million people—including 168 million in India, 52 million in Pakistan, 33 million in Bangladesh, and 14 million in Indonesia—still lacked access to electricity, most in remote mountainous areas or islands. The challenge for developing Asia is to deal with the "energy trilemma," making energy available, affordable, and clean. The region must achieve these three goals simultaneously.

The trilemma can only be resolved by deploying new, advanced technologies such as renewable mini-grids with battery storage, smart grids to integrate more renewable energy, and ocean energy (tidal, wave, and thermal energy from oceans). Power networks will be improved by installing energy storage systems for renewable energy integration. Carbon capture and storage technology holds the potential to reduce carbon emissions from the existing systems still using fossil fuels. Hydrogen produced by renewable energy can be used for automobiles as well as for energy storage.

To reach the last miles of rural electrification, off-grid solutions using solar, wind, and small hydropower units may be the answer. ADB and other multilateral development banks are actively supporting Pacific island countries with these technologies.

The energy sector can also benefit from artificial intelligence (AI) and digital technologies. AI can transform cities into smart cities, and within cities, make buildings and transport systems "intelligent." Hence, they use the minimum amount of energy for the same level of comfort, mobility, and services. These "smart" cities use innovative business models and demand-response technologies to improve the energy efficiency of heating and cooling systems using smart thermostats. Also, vehicle-to-grid (V2G) systems will be developed to optimize the mobility, use, and production of electricity by turning electric cars into "virtual power plants."

The new wave of energy sector reforms should reorient the private sector and markets toward low-carbon solutions. With the significant decline in renewable energy costs, most investment will come from private investors and commercial funding, while public sector subsidies for wind and solar through feed-in tariffs will be gradually phased out. The future of renewable energy depends on its market maturity and cost competitiveness compared with conventional sources. Appropriate carbon pricing and regulations can effectively scale up the use of technological innovation. Policy makers, regulators, investors, financiers, and other stakeholders across the region must also innovate their business models, financing instruments, and procurement methods.

8.3 Transport

The transport sector has always played a dominant role in supporting economic growth. It aids development and provides access to employment, education, and social services. National network development has primarily focused on roads and railways. Investments in other modes, such as aviation and shipping, have enhanced regional connectivity, with airport and port development supporting international trade. Urban transport has also required considerable investment to support rapidly urbanizing populations across the region. This section focuses on changes in long-distance, land-based transport infrastructure as well as development of urban transport.

Since 1950, there has been a marked shift from rail- to road-based transportation across Asia (Figure 8.2). In almost all countries, the length of rail networks (per million people) fell by approximately half over the 50 years covered due to a decrease in railway kilometers combined with an increase in population. The notable exception is the PRC, which continued to invest in its rail network. By contrast, the growth of road network length per million people doubled or even quadrupled over the same period.

Figure 8.2: Transport Infrastructure Stock, 1965 and 2014

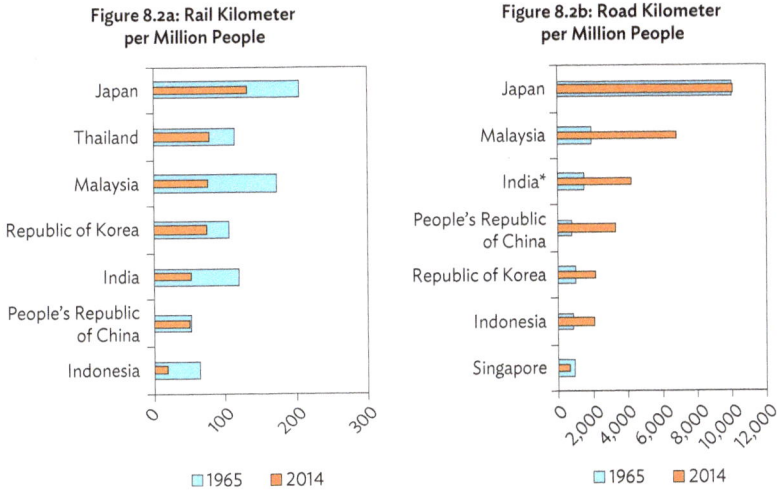

Figure 8.2a: Rail Kilometer per Million People

Figure 8.2b: Road Kilometer per Million People

km = kilometer.

Note: Asterisk (*) indicates interpolated values.

Sources: Asian Development Bank (ADB). 2007. *ADB's Infrastructure Operations: Responding to Client Needs.* Manila; International Road Federation. 2016. *World Road Statistics.* Alexandria, VA; Government of India, Ministry of Road Transport and Highways. 2014. *Basic Road Statistics of India.* https://morth.nic .in/basic-road-statistics-india; and World Bank. 2014. World Development Indicators. https://data.worldbank.org (accessed 29 October 2019).

The fundamental shift from railways to roads, along with rapid motorization, happened simultaneously in many countries (Figure 8.3). Vehicle ownership has increased across developing Asia since 2000, especially in countries with rapidly growing economies such as the PRC, India, and Indonesia.

There were several distinct periods that defined the shift in type and dominance of transport mode as well as government priorities, policies, and development plans. They can roughly be categorized as the postwar years up to the 1970s, the road boom years of the 1980s and 1990s, the emergence of congestion in the 2000s, and a more balanced approach to transport infrastructure during the 2010s.

While countries vary due to their respective stages in economic development and wealth, the overall pattern of transport infrastructure prioritization still holds. It often starts with a neglect of the traditional long-distance modes such as rail and water transport,

Figure 8.3: Vehicle Registration, Selected Asian Economies

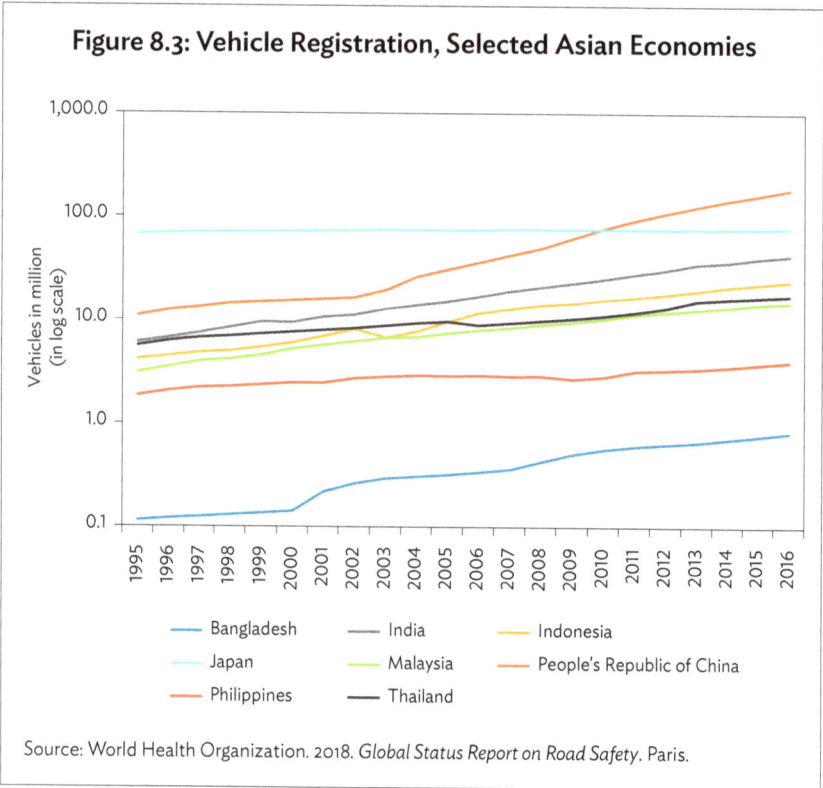

Source: World Health Organization. 2018. *Global Status Report on Road Safety*. Paris.

and the dominance of investment and support for road-based transport. However, more recently, congestion and the need to mitigate carbon emissions led to a resurgence of attention to the technological potential of railways, including high-speed trains, metros, and other urban railway systems. Many countries are now pursuing development of a more balanced multimodal transport system.

1950–1970s: Emergence from World War II

Asia and the Pacific went through several fundamental changes from 1950 into the 1970s. Many former colonies inherited their colonial-era transport infrastructure and institutions, especially railways. Some of the largest government agencies were railway authorities—such as Indian Railways. SOEs played an important role. Also, independence and the redrawing of national boundaries brought changes, as some rail networks and operating services were split between countries.

Japan's first railway was built between Tokyo and Yokohama in 1872 based on British technology. The country began heavily investing in railway systems, increasingly based on its own technology. The first subway in Tokyo was launched in 1927. The first high-speed train began operations between Tokyo and Osaka in 1964. Investment in roads and highways was far behind the West in the early postwar period. Germany had the autobahn in the 1930s, and the US began building its interstate highway system in the 1950s. Japan's first expressway opened in 1963 with the help of the World Bank.

In much of developing Asia, the 1950s to 1970s saw early road network development, often supported through international assistance, such as the Seoul–Incheon Expressway in 1968, ADB's third loan after it was founded in 1966. In the 1950s and 1960s, most countries in the region had few private vehicles, often US or German made, almost exclusively owned by the rich.

That changed when Asia's car manufacturing began reaching industrial scale in the late 1960s. The Japanese automobile industry became a dominant force in vehicle sales during the 1980s and 1990s, exporting many vehicles across the region. This expanded private vehicle ownership in the region, creating demand for new and better roads. Also, Asia is distinct due to its widespread use of motorcycles and three-wheeled vehicles. In 2018, Asia accounted for some 80% of motorcycle ownership worldwide. A variety of three-wheeled vehicles are used as private vehicles, small taxis, or delivery vehicles.

During the 1950s–1970s, a fledgling trucking industry started, taking advantage of the emergence of new highways and their wider coverage relative to limited fixed rail or river transport routes. Governments were also focused on expanding roads, which made cars and trucks the dominant mode of transport. Programs addressed missing road links, added bridges, and extended road networks generally. Many governments prioritized improving transportation networks and reducing travel time, with road access seen as the best way to support economic growth and development.

During the 1950s and 1960s, many railroad networks suffered from political neglect, leading to a deterioration of service and operations. In the 1970s, railways fell into a period of significant underinvestment—which led to a vicious spiral of decline as less financial support reduced service quality, which then lowered demand, requiring more subsidies. Therefore, there was much less support within governments for railway investment especially when the road network was expanding. One notable example was the Philippines, where the length of railways decreased from 797 kilometers (km) at its peak to 28 km due to natural disasters, underinvestment, and reduced frequency of operations combined with more road construction and bus services. As a result, railways became a poor option for moving between cities and commuting within urban areas.

1980s–1990s: The road boom years

During the 1980s–1990s, roads solidified their place as the dominant mode of transport across Asia. As economies grew rapidly, the demand for travel and shipment of goods increased. Many Asian countries undertook dramatic investment programs during this period, as their financial resources and budgets grew. Malaysia started an expressway network that greatly improved connectivity and supported growth. All newly industrialized economies invested heavily in the road subsector.

Economies such as Malaysia; the ROK; and Taipei,China began embracing PPPs to expand their road networks. The North–South Expressway in Malaysia—which runs from the Thai border to Singapore—adopted a BOT approach and is one of the most well-known examples. The Philippines also has had long experience with PPPs, since it introduced a BOT law in 1991, and now boasts several expressways that were completed on time and within budget. The PRC began massive investment during this period to develop national expressway networks and introduced toll roads as well as corporatized road services and construction.

Japan's high-speed railways started to change the perception of railways in many developed countries. However, the rest of Asia continued to allow rail networks and services to decline during the period. Some institutional changes, such as commercializing SOEs, occurred in the rail subsector to address the decline and poor performance. In many cases, however, they did not go as far as required in terms of operational and institutional reforms—and, as a result, were not so successful. Japan also saw a decline in demand and level of services on their traditional railways. In 1987, the Japanese National Railways was broken up into six entities and privatized, which offered the opportunity to terminate loss-making routes, and induce incentives for better services.

2000s: Wide-scale congestion appears

Government support to the road subsector and the development of Asian car industries, coupled with economic growth, allowed many more people to buy private vehicles. In Asian developing countries, congestion began to appear in urban areas, with some experiencing acute congestion in the 1990s. Large-scale congestion in major road networks started in the 2000s, as these expanded networks were unable to keep pace with the increase in vehicle ownership and use. Vehicle pollution has also become a serious problem in many areas. Since the UN Earth Summit in 1992, reducing carbon emissions has become a priority. This led to a rethink in investment priorities and the emergence of a more balanced approach to transport investments.

During this period, a shift began toward a new age of railways in some developing economies. The PRC; the ROK; and Taipei,China started to show interest in modern railway systems, beginning to deploy high-speed rail systems (Figure 8.4). Launching these new systems triggered a broad revival of railways across Asia.

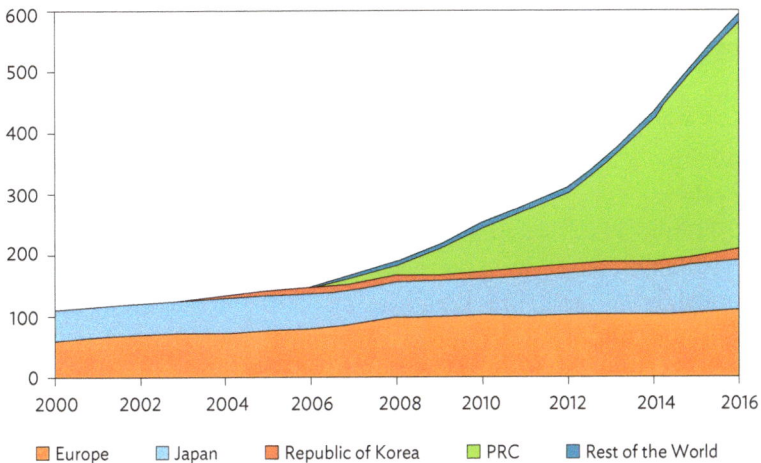

Figure 8.4: High-Speed Rail Activity in Key Regions, 2000–2016
(billion passenger-kilometer)

PRC = People's Republic of China.

Source: International Energy Agency. 2019. *The Future of Rail*. Paris.

2010s: Pursuing a more balanced approach

The 2010s saw a much more balanced approach to transportation system investment and operations. Road investments no longer dominated, while investment in railways continued to grow. New railway opportunities also emerged during this period. Many Asian countries, such as India and Bangladesh, started to heavily invest in railways. Strong growth and development throughout Asia, along with the growing problems of traffic congestion, air pollution, and the impact on climate change, brought the need for more efficient freight and public transport services.

In 2013, China Railway was established as an SOE to operate more commercially, replacing direct management by the railway ministry. International organizations often support railway subsector reform and network development projects. In 2019, ADB committed its largest project loan ($2.75 billion) for the Malolos–Clark railway (51.2 km from Malolos to Clark and Clark International Airport, and 1.9 km connecting Solis and Blumentritt stations in the City of Manila) in the Philippines. As part of expanding regional cooperation and integration, railways are now also important for cross-border connectivity.

The development of urban transport

Some cities in developing Asia, including in India, the Philippines, the PRC, the ROK, and others, had trams or suburban railway systems even before World War II. Nonetheless, most activities, such as employment opportunities, were limited to around 3–4 km of the home, a distance that could comfortably be traveled on foot or by bicycle.

Rapidly urbanizing populations began to place immense pressure on cities to address increasing travel demand. The combination of motorization and urbanization resulted in severe congestion, aside from deteriorating air quality from vehicle emissions. Some cities attempted to build their way out of congestion with elevated expressways and grade-separated junctions aimed to accommodate the growing number of private vehicles, but any new capacity was soon occupied by the ever-growing number of cars.

Since the turn of the 21st century, there has been a significant increase in investments in public transport such as metros and buses.

Asia's megacities now lead the world in subway networks, with four of the longest—which carry the most passengers of systems worldwide—in Beijing, Shanghai, Seoul, and Tokyo. Metros are now being constructed in many cities in Asia. Georgia, Kazakhstan, and Uzbekistan had subway systems from the Soviet period and are investing to modernize and expand them.

ADB has been supporting urban public transport in such areas: subways (in Bangladesh, Georgia, India, Thailand, and Viet Nam); bus rapid transit systems (in the Lao People's Democratic Republic, Pakistan, and the PRC), and integrated multimodal transport (in Mongolia, Nepal, and Sri Lanka).

Future trends: Safety, sustainability, and technology innovations

The ongoing dramatic increase in vehicle ownership across much of Asia, together with better road networks, has given new mobility to a large part of the population, and has reduced travel times and freight costs. But congestion remains, or is even increasing, in many Asian urban areas.

Worsening road safety has also attracted more attention. Road traffic crashes are now the leading cause of death for those aged 5–29 years worldwide. Asia accounts for 53% of worldwide traffic accident fatalities.[9] Countries are now investing more in road safety through road structures such as guardrails, barriers, and pedestrian crossings. Regulations on speed and drunk driving are being enforced more than before. Car vehicle standards, including seatbelts and airbags, are now mandatory. And emergency response and postaccident medical care are better and increasingly available. Within the road subsector, there is also increasing attention paid to operating and maintaining existing road assets efficiently.

Transport infrastructure and operations will continue to require investment in both new and existing assets, with new technologies playing an increasingly important role. Large datasets will enable system operators to manage transport networks, share information, and enhance traffic control centers. Travel applications and car-share schemes will allow users to make better informed travel decisions and maximize use of available infrastructure options. In Guizhou Province in the PRC, ADB is supporting advanced technology

---

[9] World Health Organization. 2018. *Global Status Report on Road Safety*. Paris.

use for Intelligent Transport Systems, such as vehicle-to-vehicle and vehicle-to-infrastructure communication, to improve traffic flow as well as road safety.

Over the next 20–40 years, the sector could see wholesale decarbonization. Electric vehicles (e-vehicles) will most likely replace combustion engines over time, which is starting to happen and most of the change has been in Asia. The future of mobility solutions may not be traditional, with the sector using new technologies and better institutions.

8.4   Urban water supply

Adequate water supply has been the mainstay of every city from the earliest civilizations. Before the development of engineered water systems, people got their water supply directly from rivers, lakes, springs, underground sources, and rainwater, among others. These sources varied depending on topography and local climatic and hydrological conditions. For instance, atoll and small island settlements in the Pacific rely heavily on rainwater due to limited groundwater supply. The development of urban water systems in Asia and the Pacific has been an interesting journey from the basic aqueduct systems of the Indus Valley Civilization in South Asia around 3000 BC, to the development of engineered gravity and mechanized bulk water supply systems, to the emergence of today's digital technology water management systems.

The development of urban water supply over the past 50 years in many Asian developing countries initially involved management transition from colonial to national and local government systems. From the 1980s to the present, inefficient management and high utility losses led to the establishment of ways to involve the private sector in management to address these inefficiencies. Moreover, rapid urbanization required better responses using technological and management innovations to an ever-increasing demand for water in both major urban centers and secondary cities and towns.

Pre-1960s: Legacy of colonial urban water supply systems

Urban water systems were infrastructure intensive, featuring engineered reservoirs, piped transmission, and distribution networks. These early systems included one in London in 1822, which used steam engines to pump water from the River Thames onto a 60-foot-

Figure 8.5: Proportion of Population with Access to Safely Managed Piped and Non-Piped Water in Selected Asian Economies

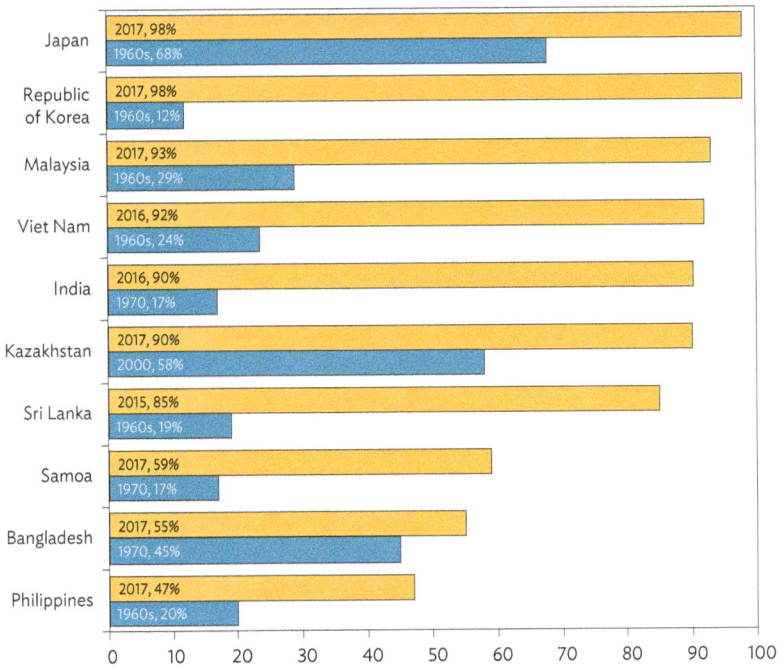

Economy	Recent	Historical
Japan	2017, 98%	1960s, 68%
Republic of Korea	2017, 98%	1960s, 12%
Malaysia	2017, 93%	1960s, 29%
Viet Nam	2016, 92%	1960s, 24%
India	2016, 90%	1970, 17%
Kazakhstan	2017, 90%	2000, 58%
Sri Lanka	2015, 85%	1960s, 19%
Samoa	2017, 59%	1970, 17%
Bangladesh	2017, 55%	1970, 45%
Philippines	2017, 47%	1960s, 20%

Notes: Older United Nations data from the 1960s measure only households with piped water connections. World Health Organization (WHO) and United Nations Children's Fund (UNICEF) indicators for 2000–2017 used a proportion of the population with access to safely managed and improved water supply, which covers both piped and non-piped sources.

Sources: UNICEF. 2019. *Progress on Household Drinking Water, Sanitation and Hygiene 2000-2017. Special Focus on Inequalities.* New York. p. 7; Fan, M. 2015. Sri Lanka's Water Supply and Sanitation Sector: Achievements and a Way Forward. *ADB South Asia Working Paper Series.* No. 35. Manila: Asian Development Bank; General Statistics Office of Viet Nam. 2016. *Viet Nam Household Living Standards Survey 2016.* Ha Noi; International Institute for Population Sciences (IIPS) and Inter City Fund. 2017. *National Family Health Survey (NFHS-4), 2015-16: India.* Mumbai: IIPS; Pacific Institute. 2013. *The World's Water: Access to Safe Drinking Water by Country, 1970-2008.* Oakland, CA; United Nations (UN). 1967. *Statistical Yearbook.* New York; and UN. 1973. *Statistical Yearbook.* New York.

high tower, which used gravity to distribute to communities. This was followed by the development of extensive city water supply networks using cast iron materials that allowed piped water connections to buildings. In the late 19th century, the development of microbiology led to chemical disinfection of drinking water using chlorination and later ozone.

These gravity systems were replicated starting from the 1850s in Asian cities—such as Calcutta (now Kolkata) in 1870 and Singapore between 1878 and 1928 under British rule. Other colonial water systems were built by the Spaniards in Manila in 1882, the Dutch in Jakarta between 1870 and 1920, and the French in Phnom Penh in 1895. In former Soviet republics, the first water supply system was developed in St. Petersburg in 1846 and later replicated in Central Asia. In Pacific island developing countries, conventional systems included rainwater collection and groundwater. They also used evaporative desalination facilities during droughts.

In the PRC, the Grand Canal—built by the Sui Dynasty in the sixth century for transportation between Beijing in the north and Hangzhou in the south—was also used for drinking water. Early water supply systems progressively expanded by establishing village-based water management systems and eventually supply to meet 20th century industrial demand. Tokyo completed its first modern water supply system in 1911, increasing capacity and coverage through purification plants and iron pipes, which replaced 19th century aqueducts, deep wells, and water vendors.

1960s–1980: Transition to decentralized and local water utility management

After independence, many countries transferred urban water supply management to national or provincial governments, or to local water utilities. This was mainly to continuously operate and later expand these colonial water systems to service demand from growing urban populations. At that time, systems were designed and built without much thought given to operation and maintenance. By 1975, the urban population in Asia and the Pacific had reached more than 670 million, more than double the urban population 20 years earlier.[10] Many cities were unable to keep up with the water supply demands of new residents.

Some cities that overcame these challenges were supported by central governments with better policy, management, and technological solutions. Singapore, for example, has done well since independence in 1965 by reducing its water supply reliance on outside sources. The city-state successfully strengthened its internal water capacity and expanded its system into "Four National Taps" (local catchment water, reclaimed wastewater, desalinated water, and imported water). It used systematic

---

[10] United Nations Framework Convention on Climate Change. 2015. *Adoption of the Paris Agreement*. Paris.

planning, committed leadership, interagency efforts, and consistent investment.[11]

In Tokyo, World War II devastated water supply systems and resources, leaving nonrevenue water (NRW) as high as 80%.[12] A series of dam and water treatment projects helped the city's water supply recover swiftly. More efficient management brought Tokyo's NRW down to 22% by 1960, with massive investments in water supply infrastructure. Today, Tokyo has one of the lowest NRW rates in the world (3.8%).[13] Tokyo and Singapore served as models for water utility management reform in many cities in the region.

1980–today: Global trends and institutional reform

Involving the private sector through PPPs to reform urban water services in developing countries gained ground during the 1990s—they would help solve inefficiencies in operating and managing government-run water utility systems. In the Philippines, two successful PPPs in Metro Manila in the 1990s provided continuous water supply to millions of households.

More recently, there has been a shift in thinking from privatization to corporatization of publicly owned water utilities. This reform strategy became common as cities in many developing countries often resisted privatization. Aside from the idea that water supply is a basic public service that includes safety and security, many believed water tariffs would rise beyond the capacity of customers to pay. Many private companies shied away from investing in water utilities, as they found them unprofitable given regulatory environments that made cost recovery difficult.

Corporatization was designed to reform the institutional structure of public water utilities. It would make them financially efficient and perform better using advanced management systems, technologies, and operational practices from private companies, while the government oversees customer welfare. The structure is also seen as a useful strategy as water utility management advances with more sophisticated technology.

---

[11] Tortajada, C., Y. Joshi, and A. K. Biswas. 2013. *The Singapore Water Story: Sustainable Development in an Urban City State*. London: Routledge.

[12] Nonrevenue water is the percentage of non-billed water against total water supplied to customers.

[13] Japan International Cooperation Agency. 2018. *Water Supply: The Foundation for Previous Lives and Livelihoods, Safe Water for All*. Tokyo.

Box 8.2: Reforming the Dhaka Water Supply and Sewerage Authority

The Dhaka Water Supply and Sewerage Authority (DWASA) was established in 1963 with a mandate to manage water supply and sewerage in the Bangladesh capital. The WASA Act of 1996 began a corporatization process that ultimately professionalized DWASA and made it profitable.

DWASA had substantial water losses and poor service delivery until about 2008. Physical losses due to leakage from pipes were over 50% and collection efficiency (percentage of water bills collected) was just 62%. A Turnaround Program in 2009–2010 was supported by an Asian Development Bank project. When completed in 2016, about 5.44 million people had continuous potable water supply from taps without requiring further treatment, with pressure sufficient for two-story houses.

The turnaround was anchored on infrastructure investments and policy reforms combined with visionary leadership, technical innovation, social inclusion (by supplying potable water to informal settlements), and a strong focus on public education programs and civil society involvement.

In 2018, overall nonrevenue water in Dhaka had fallen to 20%, with levels of less than 10% in established District Metering Areas in project areas. Collection efficiency reached 97.5%, with continuous pressurized water supplied to all customers. DWASA's success story has been closely followed by its South Asian neighbors and has served as a role model for other water utilities in the region.

Sources: Asian Development Bank. 2016. *Dhaka Water Supply Network Improvement Project.* Manila; and DWASA. 2019. https://dwasa.org.bd/.

Dhaka in Bangladesh and Phnom Penh in Cambodia have turned low-performing institutions and inefficient systems into high-performing and profitable water utilities through corporatization. They have become models for other water utility reform initiatives in the region. Measures involved capital investments and adopting appropriate technical innovations, along with sustained programs for NRW management. These combined institutional reforms and capacity building through staff training, customer orientation, and public awareness campaigns for demand management and water conservation (Box 8.2).

Ever-increasing global water demand has spawned numerous frameworks and global actions. In 1977, a UN conference stated that "all people have the right to have access to drinking water in quantity and quality equal to their basic needs."[14] This triggered the launch of the 1981–1990 International Drinking Water Supply and Sanitation Decade. When it ended, about 700 million additional people were estimated to have access to drinking water and 500 million with access to sanitation. However, rapid population increases in many developing countries in the region precluded reaching 100% coverage. The Millennium Development Goals and Sustainable Development Goals also specifically target water supply. Yet, as of 2017, around 300 million people in Asia and the Pacific still did not have access to safe sources of drinking water.[15]

Future trends: Integrated solutions for a water-secure future

Approximately one-third of countries globally have medium or high levels of water stress—meaning groundwater is scarce—with many in Central Asia and South Asia. High groundwater dependency and unsustainable extraction are major concerns. In fact, of the world's 15 largest groundwater users, seven are in Asia and the Pacific.[16] Managing water resources more carefully and balancing competing demand from domestic, irrigation, and industrial use have become a priority. In addition, with rapid urbanization, the demand for clean and safe water supply will continue to rise significantly.

Water supply continues to be a challenge in many cities. In some, distribution networks extended to new areas overstretch the designed system capacity, resulting in intermittent water supply and increased contamination risks. Many Asian cities commonly experience high water loss in distribution networks that increase costs (to pump additional water), lower revenues, and reduce financial sustainability. Fixing these issues requires improved governance by top management and applying specific technologies—such as advanced leak detection and network management systems ranging from forming District Metering Areas to applying pressure management techniques.

Using advanced technology has always been crucial for improving urban water service efficiency, such as geographic information systems to support water utility asset management. Smart networks and metering technologies are now widely used by advanced

---

[14] Bays, L. 1994. Short Overview of Water Supply Situations in the World, Water Philippines '94. *Technical Papers, 9th IWSA-ASPAC Regional Conference and Exhibition*. Manila: Philippine Water Works Association.

[15] ADB. 2017. *Meeting Asia's Infrastructure Needs*. Manila.

[16] ADB. 2016. *Dhaka Water Supply Network Improvement Project*. Manila.

water utilities such as Arisu in Seoul, one of the most well-managed water utilities in Asia.[17]

Governments, the private sector, and development partners all have a role in financing water infrastructure. And the sector must be integrated with bulk water supply, wastewater management, flood risk management, solid waste management, source protection, and integrated water resources and drought management. Governments are also expected to play a critical role in creating an enabling ecosystem of appropriate policies, regulations, and taxes—including environmental charges.

8.5 Telecommunications and information and communication technology

Electrical telecommunications systems began in the 19th century, starting with Samuel Morse's telegraph in 1837. It was followed by the telephone, radio, and television. Radio, invented in the 1890s, was widely used as a one-way broadcast technology after the 1920s. Television broadcasting was invented in the 1920s and became widely commercialized in the 1950s. Beginning in the late 1950s, satellite communications were developed after the Soviet Union's 1957 Sputnik satellite launch—from what is now Kazakhstan. By the end of the 1970s, satellites allowed voice and video broadcasts to reach living rooms across the world. The internet made data more accessible from the late 1980s, and by the mid-1990s, the World Wide Web let people communicate across global networks more easily and inexpensively.

Each of these new technologies opened new development opportunities. The telephone allowed people to stay connected over long distances, and improved access to health care and commerce, among others. The internet also enabled digital learning, e-commerce, and online employment. The digital infrastructure and investments require appropriate government policy and regional cooperation. The private sector rapidly commercialized these new technologies, and government regulation followed to maintain competition and ensure benefits reached the broader population.

Asia and the Pacific adopted telecommunications and ICT both as an input for development and as an outcome of economic prosperity. Until the 1960s, the region had limited telecommunications capability. But from then onward, wider telecommunications use and later, ICT,

---

[17] Seoul Metropolitan Government. 2017. *Seoul Tap Water Arisu*. Seoul. http://susa.or.kr/en/files/seoul-tap-water-arisu-englishpdf?ckattempt=1.

developed rapidly. This section discusses infrastructure development for telephones, computing, and for internet use. This chapter complements the broader description of technological innovation in Chapter 5.

Telephone infrastructure

Alexander Graham Bell invented the telephone in 1876. Service expanded rapidly, but the need for dedicated wiring infrastructure limited growth to mostly urban and high-income areas. Those without household landlines could use public phones or travel to the nearest town to find service. Japan had its first telephone service in 1890 and, by the mid-1960s, had 15 telephones per 100 inhabitants, compared with the US (the global leader) with 52 and Australia with 27. Meanwhile, India had only 2 telephones per 1,000 inhabitants.

Early telephone service was based on fixed-line analog infrastructure that was expensive to lay out and maintain, with limited speed and data transmission rates. Typical telephone service was delivered through SOEs or regulated monopolies given the heavy infrastructure investment required. This limited opportunities for effective competition, similar to power infrastructure.

Asian economies rapidly developed fixed telephone infrastructure in the 1960s and continued to expand through the mid-2000s, when mobile phones became widely available (Figures 8.6 and 8.7). In Japan, fixed phone service peaked at 52 lines per 100 inhabitants in 1997, while in the PRC, it peaked at 28 lines per 100 inhabitants in 2006. In India, it reached 4.4 lines per 100 inhabitants in 2005.

The mobile phone was invented in the US by Motorola in 1973. This analog mobile phone service was expensive and not widely used. By the 1990s, however, mobile phones became widely available given advances in semiconductor technology and the development of digital wireless networking. This increased both speed and accuracy. In 1999, the Nippon Telegraph and Telephone Corporation (NTT) was the first provider globally to offer full mobile internet service. High-speed 3G services became available in Japan in 2001 and in the ROK a year later.

The transition to mobile phones brought a change in regulatory structure in most countries. As mobile networks do not require fixed lines, they could support multiple competitors. Most countries in Asia today have two or more private mobile operators. However, regulations

Figure 8.6: Fixed Telephone Subscriptions per 100 Inhabitants

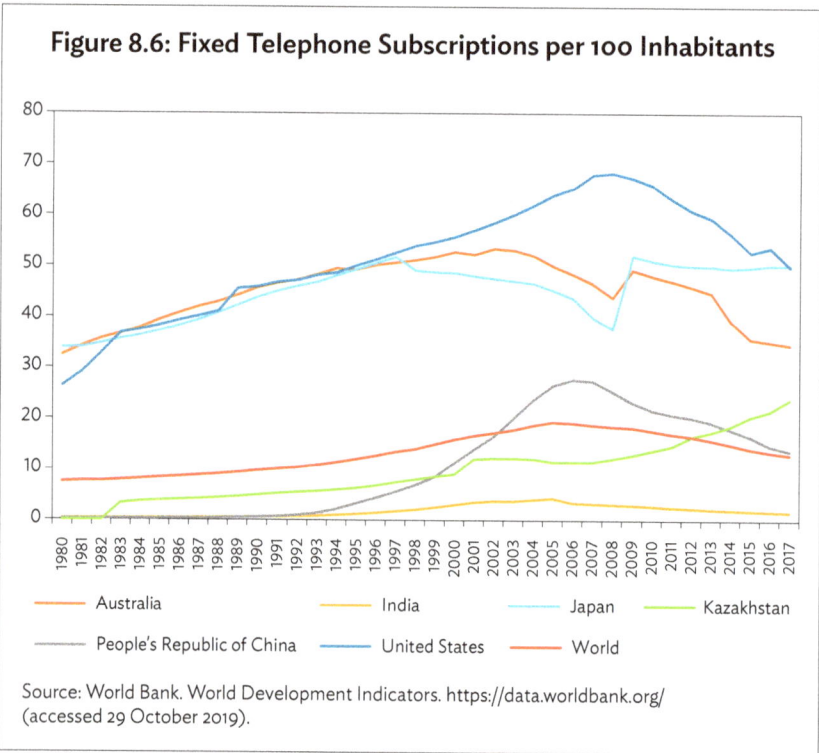

Source: World Bank. World Development Indicators. https://data.worldbank.org/ (accessed 29 October 2019).

are still needed to encourage greater use in some rural areas as investment in cell towers is not profitable given low user density and lower incomes. ADB and other development agencies funded submarine fiber-optic cables across Pacific island countries, as well as communications projects to remote areas using satellites, to enable access for underserved populations.

Apple launched its iPhone in 2007, starting the smartphone era. It was a fundamental advance by combining a handheld computer with broadband internet, featuring a large display, global positioning system (GPS) capability, integrated camera, and touch-screen user interface. While Apple has focused on high-end phones, ROK and PRC companies now lead in overall sales, including low-cost smartphones for developing countries. Since 2010, the ROK's Samsung Electronics has been the global sales leader, with PRC manufacturers following. The availability of low-cost mobile phones spread use phenomenally, today reaching most of the population worldwide (Figure 8.7). For example, India, after failing to reach even five fixed-landline

Figure 8.7: Mobile Telephone Subscriptions per 100 Inhabitants

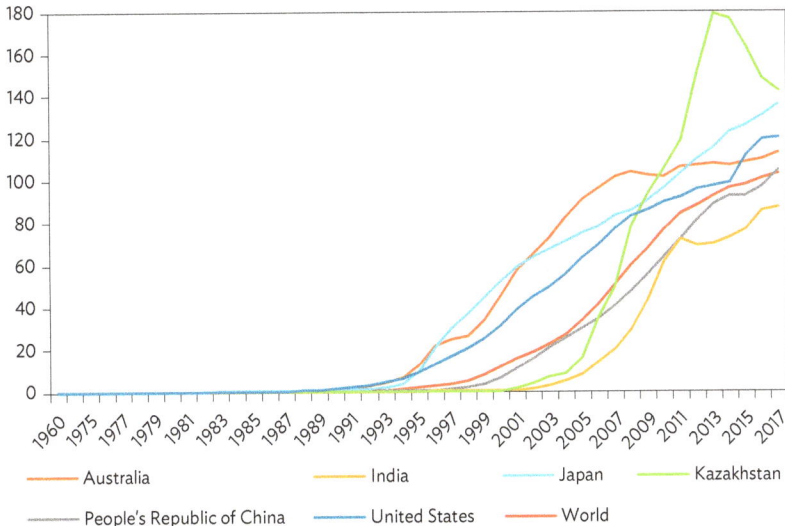

Source: World Bank. World Development Indicators. https://data.worldbank.org/ (accessed 29 October 2019).

subscriptions per 100 inhabitants, grew from 0 in 2000 to 87 mobile subscriptions per 100 inhabitants in 2017. The smartphone has become the default communication device for most of the world's population.

Widespread smartphone use has opened new opportunities for development purposes, including in health, education, employment, social services, and finance. They can be used by farmers for pricing and weather forecasts. Students can access online courses. Digital finance can be used for payments, remittances, and other financial services. Smartphones also allow access to digital medical records, remote diagnoses, and online access to doctors and nurses.

Computing and internet infrastructure

The transistor, invented in the 1940s, and the integrated circuit, invented in the 1950s, helped develop digital computers. The modern semiconductor industry began in the US in the 1970s when advances in computer chip manufacturing allowed miniaturization, mass production, and increased processing speed. Japanese firms became leaders in the industry in the 1980s. The Nippon Electric Company (NEC) invented the first digital signal processor in 1980, speeding up communications equipment by converting analog signals to digital format. TSMC, founded in Taipei,China in 1987, became an early leader in commercial semiconductor manufacturing, called foundry services, where the manufacturing process is standardized to support different component designs. The ROK has also become a leader in semiconductor manufacturing since the mid-1990s by focusing on components for mobile phones and smartphones. Government support for research and development as well as regulatory policies for intellectual property were important in fostering Asian leadership in the industry.

Advances in semiconductor technology rapidly increased computing speeds beginning in the 1970s. Moore's Law, coined in 1965 by Gordon Moore, cofounder of Intel Corporation, predicted that the number of components in an integrated circuit would double every 18 to 24 months. This held true for over 40 years, with components increasing by 1 million times because of the reduction in component size. This increased processing speed and reduced the processing power required. This exponential increase in performance was one of the most fundamental drivers of new technology, as semiconductors became the foundation for all communications and computing infrastructure.

As performance grew, desktop computers became widely available in the 1990s. Portable laptops followed later in the decade, becoming essential infrastructure for businesses and households by the mid-2000s.

In 1969, the precursor to the modern internet, called ARPANET, was activated by US researchers, supported by the Defense Advanced Research Projects Agency (DARPA). They were interested in developing communication technology (more flexible and decentralized compared with previous technologies) to connect universities and research labs globally. In 1973, several institutions in Australia and Japan were connected to the ARPANET. It was in the late 1980s when the modern internet age was born, i.e., when Tim Berners-Lee at the European Organization for Nuclear Research (CERN) created a system known as the World Wide Web—a combination of the first web browser and hypertext markup language (HTML). In 1994, the free Netscape browser began the internet revolution and the "Dotcom Boom" in Silicon Valley. Amazon launched its e-commerce service in 1994, Google began its internet search service in 1998, and Facebook started its online social network in 2003. Google and Facebook also pioneered internet advertising as a business model to monetize their free online services.

Based on free services and growing internet access, Google and Facebook quickly became the dominant platforms across Asia—with over 80% market share in search and social networking outside the PRC. The PRC developed its own versions of most services, with Alibaba launching e-commerce in 1999, Baidu starting its internet search engine in 2000, and Tencent beginning the WeChat social network in 2000.

The internet's explosive rise required a massive increase in global data centers connected by fiber-optic cables—a new form of basic infrastructure. Since the mid-2000s, cloud computing has evolved as a new form of computing infrastructure. Cloud computing enables companies to build digital services without deploying on-site hardware, but rather rent services based on usage. This has dramatically reduced the cost of computing infrastructure and enables new digital services to be launched with minimal up-front investment. ADB has supported development of cloud-based banking services to provide financial services to underserved populations where traditional financial infrastructure is not economically feasible.

By 2018, more than 50% of the world's population had internet access, mostly via smartphones, making it the default platform for digital services (Figure 8.8). In India, internet access reached almost 50% of the population by early 2019, based on the availability of low-cost smartphones and wireless broadband service.

In Asia, there is a rapid expansion of the digital economy. In the PRC, Tencent's WeChat app includes the world's largest digital payments service and is so widely used that many merchants no longer accept cash. Southeast Asia has launched two digital economy leaders, Grab, which was started in Malaysia and is now located in Singapore, and Gojek in Indonesia, both starting with ride-sharing and expanding into e-commerce and payments. India is also rapidly transitioning to the digital economy. In India, the government launched Aadhaar, a biometrics-based identity service in 2016, which now covers 99% of the adult population and dramatically increased opportunities for financial services and access to health.

The digital economy extends into digital employment and online education. India and the Philippines are regional leaders in the digital service economy, such as business process outsourcing. At the University of the South Pacific, the world's first regional university,

Figure 8.8: Internet Users
(% of population)

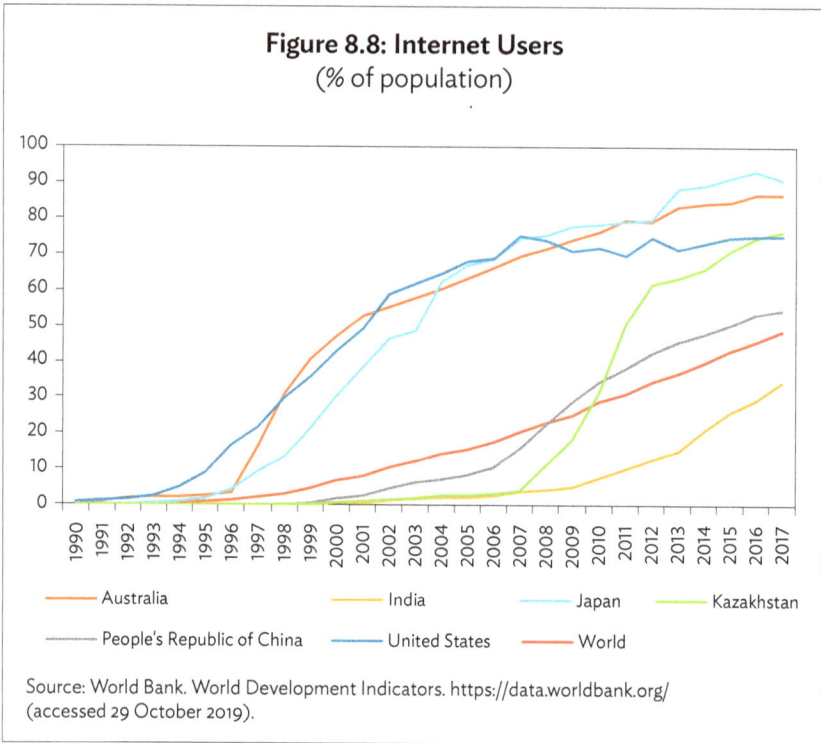

Source: World Bank. World Development Indicators. https://data.worldbank.org/
(accessed 29 October 2019).

ADB-funded submarine fiber-optic cables in the Pacific island countries further improved ICT-enabled distance learning programs.

The rise of the digital economy has created opportunities and challenges for development and governance. The rapid pace of change can create social disruption and can accelerate the obsolescence of routine jobs. On the other hand, the digital economy will enable many new opportunities for social engagement and will create many new job categories. Successfully managing the transition will require significant investments as well as new policy frameworks—to support human capital development, foster effective competition, and enable consumer protection.

Future trends

Going forward, there are several digital infrastructure trends that will continue to transform Asia's economy. These include the Internet of Things (IoT), AI, and cybersecurity and privacy protection. Each will require significant public investment and effective regulatory policies.

The IoT is infrastructure for interconnecting things based on interoperable ICT. IoT devices communicate and interact over the internet. They can be remotely monitored and controlled. For instance, IoT infrastructure can improve agriculture by remotely monitoring soil conditions and support reductions in air pollution using low-cost air-quality sensors.

AI imitates human cognitive functions to tackle increasingly complex real-world problems. Recent AI advances were enabled by increased computational capacity and the availability of large data sets. It has significantly advanced image recognition, machine translation, voice recognition, and autonomous vehicles, among others. These advances are especially promising for new services such as optimizing crop inputs for farmers, fine-tuning medical diagnosis, translating documents using smartphones, and tailoring education for students through adaptive learning.

Cybersecurity is important to protect users, data, networks, and computer systems. Cybersecurity includes technical, organizational, and regulatory aspects such as security systems, process definitions, legal frameworks and regulations, and protection of physical infrastructure. As more and more human activities are digitized, privacy protection will grow in importance.

8.6 Looking ahead

There are many people in Asia and the Pacific who still do not have access to energy, transport, urban water supply, and telecommunications and ICT. In general, developing Asian countries need to address infrastructure in the following ways, in addition to specific points raised in the future trends subsection of each previous section.

First, more investment is needed in infrastructure. ADB estimates that total investments of nearly $26 trillion are needed from 2016 to 2030 in transport, energy, urban water supply, and telecommunications.[18]

To maximize the potential for infrastructure investment to strengthen sustainable economic growth, several important investment criteria should be considered. These include a strong economic rationale, efficient life-cycle costs, positive social and environmental benefits, safety, resilience against natural disasters, climate change

---

[18]   ADB. 2017. *Meeting Asia's Infrastructure Needs*. Manila.

mitigation and adaptation, and improved governance and debt sustainability. New investment should incorporate advanced technologies. These are key elements of the "Quality Infrastructure Investment Principles," adopted at the 2019 Group of Twenty (G20) Summit.

Second, continuing capacity development and institutional reform are needed to boost efficiency and deliver high-quality services. Appropriate tariffs for utilities should be ensured to recover investment and avoid inefficient use of services.

If needed, targeted subsidies for poor households can replace subsidized tariffs. Governments can corporatize utilities and railways, which have been part of government, to improve efficiency. Governments must continue to reform SOEs (already corporatized) using better regulations and governance, and make them more commercially viable. Privatization can be an option when appropriate.

Third, private sector participation is essential to cover the infrastructure gap. The private sector can mobilize knowledge, operational efficiency, and additional financing to help develop infrastructure projects. Government has an important role to play in creating the right policy environment and setting priorities to encourage private sector participation.

PPPs for infrastructure projects can be an effective tool to attract private capital into infrastructure. Governments must improve the regulatory environment, help identify bankable projects, prepare credible estimates of cash flow, set appropriate risk-sharing arrangements, ensure reliable dispute resolution mechanisms, and develop capital markets for supporting project finance. While PPPs are not a panacea, when designed and executed well, they can deliver good infrastructure services.[19]

Finally, regional cooperation to improve connectivity across Asia and the Pacific is essential to unleash the region's potential, and to promote growth and stability. Technological advances can strengthen cross-border connectivity in the region through cross-border transport, digital links, and electricity transmission networks. This will help attract investment, build value chains to promote trade and growth, and promote sustainability through regional public goods. Cross-border trade of renewable energy also contributes to climate change mitigation and environment protection.

---

[19] ADB. 2019. *How PPP Advisory Services Can Narrow Asia's Infrastructure Gap.* Manila.

CHAPTER 9

TRADE, FOREIGN DIRECT INVESTMENT, AND OPENNESS

9.1   Introduction

Asia has a long history in international trade, spanning thousands of years.[1] Over the past 50 years, in particular, Asia's economic reemergence was driven by a system that gradually embraced open trade and investment. Developing Asia's rapid growth in trade and foreign direct investment (FDI)—and the corresponding 42-fold increase in gross domestic product (GDP, in constant 2010 United States [US] dollars)—helped narrow the development gap with industrialized countries and contributed to reducing poverty.

In general, Asia's economies passed through three evolutionary stages of external economic policy regimes over the past 5 decades, although with large variations in speed and substance between countries: first, many countries adopted a post-independence import substitution strategy to build self-reliance; second, many of the Asian economies became outward oriented; and third, they deepened integration into global value chains (GVCs) and embraced regional trade arrangements.

---

[1]   Pomeranz, K. 2001. *The Great Divergence: China, Europe, and the Making of the Modern World Economy.* Princeton: Princeton University Press; and Sugihara, K. 1996. *Japan, China, and the Growth of the Asian International Economy, 1850–1949.* Volume 1. Oxford: Oxford University Press.

In the 1950s and 1960s, many Asian economies adopted an import substitution strategy—but with limited success. By the mid-1960s, a few economies— Hong Kong, China; the Republic of Korea (ROK); Singapore; and Taipei,China (later the newly industrialized economies [NIEs])—started export promotion as a growth strategy. This was driven by a desire to industrialize, earn the foreign exchange needed to import capital goods, and access foreign markets. More Asian countries followed in the 1970s and 1980s because of the failure of import substitution strategies.

Special economic zones (SEZs) allowed export-led growth strategies to be tested in a controlled way for countries such as the People's Republic of China (PRC), which had little experience with market-based policies before beginning to open its economy in 1978. Also, after the 1985 Plaza Accord and the resulting sharp appreciation of the Japanese yen, there was a surge in FDI from Japan to the region, especially Southeast Asia, helped by Japan's substantial official development assistance in infrastructure.

Trade entered a new phase in the early 2000s, as tariffs worldwide fell dramatically, free trade agreements (FTAs) proliferated, and the PRC joined the World Trade Organization (WTO). Outward-oriented trade reforms and increased competition reinforced the increasing trend of FDI inflows to Asia and boosted the region's trade. As a result, global and regional multinational firms intensified outsourcing production to Asia, incorporating the region's economies more deeply into GVCs.

Asia's rapid trade and FDI growth underscores the region's successful transition to outward-oriented policies. Both merchandise exports and merchandise imports grew annually by 11% during 1960–2018, with the ratio of trade (exports plus imports) to GDP rising from 20% to 53%. There was also a significant shift in export composition, from mostly raw materials to manufactured goods, and from light industry to heavy industrial products, with an increasing share of high-technology exports.

Conventional trade theories by Ricardo and Heckscher-Ohlin argue that an economy benefits from trade through comparative advantage and efficiency gains from reallocating resources, especially using interindustry international trade (trade among different industries between countries). Japan's Meiji restoration in the 19th century is an example of these classical gains from trade—around 65% of Japan's increase in real income between 1858 (when Japan's self-imposed economic isolation ended) and the 1870s (when Japan embraced free trade) came from renewed trade.[2]

Intra-industry trade—trade in the same industry between countries, such as a horizontal trade of cars exported and imported between two countries, and the vertical trade of cars and their parts between two countries—deepened in Asian economies. This is explained by trade theory that emphasizes gains from scale economies,[3] the first-mover advantage, knowledge spillovers, and greater consumer welfare from the wider variety of goods and services available.[4]

The more recent trade model of firm heterogeneity[5] shows that trade liberalization enhances overall economic productivity, because only sufficiently productive firms can survive market competition after liberalization.[6] Asian economies captured these benefits initially through interindustry trade and later through intra-industry trade. In addition, FDI inflows brought further benefits: access to capital, new technologies, and management know-how. This trend also helped trigger broad and deep domestic structural reforms in the region, including greater market competition and product innovation.

This chapter revisits the role an open economic system of trade and FDI played in driving the past 50 years of Asia's rapid economic growth and structural transformation. Section 9.2 examines how Asia's trade and FDI grew across economies and over time, drawing out empirical regularities between trade and FDI and economic growth. Section 9.3 discusses the evolution of Asia's trade and FDI policies, focusing on the key policy and institutional drivers of trade and FDI

[2] Huber, R. 1971. Effect on Prices of Japan's Entry into World Commerce after 1858. *Journal of Political Economy*. 79 (3). pp. 614–628; and Latham, A. J. H., and H. Kawakatsu, eds. 2009. *Intra-Asian Trade and Industrialization: Essays in Memory of Yasukichi Yasuba*. London and New York: Routledge.

[3] Ethier, W. J. 1979. Internationally Decreasing Costs and World Trade. *Journal of International Economics*. 9 (1). pp. 1–25; Krugman, P. R. 1979. Increasing Returns, Monopolistic Competition and International Trade. *Journal of International Economics*. 9 (4). pp. 469–479; and Grossman, G., and E. Helpman. 1991. Trade, Knowledge Spillovers, and Growth. *European Economic Review*. 35 (2–3). pp. 517–526.

[4] Broda, C., and D. Weinstein. 2006. Globalization and the Gains from Variety. *The Quarterly Journal of Economics*. 121 (2). pp. 541–585.

[5] Melitz, M. 2003. The Impact of Trade on Intra-Industry Reallocations and Aggregate Industry Productivity. *Econometrica*. 71 (6). pp. 1695–1725.

[6] McCaig, B., and N. Pavcnik. 2018. Export Markets and Labor Allocation in a Low-Income Country. *American Economic Review*. 108 (7). pp. 1899–1941; Zhai, F. 2008. Armington Meets Melitz: Introducing Firm Heterogeneity in a Global CGE Model of Trade. *Journal of Economic Integration*. 23 (3). pp. 575–604; and Yu, M. 2015. Processing Trade, Tariff Reductions and Firm Productivity: Evidence from Chinese Firms. *The Economic Journal*. 125 (585). pp. 943–988.

growth. Section 9.4 focuses on the growing opportunities offered by GVCs and regional value chains (RVCs). Section 9.5 examines the growing importance of services trade. Section 9.6 discusses the proliferation of global and regional trade arrangements. Section 9.7 looks at the future of trade and FDI growth in Asia and its policy implications.

9.2   Trends in Asia's trade and foreign direct investment[7]

Trade

Asia's trade has grown substantially over the past 50 years, driven by the region's proactive outward-oriented development policies. As a result, most Asian economies have seen a higher export-to-GDP share in the 2010s (shown along the horizontal axis of Figure 9.1) compared to the 1980s (shown in the vertical axis). Hong Kong, China and Singapore are the most open economies in the region and globally, given their relatively small economic size.

The PRC's share of exports in goods and services increased from an annual average of 10% of GDP in the 1980s to a peak of 36% in 2006, stabilizing around 23% during 2010–2018 after the global financial crisis. India's export share more than tripled from 6% in the 1980s to 22% in the 2010s. These are dramatic, especially given the size of the two economies. The PRC's accession to the WTO in 2001 and India's economic liberalization reform beginning in 1991 provided further impetus to their outstanding export growth. For relatively smaller economies in Southeast Asia and the Pacific, the ratio increased even more dramatically. Viet Nam's export-to-GDP share soared almost nine times from 10% in the 1980s to 87% in the 2010s. Over the same period, the export share rose eight times (to 27%) in the Federated States of Micronesia and five times (to 37%) in the Lao People's Democratic Republic.

While Asia's global trade was growing fast, initial interindustry trade based on comparative advantage switched to intra-industry GVC trade spurred by scale economies as well as product differentiation and sophistication. As a corollary, while Europe and the United States (US) are important destinations for Asia's exports, Asia's market has continuously expanded, making it an important destination for European and US products.[8]

---

[7]   In this section, Asia includes developing Asia and the three advanced economies of Australia, Japan, and New Zealand.

[8]   Helble, M., and B. Ngiang. 2016. From Global Factory to Global Mall? East Asia's Changing Trade Composition. *Japan and the World Economy*. 39 (September). pp. 37–47.

Figure 9.1: Exports of Goods and Services
(% of GDP)

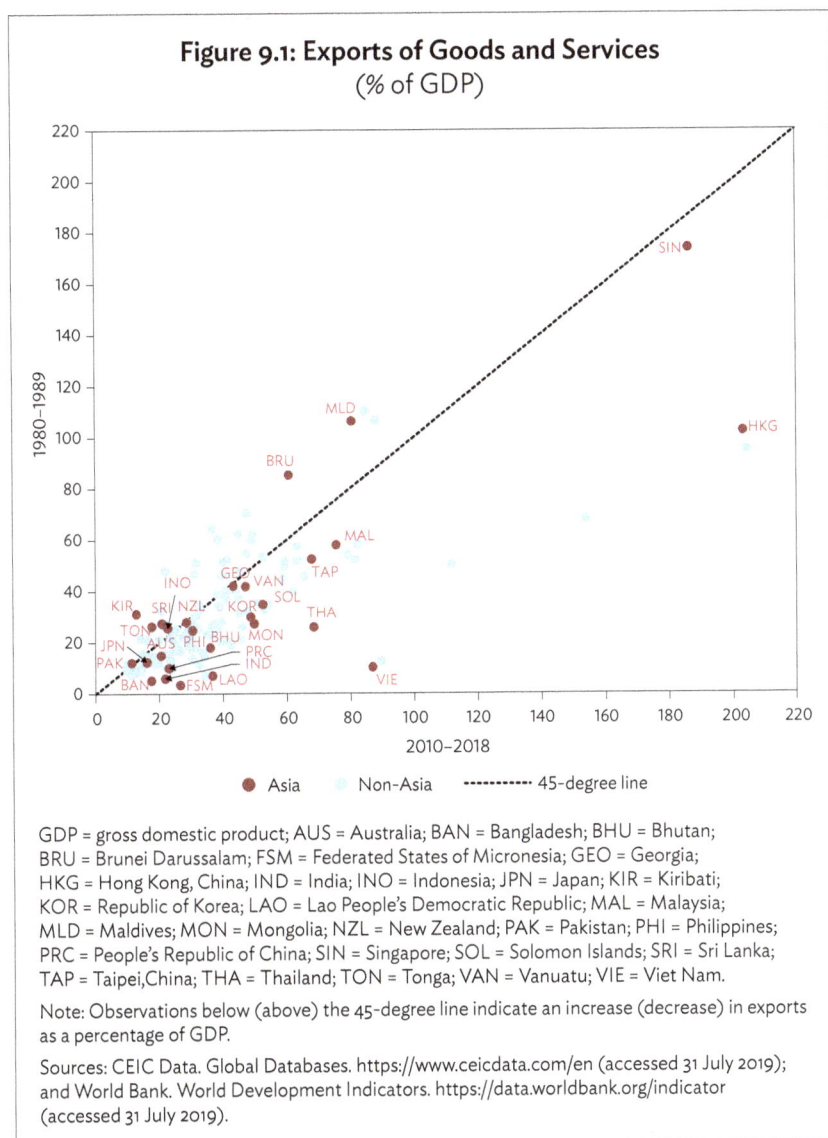

GDP = gross domestic product; AUS = Australia; BAN = Bangladesh; BHU = Bhutan; BRU = Brunei Darussalam; FSM = Federated States of Micronesia; GEO = Georgia; HKG = Hong Kong, China; IND = India; INO = Indonesia; JPN = Japan; KIR = Kiribati; KOR = Republic of Korea; LAO = Lao People's Democratic Republic; MAL = Malaysia; MLD = Maldives; MON = Mongolia; NZL = New Zealand; PAK = Pakistan; PHI = Philippines; PRC = People's Republic of China; SIN = Singapore; SOL = Solomon Islands; SRI = Sri Lanka; TAP = Taipei,China; THA = Thailand; TON = Tonga; VAN = Vanuatu; VIE = Viet Nam.

Note: Observations below (above) the 45-degree line indicate an increase (decrease) in exports as a percentage of GDP.

Sources: CEIC Data. Global Databases. https://www.ceicdata.com/en (accessed 31 July 2019); and World Bank. World Development Indicators. https://data.worldbank.org/indicator (accessed 31 July 2019).

Exports

Intraregional exports have expanded over time across Asia. The region's annual average share of intraregional exports to total exports increased from 36% in the 1960s to 56% in 2010–2018 (Figure 9.2). Whereas the US and the European Union (EU) accounted for almost half of Asia's exports in 1960, they now absorb just 27%. From being Asia's top

Figure 9.2: Destination of Asia's Merchandise Exports
(% of total, average over the specified period)

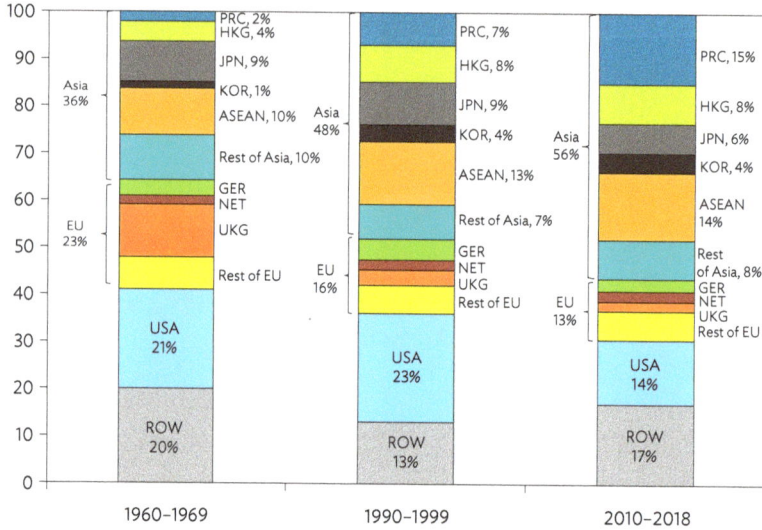

ASEAN = Association of Southeast Asian Nations; EU = European Union (28 members); GER = Germany; HKG = Hong Kong, China; JPN = Japan; KOR = Republic of Korea; NET = Netherlands; PRC = People's Republic of China; ROW = rest of the world; UKG = United Kingdom; USA = United States.

Note: In 2010–2018, out of the PRC's 15% share in Asia's exports, 4% came from Hong Kong, China; and out of Hong Kong, China's 8% share, 5% is from the PRC.

Source: International Monetary Fund. Direction of Trade Statistics. http://data.imf.org (accessed 26 July 2019).

export destination in the 1960s with an average 23% share, the EU's share dropped to 13% in the 2010s mainly due to the significant drop in exports to the United Kingdom. Exports to the US declined steadily from a 26% peak in the 1980s to 14% in the 2010s. Following the 2008–2009 global financial crisis, Asia's strong intraregional exports provided a buffer amid the slowdown in demand from advanced economies.

Within Asia, Japan was the major export destination until the 1990s, accounting for around 9% of Asian exports. Then the PRC took over with an annual average share of 15% in 2010–2018, up from just 2% in the 1960s. Over the period, the PRC became the regional hub for global production networks, built on low labor costs in early years and its massive production assembly capacity.[9] Asian economies quickly

---

[9] Asian Development Bank (ADB). 2008. *Emerging Asian Regionalism: A Partnership for Shared Prosperity*. Manila.

incorporated into global and regional supply chains and thus thrived in exports of both intermediate and final goods, which cross borders multiple times within the same industry. This was likely behind the rise in the share of the Association of Southeast Asian Nations (ASEAN) in Asian exports—from 10% in the 1960s to 14% in the 2010s. The ROK's share likewise increased from 1% to 4%.

The composition of exports shifted from mostly labor-intensive raw materials (such as textiles and garments) in the 1960s to higher value-added, capital-intensive products (such as electrical machinery and appliances) in the 2010s. This was partly due to the shift from interindustry to intra-industry trade (Figure 9.3). Today, for instance, in automobile and electronics industries, final products, intermediate goods, and parts are traded between countries along production networks. Export product diversity also grew

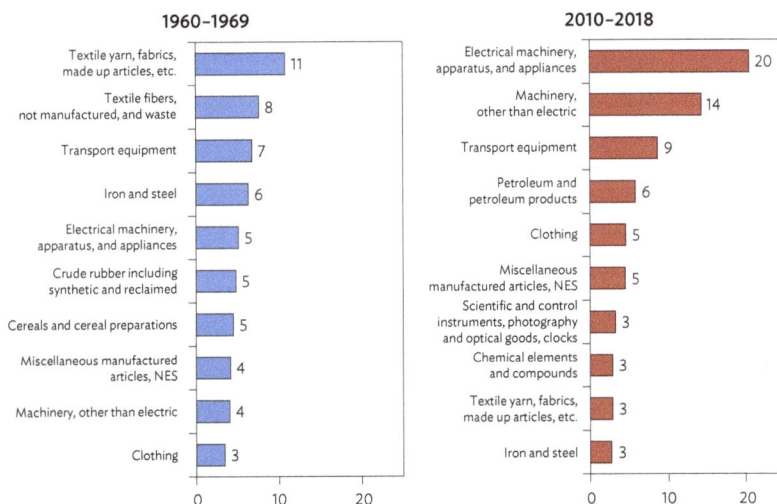

Figure 9.3: Asia's Top Merchandise Exports
(% of total)

NES = not elsewhere specified.

Notes: Commodity classification is based on SITC Rev 1 (2-digit commodity codes).
The category "miscellaneous manufactured articles, NES" includes the following: musical instruments, sound recorders and parts; printed matter; articles of artificial plastic materials, NES; perambulators, toys, games, and sporting goods; office and stationery supplies, NES; works of art, collectors' pieces, and antiques; and manufactured articles, NES.

Source: World Bank. World Integrated Trade Solution. https://wits.worldbank.org/ (accessed 4 November 2019).

dramatically. And the variety of imported products also expanded significantly. Tariff reductions allowed many previously unavailable consumer goods to enter Asian markets.

Also, there was a general positive relationship between export growth and economic growth in the world over the past 57 years (Figure 9.4). Several points are noteworthy. First, the positive relationship between export growth and economic growth is salient among the NIEs as well as other Asian economies, which have cultivated a broader manufacturing industrial base. Second, economies like the NIEs—with a high degree of economic openness (measured by

Figure 9.4: Export Growth and Economic Growth, 1960–2017

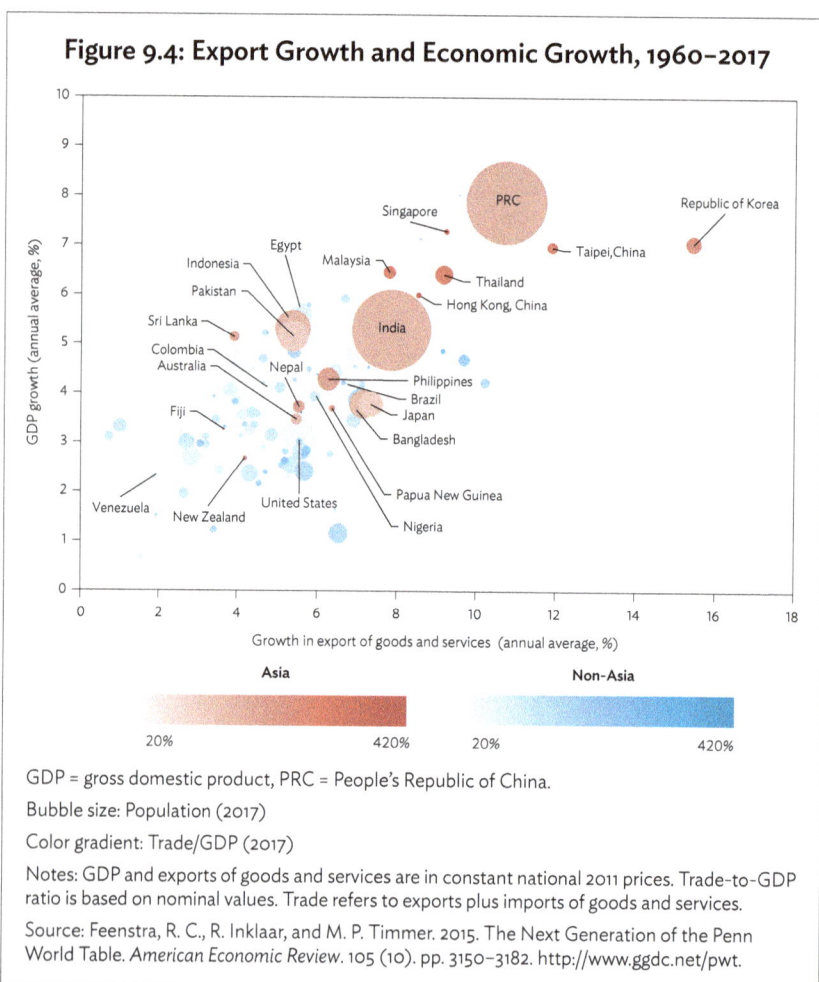

GDP = gross domestic product, PRC = People's Republic of China.

Bubble size: Population (2017)

Color gradient: Trade/GDP (2017)

Notes: GDP and exports of goods and services are in constant national 2011 prices. Trade-to-GDP ratio is based on nominal values. Trade refers to exports plus imports of goods and services.

Source: Feenstra, R. C., R. Inklaar, and M. P. Timmer. 2015. The Next Generation of the Penn World Table. *American Economic Review*. 105 (10). pp. 3150–3182. http://www.ggdc.net/pwt.

the ratio of exports plus imports to GDP in 2017), had faster economic growth in general over the past decades. Third, countries such as the PRC and India, despite their large economic size, have a fairly high level of external openness which is associated with high economic and export growth rates.

Foreign direct investment

FDI inflows (in US dollars) to the region increased steadily, especially after the 1985 Plaza Accord, until disrupted by the 1997–1998 Asian financial crisis (Figure 9.5). Then the inflows recovered rapidly until the 2008–2009 global financial crisis, after which inflow growth remained stable. Overall, inward FDI to Asia increased from 10% of GDP in 1980 to 28% in 2017. Asia's share of global FDI inflows likewise increased from 14% to 35%.

FDI inflows, along with tourism receipts and remittances, are now the major source of financial inflows to developing economies in the region (Chapter 7). Net portfolio investment is not large compared with these three sources. From the early official development assistance dominance as main external investment financier, the region dramatically embraced a greater openness toward FDI and other forms of financial inflows, with foreign businesses looking to reap huge benefits from FDI into Asia (Chapter 7).

Developing Asia became a natural destination for FDI because of (i) relatively low labor costs (particularly during initial phases of industrial development), (ii) an improving business climate, and (iii) large market size. Many Asian governments introduced policies on export promotion, current and capital account liberalization, SEZs, and tax incentives, all playing important roles in attracting FDI to developing Asia. Over the past few decades, the development of GVCs and regional production networks—motivated by cost reductions in outsourcing and advances in information and communication technology—were also behind rapid FDI growth.

Initially, agriculture and mining attracted most FDI, particularly in countries with abundant natural resources. Then FDI was focused on labor-intensive light industry. Liberalized FDI regulations, along with a gradually improved business environment, also spurred the acceleration of foreign capital inflows. Over time, FDI shifted toward heavy and high-technology manufacturing and services. As Asian incomes rose, its attractiveness as an FDI destination increasingly shifted toward the large and growing domestic consumption market.

Figure 9.5: Asia's Foreign Direct Investment Inflows and Outflows

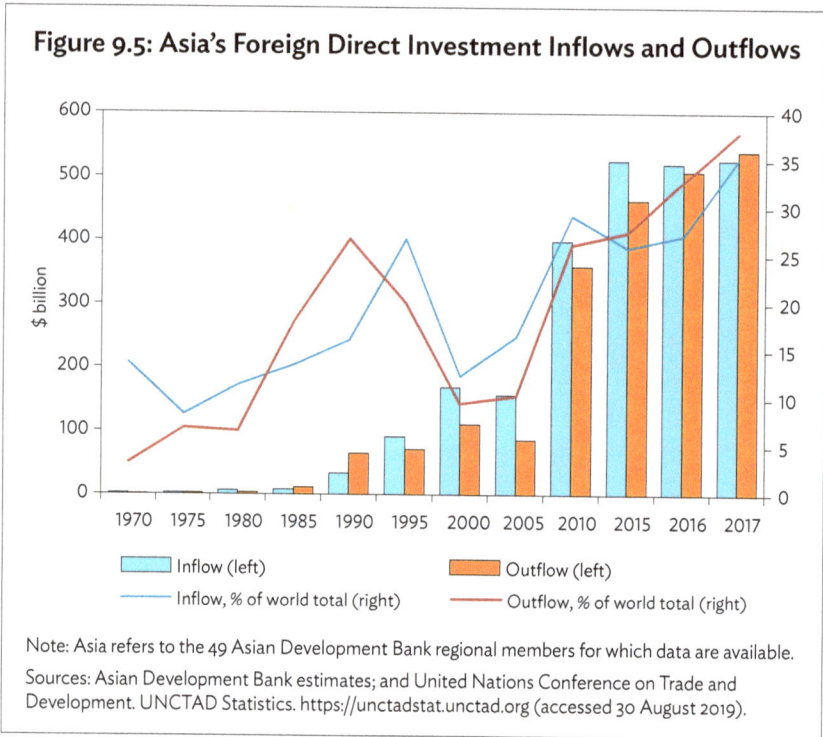

Note: Asia refers to the 49 Asian Development Bank regional members for which data are available.

Sources: Asian Development Bank estimates; and United Nations Conference on Trade and Development. UNCTAD Statistics. https://unctadstat.unctad.org (accessed 30 August 2019).

In 2017, Hong Kong, China; the PRC; and Singapore remained Asia's top FDI recipients (Figure 9.6). As a percentage of GDP, FDI was highest in the more open smaller economies, particularly Hong Kong, China (30.6%) and Singapore (19.1%). Other Asian economies—such as Cambodia, Georgia, the Lao People's Democratic Republic, Maldives, Mongolia, and Palau—also tend to rely heavily on FDI, with FDI inflows accounting for around 10% of GDP (Figure 9.6).

Firm-level data suggest that, historically, greenfield investments were the dominant mode of entry for multinationals investing in Asia, accounting for an annual average of 65% of total investments in 2003–2017.[10] Mergers and acquisitions increased rapidly in recent years, with its share of total investments more than tripling from 13% in 2003 to 48% in 2017. In terms of sectors, greenfield FDI has been the more common mode of entry in manufacturing and primary sectors since

---

[10] ADB estimates; Financial Times. fDi Markets. https://www.fdimarkets.com (accessed 1 April 2019); and Bureau van Dijk. Zephyr M&A Database. https://www.bvdinfo.com (accessed 1 April 2019).

Figure 9.6: Top 10 Asian Foreign Direct Investment Recipients

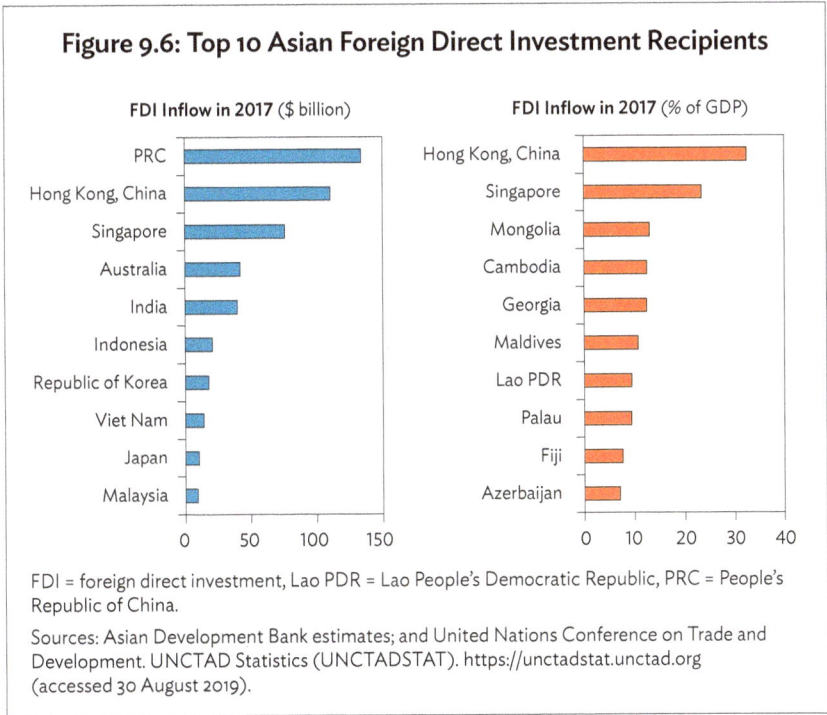

FDI Inflow in 2017 ($ billion)

FDI Inflow in 2017 (% of GDP)

FDI = foreign direct investment, Lao PDR = Lao People's Democratic Republic, PRC = People's Republic of China.

Sources: Asian Development Bank estimates; and United Nations Conference on Trade and Development. UNCTAD Statistics (UNCTADSTAT). https://unctadstat.unctad.org (accessed 30 August 2019).

the early 2000s, while mergers and acquisitions gradually became prominent in business and financial services as well as transportation and communications.

Traditionally, most FDI to Asia came from Japan and advanced countries in Europe and North America (Figure 9.7). In more recent years, however, emerging Asian economies, in particular Hong Kong, China; the PRC; the ROK; and Singapore, have rapidly become important sources of FDI to Asia. In fact, intraregional FDI currently accounts for more than 45% of developing Asia's FDI inflows.[11] In 2017, East Asia accounted for the largest share of intraregional FDI (receiving 56.1%), followed by Southeast Asia (27.2%). Closer trade linkages within the region are also backed by steadily growing intraregional FDI, particularly from Japan, the PRC, and the ROK to the rest of Asia—especially ASEAN. Many investments target local or regional markets. A fast-growing middle class and strong purchasing power makes the ASEAN market a favorite. Increasingly, goods and

---

[11] Fifty percent including Australia, Japan, and New Zealand.

Figure 9.7: Top Global Investors into Asia
($ billion)

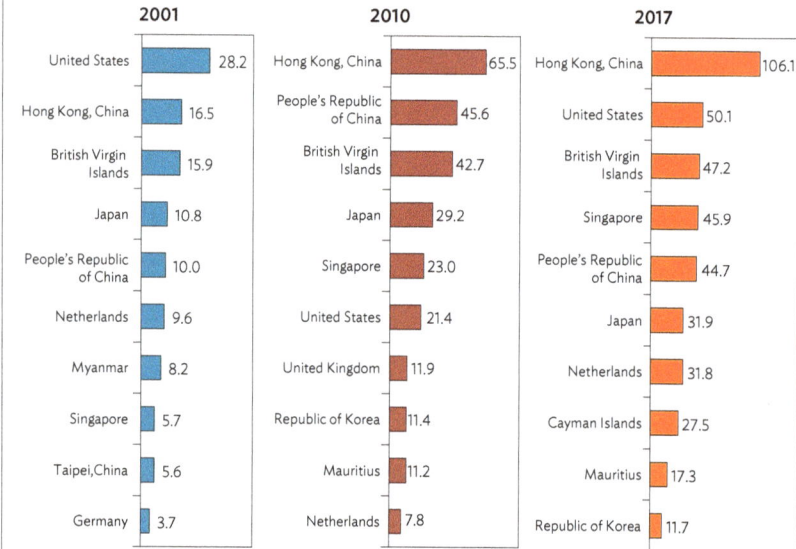

2001	
United States	28.2
Hong Kong, China	16.5
British Virgin Islands	15.9
Japan	10.8
People's Republic of China	10.0
Netherlands	9.6
Myanmar	8.2
Singapore	5.7
Taipei,China	5.6
Germany	3.7

2010	
Hong Kong, China	65.5
People's Republic of China	45.6
British Virgin Islands	42.7
Japan	29.2
Singapore	23.0
United States	21.4
United Kingdom	11.9
Republic of Korea	11.4
Mauritius	11.2
Netherlands	7.8

2017	
Hong Kong, China	106.1
United States	50.1
British Virgin Islands	47.2
Singapore	45.9
People's Republic of China	44.7
Japan	31.9
Netherlands	31.8
Cayman Islands	27.5
Mauritius	17.3
Republic of Korea	11.7

Source: Asian Development Bank, Asia Regional Integration Center. Integration Indicators. https://aric.adb.org/integrationindicators (accessed 30 August 2019).

products produced by firms of these investing countries are produced and marketed within ASEAN, instead of being imported to ASEAN.[12] This partly explains why Japan's share of total ASEAN trade is declining.

Hong Kong, China is now the largest investor in Asia, both globally and regionally. It accounted for around 18% of Asia's total FDI inflows in 2017, with greenfield investments mostly going to real estate, financial services, and hotels and tourism (Figure 9.7).[13] The US—currently the second-largest investor in Asia—used to be the top investor with a share of around 20% of Asia's total FDI inflows in 2001. It was overtaken by Hong Kong, China starting in 2008. By 2017, the US share of Asia's FDI inflows more than halved to less than 10%. Japan used to be a large FDI investor, especially after the substantial yen appreciation following the 1985 Plaza Accord. It invested heavily

---

[12] ADB. 2014. *Asian Economic Integration Monitor*. Manila.

[13] However, considering that a significant portion of Hong Kong, China-sourced FDI to the PRC are investments by the PRC residents round-tripping through Hong Kong, China, the FDI share of Hong Kong, China in Asia, excluding the PRC, drops to 3%.

in ASEAN, particularly Singapore and Thailand, as well as Australia in real estate, oil and natural gas, automotive industries, and electronics. Other key regional investors in Asia are the PRC and Singapore. The bulk of Singapore's FDI went to the ASEAN real estate sector. The PRC's FDI mostly went to East Asia and ASEAN in metals, petroleum, and plastics.

More recently, Asia also strengthened its presence as a major global outward FDI investor. Asian countries are accumulating more domestic savings, augmenting supply-chain networks, and becoming important producers of new business models and technologies.

Table 9.1: Top Global Investors
($ billion)

Economy	1970	Economy	1980	Economy	1990
United States	7.6	United States	19.2	Japan	50.8
United Kingdom	1.7	United Kingdom	7.9	France	38.3
Netherlands	1.3	Netherlands	4.8	United States	31.0
Germany	1.1	Germany	4.7	Germany	24.2
Canada	0.9	Canada	4.1	United Kingdom	17.9
France	0.4	France	3.1	Sweden	14.7
Japan	0.4	Japan	2.4	Netherlands	14.4
Sweden	0.2	South Africa	0.8	Italy	7.6
Belgium	0.2	Italy	0.7	Switzerland	7.2
Italy	0.1	Sweden	0.6	Belgium	6.3
Economy	**2001**	**Economy**	**2010**	**Economy**	**2017**
United States	124.9	United States	277.8	United States	300.4
Belgium	100.6	Germany	125.5	Japan	160.4
United Kingdom	57.2	Hong Kong, China	86.2	PRC	158.3
France	52.8			United Kingdom	117.5
Netherlands	50.6	Switzerland	86.2	Germany	91.8
Germany	39.9	PRC	68.8	Hong Kong, China	86.7
Japan	38.3	Netherlands	68.4		
Canada	36.0	Japan	56.3	Canada	79.8
Spain	33.1	British Virgin Islands	56.2	British Virgin Islands	54.7
British Virgin Islands	30.1	France	48.2	Singapore	43.7
		United Kingdom	48.1	France	41.3

PRC = People's Republic of China.

Source: United Nations Conference on Trade and Development. UNCTAD Statistics. https://unctadstat.unctad.org (accessed 30 August 2019).

The region's global FDI outflows increased from a mere $0.5 billion in 1970 to $540 billion in 2017, with its share of global FDI outflows growing from just 3% to 38%. Historically, Japan has been Asia's largest outward investor, and in 2017 was the second largest globally after the US (Table 9.1). Outward FDI by firms from developing Asia also grew rapidly in recent years. The PRC's outward investment has increased steadily since 2004, primarily going to Egypt, India, Indonesia, and the US—mostly in real estate; coal, oil, and gas; and metals. India's outward FDI grew in recent years—mostly in coal, oil, and gas; renewable energy; and rubber. Indonesia and Thailand also increased outward investments in areas such as food products, real estate, and retail within and outside Asia, including Europe.

Development impact of openness

Asia's outstanding growth in trade and FDI inflows had a significant impact on development in the region. Its experience provides strong empirical evidence that greater openness helps spur economic and productivity growth through gains from trade, learning effects, and the exploitation of economies of scale. In addition to a well-established positive relationship between trade openness and economic growth (Figure 9.4),[14] FDI inflows helped the region's countries grow by helping firms overcome growth constraints such as lack of management skills and access to finance.

There is also a large and growing body of empirical evidence that suggests greater openness helps reduce poverty in the region. As economic growth promotes overall poverty reduction, trade and FDI helped reduce poverty directly by generating employment and indirectly by enhancing overall economic development.

For a positive relationship between greater openness and development to materialize, Asia's experience appears to show it is critical that countries ensure other basic conditions are in place—such as the quality of human capital and infrastructure, the level of financial and institutional development, the quality of governance, and macroeconomic stability.

---

[14] Dollar, D. 1992. Outward-Oriented Developing Economies Really Do Grow More Rapidly: Evidence from 95 LDCs, 1976–1985. *Economic Development and Cultural Change.* 40 (3). pp. 523–544; Sachs, J. D., and A. Warner. 1995. Economic Reform and the Process of Global Integration. *Brookings Papers on Economic Activity, 25th Anniversary Issue.* 1 (January). pp. 1–18; and Edwards, S. 1998. Openness, Productivity and Growth: What Do We Really Know? *The Economic Journal.* 108 (447). pp. 383–398.

9.3 Evolution of trade and foreign direct investment policies in Asia

What allowed Asia to grow fast was in part the evolution of trade and FDI policies in the region. Policies did not change overnight. They changed gradually over the years (and sometimes decades). Experimentation often preceded changes in overarching policy frameworks. The changes were promoted by critical thinking, performance evaluation, pragmatism, and competition with neighbors. As mentioned in the introduction of this chapter, since the end of World War II, Asian economies generally have passed through three stages of international economic regimes: (i) post-independence self-reliance import substitution, (ii) outward orientation, and (iii) deepening GVCs and regional trade agreements. The development thinking and diverse country experiences are already discussed in Chapter 2. The following discussion focuses on the evolution of thinking and policy regimes regarding trade and FDI.

Import substitution

The first stage included import substitution industrialization policies. After many Asian countries gained political independence in the late 1940s and 1950s, the vast majority adopted a strategy of import substitution to create a domestic industrial base (Chapter 2). These policies were widely used in the 1950s and 1960s, and they persisted in several developing Asian economies in some form until the 1980s.

There was a nationalistic element in favoring these strategies. Before independence, many countries traded mostly bilaterally with their colonial powers, exporting commodities, raw materials, and some processed agricultural products in return for some manufactured consumer products and needed capital equipment. The sentiment following independence was to create self-reliance and develop a domestic industrial base to leave the past behind. There was also a socialist or communist idea, which emphasized state-led industrialization.

There was general pessimism about the high reliance on the export of primary goods in the 1950s, justified by the Prebisch–Singer hypothesis based on "center–periphery" or dependency theory, which argues long-run terms-of-trade deterioration of primary products (decreasing relative prices of agriculture and mining compared to industrial goods). As such, import substitution strategies were advocated to spur industrialization, reduce dependency on external inputs, develop local industries, save on scarce foreign exchange, and insulate the economy from adverse terms of trade.

Import substitution strategies and policies were marked by high and complicated tariffs and taxes on imports. Protection for infant industries was a fundamental tool in allowing local industry to develop. The widespread and discretionary use of prohibitions and quantitative restrictions on imports were adopted to secure domestic markets for industrialization. At the same time, authorities provided preferential, often duty-free, imports of the capital and intermediate goods needed to produce import-substituting goods domestically. The exchange rate was kept overvalued. To assuage nationalist sentiment and help control competitive interference, several monopolies on imports and exports were created—mostly state owned. In tandem, there were restrictions on FDI—whether on commodity extraction, agricultural processing, or manufacturing—and on foreign exchange transactions (under the Bretton Woods system of mostly pegged exchange rates). Hence, exports were discouraged including through overvalued exchange rates.

While the "infant industry protection" argument was taken as a theoretical rationale for import substitution strategies, those that adopted these policies—such as Latin American countries and India—were plagued by poor economic results.[15] Although the strategy was intended to reduce reliance on external inputs, countries still needed to import raw materials and capital equipment for domestic production. Meanwhile, trade protection, lack of competition in domestic and global markets, and artificially overvalued exchange rates made these economies inefficient. As a result, export receipts and foreign currency were rarely sufficient to purchase the imports the domestic economy needed.

This triggered periodic balance of payments crises in several countries, even in some with large commodity exports. Protectionism, combined with small-scale production due to limited domestic markets, left the economy's overall productivity low, with high unit costs and no pressure to upgrade technology or innovate.[16]

---

[15] Little, I., T. Scitovsky, and I. M. Scott. 1970. *Industry and Trade in Some Developing Countries: A Comparative Study*. London, New York, Toronto: Oxford University Press.

[16] McCawley, P. 2017. *Banking on the Future of Asia and the Pacific: 50 Years of the Asian Development Bank*. Manila: Asian Development Bank.

Protection of certain industries created incentives and opportunities for unproductive rent-seeking and corruption. All these factors made it apparent that, in the end, the import substitution strategy failed to spur either industrialization or rapid economic growth.

Outward-oriented policies

The trend toward import substitution was relatively short-lived across much of Asia compared with Latin America and other regions. From early on, Japan (which adopted restrictive import policies due to severe foreign exchange constraints during the recovery period after the war) and the NIEs moved away from import substitution toward outward-oriented and market-friendly policies. The apparent failure of import substitution strategies to achieve its goals in Latin America and some Asian countries provided the impetus for Asia's second evolutionary stage. Using the NIEs model, many developing economies in Asia began adopting outward-oriented policies. Several economies quickly saw that exports held an important advantage as a means of accelerating growth while bringing in needed foreign exchange.

Instruments used to promote exports included foreign exchange allocations for necessary inputs, subsidies, tax incentives, favorable access to credit, and the establishment of export-promotion agencies. Some countries maintained undervalued exchange rates to increase export competitiveness. These export-promotion policies aimed at shifting to a more viable path toward industrialization, which would be based on the access to large external markets, and earning sufficient foreign exchange to increase import of natural resources, capital goods, and intermediate inputs. As these policies contributed to increasing both exports and imports, they should be called "outward-oriented policies" rather than export-oriented policies.

These policies were particularly important for economies with small domestic markets, or those that lacked a natural resource base (aside from agriculture) and thus could not produce much without importing raw materials and technology. In some countries, the key element of these outward-oriented policies was "performance-based" selective support for firms and/or industries that were potentially competitive internationally.

It is worth highlighting the diversity in country experience. Although most economies in Asia (with the exception of Hong Kong, China) embraced import substitution strategies, the duration and strength of these policies differed from economy to economy. For instance, India and the Philippines had very strong and extensive import substitution policies between the 1950s and 1980s. By contrast, Taipei,China's import substitution policies were in place for less than a decade (in the 1950s), and they were fairly moderate compared with those in the Philippines. Mongolia, the PRC, Viet Nam, and the former Soviet economies in Central Asia initially undertook industrialization policies with strong inward orientation to achieve domestic production of not only consumer goods, but also capital goods and industrial materials.

Export orientation also involved different starting points and speeds, with some developing Asian economies approaching the reform process cautiously. The ROK; Singapore; and Taipei,China tilted toward outward-oriented policies in the 1960s. By the 1970s and 1980s, the larger ASEAN members began emulating the export-led model to achieve rapid growth and industrialization.

In South Asia, India embarked on market-oriented reforms with trade liberalization in 1991. Sri Lanka's trade policies vacillated between open and restrictive from the time it gained independence until 1997, when restrictions were abandoned. In Central Asia, reforms began in the early 1990s after the dissolution of the Soviet Union and abandonment of centrally planned economies.

The policy mix adopted during the transition also differed, but in many countries, export-promotion policies were adopted while maintaining import substitution policies in some sectors. The shift toward export promotion did not mean the immediate dismantling of import protection. In East Asia and Southeast Asia, while tariff barriers remained in place for the economy in general, exporters were given access to inputs and capital goods at world market prices. Similarly, India's reforms initially focused on liberalizing capital inputs for industrial expansion with a more regulated approach to importing consumer goods.

SEZs were an important part of outward-oriented policies in Southeast Asia and the PRC. They are specifically designed to promote commercial export products (Box 9.1). These SEZs, insulated from the rest of the economy, allowed authorities to test whether their export-led strategies—based on incentives and a liberal regulatory environment—could work.

Box 9.1: Asia's Experiment with Special Economic Zones

A special economic zone (SEZ) is a geographic area within a country's national boundaries where taxation, regulations regarding investment and labor, and other rules and laws are more preferential to businesses than those in the rest of the country. SEZs are often used for attracting companies that import input from abroad, assemble products, and then export them to other countries.

The very first SEZ was established in New York in 1937 with the passing of the Free Trade Zone Act by the United States Congress in 1934. Puerto Rico was the second (in 1942) in an effort to industrialize the territory by luring in United States firms. A steady trickle of new zones appeared beginning in 1959 with the Shannon Free Zone in Ireland and others mostly in Western Europe amid the industrial revival after World War II. In the developing world, India was arguably the first, creating a processing zone at Kandla Port in 1965. Taipei,China's Kaohsiung Harbor was set up in 1966.

In Asia, SEZs began as a means to test new trade and foreign direct investment (FDI) policies in isolation from the general economy. In some cases, over time they became a major engine for national development through backward and forward linkages that accelerated national structural transformation. Several success stories demonstrate the effective use of SEZs as policy tools to increase employment and exports, attract FDI, and accelerate economic growth. SEZs are often supported by factors such as skills upgrading, access to infrastructure, and favorable location, among others.

The Republic of Korea and Taipei,China began using SEZs in the 1960s to drive economic development, transitioning from labor-intensive to skill- and technology-intensive production over time. The People's Republic of China officially launched SEZs in 1980 in Shenzhen, Xiamen, Shantou, and Zhuhai. By 2007, SEZs (including all types of industrial parks and zones) in the People's Republic of China accounted for about 22% of gross domestic product, 46% of FDI, 60% of exports, and generated more than 30 million jobs. Malaysia, Singapore, Thailand, and Viet Nam also succeeded in developing automobile and electronics industries through SEZs.

Source: Asian Development Bank. 2015. *Asian Economic Integration Report 2015*. Manila.

Beginning in the 1980s, more and more developing countries began embarking on reforms that both promoted exports and reduced barriers to imports. In several countries, balance of payments vulnerabilities led to large stabilization and adjustment programs, funded primarily by the International Monetary Fund (IMF) and the World Bank. These also played a role in liberalizing trade regimes. Unilateral reforms were undertaken, many based on the objective to join the General Agreement on Tariffs and Trade (GATT)—and accession to the WTO, which was founded in 1995.

In addition to broader trade liberalization, developing countries also began embracing policies that improved the investment climate to attract FDI and multinational corporations (MNCs). As with trade, most Asian economies initially pursued highly restrictive policies toward FDI. While several countries with large, valuable resource-based industries—Indonesia, for example—developed joint ventures and production-sharing contracts as early as the late 1960s and 1970s, it was outward-oriented trade reforms that paved the way for the eventual easing of FDI restrictions.

Hong Kong, China and the ASEAN4—Indonesia, Malaysia, the Philippines, and Thailand—were the first Asian economies to begin liberalizing FDI, initially in a bid to attract foreign investment from Japan. But it was the 1985 Plaza Accord that played a huge role in accelerating the process.[17] The sharp appreciation of the yen induced massive flows of Japanese outward investment, especially into Asian economies. The NIEs and the ASEAN4 responded by liberalizing their FDI regimes.[18] Restrictions on FDI continued to decline as competition for investments increased and regional production networks began to blossom throughout the region.

Investment incentives eventually became standard in most Asian economies, coming in four types: (i) fiscal (such as tax holidays and reduced corporate tax rates), (ii) financial (preferential credit

[17] The Plaza Accord was an agreement between France, Germany, Japan, the US, and the United Kingdom to intervene in exchange rates by depreciating the US dollar relative to the Japanese yen and German deutsche mark. Its purpose was to correct trade imbalances between the US and Japan (and between the US and Germany). While it did not affect the Japan–US trade imbalance much, the sharp yen appreciation did induce large flows of new outward investment.

[18] Chia, S. Y. 2010. Trade and Investment Policies and Regional Economic Integration in East Asia. *ADBI Working Paper Series*. No. 210. Tokyo: Asian Development Bank Institute; and McCawley, P. 2017. *Banking on the Future of Asia and the Pacific: 50 Years of the Asian Development Bank*. Manila: Asian Development Bank.

and loan guarantees, among others), (iii) regulatory (exemptions from certain laws or regulations), or (iv) technical/business support. Over time, more developing countries began pursuing a much broader reform agenda aimed at reforming the overall investment climate. FDI spurred further economic growth through capital accumulation, and the incorporation of new inputs and foreign technologies in the production process.

9.4 Emergence of global value chains

The surge of FDI inflows in Asia enabled Asian trade to transform from interindustry trade to intra-industry trade. Accordingly, most Asian economies entered GVCs. This was the third evolutionary stage of Asia's international economic policy regime. It also underpinned the growing connectivity and economic interdependence within the region.

GVCs were driven by a steady decline in cross-border transportation costs due to liberalized trade, and advances in transport and logistics—including containerization and improvements in the design of large container vessels, a virtual revolution in air transport, and modern communication technologies. Enhanced infrastructure connectivity allowed the seamless flow of intermediate goods trade (Figure 9.8). These helped create increasingly complex, yet cost-effective, production networks. Also, expanding economies of scale and scope in mass production as well as rapid progress in standardized processes—spurred by "compartmentalization and modularization" of production flows—prompted the pervasion of GVCs globally. Homogenization of consumer tastes borne out of an ever-expanding middle class also promoted GVCs.

The GVCs that formed in the wake of the "second unbundling"[19] offered opportunities for early movers to consolidate supplier relationships within the value chain. According to Richard Baldwin, the steam revolution drove a "first unbundling," as railroads and steamships enabled the spatial separation of production and consumption. Since the 1990s, the information and communication technology revolution has fostered a geographical dispersion of production stages through the "second unbundling." In the second unbundling, modularization of production in GVCs helped divide the production process into stages that could take place in

---

[19] Baldwin, R. 2016. The Great Convergence: *Information Technology and the New Globalization*. Cambridge, MA: Belknap Press of Harvard University Press.

Figure 9.8: Share of Asia's Intermediate Goods Trade (%)

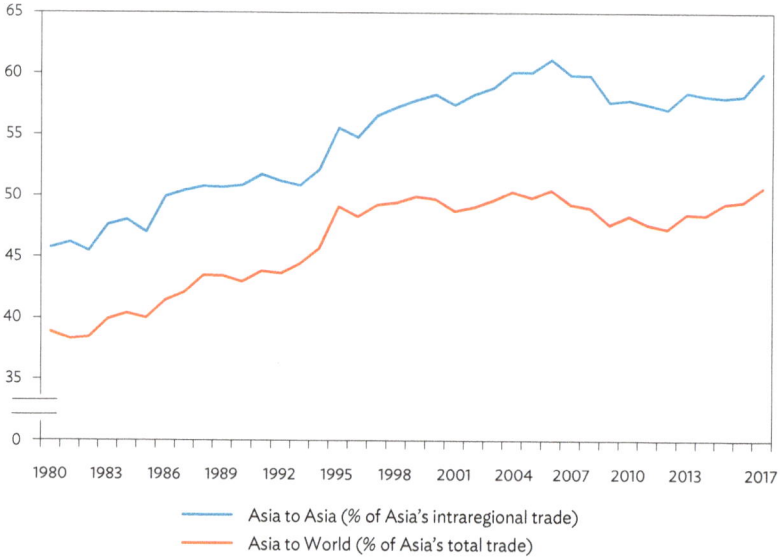

Asia to Asia (% of Asia's intraregional trade)
Asia to World (% of Asia's total trade)

Notes: Asia includes Afghanistan; Australia; Bangladesh; Bhutan; Brunei Darussalam; Cambodia; the Cook Islands; Fiji; Hong Kong, China; India; Indonesia; Japan; Kiribati; the Lao People's Democratic Republic; Malaysia; Maldives; Mongolia; Myanmar; Nauru; Nepal; New Zealand; Pakistan; Papua New Guinea; the People's Republic of China; the Philippines; the Republic of Korea; Samoa; Singapore; Solomon Islands; Sri Lanka; Taipei,China; Thailand; Timor-Leste; Tonga; Tuvalu; Vanuatu; and Viet Nam. Concordance between Standard International Trade Classification (SITC) revision 2 and Broad Economic Categories was used to define intermediate goods. Trade refers to the sum of exports and imports.

Sources: Asian Development Bank estimates; and Growth Lab at Harvard University. Atlas of Economic Complexity Database. http://atlas.cid.harvard.edu/about-data/goods-data (accessed 30 August 2019).

different locations. Meanwhile, the "third unbundling" refers to the geographical separation between labor and labor services enabled by digital technologies for "telepresence" and "telerobotics." According to Baldwin, for the first time, globalization will mostly affect the services sector. The third unbundling can also include manufacturing GVC, through the combination of internet and robotics. For example, "Japanese engineers could repair Japanese-made capital equipment in South Africa by controlling sophisticated robots from Tokyo."

GVC progress in Asia and around the globe went hand in hand with the increased capacity of MNCs to manage production, sourcing, product integration, and logistics across multiple locations.[20] MNCs had two main, possibly overlapping, market motivations. First, MNCs relocated parts of the production process where costs were lower for reexporting intermediate and/or final goods—either to their home countries (vertical FDI) or third countries (export-platform FDI). Second, they set up affiliates in a foreign country to serve the domestic market as a substitute for exports (horizontal or market-seeking FDI), replicating the production process to avoid trade costs. In either case, MNCs played a key role in transferring frontier technologies and new business models which, in turn, promoted further GVC development (Chapter 5).

Evolving patterns of a particular economy's participation in GVCs are also apparent in the transformation from the "flying geese" model of dynamic interindustry trade to Asia's more complex intra-industry trade (Box 9.2). Today, the shape of Asian economic trade relations is more like networks than flying geese.

In Asia, in terms of sectors, manufacturing attracts those MNCs engaged in GVCs: almost 70% of affiliates belonging to foreign manufacturer parents engage in international trade. The semiconductor and related device manufacturing sector attracts the most GVC–FDI in Asia as a share of affiliates (Table 9.2). GVC expansion continues to benefit from the very low average tariffs applied across industry sectors using WTO most-favored nation rates—as well as preferential tariff rates under various regional and bilateral free trade agreements (FTAs).

How fast GVCs expand depends on how open markets become. Before a final product or service is shipped, intermediate goods, as well as services, cross borders multiple times. While GVCs offer substantive efficiency gains, they cannot thrive without open markets. Rising trade barriers due to intense trade tensions could cause material harm to the global production networks, undermining production efficiency and economic gains for GVC-participating countries.

---

[20] WTO. 2008. Trade, the Location of Production and the Industrial Organization of Firms. *World Trade Report 2008*. Geneva; and Hummels, D. 2007. Transportation Costs and International Trade in the Second Era of Globalization. *Journal of Economic Perspectives*. 21 (3). pp. 131–154.

Box 9.2: From Flying Geese to Global Value Chains

Over the past 50 years, many believed Asia's development pattern evolved—and continues to evolve—from the so-called "flying geese" model that became popular in the 1960s.[a] The model proposes that certain industries and production centers will shift from a front-runner—in Asia's case, Japan—to others that have the early economic, financial, and industrial wherewithal to attract new industries and engage in higher value-added trade. It is an encompassing view of technological convergence, trade, and foreign direct investment in a way that dynamically creates new comparative advantage. The common example is Asia's "four tigers"—Hong Kong, China; the Republic of Korea; Singapore; and Taipei,China—also known as Asia's newly industrialized economies. The flock grows as technology advances and spreads.[b]

The original flying geese analogy came from Akamatsu's study of a sequential development pattern, mostly among today's developed countries. He developed his idea as early as 1935 and wrote an English-language paper in 1961. According to his study, increasing imports lead to new domestic production, which, over time, naturally leads to export promotion. This sequence thus moves beyond the process of import substitution—where "infant" industries are given protection—and, ultimately, leading to export-led growth.

Akamatsu's second flying geese pattern includes a sequence of structural changes on how industries develop. It starts with the production of consumer goods evolving into capital goods, and it also involves a progression from basic and simple labor-intensive goods to more complex and refined capital-intensive products.

The third flying geese analogy refers to the continuous relocation of industries from developed to developing countries. By trading with and attracting investment from the former, the latter can upgrade industries continuously. During this catching-up process of industrial production, less-developed economies can absorb knowledge and technology, which reinforces the catching-up process further.

While the flying geese model is powerful, especially in explaining the dynamic pattern of interindustry trade in Asia, the region began engaging in more intra-industry trade. Over the past decades, the intercountry development model has become more complex and dynamic, as regional and global value chains proliferated, with different economies sharing parts of production processes.

[a] Akamatsu, K. 1961. A Theory of Unbalanced Growth in the World Economy. *Weltwirtschaftliches Archiv.* 86 (January). pp. 196–217.

[b] Kojima, K. 2000. The "Flying Geese" Model of Asian Economic Development: Origin, Theoretical Extensions, and Regional Policy Implications. *Journal of Asian Economics.* 11 (4). pp. 375–401.

Source: Vandana, C., J. Yifu Lin, and Y. Wang. 2013. Leading Dragon Phenomenon: New Opportunities for Catch-Up in Low-Income Countries. *Asian Development Review.* 30 (1). pp. 52–84.

Table 9.2: Top Manufacturing Sectors of Foreign Affiliates Engaging in Trade in Asia, 2015

Affiliated Industry	Number of Affiliates	Number of Affiliates That Export and Import	Share of Affiliates That Export and Import (%)
Semiconductor and related device manufacturing	1,275	694	54.4
Bare printed circuit board manufacturing	819	360	44.0
Other electronic component manufacturing	3,423	1,358	39.7
Motor and generator manufacturing	960	354	36.9
Ethyl alcohol manufacturing	1,302	477	36.6
Nonferrous metal (except copper and aluminum) rolling, drawing, and extruding	806	286	35.5
Motor vehicle brake system manufacturing	5,760	1,925	33.4
Motor vehicle air-conditioning manufacturing	858	270	31.5
Plastics material and resin manufacturing	1,487	465	31.3
Textile bag mills	924	275	29.8

Source: Asian Development Bank (ADB) estimates based on data from ADB. 2016. *Asian Economic Integration Report 2016: What Drives Foreign Direct Investment in Asia and the Pacific?* Manila.

9.5 Growing importance of services trade

All Asian economies have undergone a marked structural transformation over the past 50 years. While the pace of structural transformation varied across countries, there was a clear shift toward manufacturing and, more recently, toward services. The services sector contributes about 60% of the region's economic activity and employs almost half its labor force (Chapter 3).

Figure 9.9: Growth in Asia's Exports of Goods, Services, and Travel, 2005–2017

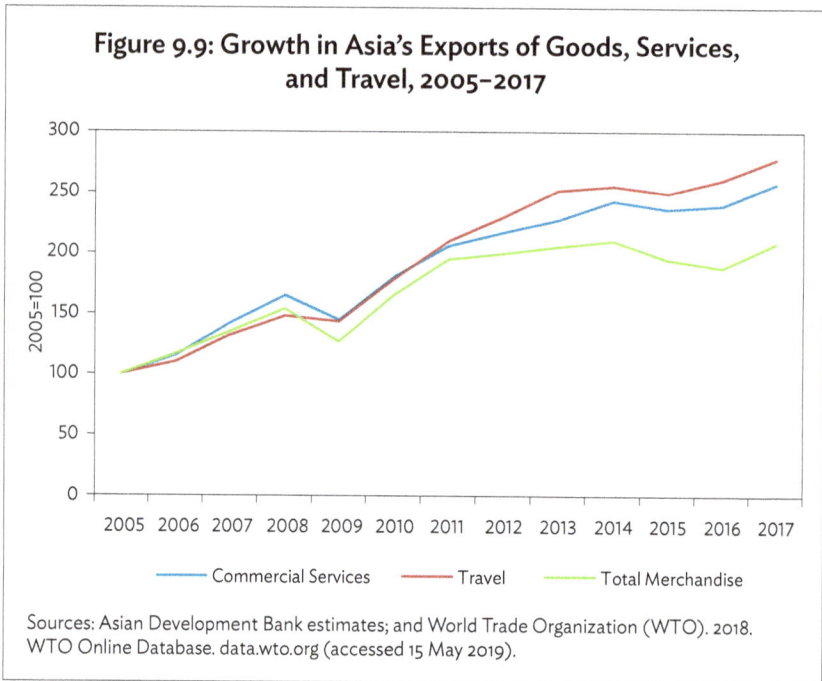

Sources: Asian Development Bank estimates; and World Trade Organization (WTO). 2018. WTO Online Database. data.wto.org (accessed 15 May 2019).

More recently, services are increasingly traded as a part of GVCs. The share of services involved in manufacturing value added in Asia varies across countries. Regionally, it has reached 43%.[21] While this share remains below the Organisation for Economic Co-operation and Development average, increasingly more complex tasks, such as research and development, are contracted to outside providers from manufacturers (Chapter 3). Indeed, more services enter the manufacturing process as intermediate inputs. For example, automobile companies increasingly outsource engineering services, logistics, and back-office operations to third-party providers. And as production is organized in regional and global value chains, services are increasingly traded. Exports of commercial services amounted to $515 billion in 2005 and more than doubled to $1,325 billion in 2017— despite the impact of the 2008–2009 global financial crisis (Figure 9.9). Continued regional integration in Asia, combined with advances in

---

[21] Mercer-Blackman, V., and C. Ablaza. 2019. The Servicification of Manufacturing in Asia — A Conceptual Framework. In Helble, M., and B. Shepherd, eds. *Leveraging Services for Development: Prospects and Policies*. Tokyo: Asian Development Bank Institute.

technology such as the introduction of 5G networks, will further help expand trade in services within GVCs and offer new opportunities.

Despite this strong growth, services remain a relatively small fraction of total trade. In 2017, Asia's services export share was just 17.2% of total exports. One of the WTO's priorities when it was created in 1995 was liberalizing services trade. However, little progress has been made since then. In contrast, an increasing number of Asian FTAs cover services, but further opening is needed to fully reap the benefits of increased services trade.

9.6 Global and regional trade arrangements

GATT became effective in 1948 as an international legal agreement to reduce tariff and other trade barriers substantially. Over the following decades, many Asian countries became members of GATT and its succeeding organization, WTO (established in 1995), embracing the global trade liberalization regime (Figure 9.10). The Uruguay Round Agreements Act in 1994 set a new stage for Asia's trade and investment policies. In accordance with the GATT and WTO rules governing tariffs, local content requirements for exports, and discriminative direct trade support including export subsidies, Asian policies shifted over time to more market-friendly support such as for research and development.

As globalization expanded in the 1990s, Asian economies became actively involved in a variety of regional trade arrangements. Broadly speaking, preferential trade arrangements (PTAs), such as free trade agreements (FTAs), have been used to strengthen cooperation in facilitating trade and investment. FTAs cover broad areas that serve as engines of trade creation, allowing them to function as "building blocks" rather than "stumbling blocks." They could also continue to progress toward multilateralization.

The first wave of Asian FTAs that surged in the 1990s was mostly traditional. They largely emphasized trade in goods and focused on tariffs and other border measures that directly affected market access (Figure 9.11). The continued reduction of trade barriers in some parts of Asia through the GATT/WTO and FTAs—especially since the PRC joined the WTO in 2001—made East Asia and Southeast Asia, in particular, even more appealing to foreign investment.

Under the WTO framework, the Doha Round, which started in 2001, has not yet concluded. Given the slow progress in multilateral trade liberalization, Asia has shifted its focus more on FTAs. Asian

Figure 9.10: Asia's World Trade Organization Accessions

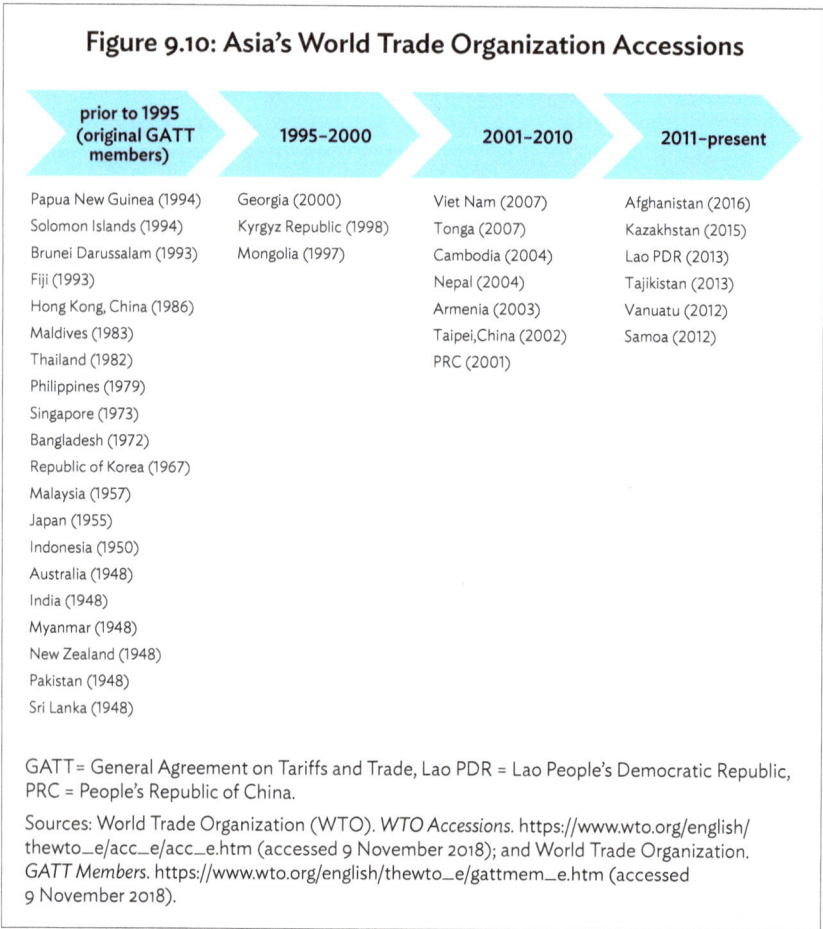

prior to 1995 (original GATT members)	1995–2000	2001–2010	2011–present
Papua New Guinea (1994)	Georgia (2000)	Viet Nam (2007)	Afghanistan (2016)
Solomon Islands (1994)	Kyrgyz Republic (1998)	Tonga (2007)	Kazakhstan (2015)
Brunei Darussalam (1993)	Mongolia (1997)	Cambodia (2004)	Lao PDR (2013)
Fiji (1993)		Nepal (2004)	Tajikistan (2013)
Hong Kong, China (1986)		Armenia (2003)	Vanuatu (2012)
Maldives (1983)		Taipei,China (2002)	Samoa (2012)
Thailand (1982)		PRC (2001)	
Philippines (1979)			
Singapore (1973)			
Bangladesh (1972)			
Republic of Korea (1967)			
Malaysia (1957)			
Japan (1955)			
Indonesia (1950)			
Australia (1948)			
India (1948)			
Myanmar (1948)			
New Zealand (1948)			
Pakistan (1948)			
Sri Lanka (1948)			

GATT = General Agreement on Tariffs and Trade, Lao PDR = Lao People's Democratic Republic, PRC = People's Republic of China.

Sources: World Trade Organization (WTO). *WTO Accessions*. https://www.wto.org/english/thewto_e/acc_e/acc_e.htm (accessed 9 November 2018); and World Trade Organization. *GATT Members*. https://www.wto.org/english/thewto_e/gattmem_e.htm (accessed 9 November 2018).

economies actively embraced bilateral FTAs, leading to a proliferation of bilateral agreements within the region and with the rest of the world—a domino effect.[22] These new bilateral FTAs cover a broader range of liberalization (Figure 9.11).

By 2018, the number of Asian FTAs (signed and in effect) reached 151, of which 70 are intra-Asia FTAs and 81 with economies from outside the region. The multitude of FTAs has helped spur further economic liberalization as well as domestic structural reforms across the region. Sometimes, they created a proliferation of rules (such as

---

[22] Baldwin, R. 1993. A Domino Theory of Regionalism. *NBER Working Paper Series*. No. w4465. Cambridge, MA: National Bureau of Economic Research.

Figure 9.11: Content of Free Trade Agreements in Asia, 1992–2015

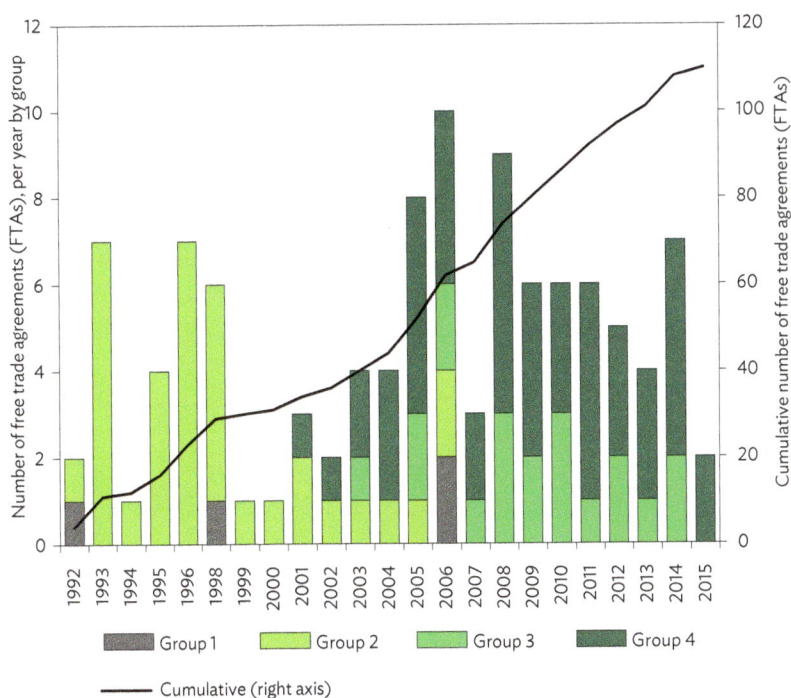

Group 1 = FTAs that only have border policies.
Group 2 = FTAs with less than five border policies and less than five behind-the-border policies.
Group 3 = FTAs with five or more border policies and less than five behind-the-border policies.
Group 4 = FTAs with five or more border policies and five or more behind-the-border policies.

Notes:
1. **Border policies** cover tariff reductions in manufacturing and agriculture, anti-dumping, countervailing measures, Agreement on Trade-Related Investment Measures, Agreement on Trade-Related Aspects of Intellectual Property Rights, customs, export taxes, sanitary and phytosanitary measures, technical barriers to trade, and the movement of capital.
2. **Behind-the-border policies** cover state enterprises, state aid, competition policy, intellectual property rights, investment, public procurement, and the General Agreement on Trade in Services.
3. The categorization of border and behind-the-border policies is based on the methodology of Hofmann, C., A. Osnago, and M. Ruta. 2017. Horizontal Depth: A New Database on the Content of Preferential Trade Agreements. *Policy Research Working Paper*. No. WPS 7981. Washington, DC: World Bank.

Source: World Bank. Content of Deep Trade Agreements. https://datacatalog.worldbank.org/dataset/content-deep-trade-agreements (accessed 4 June 2019).

technical standards and rules of origin) that companies must comply with, which is called the "noodle bowl" effect.

Asia is also intensifying efforts on trade facilitation, by incorporating provisions on customs clearance and technical regulations (including sanitary and phytosanitary measures) into FTAs. National single window systems have been widely adopted in the region to simplify administrative procedures and reduce trade costs for businesses, sometimes working with the World Customs Organization (WCO). The evolution into a subregional single window system as an integrated online platform is making good progress in ASEAN.

Asia is working toward more regional and super-regional arrangements. ASEAN countries launched the ASEAN Free Trade Agreement in 1992, the ASEAN Free Trade Area in 2003, and the ASEAN Economic Community in 2015 by gradually expanding coverage to include lowering barriers to services trade, reducing nontariff barriers, and harmonizing standards (Chapter 15).

Following the US withdrawal from the Trans-Pacific Partnership (TPP), the remaining 11 TPP members signed the Comprehensive and Progressive Agreement for Trans-Pacific Partnership (CPTPP) on 8 March 2018 in Chile. The CPTPP entered into force on 30 December 2018. Another "mega" trade deal, the Regional Comprehensive Economic Partnership (RCEP), remains under negotiation. The RCEP would cover the 10 ASEAN members and the 6 economies[23] with existing FTAs with ASEAN. If finalized, the RCEP will be the largest FTA in the world, covering 30% of global GDP and more than 3.5 billion people.

9.7 Looking ahead

Overall, by adopting market-oriented trade and investment policies, governments in the region encouraged firms to adjust to domestic and international market movements. Whether Asia will continue to reap the benefits of globalization depends on several future developments.

First, governments should continue to promote open trade and investment. Although nontariff measures, such as different rules and standards, can be justified with public policy objectives (for example, protecting public health and the environment), they may have potentially harmful effects on trade flows and undermine economic

---

[23] Australia, India, Japan, New Zealand, the PRC, and the ROK.

efficiency. Governments should work toward lowering nontariff measures, harmonizing standards, and applying mutual recognition.

Second, further opening services trade can help improve the efficiency of service providers, enhance technological spillovers, and increase the competitiveness of the entire economy. As Asian economies increasingly rely on services, governments must think about how to incorporate them into their trade and growth strategies.

Third, governments need to continue helping small and medium-sized enterprises access international markets by improving regulations, easing access to finance, and supporting capacity building, among others. While small and medium-sized enterprises play a crucial role in economic growth and employment, their access to international trade and integration into global production networks remain below potential.

Fourth, governments must keep abreast with rapidly changing technologies and the Fourth Industrial Revolution—which is fundamentally changing how goods and services are produced, traded, and consumed, including through e-commerce and digital trade.

Finally, Asia's governments should renew efforts to support the multilateral trading system. Under the growing challenges to existing global trade governance frameworks, concerted efforts by the international community to uphold the rules-based, multilateral system have become even more imperative.

CHAPTER 10

PURSUING MACROECONOMIC STABILITY

10.1 Introduction

Good macroeconomic management—using fiscal, monetary, exchange rate, and other policies to promote macroeconomic stability—is critical for development. Stable growth and low inflation make it easier for households and businesses to make consumer and investment decisions, which are the key drivers of economic growth.

Sustainable public finance allows governments to focus on critical areas such as health, education, and infrastructure, and thus provide necessary public goods and address market failures. Fair and broad tax systems are an important part of fiscal policies, as they finance expenditures and redistribute income and assets. In addition, maintaining economic stability and creating jobs contribute directly to reducing poverty (Chapter 11).

This chapter chronicles macroeconomic management in developing Asia over the past half century. Section 10.2 takes a bird's-eye view of macroeconomic performance, showing that developing Asia managed better than other developing regions over the past 50 years. The region had higher average growth, less volatility, lower average inflation, and fewer economic crises. Section 10.3 examines the conduct of fiscal, monetary, and exchange rate policies in developing Asia to see how they contributed to the region's good macroeconomic performance.

Sections 10.4–10.6 then describe macroeconomic management throughout the decades, particularly during and after crises. It examines the various shocks that affected the region and how policy makers responded. The most important to developing Asia was the 1997–1998 Asian financial crisis (AFC), which served as a wake-up call for policy makers and shaped the conduct of macroeconomic policy in the years that followed. Those changes helped Asian economies weather the 2008–2009 global financial crisis (GFC) relatively well. Section 10.7 ends the chapter with a look forward to the macroeconomic challenges facing developing Asia.

10.2 Macroeconomic performance in the past 5 decades

When viewed from several dimensions, developing Asia's macroeconomic performance was generally strong over the past 50 years. It is well-known that Asia has grown faster and had lower unemployment than other developing regions over the period (Figure 10.1). Growth has averaged close to 9% in the People's Republic of China (PRC) since the 1970s; 7% in the newly industrialized economies (NIEs) of Hong Kong, China; the Republic of Korea (ROK); Singapore; and Taipei,China; and about 6% in India and in five Association of Southeast Asian Nations (ASEAN) members (Indonesia, Malaysia, the Philippines, Thailand, and Viet Nam), or ASEAN5. These are all higher than the average growth in Latin America (3.2%) and Sub-Saharan Africa (3.3%).

The difference in growth rates created a significant divergence in economic outcomes. If a country grows by 9% a year, it can double its gross domestic product (GDP) every 8 years. If growth is 3%, GDP doubles only every 24 years. Developing Asia also had comparatively lower unemployment rates, which resulted from and contributed to its more rapid expansion. In contrast, Latin American countries frequently experienced double-digit unemployment rates.

Spanning the decades, there is a clear acceleration in growth of the region's two giants, the PRC and India. Surprisingly, despite bearing the brunt of the AFC, average growth in the 1990s among ASEAN5 remained strong due to the rapid GDP expansion prior to the crisis. The NIEs had spectacular growth in the 1970s and 1980s, and then gradually slowed, reflecting their success in achieving high-income status.

Figure 10.1: Average Growth Rates and Unemployment by Decade, 1970–2018

Figure 10.1a: Average Growth (%), 1970–2018

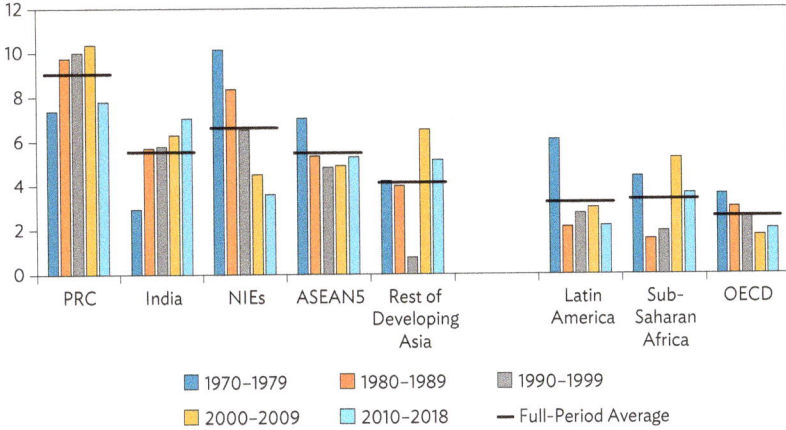

■ 1970–1979   ■ 1980–1989   ■ 1990–1999
■ 2000–2009   ■ 2010–2018   — Full-Period Average

Figure 10.1b: Unemployment (%), 1970–2018

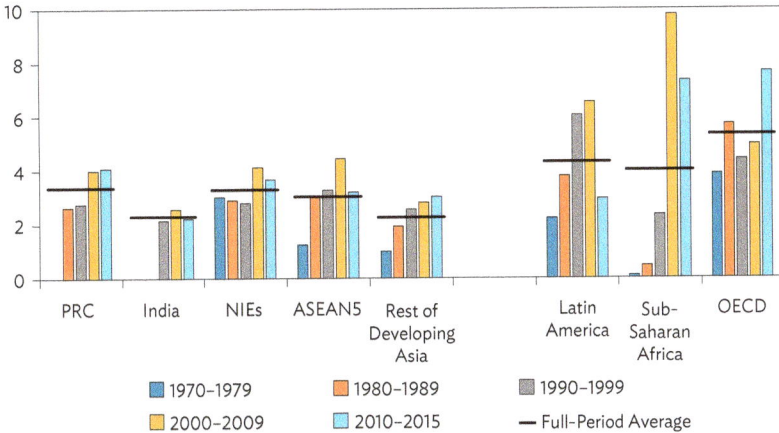

■ 1970–1979   ■ 1980–1989   ■ 1990–1999
■ 2000–2009   ■ 2010–2015   — Full-Period Average

ASEAN = Association of Southeast Asian Nations, NIEs = newly industrialized economies, OECD = Organisation for Economic Co-operation and Development, PRC = People's Republic of China.

Notes: The NIEs comprise Hong Kong, China; the Republic of Korea; Singapore; and Taipei,China. ASEAN5 comprises Indonesia, Malaysia, the Philippines, Thailand, and Viet Nam. Rest of Developing Asia refers to all Asian Development Bank developing member economies excluding the PRC, India, the NIEs, and ASEAN5.

Sources: Asian Development Bank. Key Indicators Database. https://kidb.adb.org/kidb/ (accessed 2 August 2019); and World Bank. World Development Indicators. https://databank .worldbank.org/source/world-development-indicators (accessed 2 August 2019).

Much of developing Asia was able to achieve this high average growth with substantially lower volatility than other developing regions. One measure of volatility, the coefficient of variation (standard deviation divided by the mean) of GDP growth over the past 50 years was lower in the PRC, India, the NIEs, and ASEAN5 (all had coefficients of variation between 0.34 and 0.53) than Latin America (0.78) and Sub-Saharan Africa (0.77). Low volatility and high economic growth have gone hand in hand across the region. And lower economic uncertainty provides an environment conducive for private enterprises and entrepreneurs to invest and innovate, leading to high and sustainable rates of economic growth.

Developing Asia also managed to keep inflation relatively low (Figure 10.2). The average inflation rate in the PRC and India and weighted-average inflation rates in the NIEs, ASEAN5, and the rest

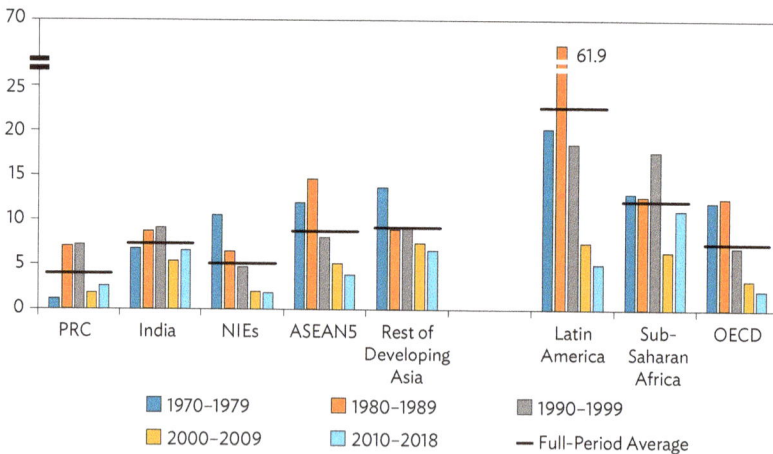

Figure 10.2: Inflation by Decade, 1970–2018
(%)

ASEAN = Association of Southeast Asian Nations, NIEs = newly industrialized economies, OECD = Organisation for Economic Co-operation and Development, PRC = People's Republic of China.

Notes: The NIEs comprise Hong Kong, China; the Republic of Korea; Singapore; and Taipei,China. ASEAN5 comprises Indonesia, Malaysia, the Philippines, Thailand, and Viet Nam. Rest of Developing Asia refers to all Asian Development Bank developing member economies excluding the PRC, India, the NIEs, and ASEAN5.

Sources: International Monetary Fund. World Economic Outlook Database. https://www.imf. org/external/pubs/ft/weo/2019/01/weodata/index.aspx (accessed 27 August 2019); and Asian Development Bank estimates.

of developing Asia were in the single digits during the past 50 years, ranging from 4% in the PRC to 9% in ASEAN5 and the rest of developing Asia. By contrast, weighted average inflation in Latin America was about 23%, due to hyperinflation episodes in some countries in the 1980s. It averaged close to 12% in Sub-Saharan Africa. Developing Asia has kept average inflation in the low single digits over the past 2 decades.

The region also managed to have fewer economic crises. Figure 10.3 plots the relative frequency of different types of crises (banking crises, currency crashes, currency conversion/debasement, defaults on external debt, defaults on domestic debt, and high inflation episodes). For the global sample, there was a rise in crisis frequency from the early 1980s, and the frequency remained high through mid-1995 before beginning to slowly decline. It spiked again with the GFC beginning in 2008, then fell back.

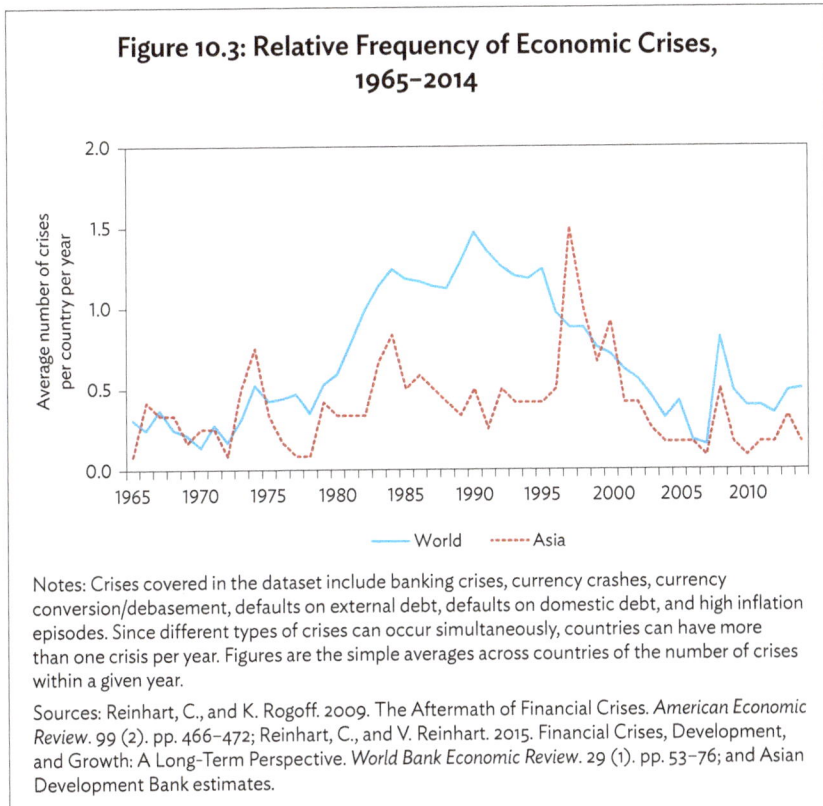

Figure 10.3: Relative Frequency of Economic Crises, 1965–2014

Notes: Crises covered in the dataset include banking crises, currency crashes, currency conversion/debasement, defaults on external debt, defaults on domestic debt, and high inflation episodes. Since different types of crises can occur simultaneously, countries can have more than one crisis per year. Figures are the simple averages across countries of the number of crises within a given year.

Sources: Reinhart, C., and K. Rogoff. 2009. The Aftermath of Financial Crises. *American Economic Review*. 99 (2). pp. 466–472; Reinhart, C., and V. Reinhart. 2015. Financial Crises, Development, and Growth: A Long-Term Perspective. *World Bank Economic Review*. 29 (1). pp. 53–76; and Asian Development Bank estimates.

10.3 The evolution of fiscal, monetary, and exchange rate policies

Good fundamentals—including the region's high savings rates, early diversification, and pursuit of greater education and regional economic integration through trade and investment—contributed to macroeconomic stability. But good macroeconomic policymaking has undoubtedly played an important role. Overall, Asia's developing economies pursued prudent fiscal policy and sound monetary management. They adopted more flexible exchange rates after the AFC. This allowed them to weather the GFC relatively well. Today, as financial markets are more liberalized, governments are more responsive to market signals such as interest rates in government bond markets (which rise when bond values drop, reflecting an economy's creditworthiness) and exchange rates (which can depreciate on market concerns, including a country's balance of payments position).

The importance of fiscal prudence

Fiscal prudence has been an important aspect of the region's relative macroeconomic stability (Figure 10.4). Many economies in the region have maintained public debt below 50% of GDP throughout the past 5 decades. Average public debt was 16% of GDP in the PRC, 29% in the NIEs, and 39% in ASEAN5. By contrast, public debt was close to or above the critical 50% threshold for Latin America and Sub-Saharan Africa following the sharp rise in debt in both regions from the 1970s to the 1990s. The generally manageable fiscal deficits allowed most of developing Asia to keep debt levels relatively low.

Just as important is how the fiscal policy stance adjusts over the business cycle, known as the cyclicality of fiscal policy. The government's fiscal stance can be used as a "countercyclical" tool to temper fluctuations—supporting the economy during periods of weak activity or cooling it down when there are signs of overheating. This can be done via "automatic stabilizers" such as lower tax revenues or larger unemployment insurance spending at the time of the economic downturn. This can also be achieved through discretionary fiscal policies. In practice, however, the fiscal policies of many developing countries (as well as developed countries) have been procyclical—stimulating the economy when it is strong (spending more) and pulling back when weak (due to fiscal constraints), thus increasing, rather than reducing, volatility.

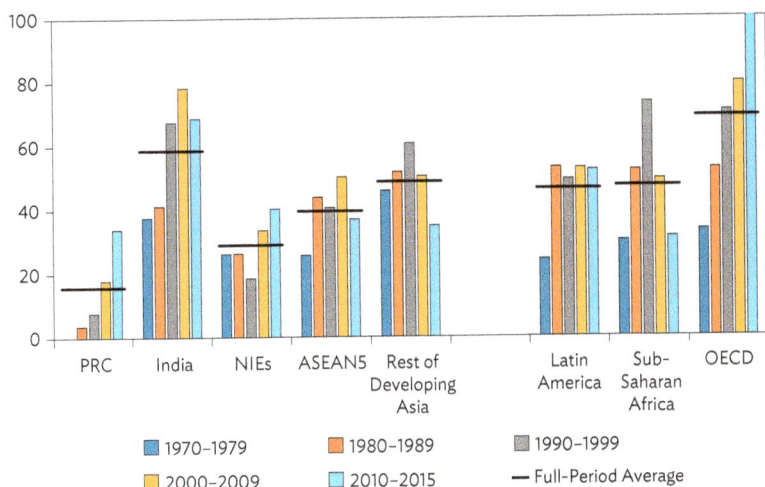

Figure 10.4: Public Debt, 1970–2015 (% of GDP)

GDP = gross domestic product, ASEAN = Association of Southeast Asian Nations, NIEs = newly industrialized economies, OECD = Organisation for Economic Co-operation and Development, PRC = People's Republic of China.

Notes: The NIEs comprise Hong Kong, China; the Republic of Korea; Singapore; and Taipei,China. ASEAN5 comprises Indonesia, Malaysia, the Philippines, Thailand, and Viet Nam. Rest of Developing Asia refers to all Asian Development Bank developing member economies excluding the PRC, India, the NIEs, and ASEAN5.

Sources: International Monetary Fund. Public Debt Database. https://www.imf.org/external/datamapper/datasets/DEBT (accessed 1 August 2019); and Asian Development Bank estimates.

Figure 10.5 shows the cyclicality of government spending in developing Asia, Latin America, and Sub-Saharan Africa. Positive numbers indicate a country had a "procyclical" fiscal policy on average—government spending increased when the economy grew and decreased when the economy contracted—while negative numbers indicate a countercyclical fiscal policy. While all three developing regions had procyclical fiscal policies from 1960 to 2016, fiscal policy was less procyclical in Asia than other regions, although it never became negative or countercyclical. In more recent decades, there has been a larger drop in developing Asia's procyclicality than in the other two developing regions.

Figure 10.5: Fiscal Policy Cyclicality

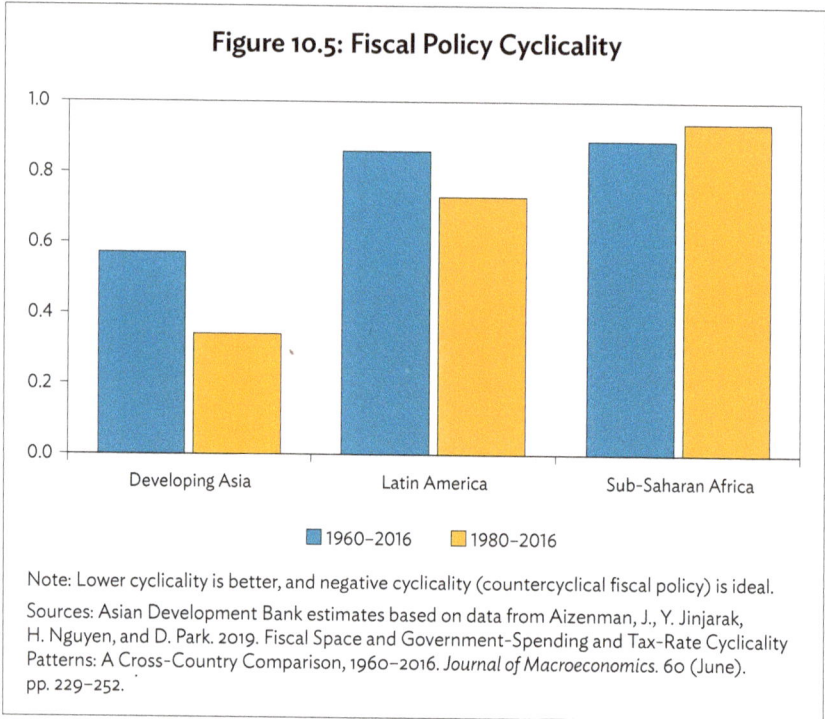

Note: Lower cyclicality is better, and negative cyclicality (countercyclical fiscal policy) is ideal.

Sources: Asian Development Bank estimates based on data from Aizenman, J., Y. Jinjarak, H. Nguyen, and D. Park. 2019. Fiscal Space and Government-Spending and Tax-Rate Cyclicality Patterns: A Cross-Country Comparison, 1960–2016. *Journal of Macroeconomics.* 60 (June). pp. 229–252.

Economies in developing Asia that rely heavily on commodities as their main export and source of income (such as Kazakhstan, Mongolia, and Papua New Guinea) face particular fiscal challenges. There were frequent large fluctuations in global commodity prices over the past 5 decades (Figure 10.6). They can be driven by sudden dramatic changes in supply, such as those caused by the 1973 oil embargo or the 1979 revolution in Iran. Price shifts can also come from changes in demand, such as during the early 2000s and after 2010 as rising emerging market demand, especially from the PRC, drove metals and other commodity prices higher.

Therefore, commodity-dependent countries are prone to greater fiscal procyclicality and much greater macroeconomic volatility. Developing Asia, as a whole, is less dependent on commodities than other developing regions, which helps explain the lower cyclicality of fiscal policy and lower volatility. Also, some commodity-dependent economies in the region use tools such as fiscal rules and sovereign wealth funds to help mitigate the effects of commodity price fluctuations (Box 10.1).

Figure 10.6: World Commodity Prices, 1960–2019
(in real terms; 2010 = 100)

Figure 10.6a: Energy and Metals

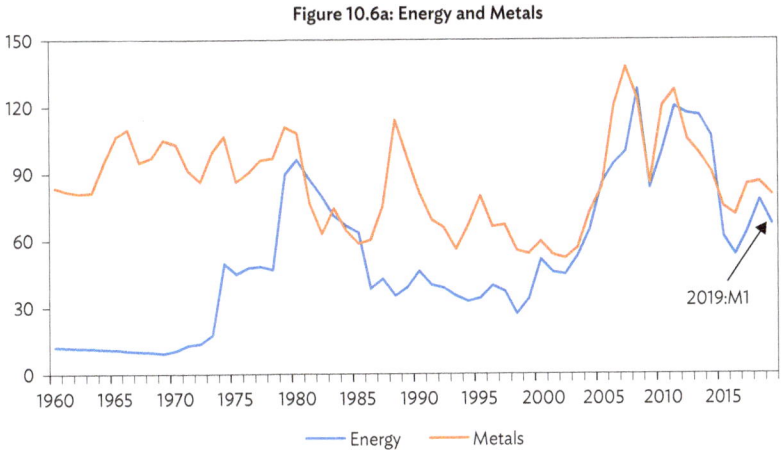

2019:M1

Energy   Metals

Figure 10.6b: Food and Raw Materials

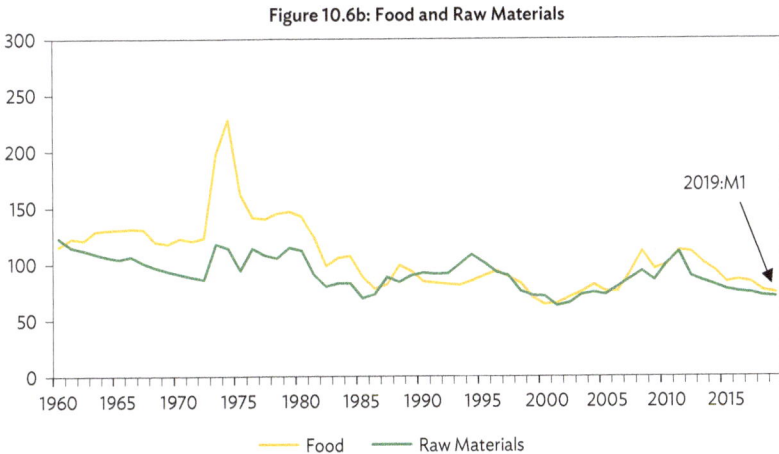

2019:M1

Food   Raw Materials

M1 = first month of the year.

Note: The real price indexes are trade-weighted averages based on 2002–2004 developing country export values deflated by United States manufacturing producer price index and normalized to 100 in 2010.

Sources: World Bank. *Pink Sheet Data*. https://www.worldbank.org/en/research/commodity -markets (accessed 22 February 2019); and Organisation for Economic Co-operation and Development (OECD). OECD Data. https://data.oecd.org/price/producer-price-indices-ppi.htm (accessed 22 February 2019).

Box 10.1: Tackling the "Resource Curse"

Resource-rich countries often experience a "resource curse" in three ways. First is the appreciated exchange rate due to large earnings from commodity exports, which leads to a loss of competitiveness, especially in manufacturing (called the "Dutch disease"). Second is the fluctuation in balance of payments and fiscal conditions, which creates economic volatility. Third is the greater possibility for rent-seeking and governance problems that distort appropriate economic incentives and damage efficiency and productivity.

Sovereign wealth funds (government-controlled investment vehicles) are an option that commodity exporters can use to mitigate the harmful effects of appreciated exchange rates and price fluctuations, and to share national wealth with future generations.

Azerbaijan and Kazakhstan effectively manage their oil revenues through the sovereign wealth funds they created in the early 2000s. Transfers to the national budget have been limited, which, to a large extent, isolated public finance from the volatility of oil-related revenues. In 2005, Timor-Leste established the Petroleum Fund to promote transparent and responsible management of its large income from offshore petroleum resources. The fund is managed by investment professionals and invested in a broad range of foreign assets—about 40% in equities and 60% in bonds. When petroleum revenues began declining in recent years, the country was still able to boost public spending using withdrawals from the fund, thus supporting economic activity.

Appropriately managing sovereign wealth funds is more important than just creating them. They cannot achieve their intended purpose if fund resources are used imprudently to finance domestic expenditure programs. Unless managed professionally and carefully, countries will lose important resources for future generations.

Sources: Asian Development Bank; and Government of Timor-Leste, Ministry of Finance, Petroleum Fund Administration Unit. 2019. *Timor-Leste Petroleum Fund: Annual Report 2018.* https://www.mof.gov.tl/wp-content/uploads/2019/08/2018-annual-report-ENGLISH.pdf.

While Asia's developing countries generally adhered to prudent fiscal policies, especially after the AFC, an important remaining issue for many countries is the low tax revenue-to-GDP ratio. This constrains current expenditures for much-needed education, health, and other public services, and lowers public investments available for infrastructure. A narrow tax base limits a government's ability to reduce inequality by redistributing income and assets.

For instance, in 2017, Indonesia's tax revenues were only 12% of GDP, Malaysia 14%, and the Philippines and Thailand about 18%. This compares with average tax revenues of 18% of GDP in Sub-Saharan Africa, 23% in Latin America, and 34% in Organisation for Economic Co-operation and Development (OECD) countries.[1] Many countries in the region are working to broaden the tax base by reducing loopholes, rationalizing preferential tax measures, and strengthening collections and enforcement.

Monetary, exchange rate, and other policy tools

Inflation has generally been lower in developing Asia than in other developing regions thanks to sound monetary policy (Figure 10.2). Maintaining price stability is typically a primary objective of central banks, often in conjunction with growth and employment.

Monetary policy in the region has evolved over the decades. In general, the main monetary policy tool in the decades up to the 1980s was direct control over monetary aggregates through credit allocation to commercial banks. As financial markets deepened over the years, there was a shift to more market-based instruments such as open market operations (purchase or sales of government bonds in the market) and setting policy interest rates.

Inflation targeting has also been increasingly used by Asian central banks. Bank Indonesia, the Bank of Korea, Bangko Sentral ng Pilipinas, and the Bank of Thailand formally adopted inflation targeting in the late 1990s and early 2000s, which helped contain persistent inflation in these countries after the AFC.

Asia's central banks have also grown more independent over time. De jure measures show that central bank independence increased across the region, especially after the AFC (Figure 10.7). Independence gives central banks greater scope to pursue price stability with less political interference. Without independent central banks, governments tend to use monetary policy to stimulate economies for political reasons and sometimes to monetize fiscal deficits, as occurred in some Latin American and Sub-Saharan African countries.

An important concept in international economics is the so-called "impossible trinity" or "trilemma"; a country cannot simultaneously have an independent monetary policy, fixed exchange rate, and free movement of capital. Until the demise of the Bretton

---

[1]   OECD. 2019. *Revenue Statistics in Asian and Pacific Economies 2019.* Paris.

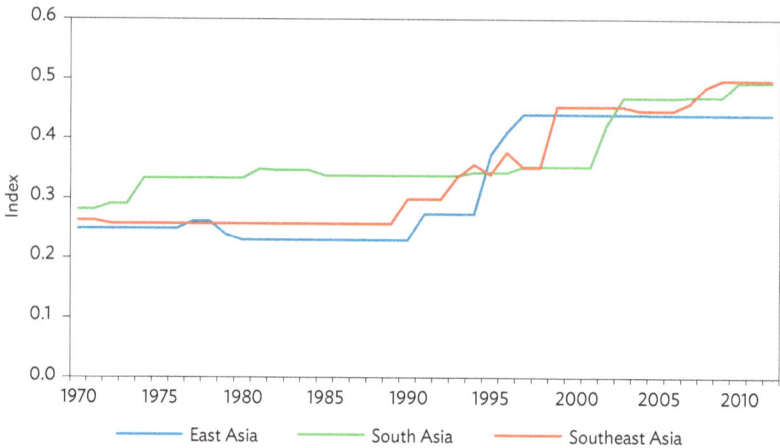

Figure 10.7: Average Central Bank Independence, 1970–2010

Source: Asian Development Bank estimates using data from Garriga, A. 2016. Central Bank Independence in the World: A New Data Set. *International Interactions*. 42 (5). pp. 849–868.

Woods system in the 1970s, while countries controlled capital flows, they had fixed exchange rate regimes and independent monetary policies (although they could not totally exclude influence from other countries' monetary conditions). In the decades since the end of the Bretton Woods system, developing Asia has faced this trilemma in different ways.

Over the past 5 decades, with the exception of a few economies such as Hong Kong, China, which uses a currency board, most developing Asian economies prioritized monetary policy autonomy. In Hong Kong, China, the exchange rate is fixed to the United States (US) dollar, with central bank base money fully backed by foreign exchange reserves. This means there is no monetary policy autonomy; the central bank cannot invest in government bonds or lend to private banks, and it cannot function as lender of last resort.

One important decision facing Asian monetary authorities has been whether to tightly manage—or even peg—the exchange rate, typically against the US dollar, or allow greater flexibility. Even after the collapse of the Bretton Woods system in the 1970s, economies in developing Asia continued to strongly manage exchange rates, with several establishing de facto pegs against the US dollar. The fact that many countries still had relatively closed capital accounts enabled exchange rate stability and monetary policy autonomy. As capital accounts opened up—gradually in the 1970s and more rapidly in the 1980s and 1990s—the ability to maintain both independent monetary policy and a fixed exchange rate became more difficult, just as the trilemma would dictate.

When capital accounts and financial sectors became more liberalized, the de facto pegs led to massive capital inflows and a buildup of imbalances. With freer movement of capital and exchange rate stability, monetary policy was ineffective in controlling domestic financial conditions. These eventually contributed to the AFC in the late 1990s (section 10.5).

As a result of the AFC, many economies shifted to more flexible exchange rate regimes, whether measured in de jure or de facto terms (Figure 10.8), while maintaining monetary policy autonomy and a high degree of capital mobility. However, this did not mean monetary policies were immune to external conditions, including monetary policies of advanced economies.

More recently, policy makers have adopted "capital flow management measures" and "macroprudential policies" to manage capital flows and address the asset price fluctuations that affect macroeconomic stability. This helps avoid systemic risks.

The use of capital flow management measures, which restrict certain types of capital flows, has picked up because global financial conditions can lead to economic overheating through sharp capital inflows, its sudden stops, and capital outflows (capital flight). The use of these tools in the region has grown in the past 2 decades—for example, minimum holding periods for government bonds by nonresidents and restrictions on external borrowing by banks. Many countries, including the PRC, keep a wide range of regulations on investments abroad by residents and onward investment by nonresidents. Generally, the restrictions on inflows are more widely accepted than restrictions on outflows, especially those of nonresident investors.

Macroprudential policies have also become an integral part of macroeconomic management globally. Measures such as caps on loan-to-value or debt-to-income ratios, or countercyclical capital requirements, aim to limit the risk of financial system distress. These measures are part of the policy framework for stabilization, as discussed by the International Monetary Fund (IMF), Financial Stability Board, and the Group of Twenty (G20).

Figure 10.8: Exchange Rate Flexibility in Developing Asia, 1990–2016

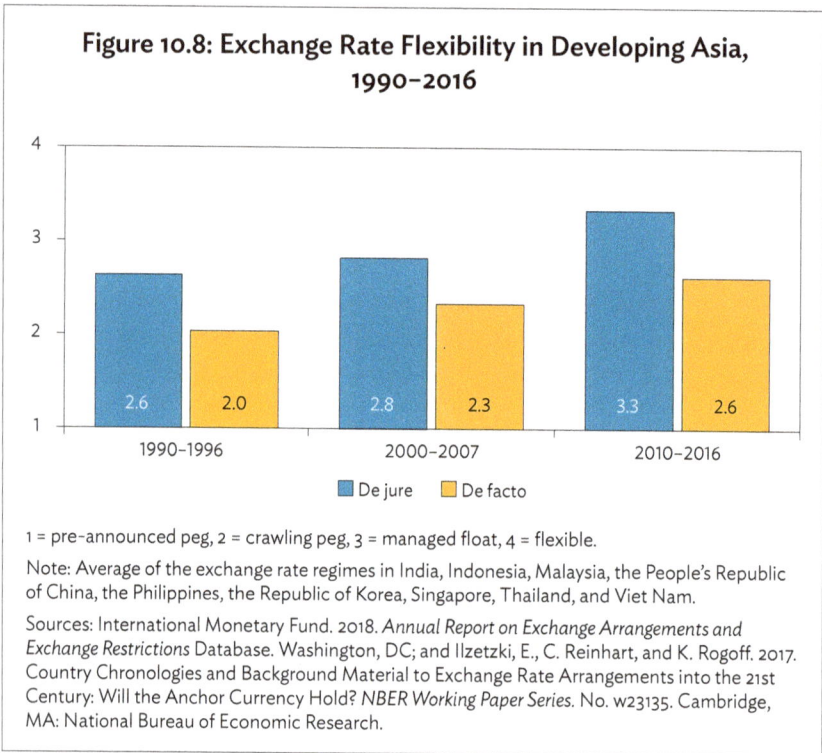

1 = pre-announced peg, 2 = crawling peg, 3 = managed float, 4 = flexible.

Note: Average of the exchange rate regimes in India, Indonesia, Malaysia, the People's Republic of China, the Philippines, the Republic of Korea, Singapore, Thailand, and Viet Nam.

Sources: International Monetary Fund. 2018. *Annual Report on Exchange Arrangements and Exchange Restrictions* Database. Washington, DC; and Ilzetzki, E., C. Reinhart, and K. Rogoff. 2017. Country Chronologies and Background Material to Exchange Rate Arrangements into the 21st Century: Will the Anchor Currency Hold? *NBER Working Paper Series.* No. w23135. Cambridge, MA: National Bureau of Economic Research.

10.4 Avoiding debt crises in the 1980s

How did most of developing Asia manage to avoid the 1980s emerging market debt crises, which afflicted most of Latin America and Sub-Saharan Africa? The debt crises in this period were based on four factors: overborrowing to finance government investment in resource-based industries, among others; overlending by US, European, and Japanese banks as they recycled petrodollars from oil-producing countries in the 1970s; falling oil prices from the early 1980s; and the abrupt, large interest rate hikes caused by the US Federal Reserve's tight monetary policy and expansionary US fiscal policies.

Simply put, most Asian economies avoided the debt crises because they did not borrow excessively. There was greater fiscal prudence in the region but also less access to credit from international banks. The Philippines was an exception as political and historical ties to the US provided greater access to borrowing from US banks. The Philippines resorted to an IMF financing program in 1983.

In many Asian countries, the gradual shift to outward, export-based strategies in the 1960s and 1970s helped earn enough foreign currency to service their external debt. The Republic of Korea (ROK) borrowed heavily in the 1970s to finance private sector investment, but the high export-to-GDP ratio supported its creditworthiness. This contrasted with many Latin American and Sub-Saharan African countries that borrowed heavily in the late 1970s and yet maintained inward-looking import substitution policies.[2]

At the end of the 1980s, India had its own balance of payments crisis. It was triggered by a combination of political events—the Gulf War and domestic political uncertainty. Prior to the crisis, India had been running fiscal deficits reaching 7%–9% of GDP, as well as trade and current account deficits in part due to its overvalued fixed exchange rate. By 1990, those persistent twin deficits led to alarmingly large short-term foreign debt relative to exports and foreign reserves. A loss in confidence brought intense speculative pressure on the rupee in early 1991. Defending the exchange rate resulted in a rapid depletion of foreign exchange reserves. The government responded decisively by starting comprehensive reforms supported by an IMF program and rescue package by multilateral and bilateral partners (Chapter 2). The rupee significantly devalued as part of a transition to a more market-based exchange rate system, and the fiscal deficit fell significantly.

10.5 The Asian financial crisis and responses

The AFC was one of the most painful economic crises since World War II. It was initially characterized as a "currency crisis." There were rapid international capital reversals—from large inflows to massive outflows—that caused a sharp depletion of foreign exchange reserves and the collapse of the de facto fixed exchange rate system. The currency crisis then metastasized into a domestic banking crisis in several countries due to pervasive currency and maturity mismatches.

The crisis that began in July 1997 in Thailand ignited a full-blown economic recession with deep contractions in GDP, especially in the four most affected countries—Indonesia, Malaysia, the ROK, and Thailand. It also affected other major economies in East Asia and Southeast Asia including Hong Kong, China; the Philippines; Singapore; and Taipei,China; and spread to other parts of the world.

---

[2] World Bank. 1993. *The East Asian Miracle: Economic Growth and Public Policy.* New York: Oxford University Press.

Several factors converged to spark the AFC.[3]

One was premature liberalization of capital markets. This invited massive foreign capital inflows—especially short-term bank credit at relatively low interest rates—as investors were attracted by the region's strong economic growth and de facto dollar pegs in many countries that masked exchange rate risk. Poor risk management by banks, weak corporate governance, and the lack of financial transparency led to excessive borrowing and highly inefficient domestic investment financed by borrowed foreign capital—in real estate, for example, instead of productive ventures. The massive capital inflows overheated economies, generated asset bubbles, and eventually created large current account deficits.

Another related factor was the double mismatch of currencies and maturities. Stable exchange rates encouraged banks to borrow heavily in US dollars to lend in local currency. At the same time, bank balance sheets had maturity mismatches between increasingly short-term liabilities (funded by unhedged foreign inflows) invested in long-term, often illiquid projects with revenues in local currency.

When it became clear that the situation was no longer sustainable, overseas lenders' confidence waned in Southeast Asia and the ROK, and they began refusing to roll over short-term debt. This sharply reduced private capital inflows and exacerbated currency pressure. The ensuing large devaluations further undermined economic confidence, leading to a fall in equity and real estate prices, in turn leading to corporate failures and a huge rise in nonperforming bank loans. Asia's financial crisis was a currency crisis that developed into a banking crisis and full-blown economic crisis.

In response, badly affected economies such as Indonesia, Malaysia, the ROK, and Thailand tried to stabilize their economies using varying approaches. Indonesia, the ROK, and Thailand opted for IMF programs supported by bilateral and multilateral partners (including the Asian Development Bank [ADB]) (Table 10.1), which were tied to conditions such as raising interest rates and cutting government spending. Malaysia, in contrast, under the leadership of Prime Minister Mahathir Mohamad, decided not to go to the IMF for help and instead resorted to capital controls and a pegged exchange rate.

---

[3] See Park, C., et al. 2017. 20 Years after the Asian Financial Crisis: Lessons Learned and Future Challenges. *ADB Briefs*. No. 85. Manila: Asian Development Bank.

This approach by Malaysia was criticized as unorthodox, but it turned out to be effective in containing the damage. IMF programs were regarded by many Asian countries as demanding more onerous conditionality than necessary. Most now realize that fiscal consolidation consequently limited a country's capacity to stimulate its way out of crisis. In Indonesia, the IMF required the liquidation of many problem banks, even without full deposit guarantees, causing bank runs and thus exacerbating the banking crisis. In the ROK, the IMF called for public spending cuts despite the fact that they were already running fiscal surpluses, thus aggravating the downturn and leaving a lasting social impact. At the 12 July 2010 press conference in Daejeon, ROK, then-IMF Managing Director Dominique Strauss-Kahn said, "... we have made some mistakes. But we have also learned lessons from our experience during the Asian Crisis."[4] Since the AFC, the IMF has adopted more realistic and pragmatic approaches, including capital flow management. On the other hand, some may argue that IMF programs prompted necessary reforms for Asian countries.

Crisis-affected countries all began a wide array of deep-seated reforms. These included (i) strengthening financial supervision, consolidating the banking sector, and replenishing bank capital—in many countries by resolving nonperforming loans through public asset management companies; (ii) making exchange rates more flexible (with a delay in Malaysia, which maintained its fixed exchange rate from 1998 to 2005); (iii) increasing central bank independence to support prudent monetary policies; (iv) setting a framework for ensuring fiscal soundness; and (v) instituting a broad set of reforms that included strengthening corporate governance, dissolving and restructuring corporate groups, and strengthening bankruptcy and competition laws.

As a part of the IMF-led international rescue package for the AFC, ADB provided substantial quick-disbursing, policy-based lending to crisis-affected countries—Indonesia, the ROK, and Thailand—with technical assistance for necessary reforms. As the crisis unfolded, ADB continued to provide tailored loans to meet the needs of affected countries, by blending support for structural reform (public sector and financial market reforms) and assistance to maintain social services.

---

[4] IMF. 2010. *Asia and the Global Economy: Leading the Way Forward in the 21st Century.* Opening Remarks by Dominique Strauss-Kahn, Managing Director of the IMF, at the Asia 21 Conference. Daejeon. 12 July. https://www.imf.org/en/News/Articles/2015/09/28/04/53/sp071210.

Table 10.1: Currency Stabilization Support Programs during the Asian Financial Crisis[a]
($ billion)

	Thailand	Indonesia	Republic of Korea[b]
Multilateral Agencies	**6.7**	**18.0**	**35.0**
IMF	4.0	10.0	21.0
World Bank	1.5	4.5	10.0
ADB	1.2	3.5	4.0
Bilateral Support	**10.5**	**NA**	**NA**
Japan	4.0	NA	NA
PRC	1.0	NA	NA
Australia	1.0	NA	NA
Hong Kong, China	1.0	NA	NA
Malaysia	1.0	NA	NA
Singapore	1.0	NA	NA
Republic of Korea	0.5	NA	NA
Indonesia	0.5	NA	NA
Brunei Darussalam	0.5	NA	NA
Indonesia: Emergency Reserve	**NA**	**5.0**	**NA**
Subtotal	17.2	23.0	35.0
Second-Line Defense[c]	**NA**	**16.2**	**23.0**
Japan	NA	5.0	10.0
United States	NA	3.0	5.0
Singapore	NA	5.0	NA
Others	NA	3.2	8.0
Total	**17.2**	**39.2**	**58.0**

NA = not applicable, ADB = Asian Development Bank, IMF = International Monetary Fund, PRC = People's Republic of China.

[a] The composition of financial packages was complex and subject to agreements reached with agencies providing support. Timing also varied. For these reasons, different sources may record the size of the packages differently.

[b] In addition to the official programs shown here, support to the Republic of Korea was strengthened by the agreement of private sector international banks in the United States and Europe to support the efforts to restore stability in its financial markets.

[c] To be used if needed.

Source: McCawley, P. 2017. *Banking on the Future of Asia and the Pacific: 50 Years of the Asian Development Bank.* Manila: Asian Development Bank.

The AFC also prompted Asian policy makers to consider alternative regional arrangements and institutions, which complemented IMF support. One early suggestion in mid-1997 was Japan's proposal to create an Asian Monetary Fund. This did not materialize, in part due to US opposition on the ground that such a new system could compromise the role of the IMF and create a moral hazard. On 25 November 1997, the Manila Framework (New Framework for Enhanced Asian Regional Cooperation to Promote Financial Stability) was endorsed by 18 Asia-Pacific Economic Cooperation leaders (including the US). It comprised mutual foreign exchange financing during the crisis, surveillance among members, and technical assistance for capacity building. Manila Framework meetings were held periodically until it was terminated in 2004. By then, other initiatives based on similar ideas as the Manila Framework had grown more important, such as the ASEAN plus Japan, the PRC, and the ROK (ASEAN+3) Chiang Mai Initiative, a network of bilateral swap arrangements among ASEAN+3 countries—a first for the region. The Chiang Mai Initiative became the Chiang Mai Initiative Multilateralization in 2010, a multilateral currency swap arrangement under a single contract between countries, initially totaling $120 billion and expanding to $240 billion in 2012 (Chapter 15).

In sum, a wave of major economic and financial policy reforms in the aftermath of the AFC reinforced a foundation for sustained high growth. Most crisis-affected countries reduced dependence on external finance and strengthened their overall financial stability, with sound macroeconomic fundamentals and policies, stronger financial regulations, flexible exchange rates, adequate foreign exchange reserves, and closer regional financial cooperation. Together with buoyant external conditions, these reforms helped Asian economies emerge stronger from the AFC and enjoy high growth until the onset of the GFC.

10.6 The global financial crisis and responses

The GFC was a period of extreme stress in global financial markets and banking systems. The initial catalyst for the global shock was a crisis in US subprime mortgage markets in 2007. After the collapse of one of the world's largest investment banks, Lehman Brothers, in September 2008, the crisis ballooned quickly. At its depth, global output contracted by 0.1% in 2009, a sharp contrast from the 3.0% expansion in 2008.

The collapse in global demand hit commodity markets as well, with international oil prices plunging 36% in 2008–2009.

There were both macroeconomic and microeconomic factors behind the GFC. In macroeconomic terms, economic and financial distortions grew due to rising asset prices and widening current account imbalances during a period of relative US macroeconomic stability—an interval the US Federal Reserve dubbed "the Great Moderation" (from roughly the mid-1980s to the summer of 2007). During this period, the US and several European countries had relatively stable growth with low inflation and interest rates compared to the previous decades. This encouraged financial institutions to keep taking on greater risk, leverage, and credit. At the same time, there were existing inadequacies in financial systems, regulations, and supervision, as exemplified by subprime mortgage problems.

The intensity of the GFC brought the international community together in response, notably through the G20—an expansion of the Group of Seven (G7) countries by including emerging economies as well as Australia.[5] At the first G20 Summit in Washington, DC in November 2008, participants openly admitted their regulatory and supervisory responsibilities, stating that "policy-makers, regulators and supervisors, in some advanced countries, did not adequately appreciate and address the risks building up in financial markets, keep pace with financial innovations, or take into account the systemic ramifications of domestic regulatory actions."

The G20 response spanned across multiple fronts; some focused on immediate crisis response with others on future crisis prevention. Five points summarize the international response.[6]

First was the urgency to stabilize the global financial system. The G7 adopted an emergency action plan at its October 2008 meeting in Washington, DC—held immediately after the Lehman Brothers collapse triggered the crisis. Under the plan, government actions

---

[5] The G20 framework was first introduced at the meeting of financial ministers and central bank governors in September 1999 in the aftermath of the AFC. The G7 (Canada, France, Germany, Italy, Japan, the United Kingdom, and the US) decided on the new expanded framework believing global economic affairs should not be effectively discussed without involving emerging economies. The G20 includes the G7 and Australia, India, Indonesia, the PRC, and the ROK (from Asia and the Pacific), as well as Argentina, Brazil, Mexico, the Russian Federation, Saudi Arabia, South Africa, the European Union, and Turkey.

[6] Nakao, T. 2010. *Response to the Global Financial Crisis and Future Policy Challenges.* Keynote address at the symposium cohosted by Harvard Law School and the International House of Japan. Hakone. 23 October.

included the massive supply of liquidity by central banks, expansion of deposit insurance, guarantees for bank debt, capital injections using public funds, separation of toxic assets from balance sheets, and governmental control of troubled financial institutions.

Second, the international community responded to the drop in global demand with coordinated macroeconomic policies. By the February 2009 G7 finance ministers and central bank governors meeting in Rome, the drastic deterioration of the real economy was evident, particularly in advanced countries. International trade was down, production collapsed, and unemployment was rising rapidly. Governments agreed to coordinate on expansionary fiscal and accommodative monetary policies—including "unconventional" monetary measures such as large-scale quantitative easing. It was expected that simultaneous, harmonized actions would produce greater synergy and be more effective than countries acting separately. This approach would also prevent "free riding" on other country policies.

Third, there was a need to support developing countries that might be affected by the GFC. Many developing countries had sustained high growth prior to the crisis, using prudent macroeconomic policies and expanded global capital flows. However, capital flow reversals, contracting trade, and lower confidence during the crisis threatened this growth. The second G20 Summit in London in April 2009 agreed to mobilize funds from international financial institutions—such as the IMF, the World Bank, and ADB—and bilateral assistance from advanced countries to support trade, infrastructure development, and stimulus measures in developing countries. By assisting developing countries, they also tried to alleviate the decline in international trade and help advanced countries recover.

Fourth, as the discussion moved from crisis response to crisis prevention, policies to strengthen financial sector regulation and supervision were adopted. These included regulations covering capital adequacy, liquidity and leverage, more stringent regulations of "systemically important" financial institutions, cross-border bank resolution, a review of credit-rating agencies, and central clearing of over-the-counter derivatives.

And fifth, to prevent future crises, international financial institutions needed reform. World leaders agreed to (i) increase the financial resources of the IMF, the World Bank, and other multilateral development banks such as ADB; (ii) strengthen governance of these institutions; (iii) use the G20 as the premier forum for international economic cooperation; and (iv) reinforce the Financial Stability Board consisting of finance ministries, financial regulatory authorities, and central banks.

Actions were taken to implement these agreements to prevent future crises.[7] As one of the measures to strengthen global financial safety nets, the IMF's Flexible Credit Line (FCL) was enhanced, including the extension of its duration and removal of its access cap. The IMF's Precautionary Credit Line (PCL) was also created in August 2010 as a new preventive tool.[8]

ADB also enhanced its crisis response tool kit further to respond to GFC challenges. Crisis response assistance was provided mostly through loans from ADB's newly introduced quick-disbursing Countercyclical Support Facility (CSF) to support specific countercyclical fiscal expenditures. In 2009, ADB provided CSF loans of $500 million each to Bangladesh, Indonesia, Kazakhstan, the Philippines, and Viet Nam. ADB also expanded its Trade Finance Program to maintain international trade by small and medium-sized enterprises by addressing the shortage of dollar liquidity through lending to commercial banks in 16 member countries. Later in the 2010s, ADB again used the CSF when Azerbaijan and Kazakhstan suffered from sharp declines in commodity prices.

Strengthening regional financial safety nets also became an important part of global governance and the global financial architecture. The Chiang Mai Initiative Multilateralization was strengthened with the establishment of the ASEAN+3 Macroeconomic Research Office in 2011 to provide macro-surveillance. In addition, Asian countries actively used bilateral currency swap arrangements to stabilize stress in financial and exchange rate markets: Japan, the ROK, and Singapore entered into agreements to establish swap lines with the US in 2008; and Indonesia did so with Japan, the PRC, and the ROK in 2013. The ROK also resorted to bilateral swap arrangements with Japan and the PRC.

---

[7]   See Nakao, T. 2012. *Challenges in International Finance and Japan's Responses.* Keynote address at the International Financial Symposium hosted by the Institute for International Monetary Affairs. Tokyo. 15 March.

[8]   The FCL was created in March 2019 for IMF-supported programs. Countries with strong fundamentals and policy frameworks were able to access a refined FCL with enhanced predictability and effectiveness in August 2010. For the PCL, this allows countries with sound fundamentals and institutional policy framework, yet moderate vulnerabilities, to benefit from the IMF's precautionary liquidity provisions (IMF. 2010. *The Fund's Mandate—The Future Financing Role: Revised Reform Proposals.* August. Washington, DC).

In contrast to the severity of the GFC's impact on advanced economies and some regions of the world, the damage in Asia was lower. Developing Asia's growth and financial stability were disrupted only briefly. While GDP in advanced economies continued to shrink into 2009, declining by 3.3%, developing Asia recovered quickly with an average 6.1% growth.[9]

After the 1997–1998 AFC, Asia's policy makers pursued sound macroeconomic policies and comprehensive structural reforms. Macroprudential policies implemented after the AFC helped boost Asia's resilience, enabling the region to cushion the GFC shock. Over the past decade, Asia has used macroprudential policies more than any other region. The most important ones have been loan-to-value ratios for lending to the housing sector by banks, caps on debt-to-income ratios, and caps on foreign currency exposure.[10]

10.7 Looking ahead

One important lesson from the GFC was renewed awareness of the critical role governments play as the final backstop for economic and financial stability. Governments have the unique capacity to mobilize taxpayer funds based on democratic processes as well as legislate and enforce financial regulations with their associated penalties. Just as there are government failures (macroeconomic policy mistakes, over- or insufficient regulation, and various inefficiencies), so too are there market excesses such as aggressive risk-taking and overleveraging.

Looking ahead, Asia will face several important macroeconomic policy challenges.

First, Asian economies should strengthen public finance. Fiscal stimulus in the years since the GFC eroded fiscal balances, and many economies must rebuild buffers to protect against future shocks. They can also move further toward countercyclical fiscal policy. For instance, they could increase the use of social safety nets (such as unemployment insurance), which act as automatic stabilizers. Countries with a low tax revenue-to-GDP ratio should broaden the tax base, raise rates as appropriate, and strengthen collection and

---

[9] Global and advanced economy GDP data plus international oil prices from IMF. World Economic Outlook Database. https://www.imf.org/external/pubs/ft/weo/2019/02/weodata/download.aspx (accessed 20 August 2019); Developing Asia data from ADB. 2013. *Asian Development Outlook 2013: Asia's Energy Challenge*. Manila.

[10] Khan, F., A. Ramayandi, and M. Schröder. Forthcoming. Conditions for Effective Macroprudential Policy Interventions. *ADB Economics Working Paper Series*. Manila: ADB.

enforcement. Also, policy makers should consider the long-term challenges of climate change, social equity, and aging populations, given their implications for fiscal positions.

Second, independent monetary policy and a flexible exchange rate remain important for macroeconomic stability. These helped the region weather various shocks over the past 2 decades.

Third, policy makers should continue to use capital flow management measures and macroprudential policies as appropriate. It is clear that conventional macroeconomic policies are not enough to ensure financial stability. Monetary policy is often a blunt tool for addressing vulnerabilities such as asset bubbles. In addition, external factors can induce capital flow and exchange rate volatility.

Fourth, financial regulators should respond to the changing landscape of financial services which is evolving in nontraditional and innovative ways, including expansion of new services by nonbank financial institutions using new technologies. Asia's financial crises exposed the deep links between finance and the real economy, while reaffirming the fragility of an inadequately regulated financial system. "Shadow banking" is one of those issues.

Fifth, policy makers need to further coordinate fiscal, monetary, exchange rate, and financial policies—along with those covering trade and competition—to enhance policy effectiveness, aiming at the multiple objectives of price stability, employment, soundness of the financial sector, and external balance.

Sixth, it is important to enhance policy dialogue and coordination between countries in the region as economic conditions and policies spill across borders through trade, financial, and sentiment channels. Policy makers should cooperate to mitigate the potential for harmful contagion—whether during normal times or in times of crisis.

Finally, as economies in the region and the world face many emerging challenges, including the potential impact from digital technologies, policy makers should remain vigilant and agile. They can also continue to learn from history and quickly reverse any missteps.

CHAPTER 11

POVERTY REDUCTION AND INCOME DISTRIBUTION

11.1 Introduction

The past half century has seen a dramatic reduction in extreme poverty across developing Asia. This has not only improved people's welfare, but also helped create a stable environment for economic growth and development.

From 1981 to 2015, the proportion of developing Asia's population living below the $1.90 per day international poverty line (in 2011 purchasing power parity [PPP] terms) declined from 68% (1.6 billion out of 2.4 billion) to 7% (264 million out of 3.8 billion). The region contributed most to global poverty reduction. According to Asian Development Bank (ADB) projections, developing Asia could eradicate extreme poverty by 2025 if its recent growth trajectory continues.[1] At $3.20 per day, typical of national poverty lines used in lower-middle-income countries, the region's poverty rate will fall from 29% to 13% during 2015–2025.

Rapid economic growth has been the key driver of poverty reduction in Asia by generating better-quality jobs for the poor. At the same time, policies such as land reform; use of Green

---

[1] According to ADB projections, developing Asia's extreme poverty at $1.90 per day will fall to 3% by 2020 and 1% by 2025.

Revolution technologies; open trade and investment; education and health programs; and measures that broaden access to finance, infrastructure, and markets have helped raise the income-earning capacity of the population, including poor and low-income households.

However, developing Asia's progress in improving income distribution has been uneven. During the 1960s–1980s, most developing Asian economies managed to keep income inequality stable, regardless of its initial level, despite large differences in the pace of economic growth. Many economies in East Asia and Southeast Asia grew rapidly, while income inequality remained stable or even declined somewhat—a pattern referred to as "growth with equity," due to the expansion of labor-intensive manufacturing exports and inclusive policies. During the same period, South Asia saw generally stable inequality levels with slow growth.

Since the 1990s, rapid growth and poverty reduction have been accompanied by rising income inequality in many Asian countries. Technological progress and globalization have led to rising wage differentials between skilled and less-skilled workers—although they have increased incomes for both. They also increased capital earnings more than labor income. Further, technological progress and globalization have created opportunities for entrepreneurs to gain from the "first mover effect," and for large landowners in newly favored locations to benefit from appreciation of land values. Widening urban–rural income gaps, increasing regional disparity, and unequal access to opportunity have also contributed to rising income inequality. In response, developing Asia has launched major policies in recent years to make the benefits of growth more widely shared.

This chapter looks at developing Asia's experiences in reducing poverty and its changing income distribution over the past half century. Section 11.2 discusses Asia's approach to tackling poverty and inequality. Section 11.3 reviews Asia's success in poverty reduction. Section 11.4 describes the experience of stable inequality in the 1960s–1980s. Section 11.5 examines why income inequality has widened in many countries since the 1990s. Section 11.6 looks at what policy actions can address poverty and income inequality in the future.

11.2 Asia's approach to poverty and inequality

Why poverty and inequality matter

Economic growth, poverty reduction, and income distribution are among the most important dimensions of development, as they determine people's well-being and a country's prosperity. Eliminating poverty and making income distribution equitable have both intrinsic and instrumental values. The intrinsic value is based on justice, fairness, and human rights as desirable goals a human society pursues. People also prefer to live in societies with less deprivation, poverty, and inequality. This idea of altruism features prominently in many cultures and religions. The instrumental value is related to the importance of poverty reduction and equitable income distribution to sustaining growth. Growth may not be sustained if its benefits are not widely shared.

More specifically, persistently high poverty and inequality can undermine growth through several channels. One is to constrain an economy from achieving its full potential, as poor and low-income households—with fewer resources and opportunities—are less able to invest in human and productive capital. Another is to constrain the growth of a middle class, a key source of domestic consumption. A further channel is to create social tension and conflict, which are detrimental to sustained growth. Finally, high poverty and inequality can undermine the quality of institutions, for instance, by leading to "elite capture" (for example, regulations and public services biased to those in power), or by pressing politicians to enact populist policies that often distort resource allocation and hamper macroeconomic stability.

Poverty is often measured by the number of people or proportion of the population belonging to households with per capita income or consumption expenditure below a threshold, or poverty line. This chapter uses two types of poverty lines. One is international poverty lines. These are useful for comparing poverty across countries. A prominent example is the $1.90 per day per person threshold (in 2011 PPP) used by the international community to measure the level of extreme poverty. This poverty line reflects the expenditures required to meet a person's minimum food and nonfood needs. The other type is national poverty lines set by individual countries. National poverty lines typically represent different levels of consumption and/or income and are often used for country-specific poverty analyses. A key advantage of poverty estimates based on national poverty lines is that they are more often available over long periods of time.

Income inequality, on the other hand, refers to how income is distributed across individuals or households. A commonly used measure of income inequality is the Gini coefficient, which is 0 when everyone receives the same level of income in a society, meaning perfect equality, and 100 when all incomes go to one person, meaning perfect inequality. Other widely used measures are income (or wealth) shares of the richest 1%, 5%, 10%, or 20% of the population; those of the poorest 1%, 5%, 10%, or 20%; or the ratio of the two. Income inequality can be measured either on a pre-tax and pre-transfer basis, which captures inequality in market income, or on a post-tax and post-transfer basis, which incorporates income redistribution by government.

While data on the distribution of individual or household incomes within a country are a natural source for estimating income inequality, in many developing countries they are unavailable, and hence, data on household consumption expenditures are often used. There is also an argument in favor of measuring consumption expenditure inequality because consumption is more closely related to human well-being. Further, in aging societies, a consumption-based inequality measure may better capture true inequality as incomes of individuals and households will fall when they grow old even if they consume more based on their wealth.

Although poverty and inequality are distinct concepts, they are related to one another as well as with the pattern of economic growth. While inequality concerns the distribution of incomes of the entire population, poverty focuses on the lower end of that distribution—specifically on those who fall below the poverty line. For example, when growth creates more jobs for the poor, both poverty and income inequality will fall. In contrast, when growth is driven by skill- and capital-intensive production, the incomes of people who have skills and own capital are likely to rise more, leading to increased income inequality. In these situations, poverty may still decline as the benefits of growth trickle down. As will be shown, Asia has witnessed both patterns over time.

It is often suggested that a country's income inequality is related to its stage of development. According to the so-called

Kuznets hypothesis,[2] a country's income inequality is likely to rise in the initial stage of development, stabilize when its income reaches a certain level, and fall when the country becomes more developed (the "inverted U-curve").

There can be several reasons for this inverted U-curve. Kuznets noted that urbanization could raise a country's inequality initially when workers begin to move to higher-income urban industrial and services sectors—away from the traditional, lower-income and more equal rural agriculture sector. This is especially the case when there is abundant surplus labor in rural areas (Chapter 3). Others noted that economic takeoff often starts with a small number of entrepreneurs investing in new technologies and productive assets and accumulating capital before generating higher incomes for the wider population. Some argued that this process of capital accumulation in the early stage and its usage for further investment in productive assets contributed to industrialization.

As more people move from lower-income rural farming to higher-earning urban industries, surplus labor in rural areas becomes exhausted, leading to even higher wages in industries. Farmers' income also increases because of improved productivity associated with the availability of more land per capita. This urbanization process and ensuing decline in the urban–rural income gap can lead to a decline in overall income inequality. Moreover, as countries become rich, inequality can decline due to political pressures for greater income redistribution through taxes and transfers, often associated with an expanding middle class and more egalitarian ideas. But this process is not automatic, necessitating appropriate government actions.

The Kuznets hypothesis was based on empirical data largely observed in Germany, the United Kingdom, and the United States in selected years between 1875 and 1950. However, it has been noted that the decline in inequality in the United States in the early 20th century (from 1915 to 1945) was mostly due to the adverse effects of World War I, the Great Depression, and World War II on capital incomes, instead of following the process in the hypothesis.[3]

---

[2] Kuznets, S. 1955. Economic Growth and Income Inequality. *American Economic Review*. 45 (March). pp. 1–28.
[3] Piketty, T. 2006. The Kuznets Curve: Yesterday and Tomorrow. In Banerjee, A. V., R. Bénabou, and D. Mookherjee, eds. *Understanding Poverty*. New York: Oxford University Press. pp. 63–72.

Evolution of thinking on poverty, inequality, and growth

In the 1950s and 1960s, throughout developing Asia, countries placed improving standards of living for all and eradicating poverty at the core of nation-building strategies and development. Poverty reduction would come through rapid industrialization and accelerated economic growth. That approach was necessary with widespread poverty and 80%–90% of the population living in rural areas relying on subsistence agriculture. In the People's Republic of China (PRC), for example, Premier Zhou Enlai stated in his government report at the first National People's Congress in 1954 that the PRC "would not be able to escape from backwardness and poverty without modernizing its industry, agriculture, and transport and communications." In India, under Prime Minister Jawaharlal Nehru, the First Five-Year Plan for 1951–1956 noted widespread poverty and inequalities in income, wealth, and opportunity afflicting the country and called for a simultaneous advance in raising production, eliminating poverty, and removing inequality.

While most countries stressed industrialization and accelerated economic growth to eradicate poverty, the path to achieve these goals differed significantly across countries. One group of countries, including Mongolia, the PRC, Viet Nam (the northern part before 1975), and all Central Asian countries (former Soviet republics), adopted a socialist centrally planned model with public ownership of land, factories, and natural resources. The model held until the 1980s or 1990s when market-oriented reforms began (Chapter 2).

Most other developing countries, on the other hand, adopted a mixed-economy model that relied on both market forces and state intervention in resource allocation. But within this group, there were also large variations, especially in the early stage of development. Economies in South Asia (Bangladesh, India, Pakistan, and Sri Lanka) leaned more toward socialist policy with greater reliance on state-owned enterprises (SOEs), state control over industries, and an inward orientation that restricted trade and foreign investment. On the other hand, many economies in East Asia and Southeast Asia leaned more toward market-friendly policies, greater reliance on the private sector, and an outward orientation that promoted trade and attracted foreign investment.

In economies adopting the mixed-economy model, efforts to reduce poverty through accelerated growth were often supplemented by various programs to broaden access to land, education, health, and infrastructure for the general population. In East Asia, for example, land reform programs were implemented in the Republic of Korea (ROK) and Taipei,China in the late 1940s and early 1950s to redistribute land from richer landowners to poor landless peasants. India and the Philippines also undertook land reform, although implementation was more limited (Chapter 4). Many countries also worked hard to improve rural infrastructure such as roads, irrigation, and electrification.

In the 1960s and 1970s, there was wide acceptance across developing Asia of the need for the public sector to expand access to health care, nutrition, and education (Chapter 6)—factors that create greater equality of opportunity. In the newly industrialized economies, for example, pro-market and pro-business policies led to the rapid growth of labor-intensive manufacturing in the 1960s and 1970s, and the expansion of basic education equipped the labor force with the ability to learn skills needed by manufacturing firms, significantly contributing to poverty reduction.

By the 1980s, a consensus emerged in global development thinking that growth would be better promoted by a market-oriented approach (Chapter 2). This would imply more focus on using available labor resources and less on promoting capital-intensive industries. Thinking on poverty reduction began to emphasize two equally important elements. One was to promote market-based growth drawing on the productive use of labor.

The other element, in line with the idea of "basic human needs" popular at the time, was to provide essential public services to the poor, including basic education and primary health care. This was also influenced by the "capability approach" developed by Nobel laureate Amartya Sen.[4] This approach argued for going beyond gross domestic product (GDP) to measure economic welfare. It emphasized the importance of "empowering people" to choose a life that they themselves value. Critically, human beings need access to good health care, education, markets, and finance.

The capability approach also inspired the development of the United Nations Human Development Index in 1990. It led to a broadening of the scope of poverty to include non-income dimensions. The Millennium Development Goals adopted in 2000 included health, education, water and sanitation, and gender equality as targets

---

[4]   Sen, A. 1985. *Commodities and Capabilities*. Amsterdam: North-Holland.

for poverty reduction on top of eradicating income poverty. The subsequent Sustainable Development Goals adopted in 2015 further expanded the development agenda by adding targets on climate action, clean water, life on land, sustainable cities, and "decent" work. The Global Multidimensional Poverty Index, developed in 2010 by the Oxford Poverty and Human Development Initiative and the United Nations Development Programme, also aims to measure non-income poverty.

A market-oriented approach to development meant that growth was the priority, especially if rapid growth would lead to rapid poverty reduction—as many believed. Thus, in 1978, the PRC started to shift to the model that allowed markets to determine prices, encourage private sector development, and promote trade and foreign investment. According to the PRC leader Deng Xiaoping, by "allowing some people to get rich first," this policy shift can bring prosperity for all. After 1986, Viet Nam followed. India launched major liberalization reforms beginning in 1991 on trade and investment. Market-oriented reforms were implemented in many other countries in South Asia, Southeast Asia, Central Asia (after the collapse of the Soviet Union), and the Pacific (Chapter 2).

These market-oriented reforms unleashed powerful incentives for private firms and entrepreneurs to expand trade and investment. They allowed many Asian countries to benefit from technological progress (for example, information and communication technology, and automation), globalization (in trade, investment, and finance), and increased exchange of knowledge and ideas across countries. But growth and poverty reduction since the 1990s have been accompanied by rapidly rising income inequality in many countries. As a result, addressing income inequality has become a key policy focus across developing Asia.

11.3 Asia's success in reducing poverty

The broad trend in poverty reduction

There were two waves of dramatic poverty reduction in Asia during the past half century. The first was in the 1960s, 1970s, and 1980s (especially the early 1980s), coinciding with rapid economic growth in the newly industrialized economies and several Southeast Asian economies (Figure 11.1). Faster-growing economies had larger reductions in poverty.

Figure 11.1: Economic Growth and Poverty Reduction, 1960s–1980s

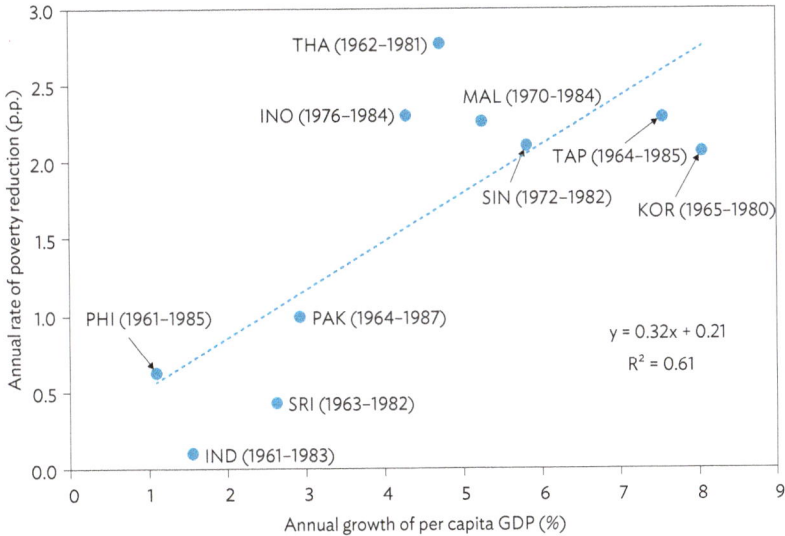

GDP = gross domestic product; p.p. = percentage point; IND = India; INO = Indonesia; KOR = Republic of Korea; MAL = Malaysia; PAK = Pakistan; PHI = Philippines; SIN = Singapore; SRI = Sri Lanka; TAP = Taipei,China; THA = Thailand.

Note: Poverty rates are measured using national poverty lines.

Sources: For India: Datt, G. 1998. Poverty in India and Indian States: An Update. *The Indian Journal of Labour Economics.* 41 (2). pp. 191–211; for Indonesia: Tjiptoherijanto, P., and S. Remi. 2001. *Poverty and Inequality in Indonesia: Trends and Programs.* Paper presented at the International Conference on the Chinese Economy "Achieving Growth with Equity." Beijing. 4–6 July; for Malaysia: Abhayaratne, A. 2004. *Poverty Reduction Strategies in Malaysia, 1970–2000: Some Lessons;* for Pakistan: Kemal, A. R. Undated. *State of Poverty in Pakistan: Overview and Trends.* http://siteresources.worldbank.org/PAKISTANEXTN/Resources/pdf-Files -in-Events /Briefing-on-PRSP/OverviewAndTrends.pdf; for the Philippines: World Bank. 1995. *Philippines: A Strategy to Fight Poverty.* http://documents.worldbank.org/curated/en/340011468758997924/ pdf/multiopage.pdf; for the Republic of Korea: Kwon, H. J., and I. Yi. 2009. Economic Development and Poverty Reduction in Korea: Governing Multifunctional Institutions. *Development and Change.* 40. pp. 769–792; for Singapore and Sri Lanka: World Bank. 1993. *The East Asian Miracle: Economic Growth and Public Policy.* New York: Oxford University Press; for Taipei,China: Warr, P. 2000. *Poverty Reduction and Economic Growth: The Asian Experience.* Manila: Asian Development Bank; and for Thailand: Warr, P. 2004. Globalization, Growth, and Poverty Reduction in Thailand. *ASEAN Economic Bulletin.* 21 (1). 1–18.

The second wave occurred from the 1980s and continues today. This wave includes India, the PRC, and many other countries, broadly coinciding with economic reforms and acceleration in economic growth (Figure 11.2). As a result, there has been a dramatic decline in both the number of poor as well as the share of poor (Table 11.1).

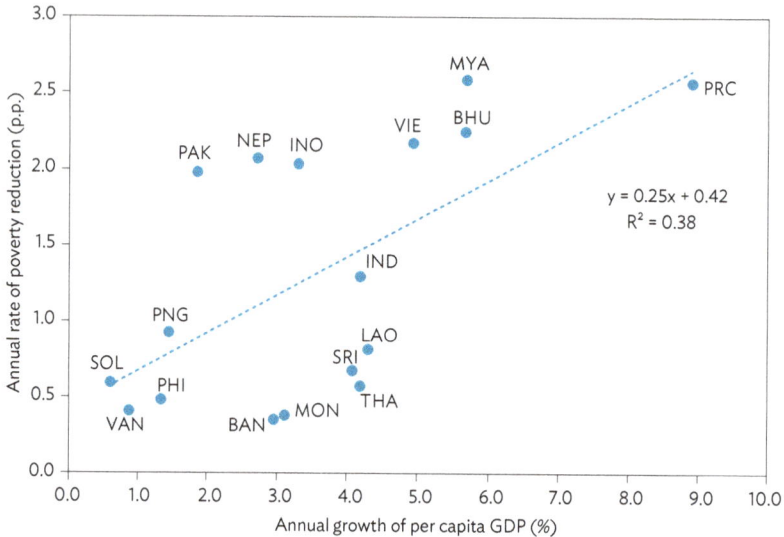

Figure 11.2: Economic Growth and Poverty Reduction, 1981–2015
(based on international poverty lines)

$y = 0.25x + 0.42$, $R^2 = 0.38$

GDP = gross domestic product, p.p. = percentage point, BAN = Bangladesh, BHU = Bhutan, IND = India, INO = Indonesia, LAO = Lao People's Democratic Republic, MON = Mongolia, MYA = Myanmar, NEP = Nepal, PAK = Pakistan, PHI = Philippines, PNG = Papua New Guinea, PRC = People's Republic of China, SOL = Solomon Islands, SRI = Sri Lanka, THA = Thailand, VAN = Vanuatu, VIE = Viet Nam.

Notes: Poverty rates are measured using the $1.90 per day international poverty line for extreme poverty. The initial year is 1981 for most economies, but 1984 for the Lao People's Democratic Republic and 1990 for Solomon Islands.

Sources: World Bank. PovcalNet Database. http://iresearch.worldbank.org/PovcalNet/home.aspx (accessed 7 November 2019); and World Bank. World Development Indicators. https://data.worldbank.org (accessed 2 August 2019).

India and the PRC together contributed 82% of the total poverty reduction for developing Asia from 1981 to 2015. For developing Asia as a whole, 68% of the population (or 1.6 billion people) lived below the $1.90 per day poverty line in 1981. By 2015, the extreme poverty rate had fallen to about 7% (or 264 million people).

Strong economic growth in Asia over the past decades was also accompanied by the emergence of a sizable middle class.[5]

---

[5] Asian Development Bank (ADB). 2010. *Key Indicators for Asia and the Pacific 2010: Asia's Emerging Middle Class: Past, Present, and Future.* Manila.

Table 11.1: Poverty Reduction in Developing Asia, $1.90 per Day International Poverty Line, 1981–2015[a]
(number of poor in million; headcount ratio in % in parentheses)

	1981	1990	2002	2010	2015
Developing Asia	1,604.8 (68.1)	1,503.8 (53.6)	1,107.2 (33.1)	620.3 (17.0)	263.9 (6.9)
Central Asia	6.3 (11.4)	8.1 (12.3)	22.3 (31.1)	10.1 (12.8)	5.3 (6.2)
East Asia	876.5 (84.7)	752.2 (63.7)	405.7 (30.5)	149.9 (10.8)	10.1 (0.7)
People's Republic of China	875.3 (88.1)	751.8 (66.2)	405.4 (31.7)	149.6 (11.2)	10.0 (0.7)
South Asia[b]	506.4 (55.7)	530.0 (47.3)	546.4 (38.6)	393.8 (24.6)	212.4 (12.4)
India	409.4 (57.4)	412.4 (47.4)	445.4 (40.9)	342.9 (27.9)	175.7 (13.4)
Southeast Asia	213.4 (60.1)	210.4 (48.8)	128.8 (24.7)	63.2 (11.0)	33.1 (5.4)
The Pacific[c]	2.2 (49.9)	3.0 (51.1)	4.0 (45.7)	3.3 (32.3)	2.9 (25.7)
Latin America and the Caribbean	49.5 (13.5)	65.5 (14.8)	63.1 (11.8)	36.7 (6.2)	24.3 (3.9)
Sub-Saharan Africa	193.9 (48.8)	280.2 (54.7)	390.9 (55.3)	408.5 (46.5)	416.4 (41.4)
Developing World[d]	1,897.8 (51.7)	1,892.6 (43.2)	1,595.9 (30.2)	1,084.9 (18.4)	727.1 (11.6)

a   Subregional estimates are derived using World Bank's PovcalNet common reference year data, which are based on either actual surveys or extrapolation/interpolation methods.

b   Data for 1981 and 1990 for Maldives are not available.

c   Data for 1981 for the Federated States of Micronesia, Samoa, Timor-Leste, and Tuvalu are not available.

d   Developing World refers to "world less other high income."

Sources: Asian Development Bank estimates; and World Bank. PovcalNet Database. http://iresearch.worldbank.org/PovcalNet/home.aspx (accessed 7 November 2019).

Defining the middle class as those in households with per capita expenditures from $3.20 per day to $32 per day (in 2011 PPP), only 13% of developing Asia's population could be considered as middle class in 1981.[6] By 2015, this had increased to almost 69% of the population. Consumer expenditures in developing Asia increased rapidly reflecting the growing middle class, supporting regional and global growth.[7]

Country experiences in poverty reduction

Country examples show more clearly the importance of economic growth for poverty reduction.

The ROK provides one of the most celebrated success stories of poverty reduction. The economy was among the poorest in the 1950s with most people relying on subsistence farming. There was widespread hunger and deprivation with much of the infrastructure destroyed during the 1950–1953 Korean War. Even as late as the mid-1960s, between 60% and 70% of the population was estimated to be living below the national poverty line. Over the following 3 decades, the ROK's GDP grew about 10% annually and, by the mid-1990s, the absolute poverty rate had declined to 3.4%. The decline was accompanied by significant gains in human development.[8]

In the PRC, after nearly 30 years of Soviet-style central planning, extreme poverty at the $1.90 per day international poverty line in 1981 remained at 88.1% (Table 11.1). But the following 40 years of reform led to rapid economic growth (close to 10% annually) and a dramatic reduction in the poverty rate (to 0.7%). Half of this decline occurred before 1995, coinciding with major reforms in agriculture. These included the introduction of the household responsibility system in 1978–1984 and rounds of price liberalization for agricultural products, which significantly increased farming household income. Also, rural incomes rose from the shift of surplus labor from agriculture to manufacturing and services.

---

[6] ADB estimates based on PovcalNet data for 29 developing Asian economies in 1981 and 2015. The range of $3.20–$32 per day in 2011 PPP is more or less equivalent to the range of $2–$20 per day in 2005 PPP, which was used by ADB in estimating the size of the middle class in its *Key Indicators for Asia and the Pacific 2010*.

[7] ADB. 2019. *Asian Development Outlook 2019 Update: Fostering Growth and Inclusion in Asia's Cities*. Manila.

[8] Henderson, J., et al. 2002. Economic Governance and Poverty Reduction in South Korea. *Working Paper*. 439. Manchester Business School.

In Viet Nam, extreme poverty declined from 76.3% in 1981 to 2.4% in 2015, with the underlying reasons similar to the PRC. Economic reforms, which began in 1986 and accelerated in 1989, also focused initially on agriculture through de-collectivization, land reform, and lifting price controls. A major beneficiary of this reform was rice production. Viet Nam quickly became the world's third-largest rice exporter after years of importing the grain. The reform increased rural incomes, leading to a large reduction in poverty. As reforms broadened to cover the urban and industry sectors, it created jobs for urban residents and rural surplus labor.

In Indonesia, the poverty rate measured at the national poverty line declined from 60% to 15% from 1970 to 1990. The drop was supported by strong economic growth (averaging 6.6% a year), with rapidly expanding labor-intensive manufacturing absorbing surplus labor from rural areas. The 1970s Green Revolution also played a critical role in reducing rural poverty. But the 1997–1998 Asian financial crisis disrupted the poverty reduction process. Growth contracted 13% in 1998, which led to massive unemployment and a surge in poverty—from 17.5% in 1996 to 23.4% in 1999. With a speedy economic recovery from 2000, supported by macroeconomic stabilization policies and structural reform, poverty reduction resumed. The poverty rate at the national poverty line declined to 14% in 2009 and 9% in 2019.

In India, from 1951 to the early 1970s, growth was slow and volatile, with the poverty rate based on national poverty lines showing no discernible trend, fluctuating between 40% and 60%.[9] This began to change from the mid-1970s, first as a result of the effects of the Green Revolution, and subsequently due to more stable and higher growth as early trade and industrial reforms took effect. Poverty reduction accelerated further when India began major economic liberalization in 1991. The poverty rate at the national poverty line declined from 55% in 1970 to 22% in 2011. After 1991, growth in urban areas and in manufacturing became important contributors to poverty reduction.

In Bangladesh, the poverty rate at the national poverty line was estimated at 70% in 1971 when it gained independence. It fell to around 50% by 2000 and further to 22% in 2018. After a period of inward orientation and heavy state control, the country introduced

---

[9]   Panagariya, A. 2008. *India: The Emerging Giant*. New Delhi: Oxford University Press.

market-oriented reforms—including liberalizing agriculture input markets in the late 1970s, industrial deregulation in the 1980s, and a more liberal trade policy from the early 1990s benefiting the garment industry. Nongovernment organizations and community-based organizations played a crucial role in poverty reduction.[10]

Central Asian countries (Armenia, Azerbaijan, Georgia, Kazakhstan, the Kyrgyz Republic, Tajikistan, Turkmenistan, and Uzbekistan) gained independence in 1991. Despite large variations among these countries in extreme poverty during the Soviet era, data show rising extreme poverty after independence, reaching 31.3% for the subregion as a whole in 2002, compared with around 12.3% in 1990 and 11.4% in 1981. Extreme poverty dropped sharply to 12.8% by 2010 and to 6.2% in 2015 (Table 11.1).

In the Pacific, after 2 decades of generally poor economic performance in the 1980s and 1990s, and fairly rapid population growth, extreme poverty (at the $1.90 per day international poverty line) was 45.7% in 2002 for the subregion. Better growth since, partly driven by resource exports, helped reduce extreme poverty to 25.7% in 2015 (Table 11.1). While Pacific island countries are targeting poverty reduction in remote rural areas, they are vulnerable to natural disasters and external economic shocks, often interrupting progress in poverty reduction.[11] Development assistance plays an important role in poverty reduction in the subregion.

11.4 Stable levels of inequality in the 1960s–1980s

The limited data available suggest that, in the 1960s, several East Asian economies including Japan; the ROK; and Taipei,China had relatively low income inequality as measured by the Gini coefficient of per capita disposable income (in the 31–34 range). In the PRC, as a socialist country, income inequality was also believed to be low, although no data are available. However, several Southeast Asian economies—including Malaysia, the Philippines, and Thailand—had higher income inequality with a Gini coefficient in the 40–50 range. South Asian

---

[10] World Bank. 2003. *Bangladesh - Development Policy Review: Impressive Achievements but Continuing Challenges*. Washington, DC.

[11] Although poverty, as measured by daily monetary consumption, comes out high in the Pacific, extreme hardship is rare in the subregion as large segments of the population are supported by subsistence agriculture and informal community-based social safety nets. Nonetheless, vulnerability to sudden episodes of hardship—brought about by environmental or economic shocks, particularly in remote outer island communities— remains a predominant concern.

countries including Bangladesh, India, Pakistan, and Sri Lanka were in the middle, with a Gini coefficient ranging from 30 to 40.[12]

World War II, its aftermath, and postwar reforms can largely explain the low levels of inequality in Japan; the PRC; the ROK; and Taipei,China in the 1950s. Land reform allowed poor and low-income farmers to acquire land from richer landowners at low prices (Chapter 4). In the PRC, land was confiscated from landowners and redistributed to poor peasants. In Southeast Asia and South Asia, former colonies were left with different property systems and agrarian structures; and land reform was not as sweeping as in East Asia. Implementation proved difficult and slow, and its impact on income distribution was far more limited.

Since the 1960s up to the 1980s, most developing Asian economies managed to keep income inequality stable, regardless of its initial level, despite large differences in the pace of economic growth. Many economies in East Asia and Southeast Asia grew rapidly while income inequality remained stable or even declined somewhat—a pattern referred to by many as "growth with equity." The eight high-performing Asian economies representing the "East Asian Miracle," including Hong Kong, China; Indonesia; Japan (Box 11.1); Malaysia; the ROK; Singapore; Taipei,China; and Thailand, grew by 5.5% on average in per capita GDP during 1965–1990. Over this period, their Gini coefficients declined or remained stable at low levels.

The pattern of "growth with equity" has been attributed to two major factors. One is that growth in East Asia and Southeast Asia during the period was broad-based and supported by a dynamic agriculture sector, vibrant labor-intensive manufacturing, expanding trade, and the development of small and medium-sized enterprises.[13] This growth pattern created jobs for a wide swath of the population and increased earnings of the low-income rural population and urban workers. The other major contributing factor was inclusive social policies and rural development.

By comparison, in most South Asian countries, while levels of income inequality remained moderate and stable from the 1960s to the 1980s, economic growth was slow. For example, in India, inequality in household expenditures fluctuated mildly around an

---

[12] World Bank. 1993. *The East Asian Miracle: Economic Growth and Public Policy*. New York: Oxford University Press.

[13] World Bank. 1993. *The East Asian Miracle: Economic Growth and Public Policy*. New York: Oxford University Press.

Box 11.1: Japan's Economic Inequality Over the Past 50 Years

Japan has often been considered a society with relatively low income inequality. However, prior to World War II, the country had very unequal income distribution. The Gini coefficient of market incomes was estimated at 53 in 1920 and 57 in 1937 (Box Figure). The income share of the top 1% income earners was around 20% in 1937.[a] Prewar industrialization led to dramatic increases in income gaps between rich and poor.

Box Figure: Japan's Gini Coefficient, 1895–2015

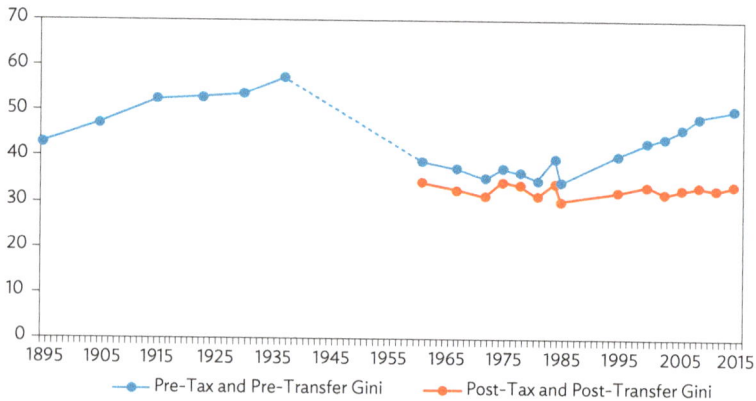

Pre-Tax and Pre-Transfer Gini
Post-Tax and Post-Transfer Gini

Sources: For 1895 to 1939: Minami, R. 2008. Income Distribution of Japan: Historical Perspective and Its Implications. *Japan Labor Review.* 5 (4). pp. 5–20; for 1960 to 1984: Tachibanaki, T. 2006. *Kakusa Shakai: Nani ga mondai nanoka* [The Divided Society: What Are the Issues?] Tokyo: Iwanami Shoten; and for 1986–2015: Organisation for Economic Co-operation and Development (OECD). OECD Statistics. https://stats.oecd.org/ (accessed 21 June 2019).

Japan's income inequality fell sharply after World War II. The top 1% income share fell to 8% in 1948 with capital earnings almost nil. The Gini coefficient of market incomes was estimated at 39 in 1961. The dramatic decline in income inequality was due to war-related destruction, high inflation, and policies implemented immediately after the war, including drastic land reform and dissolving family-owned zaibatsu (large business conglomerate).

During the 1960s and 1970s, despite rapid economic growth, income inequality remained stable and actually declined somewhat. This pattern of growth with equity was due to several factors, including (i) broad-based growth; (ii) agricultural policies such as administered rice prices and government support to increase farmers' access to credit and technology; (iii) large public infrastructure investment in rural areas to promote the

continued on next page

Box 11.1 *continued*

"harmonized development of the whole nation"; (iv) central government fiscal transfers to poorer local authorities; (v) good public education, the introduction of universal health coverage (in 1961), and an improved social security system; (vi) increased influence from trade unions after labor law reform; and (vii) highly progressive personal income and inheritance taxes (until the late 1980s, with the maximum marginal rate of as high as 70% for national income tax and 18% for local income tax, adding up to 88%, and the maximum marginal rate of 75% for inheritance tax, before reducing them).

However, Japan's income inequality has been rising, following the trend in most advanced economies. The Gini coefficient of market incomes increased from 34.5 in 1985 to 50.4 in 2015. The Gini coefficient of disposable incomes post-tax and post-transfer increased from 30.4 to 33.9.

Like many other countries, technological progress and globalization likely have contributed to rising income inequality since the 1980s. Other important contributors include changes in labor market practices such as the increased use of fixed-term labor contracts and part-time workers—especially after the asset bubble burst in 1990—and population aging. Estimates show half of the increase in income inequality in Japan since the 1980s can be attributed to population aging.[b] Compared with younger generations, older people tend to have lower incomes. Higher inequality among them also contributes to income inequality.

[a] Moriguchi, C., and E. Saez. 2008. The Evolution of Income Concentration in Japan, 1886–2005: Evidence from Income Tax Statistics. *The Review of Economics and Statistics.* 90 (4). pp. 713–734.

[b] Ohtake, F., and M. Saito. 1998. Population Aging and Consumption Inequality in Japan. *Review of Income and Wealth.* 44 (3). pp. 361–381.

Sources: Asian Development Bank; Moriguchi, C., and E. Saez. 2008; and Ohtake, F. and M. Saito. 1998.

average Gini coefficient of 32 from 1961 to 1988,[14] while per capita GDP grew a little less than 2% annually. The weak growth in most South Asian countries during that period was, to a large extent, attributed to inward-looking economic policies and heavy state control in the economy (Chapter 2). This constrained the growth of modern labor-intensive manufacturing, among others.

---

[14] Chancel, L., and T. Piketty. 2017. Indian Income Inequality, 1922–2014: From British Raj to Billionaire Raj? *CEPR Discussion Paper.* No. DP12409. Washington, DC: Center for Economic and Policy Research.

11.5 Rising income inequality since the 1990s

Recent trends of income inequality

Since the 1990s, growth in developing Asia has accelerated and has become more widespread, leading to further poverty reduction. However, in contrast with the "growth with equity" pattern in the 1960s–1980s, income inequality increased in many countries, including the three most populous: the PRC, India, and Indonesia (Figure 11.3). Based on household consumption expenditure data, India's Gini coefficient increased by 4 points between 1993 and 2012 and Indonesia's increased by 7 points between 1990 and 2017. In the PRC, the Gini coefficient of per capita household disposable income increased by nearly 12 points between 1990 and 2017.[15]

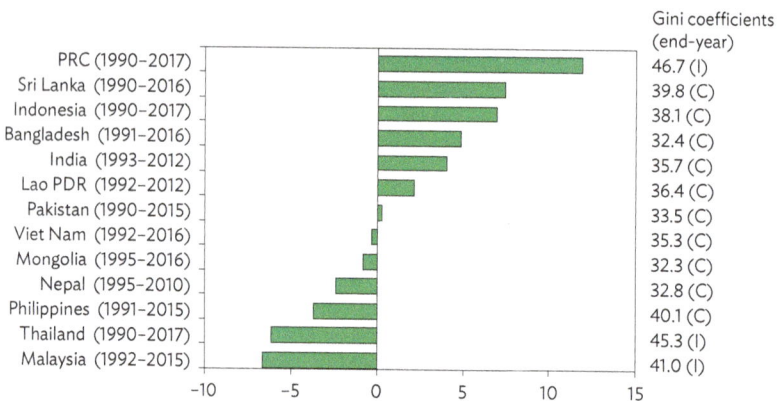

Figure 11.3: Changes in Gini Coefficients, Selected Economies in East Asia, South Asia, and Southeast Asia, 1990s–2010s

Economy	Gini coefficients (end-year)
PRC (1990–2017)	46.7 (I)
Sri Lanka (1990–2016)	39.8 (C)
Indonesia (1990–2017)	38.1 (C)
Bangladesh (1991–2016)	32.4 (C)
India (1993–2012)	35.7 (C)
Lao PDR (1992–2012)	36.4 (C)
Pakistan (1990–2015)	33.5 (C)
Viet Nam (1992–2016)	35.3 (C)
Mongolia (1995–2016)	32.3 (C)
Nepal (1995–2010)	32.8 (C)
Philippines (1991–2015)	40.1 (C)
Thailand (1990–2017)	45.3 (I)
Malaysia (1992–2015)	41.0 (I)

Lao PDR = Lao People's Democratic Republic, PRC = People's Republic of China.

Notes: Green bars refer to changes in Gini coefficients between the two indicated periods. Numbers in the column on the right refer to levels of Gini coefficients for the final year. Symbols in parentheses indicate whether a Gini coefficient is income-based (I) or consumption expenditure-based (C).

Sources: World Bank. PovcalNet Database. http://iresearch.worldbank.org/PovcalNet/home.aspx (accessed 1 October 2019); for the PRC: National Bureau of Statistics of China. *China Statistical Yearbook*. http://www.stats.gov.cn/english/Statisticaldata/AnnualData/ (accessed 1 March 2019); and for Thailand: National Economic and Social Development Board. *Social Development Indicators*. https://www.nesdb.go.th/nesdb_en/main.php?filename=social_dev_report (accessed 1 March 2019).

---

[15] The PRC's income inequality started to rise in the mid-1980s.

In some countries—such as Malaysia, the Philippines, and Thailand—the Gini coefficient declined between 1990 and 2017. However, the Gini coefficient may not adequately capture the inequality due to the very rapid income growth for top earners. In Thailand, for example, estimates show that incomes of the top 1%, a group consisting mostly of households headed by business and property owners and company executives, grew almost three times as fast as average incomes in 1988–2011,[16] even though its Gini coefficient declined during more or less the same period. In Malaysia, it has been suggested that the decline in the Gini coefficient in recent decades was mainly due to affirmative actions associated with the New Economic Policy, which narrowed income gaps between ethnic groups.[17]

The Gini coefficient of per capita wealth, another key measure of inequality but available only for a much smaller set of economies, shows that the wealth distribution is much more unequal than income distribution (Figure 11.4). In 2018, the wealth Gini coefficient was

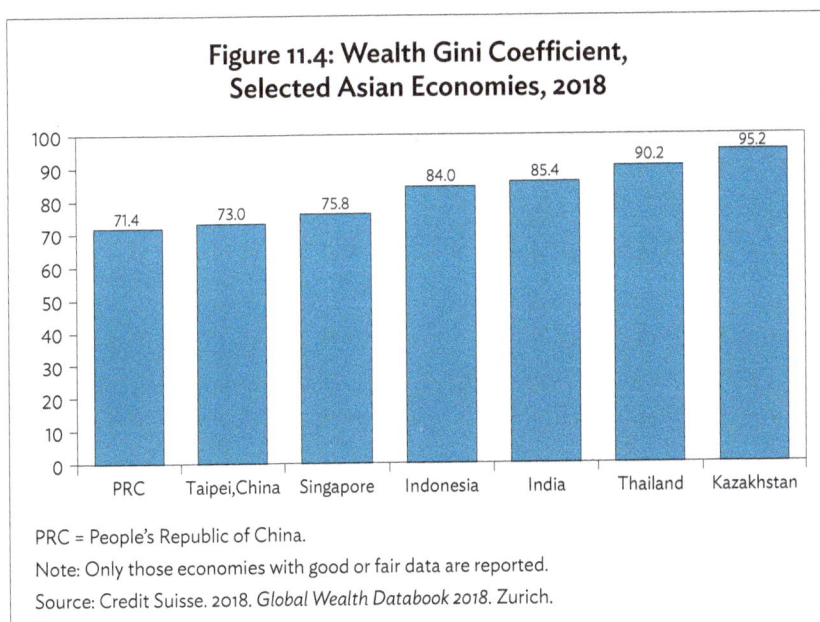

Figure 11.4: Wealth Gini Coefficient, Selected Asian Economies, 2018

PRC = People's Republic of China.
Note: Only those economies with good or fair data are reported.
Source: Credit Suisse. 2018. *Global Wealth Databook 2018.* Zurich.

---

16 Pootrakul, K. 2013. *Khunaphap kan charoen toepto jak miti khong kan krajai raidai panha lae thang ook* [The Quality of Growth from the Perspective of Income Distribution: Problems and Solutions]. Paper presented at the Bank of Thailand Annual Seminar. 19 September.
17 Ravallion, M. 2019. Ethnic Inequality and Poverty in Malaysia Since 1969. *NBER Working Paper Series.* No. w25640. Cambridge, MA: National Bureau of Economic Research.

higher than 80 in India, Indonesia, Kazakhstan, and Thailand; and in the range of 70–76 in the PRC; Singapore; and Taipei,China.

Empirical studies show that wealth inequality has also been on the rise in some Asian countries. In the PRC, for example, the share of wealth owned by the top 10% of households increased from 41% in 1990 to 67% in 2015. In India, the same share increased from 51% to 63% during 1991–2012.[18] Consistent with these trends, developing Asia has seen a sharp rise in the number of billionaires. According to Forbes, developing Asia had 14 billionaires in 1987 (in terms of net worth). The number increased to 47 in 2000 and 698 by 2019.[19]

Why income inequality has risen

Developing Asia is not alone when it comes to rising inequality. Most Organisation for Economic Co-operation and Development (OECD) countries also saw inequality rise in recent decades. Research and policy discussions cite technological progress and globalization, despite their beneficial impact on rapid growth in Asia and worldwide, as key drivers of rising inequality globally.

Technological progress can affect income distribution through two channels. One is to reduce demand for labor relative to that for capital, leading to rising returns to capital relative to wages. According to one ADB study,[20] in India; Indonesia; the PRC; the ROK; Singapore; and Taipei,China, the share of labor incomes in total manufacturing value added declined (implying an increase in the share of capital earnings) between the early 1990s and mid-2000s. As capital earnings go mostly to wealthier individuals and households, a rising share of capital earnings worsen income distribution. Many OECD countries, including Japan, have also seen a rising share of capital earnings and falling share of labor incomes in recent decades.[21]

The second channel is to increase demand for skilled (or better educated) labor relative to that for less-skilled labor. This leads to a widening wage differential between the two—the

---

[18] Wid.World. World Inequality Database. https://wid.world/wid-world/ (accessed 26 April 2019).

[19] Forbes' billionaires list is based on wealth measured using stock prices and exchange rates on 8 February 2019 (Forbes. *Billionaires: The Richest People in the World*. https://www.forbes.com/worlds-billionaires).

[20] ADB. 2012. *Asian Development Outlook 2012: Confronting Rising Inequality in Asia*. Manila.

[21] In many OECD economies, a rising share of capital earnings and falling share of wage earnings since the 1980s have also been attributed to weakening worker bargaining positions due to policies that curtail the power of labor unions.

so-called "skill premium." Wage gaps between skilled and less-skilled labor increased over the past 2 to 3 decades in both developed countries and developing countries.

In the PRC, for instance, the hourly earnings premium of workers with a college education or above over those with high school education or below increased from 41% to 58% between 1999 and 2005.[22] The same comparison in Viet Nam between 1992 and 2006 shows a jump from 23% to 57%. In India, among salaried workers, earnings of managers and professionals have grown fastest.[23]

While there is broad agreement on how technical progress contributed to recent increases in income inequality, there are mixed views about how globalization has affected income distribution. Standard trade theory predicts that, for developing countries with abundant unskilled labor, opening up the economy should raise wages of unskilled labor relative to skilled workers, because these countries will concentrate on producing and exporting goods that are unskilled-labor intensive. According to this theory, trade globalization should help reduce income inequality in developing countries. The earlier "growth with equity" story of East Asia and Southeast Asia is consistent with this thesis.

However, more recently, studies found that trade does not necessarily lead to lower income equality in developing countries. One explanation is that trade today is often accompanied by the use of new technologies, especially when associated with foreign direct investment and global value chains. As new technologies usually require more skilled workers relative to those less skilled, greater trade openness can increase demand for skilled labor relative to unskilled workers in developing countries. This causes widening wage gaps, even if wages of unskilled workers also go up and contribute to poverty reduction. Also, as new technologies and capital often work together due to their complementarity, trade liberalization can also affect income distribution between capital and labor earnings: increasing capital's share and reducing labor's share. This is especially true when foreign companies investing in developing countries partner with local businesses that are familiar with local situations. There are also cases where foreign share of investment is limited by investment laws of

---

[22] Di Gropello, E., and C. Sakellariou. 2010. Industry and Skill Wage Premiums in East Asia. *World Bank Policy Research Working Paper*. No. 5379. Washington, DC: World Bank.

[23] Cain, J., et al. 2010. Accounting for Inequality in India: Evidence from Household Expenditures. *World Development*. 38 (3). pp. 282–297.

recipient countries, and foreign direct investment investors are obliged to find local partners.

In addition, technological progress and globalization create many new economic opportunities, whether in manufacturing, services, property, or finance. Success often comes with substantial economic rents in the form of excessive executive pay or windfall profits. Those able to capitalize on these new opportunities include both entrepreneurs who are the first movers (such as the e-commerce billionaires noted by Forbes) and those with large landholdings in newly favored locations. The increasing number of superrich has been a key contributor to rising income and wealth inequality in Asia and globally.[24] When the tax system is ineffective, this can become a source of social tension.

Technological progress and globalization have not only affected income distribution between capital and labor and between skilled and unskilled workers, but also between urban and rural areas and among different regions. This is because growth driven by technological progress and globalization, as well as market-oriented reforms, usually occurs first in coastal regions (which are closer to trade routes and world markets) and urban cities (which have better infrastructure) before spreading to other areas. This growth pattern can lead to rising spatial inequality, especially in the early stage of development. The dual economic structure and barriers to labor mobility (such as the household registration system in the PRC) can exacerbate these forces. In the PRC, rising urban–rural income gaps and growing regional disparity have been among the key drivers of rising income inequality over the past 3 decades.

Another important contributing factor to rising or persistently high income inequality in developing Asia is the limited role income redistribution plays through taxes and social security transfers, especially compared with developed countries. Income redistribution plays a very important role in reducing inequality in developed countries (Table 11.2). For instance, taxes and transfers reduced the mean Gini coefficient by 33.2% (15.4 Gini points) for OECD countries in 2015, while the reduction was only 6.3% (2.6 Gini points) for developing Asia. The greater role of income redistribution as a country becomes wealthier is one of the underlying assumptions of the Kuznets inverted-U hypothesis.

---

[24] Piketty, T. 2017. *Capital in the Twenty-First Century*. Cambridge, MA: Harvard University Press.

Table 11.2: Asia's Income Inequality in the Global Context, 2015

Region	Pre-Tax and Pre-Transfer Gini (mean)	Post-Tax and Post-Transfer Gini (mean)	% Difference
Developing Asia	40.0	37.4	(6.3)
Japan, Australia, and New Zealand	45.7	32.6	(28.6)
Latin America and the Caribbean	47.1	43.4	(7.7)
Sub-Saharan Africa	45.9	45.0	(1.8)
European Union	46.8	29.9	(36.0)
North America	48.6	34.5	(29.1)
OECD	46.4	31.0	(33.2)

( ) = negative, OECD = Organisation for Economic Co-operation and Development.

Note: Mean refers to the simple average of Gini coefficients of the countries in the region.

Source: Solt, F. 2019. Measuring Income Inequality across Countries and over Time: The Standard World Income Inequality Database, Version 8. https://dataverse.harvard.edu/dataset .xhtml?persistentId=doi:10.7910/DVN/ LM4OWF (accessed 1 August 2019).

Country experiences

The PRC's Gini coefficient of per capita disposable income was below 31 in 1981, among the lowest in developing Asia. It declined briefly in the early 1980s, benefiting from the first round of rural reforms. As reforms extended to urban areas from 1984 and industrial growth accelerated, the Gini coefficient started to rise. In the late 1980s and early 1990s, the government introduced its second round of rural reforms, including the decontrol of grain procurement and sales prices, leading to a large increase in rural incomes and a reduction in the Gini coefficient.

From 1997, the Gini coefficient started to climb again, as growth accelerated, supported by deepening SOE reform, rapid trade expansion after PRC accession to the World Trade Organization in 2001, and the emergence of innovative private companies. The coefficient peaked at 49 in 2008. Since then, it has been declining, although very moderately, due to government policy measures such as increases in minimum wages, expanding social protection in rural areas, increased support for poorer provinces, and structural factors such as the shrinking rural surplus labor that increased agricultural productivity and pushed up urban wages.

In India, consumption expenditure surveys show the Gini coefficient fluctuating around an average value of 32 from 1965 to 1993,[25] but rising steadily afterward to reach around 36 by 2011. The increase in inequality since the early 1990s has been driven by rising urban inequality, especially due to a more rapid increase in wages of higher-educated workers. Industrial deregulation and trade liberalization since 1991 have led to a significant increase in exports of skill- and capital-intensive goods (such as auto parts and generic pharmaceuticals) and information technology-related services (such as business process outsourcing). The increase may have been even higher without government initiatives that expanded India's rural road and highway network and introduced a national employment guarantee scheme in the early to mid-2000s.

Indonesia's Gini coefficient of per capita household consumption expenditure was broadly stable in the 1980s. It began to rise in the early 1990s, but was interrupted by the 1997–1978 Asian financial crisis that affected the rich more than the poor. It started to climb again from 2000 as the economy recovered from the crisis. The Gini coefficient rose from 29 in 2000 to 36 in 2007 and 40 in 2013. While it has been declining since, the 2017 estimate of consumption-based Gini coefficient remained high at 38. Rising income inequality is, like in many other countries, driven by rising skill premiums, the rise of skill-intensive services, and uneven gains from recent commodity booms.

Not all economies in developing Asia have had increasing Gini coefficients since the 1990s. In Cambodia, for example, the movement of labor toward light and labor-intensive manufacturing and services gave more job opportunities for the rural poor, decreasing overall inequality. In Singapore, improved social safety nets reduced inequality in recent years. In Malaysia, the Philippines, and Thailand, pro-poor policies have helped narrow the income divide between rich and poor. In the Philippines, one example of these measures was the launch of a nationwide conditional cash transfer program in 2008.

---

[25] Chancel, L., and T. Piketty. 2017. Indian Income Inequality, 1922-2014: From British Raj to Billionaire Raj? *CEPR Discussion Paper*. No. DP12409. Washington, DC: Center for Economic and Policy Research.

In Central Asia, following the Soviet collapse, Gini coefficients increased substantially in newly independent countries as fiscal spending and welfare transfers were cut and economies contracted. The Gini coefficient of per capita consumption during 1988–1992 ranged between 25 and 28, but shot up to 52 for the Kyrgyz Republic in 1996, 45 for Uzbekistan in 1998, and 40 for Georgia in 1997.[26] But once economic stability was restored from the late 1990s, income inequality began declining. While the overall declining trend in inequality continued until 2010 for the majority of Central Asian countries, most recent data show inequality is again on the rise in some countries such as Armenia and Tajikistan.

A similar pattern occurred in Mongolia. Before 1990, Mongolia had a comprehensive social security program that included free education, universal health coverage, and high pension benefits. This was disrupted by budget cuts and the end of subsidies from the Soviet Union in the early 1990s. New social security welfare programs introduced from 1994 onward helped reduce inequality.

11.6 Looking ahead

Developing Asia has made impressive progress in reducing poverty over the past 50 years, with most countries expected to eradicate extreme poverty by 2025 (using the $1.90 per day international poverty line in 2011 PPP terms). Asia's poverty reduction has been driven by rapid economic growth and various programs to support the poor more directly. Poverty reduction, in turn, has helped create a stable environment for further development. However, poverty reduction remains an unfinished agenda in Asia. The region's poverty rate in 2015 remained at 29% at the $3.20 poverty line that is typical of lower-middle-income countries.

In addition, in many countries, especially those with rapid growth, income and/or wealth inequalities have risen in recent decades. In others, although inequalities declined or stayed unchanged, they remain high.

Looking ahead, developing Asian economies should continue efforts to eradicate (both income and non-income) poverty, and share the benefits of growth more widely, with the following policy priorities.

---

[26] Mitra, P., and R. Yemtsov. 2006. Increasing Inequality in Transition Economies: Is There More to Come? *Policy Research Working Paper Series.* No. WPS 4007. Washington, DC: World Bank.

The first is to promote sustained and inclusive growth to create quality jobs. This requires sound macroeconomic management, a continued commitment to open trade and investment, adequate investment in infrastructure and human capital, and promotion of technological adoption and innovation.

The second is to make greater use of fiscal policy for income redistribution. On the expenditure side, there is large scope in developing Asia to increase spending on education, move toward universal health coverage, and strengthen social protection—including national pension systems, unemployment insurance schemes, and social assistance programs. On the revenue side, policy options include broadening the tax base, making income taxes more progressive, introducing inheritance and property taxes, and strengthening tax administration and collection.

The third is to reduce the urban–rural income gap and regional disparity. Policy options include continued infrastructure investment to improve regional connectivity, and measures to increase agricultural productivity, and fiscal reforms to increase transfer to poor localities or revenue sharing among the regions. In countries such as the PRC, continued reform in the household registration system would promote labor mobility and give equal opportunity for migrant workers in education, health care, and social protection.

Lastly, developing Asian economies should continue governance reforms to ensure the entire population enjoys adequate public services, a level playing field, and equal access to opportunity. Continued efforts are needed to eliminate social exclusion and discrimination based on gender, ethnicity, location, and other individual circumstances, and fight against corruption.

CHAPTER 12

GENDER AND DEVELOPMENT

12.1 Introduction

Gender equality is a basic human right: women and men should have equal rights, resources, and voice. It also has an instrumental value in nurturing sustainable and inclusive economic development by enhancing productivity and improving development outcomes. Development can foster women's empowerment; at the same time, empowering women can benefit development.[1]

Gender equality is considered central to development and an objective in its own right internationally. Indeed, the Sustainable Development Goals (SDGs) recognize the importance of gender equality through a stand-alone goal (SDG 5) aiming to "achieve gender equality and empower all women and girls."

The gender equality agenda has achieved several important milestones since the United Nations (UN) set up the Commission on the Status of Women in 1946. The Women in Development (WID) paradigm emerged in the mid-1970s around the First World Conference on Women in Mexico City in 1975, aiming to ensure that women can benefit from economic development. The Convention on the Elimination of All Forms of Discrimination against Women (CEDAW)

---

[1] Duflo, E. 2012. Women Empowerment and Economic Development. *Journal of Economic Literature.* 50 (4). pp. 1051–1079.

was adopted at the UN General Assembly in 1979. CEDAW was followed by the 1995 Fourth World Conference on Women. The outcome document, the Beijing Declaration and Platform for Action, reaffirmed state parties' commitment to pursuing gender equality across 12 areas, establishing gender mainstreaming as a strategy across all policy areas at all levels of governance for achieving gender equality. Growing recognition among development practitioners, academics, and advocates of the limitations of a WID approach led to a shift toward the Gender and Development (GAD) paradigm. GAD stresses that the benefits of economic development accrue differently between women and men, and even among women depending on their class, age, marital status, religion, ethnicity, and race.

In Asia and the Pacific, the past 5 decades have seen unprecedented gains in terms of narrowing of gender gaps. For example, female education levels in developing Asia improved considerably: school enrollment rates of girls rose faster than those of boys, leading to gender parity in primary and secondary school enrollment. In terms of health, life expectancy of women improved significantly with a consistent decline in maternal mortality, narrowing the health gender gap.

There are three key drivers of gender equality trends in Asia and the Pacific. First, rapid economic growth broadened employment and economic opportunities for women. Second, policy measures on health and education—such as scholarships and, more recently, conditional cash transfer (CCT) programs for disadvantaged women— helped boost their human capital development, improving their chances for upward income mobility. Third, legal and regulatory reforms by governments created an enabling institutional environment for narrowing gender gaps on basic rights, voice, and decision-making power within households, firms, markets, and societies.

However, gender biases in favor of men across a variety of social, institutional, and economic aspects remain in the region. These are reflected in the persistently low literacy rates among women in some countries; women's high unpaid care and domestic work burden, resulting in their lower labor force participation rates; women's disproportionate engagement as informal workers; a systematic difference in male–female wage ratios; sex segregation in markets (such as access to credit and finance, and certain occupations, among others); and low levels of political representation, importantly in the share of seats women hold in national legislatures. Behind these biases are overarching societal norms that define women's position in households, firms, labor markets, and politics.

This chapter discusses developing Asia's achievements and challenges in gender and development. Section 12.2 examines improvements in women's education. Section 12.3 looks at achievements in women's health. Section 12.4 investigates changing women's labor force participation. Section 12.5 reviews women's status within the household and in public life. And section 12.6 outlines the challenges and priority areas in correcting persistent gender gaps.

12.2 Improvements in women's education

In education, girls' participation in school improved considerably over the past 50 years, leading to gender parity in primary and secondary school enrollment rates. In some countries, the previous bias toward boys in the tertiary level was reversed. In the past 5 decades, the number of girls enrolled in primary schools in developing Asia rose 10 times, 65 times in secondary schools, and 400 times at the tertiary level.[2] In contrast, school participation for boys multiplied 7 times in primary schools, 40 times in secondary schools, and 100 times at the tertiary level.

In all 31 Asian economies with available data, women obtained fewer years of schooling in 1960.[3] Pro-female bias appeared in 2010, when women completed more years in school than men in 19 of those economies (Table 12.1). Women in the Republic of Korea (ROK) were the most spectacular performers. Average years of schooling completed by ROK women aged 25–29 years rose from 4.2 years in 1960 to 14.9 years in 2010. Women in Malaysia; the ROK; Singapore; and Taipei,China on average obtained more than 10 years of additional schooling between 1960 and 2010.

As a result, female literacy rates improved considerably in regions that started with low levels of female literacy although the improvement took time to cover the entire population (Figure 12.1).

---

[2] United Nations Educational, Scientific and Cultural Organization Institute for Statistics (UIS). UIS Stat Database. http://data.uis.unesco.org/ (accessed 1 April 2019).
[3] Barro, R., and J.-W. Lee. 2013. A New Data Set of Educational Attainment in the World, 1950–2010. *Journal of Development Economics*. 104 (September). pp. 184–198.

Table 12.1: Mean Years of Completed Schooling, Population Aged 25–29, by Gender

	1960			2010		
	Male	Female	Male–Female Ratio	Male	Female	Male–Female Ratio
Developing Asia	3.1	1.7	1.5	8.8	7.9	0.9
Central Asia	6.0	5.0	0.9	10.6	11.3	(0.7)
Armenia	8.2	7.7	0.6	10.5	10.5	(0.0)
Kazakhstan	5.1	4.4	0.8	11.2	11.6	(0.4)
Kyrgyz Republic	6.1	5.0	1.1	11.4	11.6	(0.3)
Tajikistan	7.3	5.2	2.1	8.7	10.7	(2.0)
East Asia	4.3	2.6	1.7	9.1	9.0	0.1
Hong Kong, China	7.6	5.1	2.6	14.1	13.9	0.2
Mongolia	3.1	2.1	1.0	9.1	10.5	(1.4)
People's Republic of China	4.2	2.6	1.7	8.8	8.6	0.1
Republic of Korea	7.3	4.2	3.1	14.5	14.9	(0.3)
Taipei,China	4.9	2.6	2.3	13.1	13.5	(0.4)
South Asia	1.7	0.5	1.2	8.5	6.6	1.9
Afghanistan	0.7	0.0	0.6	8.0	2.2	5.9
Bangladesh	1.5	0.2	1.3	8.1	8.6	(0.5)
India	1.8	0.5	1.2	8.8	6.7	2.1
Maldives	4.6	3.6	0.9	8.5	8.7	(0.2)
Nepal	0.2	0.0	0.2	5.5	4.6	0.9
Pakistan	1.4	0.3	1.1	7.3	4.6	2.7
Sri Lanka	5.2	3.8	1.4	11.7	12.3	(0.6)
Southeast Asia	2.7	1.4	1.3	8.9	9.1	(0.2)
Brunei Darussalam	4.4	1.7	2.7	9.4	9.7	(0.2)
Cambodia	2.5	0.5	2.1	6.2	4.5	1.7
Indonesia	2.2	0.8	1.3	9.3	9.2	0.2
Lao PDR	2.5	0.4	2.1	5.8	5.1	0.7

continued on next page

Table 12.1 continued

	1960			2010		
	Male	Female	Male–Female Ratio	Male	Female	Male–Female Ratio
Malaysia	4.3	1.6	2.8	12.1	12.6	(0.5)
Myanmar	1.6	1.0	0.7	5.8	6.9	(1.1)
Philippines	3.4	2.7	0.7	9.0	9.8	(0.8)
Singapore	5.1	2.4	2.7	14.3	14.5	(0.2)
Thailand	3.5	2.8	0.7	10.1	10.9	(0.9)
Viet Nam	3.1	1.4	1.7	8.5	8.4	0.1
The Pacific	**1.6**	**1.0**	**0.6**	**6.3**	**5.7**	**0.6**
Fiji	5.8	4.3	1.5	10.6	11.2	(0.6)
Papua New Guinea	0.7	0.3	0.4	5.6	4.8	0.8
Tonga	7.0	6.5	0.5	11.9	12.4	(0.5)
Developed Asia	**9.4**	**8.1**	**1.3**	**12.8**	**13.5**	**(0.7)**
Australia	9.9	9.5	0.4	11.7	12.4	(0.7)
Japan	9.3	8.0	1.3	13.1	13.7	(0.7)
Latin America and the Caribbean	**3.6**	**3.1**	**0.5**	**9.7**	**10.0**	**(0.3)**
Sub-Saharan Africa	**2.2**	**1.2**	**1.1**	**6.7**	**5.9**	**0.8**
OECD	**7.7**	**7.1**	**0.6**	**12.3**	**12.6**	**(0.3)**
World	**4.4**	**3.4**	**1.0**	**9.3**	**8.8**	**0.5**

( ) = negative, 0.0 = magnitude is less than half of unit employed, Lao PDR = Lao People's Democratic Republic, OECD = Organisation for Economic Co-operation and Development.

Note: Barro–Lee dataset version 2.2, updated June 2018, was used in preparing this table.

Source: Barro, R., and J.-W. Lee. 2013. A New Data Set of Educational Attainment in the World, 1950–2010. *Journal of Development Economics.* 104 (September). pp. 184–198.

In the 2010s, as literacy rates reached more than 90% for females, gender parity was nearly achieved in East Asia and Southeast Asia. Central Asia reached nearly 100% literacy for both females and males in the 1980s. Data in the Pacific, while scant, show significant variations in literacy rates. In South Asia, in the 1980s, one in four women could read and write; in 2010, the number rose to one in two women. Despite substantial progress, female literacy and enrollment rates in primary school remain low in South Asia.

Figure 12.1: Literacy Rates by Gender

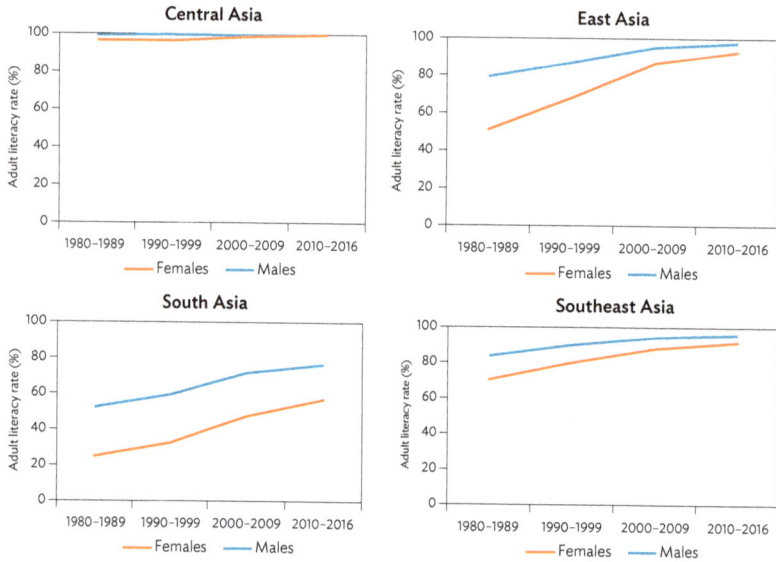

Notes: In the 1980s to 1990s, Central Asia does not include Uzbekistan. East Asia only includes the People's Republic of China for the 1980s to 1990s. Adult literacy is the share of population that is defined as those people aged 15 years and above who have the ability to read and write, and understand a short simple statement in his or her everyday life. This definition also includes "numeracy," the ability to make simple arithmetic calculations.

Source: Asian Development Bank estimates using data from United Nations Educational, Scientific and Cultural Organization Institute for Statistics (UIS). UIS Stat Database. https://data.uis.unesco.org/ (accessed 1 April 2019).

What are the underlying reasons for women's rising school enrollment and improving literacy rates? First, along with the structural transformation from the agriculture to nonagriculture sectors, emerging labor-intensive manufacturing tended to offer higher returns to female education, absorbing many female workers. That stimulated girls' schooling. For example, the explosive growth in Bangladeshi ready-made garments generated large employment for the female labor force, which created large demand for education as well as delays in girls' marriage and childbirth.[4]

---

[4] Heath, R., and A. M. Mobarak. 2015. Manufacturing Growth and the Lives of Bangladeshi Women. *Journal of Development Economics*. 115 (July). pp. 1–15. They also found that the impact on women's schooling has been larger from this growth in ready-made garments than what has been achieved by the government's scholarship program.

More recently, work opportunities brought by new technologies and globalization, such as business process outsourcing (BPO), created new job options for women, and made investments in their education more rewarding, creating another incentive for parents and guardians to invest in girls' schooling. For example, in Indian villages where there are work opportunities in the BPO industry, women are significantly less likely to get married or have children early, choosing instead to obtain more schooling and/or enter the labor market.[5] Higher household income from rapid growth and lower fertility rates have allowed parents to send both girls and boys to school.

Second, public policy, such as mandatory free primary education and cash or in-kind transfer (especially food) programs conditional on schooling, decreased the effective schooling costs shouldered by parents. These policies reduced the need for households to discriminate on school investment between boys and girls. For example, a CCT or in-kind transfer program—in which cash or food is given to households only if their children attend school for a minimum number of days a month—has proven an effective way to send children to school and keep them there for longer periods.

In Bangladesh, the government's Food for Education (FFE) Program, launched in 1993, was one of the first conditional transfer programs. The FFE, which provided a monthly ration of food grains to poor families if their children attend primary school, increased enrollment by 44% for girls and by 28% for boys.[6] The Philippines' "4Ps," *Pantawid Pamilyang Pilipino Program* (Bridging Program for the Filipino Family), supported by the World Bank and the Asian Development Bank (ADB), promotes women's use of health-care services. It improved school attendance and men's participation in family sessions on reproductive rights and gender-based violence. Another example is a program in Cambodia supported by the Japan Fund for Poverty Reduction (JFPR), an ADB trust fund. The program awarded scholarships to girls from poor families in their last grade of primary school. It increased enrollment and attendance at program

5   Jensen, R. 2010. Economic Opportunities and Gender Differences in Human Capital: Experimental Evidence for India. *NBER Working Paper Series*. No. w16021. Cambridge, MA: National Bureau of Economic Research.
6   Ahmed, A., and C. del Ninno. 2003. Food for Education in Bangladesh. In Quisumbing, A., ed. *Household Decisions, Gender, and Development*. Baltimore: Johns Hopkins University Press.

schools by about 30 percentage points, with the largest impact for girls with the lowest socioeconomic status.[7]

12.3 Achievements in women's health

In 1960, female life expectancy in developing Asia was 46 years, shorter than the world average of 54 years (Table 12.2). In 2018, female life expectancy rose to 74 years, almost on par with the world average. The largest increase was in East Asia (33 years), higher than the rise in female life expectancy globally (21 years). In 2018, women in developing Asia lived 3.8 years longer than men on average, more than the gap of 1.8 years in 1960. Healthy life expectancy[8] for females rose by 5 years from 2000 to 2016.

The rise in female life expectancy can be attributed to the decline in female mortality at two critical stages of a woman's life: during early childhood (0–5 years old) and reproductive years (aged 15–49 years). Female under-five mortality rate declined by 85% from 207 deaths per 1,000 live births in 1960 to 31 in 2018, or 177 children saved for every 1,000 born.

The maternal mortality ratio, defined by maternal deaths per 100,000 live births, declined by 67% from 369 in 1990 to 121 in 2015; the corresponding decline worldwide was 44%. Countries with high levels of maternal mortality—Bhutan, Cambodia, the Lao People's Democratic Republic, and Nepal—saw the greatest declines.

What drives the improvement in women's health? Better living standards overall included better nutrition and increased access to health services. These played a critical role. Large public health investment, especially clean water and sanitation, effectively reduced the spread of infectious diseases. The improved delivery of health services to pregnant women (antenatal care and skilled birth attendants) along with expectations to deliver in hospitals rather than at home, as well as the drop in fertility, were keys to the decline in maternal deaths (Chapter 6).

---

[7]   Filmer, D., and N. Schady. 2008. Getting Girls into School: Evidence from a Scholarship Program in Cambodia. *Economic Development and Cultural Change.* 56 (3). pp. 581–617. The program is considered a CCT because each family received cash transfers given their daughter attended school with a good grade.

[8]   Health-adjusted life expectancy (HALE) is a form of health expectancy that applies disability weights to health states to compute the equivalent number of years of good health that a newborn can expect.

Table 12.2: Life Expectancy at Birth
(years)

Subregion/Economy	Life Expectancy at Birth						Health-Adjusted Life Expectancy at Birth					
	1960			2018			2000			2016		
	Male	Female	Female–Male Gap	Male	Female	Female–Male Gap	Male	Female	Female–Male Gap	Male	Female	Female–Male Gap
Developing Asia	**44.1**	**45.9**	**1.8**	**70.0**	**73.7**	**3.8**	**57.0**	**58.0**	**1.0**	**61.3**	**63.0**	**1.7**
Central Asia	54.8	62.6	7.8	68.8	74.7	5.9	56.6	61.7	5.1	61.6	66.2	4.6
East Asia	43.2	46.2	3.1	74.7	79.3	4.6	62.9	64.5	1.6	66.9	68.2	1.3
People's Republic of China	42.4	45.2	2.8	74.5	79.1	4.5	64.1	65.6	1.5	68.0	69.3	1.3
South Asia	42.8	41.4	(1.4)	68.0	70.5	2.5	53.9	53.8	(0.1)	58.7	59.9	1.2
India	42.3	40.5	(1.7)	68.2	70.7	2.5	53.6	53.4	(0.2)	58.7	59.9	1.2
Southeast Asia	49.0	53.8	4.8	69.2	75.1	5.9	57.5	61.0	3.6	60.9	64.6	3.8
The Pacific	41.8	43.4	1.5	64.5	67.5	3.0	53.8	56.4	2.6	57.5	60.3	2.8
Developed Asia	**65.9**	**70.8**	**5.0**	**81.3**	**86.8**	**5.5**	**69.6**	**74.4**	**4.8**	**72.4**	**76.1**	**3.7**
Australia	67.8	74.0	6.3	81.3	85.3	4.0	68.5	72.0	3.5	71.8	74.1	2.3
Japan	65.5	70.3	4.8	81.3	87.5	6.2	69.9	75.0	5.1	72.6	76.9	4.3
Latin America and the Caribbean	**55.4**	**58.2**	**2.8**	**72.1**	**77.6**	**5.6**	**60.3**	**65.1**	**4.7**	**64.0**	**68.6**	**4.6**
Sub-Saharan Africa	**43.0**	**45.9**	**2.9**	**62.3**	**66.6**	**4.4**	**42.8**	**44.6**	**1.8**	**52.3**	**54.5**	**2.2**
OECD	**67.5**	**72.8**	**5.3**	**78.9**	**83.5**	**4.6**	**65.6**	**69.6**	**4.0**	**68.5**	**71.8**	**3.3**
World	**50.8**	**54.0**	**3.2**	**69.9**	**75.1**	**5.2**	**57.2**	**59.9**	**2.7**	**62.0**	**64.8**	**2.8**

( ) = negative, OECD = Organisation for Economic Co-operation and Development.

Sources: United Nations, Department of Economic and Social Affairs, Population Division. 2019. *World Population Prospects 2019. World Population Prospects 2019.* Online Edition. https://population.un.org/wpp/; and World Health Organization. Global Health Observatory Data. https://www.who.int/gho/en/.

In Indonesia, the *Bidan di Desa* (village midwife) program, which has trained more than 50,000 midwives since 1989, led to the significant rise in the proportion of births attended by skilled personnel, especially in rural areas. Over the past decade, Cambodia had one of the most dramatic declines in maternal mortality globally. The success was due to a national campaign to increase health visits during pregnancy and giving special attention to childbirth care.[9]

Japan's *Boshi Techo* (Mother and Child Health Handbook) was launched in 1947. It explains how to monitor and improve maternal and child health, and has been used in other countries such as Indonesia. It contains home-based records on pregnancy, prenatal immunization, delivery, child immunization, and child health, and helps provide continuous care needed.

Although female mortality and life expectancy improved across developing Asia, the high ratio of boys to girls at birth remains. The natural sex ratio at birth is 105–106 boys for every 100 girls. This ratio in developing Asia is higher than normal and has gone up in some economies (Figure 12.2). The availability of affordable ways to detect the sex of an unborn child, a strong preference for boys, and the desire and policy for fewer children are compounding factors. Sons are traditionally preferred over daughters in some cultures because of their perceived income-earning capacity, and roles in caring for parents and continuing the family line following a patriarchal tradition. In some cultures, dowry could be one reason for son preference due to perceived economic burden associated with girls.

In some countries, the sex ratio bias has started to decline. In the ROK, where in the 1990s the boy-to-girl ratio at birth was one of the highest in the region, the ratio declined sharply in the 2000s to normal levels. In the People's Republic of China (PRC), the ratio increased from 1.12 in 1990–1995 to 1.21 in 2008, but declined to 1.13 in 2015. Government interventions, such as the ban on ultrasound use for sex selection, and changing social norms from rising income helped correct the bias in these countries. In the ROK, the rise of the feminist movement in the 1990s led to the 2005 amendment to the family law, which abolished the head-of-family registration system, also reducing the preference for boys.

[9] United Nations Population Fund (UNFPA). 2013. *Cambodia: A Success Story in Reducing Maternal Mortality.* Phnom Penh. https://cambodia.unfpa.org/sites/default/files/pub-pdf/Poster-RH.pdf.

Figure 12.2: Sex Ratios at Birth in Asia
(male birth per female birth)

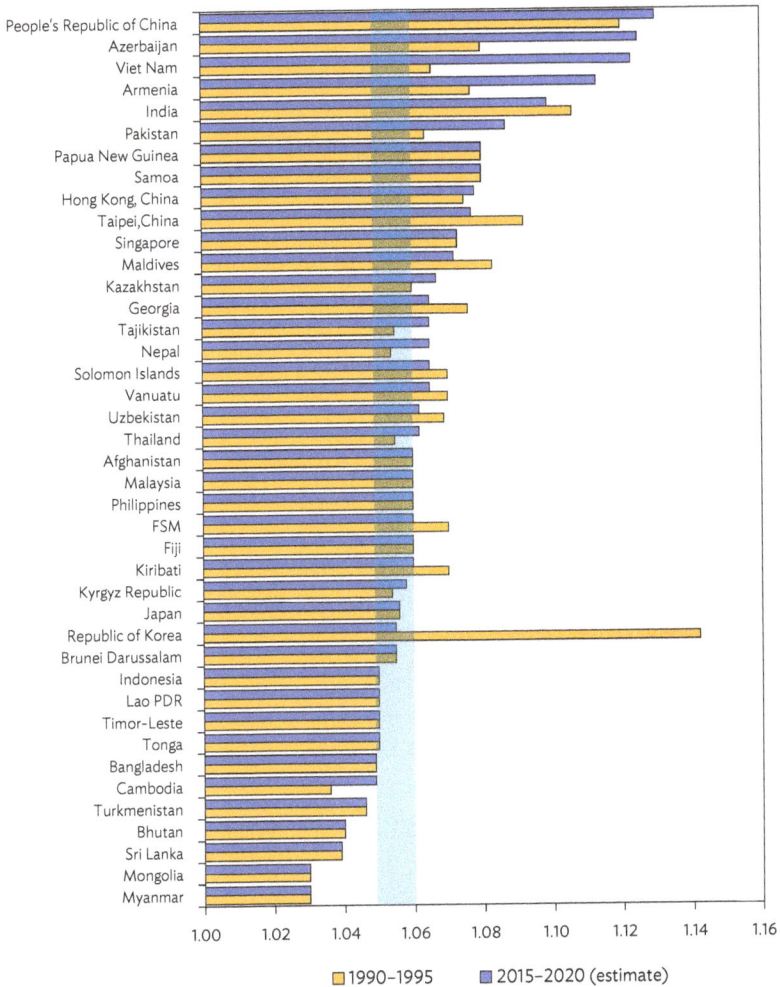

FSM = Federated States of Micronesia, Lao PDR = Lao People's Democratic Republic.

Note: The vertical blue bar refers to the natural sex ratio at birth of 105–106 boys for every 100 girls.

Source: United Nations, Department of Economic and Social Affairs, Population Division. 2019. *World Population Prospects 2019*. Online Edition. https://population.un.org/wpp/ (accessed 1 June 2019).

12.4 Women's labor force and market participation

Long-term progress in female labor force participation

Along with the enormous advances in women's education and health across the region, women's working-age labor force participation increased substantially over the past half century. Strong economic growth, women's higher school attainment, and lower fertility explain the positive long-term trend in female labor force participation rates. As many economies developed rapidly, the transformation from agriculture to manufacturing and services created many jobs for women, especially in urban areas.

Greater trade openness and economic integration contributed to the significant growth of export production, with some industries such as garments and electronics employing large numbers of women in the last few decades. For instance, in the PRC, women employment in export-oriented manufacturing increased markedly after World Trade Organization (WTO) accession in 2001.[10] In Bangladesh, job creation in the export-oriented garment industry has seen large growth in labor demand since the early 1980s, more than 75% filled by women as of 2015—mostly first-time workers from poor families.[11] Recently, the services sector has been the main driver of increased economic participation of women across all subregions, absorbing 50.6% of the female workforce in 2017 (up from 26.9% in 2000). In the Philippines, the majority of the 1.3 million BPO employees in 2016 were women.[12]

Women's labor force participation is an important driver and outcome of economic development. First, with women comprising about half of Asia's working-age population, it is important for economies to tap the full potential of their female labor force. With the pace of demographic transition and aging in many economies accelerating, creating a "gender dividend" (by promoting gender equality and increasing female labor force participation) will be increasingly important.

---

[10] Cai, F., and Y. Du. 2014. Exports and Employment in the People's Republic of China. In Khor, N., and D. Mitra, eds. *Trade and Employment in Asia.* Abingdon, United Kingdom: Asian Development Bank and Routledge.

[11] Government of Bangladesh. 2015. *Seventh Five-Year Plan FY2016–FY2020: Accelerating Growth, Empowering Citizens.* Dhaka: General Economics Division, Planning Commission.

[12] Errighi, L., C. Bodwell, and S. Khatiwada. 2016. *Business Process Outsourcing in the Philippines: Challenges for Decent Work.* Bangkok: International Labour Organization.

Second, greater female labor force participation can also enhance overall economic productivity. At the firm level, evidence shows gender-diverse working environments are more productive.[13]

Third, women's earning potential advances social development for women and girls. For instance, a study in rural PRC shows that increasing prices for tea in the early 1980s, which women produced with comparative advantage, both increased women's incomes and enhanced girls' health—it also improved the sex ratio in tea-producing regions.[14]

Fourth, where women have the opportunity for paid work and financial decision-making, their spending, saving, and investment patterns (different from men) can lead to higher human and physical capital accumulation and intergenerational spillovers.[15]

Persistent gender inequality in labor force participation

Nonetheless, women's labor force participation rate remains stubbornly, and considerably, lower than men's globally—at around 50% of the economically active female population in 2017 (Figure 12.3). Asia is no exception. Currently, women in developing Asia are, on average, 30% less likely than men to be in the workforce, with considerable cross-country variations. This gap persists despite economic growth, decreasing fertility rates, and increasing education.

While the female labor force participation rate (FLFPR) has increased in most countries since the late 1960s, more recent data show it is declining in Asia and the Pacific, visibly dropping in some subregions, where the male participation rate is declining as well.[16] On average, the FLFPR in Asia fell from 57.2% in 1990 to 50.3% in 2017, with marked variations across countries and subregions. Between 1990 and 2017, the FLFPR fell sharply in East Asia and the Pacific, and the gap between the labor force participation rate of women and men in East Asia widened.

[13] Azmat, G., and B. Petrongolo. 2014. Gender and the Labor Market: What Have We Learned from Field and Lab Experiments? *Labour Economics*. 30 (October). pp. 32–40.
[14] Qian, N. 2008. Missing Women and the Price of Tea in China: The Effect of Sex-Specific Income on Sex Imbalance. *Quarterly Journal of Economics*. 123 (3). pp. 1251–1285.
[15] There are many studies on intergenerational spillover effects of education and income. For example, see Lee, H., and J.-W. Lee. 2019. Patterns and Determinants of Intergenerational Educational Mobility: Evidence Across Countries. *Asian Growth Research Institute Working Paper Series*. No. 2019-02. Seoul: Asian Growth Research Institute.
[16] The recent declining trend in female labor participation is not necessarily driven by the rising female enrollment in secondary and tertiary schools, because there is a similar qualitative pattern using working-age (aged 25–54 years) population data.

Figure 12.3: Labor Force Participation in Asia and the Pacific

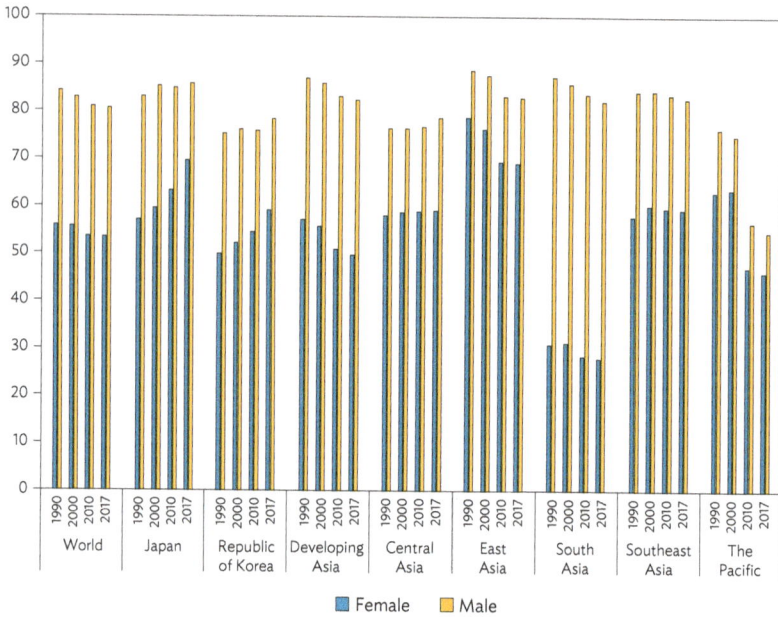

Notes: Working-age population includes those aged 15–64 years. Figures are based on International Labour Organization modeled estimates. East Asia excludes Japan and the Republic of Korea. Data for the Pacific include Fiji, Papua New Guinea, Samoa, Solomon Islands, Timor-Leste, Tonga, and Vanuatu, with Papua New Guinea driving most of the fall in the female labor force participation rate in the Pacific.

Source: Asian Development Bank calculations using data from the International Labour Organization. ILOSTAT. https://www.ilo.org/ilostat/ (accessed 1 August 2019).

Does economic development affect women's participation in the labor market? The relationship between the FLFPR and national income per capita follows a U-shape (Figure 12.4).[17] The FLFPR is high at earlier stages of development when income is low and agriculture is important. It then falls somewhat as greater household income allows some women to exit the labor market and specialize in household work. It rises again as societies become wealthier.

---

[17] Several cross-country or time-series studies have shown that the relationship between the FLFPR and economic development is not necessarily monotonic but rather represents a U-shaped curve in the process of economic development (Durand, J. D. 1975. *The Labor Force in Economic Development: A Comparison of International Census Data, 1946–1966.* Princeton: Princeton University Press).

Figure 12.4: U-Shaped Female Labor Force Participation with Economic Development in the World, 1990 and 2017

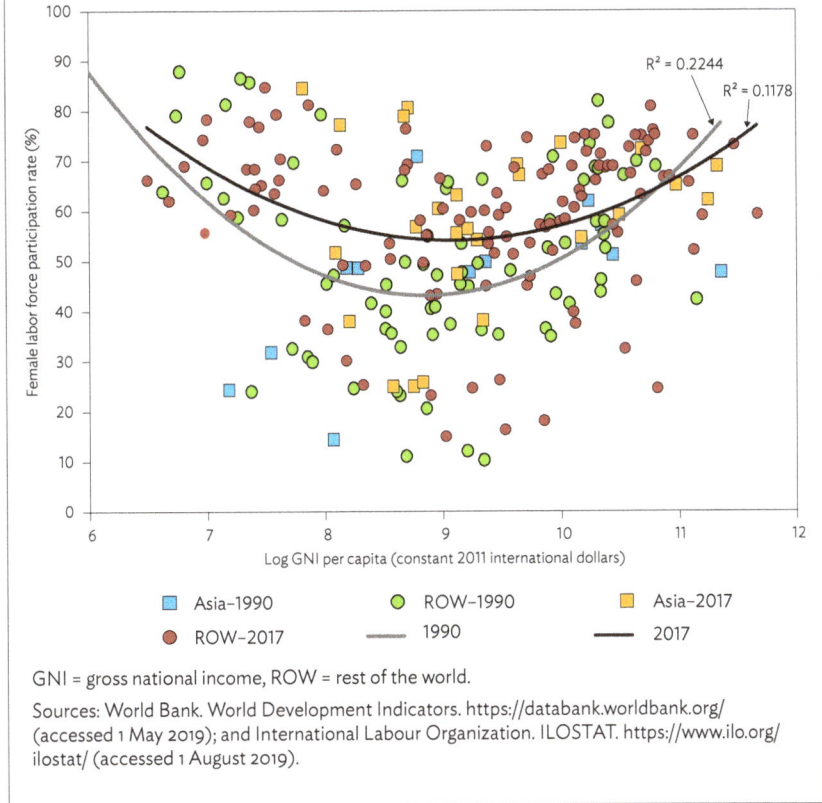

GNI = gross national income, ROW = rest of the world.

Sources: World Bank. World Development Indicators. https://databank.worldbank.org/ (accessed 1 May 2019); and International Labour Organization. ILOSTAT. https://www.ilo.org/ilostat/ (accessed 1 August 2019).

As more girls attain higher education, their desire to pursue a career may also increase.[18] In more developed economies, women's career aspirations, as well as their desire for greater economic freedom and independence, can raise female labor force participation.[19] Yet women's labor participation is determined by a variety of factors such as household income, marital status, childcare and other domestic

---

[18]   Blau, F., M. Ferber, and A. Winkler. 2001. *The Economics of Women, Men, and Work.* New Jersey: Prentice Hall.

[19]   In India, the increased quota for female representation in elected positions led to more education for girls, presumably by raising girls' own aspirations and their parents' aspirations for them (Beaman, L., et al. 2012. Female Leadership Raises Aspirations and Educational Attainment for Girls: A Policy Experiment in India. *Science.* 335 (6068). pp. 582–586).

responsibilities, labor market conditions, the availability of time-saving devices at home, institutional support, along with social and cultural norms.

The U-shaped relationship may help explain the drop in the average FLFPR across Asia since 1990, even compared with a similar global trend (Figure 12.4). As most economies in the region have reached middle-income stage, women drop out of low-paid employment in favor of home production and childcare, leading to a fall in their labor force participation. For example, average per capita income grew nearly eightfold from $1,327 to $10,414 in purchasing power parity terms, creating a strong income effect that enabled women to spend more time at home.

A disruption in a woman's labor market participation and career progression around the time of marriage, childbearing, and/or child-rearing leads to a steep decline in the FLFPR in the life cycle's middle stage, creating an M-shaped labor supply curve. Social norms and cultural influences that place a disproportionately large burden on childcare and domestic work on women reinforce the M-shaped relationship in some economies and subregions at a particular development stage (Figure 12.5).

Over the years, some economies witnessed a smoothing out of the M-shape. Governments and companies can help reduce women's labor market intermittency by increasing affordable and quality childcare options; flexible work arrangements both for women and men; maternity, paternity, and parental leaves; incentives for women's reentry into the workforce; and overall emphasis on gender equality in the workplace. The change in social norms that encourages men to share care and family responsibilities more equally can also help.

Gender gap in quality of work and lingering wage gaps

While female labor force participation is one important dimension of tracking progress in women's economic participation, perhaps even more important is to look at the quality of employment and labor conditions. In 1991–2017, the share of female workers in developing Asia was highest in medium-skill occupations in services, particularly in clerical support (47.7%) and service and sales workers (41.4%). It was lowest in high-skill occupations (20.4% in managerial occupations).[20]

---

[20] International Labour Organization (ILO). ILOSTAT Database. https://www.ilo.org/ilostat/.

Figure 12.5: Female Labor Force Participation Rate over the Life Cycle by Pseudo-Cohort—Selected Asian Economies

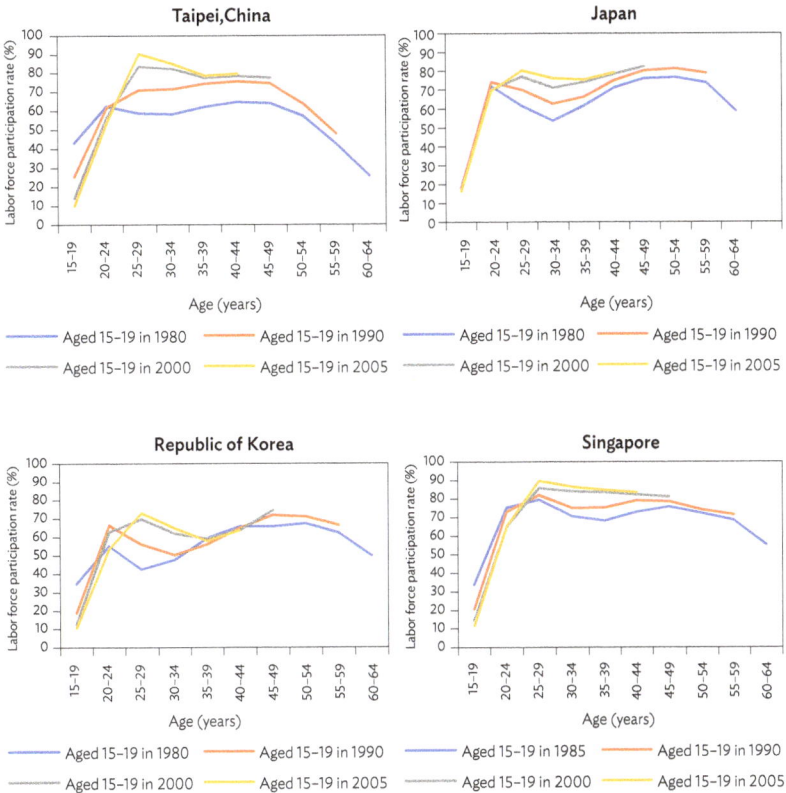

Note: Figures prior to 1990 are based on national survey data, while figures for 1990 onward are based on International Labour Organization modeled estimates.

Source: International Labour Organization. ILOSTAT. https://www.ilo.org/ilostat/ (accessed 1 July 2019).

While services helped increase women's economic participation as part of a longer-term structural shift, it also reflected the participation of women in lower-paying jobs with limited capital and skill accumulation potential. Even in modern services, such as finance, information technology (IT), and business services, international evidence shows persistent occupational differences by gender. For example, in the IT sector, women are mostly in data processing, while men dominate the better paid, high-skilled positions such as programming.[21]

In most Asian economies, women are mostly employed in the informal sector, often in micro and small enterprises, frequently in rural areas. The lack of decent labor standards and regulations in informal settings leaves them open to poor working conditions.

Also, even when in formal employment, women tend to work in jobs classified as vulnerable—short-term or part-time contracts without adequate social security and a voice at work.[22] Despite the significant progress made, more than half of women in developing Asia remain in vulnerable jobs such as informal street vendors (Figure 12.6). The pattern of vulnerable employment also shows pronounced subregional variations in tandem with the slow pace of structural transformation. In South Asia, women make up a disproportionately large share of workers in the informal sector, as they remain mostly employed in agriculture, particularly subsistence agriculture. In the Pacific, most jobs in services—which drove the increase in women's economic participation—are informal and often associated with low value-added activities.

Even when women find opportunities for non-vulnerable employment, they earn less than men for doing comparable work. Globally, women tend to receive lower wages (Figure 12.7) and fewer benefits for work than do men. The gender wage gap is largest in high-skill occupations (managerial and professional occupations). The gender wage gap can be explained more by cultural and social norms as well as institutional settings rather than income per capita of economies.

The pay gap has important consequences for closing other gender gaps. Lower pay may discourage working-age women from entering the workforce, disrupting the positive feedback loop by which paid work strengthens women's position in the household and society. It may also deter young women from investing in education and training, limiting their future options.

---

[21] See, for example, Wajcman, J., and L. A. P. Lobb. 2007. The Gender Relations of Software Work in Vietnam. *Gender, Technology and Development*. 11 (1). pp. 1–26; and Patel, R., and M. J. Parmentier. 2005. The Persistence of Traditional Gender Roles in the Information Technology Sector: A Study of Female Engineers in India. *Information Technologies and International Development*. 2 (3). pp. 29–46.

[22] Under the ILO's definition, workers in vulnerable employment include own-account workers (self-employed persons without engaging employees) and contributing family workers (self-employed persons working in an establishment operated by a relative of the same household).

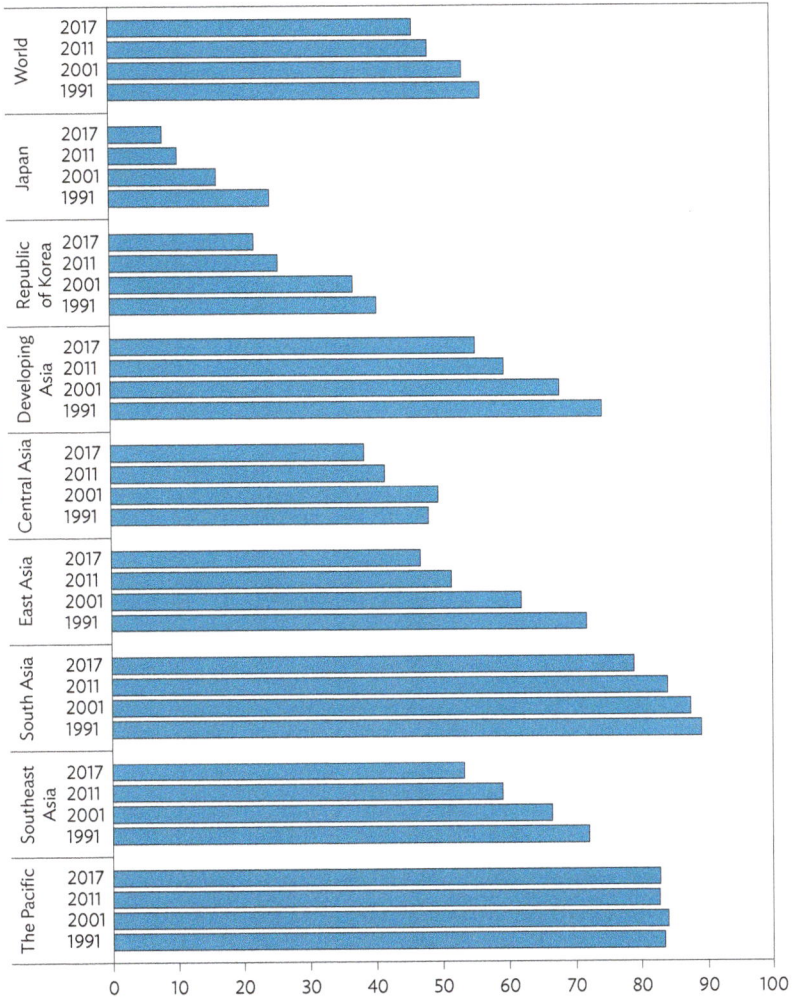

Figure 12.6: Share of Vulnerable Employment of Women
(% of total female employment)

Notes: East Asia excludes the Republic of Korea. Workers in vulnerable employment include own-account workers (self-employed persons without engaging employees) and contributing family workers (self-employed persons working in an establishment operated by a relative of the same household).

Source: Asian Development Bank calculations using data from International Labour Organization. ILOSTAT. https://www.ilo.org/ilostat/ (accessed 1 March 2019).

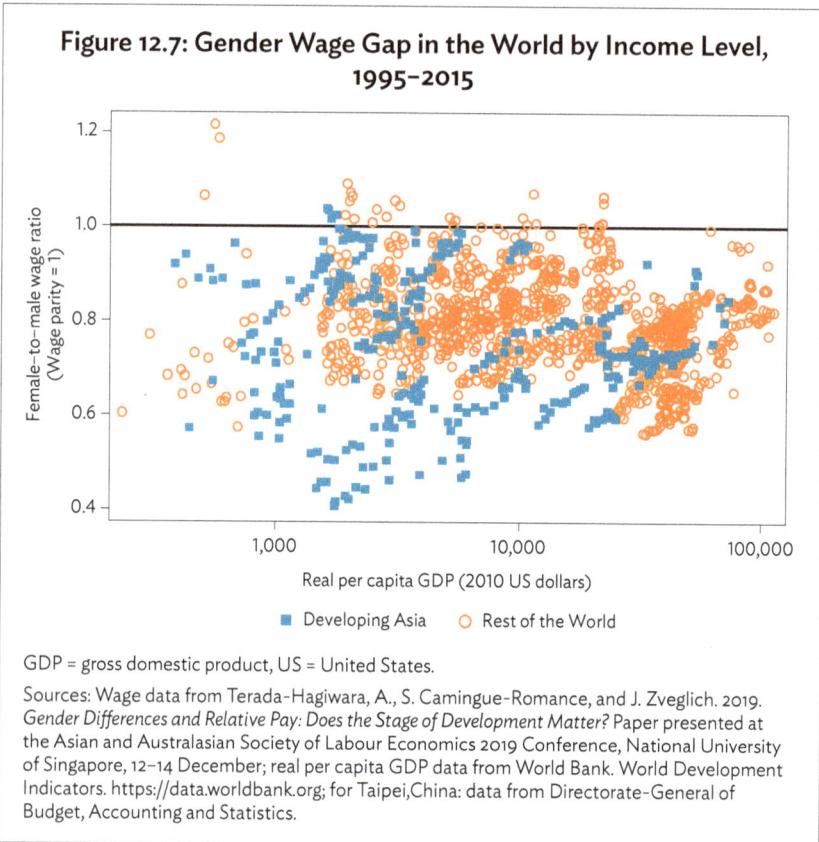

Figure 12.7: Gender Wage Gap in the World by Income Level, 1995–2015

GDP = gross domestic product, US = United States.
Sources: Wage data from Terada-Hagiwara, A., S. Camingue-Romance, and J. Zveglich. 2019. *Gender Differences and Relative Pay: Does the Stage of Development Matter?* Paper presented at the Asian and Australasian Society of Labour Economics 2019 Conference, National University of Singapore, 12–14 December; real per capita GDP data from World Bank. World Development Indicators. https://data.worldbank.org; for Taipei,China: data from Directorate-General of Budget, Accounting and Statistics.

In developing Asia, women earned, on average, about 75% of men's wages during 1995–2015, slightly less than the 79% global average (Figure 12.7). The wage gap is surprisingly persistent across countries and over time, such that rising aggregate incomes do not necessarily result in more equality for women. The chronic gender wage gap remains a key development challenge.

Trends in the gender wage gap differ widely across the region. Women have made considerable progress closing the wage gap in India and Taipei,China, and moderate gains in Indonesia. In India, women earned about half of the male average even in 2004, but the ratio rose to 61% by 2011. In the Philippines, women made more in 2001 than men on average (105%), the earliest available wage data, but dipped slightly below parity by 2013 (98%).[23]

[23] ADB. 2015. *Asian Development Outlook 2015 Update: Enabling Women, Energizing Asia.* Manila.

One important determinant of the earnings gap is differences in educational attainment, work experience, type of employment, and occupation or industry type. Rising incomes and globalization provided opportunities for girls to pursue education, and for women to pursue careers (previously blocked by traditional institutions). While education gaps narrowed significantly in most economies as they developed, working-age women as a whole in most countries are less educated than working-age men on average because of the gap among older workers.

Furthermore, men's human capital accumulated from work may have a role to play in the disparities between male and female wages. Different responsibilities in the household—particularly when it comes to children—may cause women to accrue less work experience than men or devote less time to paid work. Women may be inclined to accept lower wages in return for physical security or job flexibility.

Equal pay for work of equal value is widely recognized as a right to which men and women are both entitled. Yet not all countries have laws ensuring the equal pay principle in practice. Among economies reporting on gender discrimination in the World Bank's database,[24] 36 economies in developing Asia do not have laws guarding against wage difference based on gender. Beyond this high-level principle, policies should promote science, technology, engineering, and mathematics (STEM) education for girls; strengthen skills development for women in the workplace; and support the provision of child and elderly care.

Significant gender gaps in firm ownership and management

Women generally remain underrepresented in firm ownership and management. Enterprises owned or managed by women are often characterized as small firms with a low capital base and low productivity, and often simply try to survive. As of 2011, more than 90% of female-owned micro, small, and medium-sized enterprises in Asia and the Pacific were in the informal sector. By nature, these female-owned firms are constrained by access to finance and other disadvantages associated with the informal sector.[25]

---

[24] World Bank. Women, Business, and the Law Database. https://wbl.worldbank.org/en/data/exploretopics/getting-paid (accessed 10 November 2019).

[25] WTO, Australian Aid, and ADB. 2019. *Aid for Trade in Asia and the Pacific: Promoting Economic Diversification and Empowerment*. Manila: ADB.

Microcredit and microfinance programs supported by nongovernment organizations, governments, ADB, and other multilateral development banks have made important inroads in improving women's financial inclusion and access to finance. Women are regarded as being more credit-constrained but more reliable than men in repaying loans. Thus, rural women have been targeted by microfinance institutions. Grameen Bank in Bangladesh, founded by Nobel laureate Professor Muhammad Yunus, was an early example of closing gender gaps in financial inclusion through the rapid expansion of microcredit programs in rural areas. These programs enabled women to work on income-generating, market-based activities and enhanced their bargaining power within households.[26]

Emerging evidence indicates that the rapid digitalization of trade and growth of e-commerce offers opportunities for women entrepreneurs.[27] Applying a gender lens to information and communication technology initiatives can promote women's entrepreneurship, allowing them to take advantage of online networking and outsourcing opportunities even in geographically challenged economies of the Pacific.

12.5 Women's status in the household and in public life

Over the past 50 years, while notable improvements were made in women's legal and citizenship rights, participation in public and political life remains restricted. An important factor explaining this mixed progress on women's status is social norms and attitudes that restrict women's roles in the household, with limited access to "nontraditional" roles in society and the economy.

Progress and challenges of women's status within the household

A woman's status within the household has traditionally been defined by their reproductive and family roles: as mothers, daughters, or sisters, their roles and responsibilities primarily confined to unpaid care activities—such as caring for family members, cooking, cleaning, and fetching water and firewood, among others. While this varies

---

[26] Pitt, M. M., S. R. Khandker, and J. Cartwright. 2006. Empowering Women with Micro Finance: Evidence from Bangladesh. *Economic Development and Cultural Change.* 54 (4). pp. 791–831; and Schuler, S. R., and E. Rottach. 2010. Women's Empowerment across Generations in Bangladesh. *Journal of Development Studies.* 46 (3). pp. 379–396.

[27] WTO, Government of Australia, and ADB. 2017. *Aid for Trade in Asia and the Pacific: Promoting Connectivity for Inclusive Development.* Manila: ADB.

among subregions in Asia and the Pacific, the unequal share of unpaid work performed by women and girls is common across countries at different income levels. The increased use of household appliances such as refrigerators, washing machines, microwaves, and dryers (Figure 12.8) has helped reduce the time for domestic chores, but the burden of unpaid care and domestic work still falls disproportionately on women (Figure 12.9).

Figure 12.8: Possession of Appliances, Selected Asian Economies
(% of households)

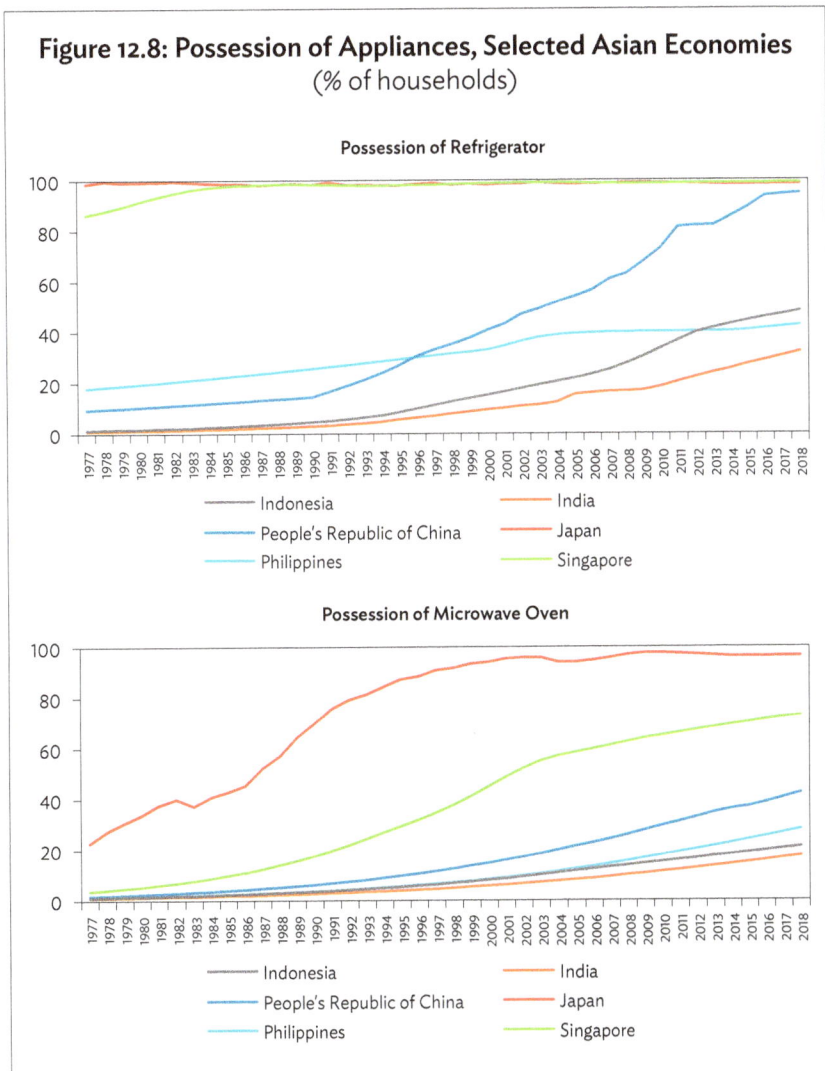

Possession of Refrigerator

Indonesia — India
People's Republic of China — Japan
Philippines — Singapore

Possession of Microwave Oven

Indonesia — India
People's Republic of China — Japan
Philippines — Singapore

continued on next page

Figure 12.8 *continued*

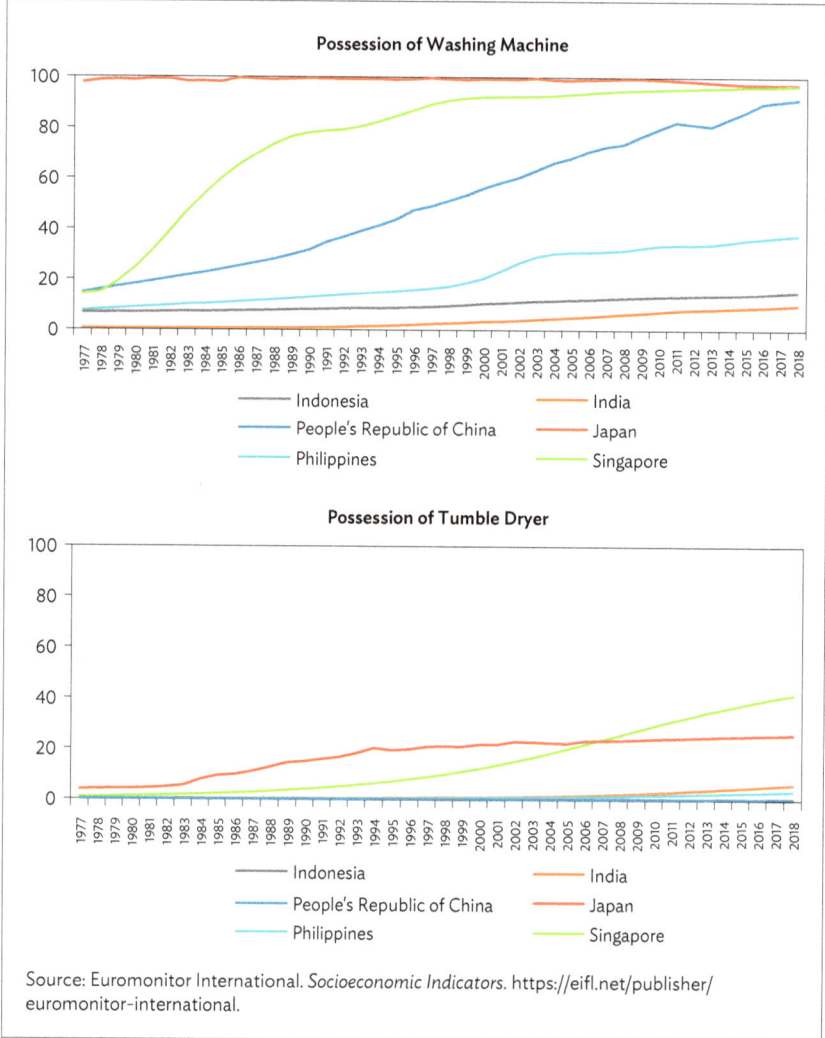

Possession of Washing Machine

Possession of Tumble Dryer

Source: Euromonitor International. *Socioeconomic Indicators*. https://eifl.net/publisher/euromonitor-international.

While women's disproportionate unpaid care work responsibilities persist, reforms to laws covering land and property, inheritance, and marriage and the family have strengthened their legal rights and status within the family. The Asia and Pacific region has made progress in eliminating sex-based discrimination in legal frameworks, particularly laws covering access to jobs and prevention

Figure 12.9: Women's Time Spent on Unpaid Care and Domestic Work, 2010–2017
(ratio of men's time)

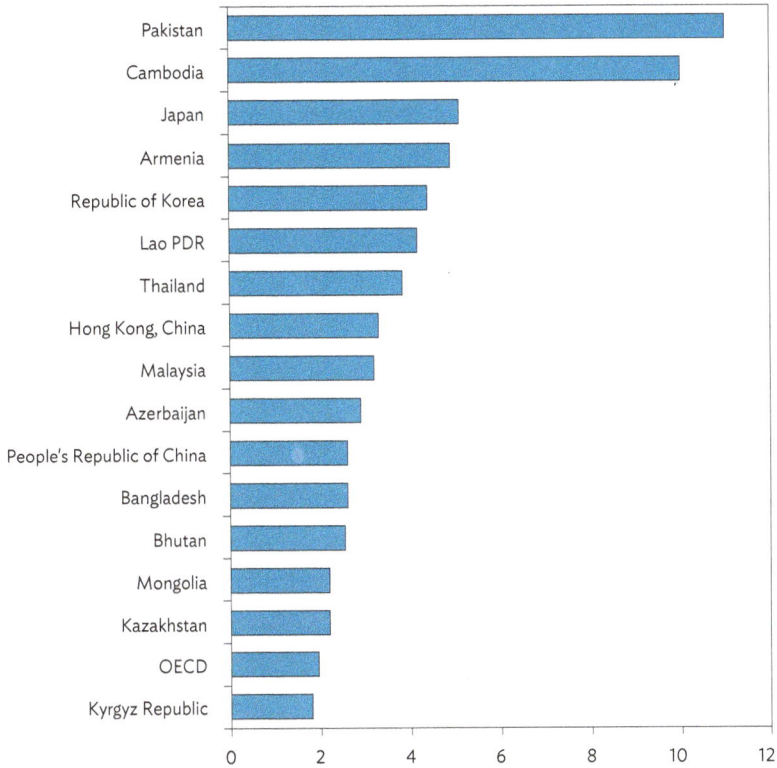

Pakistan	11
Cambodia	10
Japan	5
Armenia	4.8
Republic of Korea	4.3
Lao PDR	4.1
Thailand	3.8
Hong Kong, China	3.3
Malaysia	3.2
Azerbaijan	2.9
People's Republic of China	2.6
Bangladesh	2.6
Bhutan	2.5
Mongolia	2.2
Kazakhstan	2.2
OECD	2
Kyrgyz Republic	1.9

Lao PDR = Lao People's Democratic Republic, OECD = Organisation for Economic Co-operation and Development.

Note: Data are based on national time use surveys, covering yearly range of 2010–2017.

Sources: Asian Development Bank and UN Women. 2018. Gender Equality and the Sustainable Development Goals in Asia and the Pacific. Bangkok; United Nations, Department of Economic and Social Affairs, Statistics Division. Gender Statistics. https://genderstats.un.org/ (accessed 20 May 2019); and OECD. OECD Statistics. https://stats.oecd.org/ (accessed 15 August 2019).

of violence against women.[28] Greater equality in rights within the family, such as equal property and asset ownership, is linked to stronger bargaining power within the household.[29]

Examples of legal reform includes constitutional and/or legal recognition of women's equal land rights (for example, constitutions of the Central Asian republics during the 1990s, and Cambodia's Land Law of 2001), equal rights to inheritance (India's Hindu Succession Act Amendment of 2005), joint titling for married couples (Philippine Presidential Decree of 1978), and the right for married women to open individual bank accounts (Indonesia's Law on Marriage of 1974).[30]

There are also legal reforms that raise the minimum legal age of marriage to protect child rights and secure opportunities for girls' education. By 2016, almost all countries in Asia and the Pacific had raised the minimum legal age of marriage to 18 (with exceptions for customary or religious laws).[31] Legal reforms, combined with socioeconomic changes, led to an increase in the median age of marriage for women across many countries.

Women's decision-making within the household appears to have increased over the period, mirroring broader trends in human capital development, the ability to earn independent income, and stronger legal rights on productive assets. Although varying across the region, married women are increasingly able to participate in decision-making on major household purchases such as houses and automobiles (Figure 12.10). However, the "cost" of the combination of paid and unpaid work often leads to women's increased "time poverty"—less time available for leisure, education, and joining public and political life.[32] Achieving work–family balance is one of the biggest challenges identified by women in developing Asia.[33]

[28] As defined by the World Bank. 2018. *Women, Business, and the Law 2018*. Washington, DC.
[29] ADB. 2018. *Measuring Asset Ownership and Entrepreneurship from a Gender Perspective. Methodology and Results of Pilot Surveys in Georgia, Mongolia, and the Philippines*. Manila.
[30] World Bank. 2018. *Women, Business, and the Law 2018*. Washington, DC.
[31] Inter-Parliamentary Union and the World Health Organization. 2014. *Child, Early and Forced Marriage Legislation in 37 Asia-Pacific Countries*. Tignieu-Jameyzieu: Courand et Associés.
[32] ADB and UN Women. 2018. *Gender Equality and the Sustainable Development Goals in Asia and the Pacific*. Bangkok.
[33] ILO and Gallup. 2017. *Towards a Better Future for Women and Work: Voices of Women and Men*. Geneva and Washington, DC.

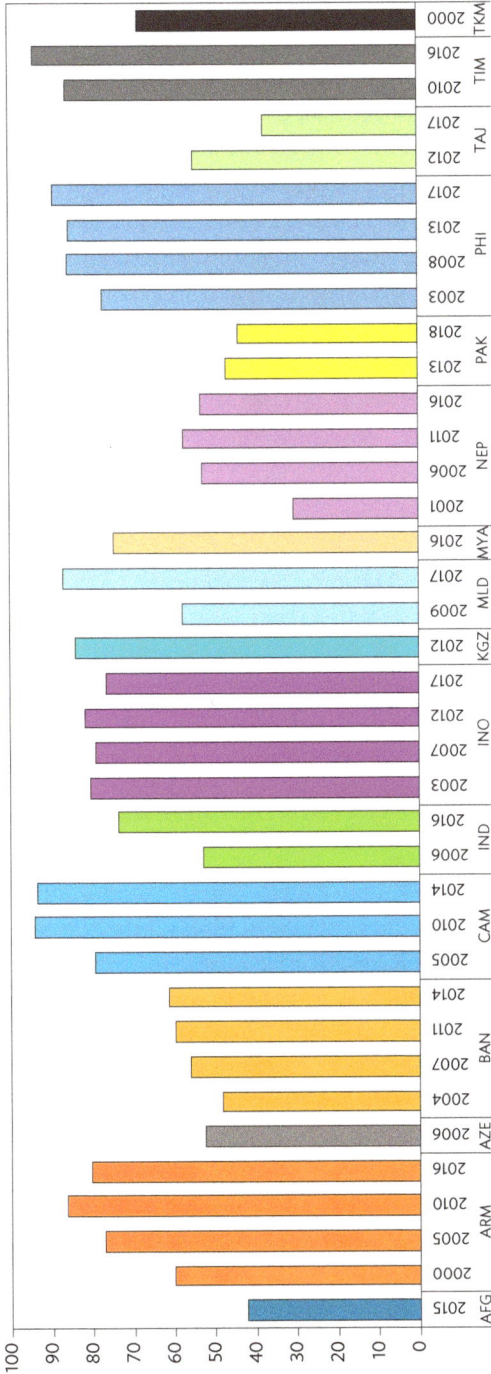

Figure 12.10: Decisions on Major Household Purchases, Selected Developing Asian Economies
(% of women who make decisions on major household purchases by themselves or jointly with their husband/partner)

AFG = Afghanistan, ARM = Armenia, AZE = Azerbaijan, BAN = Bangladesh, CAM = Cambodia, IND = India, INO = Indonesia, KGZ = Kyrgyz Republic, MLD = Maldives, MYA = Myanmar, NEP = Nepal, PAK = Pakistan, PHI = Philippines, TAJ = Tajikistan, TIM = Timor-Leste, TKM = Turkmenistan.

Source: United States Agency for International Development. Demographic and Health Surveys. https://statcompiler.com/en/ (accessed 3 January 2020).

Gains and remaining gaps in women's public and political status

The past half century has seen some leaps forward in women's public and political participation in the Asia and Pacific region (including Australia, Japan, and New Zealand). Two countries were among the first globally to grant female suffrage (New Zealand in 1893; Australia in 1902—earlier than either the United States or the United Kingdom). By 1970, just seven countries in the region had yet to grant women the right to vote or run for office. Today, all countries in the region have female suffrage. The region was also the first globally to have a female head of government, with the election of Prime Minister Sirimavo Bandaranaike in Sri Lanka in 1960. There has also been a positive trend in the share of women sitting as members of Parliament (MPs) (Figure 12.11). In 2000, 13.3% of MPs were women, increasing to 19.8%

Figure 12.11: Proportion of Seats Held by Women in National Parliaments
(%)

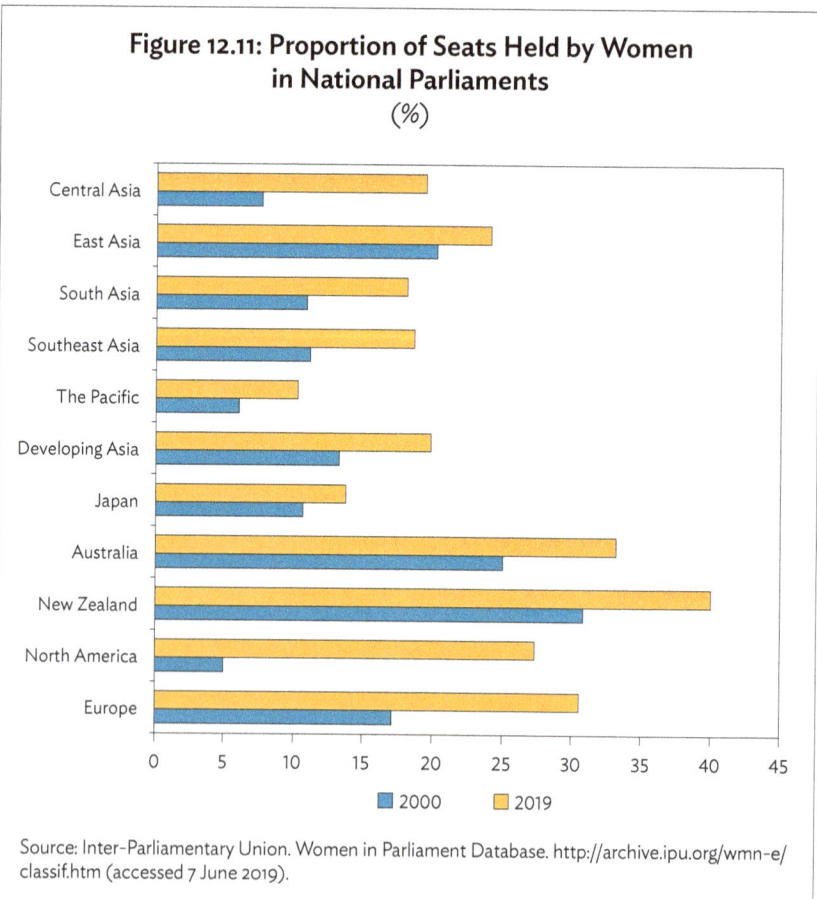

Source: Inter-Parliamentary Union. Women in Parliament Database. http://archive.ipu.org/wmn-e/classif.htm (accessed 7 June 2019).

Figure 12.12: Attitudes toward Women as Political Leaders, 2010–2014
(%)

On the whole, men make better political leaders than women do

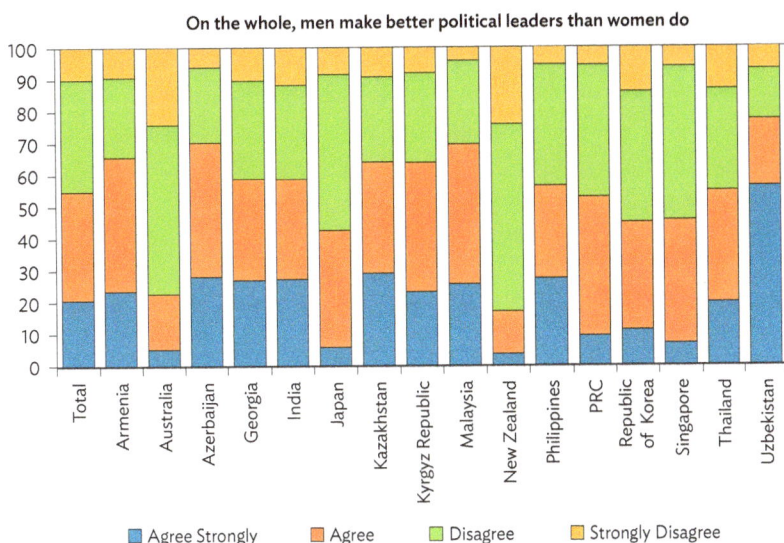

Agree Strongly ■ Agree ■ Disagree ■ Strongly Disagree

PRC = People's Republic of China.

Source: Institute for Comparative Survey Research. World Values Survey. http://www.worldvaluessurvey.org/WVSContents.jsp (accessed 23 August 2019).

in 2019. However, the regional average remains below the global average (24.3%), with the Pacific having the lowest share of women MPs worldwide.

Different factors can explain the region's rise in female political participation, albeit still lower than the world average. Quotas or temporary special measures have helped increase women's political participation.[34] In Mongolia, for example, the percentage of women MPs increased from 7% in 2005 to 15% in 2015 after the introduction of quotas.[35] On the other hand, widespread voter bias favoring male leaders persists, suggesting public attitudes must shift for women political leaders to continue making progress (Figure 12.12).

[34] ADB. 2012. *Guidance Note: Gender and Law – Temporary Special Measures to Promote Gender Equality*. Manila.

[35] International Institute for Democracy and Electoral Assistance. Gender Quotas Database. https://www.idea.int/data-tools/data/gender-quotas/quotas#different (accessed 21 June 2019).

Violence against women

Violence against women is a violation of their basic human rights, and an obstacle to socioeconomic and political empowerment. The cost of violence against women goes beyond individual survivors; it also has huge economic costs. Viet Nam recently estimated the cost at 1.4% of GDP. These estimates look at direct costs (such as medical services, justice-related services such as police and judiciary, and counseling) as well as indirect costs (for example, psychological trauma, workdays lost, and impact on the well-being of survivors).[36]

National legal reforms continue to prioritize the elimination of violence against women, spurred by the momentum of the UN General Assembly adoption of the Convention on the Elimination of All Forms of Discrimination against Women (CEDAW) in 1979, and in particular since the 1995 UN Fourth World Conference on Women was held in Beijing. Domestic or intimate partner violence legislation has been adopted among most countries in Asia and the Pacific. Countries that accede and ratify CEDAW are obliged to recognize intimate partner violence as a human rights violation and introduce domestic laws against it.[37] Other legislation, such as addressing sexual harassment, remains patchy across the region.

Social norms as a catalyst for gender equality

Social norms are the underlying factors explaining the mixed progress and "glass ceilings" that remain across the region—in the labor market, education, family, community, and public leadership.

Social norms may be "sticky" but far from static. Legal reforms, community awareness campaigns and social movements, and other factors have proven to lead to positive changes in social norms in favor of gender equality.[38] For example, in India, a 1993 law on reserved leadership positions for women in village councils significantly

---

[36] ADB and UN Women. 2018. Gender Equality and the Sustainable Development Goals in Asia and the Pacific. Bangkok. For an overview of existing methodologies on costing gender-based violence, see Duvvury, N., C. Grown, and J. Redner. 2004. Costs of Intimate Partner Violence at the Household and Community Levels: An Operational Framework for Developing Countries. Washington, DC: International Center for Research on Women.

[37] UN Women. 2013. Domestic Violence Legislation and Its Implementation. Bangkok.

[38] Heise, L., et al. 2019. Gender Inequality and Restrictive Gender Norms: Framing the Challenges to Health. The Lancet. 393 (10189). pp. 2440–2454.

enhanced aspirations and education for girls, and also altered perceptions of women in leadership.[39]

Community awareness-raising programs and media campaigns are also associated with the transmission and adoption of more positive gender norms. Cable and satellite television, which have spread rapidly throughout Asia and the Pacific, expose viewers to new values and other ways of life, affecting attitudes, behavior, and broader social norms.[40] In Mongolia, a multimedia campaign produced with the help of ADB raised awareness to challenge gender stereotypes and gender-based violence (Box 12.1).[41]

12.6 Looking ahead

Despite remarkable economic growth and poverty reduction across the region, gender equality is an unfinished agenda. Remaining gender gaps in the labor market, access to economic resources, and broader social and public life must continue to narrow. There are several ways this can be done.

First, while there has been dramatic progress in women's education and health, continued work is needed in areas such as STEM, technical and vocational education, and training in higher value-added sectors targeting women, along with improved access to reproductive health.

Second, providing basic infrastructure remains essential. Electricity, transport, safe drinking water, and sanitation all help mitigate women's time poverty, providing greater opportunities for education and paid jobs. Infrastructure can be designed and implemented to better meet the needs of women.

Third, countries should increase support to bolster women's labor market participation. Governments and the private sector can work together to promote affordable childcare services, family-friendly work practices, and legal and regulatory reforms to eliminate gender-based discrimination in recruitment and promotion.

---

[39] Beaman, L., et al. 2012. Female Leadership Raises Aspirations and Educational Attainment for Girls: A Policy Experiment in India. *Science*. 335 (6,068). pp. 582–586.

[40] Jensen, R., and E. Oster. 2009. The Power of TV: Cable Television and Women's Status in India. *Quarterly Journal of Economics*. 124 (3). pp. 1057–1094.

[41] Serafica, P., and T. Begszuren. *Communication Strategies to Enforce Gender Equality Legislation in Mongolia*. https://development.asia/case-study/communication-strategies -enforce-gender-equality-legislation-mongolia.

Box 12.1: ADB's Role in Gender and Development

The Asian Development Bank (ADB) has a long history of working toward gender equality. In 1985, it adopted a policy on the role of women in development. This has been strengthened over time. In 2018, ADB adopted Strategy 2030, where accelerating progress in gender equality is one of seven operational priorities. Under the strategy, by 2030, 75% of ADB's operations at entry will promote gender equality.

ADB continues to support women's economic empowerment through technical and vocational education and skills training programs, finance and training of women-led enterprises, and agriculture and agribusiness projects. In 2018–2019, ADB received grants from the Women Entrepreneurs Finance Initiative which are enabling commercial banks in Fiji, Sri Lanka, and Viet Nam to target their financial services to women-led enterprises in urban and rural areas.

ADB's support to social protection, health, and education remains crucial. In Pakistan, ADB financial support to the national Benazir Income Support Programme substantially increased the issuance of computerized national identity cards and cash cards for poor women, enabling them access to financial services for the first time.

ADB is helping build basic infrastructure—such as energy, transport, and water—which reduce women's heavy burdens of household maintenance and support their participation in work, education, and health. In its infrastructure projects, ADB promotes gender-responsive designs such as improving sanitary facilities in communities, having more lights on roads and stations, and having a separate space for women in public transportation. In some electrification and road connection projects, ADB is also providing facilities (such as marketplaces) and training programs (such as for technical and managerial skills) to improve income opportunities for women. In the energy sector in South Asia, ADB promotes professional networks to help women access nontraditional occupations such as frontline engineers.

ADB continues to provide technical assistance for removing gender-based discrimination within legal frameworks and justice systems. It has supported enacting gender equality laws in Maldives, Mongolia, and Viet Nam; training judges in Pakistan; and combating gender-based violence through shelters in Bangladesh and Nepal.

Source: ADB. 2019. *Strategy 2030 Operational Plan for Priority 2: Accelerating Progress in Gender Equality, 2019–2024.* Manila.

Fourth, to nurture female entrepreneurship and corporate leadership, more investment is needed to increase women's access to finance and other resources. Training in business management skills and corporate leadership is essential.

Fifth, legal and regulatory reforms that promote change in social norms to eliminate gender gaps in social, economic, and overall political rights must continue, as enshrined in SDG 5 targets (SDG 5.1). These will lead to women's greater decision-making power in the public and private spheres.

Sixth, it is becoming more important to address the new gender challenges arising from rapid aging in some countries in the region. As aging may enhance the unpaid care burden shouldered predominantly by women, governments must alleviate the burden by developing affordable, adequate, and sustainable pension, health insurance, and elderly care systems for both women and men.

Finally, more resources can be generated and partnerships fostered for gender equality among governments, the private sector, development agencies, and civil society organizations. Gender-responsive budgets, gender-focused domestic resource mobilization, and innovative products (such as gender bonds) are promising avenues to finance projects that promote gender equality. Multilateral organizations, including ADB, can play an important role.

CHAPTER 13

ENVIRONMENTAL SUSTAINABILITY AND CLIMATE CHANGE

13.1 Introduction

Asia's economic transformation over the past half century has been dramatic. This has also meant that rapid industrialization, more material and energy consumption, and a larger, more urban population have exerted escalating pressure on the environment. The focus of policies in the region for most of the earlier part of the past 50 years has been "growth first, cleanup later," in which environmental considerations had low salience and low policy priority. This led to the deterioration of forests, soil quality, freshwater ecosystems, ocean health, air quality, and biodiversity. The result has been millions of premature deaths[1] annually from pollution, declining natural capital to sustain future production, increased ecosystem fragility, and other environmental imbalances.

Climate change has emerged as a critical global issue. Although developing Asia, historically, was not a major source of greenhouse gas (GHG) emissions (carbon dioxide plus nitrous oxide, methane, and others) on a per capita basis, emissions have been growing much more

---

[1]   Health Effects Institute. 2018. *State of Global Air 2018. Special Report*. Boston.

rapidly than the global average as Asia's growth accelerated, and energy systems have been fossil fuel dependent and carbon intensive. In 2014, Asia produced 44% of global carbon dioxide (CO_2) equivalent emissions, well above its share of global gross domestic product (GDP) (21%) and close to its share of global population (54%). In the same year, the annual per capita CO_2 emissions based on primary energy consumption were 11.6 tons for the Republic of Korea (ROK), 9.5 tons for Japan, and 7.5 tons for the People's Republic of China (PRC), as compared with 16.5 tons for the United States and 9.6 tons for the Organisation for Economic Co-operation and Development (OECD) average (Chapter 8, Table 8.1). Asia's natural resources are facing additional risks due to climate change, as rising global temperatures and acidification have worsened resource degradation and water stress. Asia is especially susceptible to extreme weather events such as droughts, hurricanes, and floods, as well as rising sea levels, loss of glacial water reserves, and coastal erosion.

As the effects of environmental problems and climate change amplified, Asian policy makers have taken steps to respond. Key environmental policies have been adopted across the region, including framework legislation, safeguard policies, and air and water quality standards. Environmental and climate change policies have made greater use of market-based instruments. Asia deepened its engagement in international environmental agreements, including submissions of ambitious "nationally determined contributions" (NDCs) under the Paris Agreement on climate change. The region is also becoming a leading exporter of green products and services, which help environmental performance globally.

Despite important steps to addressing environmental and climate change challenges, many gaps remain. Countries in Asia and the Pacific need appropriate price signals and stronger governance and institutions to make environmental policies work. Greater investment needs to be mobilized in infrastructure including for wastewater and solid waste management, air quality, clean energy and public transport, and sustainable land and water management practices (Chapter 8).

This chapter presents an overview of Asia's environmental history, its current situation, and options for the future. Section 13.2 reviews key environmental subsectors, including terrestrial ecosystems, water resources, ocean health, solid waste, and air pollution. Section 13.3 looks at the issue of climate change. Section 13.4 discusses Asia's environmental policy responses, including framework legislation, standards, regulations, and market-based approaches. Section 13.5 describes Asia's engagement in international environmental and climate change agreements. Section 13.6 assesses the green industry's role in environmental solutions. Section 13.7 concludes and presents remaining challenges to enhance Asia's transition to sustainability.

13.2 Increased environmental pressure

Forests and land

Forests and terrestrial ecosystems (such as wetlands, grasslands, and riverine systems) have faced pressure during Asia's development. Forest transition theory posits that in the early stages of economic development and high levels of forest cover, deforestation is most rapid.[2] With widespread forests, timber is accessible and has low transport costs, so that profits from extraction can be substantial. At that stage, agriculture has a high share of economic activity, and its relative returns are high, so there is incentive to expand cultivation into new areas. This is compounded by traditional extensive and shifting slash-and-burn cultivation practices, as well as rising population and food demand.

According to this theory, as economic development progresses, incentives for deforestation should fall. With technological improvements, labor and capital serve as more effective substitutes for land in agriculture. At the same time, structural transformation draws people out of agricultural production and rural areas. When accessible timber becomes depleted, transportation costs for extraction and transport rise, reducing deforestation benefits. At the same time, high income elasticity for recreation in natural areas can increase demand for forest preservation and visitation. The combination of these dynamics means that forest cover is often expected to follow a U-shaped pattern relative to economic development, with a rapid initial decline followed by reducing rates of decline and eventual afforestation.

Asia has experienced this pattern in part, but with strong regional differences (Figure 13.1). The PRC and Viet Nam have made reforestation efforts for several decades, starting at low levels of GDP. National logging bans, coupled with intensive state-driven reforestation policies from the 1980s onward, have helped increase forest cover and preserve natural forest in the countries. Yet this

---

2   Rudel, T. K., et al. 2005. Forest Transitions: Towards a Global Understanding of Land Use Change. *Global Environmental Change*. 15 (1). pp. 23–31.

has also led to increased demand for timber from neighboring countries with looser harvesting controls.[3] In South Asia, forest cover has largely stabilized, with little change over recent decades. However, Southeast Asia has had continuing deforestation, as loss of natural forest cover was substantial at 41.6 million hectares from 1990 to 2015. Issuance of forest concessions on public land has been an important driver of this loss, much of which has been in areas of high biodiversity and carbon storage.[4] These concessions have transferred valuable timber to concessionaires who often have reimbursed the state less than the market value of wood that is harvested, so that forest clearance is implicitly subsidized.

Forestlands allocated for concessions are often inhabited by indigenous populations without recognized tenure, so that the

Figure 13.1: Natural Forest Cover, Developing Asia, 1990–2015

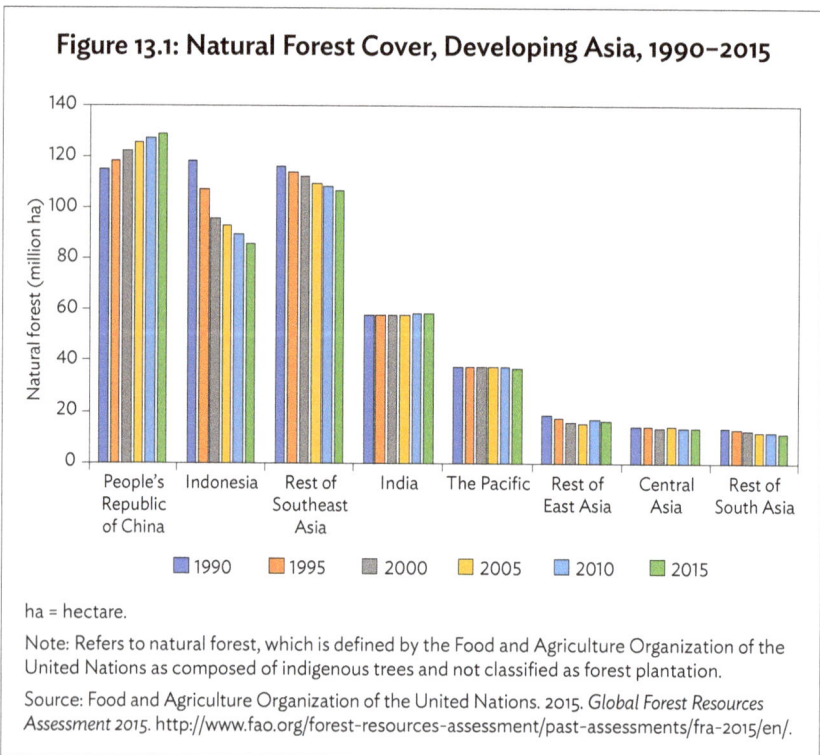

ha = hectare.

Note: Refers to natural forest, which is defined by the Food and Agriculture Organization of the United Nations as composed of indigenous trees and not classified as forest plantation.

Source: Food and Agriculture Organization of the United Nations. 2015. *Global Forest Resources Assessment 2015*. http://www.fao.org/forest-resources-assessment/past-assessments/fra-2015/en/.

[3] Lang, G., and C. H. W. Chan. 2006. China's Impact on Forests in Southeast Asia. *Journal of Contemporary Asia*. 36 (2). pp. 167–194.
[4] Imai, N., et al. 2018. Factors Affecting Forest Area Change in Southeast Asia during 1980–2010. *PLoS ONE*. 13 (5): e0197391.

allocation often leads to conflicting claims of ownership and loss of customary lands.[5] Many populations who customarily used concession areas practiced slash-and-burn cultivation, which entails cycles of forest burning followed by cropping and fallow periods for natural forest regeneration that are sustainable if carried out at low frequency. However, for those pushed aside by concessions, regeneration cycles become compressed on their remaining areas, making slash-and-burn cultivation unsustainable.[6]

With ownership contested, concessionaires also faced uncertainty about the ability to capture future returns from forests, and this uncertainty incentivizes rapid timber extraction.[7] Improved infrastructure also lowered transport costs to forest areas over time, further raising the value of standing timber and incentives for logging. As a result, although planted and secondary forest cover has expanded in Asia overall, reforestation has not restored the ecological functions of natural forests in terms of biodiversity and carbon storage.[8]

Where deforestation is widespread, biodiversity has been lost rapidly. However, even where overall natural forest cover remained stable, biodiversity is still threatened due to climate change, pollution, and destruction of other important ecosystems. Projected levels of mean species abundance are falling across the region (Figure 13.2).

Beyond forests, land has been increasingly degraded, via loss of productive potential through removal of nutrients, topsoil erosion, or contamination, with Asia accounting for more degraded land than any other world region.[9] The region also has a higher share of rural population residing on degrading agricultural land than the rest of the world, with particularly high shares in East Asia, Southeast Asia, and Central Asia (Table 13.1).

[5] Yasmi, Y., J. Guernier, and C. J. Colfer. 2009. Positive and Negative Aspects of Forestry Conflict: Lessons from a Decentralized Forest Management in Indonesia. *International Forestry Review.* 11 (1). pp. 98–110.

[6] Mertz, O., et al. 2009. Swidden Change in Southeast Asia: Understanding Causes and Consequences. *Human Ecology.* 37 (3). pp. 259–264.

[7] Abood, S. A., et al. 2015. Relative Contributions of the Logging, Fiber, Oil Palm, and Mining Industries to Forest Loss in Indonesia. *Conservation Letters.* 8. pp. 58–67.

[8] Howes, S., and P. Wyrwoll. 2012. Asia's Wicked Environmental Problems. *ADBI Working Paper Series.* No. 348. Tokyo: Asian Development Bank Institute.

[9] Prince, S., et al. 2018. Chapter 4: Status and Trends of Land Degradation and Restoration and Associated Changes in Biodiversity and Ecosystem Functions. In Montanarella, L., R. Scholes, and A. Brainich, eds. *The IPBES Assessment Report on Land Degradation and Restoration.* Bonn: Secretariat of the Intergovernmental Science-Policy Platform on Biodiversity and Ecosystem Services.

Figure 13.2: Projected Mean Species Abundance, Developing Asia, 2000–2050

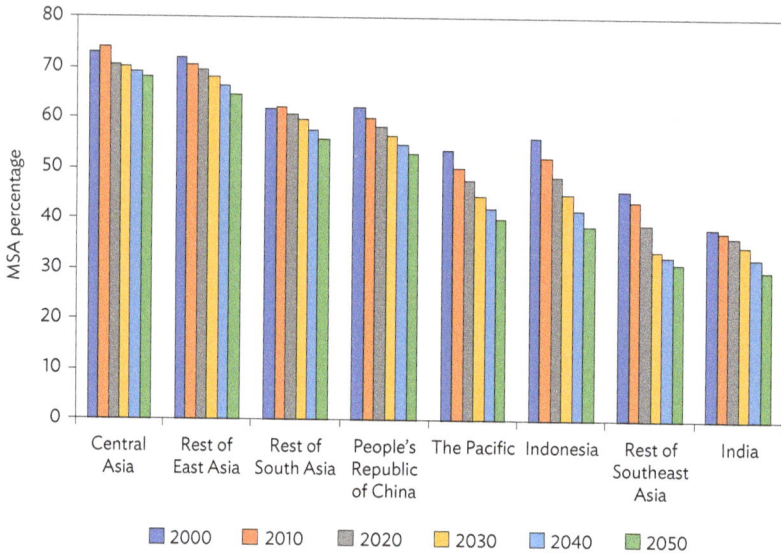

MSA = mean species abundance.

Notes: MSA is defined as the mean abundance of the original species relative to their abundance in undisturbed ecosystems. An area with an MSA of 100% means a biodiversity that is similar to a natural situation. An MSA of 0% means a completely destroyed ecosystem, with no original species remaining. Subregional averages are simple averages.

Source: PBL Netherlands Environmental Assessment Agency. *IMAGE 2.4–2.5 using GLOBIO for RIO+12 Global Integrated Assessments, Baseline Scenario.* The Hague.

Land degradation includes human-induced processes that reduce the productivity of land or level of environmental services. Erosion is the most widespread process, and water is the main mechanism of erosion, followed by wind. Agriculture is a major driver of erosion, as most crop production in the region remains under intensive tillage with limited use of cover crops or other soil conservation techniques, and large areas of public pasture remain with limited governance of livestock density.[10] Many riparian areas have been highly degraded and eroded due to urban encroachment and unregulated cropping. Wetland area declined in Asia by 30% from 1970

---

[10] Blaikie, P. 2016. *The Political Economy of Soil Erosion in Developing Countries.* London: Routledge.

to 2015.[11] This accumulated impact from degradation has made much of developing Asia more vulnerable to water stress and flooding, with reduced agricultural productivity potential.

Table 13.1: Rural Population Residing on Degrading Agricultural Land by Region, 2010
(million)

Regional Classification	Total Population	Rural Population	Rural Population on Degrading Agricultural Land	Percentage Share of Rural Population on Degrading Agricultural Land (%)
Developing Asia	3,669.0	2,824.3	1,121.6	39.7
Central Asia	79.4	50.2	23.0	45.8
East Asia	1,395.7	1,068.3	595.2	55.7
South Asia	1,597.3	1,284.0	336.1	26.2
Southeast Asia	588.9	414.8	166.9	40.2
The Pacific	7.7	7.0	0.4	5.9
Developed Asia	153.3	33.9	4.5	13.1
Latin America and the Caribbean	592.2	335.7	48.2	14.4
Africa	994.1	812.0	184.0	22.7
North America	346.1	71.5	11.4	15.9
Europe	778.1	375.0	90.7	24.2

Note: Africa includes both Sub-Saharan Africa and North Africa.

Source: Based on Appendix data from Barbier, E. B., and J. P. Hochard. 2014. Land Degradation, Less Favored Lands and the Rural Poor: A Spatial and Economic Analysis. *A Report for the Economics of Land Degradation Initiative.* Laramie: Department of Economics and Finance, University of Wyoming.

Chemical contamination of land has increased dramatically.[12] This occurred through several processes. Uncontrolled dumping of hazardous waste occurred due to both poor regulatory enforcement

---

[11] Ramsar Convention Secretariat and United Nations Environment Programme World Conservation Monitoring Centre. 2017. *Wetland Extent Trends (WET) Index – 2017 Update. Technical Update 2017.* Gland, Switzerland: Ramsar Convention Secretariat.

[12] Lu, Y., et al. 2015. Impacts of Soil and Water Pollution on Food Safety and Health Risks in China. *Environment International.* 77. pp. 5–15.

and by accidents, and watercourses and wind have carried this waste over large areas of land. As agriculture became more input intensive, pesticide and fertilizer application rates rose to levels far above the world average in many Asian countries, which spread chemical contamination problems to large areas.

Quantities of untreated sewage in Asia's waterways have grown rapidly, along with use of sewage wastewater for irrigation, which has introduced heavy metal contamination problems.[13] Irrigation using groundwater in arid conditions also led to substantial soil salinization in South Asia and Central Asia.

Water resources

In Asia, water supply has improved over time to better meet agricultural, household, and industrial demand. Irrigated area has expanded greatly, contributing to agricultural development, and water supply infrastructure has expanded. Improved water access has meant that water withdrawal also rapidly increased, with growing competition for consumption among agricultural, energy, industrial, and household users. Rising withdrawals have led a number of countries, especially in Central Asia, to use more water resources than are renewed each year.

A majority of water supply, especially for irrigation, is under direct and indirect subsidies, which further encourages overuse. Water-intensive activities, such as rice cultivation, have also been subsidized, intensifying demand.[14] In arid and semiarid areas of South Asia, wells are a primary source of fresh water, and they often operate under electricity subsidies. Overextraction of groundwater has led to arsenic contamination of groundwater resources, and excess use of irrigation has led to soil salinization. It has also caused falling groundwater tables, increasing economic costs for water access, and greater scarcity.

Pollution pressure on surface fresh water has been rising. Overuse of chemical fertilizers, encouraged by subsidies, has led to nutrient runoff, driving freshwater eutrophication.[15] Industries developed with little effluent control also deteriorated water quality.

---

[13] Mohapatra, D. P., et al. 2016. Application of Wastewater and Biosolids in Soil: Occurrence and Fate of Emerging Contaminants. *Water, Air, & Soil Pollution.* 227 (3). pp. 1–14.

[14] World Bank. 2006. Do Current Water Subsidies Reach the Poor? *Series on Water Tariffs and Subsidies in South Asia.* No. 4. Washington, DC.

[15] Good, A. G., and P. H. Beatty. 2011. Fertilizing Nature: A Tragedy of Excess in the Commons. *PLoS Biology.* 9 (8): e1001124.

Even with growing household water supply and wastewater collection, only one-third of wastewater is treated (Table 13.2).[16] This means that severe pathogen pollution is estimated to affect about one-third to one-half of Asian river stretches.[17]

Table 13.2: Proportion of Wastewater Receiving Treatment, Selected Economies, Developing Asia, 2011

0%–5%	6%–19%	20%–60%	61%–90%	91%–100%
Afghanistan	Fiji	Azerbaijan	Malaysia	Hong Kong, China
Armenia	Mongolia	India		
Cambodia	Philippines	People's		Palau
Bangladesh	Viet Nam	Republic		Republic
Bhutan		of China		of Korea
Indonesia		Taipei,China		Singapore
Lao PDR		Thailand		
Myanmar		Turkmenistan		
Nepal				
Pakistan				
Papua New Guinea				
Solomon Islands				
Sri Lanka				
Tajikistan				
Timor-Leste				
Uzbekistan				

Lao PDR = Lao People's Democratic Republic.

Notes: Only economies with available data are included. Reporting year is latest year with available data from 2006 to 2015. Most data are from 2011.

Sources: For India (2011), Malaysia (2009), the Republic of Korea (2011), and Viet Nam (2012): Food and Agriculture Organization of the United Nations. AQUASTAT Database. http://www.fao.org/nr/water/aquastat/data/query/ index.html?lang=en (accessed 6 June 2018). For Taipei,China (2019): Environmental Protection Administration. *Water*. All other data derived from Socioeconomic Data and Applications Center. Environmental Performance Index. http://sedac.ciesin.columbia.edu/data/set/epi-environmental-performance-index-2016/data-download.

---

[16]   Evans, A., et al. 2012. Water Quality: Assessment of the Current Situation in Asia. *Water Resources Development*. 28 (2). pp. 195–216.

[17]   The study defines severe pathogen pollution as fecal coliform concentrations of over 1,000 units per 100 milliliters. United Nations Environment Programme. 2011. *Towards a Green Economy: Pathways to Sustainable Development and Poverty Eradication*. Nairobi.

Ocean health

With rising incomes, Asia's demand for fish and seafood rose rapidly, even as marine resources have deteriorated. Although fish farming also expanded quickly, most fish supply originates from capture fisheries, which face falling maximum sustainable yields. Annual fish catches have grown nine times over the past 50 years, and have utilized increasingly effective techniques (Figure 13.3). This is further compounded by increasingly globalized fishing fleets that operate in areas far from their countries of registration, so that there is more competition to harvest fish from open-access common marine resources.

Figure 13.3: Capture Fisheries Production, Developing Asia, 1960–2017

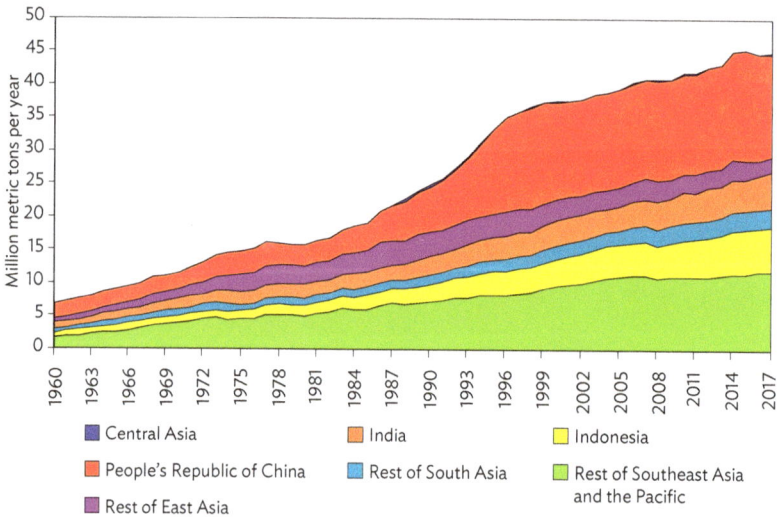

Notes: Data availability varies across countries over time. Fish catches are reported by country of the vessel performing the catch.

Source: Food and Agriculture Organization of the United Nations. 2019. Global Capture Production 1950–2017. http://www.fao.org/fishery/statistics/global-capture-production/query/en (accessed 31 October 2019).

By 2013, 90% of marine areas globally were considered overfished, and global fish catches peaked in the 1990s, even as fishing effort intensified.[18] The decline in fish production has been particularly pronounced in East Asia, with the decline driving fleets from the subregion into other Asian and Pacific waters to capture fish.[19] Underreporting of fish catches in the region hampers governance of fisheries. Enforcement of regulations has proven difficult, particularly in areas beyond national jurisdictions.

Capture fisheries have relied partially on the use of indiscriminate nets (often prohibited) and illegal explosives in blast fishing, which have destroyed ocean habitat and coral resources. Coastal developments and pollution have further aggravated the loss of key habitats and biodiversity areas.

Ocean health continues to suffer from uncollected and inappropriately disposed waste, leading to accumulated plastic and other waste materials that threaten marine ecosystems. By one estimate, nearly 25% of plastic waste in the oceans is deposited by 10 river systems, of which seven are in developing Asia.[20] Another set of estimates (Figure 13.4) show that 55%–60% of the 8 million tons of plastic entering oceans annually comes from five developing Asian countries.[21] These plastics degrade into microplastics that threaten a range of organisms when ingested and passed through the food chain. This is of particular risk to plankton, as microplastics displace normally ingested food sources and reduce reproductive ability, and loss of plankton has effects that cascade across marine food chains.[22]

Solid waste

As rapid growth and urbanization led to increasing material production and consumption, the ability to deal with the collection, disposal, and treatment of waste by-products has not kept pace. The result is a mounting solid waste problem, especially in urban areas. Waste

[18] Food and Agriculture Organization of the United Nations. 2016. *The State of World Fisheries and Aquaculture: Contributing to Food Security and Nutrition for All*. Rome.
[19] Pauly, D., and D. Zeller. 2016. Catch Reconstructions Reveal that Global Marine Fisheries Catches Are Higher than Reported and Declining. *Nature Communications*. 7. 10244.
[20] Schmidt, C., T. Krauth, and S. Wagner. 2017. Export of Plastic Debris by Rivers into the Sea. *Environmental Science & Technology*. 51 (21). pp. 12246–12253.
[21] Ocean Conservancy. 2017. *Stemming the Tide: Land-Based Strategies for a Plastic-Free Ocean*. Washington, DC.
[22] Lin, V. S. 2016. Research Highlights: Impacts of Microplastics on Plankton. *Environmental Science: Processes & Impacts*. 18 (2). pp. 160–163.

Figure 13.4: Plastic Waste Disposal in Oceans, 2010
(million tons)

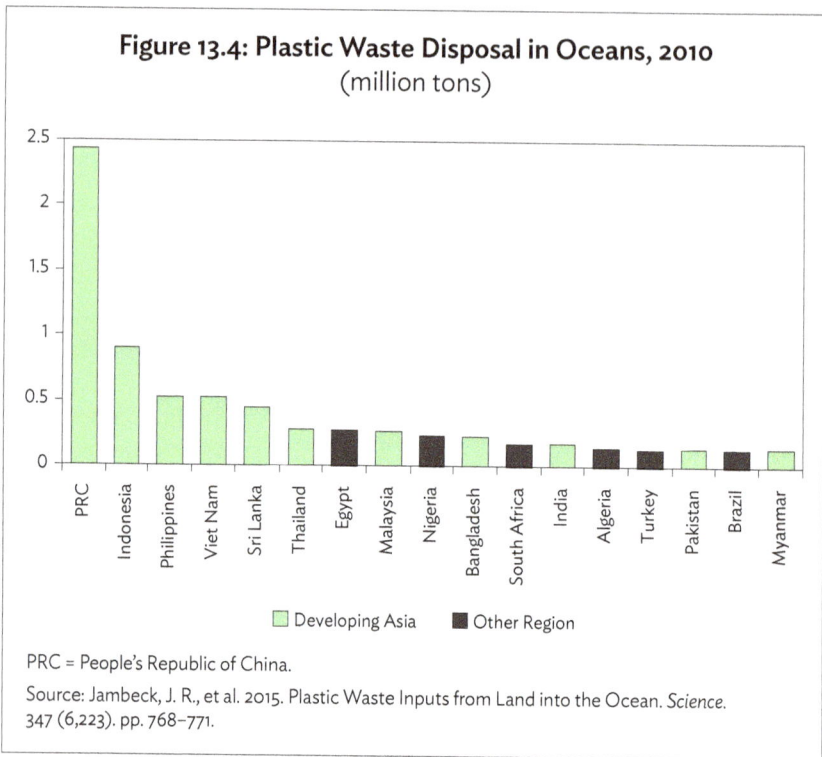

PRC = People's Republic of China.

Source: Jambeck, J. R., et al. 2015. Plastic Waste Inputs from Land into the Ocean. *Science*. 347 (6,223). pp. 768–771.

pressure has grown rapidly, as material consumption escalated in the region from 15 billion tons of material in 1992 to 52 billion tons in 2017.[23] As of 2010, only around half of waste was collected in the region with a small share disposed of appropriately (Figure 13.5).

Generation of hazardous waste, such as those in disposed electronics, has grown even faster than overall waste levels.[24] Recycling rates of collected municipal solid waste have also remained low. These statistics show how far the region remains from a "circular economy." The social costs of waste are rarely recovered from user charges, so that excess waste generation is implicitly subsidized.

---

[23] International Resource Panel. Global Material Flows Database. 2018. http://www .resourcepanel.org/global-material-flows-database (accessed 24 October 2019).

[24] Chakraborty, P., et al. 2016. E-Waste and Associated Environmental Contamination in the Asia/Pacific Region (Part 1): An Overview. In Loganathan, B. G., et al., eds. *Persistent Organic Chemicals in the Environment: Status and Trends in the Pacific Basin Countries I Contamination Status*. Washington, DC: American Chemical Society and Oxford University Press.

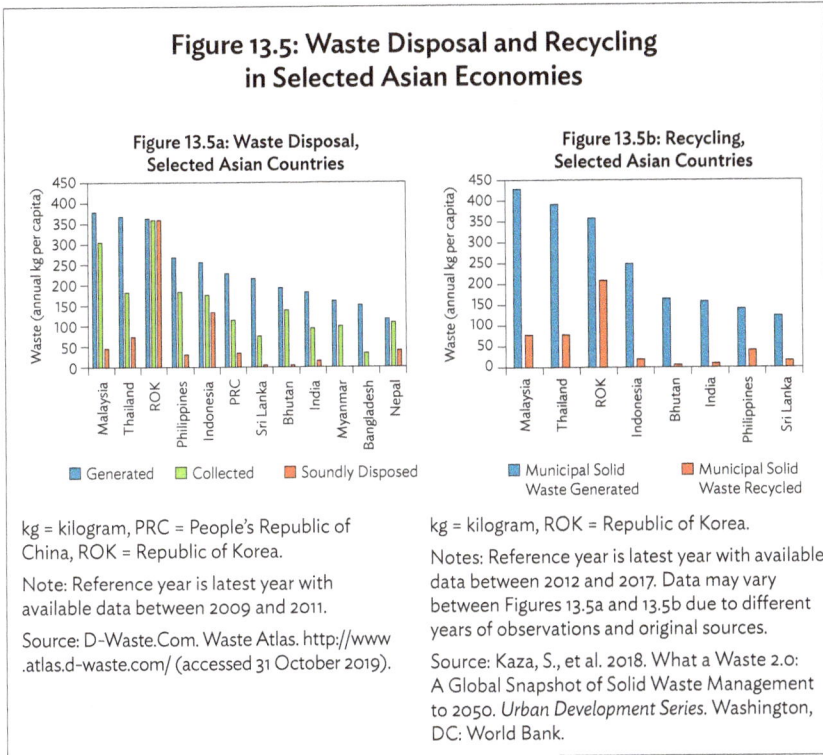

Figure 13.5: Waste Disposal and Recycling in Selected Asian Economies

Figure 13.5a: Waste Disposal, Selected Asian Countries

Figure 13.5b: Recycling, Selected Asian Countries

kg = kilogram, PRC = People's Republic of China, ROK = Republic of Korea.

Note: Reference year is latest year with available data between 2009 and 2011.

Source: D-Waste.Com. Waste Atlas. http://www.atlas.d-waste.com/ (accessed 31 October 2019).

kg = kilogram, ROK = Republic of Korea.

Notes: Reference year is latest year with available data between 2012 and 2017. Data may vary between Figures 13.5a and 13.5b due to different years of observations and original sources.

Source: Kaza, S., et al. 2018. What a Waste 2.0: A Global Snapshot of Solid Waste Management to 2050. *Urban Development Series*. Washington, DC: World Bank.

Air pollution

Much of Asia's economic growth has been fueled by increasing reliance on coal, oil, and gas-based energy for an expanding array of uses. Until recently, most fossil fuel consumption was combusted with limited pollution control, with large amounts of sulfur dioxide (SO_2), nitrogen oxides (NOx), volatile organic compounds, ozone, carbon monoxide, and particulate matter released. These emissions were most intense in urban areas, where high population densities live in close proximity to pollution.

In developing Asia, fine particulate matter (PM2.5) emissions increased by 121% from 1970 to 2010 (Figure 13.6), while NOx rose 168% and SO_2 grew by 238%. Overall, in low- and middle-income countries, 97% of cities with more than 100,000 inhabitants do not meet the air quality guidelines of the World Health Organization.[25] Asian cities in

---

[25] World Health Organization. 2018. WHO Global Ambient Air Quality Database. https://www.who.int/airpollution/data/cities/en/ (accessed 23 May 2019).

Bangladesh, India, Pakistan, and the PRC are among the world's most polluted.[26]

Trends are slightly better for coarser particulate matter (PM10), as improved roads reduced dust, and indoor air pollution dropped due to greater ventilation and greater use of cooking gas. However, the overall health impact of air pollution has risen, with 4.2 million premature deaths estimated in 2016 in developing Asia.[27] In addition, SO_2 and NOx have driven escalating levels of acid rain, which damaged forests and aquatic ecosystems in the region.[28]

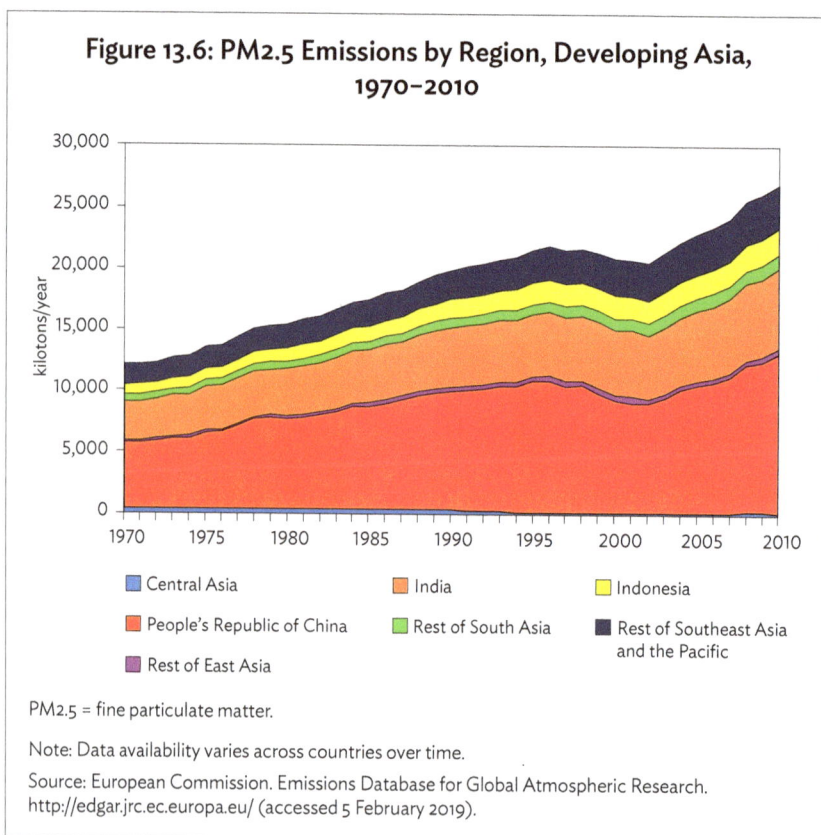

Figure 13.6: PM2.5 Emissions by Region, Developing Asia, 1970–2010

PM2.5 = fine particulate matter.

Note: Data availability varies across countries over time.

Source: European Commission. Emissions Database for Global Atmospheric Research. http://edgar.jrc.ec.europa.eu/ (accessed 5 February 2019).

---

[26] Based on annual average PM2.5 levels. AirVisual 2018. World Most Polluted Cities 2018. https://www.airvisual.com/world-most-polluted-cities (accessed 27 May 2019).

[27] Health Effects Institute. 2018. *State of Global Air 2018. Special Report*. Boston.

[28] Duan, L., et al. 2016. Acid Deposition in Asia: Emissions, Deposition, and Ecosystem Effects. *Atmospheric Environment*. 100 (146). pp. 55–69.

13.3 Climate change

A more fossil fuel-intensive energy mix has meant that GHG emissions have risen rapidly with economic growth (Chapter 8). This was driven by expanded electrification, coal's dominance in power generation mixes, and expanded use of gasoline-powered transport. These trends have been underpinned by subsidies given for fossil fuels during much of the past 50 years, although progress has been made in subsidy reduction during the past decade. More recently, many countries have developed ambitious plans for renewable energy development, but as in many developed countries, power development patterns often remain more fossil fuel-based in practice. In Southeast Asia, deforestation also became a major source of emissions, as a substantial share of forest clearance occurred on peatlands that contain thousands of tons of carbon per hectare, which are emitted as the forest is lost.

As a result, GHG emissions rose faster in developing Asia than in any other region globally between 1990 and 2014 (Figure 13.7), with its share in global emissions increasing from 23% to 44% during the same period (Figure 13.8). Developing Asia is projected to increase this to half of global emissions by 2030.[29] Historically, per capita emissions in developing Asia were well below the rest of the world, although by 2014, they were approaching the global average.[30]

Developing Asia is one of the world's most vulnerable regions to the impact of climate change, so these trends place the region's future at peril.[31] Asia's substantial population dependent on agriculture and natural resources will be affected by more droughts, floods, salinity intrusion, and pest and disease epidemics for crop production under climate change. Reduced water availability for irrigation and increased water demand under higher temperatures will increasingly constrain production. Hundreds of millions of people in the region work in manual labor that is already limited by temperatures during hot seasons. As peak temperatures rise even further, productivity will be lost in sectors where cooling is not possible, and elsewhere additional cooling will be at the expense of substantial energy consumption.

---

[29] Reis, L. A., et. al. 2016. The Economics of Greenhouse Gas Mitigation in Developing Asia. *ADB Economics Working Paper Series.* No. 504. Manila: Asian Development Bank.

[30] World Resources Institute. CAIT Climate Data Explorer. http://cait.wri.org (accessed 26 October 2019).

[31] Asian Development Bank (ADB). 2017. *A Region at Risk: The Human Dimensions of Climate Change in Asia and the Pacific.* Manila.

Figure 13.7: Greenhouse Gas (Carbon Dioxide Equivalent) **Average Annual Emissions Growth in World Regions, 1990–2014** (%)

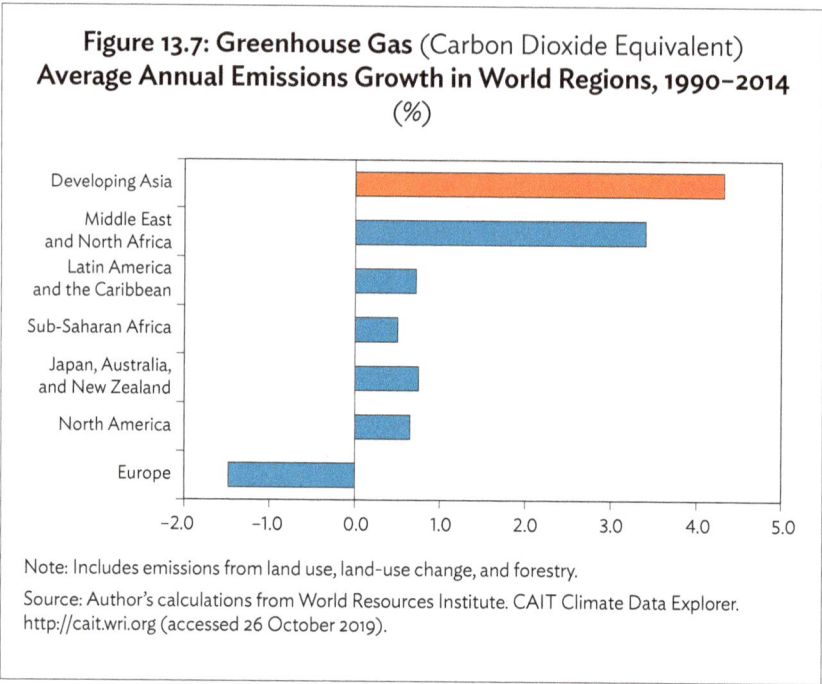

Note: Includes emissions from land use, land-use change, and forestry.

Source: Author's calculations from World Resources Institute. CAIT Climate Data Explorer. http://cait.wri.org (accessed 26 October 2019).

Human health will also be impacted by increased cardiovascular mortality from heat stress and the induced spread of mosquito-borne diseases such as malaria and dengue.

Asia has very densely populated lowland delta areas that are at high risk from sea-level rise, as are low-lying atolls in the Pacific. Increased storm surges during high magnitude cyclones, which are expected to increase in frequency under climate change, will compound these effects and salinize fresh water, including groundwater. More frequent floods and landslides from intensified rainfall and storms will expose other populations to increased disaster risk as well.

Rising global temperatures have exacerbated natural resource degradation. Approximately 95% of coral reef area in Southeast Asia is considered highly threatened by rising ocean temperatures and acidification.[32] Tropical Asian forests will be severely affected by increasing frequency of fires and by water stress.[33] Under climate

---

[32] Burke, L., et al. 2011. *Reefs at Risk Revisited*. Washington, DC: World Resources Institute.

[33] Huntingford, C., et al. 2013. Simulated Resilience of Tropical Rainforests to CO_2-Induced Climate Change. *Nature Geoscience*. 6 (4). pp. 268–273.

Figure 13.8: Global Shares of Greenhouse Gas (Carbon Dioxide Equivalent) **Annual Emissions, 1990 and 2014**

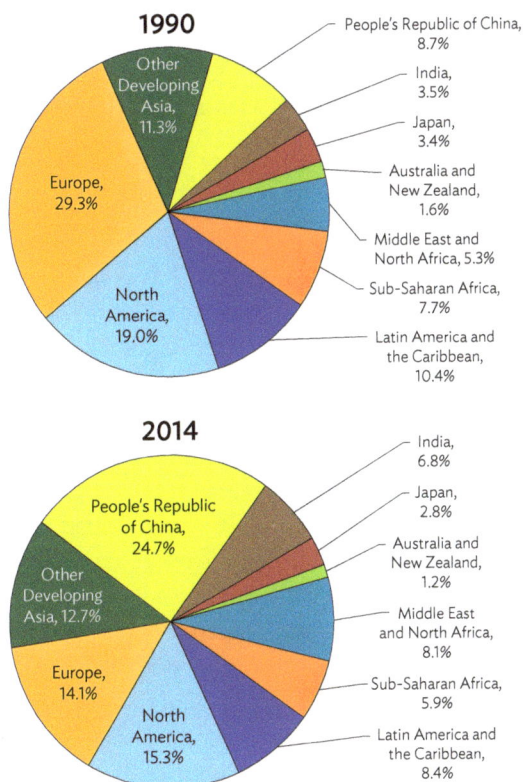

1990

- People's Republic of China, 8.7%
- India, 3.5%
- Japan, 3.4%
- Australia and New Zealand, 1.6%
- Middle East and North Africa, 5.3%
- Sub-Saharan Africa, 7.7%
- Latin America and the Caribbean, 10.4%
- North America, 19.0%
- Europe, 29.3%
- Other Developing Asia, 11.3%

2014

- India, 6.8%
- Japan, 2.8%
- Australia and New Zealand, 1.2%
- Middle East and North Africa, 8.1%
- Sub-Saharan Africa, 5.9%
- Latin America and the Caribbean, 8.4%
- North America, 15.3%
- Europe, 14.1%
- Other Developing Asia, 12.7%
- People's Republic of China, 24.7%

Note: Includes emissions from land use, land-use change, and forestry.

Source: Authors' calculations from World Resources Institute. CAIT Climate Data Explorer. http://cait.wri.org (accessed 26 October 2019).

change projections, water scarcity will likely rise from affecting 1.2 billion people in Asia in 2010 to 1.9 billion by 2050,[34] as rainfall declines over large portions of already semiarid South Asia. Rainfall will become more concentrated and variable in other regions.

Asian Development Bank (ADB) estimates of potential climate change impacts in developing Asia range from annual losses of 5% of

---

[34] Satoh, Y., et al. 2017. Multi-Model and Multi-Scenario Assessments of Asian Water Futures: The Water Futures and Solutions (WFaS) Initiative. *Earth's Future*. 5 (7). pp. 823–852.

GDP by 2100 in East Asia to 9% in South Asia and 11% in Southeast Asia.[35] A recent ADB econometric analysis, based on historical relationships between temperature fluctuations and growth, suggests potential losses of 10% of GDP annually for developing Asia, as a whole, by 2100 in the absence of policies to mitigate climate change.[36]

13.4 Asian efforts to address environmental and climate challenges

Drivers of policy development

Although Asia's environment has many negative trends, problems could have been even worse without the concerted actions of countries in the region. Important improvements have come from improved environmental governance that addresses market and institutional failures, such as externalities, inadequate regulatory and enforcement capacities, and other policy constraints.

The positioning of a country with regard to environmental policies can logically be related to the costs and benefits that the country experiences from environmental protection actions. When environmental problems are not perceived as having large detrimental effects and abatement costs are considered high, environmental action appears unwarranted, and this may induce environmental policies that are neither ambitious nor binding. Conversely, the larger the perceived effects, and the lower the abatement costs, the more environmental action will be justified with environmental policies expected to have greater effect.

Over time, these two elements have shifted in Asia. The effects of environmental problems have grown dramatically, with more populations exposed to air and water pollution, and are increasingly recognized by the public. Increased demand for environmental amenities as superior goods (meaning income increases led to greater demand) amplifies how environmental effects are perceived and valued. At the same time, technological improvement has reduced the cost of many environmental protection measures, especially those implemented by adopting technologies already available in developed markets. Thus, the shift in perceived costs and benefits of

---

[35] ADB. 2016. *Asian Development Outlook 2016 Update: Meeting the Low-Carbon Growth Challenge.* Manila.

[36] Lee, M., M. L. Villaruel, and R. Gaspar. 2016. Effects of Temperature Shocks on Economic Growth and Welfare in Asia. *ADB Economics Working Paper Series.* No. 501. Manila: Asian Development Bank.

environmental policies induced a transition toward more meaningful environmental protection in the region.

This dynamic was initially most visible in the most advanced economies of Asia. Japan in the 1960s experienced a number of high-profile mercury and cadmium poisoning incidents that drew serious attention to industrial pollution problems.[37] Affected people, including many mothers, advocated for action. Within a decade or so, important court decisions were issued, major environmental legislation was passed, and polluting industries were liable to compensate those affected. In the 1970s, action moved on to air pollution and wastewater effluents, and progressively tackled more complex challenges. The ROK and Taipei,China also began to forcefully implement similar environmental measures in the 1980s.

In parallel to these domestic developments, a series of international events drew increasing attention to environmental problems and helped spur responses. In 1972, the Club of Rome released *Limits to Growth,* which showed the consequences of natural resource depletion, and in the same year, the United Nations (UN) Conference on the Human Environment resulted in the first international declaration on the environment. The Brundtland Commission released *Our Common Future* in 1987, which provided the first internationally recognized definition of "sustainable development" and agreement on a multilateral approach to environmental policy.

At the UN Conference on Environment and Development in Rio de Janeiro in 1992, the Convention on Biological Diversity, UN Framework Convention on Climate Change, and UN Convention to Combat Desertification were signed, and Agenda 21 was agreed. This laid the foundation for intensified actions and agreements at the Earth Summits in 2002 and 2012, the 1997 Kyoto Protocol and 2015 Paris Agreement on climate change, and the Millennium Development Goals (2000) and Sustainable Development Goals (2015).

Throughout these international processes, representatives from Asia and the Pacific played active roles. For example, since 2015, the Philippines, Fiji, and the Marshall Islands have successively chaired the Climate Vulnerable Forum that advocates ambitious climate action under the Paris Agreement.

---

[37] Tani, M. 2015. Japan's Environmental Policy. *Policy Update.* No. 059. Tokyo: Research Institute of Economy, Trade and Industry.

Progress in implementing key policies and measures

International developments and the recognition of both the benefits of environmental action and costs of inaction helped spur improvements in developing Asia. Starting in the 1970s, developing Asian countries established laws, regulations, risk-appraisal procedures, and administrative agencies focused on environmental protection. Most of the early approaches focused on defining aspirational goals and creating command-and-control regulations in what may be termed a "do no harm" approach.[38] However, uncoordinated regulations, weak incentives, and limited enforcement capacity reduced the effectiveness of environmental policies.

To address this, environmental laws and policies were revised, reformed, and strengthened from the early 1990s onward, although the process still remains partial and ongoing. By early 1990s, nearly all developing Asian economies had framework environmental legislation (Table 13.3). In parallel to the establishment of this legislation, line ministries on the environment also emerged and enforcement capacity was strengthened. Approaches became more proactive and included increasing numbers of incentives for environmentally friendly actions, in addition to restrictions on activities with greater environmental risks.

Environmental quality standards have been established by almost all developing Asian economies. For air quality, standards are almost universal for SO_2 and NOx, and most economies have standards for ozone and fine particulate matter (PM2.5). Most standards were introduced in the 1990s. Water quality standards were adopted after air quality standards in much of the region. However, almost all of the standards are less strict than those recommended by the World Health Organization.

The diffusion of environmental safeguard policies for infrastructure investments has followed a similar path. While only 11 economies in developing Asia had environmental impact assessment requirements before 1990, most had established these requirements a decade later.

The threat of climate change has also been recognized by all economies in the region, as they quickly established national climate change policies. Within developing Asia, the ROK was the only country in 1999 that had established overarching cross-sectoral climate policies,

---

[38] Harashima, Y. 2000. Environmental Governance in Selected Asian Developing Countries. *International Review for Environmental Strategies.* 1 (1). pp. 193–207.

in addition to climate change-related policies for particular sectors such as energy. By 2012, a majority of developing economies in Asia and the Pacific had adopted climate change policies.

Economies in the region have proactively engaged in international climate finance mechanisms such as the Clean Development Mechanism (CDM) (which enabled selling of emission reduction offsets from mitigation projects in developing countries to help developed countries meet Kyoto Protocol commitments). Almost 80% of certified emission reduction credits under the CDM have originated from the region. The CDM is the first international market-based mechanism that incentivized the private sector in developing Asia to invest in climate action. Going forward, countries have also committed ambitious climate targets under the Paris Agreement, including peaking their GHG emissions (for example, the PRC by 2030), and aiming for up to 100% renewable energy electricity generation (the Cook Islands by 2020, Tuvalu by 2025, and Fiji and Vanuatu by 2030) and carbon neutrality (Bhutan).

Evolving approaches to environmental policy

Policy makers in the region have increasingly mainstreamed attention to the environment in their development strategies. For example, the Government of Indonesia put environmental sustainability as one of its three development pillars in its 2010–2014 Medium-Term Development Plan. Similarly, the PRC's 13th Five-Year Plan (2016–2020) also placed "eco-civilization" at the center of its development path. The Government of India made sustainable development a core pillar in its 2017–2020 Action Agenda, creating a new central body to oversee achievement of the Sustainable Development Goals.

As environmental regulation matured in developing Asia, market-based policy instruments emerged as a means of directly addressing incentive problems related to outcomes, in addition to regulations. Market-based instruments used in the region include taxes, fees, or charges; subsidies; tradable permits; cap-and-trade and emission trading schemes; payments for ecosystem services; and information provision, labels, and voluntary agreements.

For air pollution and climate change mitigation, market-based policy instruments are already used by some countries to control emissions, and promote energy efficiency and renewable energy. For example, tradable permit schemes are in place to control CO_2 and

Table 13.3: Water and Air Quality Standards, and Establishment of Environmental Ministries in Developing Asia

Policy	1960–1969	1970–1979	1980–1989	1990–1999	2000–2009	2010–2016
Establishment of water quality standards	Brunei Darussalam	India Malaysia Philippines Taipei,China	Hong Kong, China	Azerbaijan Bangladesh Cambodia Kyrgyz Republic Lao PDR Nepal Republic of Korea Timor-Leste Uzbekistan	Afghanistan Armenia Bhutan Indonesia Kazakhstan Papua New Guinea People's Republic of China Samoa Tajikistan Vanuatu	Cook Islands Maldives Mongolia Nauru People's Republic of China Turkmenistan Tuvalu Pakistan
Establishment of air quality standards	Hong Kong, China	Taipei,China	India	Armenia Cambodia Georgia Indonesia Kyrgyz Republic Maldives Pakistan Philippines Republic of Korea Tajikistan Uzbekistan	Azerbaijan Mongolia Sri Lanka	Afghanistan Malaysia People's Republic of China Turkmenistan

continued on next page

Table 13.3 *continued*

Policy	1960–1969	1970–1979	1980–1989	1990–1999	2000–2009	2010–2016
Establishment of dedicated environment ministries and/or departments		Bangladesh Indonesia Marshall Islands People's Republic of China Singapore	Hong Kong, China India Papua New Guinea Philippines Samoa Sri Lanka Taipei,China Tajikistan	Armenia Bhutan Georgia Kyrgyz Republic Pakistan Republic of Korea	Afghanistan Azerbaijan Cook Islands Kazakhstan Malaysia Myanmar Palau Solomon Islands Thailand Viet Nam	Cambodia Federated States of Micronesia Lao PDR Mongolia Turkmenistan Uzbekistan

Lao PDR = Lao People's Democratic Republic.

Notes: Economies with environment ministries merged with other functions and those with unclear establishment dates are not included. Year used for legislation is the year when separate legislation was adopted for air quality and water quality.

Sources: Environment ministry websites of listed governments, various sources; primary source materials from available databases in environment legislation.

SO_2 emissions in the PRC, while taxes are put on coal inputs in India. Kazakhstan and the PRC are introducing national or subnational greenhouse gas emissions trading schemes. For water resources management, volumetric pricing and markets for irrigation water have developed in selected locations. Tradable discharge permits are being piloted in the PRC. Successful eco-compensation schemes have also emerged in the PRC and Viet Nam. Extended producer responsibility policies are emerging to reduce waste at the source. By obligating producers and importers of electrical and electronic equipment to pay for related waste disposal costs, the PRC increased the quantities of recycling of iron, copper, aluminum, and plastics by more than three times between 2013 and 2016.[39]

Civil society has been increasingly playing the role of monitoring environmental actions. For example, in the 1990s, Indonesia, the ROK, and Thailand gave official status to environmental nongovernment organizations in their framework legislation.[40] Courts in developing Asia have more stringently interpreted environmental regulations and the rights of affected parties over time to support enforcement.[41]

Effectiveness of policy measures and remaining challenges

Although many policy steps have been taken to address environmental problems, the steps often remain partial. Many strategies and plans contain ambitious targets that do not necessarily correspond with sector plans or actions, and policies have important gaps.

At the most basic level, an important question is whether Asia is able to have "decoupling" or whether environmental degradation is slowing relative to economic development. Trends suggest this is happening, even though it may be masked when worsening environmental outcomes are considered in isolation. As shown in Figure 13.9, developing Asia's use of energy and material per unit of GDP has been in decline over time.

---

[39] Grainger, C., et al. 2019. Opportunities for Scaling Up Market-Based Approaches to Environmental Management in Asia. *Technical Assistance Consultant's Report.* Manila: Asian Development Bank.

[40] Institute for Global Environmental Strategies. 2001. *Report of the First Phase Strategic Research.* Kanagawa.

[41] For example, a 1993 Philippine Supreme Court ruling reinforced "intergenerational equity" by recognizing future generations as legal persons, and a 2013 ruling of Indonesia's Constitutional Court ruled that customary forests should belong to indigenous peoples rather than the State.

Figure 13.9: Energy and Material Intensity in Developing Asia

Figure 13.9a: Energy Intensity,
Developing Asia, 1990–2014

Figure 13.9b: Material Intensity,
Developing Asia, 1992–2017

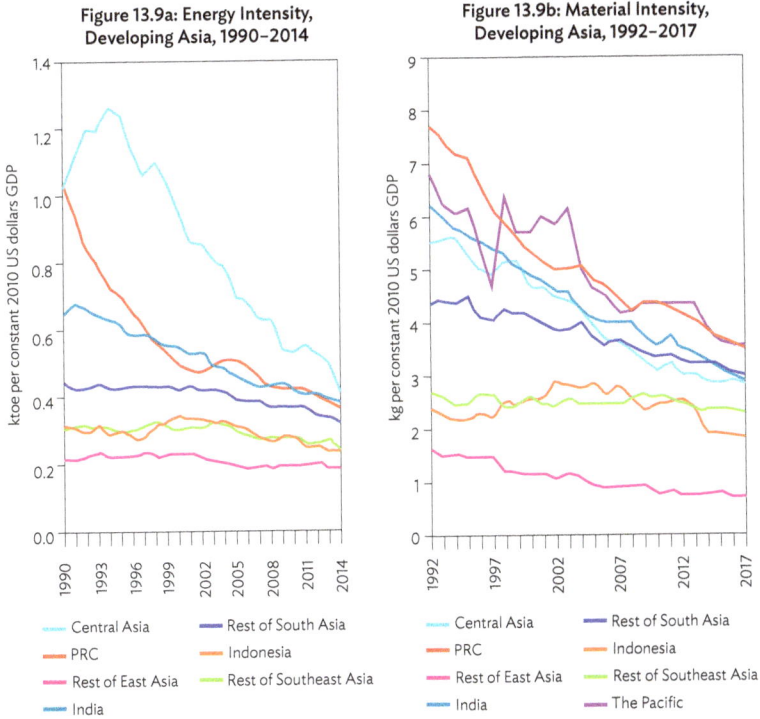

Legend:
- Central Asia
- PRC
- Rest of East Asia
- India
- Rest of South Asia
- Indonesia
- Rest of Southeast Asia
- The Pacific

GDP = gross domestic product, kg = kilogram, ktoe = kiloton of oil equivalent, PRC = People's Republic of China.

Note: Data availability varies across countries over time.

Sources: World Bank. World Development Indicators. https://data.worldbank.org (accessed 24 October 2018); and for domestic material consumption: International Resource Panel. Global Material Flows Database. https://www.resourcepanel.org/global-material-flows-database (accessed 2 November 2018).

Decoupling, however, is not sufficient to reverse environmental degradation. A stronger test is the Environmental Kuznets Curve (EKC) hypothesis, which posits that degradation may slow and ultimately reverse after a per capita income turning point. This could occur if development over time is associated with stronger regulations and institutions.[42]

---

[42] Levinson, A. 2000. The Ups and Downs of the Environmental Kuznets Curve. Paper prepared for the UCF/CentER conference on Environment. 30 November–2 December. Orlando.

A new analysis[43] estimates the EKC for major developing countries in Asia for four outcomes: (i) deforestation (natural forest loss), (ii) PM2.5 air pollution, (iii) SO_2 air pollution, and (iv) and GHG emissions (CO_2 equivalent). The analysis finds turning point estimates for PM2.5 at a relatively low $8,400 per capita GDP in purchasing power parity terms and SO_2 emissions at $10,800, which is consistent with many previous studies globally and in other regions.[44] The analysis also finds increasing effects of regulations over time on SO_2 and NOx pollution, which is consistent with the EKC findings.

However, there is no evidence of an EKC or effects of regulatory improvements for CO_2 equivalent emissions or loss of natural forest cover in developing Asia, which mirrors patterns in the rest of the world. This difference in results suggests that Asia is increasingly able to address environmental challenges with mature technological solutions, but that more complex challenges require more fundamental shifts such as natural ecosystem preservation. Furthermore, climate change mitigation falls behind measures to address pollution and needs additional efforts.

13.5 Engagement in international agreements and roles of development partners

Engagement in international agreements

Developing Asia has been increasingly engaged in international efforts to solve global environmental challenges, most notably climate change. This is critically important, as the region can benefit substantially from coordinated approaches to global climate challenges (Box 13.1). Nearly all countries in the region are party to the three major conventions and agreements on climate change—the 1992 UN Framework Convention on Climate Change (UNFCCC), the 1997 Kyoto Protocol, and the 2015 Paris Agreement. Under the nationally determined contributions to the Paris Agreement,

---

[43] Raitzer, D. A., et al. Forthcoming. *The Environmental Sustainability of Asia's Development.* Manila: Asian Development Bank. The study takes a panel of 23 to 43 developing countries in Asia, with observations dating as far back as 1960 for GHG, and to 1990 for other air pollutants.

[44] Borghesi, S. 1999. The Environmental Kuznets Curve: A Survey of the Literature. *FEEM Working Paper Series.* No. 85–99. Milan: Fondazione Eni Enrico Mattei.

Box 13.1: Benefits of International Cooperation on Climate Change

Effective international cooperation is important to address climate change for several reasons. First, as each country only internalizes a small share of the global effects of their actions, each has little incentive to solve global problems unless it is assured that other countries act as well. Second, the marginal costs of mitigating emissions problems are often different across countries and actors. An effective international cooperation mechanism can help abatement occur where these costs are lowest, increasing efficiency. Third, international cooperation can help realize important economies of scale in technological development and piloting.

Modeling climate mitigation costs illustrates the potential gains of effective international cooperation. In one recent study, developing a coordinated global carbon market under the Paris Agreement was found to potentially reduce the 2050 policy costs of limiting global warming to 2° Celsius by nearly 50% for Asia (Box Figure). This is because abatement can occur where it is least expensive, there are potential synergies in deploying advanced low-carbon energy technologies, and there is potential for the region to export carbon credit.

Box Figure: Asian Policy Costs of Global Emissions Pathways Relative to Business as Usual
(% of GDP)

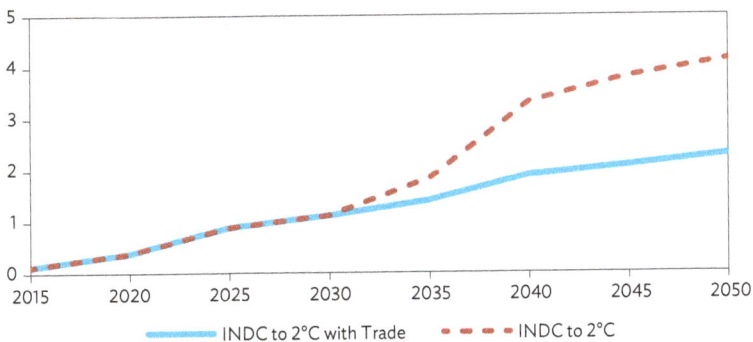

C = Celsius, GDP = gross domestic product, INDC = intended nationally determined contribution.

Notes: "Business as usual" refers to a scenario absent of specific climate policies post-2015, with economic development according to unconstrained optimal growth. The emissions trajectory is slightly lower than the Representative Concentration Pathway 8.5 of the Intergovernmental Panel on Climate Change.

Source: Reis, L. A., et al. 2016. The Economics of Greenhouse Gas Mitigation in Developing Asia. *ADB Economics Working Paper Series*. No. 504. Manila: Asian Development Bank.

89% of Asia's developing countries identified adaptation and mitigation contributions, while 11% identified only mitigation contributions.[45]

Developing Asia has become an active participant in many other international environmental agreements and processes, including the Ramsar Convention on Wetlands, the Montreal Protocol (for the ozone layer), and the Aichi Targets of the Convention on Biological Diversity. The Sustainable Development Goals, which integrate environmental goals into national and subnational policies, plans, and programs, are shared objectives in national strategies across Asia.

Asia also has a long history of transboundary agreements within the region related to natural resources, such as the 1960 Indus Water Treaty, which coordinated water resource development between Pakistan and India. The Mekong River Commission in Southeast Asia is an intergovernmental organization devoted to coordinating water resource use among Cambodia, the Lao People's Democratic Republic, Thailand, and Viet Nam. At the same time, these bodies and their agreements have struggled to balance rising competition for water and other resources among members as domestic demand has grown. There have been regional treaties established to tackle more recent problems such as transboundary haze, but supporting international bodies still need to be created to support actions.

Role of bilateral and multilateral development partners

Support from the international community to help address environmental and climate challenges has played a critical role in shaping the evolution of the region's policies. International nongovernment organizations have often been instrumental in raising awareness on specific environmental issues and climate change, and spurring domestic advocacy. Environmental impact assessment requirements and environmental quality standards have been developed with international technical assistance. In addition, the development of climate policies has benefited from both bilateral and multilateral support.

Multilateral development banks, including ADB, and bilateral development partners have increasingly aligned their strategies to support environment and climate change goals and have provided financial support for investing in climate change mitigation and

---

[45] ADB analysis of submission of nationally determined contributions to the UNFCCC Secretariat.

adaptation. Of the $43.1 billion in climate finance from multilateral development banks in 2018, about a third went to countries in Asia and the Pacific.[46]

ADB has long prioritized addressing environmental and climate challenges. Its Strategy 2030, adopted in 2018, further expands finance targets for both climate change mitigation and adaptation. Together with other multilateral and bilateral partners, ADB has been supporting developing Asia by (i) providing a range of financial assistance including policy-based lending with policy matrices of a country's climate actions; (ii) replenishing lending resources by issuing green bonds; (iii) helping mobilize private sector resources for climate investment; (iv) supporting countries in implementing nationally determined contributions; and (v) providing technical assistance for policies, regulations, and judicial system regarding environment and climate change. In 2019, ADB launched an action plan to promote ocean health.

13.6 Green industry contribution to environmental solutions

Asia's private sector also plays an increasingly important role in generating environmental solutions via green industries, particularly for renewable energy, energy efficiency, GHG mitigation, pollution abatement, and material recycling. The size of the environmental market in Asia and the Pacific is growing faster than that of other regions globally, both in terms of actual value and as a share of global trade, with Japan and the PRC as the largest contributors.[47]

In addition, Asian countries show large potential for leading green innovation, with major investments in deploying green technologies. Asia accounted for 44% of global exports of climate change mitigation technologies—such as solar panels and efficient lighting—and filed more high-value patents for these technologies than Europe and Latin America combined.

---

[46] African Development Bank, ADB, European Bank for Reconstruction and Development, European Investment Bank, Inter-American Development Bank Group, Islamic Development Bank, and the World Bank Group. 2019. *2018 Joint Report on Multilateral Development Banks' Climate Finance*. London: European Bank for Reconstruction and Development. https://www.adb.org/news/mdb-climate-finance-hit-record-high-431-billion-2018.

[47] Fankhauser, S., A. Kazaglis, and S. Srivastav. 2017. Green Growth Opportunities for Asia. *ADB Economics Working Paper Series*. No. 508. Manila: Asian Development Bank.

Globally, the PRC and India are making the largest investments in renewables and receive the largest inflows of greenfield foreign direct investment. There is growing pressure from consumers and nongovernment organizations for corporations, especially multinationals, to adopt "green supply chains." Many companies in the region use environmental management systems, and modify processes and products to reduce environmental impact. This is increasingly accompanied by certification and eco-labeling of products as part of their international trade strategy.

Private sector investment in environmental projects will be increased by addressing the risks associated with the changes of policies and technological uncertainties. Green finance is emerging as a way to accelerate environmentally oriented investment. Green investment by financial institutions in the region has grown steadily over the past few years. To accelerate this, environmental concerns are being mainstreamed into banking systems.[48]

Green or climate-aligned bonds are important green financing instruments, and developing Asia is at the forefront of their use. These bonds seek to raise capital for environment-related projects. They may be "labeled" and subjected to third-party certification concerning their environmental contributions. Asia was the largest region in outstanding climate-aligned bonds with a 2017 global market share of 42%. This was dominated by issuance from the PRC, which accounts for 82% of the region's total.[49] Indonesia pioneered the use of sovereign Islamic green bonds with an issue in early 2018, and Fiji pioneered the use of green bonds for climate resilience.

13.7 Looking ahead

Developing Asia has begun to take important steps toward addressing its profound environmental challenges. At the same time, the pace of progress has not yet matched the enormity of the threats facing the region. If trends continue, the region will not be able to sustain the economic progress achieved over the past 50 years far into the 21st century, as resources will be too depleted and degraded and ecological systems too disrupted. Although the region's energy and carbon intensity

---

[48] ADB. 2017. *Catalyzing Green Finance: A Concept for Leveraging Blended Finance for Green Development*. Manila.

[49] Khanna, M. 2018. *Greening Businesses in the Asia and Pacific Region: Opportunities and Challenges*. Manila: Asian Development Bank.

of economic output have fallen, further efforts are needed to align with the Paris Agreement goals to keep mean global warming below 2° Celsius above preindustrial levels.

To put the region on a sustainable path, it needs to redouble the following policy efforts.

First, ensure prices reflect the costs of environment and climate change externalities. "Perverse" price signals that encourage the unsustainable use of natural capital and ecosystem services remain a major impediment to green growth. Removing fossil fuel and other perverse subsidies and replacing them with progressive alternatives such as means-tested household subsidies is an essential first step. Both environmental taxes and fees, such as timber royalties and water charges, are important to reform.

Second, enhance governance for better environmental management. Environmental problems are essentially externalities, and thus appropriate public intervention is needed to resolve them. Further strengthening regulations and enforcement is crucial. Regulations can benefit from higher levels of ambition and scope. Monitoring by civil society may help to augment limited governance capacity.

Third, substantially invest in environmentally friendly, low-carbon, and climate-resilient infrastructure. This includes investing in renewable energy, energy efficiency, and sustainable public transport, and also fortifying existing infrastructure to be climate-friendly. Effective collection, disposal, and treatment of waste depends on new investment in new and existing facilities using the latest technologies to avoid pollution.

Fourth, attract private investment in sustainability. More investment is needed than the public sector can offer. The viability of private investment often depends on the incentives set by governments and political risk. Public investors can signal their public commitment to private investors. Governments and multilateral development banks can offer products such as risk guarantees for technological, contractual, and political risks. Expansion of green bonds and green banks can help mobilize environmentally friendly finance.

Fifth, advance transformative technologies. The successful transition to low-carbon development depends on technologies such as advanced biofuels and energy storage. Managing Asia's waste requires innovations in recycling, composting, and disposal. Intelligent transport systems have the potential to reduce the environmental impact in urban centers. Governments can support innovation by investing in research, pilot, and demonstration projects, and enhancing access to finance.

Finally, intensify international cooperation. Many of the region's most pressing environmental challenges are transboundary. Governments can further strengthen cross-border collaboration and collective action in areas such as air and water pollution, ocean health and fisheries management, water resources management, biodiversity, disaster risk management, and coastal protection. They can also enhance cooperation in addressing the global agenda of climate mitigation and adaptation and can collaborate to exploit economies of scale in developing technological solutions.

CHAPTER 14

THE ROLE OF BILATERAL AND MULTILATERAL DEVELOPMENT FINANCE

14.1 Introduction

The preceding chapters document how financing development has been a major challenge in Asia and the Pacific over the past 50 years. Export receipts, remittances, foreign direct investment (FDI), bank loans, bond purchases, and portfolio equity investments by nonresidents were important sources of external finance (Chapter 7). Bilateral and multilateral development finance also played a key role in many aspects of Asia's economic and social development.

In the early years, countries in the region had shortages of domestic savings and foreign exchange. They were less creditworthy to borrow from abroad, and domestic capital markets were not developed. At that moment, external development finance from bilateral aid agencies of developed countries as official development assistance (ODA) was critical.[1] Large amounts of development finance were also provided as concessional (including grants) and non-concessional

---

[1] ODA is defined by the Organisation for Economic Co-operation and Development (OECD) as financial flows provided by official agencies intended to promote economic development and welfare of the recipient, and sufficiently concessional in character (grants, and lower interest rate and longer maturity loans).

flows from multilateral development banks (MDBs) such as the Asian Development Bank (ADB) and the World Bank, and United Nations (UN) agencies such as the United Nations Development Programme (UNDP), United Nations Children's Fund (UNICEF), and International Fund for Agricultural Development (IFAD).

There is a large and growing volume of literature on aid effectiveness.[2] Findings and conclusions tend to differ and diverge depending on the context, situation, and type of aid because the complexity of the overall economic development process makes it difficult to generalize and precisely attribute development results to development finance. But in Asia, it is generally agreed that development finance played an important role in supporting country development.[3] Recipients of development finance—through programs and projects— benefited from finance combined with the transfer of technology and ideas. Countries worked to enhance their absorptive capacities, aligning external finance with country strategies, and maintaining "ownership." Bilateral and multilateral development finance remains important today, especially for supporting such areas as persistent poverty, gender equality, climate change, and quality infrastructure.

In general, there are three instruments of bilateral and multilateral assistance.

The first is loan financing to bridge gaps in necessary funding resources for development. A developing country, for many reasons, often faces constraints in financing, in particular large investment requirements in physical infrastructure.[4] Development finance plays a fundamental role in loosening constraints by filling financing gaps, enabling a country to undertake projects that promote economic growth and enhance its repayment capacity. Also, large loans from bilateral and multilateral development partners often come with the

---

[2] For example, Roodman, R. 2007. The Anarchy of Numbers: Aid, Development, and Cross-Country Empirics. *World Bank Economic Review*. 21 (2). pp. 255–277; Bourguignon, F., and M. Sundberg. 2007. Aid Effectiveness – Opening the Black Box. *The American Economic Review*. 97 (2). pp. 316–321; and Quibria, M. G. 2014. Aid Effectiveness: Research, Policy, and Unresolved Issues. *Development Studies Research*. 1 (1). pp. 75–87.

[3] Kimura, H., Y. Mori, and Y. Sawada. 2012. Aid Proliferation and Economic Growth: A Cross-Country Analysis. *World Development*. 40 (1). pp. 1–10; and Hino, H., and I. Atsushi. 2008. Aid Effectiveness Revisited: Comparative Studies of Modalities of Aid to Asia and Africa. *Discussion Paper Series*. No. 218. Kobe: Research Institute for Economics & Business Administration, Kobe University.

[4] Lucas, R. E., Jr. 1990. Why Doesn't Capital Flow from Rich to Poor Countries? *American Economic Review*. 80 (2). pp. 92–96.

transfer of knowledge, ideas, governance, and policies. In addition, recipient countries and loan providers tend to pay more attention to the economic grounds of projects than grants.

The second instrument is grant assistance, especially for social infrastructure such as health and education, humanitarian assistance, and other social programs. Grant aid is a form of financial assistance without repayment obligations. Grant is effective to support the poorest countries and those in fragile and conflict-affected situations. Grant is also used for severely debt-distressed countries. ADB's operations had been in the form of loans (non-concessional and concessional) in addition to technical assistance since its establishment in 1968. ADB began grant operations in 2005.

The third instrument is technical assistance. It is used to deliver technical and managerial skills in health, education, agriculture, forestry, and others. Technical assistance helps design and prepare projects. It also supports effective policies and structural reforms in such areas as public finance, social security, the financial sector, the education system, health service delivery, and environmental protection. There are broader knowledge spillover effects of international technology transfers through technical cooperation (Chapter 5).

In general, the use of resource inflows from abroad for development evolves in relative importance depending on the stage of development: initially, grant aid for less-developed countries, moving to concessional loans, and then non-concessional finance from bilateral partners (including export credit agencies) and MDBs (including loans and equity investments to private companies). As countries become more developed, private capital inflows, including FDI, commercial loans, portfolio bonds, and equity investments, increase their importance. Since the mid-1970s in developing Asia, the share of bilateral and multilateral development finance has gradually declined as other modes of external finance expanded significantly (Chapter 7).

This chapter discusses bilateral and multilateral development finance in Asia and the Pacific. Section 14.2 gives an overview of bilateral ODA for Asia, while section 14.3 presents an overview of multilateral development financing. Section 14.4 offers a summary of the experience in selected recipient countries. Section 14.5 discusses experiences of several Asian bilateral development finance providers. Section 14.6 looks at future challenges and priorities.

14.2 Bilateral official development assistance flows

In developing Asia, the United States (US) was the largest ODA provider in the 1960s and early 1970s (Figure 14.1). Since the late 1970s, Japan has consistently increased ODA and has become the single largest bilateral aid provider, using large concessional lending ("yen credit").

ODA flows from Europe, including European Union (EU) institutions, account for around one-third of total ODA flows to developing Asia, with countries targeted changing over time. Australia and New Zealand have prioritized their ODA allocations for

Figure 14.1: Inflows of Bilateral Official Development Assistance, Developing Asia
(gross disbursement, $ billion)

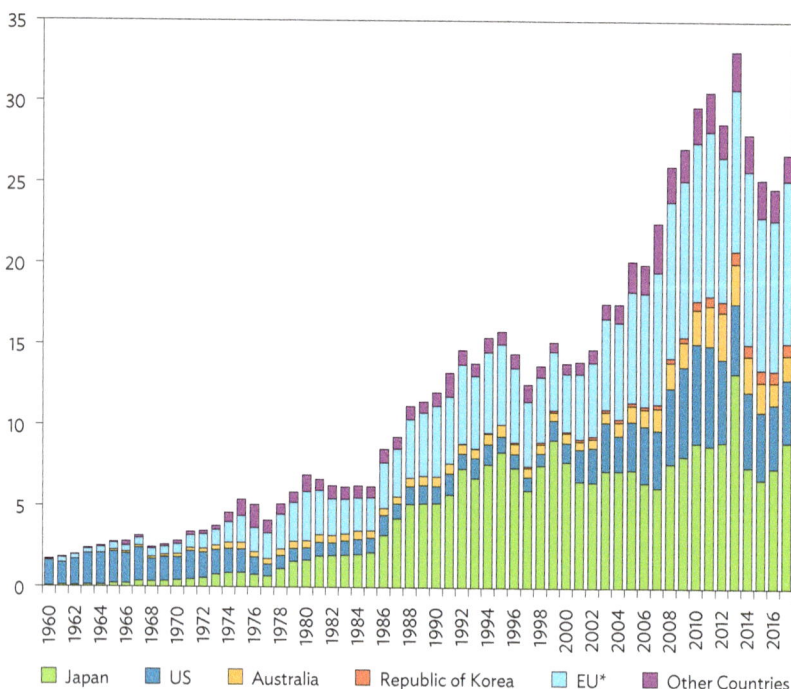

Japan   US   Australia   Republic of Korea   EU*   Other Countries

EU = European Union, US = United States.

Notes: EU* includes Development Assistance Committee (DAC) EU member countries and EU institutions. Other countries include non-DAC countries such as Thailand, which reports to DAC.

Source: Organisation for Economic Co-operation and Development (OECD). *OECD Data.* https://data.oecd.org/ (accessed 22 July 2019).

the Pacific region. The Republic of Korea (ROK) has become an ODA provider in developing Asia since the late 1980s, with the volume of assistance rising steadily.

Japan, the US, Australia, New Zealand, the ROK, and the EU are all members of the Organisation for Economic Co-operation and Development (OECD), guided by the policies of the OECD Development Assistance Committee (DAC). Emerging economies, such as the People's Republic of China (PRC), Thailand, and India, are increasingly becoming "emerging donors," providing assistance to other developing countries in Asia and the Pacific.

The large numbers of donors and projects may potentially overwhelm a recipient government's capacity to manage and administer aid inflows, undermining the efficiency of official development finance, and leading to a situation called "aid proliferation." But in Asia, this problem has generally been controlled as there were fewer aid providers operating in each recipient country, for instance, compared with Africa.[5] Also, aid providers coordinate among themselves and work together with recipient countries based on their strong ownership, which enhances aid effectiveness.

14.3 Multilateral development banks

Postwar multilateral development assistance began with the establishment of the International Bank for Reconstruction and Development (IBRD), or the World Bank, and the International Monetary Fund (IMF) based on the Bretton Woods Conference in 1944. Originally, the IBRD loans helped rebuild countries devastated by World War II. In time, the focus shifted from reconstruction to development. IBRD started lending to developing countries beginning with Chile in 1948. Its first loan to Asia was to India in 1948 for railway rehabilitation. In 1960, the International Development Association (IDA) was established as a member of the World Bank Group to provide concessional loans and grants to the poorest developing countries. The first IDA loan to Asia was to India in 1961.

In 1966, ADB was established "to foster economic growth and co-operation in the region of Asia and the Far East ... and to contribute to the acceleration of the process of economic development of the developing member countries in the region, collectively and

---

[5]   Kimura, H., Y. Mori, and Y. Sawada. 2012. Aid Proliferation and Economic Growth: A Cross-Country Analysis. *World Development*. 40 (1). pp. 1–10.

individually."[6] The 31 original ADB members increased to 68 by 2019, of which 49 are regional members and 19 are nonregional. ADB provided its first loan to Thailand in 1968 (a $5 million financial sector loan to support industrial development). Its first concessional loan (Indonesia irrigation project) was also provided in 1968 from its Agricultural Special Fund. The Asian Development Fund (ADF) was established in 1974 to support concessional lending. And in 2005, ADF donors agreed to establish a grant program under ADF. It has helped reduce the debt burden in the poorest countries, assisted poor countries in transition from post-conflict situations, and supported countries' social programs such as health and education.

Initially, ADB's focus was on food production and rural development in its developing member countries. Lending and technical assistance increasingly covered power, transport, and urban development, later adding the social sectors such as health and education. Over the years, ADB developed policy-based lending to support reforms, grants for the poorest countries, and private sector operations.[7]

Gross disbursement of multilateral development finance flows to developing Asia surged in 1997 and 1998 to assist countries affected by the Asian financial crisis (Figure 14.2). It has increased again since 2005. The ADB share has increased steadily. As a result of combining concessional ADF lending operations with its ordinary capital resources (OCR) balance sheet in 2017, ADB's lending capacity for both non-concessional and concessional loans expanded substantially—because of the large combined equity and use of leverage for concessional lending. ADB's new commitment increased from $13.9 billion in 2014 to $19.7 billion in 2017. ADB's gross disbursement reached $11.4 billion in 2017, a record high, or 30% of total multilateral financing in developing Asia.

Infrastructure for transport, energy, and water accounted for a large share of ADB's development finance from 1968 to 2017 (Figure 14.3). But the sector focus shifted over time. The share of agriculture declined, while transport increased. The energy share remained at 25%, although today it is predominantly for renewable energy and energy efficiency. During 1997–2006, the share of the

---

[6] ADB. 1965. *Agreement Establishing the Asian Development Bank.* https://www.adb.org/documents/agreement-establishing-asian-development-bank-adb-charter.

[7] McCawley, P. 2017. *Banking on the Future of Asia and the Pacific: 50 Years of the Asian Development Bank.* Manila: Asian Development Bank.

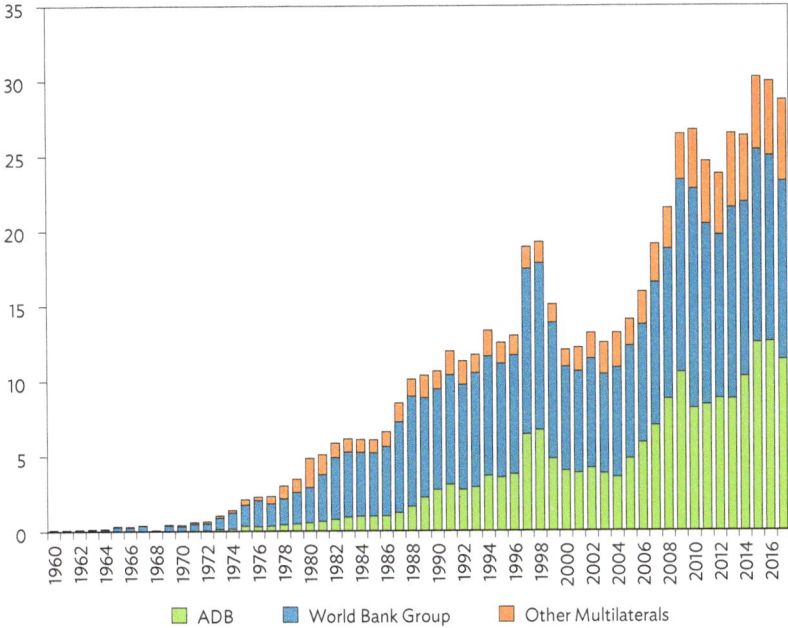

Figure 14.2: Inflows of Multilateral Development Finance, Developing Asia
(gross disbursement, $ billion)

ADB = Asian Development Bank.

Note: European Union institutions are not included in this figure.

Sources: Organisation for Economic Co-operation and Development (OECD). *OECD Data.* https://data.oecd.org/ (accessed 22 July 2019); and for flows from ADB: ADB, Controller's Department. *Disbursements Data.* Manila.

finance and public sectors more than doubled over the earlier period, as there was a concerted effort globally to provide countercyclical support to developing countries in the aftermath of the 1997–1998 Asian financial crisis.

Reflecting the changing needs and priorities of developing member countries, MDBs broadened the scope of their assistance to new areas such as governance, fragility, and post-conflict assistance. They developed new modalities such as policy-based financing (budget support finance based on certain reform measures), results-based financing (disbursements linked to performance indicators such as in education and health), and contingency disaster risk financing.

They are also increasing climate finance to support climate change mitigation and adaptation. Nonsovereign operations (lending to and equity investment in private companies) have been expanding. MDBs have extended their country presence by opening field offices, and continue to enhance the quality of engagement by aligning country strategies with those of recipient countries. With their unique cross-country perspective, MDBs can promote learning and knowledge sharing of comparative development experiences.

Figure 14.3: Evolution of ADB Loan and Grant Approvals, 1968–2016
(%)

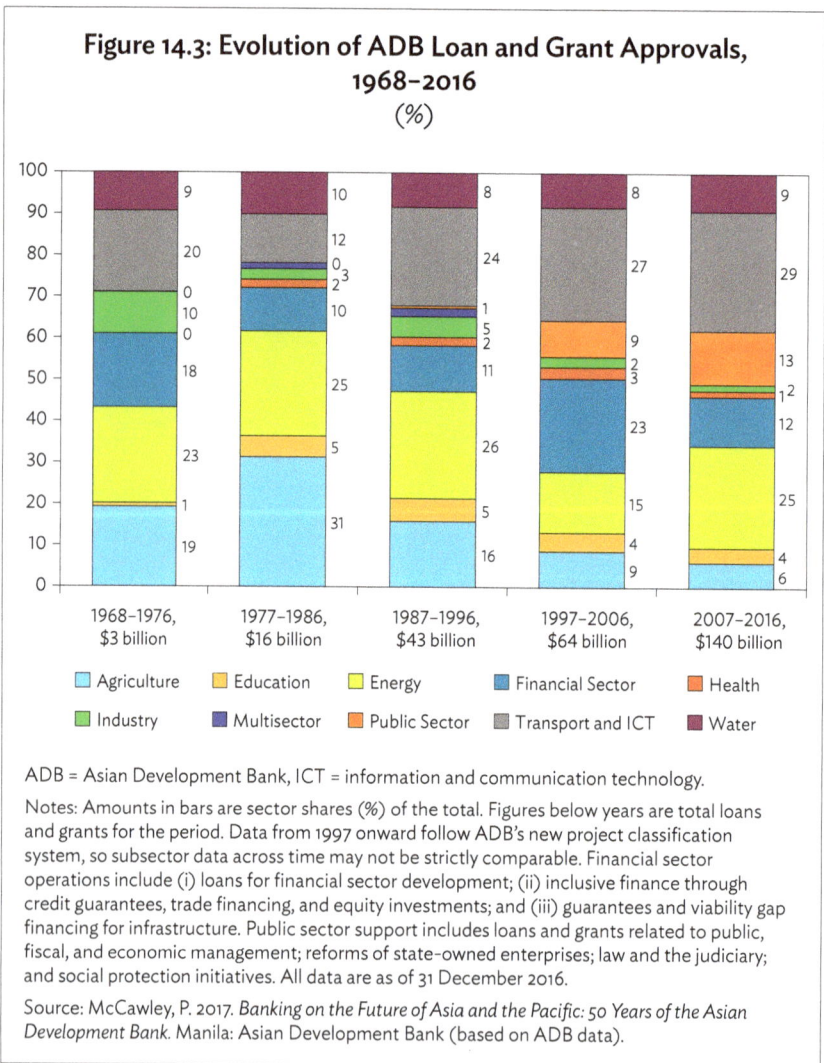

ADB = Asian Development Bank, ICT = information and communication technology.

Notes: Amounts in bars are sector shares (%) of the total. Figures below years are total loans and grants for the period. Data from 1997 onward follow ADB's new project classification system, so subsector data across time may not be strictly comparable. Financial sector operations include (i) loans for financial sector development; (ii) inclusive finance through credit guarantees, trade financing, and equity investments; and (iii) guarantees and viability gap financing for infrastructure. Public sector support includes loans and grants related to public, fiscal, and economic management; reforms of state-owned enterprises; law and the judiciary; and social protection initiatives. All data are as of 31 December 2016.

Source: McCawley, P. 2017. *Banking on the Future of Asia and the Pacific: 50 Years of the Asian Development Bank*. Manila: Asian Development Bank (based on ADB data).

In its corporate strategy, Strategy 2030, adopted in 2018, ADB set remaining poverty, gender equality, climate change, livable cities, rural development and food security, governance, and regional cooperation and integration as priority areas. ADB will increase private sector operations (aiming at one-third of ADB's operations in number by 2024) and mobilize more private sector resources including through public–private partnership.

Cooperation and coordination among MDBs and bilateral donors have strengthened too. Project cofinancing is a common form of cooperation, especially for financing large infrastructure projects. For example, ADB, the World Bank, and Japan cofinanced megaprojects such as the Jamuna Bridge in Bangladesh. The Nam Theun 2 Hydropower Project in the Lao People's Democratic Republic was another mega-infrastructure investment that involved multilateral and bilateral cofinancing. In addition, MDBs and bilateral partners have conducted regional studies. For instance, in 2005, ADB, the Japan Bank for International Cooperation (JBIC), and the World Bank jointly produced a regional flagship study, *Connecting East Asia: A New Framework for Infrastructure.*[8]

MDBs cooperate with the IMF to support countries in implementing policy and institutional reforms and to mitigate the socioeconomic impact of external shocks. In the aftermath of the 1997–1998 Asian financial crisis and 2008–2009 global financial crisis, MDBs and the IMF worked closely to support affected countries by providing larger amounts of finance. When there is a balance of payments crisis, MDBs participate in IMF-led programs—the IMF provides foreign exchange financing based on conditionalities on macroeconomic policies and structural reforms, and MDBs provide policy-based, budget support loans for social sector expenditures and structural reforms.

MDBs cooperate with other development partners including UN agencies. ADB has worked with the World Health Organization (WHO) in Asia to help address regional health security related to malaria, HIV/AIDS, and avian influenza. ADB also cofinanced projects with the Global Environment Facility (GEF) to support environmental protection and biodiversity, and the Green Climate Fund (GCF) for climate change mitigation and adaptation.

---

[8] ADB, JBIC, and the World Bank. 2005. *Connecting East Asia: A New Framework for Infrastructure.* Washington, DC: World Bank.

More recently, in 2016, the Asian Infrastructure Investment Bank (AIIB) and the New Development Bank (NDB) began operating as new MDBs. ADB and the World Bank have been working closely with them, including through cofinancing in several Asian developing countries.

14.4 Experiences of recipient countries

How well recipient countries used bilateral and multilateral development finance differed. Most Asian countries benefited from development finance as they worked simultaneously to build their absorptive capacity to design and implement projects, and have complementary policies to maximize the impact of external support and, most importantly, keep a strong sense of ownership. They avoided aid dependency.

Japan

Japan received humanitarian and economic aid immediately after World War II from the US government and nongovernment organizations (NGOs). These included the Government Aid and Relief in Occupied Areas (GARIOA), Licensed Agencies for Relief in Asia (LARA), and Economic Rehabilitation in Occupied Areas (EROA). From CARE International, a US-based NGO, the country received aid for necessities such as food and clothing, farm implements, and seeds.

IBRD provided large investment loans from 1951 to 1966— $863 million for 31 loan programs—with repayments completed in July 1990.[9] Japan used the resources to fill financing gaps in domestic investments and development programs, particularly focusing on the "Pacific Belt Zone"—the organic link of industrial clusters between Tokyo and Fukuoka.[10] Examples include the steel-plate production facilities of Yawata Iron & Steel Co. Ltd. (1955), Koromo Plant truck and bus machine tools of Toyota Motor Co. Ltd. (1956), Kurobe No. 4 hydroelectric power station of Kansai Electric Power Co. Ltd. (1958), Tokaido Shinkansen (the first high-speed train) line of Japanese

---

[9]   World Bank. 2005. *World Bank's Loans to Japan*. Washington, DC. http://www.worldbank
      .org/en/country/japan/brief/world-banks-loans-to-japan.
[10] ADB, Department for International Development of the United Kingdom (DFID), Japan
      International Cooperation Agency (JICA), and World Bank Group. 2018. *The WEB of
      Transport Corridors in South Asia*. Washington, DC: World Bank.

National Railways (1961), and Tomei Expressway of Japan Highway Public Corporation (1964).[11]

The IBRD loans were extremely important for Japan, providing much-needed foreign exchange and financial resources more generally, but also to transfer knowledge and new technology. The Shinkansen railway was based primarily on Japanese technology as the country had long prioritized railway systems. For its road systems, the Japanese construction ministry drew on a German consultant engaged by IBRD to design and construct toll-based highways.

Republic of Korea

Devastated by the 1950–1953 Korean War, the ROK relied heavily on foreign assistance for development finance and external payments. In the 1950s, foreign aid inflows, especially from the US, financed about 70% of crucial imports. Foreign aid was also used for the rehabilitation and reconstruction of war-damaged infrastructure. Aside from import and infrastructure financing, emergency relief and military aid, US aid went to higher education (including scholarships to study in the US) and capacity building of public administration that supported industrialization.[12] After normalizing diplomatic relations between the ROK and Japan in 1965, bilateral ODA from Japan increased significantly.

Overall, foreign aid was an important source of investment financing during the country's early economic development. Foreign aid accounted for 42% of overall fixed capital formation during 1965–1974. The ROK used ODA effectively to promote rapid industrialization. Although the World Bank turned down a plan for constructing a new steel mill due to the size of the ROK economy, the government built it in 1969 with Japanese assistance.[13]

Multilateral support played an important role in economic development. ADB's first loan to the ROK was for the Seoul–Incheon highway project in 1968. While construction was already underway when ADB was approached for financing, ADB's technical contribution was critical to ensure a high design standard and effective

---

[11] World Bank. 2005. *World Bank's Loans to Japan*. Washington, DC. http://www.worldbank
    .org/en/country/japan/brief/world-banks-loans-to-japan.
[12] Suh, J. J., and J. Kim. 2017. Aid to Build Governance in a Fragile State: Foreign Assistance
    to a Post-Conflict South Korea. In Howe, B. M., ed. *Post-Conflict Development in East Asia*.
    Surrey, UK: Ashgate Publishing Limited.
[13] Kim, J. K. 2011. *Modularization of Korea's Development Experience: Impact of Foreign Aid
    on Korea's Development*. Seoul: Ministry of Strategy and Finance, and KDI School.

implementation, closely engaging authorities and local consultants. The ROK graduated from ADB assistance in 1988. But during the 1997–1998 Asian financial crisis, ADB approved a large policy-based loan to support reform and recovery.

The People's Republic of China since 1978

Following the 1978 reforms and move toward opening its economy, the PRC began receiving significant bilateral and multilateral development finance together with the transfer of knowledge and technology. Japan was the largest bilateral aid provider between the early 1980s and early 2000s. In 1979, it started to support PRC policy reforms based on the Treaty of Peace and Friendship between Japan and the PRC. During the period, Japan provided 367 concessional loans (yen credit) totaling ¥3.3 trillion, based on the "round modality" in which Japan pledged a lump sum every 5 years to support the PRC's five-year plans.[14] Assistance from other bilateral donors, the World Bank, and, later, ADB also increased.

In the 1980s, bilateral and multilateral partners supported the PRC on major development goals such as alleviating infrastructure bottlenecks and improving health. Knowledge was also critical. In 1985, the World Bank sponsored the 6-day International Symposium on Macroeconomic Management—a river cruise conference along the Yangtze River—which brought together senior officials and many world-renowned economists. Today, it is considered a symbolic event that inspired future market-driven reforms. In the 1990s, donors started paying more attention to supporting PRC efforts to cope with emerging challenges such as urban reform, environmental protection, and poverty reduction.

Sharing development experience and absorbing technology from abroad were essential for the PRC's rapid economic development, both for building highways, bridges, and urban infrastructure, and for macroeconomic policy, city planning, and environmental protection. The Ministry of Finance and the State Development Planning Commission (the predecessor of the National Development and Reform Commission) were the central government agencies for engaging with bilateral and multilateral development partners.

---

[14] Government of Japan, Ministry of Foreign Affairs. 1978. *Treaty of Peace and Friendship between Japan and the People's Republic of China.* https://www.mofa.go.jp/region/asia -paci/china/treaty78.html.

The PRC joined ADB in 1986 and became a large borrower together with India (which also began borrowing from ADB in 1986, although it was a founding member). The focus of ADB lending was initially to support industrial development in coastal areas, but over time, it shifted to transport and urban development in poorer inland provinces. ADB's operations supported capacity building of public institutions to develop, implement, and operate public projects. They included best practices for international competitive bidding, contract awards, and safeguard policies against adverse environmental and social impacts. ADB's country partnership strategy for the PRC (2016–2020), aligned with the 13th Five-Year Plan, prioritized climate change, environmental protection, institution building for inclusive growth, and regional cooperation.

Thailand

ODA flows to Thailand played a critical role in facilitating economic growth and development. Since the mid-1970s, Japan has been a major provider of ODA (approximately 60%–80% of assistance from DAC countries) by way of grants, technical assistance, and concessional loans. The Eastern Seaboard Development Program shows how Thailand successfully leveraged bilateral and multilateral development finance to industrialize (Figure 14.4). The Government of Thailand also used external finance for integrated rural development initiatives, including small-scale irrigation programs, rural finance through the public Bank for Agriculture and Agricultural Cooperatives, and vocational education such as an industrial college in Chiang Mai.[15]

Thailand actively promoted FDI-led industrialization by using development assistance to crowd-in private investment. Bilateral and multilateral development finance together contributed to attracting FDI.[16] There is an "infrastructure effect" that improves physical infrastructure; and a "vanguard effect" whereby foreign aid from a particular country promotes FDI by bringing its own specific business practices, rules, and systems into recipient countries. Over time, the country benefits from an improved business climate.

---

[15] Kitano, N. 2014. Japanese Development Assistance to ASEAN Countries. In Shiraishi, T., and T. Kojima, eds. *ASEAN-Japan Relations*. Singapore: Institute of Southeast Asian Studies.

[16] Kimura, H., Y. Todo, and Y. Sawada. 2010. Is Foreign Aid a Vanguard of Foreign Direct Investment? A Gravity-Equation Approach. *World Development*. 38 (4). pp. 482–497.

Figure 14.4: Infrastructure Development of Thailand's Eastern Seaboard

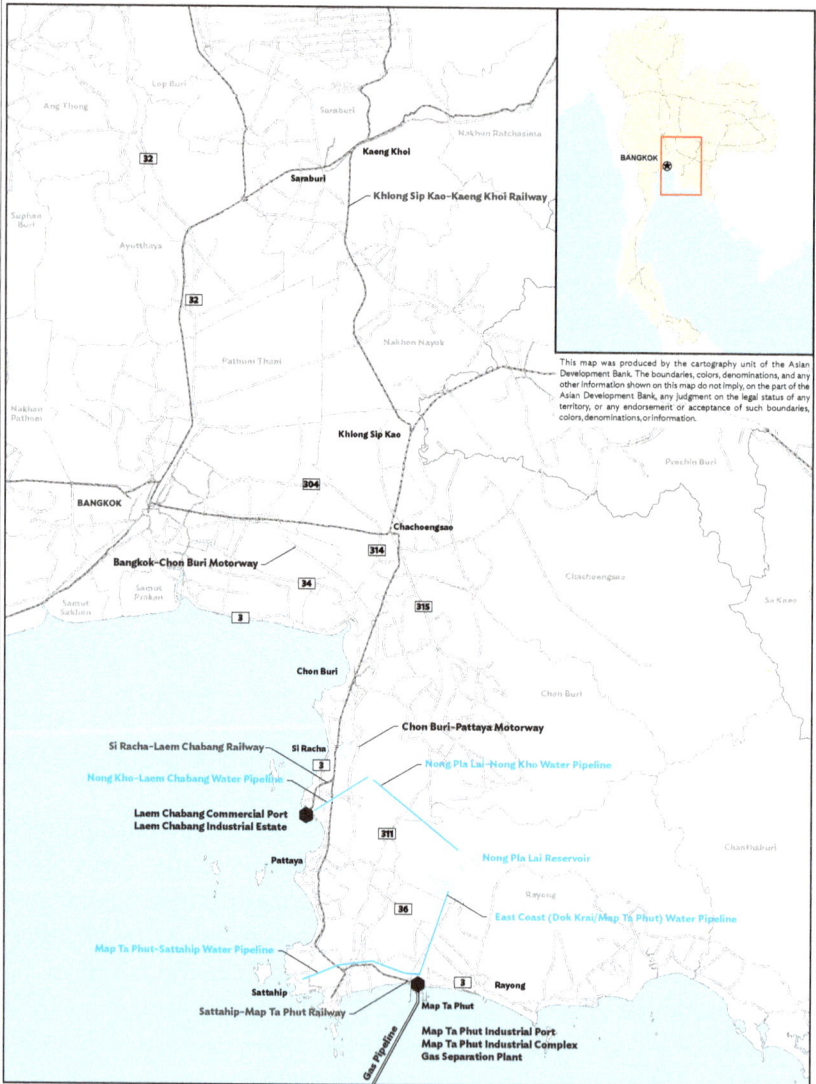

Source: Reproduced from Ariga, K., and S. Ejima. 2000. Post-Evaluation for ODA Loan Project – Kingdom of Thailand: Overall Impact of Eastern Seaboard Development Program. *JBIC Review*. 2 (Nov). pp. 81–115.

FDI-led agglomerations, including the automobile and auto parts industry, expanded formal employment opportunities, improved education in rural areas, and narrowed the urban–rural income gap.

Bangladesh

Soon after Bangladesh became independent in 1971, ADB, the World Bank, and bilateral donors began supporting its socioeconomic development (Figure 14.5). In the 1970s, the country was heavily dependent on foreign aid due to a lack of domestic resources needed

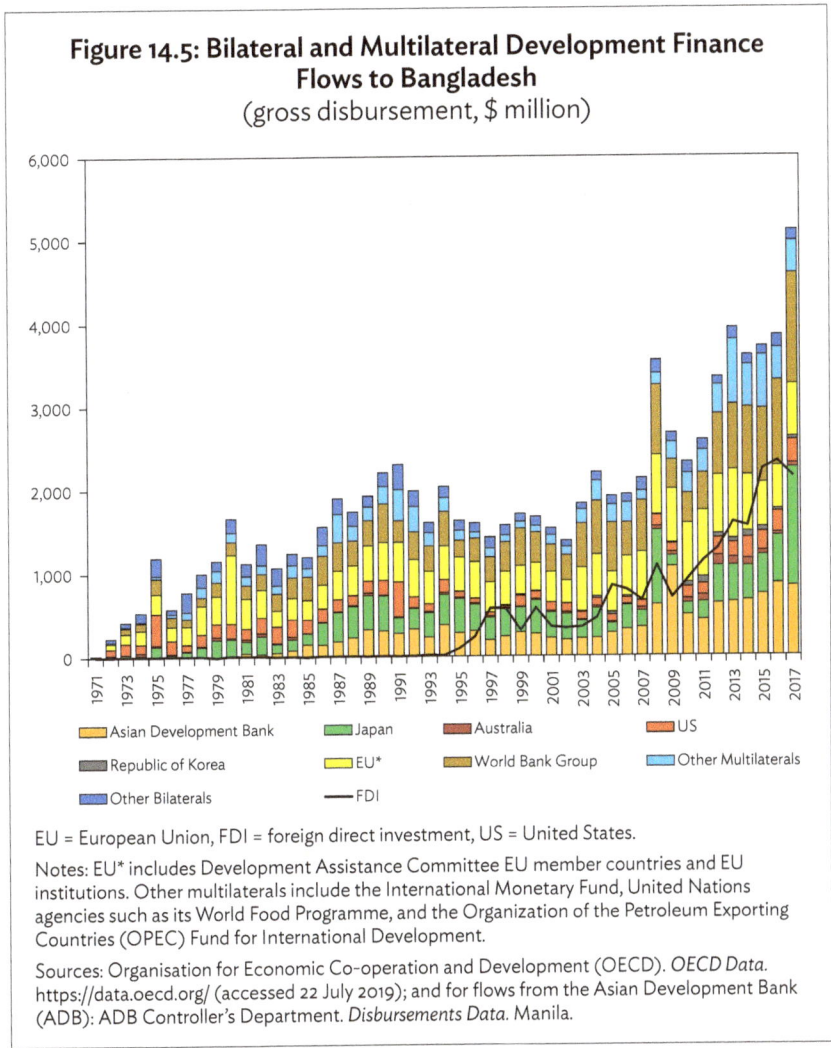

Figure 14.5: Bilateral and Multilateral Development Finance Flows to Bangladesh
(gross disbursement, $ million)

EU = European Union, FDI = foreign direct investment, US = United States.

Notes: EU* includes Development Assistance Committee EU member countries and EU institutions. Other multilaterals include the International Monetary Fund, United Nations agencies such as its World Food Programme, and the Organization of the Petroleum Exporting Countries (OPEC) Fund for International Development.

Sources: Organisation for Economic Co-operation and Development (OECD). *OECD Data.* https://data.oecd.org/ (accessed 22 July 2019); and for flows from the Asian Development Bank (ADB): ADB Controller's Department. *Disbursements Data.* Manila.

for capital formation: the savings rate stayed below 5% of gross domestic product.[17] External aid initially came in the form of food aid and then mostly as project aid. Both bilateral and multilateral aid played a critical role in financing physical infrastructure, especially in energy and transportation as well as innovative social development projects and programs such as microfinance.

Jamuna Bridge, cofinanced by ADB, the World Bank, and Japan, is the longest and largest multipurpose bridge in Bangladesh. It carries gas pipelines, a railway, power cables, and a two-lane dual highway. The bridge both improves national connectivity as a strategic link between the eastern and western parts of Bangladesh and helps reduce poverty in the surrounding region.[18] Even though ODA has been a significant source of foreign exchange and domestic investment, its relative importance declined over the years as other sources of foreign exchange, such as exports and worker remittances, grew.[19]

Viet Nam

After several decades of war and reunification, in 1986 Viet Nam began the *Doi Moi* reform process, covering a broad range of economic policies—to move from a centrally planned economy to one more market-oriented. During this transition, bilateral and multilateral donors both supported infrastructure development and the social sectors such as health, education, and rural development (Figure 14.6). Physical infrastructure helped develop a wide range of manufacturing and improved linkages to global and regional supply chains. Ensuing strong economic growth led Viet Nam to middle-income status in 2009.

Large amounts of bilateral and multilateral development finance were combined with advice for reform policies and capacity building. The ROK is an important ODA provider to Viet Nam. Since 1993, it has provided $2.7 billion for Viet Nam for about 60 projects in priority areas such as transport and energy infrastructure,

[17] Taslim, M. A. 2008. Governance, Policies and Economic Growth in Bangladesh. In Islam, N., and M. Asaduzzaman, eds. *A Ship Adrift: Governance and Development in Bangladesh.* Dhaka: Bangladesh Institute of Development Studies.
[18] Sawada, Y., M. Mahmud, and N. Kitano, eds. 2018. *Economic and Social Development of Bangladesh: Miracle and Challenges.* London: Palgrave Macmillan.
[19] Quibria, M. G., and S. Ahmad. 2007. Aid Effectiveness in Bangladesh. *MPRA Paper.* No. 10299. Munich: Munich Personal RePEc Archive.

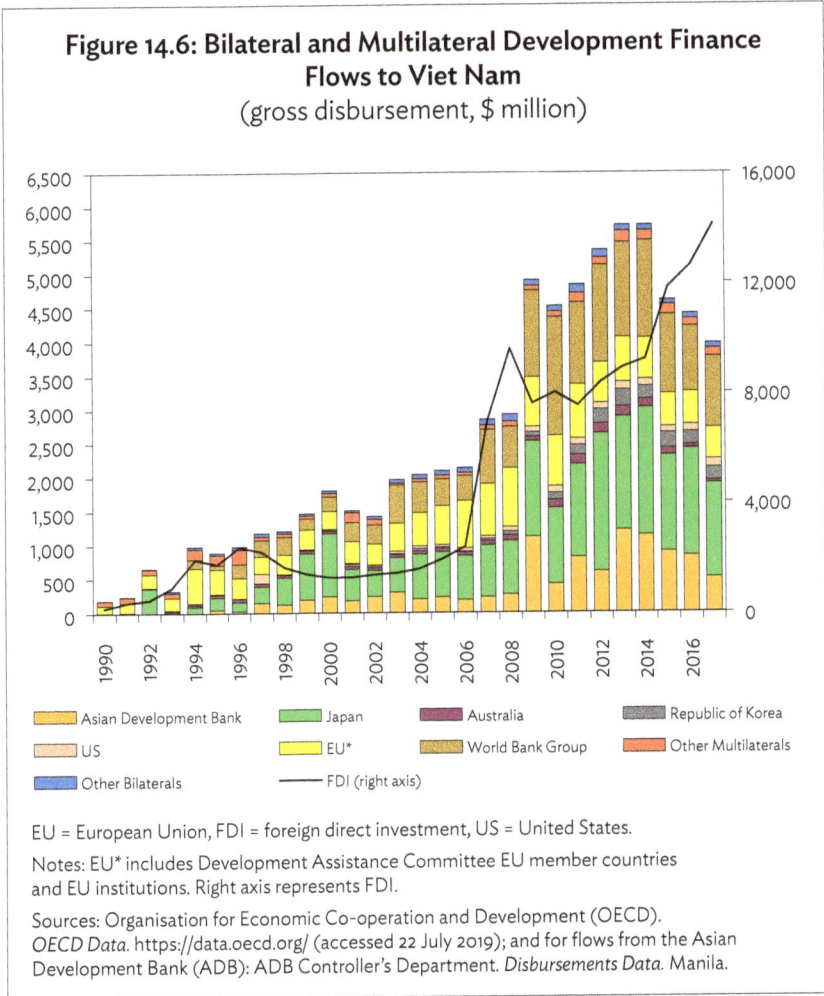

Figure 14.6: Bilateral and Multilateral Development Finance Flows to Viet Nam
(gross disbursement, $ million)

EU = European Union, FDI = foreign direct investment, US = United States.

Notes: EU* includes Development Assistance Committee EU member countries and EU institutions. Right axis represents FDI.

Sources: Organisation for Economic Co-operation and Development (OECD). *OECD Data.* https://data.oecd.org/ (accessed 22 July 2019); and for flows from the Asian Development Bank (ADB): ADB Controller's Department. *Disbursements Data.* Manila.

health, water supply, and drainage.[20] These ODA projects met both Viet Nam's development needs and matched sectors where the ROK is strong. Korean partners work directly with their Vietnamese counterparts to share technical knowledge and implementation experience to strengthen local capacity.[21]

---

[20] Government of Viet Nam, Ministry of Planning and Investment. 2017. *Thúc đẩy giải ngân vốn ODA và vốn vay ưu đãi.* [in Vietnamese]. http://www.mpi.gov.vn/Pages/tinbai .aspx?idTin=37705&idcm=188.

[21] Stallings, B., and E. M. Kim. 2017. *Promoting Development: The Political Economy of East Asia Foreign Aid.* Singapore: Palgrave Macmillan.

Through ODA support, the ROK also assists Viet Nam in structuring public–private partnership finance for infrastructure projects with ROK private companies. Viet Nam is an important production base and network for a wide range of East Asian multinational firms such as Canon, LG, Panasonic, and Samsung. ODA-supported investments in constructing various sections of the North–South and East–West corridors benefit both Viet Nam and its subregional neighbors. Infrastructure connectivity increased mobility and lowered transportation costs, strengthening regional integration.

Central Asia

Since the 1990s, the Central Asia and South Caucasus region has begun a drastic transition from central planning to market-based systems. Bilateral and multilateral development partners provided technical assistance on policy analysis and capacity building, including price liberalization and reforming state-owned enterprises. They also provided special financial assistance to ensure imports of essential goods and help mitigate the adverse impacts from the sudden disruption of trade and financial flows after the breakup of the Soviet Union. By the end of the 1990s, the World Bank, ADB, the European Bank for Reconstruction and Development, and bilateral ODA partners started financing development priorities such as infrastructure, human capital, agriculture and rural development, the financial sector, and social protection.

A main barrier to development in Central Asia was the shortage of connectivity between neighboring countries and beyond. The ADB-led Central Asia Regional Economic Cooperation (CAREC) Program was formally established in 2001 to enhance cooperation and connectivity between members (Chapter 15). The program provides financing for cross-border energy and transport infrastructure, and trade facilitation such as customs. It is now expanding its scope under a new long-term strategic framework, CAREC 2030, by including economic and financial stability, environment, agriculture and water, tourism, and regional human capital development.

The Pacific

Small Pacific island countries face a set of development challenges very different from those of other countries in developing Asia. Pacific nations are particularly vulnerable because of their small populations, geographical isolation and dispersion, exposure to shocks such as natural hazards, climate change, and abrupt fluctuations in food and fuel prices. High production and transportation costs severely limit private sector development along with the potential for export-led growth and resulting job creation. They also lack sufficient resources to produce and deliver a wide range of public services.

In the Pacific, bilateral partners such as Australia and New Zealand and multilateral agencies such as ADB and the World Bank provide assistance tailored to Pacific island country needs. Assistance supports building infrastructure and improving education, health, and small and medium-sized enterprise finance to foster inclusive growth. Development partners help countries take advantage of technologies, such as digital connectivity, to encourage private sector activity and promote women's participation in the workforce. They also prioritize disaster risk management and adaptation to climate change. Australia and New Zealand have seasonal worker schemes in the Pacific that both help address employment challenges in the island countries and alleviate labor shortages in the two host countries.[22]

14.5 Experiences of Asian official development assistance providers

As providers, Japan and the ROK share some common characteristics of emphasizing economic infrastructure, supportive concessional loans, and the idea of self-reliance. These principally reflect their experience in using external development finance to support their own economic development. Australia and New Zealand have become important ODA providers and use grants to support Pacific island countries, especially in social and private sector development. Emerging donors in Asia are also becoming important providers of official development finance to other Asian countries.

---

[22] ADB and International Labour Organization (ILO). 2017. *Improving Labour Market Outcomes in the Pacific: Policy Challenges and Priorities*. Suva: ILO. https://www.adb.org/sites/default/files/publication/409216/improving-labour-market-outcomes-pacific.pdf.

Japan

Historically, Japan's development assistance can be divided into three eras. The first ran from the mid-1950s to the mid-1970s. During the postwar period, Japan started reparations and joined the Colombo Plan in 1954. Even prior to this, it provided technical assistance under the Third Country Training (3CT) Program sponsored by the US International Cooperation Administration (ICA) for Southeast Asian countries in the 1950s. Through this technical assistance program, Japanese experts were sent to developing countries and trainees were brought to Japan.

Through the 1960s, Japan used a four-pillar system of developing country assistance—grant aid, concessional loans, technical assistance, and contributions to international organizations. During this period, Japan established aid delivery institutions such as the Overseas Economic Cooperation Fund (OECF) (formed in 1961) to manage ODA loans (yen credit). In 1964, Japan joined the OECD DAC. The Japan International Cooperation Agency (JICA) was established for technical assistance and grant operations in 1974, succeeding the Overseas Technical Cooperation Agency.

The second era spanned from the mid-1970s to the 1980s. Japan's economic vitality in the 1980s and the yen appreciation following the 1985 Plaza Accord led to consecutive plans that aimed to double the volume of ODA (for instance, in 3 years from 1978). The idea was to support Asia's industrialization, trade, and overall economic development using aid, trade, and FDI—functioning as a comprehensive economic cooperation package. The large growth of Japanese ODA by the 1990s was supported by three underlying factors: (i) Japan's strong economic growth and healthy fiscal position, (ii) large current account surpluses, and (iii) the idea of contributing to the international community under its pacifist constitution.

The third era began in the 1990s. The first ODA Charter in 1992 clarified Japan's policy more clearly, highlighting, among others, its geographical focus on Asia, the dual targets of environmental and economic development, tackling global issues, basic human needs, infrastructure development, and the principle of self-help. Since the early 1990s, Japan's position on ODA has changed. First, the economy entered a period of long-term tepid growth with a significantly deteriorated fiscal position. Second, the prospect of very large current account surpluses had diminished. And third, Japan felt it should enhance contributions to the international community through activities such as peacekeeping.

These changes, plus evolving global thinking on aid, shifted Japan's ODA policy in 2003 from increasing the quantity of assistance to ensuring its effectiveness and cooperation with the international aid community. Its revised ODA Charter incorporated human security as a core principle, setting poverty reduction and sustainable growth and tackling global issues as main objectives. It emphasized the need for evaluation, coherence, aid effectiveness, governance, and alignment with recipient country strategies.[23] In 2015, Japan's new Development Cooperation Charter emphasized the need to enhance synergies for development by strengthening collaboration with development partners including NGOs and the private sector.[24]

Australia

Australia's official aid work began before World War II in Papua New Guinea (which was a mandate territory under the League of Nations framework and a UN trust territory until 1975). Australian aid increased rapidly after World War II. Australia made significant contributions to UN agencies and the World Bank and provided bilateral aid, especially for supporting Pacific island countries. Australia was an ADB founding member and is today its fifth-largest shareholder in OCR and third-largest contributor to concessional resources.

In 1951, Australia helped found the Colombo Plan, which provided about 40,000 scholarships over 35 years to students from developing countries for academic degree programs at Australian educational institutions. It began to institutionalize aid delivery starting with the Australian Development Assistance Agency (ADAA) in 1974. In 2013, Australia integrated ADAA's successor, the Australian Agency for International Development (AusAID), into the Department of Foreign Affairs and Trade (DFAT) to more closely align aid with diplomacy.

---

[23] Akiyama, T., and T. Nakao. 2005. Japanese ODA Adapting to the Issues and Challenges of the New Aid Environment. *FASID Discussion Paper on Development Assistance*. No. 8. Tokyo: Foundation for Advanced Studies on International Development.

[24] Kato, H. 2016. Japan's ODA 1954–2014: Changes and Continuities in a Central Instrument in Japan's Foreign Policy. In Shimomura, Y., J. Page, and H. Kato, eds. *Japan's Development Assistance: Foreign Aid and the Post-2015 Agenda*. London: Palgrave Macmillan.

From 2004, Australia's aid budget grew significantly as part of a bipartisan effort to substantially increase Australia's contribution to international development. By 2014, it had become the second-largest bilateral donor to East Asia and the Pacific. Papua New Guinea and Indonesia are the largest recipients of Australian aid, followed by Solomon Islands.

New Zealand

New Zealand has a tradition of progressive ideas, symbolized by being the first to allow women's suffrage to the national legislature in 1893 (when it was a self-governing British colony). Since the 1960s, official aid has mostly provided budget support for newly independent states, especially in the Pacific. In the 1970s and 1980s, the New Zealand official assistance program started providing project aid and humanitarian support. Like Australia, scholarships to developing country students were an important element of New Zealand's aid program.

In recent years, New Zealand aid has become more focused on helping countries achieve sustainable development and reduce poverty. Strategic focus is a key feature. In 2017, its ODA budget was about NZ$615 million.[25] Climate change, renewable energy, agribusiness, private sector development, gender equality, and capacity building are among its priorities.

Geographically, New Zealand focuses its ODA on the Pacific island countries, with the Pacific receiving 60% of New Zealand's annual ODA budget. Modalities of ODA support in the Pacific evolved to include budget support, project investments in areas where New Zealand has comparative strength, and long-term institutional building for Pacific island-states. New Zealand works closely with MDBs such as ADB and the World Bank, and other bilateral agencies. In 1965, New Zealand hosted the United Nations Economic Commission for Asia and the Far East (ECAFE) meeting that passed the resolution supporting the creation of ADB. New Zealand became a founding member the following year.

---

[25] Government of New Zealand, Ministry of Foreign Affairs and Trade. *Aid & Development*. https://www.mfat.govt.nz/en/aid-and-development/our-approach-to-aid/.

Republic of Korea

While the ROK had early experience hosting technical training for other developing countries, its economic assistance broadened in the 1980s to include sending out ROK volunteers and providing concessional loans. In the 1990s, the current structure of its ODA system began to take shape. In 1991, the Korea International Cooperation Agency (KOICA) was established to provide grant assistance. The Korea Eximbank (established in 1987) operates and administers the Economic Development Cooperation Fund (EDCF). The ROK joined the OECD in 1996.

In 2004, the ROK launched a policy-oriented development cooperation program called the Knowledge Sharing Program (KSP) which supports developing countries by sharing its development experience. A good example is the *Saemaul Undong* (New Village Movement) program, the ROK version of community-driven development with a strong emphasis on intervillage competition and intra-village resource mobilization.

After joining the OECD DAC in 2010, the ROK hosted the Fourth High-Level Forum on Aid Effectiveness in Busan in 2011, which culminated in adopting the Busan Partnership for Effective Development Co-operation. The meeting was the most inclusive forum ever on aid effectiveness. It formally acknowledged the important roles of emerging donors.

The ROK also actively cooperates with multilateral development institutions. In 2006, it established the e-Asia and Knowledge Partnership Fund at ADB in response to the widening "digital divide" in developing member countries and to support capacity building and knowledge sharing. In Myanmar and Uzbekistan, for example, the fund developed an information and communication technology (ICT) strategy and priority action plans for e-government and public institutions. In Bhutan and the Kyrgyz Republic, the fund helped ICT-supported tax administration and revenue management information systems.

Emerging donors in Asia

Aside from the traditional bilateral donors, emerging donors in Asia include the PRC, India, and Thailand, which are increasingly active in providing development finance to other Asian countries.

The PRC sees South–South cooperation as an important external policy. It supports developing countries in Asia and beyond, based on its own development experience. It provides foreign aid in the form of grants and concessional loans, and through the Export–Import Bank of China and China Development Bank, preferential export buyer credits and other forms of finance. The PRC took the initiative of founding the AIIB, which began operations in early 2016.

India's development cooperation consists of Exim Bank lines of credit, grant assistance, small development projects, technical consultancy, disaster relief and humanitarian aid, and capacity-building programs.

Thailand also provides aid, especially to developing neighboring countries through the Thailand International Development Cooperation Agency and Neighboring Countries Economic Development Cooperation Agency.

Many other emerging Asian economies (Brunei Darussalam; Hong Kong, China; Indonesia; Kazakhstan; Malaysia; Singapore; and Taipei,China) are now becoming donors for a wide range of countries in Asia and beyond. Together with the PRC, India, the ROK, and Thailand, these economies are now contributing to the ADB concessional window—Asian Development Fund (which currently provides grant support to the lowest-income ADB members, as concessional lending was merged into OCR at the start of 2017).

While statistics on official development finance from these emerging donors are not listed in the OECD ODA reporting system (except Thailand, which reports to the DAC as a non-OECD and non-DAC country), the importance of official financing by these emerging donors has increased and is continuing to grow.

14.6 Looking ahead

In Asia, several countries graduated from ODA and assistance from MDBs, but many will still need assistance in the years ahead. Bilateral and multilateral financing partners and recipient countries must work together, focusing on the following priorities.

First, more effort is needed to address remaining and emerging challenges—including persistent poverty, increasing inequality, climate change mitigation and adaptation, disaster resilience as well as environmental sustainability, gender equality, rapid urbanization, demographic aging, rural development, and food security. Working within global agendas, such as the Sustainable Development Goals and the Paris Agreement on climate change adopted at the 21st Conference of the Parties (COP21) to the UN Framework Convention on Climate Change, is critical.

Second, quality infrastructure should be promoted using new technologies. The "Quality Infrastructure Principles" adopted by the Group of Twenty (G20) Summit in Osaka in 2019 emphasizes the importance of incorporating advanced technologies and know-how, paying attention to infrastructure maintenance and life-cycle costs, integrating environmental and social considerations, building resilience against natural hazards, and strengthening governance for debt sustainability and transparency.

Third, developing country support should pursue policy and institutional reform. Policy-based MDB financing instruments have proven effective in supporting policy reform. Technical assistance and capacity building can support project preparation; public sector management; climate action; and areas such as foreign exchange reserve management, environmental law, anti-money laundering, and legal frameworks for gender equality.

Fourth, continued attention must be given to aid effectiveness. It is necessary to enhance coordination and cooperation among recipient countries, bilateral donors, the IMF, and MDBs, including new institutions such as AIIB and the NDB. Ensuring debt sustainability should be part of this coordinated work. It is critical to closely monitor a country's debt situation and avoid excessive lending beyond its repayment capacity.

Fifth, private sector resources must be mobilized for development finance. In addition to infrastructure such as highways, water, and renewable energy, the private sector can support education, health, small and medium-sized enterprise finance, and agribusiness. MDBs should help crowd-in private sector development finance by improving the investment climate, identifying bankable projects, and advising on well-designed public–private partnerships.

CHAPTER 15

STRENGTHENING REGIONAL COOPERATION AND INTEGRATION IN ASIA

15.1 Introduction

Regional cooperation and integration (RCI) refers to policies and initiatives of countries in a region to engage in close economic cooperation and promote the integration of their economies, especially through trade and investment. RCI has played an important role in supporting Asian development over the past half century. It contributed to the region's peace and stability, promoted intraregional trade and investment, and supported the provision of regional public goods— in particular, controlling transboundary environmental pollution (for example, in rivers and the haze), combating communicable disease, and preventing financial contagion.

RCI in developing Asia has evolved significantly since World War II in terms of country coverage and the scope of cooperation. It was initially motivated by the need to ensure peace and security after years of war and conflict in the region, and to move beyond former colonial links. It was also influenced by the United Nations (UN), initially through the establishment of the Economic Commission for Asia and the Far East (ECAFE) in 1947.

Over time, RCI became homegrown and expanded to more areas, including research, education, and capacity development; development financing; trade and investment; money and finance; and responding to common regional challenges. The Asian Development Bank (ADB) continues to promote RCI across many subregions.

This chapter discusses the institutional evolution of RCI in Asia and the Pacific. Section 15.2 looks at the key motivating factors. Section 15.3 traces the changing drivers that influenced RCI's evolution in East Asia and Southeast Asia—the subregions that benefited most thus far from regional cooperation and market-driven integration. It shows how the Association of Southeast Asian Nations (ASEAN) emerged as a successful example of RCI. Section 15.4 discusses RCI across different subregions. Section 15.5 discusses the establishment of ADB as a prime example of RCI. Finally, section 15.6 highlights the future of RCI, including megaregional free trade agreements (FTAs) consistent with the region's brand of "open regionalism," and addressing the challenges of inclusive and sustainable development.

15.2 Why regional cooperation and integration?

RCI, together with private-sector, market-led actions, promotes integration among economies in trade, investment, finance, and other areas. There are different motivations and reasons for countries to undertake RCI in Asia and the Pacific.

First, RCI can contribute to peace and stability, creating an environment of mutual trust that allows countries to deepen economic cooperation and interdependence. Looking back, the 1950s–1970s was an era characterized by tensions between countries. As a result, they sought security cooperation with neighboring countries. In addition, some countries sought to promote the Non-Aligned Movement, which contributed to binding ties among 120 developing countries within the Asian region and beyond.

Regional groupings such as ASEAN, which was established in 1967, had their original motivation based on concerns over security. As political stability took root, security gradually took second place to economic cooperation. For ASEAN, this evolution was seen in the creation of the ASEAN Preferential Trading Arrangements in 1977 and the ASEAN Free Trade Agreement in 1992. ASEAN played a critical role in nurturing mutual trust at the time Cambodia, the Lao People's Democratic Republic, Myanmar, and Viet Nam began market-oriented reforms.

Second, RCI enhances cross-border economic opportunities. It can provide a wide range of opportunities to increase trade and investment by helping lower tariff barriers and removing obstacles to free trade, promoting open investment regimes, and fostering infrastructure connectivity between countries.

The resulting regional integration allows countries to exploit economies of scale by expanding markets for their goods and services. It can better allocate resources as inputs are sourced beyond national boundaries, leading to cost reductions and the introduction of new products. It also enables technology and skills transfers. This facilitates the narrowing of development gaps between countries in the Asia and Pacific region and participation in regional and global value chains for some parts of the region.

RCI also allows countries to cooperate to mitigate macroeconomic and financial risks through regional policy dialogue and mechanisms that enhance financial stability. This became evident in East Asian and Southeast Asian countries after the 1997–1998 Asian financial crisis and the 2008–2009 global financial crisis.

In addition, RCI offers a forum, through peer influence, to promote good policies on prudent macroeconomic management, open trade and investment regimes, sound financial regulations, environmental protection, and stronger governance and institutions.

Third, RCI provides for regional public goods. Increasingly, the region's economies are vulnerable to a range of new cross-border risks arising from health and environmental issues such as the spread of communicable disease, transboundary pollution, and natural disasters triggered by cross-border natural hazards. Many of these issues need to be addressed not only nationally and globally, but also regionally. RCI can support collective action on climate change mitigation and adaptation.

RCI is also needed to combat illegal cross-border activities such as drug trafficking and money laundering by coordinating laws, policies, regulations, standards, and/or institutional mechanisms. These issues require collective effort because of the possible large harmful spillovers these illegal activities can have on neighboring countries.

Fourth, RCI can be a platform for a stronger Asian voice. Asia's contribution to the global economy is increasing, and more Asian countries are participating in global forums such as the Group of

Twenty (G20).[1] It is necessary to represent the region's views in global discussions on macroeconomic policies, coordination on taxation, financial regulations on banks and securities, and global agendas such as the Sustainable Development Goals and climate change.

For Asia to be effectively represented in global forums as well as to ensure Asian views influence the global agenda, there is a need for closer regional dialogue to understand how global issues affect the countries in the region and how Asia can contribute to setting the global agenda and pursuing it.

Finally, some regional forums provide platforms to draw in countries from outside the region. For instance, ASEAN provided impetus for the establishment of the Asia-Pacific Economic Cooperation (APEC) in 1989, and the basis for ASEAN+3—ASEAN plus the People's Republic of China (PRC), Japan, and the Republic of Korea (ROK)— in the late 1990s after the Asian financial crisis, and for ASEAN+6 (including Australia, India, and New Zealand) more recently.

In addition, ASEAN facilitated the establishment in 1994 of the ASEAN Regional Forum, which fosters dialogue and consultation on peace and security with countries far beyond ASEAN, including many countries in Asia and the Pacific (such as the Democratic People's Republic of Korea), Canada, the European Union, the Russian Federation, and the United States (US). In all these initiatives, the ASEAN Plus framework provides the anchor for cohesive cooperation.

15.3 Early movers of regional cooperation and integration in East Asia and Southeast Asia

Asia and the Pacific saw many forms of RCI after World War II. At the time, most Asian countries were trying to rebuild after the devastation of war. The UN ECAFE was established in 1947 to provide research and advice on economic issues faced by the region's developing countries. It was later renamed the Economic and Social Commission for Asia and the Pacific (ESCAP), broadening its focus to social issues such as labor and human development.[2]

---

[1] Six countries from the region are G20 members—Australia, India, Indonesia, Japan, the PRC, and the ROK.
[2] United Nations Economic and Social Commission for Asia and the Pacific. 2014. *Asia and the Pacific: A Story of Transformation and Resurgence*. Bangkok.

In 1950, the Colombo Plan for Cooperative Economic Development in South and Southeast Asia[3] was established as the region's first multilateral initiative to provide finance for development. It was designed as a cooperative venture, channeling bilateral capital and technical assistance from developed countries (including Australia, Japan, the United Kingdom, and the United States) to countries in South Asia and Southeast Asia.[4]

Newly independent states in the region also sought to develop their economies beyond their colonial ties, building national identities and aspirations, and forging cooperation with other developing regions in the world—such as Africa and Latin America. These were central themes in some Asian conferences organized by developing countries in the early years.[5]

The most prominent was the 1955 Asian–African Conference in Bandung, Indonesia. The Bandung Conference was a high-water mark in propounding the notion of the "Third World" and the "South." During the conference, Asian and African leaders enunciated the principles of cooperation, self-determination, mutual respect for sovereignty, nonaggression, noninterference in internal affairs, and equality.[6] These principles paved the way for developing countries in Asia to establish the Non-Aligned Movement in 1961.[7]

In 1954, some countries in Southeast Asia and Pakistan, along with Australia, France, the United Kingdom, and the US, created a regional collective security organization, the Southeast Asia Treaty Organization (SEATO), to address the expanding communist influence in the region. However, SEATO had limited active support from the region and was dissolved in 1977.

---

[3] Later renamed as Colombo Plan for Cooperative Economic and Social Development in Asia and the Pacific.
[4] Oakman, D. 2004. *Facing Asia. A History of the Colombo Plan*. Canberra: The Australian National University Press.
[5] Acharya, A. 2005. Why Is There No NATO in Asia? The Normative Origins of Asian Multilateralism. *Weatherhead Center for International Affairs Working Paper Series*. No. 05-05. Cambridge, MA: Harvard University.
[6] CVCE.eu. *Final Communiqué of the Asian–African Conference of Bandung Signed on 24 April 1955*. http://franke.uchicago.edu/Final_Communique_Bandung_1955.pdf.
[7] Timossi, A. J. 2015. Revisiting the 1955 Bandung Asian–African Conference and Its Legacy. *South Bulletin*. 85. 15 May. Geneva: South Centre. https://www.southcentre.int/question/revisiting-the-1955-bandung-asian-african-conference-and-its-legacy/.

Other efforts such as the Association of Southeast Asia in 1961 and Maphilindo (Malaysia, the Philippines, and Indonesia) in 1963 were short-lived, primarily due to political tensions between members.[8] However, these efforts led to the creation of ASEAN in 1967. ASEAN's establishment was successful because of its strict adherence to noninterference and its adoption of informal and consensus-oriented cooperation (Box 15.1).

Box 15.1: The Successful Evolution of ASEAN into the ASEAN Economic Community

The Association of Southeast Asian Nations (ASEAN) was established in 1967 by five countries—Indonesia, Malaysia, the Philippines, Singapore, and Thailand—to overcome conflict in the Southeast Asian region. Its form of regional cooperation was based on informality, consensus building, and nonconfrontational bargaining.

During its first decade, ASEAN's agenda was dominated by political and security issues with the backdrop of the Cold War. As peace and stability were nurtured gradually, greater trust between countries facilitated economic cooperation.[a] This was embodied in the ASEAN Concord, agreed at ASEAN's first Leaders' Summit in Bali in 1976. The ASEAN Concord started cooperation on basic commodities, particularly food and energy, and industrial production in the form of technical cooperation and preferential trading arrangements.[b] It became the harbinger for subsequent agreements such as the ASEAN Preferential Trading Arrangements in 1977, ASEAN Free Trade Area (AFTA) in 1992, ASEAN Framework Agreement on Services in 1995, and ASEAN Investment Area in 1998.

Together with unilateral country policies to liberalize trade and investment, AFTA and ASEAN's other trade and investment frameworks attracted foreign direct investment and knowledge transfer, and fostered emerging regional production networks. Data show that after AFTA's creation, United States multinational activity in the subregion increased faster than in other Asian countries.[c]

continued on next page

---

[8] Acharya, A. 2014. Foundations of Collective Action in Asia: Theory and Practice of Regional Cooperation. In Capannelli, G., and M. Kawai, eds. *The Political Economy of Asian Regionalism*. Tokyo: Asian Development Bank Institute and Springer.

Box 15.1 *continued*

In 2003, ASEAN leaders agreed to establish the ASEAN Economic Community to consolidate ASEAN as a single market and production base and allow it to become more globally competitive. The ASEAN Economic Community was formally launched in 2015. It entails further economic liberalization; labor mobility; and the promotion of connectivity in transport, energy, and information and communication technology. It also aims at narrowing the development gap between members and strengthening ASEAN's relationship externally. To address financing gaps in building needed infrastructure, the ASEAN Infrastructure Fund was established in 2011 with equity investments from ASEAN members and the Asian Development Bank.

ASEAN's steadfast support for open regionalism in trade and investment is embodied in its ASEAN Plus framework. It has been central in wider regional initiatives such as ASEAN+3 (for monetary and financial cooperation) and the proposed megaregional ASEAN+6 free trade agreement—the Regional Comprehensive Economic Partnership (RCEP).[d]

[a] Acharya, A. 2014. Foundations of Collective Action in Asia: Theory and Practice of Regional Cooperation. In Capannelli, G., and M. Kawai, eds. *The Political Economy of Asian Regionalism.* Tokyo: Asian Development Bank Institute and Springer.

[b] ASEAN. The Declaration of ASEAN Concord. Bali, Indonesia. 24 February 1976. https://asean.org/?static_post=declaration-of-asean-concord-indonesia-24-february-1976.

[c] Antras, P., and C. Foley. 2011. Regional Trade Integration and Multinational Firm Strategies. In Barro, R., and J.-W. Lee, eds. *Costs and Benefits of Economic Integration in Asia.* Oxford and New York: Oxford University Press and Asian Development Bank (ADB).

[d] ASEAN+6 comprises ASEAN+3, Australia, India, and New Zealand.

Sources: McCawley, P. 2017. *Banking on the Future of Asia and the Pacific: 50 Years of the Asian Development Bank.* Box 12.3. Manila: ADB; ADB website. https://www.adb.org; and Central Asia Regional Economic Cooperation Program. https://www.carecprogram.org.

Technical and research institutions in the region were established to cater to specific priority areas—the Asian Institute of Technology in Thailand (1959) for technology, the International Rice Research Institute in the Philippines (1960) for agriculture, the Asian Productivity Organization in Japan (1961) for productivity, and the Asian Institute of Management in the Philippines (1968) for executive education.

Trade liberalization started gaining traction in the 1970s and 1980s. The spread of an open market environment, combined with declining transport costs for outsourced production, attracted multinational companies to locate to East Asia and Southeast Asia. Against the backdrop of slow-moving negotiations on the General

Agreement on Tariffs and Trade, APEC was created in 1989.[9] Leaders saw APEC as a useful informal group for supporting the General Agreement on Tariffs and Trade Uruguay Round, which was concluded in 1994.

The 1997–1998 Asian financial crisis was a turning point for East Asian and Southeast Asian regionalism. It led to further regional cooperation on monetary and financial issues, spurring innovative mechanisms built on previous initiatives such as the ASEAN Swap Arrangement.[10] ASEAN+3 developed several initiatives to strengthen resilience against financial instability, such as the Chiang Mai Initiative (2000) as a network of currency swap arrangements and the Asian Bond Markets Initiative (2002) to promote long-term financing within the region.

Asian countries weathered the 2008–2009 global financial crisis better than most because they pursued prudent macroeconomic policies, implemented comprehensive structural and financial sector reforms, and increased their foreign reserves after the Asian financial crisis. To collectively strengthen their preparedness for future crises, ASEAN+3 launched the Chiang Mai Initiative Multilateralization (CMIM) in 2010 (currently $240 billion in size) and the ASEAN+3 Macroeconomic Research Office in 2011 to monitor CMIM economies, support implementation of the CMIM, and provide technical assistance to CMIM members (Chapter 10).

15.4 Regional cooperation and integration in other subregions

RCI developed in Asian subregions at different speeds. Those outside East Asia and Southeast Asia faced challenges from their political and economic environments. They lagged behind in terms of their intrasubregional trade shares (Figure 15.1). East Asia and Southeast Asia, after adopting open trade and investment regimes, faced new

---

[9] Founding members were Australia, Brunei Darussalam, Canada, Indonesia, Japan, Malaysia, New Zealand, the Philippines, the ROK, Singapore, Thailand, and the US. Hong Kong, China; the PRC; and Taipei,China joined in 1991. Mexico and Papua New Guinea joined in 1993; Chile acceded in 1994; and Peru, the Russian Federation, and Viet Nam joined in 1998, leaving APEC with its current 21 members.

[10] Central banks and monetary authorities of the original five ASEAN members—Indonesia, Malaysia, the Philippines, Singapore, and Thailand—agreed to establish reciprocal currency or swap arrangements in August 1977. The ASEAN Swap Arrangement was created primarily to provide liquidity support for those with balance of payment problems (see Asia Regional Integration Center. https://aric.adb.org/initiative/asean -swap-arrangement). It was the historical forerunner of the Chiang Mai Initiative and the Chiang Mai Initiative Multilateralization.

Figure 15.1: Intrasubregional Trade Share, 1992–2018
(% of a subregion's total trade)

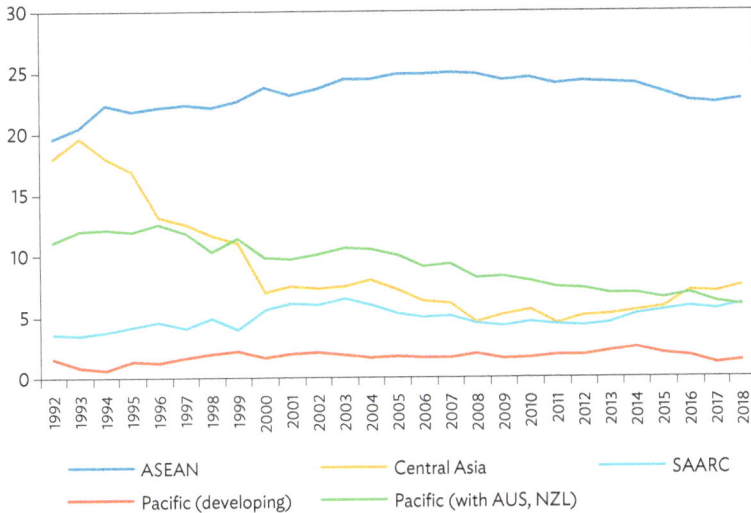

ASEAN = Association of Southeast Asian Nations, AUS = Australia, NZL = New Zealand, SAARC = South Asian Association for Regional Cooperation.

Source: Asian Development Bank calculations using data from International Monetary Fund. *Direction of Trade Statistics.* https://www.imf.org/en/Data (accessed 27 December 2019).

challenges that required a deepening of RCI, particularly in financial cooperation.

In South Asia—which for a long time struggled to secure stability, peace, and security in the subregion—RCI progress was hampered by geopolitical tensions. The South Asian Association for Regional Cooperation (SAARC) was established in 1985.[11] It launched RCI initiatives such as the SAARC Preferential Trading Arrangement (SAPTA) and the Agreement on South Asian Free Trade Area (SAFTA) signed in 1993 and 2004, respectively. However, they have had limited impact on intraregional trade thus far.[12]

Central Asia, following the collapse of the Soviet Union in 1991, began several cooperation arrangements to recover and maintain economic connectivity. The most recent is the Eurasian Economic

[11] Afghanistan, Bangladesh, Bhutan, India, Maldives, Nepal, Pakistan, and Sri Lanka.
[12] Desai, V. V. 2010. The Political Economy of Regional Cooperation in South Asia. *ADB Working Paper Series on Regional Economic Integration.* No. 54. Manila: Asian Development Bank.

Union (2015), which includes a customs union.[13] These arrangements did not include all Central Asian countries, and they represent a work in progress, with full impact on regional integration still to be assessed.

In 1971, the South Pacific Forum was initiated to foster regional cooperation, particularly on trade and economic issues. It became the Pacific Islands Forum in 1999 to denote its membership of both the north and south Pacific island countries.[14]

South Asia, Central Asia, and Pacific subregions need continued efforts to boost RCI.

South Asia needs to deepen connectivity through transport, energy, and trade facilitation. It is also important to pursue broad-based, market-oriented reforms unilaterally and collectively to further integrate the subregion economically, and integrate more with other Asian subregions and the global economy.

Central Asia needs to move beyond basic transport and energy connectivity to develop economic corridors that attract private sector participation and build value chains. To promote inclusive growth, these corridors should allow lagging border and remote areas, agriculture, and small and medium-sized enterprises to participate in private sector-led value chains. Central Asian countries should also expand regional cooperation on economic policy and structural reforms and explore working together on development of financial and capital markets.

While Pacific island countries are challenged by their small size, geographic remoteness, and vulnerability to natural hazards and climate change, RCI can help mitigate and help resolve these challenges. Examples include encouraging maritime and digital connectivity, tackling ocean health and managing shared ocean resources, promoting sustainable tourism, and fostering human capacity development. The University of the South Pacific, owned by 12 Pacific governments, was founded in 1968 and currently operates an online education platform.

---

[13] The Eurasian Economic Union came into force on 1 January 2015 with Armenia, Belarus, Kazakhstan, the Kyrgyz Republic, and the Russian Federation. It incorporates previous treaties covering the Eurasian Customs Union (2010) and the Eurasian Economic Space (2012). Uzbekistan is working toward joining the Eurasian Economic Union.

[14] Membership includes Australia, the Cook Islands, the Federated States of Micronesia, Fiji, Kiribati, the Marshall Islands, Nauru, New Zealand, Niue, Papua New Guinea, Samoa, Solomon Islands, Tonga, Tuvalu, and Vanuatu.

15.5 ADB and its role in regional cooperation and integration

ADB's founding in 1966 was itself an early example of RCI. Countries in Asia and the Pacific wanted an institution that would support Asian development. They also sought to bring in financial resources and know-how from within and outside the region with the help of nonregional members (Chapter 14).

RCI has always been an ADB priority. Its Charter mandates ADB to "foster economic growth and cooperation in the region ... and to contribute to the acceleration of the process of economic development of the developing member countries of the region, collectively and individually."

ADB promotes its RCI agenda through subregional cooperation programs (Box 15.2). The first subregional program, the Greater Mekong Subregion (GMS) Economic Cooperation Program, was established in 1992. This initiative was designed to foster economic linkages after countries launched market-oriented reforms. The GMS Program was followed by the Indonesia–Malaysia–Thailand Growth Triangle (IMT-GT) Program in 1993, and later by the Brunei Darussalam–Indonesia–Malaysia–Philippines East ASEAN Growth Area (BIMP-EAGA) Program in 1994.

In 1997, the Bay of Bengal Initiative for Multi-Sectoral Technical and Economic Cooperation (BIMSTEC) was created to support economic ties between South Asia and Southeast Asia. The Central Asia Regional Economic Cooperation (CAREC) Program was formally launched in 2001 to facilitate trade, transport, and energy linkages following the 1991 breakup of the Soviet Union. In South Asia, the South Asia Subregional Economic Cooperation (SASEC) Program was established in 2001.

15.6 Looking ahead

Asia and the Pacific have adopted RCI frameworks over the years to promote trade, investment, infrastructure connectivity, and regional public goods. These frameworks contributed to the pursuit of good policies and a sense of cooperation between countries.

Looking ahead, there remain many areas where RCI can further deepen and contribute to the welfare of the region and the world at large.

Box 15.2: ADB Subregional Cooperation Programs

Greater Mekong Subregion (GMS) Economic Cooperation Program: In 1992, six countries—Cambodia, the Lao People's Democratic Republic, Myanmar, the People's Republic of China (PRC) (Yunnan Province), Thailand, and Viet Nam—established the GMS Program. The PRC's Guangxi Zhuang Autonomous Region joined the program in 2004. The GMS Program focuses on (i) increasing connectivity through sustainable development of physical infrastructure and economic corridors; (ii) improving competitiveness through efficient facilitation of cross-border movement of people and goods, market integration, and enhancement of value chains; and (iii) building a greater sense of community through shared concerns. The GMS Program pays particular attention to building strategic alliances, especially with the Association of Southeast Asian Nations (ASEAN), ASEAN+3 (ASEAN plus the PRC, Japan, and the Republic of Korea), and the Mekong River Commission.

Indonesia–Malaysia–Thailand Growth Triangle (IMT-GT): The program began in 1993 as a subregional framework for accelerating economic cooperation and integration. The IMT-GT currently covers 14 provinces in southern Thailand, 8 states of Peninsular Malaysia, and 10 provinces of Sumatra in Indonesia. The strategic objectives are to (i) facilitate trade and investment; (ii) promote agriculture, agro-industry, and tourism; (iii) strengthen infrastructure linkages and support IMT-GT integration; (iv) address cross-sector concerns such as human resource development, labor, and the environment; and (v) strengthen institutional arrangements and mechanisms for cooperation.

Brunei Darussalam–Indonesia–Malaysia–Philippines East ASEAN Growth Area (BIMP-EAGA): The BIMP-EAGA Program was launched in 1994 to address subregional development inequality. The program includes Brunei Darussalam; the provinces of Kalimantan, Sulawesi, Maluku, and West Papua in Indonesia; Sabah and Sarawak and the Federal Territory of Labuan in Malaysia; and Mindanao and Palawan Province in the Philippines. The Asian Development Bank has been BIMP-EAGA's regional development advisor since 2001. The program focuses on five strategic pillars: (i) connectivity, (ii) a food "basket," (iii) tourism, (iv) the environment, and (v) sociocultural activities and education. Its long-term goal is to ensure that non-resource-based industries are established in the subregion. BIMP-EAGA cooperation aims to increase trade, tourism, and investment within and outside the subregion, taking advantage of the subregion's resources and existing complementarities.

continued on next page

Box 15.2 *continued*

Central Asia Regional Economic Cooperation (CAREC) Program: CAREC was formally established in 2001 to promote economic cooperation in Central Asian countries. Initial members included Azerbaijan, Kazakhstan, the Kyrgyz Republic, Mongolia, the PRC (the Xinjiang Uygur Autonomous Region; the Inner Mongolia Autonomous Region joined later), Tajikistan, and Uzbekistan. Afghanistan joined in 2005, and Pakistan and Turkmenistan in 2010, enabling a north–south route to the Arabian Sea through Pakistan. Georgia joined in 2016. The program includes a partnership between members and a group of multilateral development partners. ADB serves as CAREC secretariat, operational since 2000. CAREC has focused on transport, energy, trade (both trade facilitation and trade policy), and economic corridor development. The focus is now expanded under the CAREC 2030 strategy, approved in 2017, to include support for economic and financial stability, tourism, agriculture and water, and regional human capital development.

South Asia Subregional Economic Cooperation (SASEC) Program: SASEC was established in 2001 as a project-based initiative that initially promoted economic cooperation by enhancing cross-border connectivity and facilitating trade between Bangladesh, Bhutan, India, and Nepal. Sri Lanka and Maldives joined in 2014, and Myanmar in 2017. Priority areas for cooperation include transport, trade facilitation, energy, and economic corridor development.

Sources: McCawley, P. 2017. *Banking on the Future of Asia and the Pacific: 50 Years of the Asian Development Bank.* Box 12.3. Manila: Asian Development Bank (ADB); ADB website. https://www.adb.org; and CAREC. https://www.carecprogram.org.

First, trade and investment can be further liberalized and trade facilitated through subregional initiatives and multilateral agreements. Streamlining and harmonizing customs border procedures, for example, can ease cross-border flows. The World Trade Organization (WTO) Trade Facilitation Agreement, which came into force in February 2017, was the most recent global multilateral trade agreement. Asia's subregions should continue to work toward implementing such global agreements.

Second, megaregional FTAs that can act as building blocks for the multilateral trading system need to be promoted. The Comprehensive and Progressive Agreement for Trans-Pacific Partnership (CPTPP) and the Regional Comprehensive Economic Partnership (RCEP) (still under negotiation) are examples of this type of FTA. Megaregional FTAs can promote liberalization consistent with WTO principles and simplify complexities from the proliferation of bilateral and regional FTAs by rationalizing rules of origin.

Third, there is a need to complement hard infrastructure with "soft" connectivity institutions to more efficiently use cross-border connectivity, including digital communications. Examples in Central Asia and the GMS include railway associations for cross-border rail safety and gauge coordination, and regional power coordination centers to make cross-border transmission more efficient and boost power trade.

Fourth, greater cooperation is needed in conservation and management of shared natural resources such as rivers, oceans, and forests with large biodiversity. Collective effort is needed to achieve the targets of the 21st Conference of the Parties (COP21) to the UNFCCC. Managing transboundary rivers, as pioneered by the Indus Water Treaty agreed between India and Pakistan in 1960, is critical.

Fifth, greater cooperation is needed in agriculture, including policies, research on seed varieties, and land and water use. In addition, with the increased cross-border flow of agricultural products, cooperation should be strengthened in veterinary services to reduce the spread of contagious disease among animals, and in coordination of food quality and quarantine standards.

Sixth, a greater focus on people is required. Promoting sustainable regional tourism is one priority. Subregional initiatives can share country experiences on policies covering technical and vocational education and training, universal health coverage, and social protection, among others. Along with easing people's mobility across borders for work and tourism, enhanced cooperation on the prevention of contagious diseases, including HIV/AIDS, is also needed.

Finally, Asia's voice on global affairs should be amplified. As the economies of Asia and the Pacific and its populations continue to grow, the region becomes more important in addressing global issues, whether on the environment and climate change, population aging, or trade issues. Its voice should be commensurate with its increased economic importance in the global community.

APPENDIXES

1 Total Population (Midyear)

2 Gross Domestic Product

3 Gross Domestic Product Growth Rates

4 Gross Domestic Product Per Capita

5 Sector Shares in Output

6 Sector Shares in Employment

7 Exports of Goods and Services

8 Imports of Goods and Services

9 Current Account Balance

10 General Government Net Lending/Borrowing

11 Gross Domestic Savings

12 Gross Capital Formation

13 Public Spending on Education

14 Public Spending on Health

15 Poverty Rate

16 Net Enrollment Rate, Primary, Both Sexes

17 Gross Enrollment Ratio, Secondary, Both Sexes

18 Gross Enrollment Ratio, Tertiary, Both Sexes

19 Life Expectancy at Birth

20 Under-Five Mortality Rate (U5MR)

Appendix 1: Total Population (Midyear)
(million)

	1960	1970	1980	1990	2000	2010	2018
Developing Asia	1,524.7	1,924.6	2,381.2	2,898.8	3,363.6	3,775.3	4,082.4
Central Asia	34.1	45.6	55.4	66.3	70.9	78.8	89.0
Armenia	1.9	2.5	3.1	3.5	3.1	2.9	3.0
Azerbaijan	3.9	5.2	6.2	7.2	8.1	9.0	10.0
Georgia	4.0	4.7	5.0	5.4	4.4	4.1	4.0
Kazakhstan	9.9	13.0	14.8	16.4	14.9	16.3	18.3
Kyrgyz Republic	2.2	3.0	3.6	4.4	4.9	5.4	6.3
Tajikistan	2.1	2.9	3.9	5.3	6.2	7.5	9.1
Turkmenistan	1.6	2.2	2.9	3.7	4.5	5.1	5.9
Uzbekistan	8.5	12.1	15.9	20.4	24.8	28.5	32.5
East Asia	700.6	879.8	1,062.6	1,248.2	1,368.9	1,451.2	1,513.1
Hong Kong, China	3.0	3.8	4.9	5.7	6.6	7.0	7.4
Mongolia	1.0	1.3	1.7	2.2	2.4	2.7	3.2
People's Republic of China	660.4	827.6	1,000.1	1,176.9	1,290.6	1,368.8	1,427.6
Republic of Korea	25.3	32.2	38.0	42.9	47.4	49.5	51.2
Taipei,China	10.9	14.9	17.9	20.5	22.0	23.2	23.7
South Asia	572.8	713.7	900.6	1,133.5	1,390.9	1,638.8	1,814.0
Afghanistan	9.0	11.2	13.4	12.4	20.8	29.2	37.2
Bangladesh	48.0	64.2	79.6	103.2	127.7	147.6	161.4
Bhutan	0.2	0.3	0.4	0.5	0.6	0.7	0.8
India	450.5	555.2	699.0	873.3	1,056.6	1,234.3	1,352.6
Maldives	0.1	0.1	0.2	0.2	0.3	0.4	0.5
Nepal	10.1	12.1	15.0	18.9	23.9	27.0	28.1
Pakistan	45.0	58.1	78.1	107.6	142.3	179.4	212.2
Sri Lanka	9.9	12.5	15.0	17.3	18.8	20.3	21.2
Southeast Asia	213.5	280.8	357.0	443.7	524.1	595.9	654.0
Brunei Darussalam	0.1	0.1	0.2	0.3	0.3	0.4	0.4
Cambodia	5.7	7.0	6.7	9.0	12.2	14.3	16.3
Indonesia	87.8	114.8	147.4	181.4	211.5	241.8	267.7
Lao PDR	2.1	2.7	3.3	4.3	5.3	6.2	7.1
Malaysia	8.2	10.8	13.8	18.0	23.2	28.2	31.5
Myanmar	21.7	27.3	34.2	41.3	46.7	50.6	53.7
Philippines	26.3	35.8	47.4	61.9	78.0	94.0	106.7
Singapore	1.6	2.1	2.4	3.0	4.0	5.1	5.8
Thailand	27.4	36.9	47.4	56.6	63.0	67.2	69.4
Viet Nam	32.7	43.4	54.3	68.0	79.9	88.0	95.5

continued on next page

Appendix 1 *continued*

	1960	1970	1980	1990	2000	2010	2018
The Pacific	3.6	4.5	5.6	7.1	8.7	10.6	12.4
Cook Islands	0.0	0.0	0.0	0.0	0.0	0.0	0.0
Federated States of Micronesia	0.0	0.1	0.1	0.1	0.1	0.1	0.1
Fiji	0.4	0.5	0.6	0.7	0.8	0.9	0.9
Kiribati	0.0	0.1	0.1	0.1	0.1	0.1	0.1
Marshall Islands	0.0	0.0	0.0	0.0	0.1	0.1	0.1
Nauru	0.0	0.0	0.0	0.0	0.0	0.0	0.0
Niue	0.0	0.0	0.0	0.0	0.0	0.0	0.0
Palau	0.0	0.0	0.0	0.0	0.0	0.0	0.0
Papua New Guinea	2.3	2.8	3.6	4.6	5.8	7.3	8.6
Samoa	0.1	0.1	0.2	0.2	0.2	0.2	0.2
Solomon Islands	0.1	0.2	0.2	0.3	0.4	0.5	0.7
Timor-Leste	0.5	0.6	0.6	0.7	0.9	1.1	1.3
Tonga	0.1	0.1	0.1	0.1	0.1	0.1	0.1
Tuvalu	0.0	0.0	0.0	0.0	0.0	0.0	0.0
Vanuatu	0.1	0.1	0.1	0.1	0.2	0.2	0.3
Developed Asia	106.3	120.5	135.6	144.9	150.4	155.1	156.8
Australia	10.2	12.8	14.6	17.0	19.0	22.2	24.9
Japan	93.7	104.9	117.8	124.5	127.5	128.5	127.2
New Zealand	2.4	2.8	3.1	3.4	3.9	4.4	4.7
Asia and the Pacific	1,631.0	2,045.1	2,516.8	3,043.7	3,514.0	3,930.4	4,239.3
Latin America and the Caribbean	219.9	286.0	360.6	442.0	521.0	590.3	641.4
Middle East and North Africa	105.2	138.5	184.6	254.2	315.3	385.9	448.9
Sub-Saharan Africa	227.2	290.5	383.2	509.5	665.3	869.0	1,078.3
OECD	791.3	895.6	989.6	1,071.0	1,157.2	1,242.3	1,303.5
World	3,035.0	3,700.4	4,458.0	5,327.2	6,143.5	6,956.8	7,631.1

0.0 = magnitude is less than half of unit employed, GDP = gross domestic product, Lao PDR = Lao People's Democratic Republic, OECD = Organisation for Economic Co-operation and Development.

Sources: United Nations, Department of Economic and Social Affairs, Population Division. 2019. *World Population Prospects 2019*. Online Edition. https://population.un.org/wpp/ (accessed 23 August 2019); and Asian Development Bank estimates.

Appendix 2: Gross Domestic Product
(constant 2010 US dollars, million)

	1960	1970	1980	1990	2000	2010	2018
Developing Asia	471,881	803,588	1,442,595	3,055,580	5,838,904	12,232,653	19,850,594
Central Asia	...	9,783	17,548	188,056	127,555	294,201	419,271
Armenia	...	...		6,358	4,311	9,260	13,008
Azerbaijan	...	...		22,673	13,351	52,903	57,357
Georgia	...	9,783	17,548	16,879	6,331	11,639	16,675
Kazakhstan	...	...		96,294	66,851	148,047	204,067
Kyrgyz Republic	...	...		4,812	3,205	4,794	6,867
Tajikistan	...	...		6,781	2,583	5,642	9,765
Turkmenistan	...	...		13,680	10,754	22,583	44,747
Uzbekistan	...	...		20,578	20,169	39,333	66,785
East Asia	161,695	294,857	606,405	1,453,905	3,396,579	7,864,302	13,029,721
Hong Kong, China	10,710	22,947	54,314	104,113	153,402	228,638	288,985
Mongolia	...	...	2,497	3,847	3,837	7,189	13,308
People's Republic of China	128,268	187,317	340,606	827,732	2,232,146	6,087,165	10,800,568
Republic of Korea	23,619	58,518	141,052	362,886	710,035	1,094,499	1,381,860
Taipei,China	9,808	26,076	70,433	155,327	297,159	446,811	545,000
South Asia	183,007	286,076	385,703	657,595	1,105,406	2,061,060	3,429,830
Afghanistan	...	...		...	7,465	15,857	20,959
Bangladesh	17,863	26,411	28,627	42,421	67,013	115,279	194,146
Bhutan	...	...	165	424	689	1,585	2,394
India	148,773	219,862	295,590	507,565	873,357	1,675,615	2,846,128
Maldives	...	...		...	1,620	2,588	4,151
Nepal	2,688	3,434	4,218	6,697	10,900	16,003	22,814
Pakistan	13,684	27,481	43,430	79,876	117,555	177,407	253,935
Sri Lanka	5,924	8,888	13,672	20,612	34,272	56,726	85,303

continued on next page

Appendix 2 continued

	1960	1970	1980	1990	2000	2010	2018
Southeast Asia	**124,197**	**207,166**	**425,037**	**745,563**	**1,193,270**	**1,988,166**	**2,938,876**
Brunei Darussalam	...	...	11,519	9,594	11,971	13,707	13,485
Cambodia	...	...	...	...	5,241	11,242	19,586
Indonesia	60,581	88,635	181,537	309,821	453,414	755,094	1,146,845
Lao PDR	...	...	...	1,967	3,582	7,128	12,634
Malaysia	11,043	20,699	45,772	81,801	162,523	255,017	381,795
Myanmar	3,333	4,477	7,053	8,012	15,985	49,541	84,425
Philippines	27,832	45,006	79,972	94,520	125,348	199,591	322,301
Singapore	5,768	14,080	32,670	68,780	136,347	239,809	328,441
Thailand	15,640	34,269	66,514	141,611	217,712	341,105	441,678
Viet Nam	...	...	...	29,458	61,146	115,932	187,687
The Pacific	**2,982**	**5,704**	**7,903**	**10,461**	**16,094**	**24,924**	**32,896**
Cook Islands						240	335
Federated States of Micronesia					291	297	312
Fiji	698	1,149	1,860	2,132	2,689	3,141	4,292
Kiribati		122	129	122	145	156	204
Marshall Islands			71	124	137	165	190
Nauru						49	127
Niue						18	23
Palau					176	183	230
Papua New Guinea	2,284	4,433	5,674	6,431	9,608	14,251	20,657
Samoa			347	380	483	643	764
Solomon Islands			...	405	517	681	964
Timor-Leste					1,172	3,999	3,499
Tonga			206	242	321	369	418
Tuvalu			...	21	29	32	42
Vanuatu			239	376	526	701	838

continued on next page

Appendix 2 continued

	1960	1970	1980	1990	2000	2010	2018
Developed Asia	**995,352**	**2,334,332**	**3,528,328**	**5,400,124**	**6,311,389**	**6,992,820**	**7,797,951**
Australia	199,139	326,688	439,402	612,854	849,137	1,146,138	1,422,550
Japan	796,213	1,951,225	3,019,349	4,703,605	5,348,935	5,700,098	6,189,748
New Zealand	...	56,419	69,577	83,665	113,317	146,584	185,653
Asia and the Pacific	**1,467,233**	**3,137,919**	**4,970,923**	**8,455,704**	**12,150,293**	**19,225,473**	**27,648,544**
Latin America and the Caribbean	**809,032**	**1,390,832**	**2,490,731**	**2,897,773**	**3,915,383**	**5,347,162**	**6,125,467**
Middle East and North Africa	...	**595,950**	**1,095,972**	**1,264,310**	**1,827,940**	**2,768,123**	**3,522,083**
Sub-Saharan Africa	**252,761**	**398,185**	**575,619**	**660,407**	**807,228**	**1,369,737**	**1,786,675**
OECD	**9,099,579**	**15,255,664**	**21,444,901**	**29,278,658**	**38,167,254**	**44,700,082**	**52,058,530**
World	**11,394,358**	**19,191,755**	**27,907,493**	**37,952,345**	**50,036,361**	**66,036,919**	**82,643,195**

... = data not available, Lao PDR = Lao People's Democratic Republic, OECD = Organisation for Economic Co-operation and Development, US = United States.

Notes: Where no data are available for the specific year headings, available data for the nearest 1 or 2 years are reflected. For Hong Kong, China and Sri Lanka, 1960 refers to 1961 data. For Mongolia, the Marshall Islands, and Tonga, 1980 refers to 1981 data. For Samoa, 1980 refers to 1982 data. For Afghanistan, 2000 refers to 2002 data.

Sources: Asian Development Bank. Key Indicators Database. http://kidb.adb.org (accessed 16 September 2019); World Bank. World Development Indicators Database. http://data.worldbank.org (accessed 2 August 2019); Asian Development Bank estimates; and for Taipei,China: Directorate-General of Budget, Accounting and Statistics.

Appendix 3: Gross Domestic Product Growth Rates
(%)

	1960–1969	1970–1979	1980–1989	1990–1999	2000–2009	2010–2018
Developing Asia	4.5	6.3	7.1	6.6	7.5	6.6
Central Asia	...	...	...	(4.8)	8.9	4.8
Armenia	...	...	...	(3.4)	8.7	4.1
Azerbaijan	...	...	...	(5.9)	15.8	1.5
Georgia	5.8	6.8	1.8	(9.0)	5.9	4.8
Kazakhstan	...	...	...	(4.8)	8.6	4.5
Kyrgyz Republic	...	...	6.4	(3.4)	4.8	4.1
Tajikistan	...	...	2.4	(9.3)	8.3	7.0
Turkmenistan	...	...	3.4	1.2	7.4	9.0
Uzbekistan	...	...	6.1	(0.3)	6.5	7.0
East Asia	4.9	8.5	9.1	8.6	8.6	6.9
Hong Kong, China	8.9	9.0	7.4	3.6	4.2	3.4
Mongolia	...	...	6.0	(0.3)	6.0	7.9
People's Republic of China	3.4	7.4	9.7	10.0	10.4	7.8
Republic of Korea	9.5	10.5	8.8	7.1	4.7	3.4
Taipei,China	10.1	10.9	8.5	6.6	3.8	3.4
South Asia	4.1	3.0	5.6	5.5	6.0	6.7
Afghanistan	...	...	...	...	9.4	4.8
Bangladesh	3.9	1.5	3.5	4.7	5.6	6.6
Bhutan	...	...	10.0	5.4	8.3	6.0
India	3.9	2.9	5.7	5.8	6.3	7.0
Maldives	...	...	...	7.5	5.0	6.2
Nepal	2.5	2.6	4.1	4.8	4.1	4.6
Pakistan	6.8	4.8	6.9	4.0	4.5	4.3
Sri Lanka	4.7	4.2	4.1	5.3	5.0	5.6
Southeast Asia	5.0	7.2	5.3	5.0	5.1	5.3
Brunei Darussalam	...	12.2	(2.4)	2.1	1.4	0.1
Cambodia	...	...	...	0.4	8.5	7.0
Indonesia	3.5	7.2	5.8	4.3	5.1	5.5
Lao PDR	...	...	4.1	6.3	6.9	7.5
Malaysia	6.5	8.2	5.9	7.2	4.8	5.4
Myanmar	3.0	4.4	1.9	6.1	12.4	7.2
Philippines	5.1	5.8	2.0	2.8	4.5	6.3
Singapore	8.9	9.2	7.8	7.2	5.4	5.2
Thailand	7.8	7.5	7.3	5.2	4.3	3.8
Viet Nam	...	...	4.5	7.4	6.6	6.2

continued on next page

Appendix 3 *continued*

	1960–1969	1970–1979	1980–1989	1990–1999	2000–2009	2010–2018
The Pacific	6.0	4.4	1.2	3.8	3.6	3.8
Cook Islands	...	...	...	...	0.1	3.2
Federated States of Micronesia	...	...	2.4	2.5	0.5	0.8
Fiji	4.4	6.5	0.8	3.2	1.1	3.9
Kiribati	...	4.4	(2.0)	1.1	1.5	3.0
Marshall Islands	...	...	7.2	0.8	1.9	2.3
Nauru	...	...	...	...	21.5	13.3
Niue	...	...	...	...	...	3.1
Palau	...	...	...	...	0.5	2.7
Papua New Guinea	6.4	3.9	1.4	4.3	2.8	5.4
Samoa	...	...	2.0	1.4	3.6	2.0
Solomon Islands	...	...	...	4.6	0.8	4.7
Timor-Leste	...	...	...	...	16.9	(0.7)
Tonga	...	...	2.3	2.4	1.4	1.8
Tuvalu	...	...	...	3.8	1.2	2.8
Vanuatu	...	...	2.5	4.0	3.4	2.2
Developed Asia	9.5	4.1	4.2	1.8	1.0	1.6
Australia	4.9	3.4	3.4	3.3	3.2	2.7
Japan	10.4	4.3	4.3	1.5	0.5	1.4
New Zealand	...	2.3	2.0	2.8	2.8	2.8
Asia and the Pacific	8.0	4.7	5.1	3.7	4.5	4.9
Latin America and the Caribbean	5.5	6.1	2.1	2.7	3.0	2.2
Middle East and North Africa	11.6	8.5	0.1	4.5	4.3	3.3
Sub-Saharan Africa	4.1	4.4	1.6	1.9	5.2	3.6
OECD	5.6	3.6	3.0	2.6	1.7	2.0
World	5.5	4.0	3.0	2.7	2.8	3.0

... = data not available, ( ) = negative, Lao PDR = Lao People's Democratic Republic, OECD = Organisation for Economic Co-operation and Development.

Sources: Asian Development Bank. Key Indicators Database. http://kidb.adb.org (accessed 16 September 2019); World Bank. World Development Indicators Database. http://data.worldbank.org (accessed 2 August 2019); Asian Development Bank estimates; and for Taipei,China: Directorate-General of Budget, Accounting and Statistics.

Appendix 4: Gross Domestic Product Per Capita
(constant 2010 US dollars)

	1960	1970	1980	1990	2000	2010	2018
Developing Asia	330	445	647	1,078	1,762	3,267	4,903
Central Asia	...	...	...	2,862	1,813	3,740	4,704
Armenia	...	...	...	1,797	1,404	3,218	4,407
Azerbaijan	...	...	...	3,167	1,659	5,843	5,769
Georgia	...	2,375	3,928	3,515	1,553	3,074	4,469
Kazakhstan	...	...	...	5,890	4,492	9,070	11,166
Kyrgyz Republic	...	...	...	1,096	654	880	1,087
Tajikistan	...	...	...	1,283	415	750	1,073
Turkmenistan	...	...	...	3,713	2,381	4,439	7,648
Uzbekistan	...	...	...	1,003	818	1,377	2,027
East Asia	230	339	582	1,205	2,533	5,538	8,812
Hong Kong, China	3,381	5,796	10,727	18,251	23,016	32,550	38,785
Mongolia	...	...	1,441	1,761	1,600	2,643	4,198
People's Republic of China	192	229	347	729	1,768	4,550	7,755
Republic of Korea	944	1,815	3,700	8,465	15,105	22,087	26,762
Taipei,China	919	1,791	3,993	7,691	13,395	19,308	23,113
South Asia	331	407	435	587	807	1,258	1,890
Afghanistan	...	...	...	...	330	543	564
Bangladesh	372	411	359	411	525	781	1,203
Bhutan	...	...	406	799	1,165	2,313	3,173
India	330	396	423	581	827	1,358	2,104
Maldives	...	...	...	...	5,798	7,077	8,050
Nepal	266	284	281	354	455	592	812
Pakistan	304	473	556	742	826	989	1,197
Sri Lanka	586	712	909	1,190	1,825	2,800	3,936
Southeast Asia	718	910	1,452	1,715	2,277	3,337	4,494
Brunei Darussalam	...	...	59,413	37,081	35,932	35,270	31,437
Cambodia	...	...	...	...	431	786	1,205
Indonesia	690	772	1,231	1,708	2,144	3,122	4,285
Lao PDR	...	...	...	462	673	1,141	1,789
Malaysia	1,354	1,916	3,317	4,537	7,007	9,041	12,109
Myanmar	153	164	206	194	342	979	1,572
Philippines	1,059	1,257	1,689	1,527	1,607	2,124	3,022
Singapore	3,503	6,787	13,534	22,572	33,851	47,237	58,248
Thailand	571	929	1,404	2,504	3,458	5,076	6,362
Viet Nam	...	...	...	433	765	1,318	1,964

continued on next page

Appendix 4 *continued*

	1960	1970	1980	1990	2000	2010	2018
The Pacific	1,125	1,700	1,804	1,664	1,853	2,342	2,663
Cook Islands	...	...	...	...	...	10,144	17,985
Federated States of Micronesia	...	...	...	2,362	2,708	2,881	2,774
Fiji	1,774	2,207	2,928	2,927	3,316	3,653	4,859
Kiribati	...	2,394	2,181	1,683	1,722	1,517	1,762
Marshall Islands	...	...	2,232	2,632	2,690	2,927	3,255
Nauru	...	...	...	...	...	4,921	9,962
Niue	...	...	...	...	...	11,140	13,144
Palau	...	...	...	...	9,228	10,185	12,854
Papua New Guinea	1,012	1,593	1,589	1,393	1,643	1,949	2,400
Samoa	...	...	2,206	2,335	2,769	3,458	3,894
Solomon Islands	...	...	...	1,299	1,253	1,290	1,477
Timor-Leste	...	...	...	...	1,326	3,657	2,760
Tonga	...	...	2,206	2,547	3,279	3,553	4,055
Tuvalu	...	...	...	2,406	3,088	3,022	3,636
Vanuatu	...	...	2,071	2,566	2,841	2,967	2,863
Developed Asia	9,685	19,508	26,216	37,519	42,117	45,275	49,857
Australia	19,378	26,120	29,908	35,913	44,334	52,022	56,919
Japan	8,608	18,700	25,855	38,074	42,170	44,508	48,920
New Zealand	...	20,073	22,351	25,126	29,374	33,692	38,001
Asia and the Pacific	956	1,629	2,102	2,840	3,508	4,932	6,576
Latin America and the Caribbean	3,679	4,863	6,907	6,555	7,516	9,058	9,551
Middle East and North Africa	...	4,304	5,936	4,973	5,797	7,173	7,846
Sub-Saharan Africa	1,112	1,371	1,502	1,296	1,213	1,576	1,657
OECD	11,499	17,034	21,669	27,337	32,981	35,981	39,937
World	3,758	5,210	6,294	7,186	8,182	9,539	10,882

... = data not available, Lao PDR = Lao People's Democratic Republic, OECD = Organisation for Economic Co-operation and Development, US = United States.

Notes: Where no data are available for the specific year headings, available data for the nearest 1 or 2 years are reflected. For Hong Kong, China and Sri Lanka, 1960 refers to 1961 data. For Mongolia, the Marshall Islands, and Tonga, 1980 refers to 1981 data. For Samoa, 1980 refers to 1982 data. For Afghanistan, 2000 refers to 2002 data.

Sources: Asian Development Bank. Key Indicators Database. http://kidb.adb.org (accessed 16 September 2019); World Bank. World Development Indicators Database. http://data.worldbank .org (accessed 2 August 2019); Asian Development Bank estimates; and for Taipei,China: Directorate-General of Budget, Accounting and Statistics.

Appendix 5: Sector Shares in Output
(% of GDP)

	Agriculture						Industry						Services					
	1970–1979	1980–1989	1990–1999	2000–2009	2010–2018	2018	1970–1979	1980–1989	1990–1999	2000–2009	2010–2018	2018	1970–1979	1980–1989	1990–1999	2000–2009	2010–2018	2018
Developing Asia	31.9	23.2	**14.9**	**11.0**	**9.6**	**8.5**	33.8	36.0	**36.5**	**38.7**	**38.9**	**37.5**	34.3	40.8	**48.6**	**50.3**	**51.5**	**54.0**
Central Asia	...	...	**23.3**	**13.9**	**10.3**	**10.3**	...	...	**32.7**	**38.8**	**40.0**	**39.9**	...	...	**43.9**	**47.3**	**49.7**	**49.8**
Armenia	...	...	...	...	18.3	15.0	...	...	...	...	28.5	27.4	...	...	...	...	53.3	57.6
Azerbaijan	...	...	26.5	11.0	5.8	5.7	...	...	35.4	57.9	57.9	56.3	...	...	38.1	31.1	36.3	38.0
Georgia	...	24.7	32.8	16.1	8.6	7.6	...	37.2	26.6	23.8	24.2	25.8	...	38.1	40.6	60.1	67.3	66.6
Kazakhstan	...	...	14.4	7.2	4.8	4.5	...	...	33.9	38.9	37.0	36.7	...	...	51.7	53.9	58.2	58.7
Kyrgyz Republic	...	31.9	40.3	32.0	16.1	13.1	...	33.4	27.1	23.8	28.4	30.9	...	34.7	32.6	44.2	55.5	56.0
Tajikistan	...	32.0	31.2	23.9	24.5	23.7	...	40.1	36.4	33.4	27.5	30.1	...	27.8	32.4	42.6	47.9	46.2
Turkmenistan	...	27.5	23.4	18.7	9.2	9.3	...	37.6	45.1	44.8	60.9	57.0	...	34.9	31.5	36.5	29.9	33.7
Uzbekistan	...	29.3	32.8	29.2	27.3	32.4	...	35.5	30.1	27.2	30.0	32.0	...	35.1	37.1	43.5	42.8	35.6
East Asia	28.0	19.6	**11.2**	**8.4**	**7.3**	**6.3**	41.3	41.2	**39.1**	**40.8**	**41.3**	**39.5**	30.7	39.2	**49.7**	**50.8**	**51.4**	**54.1**
Hong Kong, China	0.9	0.6	0.2	0.1	0.1	0.1	28.2	27.0	15.9	9.3	7.3	7.6	70.9	72.4	83.9	90.6	92.7	92.3
Mongolia	...	17.1	29.0	22.5	13.1	12.2	...	28.4	32.3	32.5	36.9	42.8	...	54.5	38.7	45.0	49.9	44.9
People's Republic of China	31.9	28.9	20.1	12.0	8.5	7.2	44.2	44.1	45.0	46.1	43.1	40.7	23.9	27.0	34.9	42.0	48.4	52.2
Republic of Korea	25.9	13.0	6.2	3.3	2.3	2.2	29.6	37.3	39.0	37.0	38.5	38.7	44.5	49.7	54.9	59.7	59.2	59.1
Taipei;China	12.3	6.2	3.1	1.7	1.7	1.8	40.6	44.0	35.0	31.7	34.4	35.5	47.1	49.8	61.9	66.6	63.9	62.7
South Asia	40.5	32.3	**27.8**	**20.5**	**18.2**	**16.5**	24.0	27.8	**28.5**	**30.1**	**29.4**	**28.7**	35.6	39.9	**43.6**	**49.5**	**52.4**	**54.8**
Afghanistan	...	...	...	32.1	23.4	21.5	...	...	...	26.2	22.6	23.2	33.1	...	...	41.7	54.0	55.3
Bangladesh	54.8	33.0	27.7	20.3	15.9	13.8	12.1	20.7	23.1	24.7	27.9	30.2	...	46.3	49.3	55.0	56.2	56.0
Bhutan	...	40.8	32.2	23.2	17.5	18.3	...	20.5	30.8	39.9	43.5	42.7	...	38.7	37.1	36.9	39.0	39.1
India	39.6	32.6	28.1	20.1	17.9	16.0	25.6	29.3	30.0	31.7	30.7	29.8	34.8	38.1	41.9	48.3	51.4	54.2
Maldives	...	...	10.2	7.0	6.2	6.6	...	...	14.1	12.3	11.8	14.9	...	...	75.7	80.7	82.0	78.5

continued on next page

Appendix 5 continued

	Agriculture						Industry						Services					
	1970–1979	1980–1989	1990–1999	2000–2009	2010–2018	2018	1970–1979	1980–1989	1990–1999	2000–2009	2010–2018	2018	1970–1979	1980–1989	1990–1999	2000–2009	2010–2018	2018
Nepal	67.4	56.0	43.5	35.3	32.7	28.2	10.1	14.2	20.9	17.5	14.9	15.1	22.5	29.8	35.6	47.2	52.4	56.7
Pakistan	33.8	28.5	26.1	23.3	24.7	24.0	22.8	23.3	24.4	23.4	20.4	19.3	43.4	48.2	49.5	53.3	54.9	56.8
Sri Lanka	29.3	27.5	23.8	14.1	8.7	8.6	26.4	27.3	26.6	28.9	30.4	29.4	44.3	45.2	49.6	57.0	61.0	62.0
Southeast Asia	**27.1**	**19.3**	**12.6**	**11.1**	**11.4**	**10.4**	**31.2**	**35.8**	**36.9**	**39.1**	**37.4**	**36.4**	**41.8**	**44.9**	**50.4**	**49.8**	**51.2**	**53.2**
Brunei Darussalam	1.1	1.2	1.1	0.9	0.9	1.0	86.7	69.9	56.6	67.2	65.7	62.2	12.2	28.8	42.3	31.9	33.4	36.7
Cambodia	...	...	46.6	33.8	30.6	23.5	...	...	15.9	25.3	28.0	34.4	...	...	37.4	40.9	41.4	42.1
Indonesia	31.5	20.0	14.9	13.5	13.8	13.7	27.9	35.3	38.3	42.8	42.7	41.0	40.6	44.7	46.8	43.7	43.5	45.4
Lao PDR	...	45.1	40.9	31.2	20.1	17.7	...	12.8	18.2	23.3	33.2	35.5	...	42.2	40.9	45.5	46.7	46.8
Malaysia	29.0	20.5	12.8	9.0	9.3	7.8	35.0	39.3	41.4	44.9	39.9	39.5	36.0	40.2	45.8	46.0	50.7	52.7
Myanmar	...	...	...	48.0	28.6	24.6	...	...	...	16.8	32.8	32.3	...	...	...	35.2	38.6	43.2
Philippines	29.5	23.9	19.9	13.0	10.9	9.3	34.9	36.8	33.0	33.7	31.2	30.7	35.6	39.3	47.0	53.3	57.9	60.0
Singapore	2.2	1.0	0.2	0.1	0.0	0.0	32.1	35.0	33.5	31.6	26.0	26.6	65.7	64.1	66.3	68.3	73.9	73.3
Thailand	25.7	17.9	10.0	9.2	9.9	8.1	27.6	32.0	37.3	38.2	36.8	35.0	46.8	50.1	52.7	52.5	53.3	56.9
Viet Nam	...	41.4	30.2	21.1	19.4	16.2	...	26.3	28.9	38.3	37.0	38.1	...	32.3	40.9	40.6	43.6	45.7
The Pacific	**30.2**	**28.4**	**26.8**	**23.1**	**16.1**	**16.6**	**26.2**	**24.8**	**29.5**	**30.7**	**33.3**	**31.2**	**43.6**	**46.9**	**43.7**	**46.2**	**50.6**	**52.3**
Cook Islands	...	...	...	6.2	3.4	3.8	...	...	...	9.0	8.1	7.3	...	...	...	84.8	88.4	88.9
Federated States of Micronesia	...	...	24.0	24.9	27.6	27.1	...	...	7.6	6.2	7.2	6.1	...	...	68.4	68.9	65.3	66.8
Fiji	24.7	20.1	19.5	14.4	11.7	12.9	21.9	21.0	24.5	20.9	19.8	20.0	53.4	58.9	56.0	64.8	68.5	67.1
Kiribati	19.1	29.7	27.2	24.5	25.2	28.9	52.3	7.8	9.6	10.3	13.4	11.6	28.7	62.5	63.2	65.2	61.4	59.5
Marshall Islands	...	...	...	10.1	17.1	16.7	...	...	...	11.7	12.2	13.7	...	...	...	78.2	70.6	69.6
Nauru	...	...	...	...	3.7	...	...	...	...	...	23.5	...	...	...	...	...	72.8	...
Niue	...	...	...	23.6	21.2	19.1	...	...	...	3.5	2.7	3.7	...	...	...	72.8	76.1	77.2
Palau	...	...	...	4.2	3.8	3.5	...	...	...	15.6	9.3	8.9	...	...	...	80.2	87.0	87.6
Papua New Guinea	32.5	32.2	30.8	31.8	18.5	17.9	28.0	27.5	33.9	35.6	32.3	34.7	39.5	40.3	35.3	32.6	49.3	47.4
Samoa	...	...	18.8	12.9	9.9	10.7	...	...	25.6	28.0	24.7	21.2	...	...	55.5	59.1	65.4	68.1

continued on next page

Appendix 5 continued

	Agriculture						Industry						Services					
	1970–1979	1980–1989	1990–1999	2000–2009	2010–2018	2018	1970–1979	1980–1989	1990–1999	2000–2009	2010–2018	2018	1970–1979	1980–1989	1990–1999	2000–2009	2010–2018	2018
Solomon Islands	...	...	...	33.1	28.5	27.3	...	...	...	11.1	15.0	14.7	...	...	...	55.7	56.5	58.0
Timor-Leste	...	...	...	13.3	7.5	10.4	...	...	...	56.1	65.6	45.6	...	...	...	30.6	26.9	44.0
Tonga	38.5	32.3	25.6	17.7	17.1	17.2	10.6	12.1	15.1	17.0	17.5	17.3	50.9	55.6	59.3	65.4	65.4	65.5
Tuvalu	...	...	23.7	20.2	20.2	16.5	...	...	14.6	8.8	7.5	7.3	...	...	61.6	71.0	72.3	76.2
Vanuatu	22.0	22.5	19.0	22.1	24.8	26.6	6.0	9.6	10.9	8.8	10.0	11.4	72.0	68.0	70.1	69.1	65.2	62.0
Developed Asia	5.3	3.2	2.0	1.5	1.6	1.7	41.8	38.7	35.0	29.7	27.4	27.2	52.9	58.1	62.9	68.7	71.0	71.2
Australia	6.6	4.9	3.4	3.1	2.6	2.7	37.4	34.4	28.4	27.0	25.9	24.7	56.0	60.7	68.2	69.9	71.5	72.6
Japan	4.9	2.9	1.9	1.2	1.1	1.1	42.8	39.3	35.7	30.2	28.0	28.1	52.3	57.8	62.5	68.6	70.8	70.8
New Zealand	11.6	9.0	8.3	7.9	7.8	7.4	34.5	32.6	26.0	23.5	21.3	21.5	53.8	58.5	65.6	68.6	70.9	71.1
Asia and the Pacific	16.0	10.3	6.5	6.4	7.3	6.9	38.5	37.8	35.6	34.5	35.6	35.2	45.5	52.0	57.8	59.1	57.1	57.9
Latin America and the Caribbean	12.3	9.7	7.2	5.4	5.3	5.3	36.9	37.6	32.5	32.8	29.6	27.9	50.7	52.6	60.3	61.8	65.1	66.8
Middle East and North Africa	10.1	9.7	9.0	6.2	4.8	4.2	52.1	42.7	40.7	45.7	44.8	42.4	37.8	47.6	50.4	48.1	50.4	53.4
Sub-Saharan Africa	21.3	18.3	17.9	17.6	17.7	18.2	29.8	33.4	30.4	29.4	27.8	27.8	48.9	48.3	51.7	53.0	54.5	54.0
OECD	4.5	3.0	2.3	1.7	1.6	1.5	34.7	33.0	30.2	26.0	24.2	23.7	60.8	64.0	67.5	72.3	74.2	74.8
World	8.1	6.0	4.2	3.5	4.3	4.1	35.4	34.2	31.3	28.6	28.8	28.5	56.5	59.7	64.5	67.9	66.9	67.4

... = data not available, 0.0 = magnitude is less than half of unit employed, GDP = gross domestic product, Lao PDR = Lao People's Democratic Republic, OECD = Organisation for Economic Co-operation and Development.

Notes: Sector shares are rescaled so that the sum of shares in value added is equal to 100. Latest data refer to 2015 for Turkmenistan, Tuvalu, and Vanuatu; and 2016 for the Federated States of Micronesia, New Zealand, Papua New Guinea, and Tonga. Data for Australia; Hong Kong, China; Indonesia; and Japan are from 2017.

Sources: Asian Development Bank estimates using data from World Bank's World Development Indicators. https://data.worldbank.org (accessed 2 August 2019); for Taipei,China: Directorate-General of Budget, Accounting and Statistics; for Australia; Hong Kong, China; Indonesia; and for Japan: United Nations Statistics Division. UNSD Database. https://unstats.un.org/home/ (accessed 2 August 2019).

Appendix 6: Sector Shares in Employment
(% of total employment)

	Agriculture						Industry						Services					
	1970–1979	1980–1989	1990–1999	2000–2009	2010–2018	2018	1970–1979	1980–1989	1990–1999	2000–2009	2010–2018	2018	1970–1979	1980–1989	1990–1999	2000–2009	2010–2018	2018
Developing Asia	**71.0**	**61.6**	**54.7**	**47.5**	**36.5**	**33.5**	**14.1**	**18.5**	**20.1**	**21.7**	**25.1**	**25.5**	**14.9**	**19.9**	**25.2**	**30.8**	**38.3**	**41.0**
Central Asia	...	...	**40.2**	**37.7**	**32.2**	**29.8**	...	...	**20.0**	**21.3**	**23.2**	**23.9**	...	...	**39.8**	**41.0**	**44.5**	**46.3**
Armenia	...	...	40.7	38.2	35.7	33.3	...	...	16.6	17.8	16.5	15.8	...	...	42.7	44.0	47.7	50.9
Azerbaijan	...	...	43.0	39.4	37.0	36.1	...	...	11.0	12.0	14.2	14.4	...	...	46.0	48.6	48.8	49.5
Georgia	...	...	49.6	53.6	48.1	42.9	...	...	10.1	9.4	11.8	13.2	...	...	40.3	37.0	40.1	43.9
Kazakhstan	...	...	36.9	33.0	21.2	15.0	...	...	16.1	17.6	20.1	21.3	...	...	47.0	49.4	58.7	63.7
Kyrgyz Republic	...	...	44.3	41.3	29.6	26.5	...	...	17.7	16.4	21.3	22.2	...	...	38.0	42.2	49.1	51.3
Tajikistan	...	...	57.8	55.6	52.0	51.1	...	...	17.4	16.9	16.2	16.7	...	...	24.8	27.5	31.7	32.2
Turkmenistan	...	...	26.7	25.1	23.5	22.8	...	...	33.5	33.4	33.6	33.7	...	...	39.8	41.5	42.9	43.5
Uzbekistan	...	...	38.2	36.1	34.1	33.4	...	...	29.1	29.5	30.0	30.3	...	...	32.7	34.4	35.9	36.3
East Asia	**74.5**	**61.6**	**52.2**	**43.4**	**29.4**	**25.6**	**14.4**	**21.1**	**24.0**	**25.4**	**28.5**	**28.5**	**11.2**	**17.2**	**23.8**	**31.2**	**42.1**	**45.9**
Hong Kong, China	2.9	1.8	0.6	0.2	0.2	0.2	51.9	46.2	28.3	16.0	11.9	11.8	45.2	52.0	71.2	83.7	87.9	88.0
Mongolia	...	...	46.3	43.0	30.6	28.7	...	...	16.7	14.8	18.9	19.1	...	...	37.0	42.2	50.4	52.2
People's Republic of China	76.4	63.9	54.1	45.2	30.7	26.8	13.7	20.4	23.6	25.3	28.7	28.6	9.9	15.7	22.2	29.5	40.6	44.6
Republic of Korea	45.5	26.9	13.1	8.4	5.6	4.7	23.4	31.2	32.8	26.7	24.9	25.0	31.1	41.9	54.1	64.9	69.5	70.3
Taipei,China	19.3	10.3	7.4	5.9	4.6	4.4	33.3	37.9	34.8	33.5	33.0	32.4	47.4	51.8	57.8	60.6	62.5	63.2
South Asia	**67.4**	**64.5**	**60.9**	**55.1**	**46.2**	**43.6**	**14.4**	**15.2**	**15.6**	**18.2**	**23.1**	**23.8**	**18.1**	**20.3**	**23.6**	**26.7**	**30.7**	**32.6**
Afghanistan	...	...	64.1	62.3	40.5	38.6	...	...	10.3	11.0	17.0	17.6	...	...	25.6	26.7	42.5	43.8
Bangladesh	...	...	66.6	54.1	44.0	40.1	...	...	11.1	13.6	19.3	20.5	...	...	22.3	32.3	36.7	39.4
Bhutan	...	...	67.5	63.3	57.8	56.8	...	...	6.3	7.3	9.6	9.8	...	...	26.2	29.4	32.5	33.5
India	68.6	66.2	61.8	56.1	46.5	43.9	14.0	14.5	15.7	18.8	24.1	24.7	17.4	19.3	22.5	25.1	29.4	31.5
Maldives	...	...	19.3	16.4	10.5	9.0	...	...	24.6	23.1	19.5	18.6	...	...	56.1	60.6	70.0	72.4

continued on next page

Appendix 6 continued

	Agriculture						Industry						Services					
	1970–1979	1980–1989	1990–1999	2000–2009	2010–2018	2018	1970–1979	1980–1989	1990–1999	2000–2009	2010–2018	2018	1970–1979	1980–1989	1990–1999	2000–2009	2010–2018	2018
Nepal	...	...	79.9	74.6	71.5	70.1	...	...	5.7	10.6	12.2	13.0	...	...	14.4	14.8	16.2	16.9
Pakistan	51.8	48.6	43.8	43.0	42.4	41.7	20.1	21.5	21.1	20.7	22.9	23.6	28.1	29.9	35.2	36.3	34.7	34.7
Sri Lanka	...	...	41.3	36.2	29.1	25.9	...	...	23.0	25.0	26.7	28.3	...	...	35.7	38.8	44.2	45.8
Southeast Asia	**61.1**	**53.5**	**52.0**	**44.9**	**36.1**	**32.1**	**12.2**	**14.7**	**16.1**	**18.2**	**20.8**	**22.1**	**26.7**	**31.8**	**31.9**	**37.0**	**43.1**	**45.8**
Brunei Darussalam	...	...	1.6	1.0	0.8	1.3	...	...	23.5	20.7	18.0	16.1	...	...	74.9	78.3	81.1	82.6
Cambodia	...	...	75.2	59.3	33.3	30.4	...	...	8.2	14.5	25.4	26.9	...	...	16.6	26.1	41.3	42.7
Indonesia	60.3	52.4	47.2	43.2	34.2	30.5	11.7	14.5	17.0	18.4	21.1	22.0	28.0	33.1	35.8	38.4	44.7	47.5
Lao PDR	...	...	84.8	77.7	69.6	68.0	...	...	3.7	6.1	8.7	9.1	...	...	11.5	16.2	21.6	22.9
Malaysia	40.6	29.2	20.3	14.9	12.2	11.1	22.9	26.4	31.9	30.4	27.9	27.3	36.4	44.5	47.8	54.8	59.9	61.6
Myanmar	...	...	66.3	57.9	52.2	50.1	...	...	10.5	14.0	16.2	16.0	...	...	23.2	28.1	31.7	33.9
Philippines	53.4	49.3	43.0	35.7	29.6	25.2	14.7	14.7	16.0	15.6	16.5	18.3	31.9	36.0	41.0	48.7	54.0	56.5
Singapore	2.0	0.8	0.5	0.9	0.5	0.5	33.7	36.7	32.4	24.6	18.3	16.6	64.3	62.5	67.2	74.5	81.1	82.9
Thailand	74.3	67.4	55.0	41.6	35.5	30.7	8.8	11.1	17.7	20.9	22.1	23.5	17.0	21.4	27.3	37.4	42.4	45.8
Viet Nam	...	...	66.3	56.1	44.8	39.8	...	...	12.3	17.7	22.9	25.8	...	...	21.4	26.2	32.3	34.4
The Pacific	**...**	**...**	**66.4**	**55.6**	**55.5**	**61.7**	**...**	**...**	**6.3**	**5.9**	**7.6**	**6.9**	**...**	**...**	**27.3**	**38.5**	**36.9**	**31.4**
Cook Islands	...	...	...	6.0	4.8	5.3	...	...	...	10.1	10.9	10.1	...	...	...	83.9	84.3	84.6
Federated States of Micronesia	...	...	...	...	...	...	...	...	...	...	...	...	...	...	...	...	...	...
Fiji	...	...	47.0	44.6	41.1	39.4	...	...	14.6	14.4	13.5	13.1	...	...	38.3	40.9	45.4	47.5
Kiribati	...	...	...	7.4	23.2	...	...	...	...	8.7	17.1	...	...	...	...	83.9	59.7	...
Marshall Islands	...	...	...	6.4	9.7	6.4	...	...	...	10.0	8.7	10.3	...	...	...	83.6	81.6	83.3
Nauru	...	...	...	...	...	...	...	...	...	...	...	...	...	...	...	...	...	...
Niue	...	...	...	12.5	9.6	8.7	...	...	...	18.7	14.2	14.2	...	...	...	68.8	76.3	77.1
Palau	...	...	...	7.5	6.4	...	...	...	...	1.7	11.7	...	...	...	...	90.9	82.0	...
Papua New Guinea	...	...	72.1	72.7	68.9	67.7	...	...	3.7	3.9	4.8	5.0	...	...	24.2	23.4	26.3	27.4
Samoa	...	...	42.1	34.4	6.3	5.2	...	...	20.1	21.0	15.2	14.7	...	...	37.8	44.6	78.4	80.1

continued on next page

Appendix 6 continued

	Agriculture						Industry						Services					
	1970–1979	1980–1989	1990–1999	2000–2009	2010–2018	2018	1970–1979	1980–1989	1990–1999	2000–2009	2010–2018	2018	1970–1979	1980–1989	1990–1999	2000–2009	2010–2018	2018
Solomon Islands	...	...	65.2	64.6	62.2	61.4	...	...	9.6	8.7	9.0	9.1	...	...	25.2	26.7	28.8	29.5
Timor-Leste	...	...	53.9	52.3	50.1	50.0	...	...	9.8	8.6	9.7	9.4	...	...	36.3	39.0	40.3	40.5
Tonga	...	...	33.1	31.8	30.9	30.5	...	...	31.1	30.3	30.0	29.7	...	...	35.8	37.9	39.1	39.8
Tuvalu	...	...	...	...	...	...	...	...	...	...	...	...	...	...	...	...	...	...
Vanuatu	...	...	64.6	62.9	61.7	61.1	...	...	6.1	6.3	6.5	6.5	...	...	29.3	30.8	31.9	32.3
Developed Asia	12.8	8.7	5.9	4.6	3.6	3.4	35.9	34.1	32.3	27.7	24.7	23.6	51.3	57.2	61.8	67.8	71.7	73.0
Australia	7.2	6.3	5.2	3.9	2.7	2.6	34.6	28.2	23.0	21.2	20.3	19.4	58.2	65.6	71.8	74.9	76.9	78.1
Japan	13.4	8.9	5.9	4.6	3.7	3.4	36.1	34.8	33.7	28.8	25.6	24.5	50.5	56.3	60.4	66.6	70.7	72.1
New Zealand	...	...	9.8	7.8	6.5	6.2	...	...	24.1	22.4	20.6	20.4	...	...	66.1	69.8	72.9	73.4
Asia and the Pacific	66.4	58.1	52.2	45.6	35.2	32.2	15.9	19.5	20.7	21.9	25.1	25.4	17.8	22.4	27.0	32.5	39.7	42.4
Latin America and the Caribbean	32.6	25.4	22.0	19.0	14.9	13.9	24.4	24.0	22.3	21.5	21.4	21.0	43.0	50.6	55.6	59.5	63.7	65.0
Middle East and North Africa	50.6	42.7	27.7	23.0	17.8	16.9	18.7	21.3	24.6	24.8	26.7	26.7	30.8	36.0	47.7	52.2	55.5	56.3
Sub-Saharan Africa	61.9	56.6	61.3	60.0	55.0	53.5	13.2	12.0	10.1	10.1	10.9	11.4	24.9	31.3	28.5	29.9	34.1	35.2
OECD	11.4	8.4	8.3	5.8	4.8	4.6	35.9	31.6	28.6	25.7	23.1	22.7	52.7	60.0	63.1	68.5	72.1	72.7
World	51.1	45.6	42.0	37.3	30.1	28.2	21.0	21.8	21.7	21.6	23.0	23.0	28.0	32.6	36.3	41.1	46.9	48.8

... = data not available, GDP = gross domestic product, Lao PDR = Lao People's Democratic Republic, OECD = Organisation for Economic Co-operation and Development.

Sources: International Labour Organization (ILO). ILOSTAT Database. https://wwww.ilo.org/ilostat (accessed 28 August 2019); OECD. OECD Employment and Labour Market Statistics. https://www.oecd-ilibrary.org/employment/data/oecd-employment-and-labour-market-statistics_lfs-data-en (accessed 28 August 2019); Timmer, M. P., G. J. de Vries, and K. de Vries. 2015. Patterns of Structural Change in Developing Countries. In Weiss, J., and M. Tribe, eds. Routledge Handbook of Industry and Development. Abingdon: Routledge. pp. 65–83 (for the Groningen Growth and Development Center 10-Sector Database) (accessed 28 August 2019); and Asian Development Bank estimates.

Appendix 7: Exports of Goods and Services
(% of GDP)

	1960–1969	1970–1979	1980–1989	1990–1999	2000–2009	2010–2018	2018
Developing Asia	8.5	15.0	25.3	35.5	42.4	35.0	30.7
Central Asia	...	...	...	29.6	45.1	37.3	37.7
Armenia	...	...	...	30.9	24.2	29.6	37.5
Azerbaijan	...	...	...	39.5	53.0	49.2	54.3
Georgia	...	...	42.1	29.8	29.6	43.4	55.1
Kazakhstan	...	...	...	41.4	50.3	38.5	38.9
Kyrgyz Republic	...	...	...	34.5	44.1	40.9	32.7
Tajikistan	...	...	...	58.7	55.7	13.5	15.7
Turkmenistan	...	...	...	59.9	40.1	40.5	22.7
Uzbekistan	...	...	...	22.6	35.5	24.1	29.1
East Asia	6.6	13.9	28.3	34.0	40.1	32.4	27.5
Hong Kong, China	71.8	87.0	102.2	118.5	162.0	203.2	188.0
Mongolia	...	...	27.2	43.2	55.0	50.0	60.3
People's Republic of China	3.7	4.1	9.9	17.1	28.4	23.0	19.5
Republic of Korea	6.5	21.0	29.9	27.7	38.0	48.9	44.0
Taipei,China	18.8	43.2	52.3	44.9	59.2	68.0	66.8
South Asia	5.4	6.4	7.0	11.3	17.7	20.5	18.3
Afghanistan	7.7	12.3	...	...	28.8	14.1	8.1
Bangladesh	9.7	5.7	5.1	9.3	14.3	17.6	14.8
Bhutan	...	...	18.0	32.5	37.7	36.1	29.1
India	4.0	5.2	5.9	9.9	17.9	21.9	19.7
Maldives	...	...	106.3	77.1	79.0	80.6	67.6
Nepal	6.8	8.2	11.4	19.5	16.2	10.0	8.8
Pakistan	9.0	10.5	12.1	16.4	14.4	11.3	8.5
Sri Lanka	24.3	28.2	27.3	33.7	31.9	20.9	22.8
Southeast Asia	24.0	33.5	42.3	62.2	77.1	62.9	61.5
Brunei Darussalam	...	93.1	85.2	57.5	70.3	60.8	51.9
Cambodia	11.7	5.8	...	29.1	59.0	59.6	61.6
Indonesia	9.6	21.3	25.6	30.8	32.4	22.7	21.0
Lao PDR	...	...	7.0	23.0	30.0	36.8	34.3
Malaysia	49.0	46.6	57.9	91.2	108.3	75.6	69.7
Myanmar	...	...	...	...	0.2	13.4	20.0
Philippines	17.0	21.5	24.7	36.8	44.5	30.4	31.7
Singapore	132.5	142.0	173.8	170.5	205.8	186.3	176.4
Thailand	16.7	19.0	25.9	42.5	65.8	68.5	66.8
Viet Nam	...	...	10.1	37.6	61.5	86.9	95.4

continued on next page

Appendix 7 *continued*

	1960–1969	1970–1979	1980–1989	1990–1999	2000–2009	2010–2018	2018
The Pacific	17.6	38.0	39.8	49.1	56.5	...	...
Cook Islands	...	...	...	...	...	...	...
Federated States of Micronesia	...	...	3.4	...	19.7	26.6	26.6
Fiji	...	...	...	...	56.2	55.6	50.8
Kiribati	...	57.8	31.1	19.2	15.0	12.9	13.2
Marshall Islands	...	...	...	...	33.0	46.6	31.5
Nauru	...	...	...	...	...	59.5	48.8
Niue	...	...	...	...	...	...	...
Palau	...	...	...	...	44.8	53.8	46.7
Papua New Guinea	17.6	37.7	40.7	52.4	68.1	...	...
Samoa	...	...	...	...	29.9	29.0	31.0
Solomon Islands	...	...	34.9	35.4	31.3	52.3	50.1
Timor-Leste	...	...	...	...	62.7	85.0	61.1
Tonga	...	31.4	26.3	21.2	15.8	18.2	21.6
Tuvalu	...	...	...	...	...	...	...
Vanuatu	...	...	41.8	44.9	43.0	47.0	47.7
Developed Asia	10.7	12.0	12.8	10.6	14.4	17.6	19.5
Australia	13.1	13.6	14.9	17.7	20.0	20.6	21.7
Japan	9.9	11.4	12.3	9.7	13.4	16.5	18.5
New Zealand	...	24.5	27.9	29.5	31.1	28.5	28.3
Asia and the Pacific	9.4	13.0	17.0	19.2	28.7	29.9	28.2
Latin America and the Caribbean	10.5	12.3	15.5	16.4	22.2	21.6	23.0
Middle East and North Africa	31.7	40.8	30.0	29.9	44.5	44.9	40.5
Sub-Saharan Africa	20.8	23.4	22.3	23.3	31.2	28.3	24.7
OECD	11.8	15.3	17.9	19.6	24.0	28.1	28.8
World	12.1	16.0	18.6	21.4	27.5	29.7	29.4

... = data not available, GDP = gross domestic product, Lao PDR = Lao People's Democratic Republic, OECD = Organisation for Economic Co-operation and Development.

Sources: Asian Development Bank. Key Indicators Database. http://kidb.adb.org (accessed 16 September 2019); World Bank. World Development Indicators Database. http://data.worldbank.org (accessed 2 August 2019); Asian Development Bank estimates; and for Taipei,China: Directorate-General of Budget, Accounting and Statistics.

Appendix 8: Imports of Goods and Services
(% of GDP)

	1960–1969	1970–1979	1980–1989	1990–1999	2000–2009	2010–2018	2018
Developing Asia	9.6	15.7	25.6	34.7	38.7	32.9	29.8
Central Asia	...	...	...	37.2	41.1	31.6	32.1
Armenia	...	...	...	58.1	44.4	47.0	52.9
Azerbaijan	...	...	...	50.0	43.1	31.2	37.7
Georgia	...	...	44.2	51.6	48.9	59.3	66.7
Kazakhstan	...	...	...	45.1	42.9	27.1	26.3
Kyrgyz Republic	...	...	...	47.5	61.6	79.8	68.4
Tajikistan	...	...	...	66.0	78.4	52.4	40.9
Turkmenistan	...	...	...	62.2	33.3	41.7	12.5
Uzbekistan	...	...	...	23.8	31.2	25.9	38.7
East Asia	6.9	14.1	27.1	32.3	35.7	29.5	26.0
Hong Kong, China	73.7	81.4	96.4	116.1	153.3	201.2	188.0
Mongolia	...	...	67.2	53.7	64.0	58.5	63.5
People's Republic of China	3.1	4.1	10.5	15.0	23.9	20.6	18.7
Republic of Korea	16.6	27.5	30.0	26.7	36.0	44.3	39.0
Taipei,China	21.6	41.5	43.9	42.7	53.6	58.1	56.3
South Asia	7.4	8.3	10.6	13.3	21.1	25.5	23.6
Afghanistan	14.4	14.8	...	...	68.8	52.5	45.3
Bangladesh	11.9	12.9	13.7	14.8	19.7	24.4	23.4
Bhutan	...	...	45.3	44.5	55.9	60.8	49.6
India	5.7	5.6	7.9	10.8	20.5	25.8	23.4
Maldives	...	...	120.1	81.5	76.0	72.7	72.2
Nepal	9.5	12.0	20.4	30.2	31.3	38.9	45.5
Pakistan	15.6	18.4	22.4	20.0	18.0	18.6	19.4
Sri Lanka	26.8	32.0	40.6	42.6	40.8	29.6	30.1
Southeast Asia	26.8	33.4	41.6	60.2	68.9	57.7	57.4
Brunei Darussalam	...	17.3	19.4	50.6	32.8	35.0	42.0
Cambodia	15.7	7.8	...	43.6	67.0	64.0	63.3
Indonesia	12.9	20.0	23.5	28.1	26.9	22.3	22.1
Lao PDR	...	...	17.0	35.9	42.1	51.8	41.5
Malaysia	43.6	42.3	55.4	86.9	88.3	65.8	62.6
Myanmar	...	...	...	...	0.2	16.1	28.0
Philippines	17.5	23.6	26.3	43.6	48.7	36.5	44.4
Singapore	143.0	152.6	172.3	155.7	182.0	160.7	149.8
Thailand	18.6	22.6	28.8	43.6	60.4	60.9	56.5
Viet Nam	...	...	20.1	45.1	69.5	86.2	92.1

continued on next page

Appendix 8 *continued*

	1960– 1969	1970– 1979	1980– 1989	1990– 1999	2000– 2009	2010– 2018	2018
The Pacific	36.1	46.0	55.2	48.9	61.4	...	...
Cook Islands	...	...	...	...	...	...	...
Federated States of Micronesia	...	...	84.3	...	79.0	78.6	72.4
Fiji	...	...	...	...	67.0	61.6	56.1
Kiribati	...	38.8	68.4	98.3	94.8	89.1	92.0
Marshall Islands	...	...	...	...	95.1	98.8	88.8
Nauru	...	...	...	...	...	88.1	101.7
Niue	...	...	...	...	...	...	...
Palau	...	...	...	...	82.2	77.7	75.4
Papua New Guinea	36.1	45.9	53.7	46.7	54.8	...	...
Samoa	...	...	...	...	49.2	50.4	45.5
Solomon Islands	...	...	65.6	61.6	48.0	63.8	57.3
Timor-Leste	...	...	...	...	78.1	49.9	59.9
Tonga	...	64.5	66.8	53.0	53.5	63.9	73.4
Tuvalu	...	...	...	...	...	...	...
Vanuatu	...	...	57.8	55.8	51.3	54.4	57.9
Developed Asia	10.6	11.4	11.5	9.3	13.4	18.0	18.1
Australia	14.1	13.5	16.6	18.6	21.6	21.2	21.3
Japan	9.6	10.6	10.6	8.3	12.1	16.9	16.8
New Zealand	...	26.8	28.5	27.4	29.9	27.4	26.7
Asia and the Pacific	10.0	12.9	16.3	18.0	26.3	28.5	27.2
Latin America and the Caribbean	10.7	13.8	13.7	17.1	21.0	22.6	23.9
Middle East and North Africa	25.3	29.4	33.6	30.6	34.2	37.1	37.8
Sub-Saharan Africa	22.1	25.1	22.0	23.6	30.1	29.8	26.3
OECD	12.2	15.9	18.6	19.5	24.6	28.0	28.2
World	12.4	16.1	19.2	21.1	26.6	29.0	28.5

... = data not available, GDP = gross domestic product, Lao PDR = Lao People's Democratic Republic, OECD = Organisation for Economic Co-operation and Development.

Sources: Asian Development Bank. Key Indicators Database. http://kidb.adb.org (accessed 16 September 2019); World Bank. World Development Indicators Database. http://data.worldbank .org (accessed 2 August 2019); Asian Development Bank estimates; and for Taipei,China: Directorate-General of Budget, Accounting and Statistics.

Appendix 9: Current Account Balance
(% of GDP)

	1980	1990	2000	2010	2018
Developing Asia	(2.2)	0.1	2.2	3.2	0.8
Central Asia	...	(20.9)	1.2	4.5	0.5
Armenia	...	(46.3)	(15.8)	(13.6)	(6.2)
Azerbaijan	...	(16.6)	(3.5)	28.4	12.6
Georgia	...	...	(5.8)	(10.3)	(7.9)
Kazakhstan	...	(51.7)	2.0	0.9	0.6
Kyrgyz Republic	...	(5.7)	(4.3)	(2.2)	(9.8)
Tajikistan	...	(16.8)	(1.6)	(9.6)	(5.3)
Turkmenistan	...	0.0	8.2	(12.9)	3.1
Uzbekistan	...	(6.7)	4.0	7.0	(7.8)
East Asia	(2.7)	2.7	2.0	4.1	1.3
Hong Kong, China	(5.0)	6.2	4.4	7.0	3.5
Mongolia	...	(2.9)	(4.1)	(13.0)	(14.6)
People's Republic of China	(0.8)	3.1	1.7	3.9	0.4
Republic of Korea	(10.6)	(1.0)	1.8	2.6	4.7
Taipei,China	...	6.5	2.5	8.3	11.6
South Asia	(2.0)	(2.9)	(0.4)	(2.3)	(2.9)
Afghanistan	...	...	33.9	29.4	4.8
Bangladesh	(1.1)	(2.7)	(1.2)	0.4	(2.8)
Bhutan	11.4	(9.9)	(9.1)	(22.2)	(22.7)
India	(1.5)	(2.9)	(0.6)	(2.8)	(2.5)
Maldives	(16.1)	12.4	(6.4)	(7.3)	(24.0)
Nepal	(5.7)	(7.6)	6.4	(2.4)	(8.2)
Pakistan	(3.0)	(2.6)	(0.3)	(2.2)	(6.1)
Sri Lanka	(16.9)	(4.0)	(5.5)	(1.9)	(3.2)
Southeast Asia	(1.5)	(2.4)	5.8	5.3	2.4
Brunei Darussalam	...	60.3	45.0	36.6	11.0
Cambodia	...	(1.0)	(2.6)	(8.7)	(10.5)
Indonesia	2.9	(2.3)	4.5	0.7	(3.0)
Lao PDR	(2.2)	(4.5)	1.5	(16.5)	(17.1)
Malaysia	(1.0)	(1.9)	8.4	10.1	2.3
Myanmar	...	...	(7.0)	4.5	(5.2)
Philippines	(5.3)	(5.5)	(2.8)	3.6	(2.6)
Singapore	(13.4)	8.1	10.8	23.4	17.7
Thailand	(6.2)	(8.2)	7.4	3.4	7.7
Viet Nam	(2.0)	(4.0)	2.7	(3.8)	3.0

continued on next page

Appendix 9 *continued*

	1980	1990	2000	2010	2018
The Pacific	(4.8)	(3.7)	(1.6)	(7.6)	12.9
Cook Islands	...	...	...	15.5	2.6
Federated States of Micronesia	...	...	(14.6)	(17.8)	21.3
Fiji	(3.3)	(9.9)	(5.5)	(4.5)	(5.9)
Kiribati	27.2	(14.6)	(3.7)	(2.2)	10.3
Marshall Islands	...	...	(10.9)	(17.9)	3.8
Nauru	...	...	...	46.3	(7.7)
Niue	...	...	...	(53.9)	15.7
Palau	...	...	(50.1)	(7.4)	(17.3)
Papua New Guinea	(5.5)	(1.9)	2.6	(20.4)	23.5
Samoa	(12.9)	7.3	(1.7)	(6.7)	2.3
Solomon Islands	(3.2)	(12.6)	(8.0)	(32.9)	(6.4)
Timor-Leste	...	...	(3.5)	39.7	(2.4)
Tonga	(4.5)	(10.9)	(6.0)	(21.9)	(9.9)
Tuvalu	...	...	(57.3)	(12.0)	3.5
Vanuatu	1.0	2.7	1.1	(5.9)	(6.9)
Developed Asia	(1.2)	0.8	2.1	2.4	2.1
Australia	(2.4)	(4.9)	(4.1)	(3.7)	(2.1)
Japan	(1.0)	1.4	2.7	3.9	3.5
New Zealand	(4.0)	(2.9)	(3.3)	(2.3)	(4.0)
Asia and the Pacific	(1.6)	0.5	2.2	2.9	1.1
Latin America and the Caribbean	(3.4)	(0.4)	(2.2)	(2.0)	(1.9)
Middle East and North Africa	15.4	0.3	7.2	6.5	3.1
Sub-Saharan Africa	(1.2)	(0.3)	1.2	(0.8)	(2.6)
OECD	(1.3)	(0.6)	(1.1)	(0.4)	0.3
World	(0.5)	(0.5)	(0.4)	0.4	0.4

... = data not available, ( ) = negative, GDP = gross domestic product, Lao PDR = Lao People's Democratic Republic, OECD = Organisation for Economic Co-operation and Development.

Note: For Central Asian economies, 1990 refers to 1992 data.

Sources: Asian Development Bank. Key Indicators Database. https://kidb.adb.org/kidb/ (accessed 16 September 2019); International Monetary Fund. World Economic Outlook Databases. April 2019 Edition. https://www.imf.org/en/Publications/SPROLLs/world-economic-outlook-databases#sort=%40imfdate%20descending (accessed 25 September 2019); and Asian Development Bank estimates.

Appendix 10: General Government Net Lending/Borrowing
(% of GDP)

	1980	1990	2000	2010	2018
Developing Asia	(0.3)	(2.7)	(2.3)	(1.6)	(3.8)
Central Asia	...	...	(1.3)	3.3	1.0
Armenia	...	...	(3.4)	(5.0)	(1.8)
Azerbaijan	...	...	0.1	13.8	4.0
Georgia	...	...	(2.0)	(4.8)	(0.9)
Kazakhstan	...	...	1.9	1.5	0.5
Kyrgyz Republic	...	...	(10.7)	(5.9)	(1.3)
Tajikistan	...	...	(5.6)	(3.0)	(4.8)
Turkmenistan	...	...	(0.5)	2.0	0.6
Uzbekistan	...	9.0	(4.6)	3.2	3.1
East Asia	0.1	(1.4)	(1.3)	(0.2)	(3.8)
Hong Kong, China	2.8	0.6	(0.6)	4.1	2.0
Mongolia	(4.1)	(9.7)	(5.0)	0.4	(3.4)
People's Republic of China	0.2	(0.7)	(2.8)	(0.4)	(4.8)
Republic of Korea	...	...	4.2	1.5	2.8
Taipei,China	(2.4)	(4.0)	(5.3)	(5.1)	(1.9)
South Asia	...	(7.2)	(7.2)	(7.9)	(6.4)
Afghanistan	...	...	(0.1)	0.9	0.9
Bangladesh	(7.0)	(0.2)	(2.9)	(2.7)	(4.1)
Bhutan	(4.2)	(7.9)	(4.0)	1.6	(1.0)
India	...	(7.9)	(8.3)	(8.6)	(6.7)
Maldives	...	(12.8)	(3.9)	(13.5)	(5.3)
Nepal	...	...	(1.7)	(0.8)	(6.5)
Pakistan	...	...	(4.0)	(6.0)	(6.5)
Sri Lanka	...	(6.6)	(8.0)	(7.0)	(5.3)
Southeast Asia	...	...	(0.9)	(1.0)	(1.2)
Brunei Darussalam	...	(2.1)	6.9	7.6	(8.4)
Cambodia	...	...	(4.8)	(3.8)	(2.0)
Indonesia	...	...	(1.9)	(1.2)	(1.8)
Lao PDR	...	...	(4.1)	(2.8)	(4.6)
Malaysia	...	0.2	(6.1)	(4.4)	(3.6)
Myanmar	...	...	(4.8)	(4.8)	(2.6)
Philippines	...	(1.6)	(3.4)	(2.4)	(1.0)
Singapore	...	11.9	10.3	6.0	4.0
Thailand	...	...	(1.8)	(1.3)	(0.3)
Viet Nam	...	...	(2.0)	(2.8)	(4.6)

continued on next page

Appendix 10 *continued*

	1980	1990	2000	2010	2018
The Pacific	...	(2.2)	(0.5)	0.6	(3.7)
Cook Islands	...	...	...	2.9	8.7
Federated States of Micronesia	...	...	(3.5)	0.5	23.8
Fiji	...	(2.3)	(1.5)	(2.8)	(4.4)
Kiribati	...	(4.3)	(0.2)	(7.2)	(19.8)
Marshall Islands	...	...	8.0	3.4	1.3
Nauru	...	...	...	0.1	24.1
Niue	...	...	...	...	...
Palau	...	...	(12.6)	(1.0)	4.3
Papua New Guinea	...	(2.0)	0.3	3.1	(2.9)
Samoa	...	(10.1)	(0.6)	(5.8)	0.1
Solomon Islands	5.1	2.8	(3.9)	6.3	(3.6)
Timor-Leste	...	...	3.0	(4.4)	(17.3)
Tonga	...	...	1.8	(3.7)	0.7
Tuvalu	...	...	...	(23.9)	6.4
Vanuatu	...	(2.8)	(6.3)	(2.5)	2.9
Developed Asia	(4.5)	1.7	(7.5)	(8.7)	(2.7)
Australia	...	(0.2)	1.3	(5.1)	(1.2)
Japan	(4.5)	2.0	(8.3)	(9.5)	(3.2)
New Zealand	...	(2.9)	0.1	(5.5)	0.4
Asia and the Pacific	(3.4)	0.6	(5.4)	(4.2)	(3.5)
Latin America and the Caribbean	0.1	0.0	(2.5)	(2.8)	(4.7)
Middle East and North Africa	...	(1.0)	6.0	1.9	(2.8)
Sub-Saharan Africa	(1.2)	(1.0)	(0.3)	(3.5)	(3.7)
OECD	(1.3)	(1.2)	(1.5)	(7.7)	(2.4)
World	(1.1)	(1.1)	(1.4)	(5.7)	(2.8)

... = data not available, ( ) = negative, GDP = gross domestic product, Lao PDR = Lao People's Democratic Republic, OECD = Organisation for Economic Co-operation and Development.

Note: Where no data are available for the specific year headings, available data for the nearest 1 or 2 years are reflected.

Sources: International Monetary Fund. World Economic Outlook Databases. April 2019 Edition. https://www.imf.org/en/Publications/SPROLLs/world-economic-outlook-databases#sort=%40imfdate%20descending (accessed 25 September 2019). For Armenia (2000) and the Cook Islands (2010 and 2018): Asian Development Bank. Key Indicators Database. https://kidb.adb.org/kidb/ (accessed 16 September 2019).

Appendix 11: Gross Domestic Savings
(% of GDP)

	1960–1969	1970–1979	1980–1989	1990–1999	2000–2009	2010–2018
Developing Asia	18.0	24.9	27.4	32.9	36.6	41.0
Central Asia	...	...	...	12.8	32.7	35.5
Armenia	...	...	...	(3.5)	7.5	5.2
Azerbaijan	...	...	...	11.1	39.2	41.2
Georgia	...	...	31.0	(3.9)	7.4	13.1
Kazakhstan	...	...	...	15.9	37.1	40.1
Kyrgyz Republic	...	...	13.3	4.8	3.0	(6.3)
Tajikistan	...	...	...	33.6	(1.4)	(17.2)
Turkmenistan	...	...	...	7.1	45.5	83.5
Uzbekistan	...	...	...	20.9	29.9	26.1
East Asia	25.7	34.4	34.6	36.9	40.4	45.6
Hong Kong, China	24.0	30.8	33.6	32.0	31.6	25.0
Mongolia	...	...	19.4	30.6	22.9	33.2
People's Republic of China	27.0	36.6	35.0	39.7	44.5	48.3
Republic of Korea	8.7	22.6	33.3	38.0	33.8	35.1
Taipei,China	21.0	31.8	35.1	30.3	30.4	33.9
South Asia	8.4	11.2	14.7	21.9	26.8	28.1
Afghanistan	5.1	6.7	...	...	(31.7)	1.1
Bangladesh	8.4	1.9	12.3	15.4	20.6	22.5
Bhutan	...	...	...	...	32.6	32.3
India	8.4	12.6	15.8	23.9	29.9	31.5
Maldives	...	...	...	...	...	...
Nepal	...	12.1	11.0	12.0	10.6	11.0
Pakistan	9.9	8.2	8.3	15.1	14.1	8.1
Sri Lanka	11.8	15.2	17.8	18.0	16.9	22.9
Southeast Asia	16.1	23.6	28.7	32.9	32.2	33.6
Brunei Darussalam	...	80.1	76.7	39.3	53.7	60.5
Cambodia	12.4	10.5	...	(0.4)	11.7	17.0
Indonesia	5.1	19.9	26.7	28.4	28.3	33.9
Lao PDR	...	...	0.8	...	15.7	15.4
Malaysia	12.1	25.1	32.1	40.6	43.0	34.7
Myanmar	...	...	...	...	13.4	32.9
Philippines	20.4	26.3	23.0	15.1	16.0	15.9
Singapore	9.7	28.8	43.0	49.0	48.0	53.6
Thailand	25.7	21.4	26.0	35.7	31.5	32.3
Viet Nam	...	...	4.4	16.2	27.5	27.0

continued on next page

Appendix 11 *continued*

	1960–1969	1970–1979	1980–1989	1990–1999	2000–2009	2010–2018
The Pacific	1.2	16.5	11.1	23.5	20.4	...
Cook Islands	...	...	...	...	...	...
Federated States of Micronesia	...	...	(42.3)	...	...	...
Fiji	...	...	...	...	18.1	15.1
Kiribati	...	28.6	11.2	11.9	...	...
Marshall Islands	...	...	...	...	(39.1)	(30.5)
Nauru	...	...	...	...	...	...
Niue	...	...	...	...	...	...
Palau	...	...	...	...	(1.2)	0.3
Papua New Guinea	1.2	16.5	12.2	27.0	33.9	...
Samoa	...	...	...	...	...	...
Solomon Islands	...	...	...	(23.2)	(16.8)	...
Timor-Leste	...	...	...	...	(1.5)	51.8
Tonga	...	(7.4)	(14.5)	(12.4)	(15.9)	(15.9)
Tuvalu	...	...	...	...	...	...
Vanuatu	...	...	6.4	10.6	17.6	22.1
Developed Asia	30.5	35.6	32.4	31.5	25.9	23.4
Australia	30.5	28.8	25.5	24.3	25.1	25.7
Japan	...	37.0	33.3	32.2	26.0	22.6
New Zealand	...	22.9	23.9	23.5	24.5	23.3
Asia and the Pacific	19.8	31.2	30.6	32.1	31.7	36.2
Latin America and the Caribbean	20.0	21.2	23.4	20.1	21.3	19.8
Middle East and North Africa	30.2	36.1	21.9	25.4	38.0	37.0
Sub-Saharan Africa	...	...	30.7	23.1	23.5	20.2
OECD	...	25.2	23.7	23.4	22.1	21.4
World	...	26.0	24.8	25.1	25.5	25.1

... = data not available, ( ) = negative, GDP = gross domestic product, Lao PDR = Lao People's Democratic Republic, OECD = Organisation for Economic Co-operation and Development.

Sources: Asian Development Bank. Key Indicators Database. https://kidb.adb.org/kidb/ (accessed 16 September 2019); World Bank. World Development Indicators Database. http://data.worldbank .org (accessed 2 August 2019); Asian Development Bank estimates; and for Taipei,China: Directorate-General of Budget, Accounting and Statistics.

Appendix 12: Gross Capital Formation
(% of GDP)

	1960–1969	1970–1979	1980–1989	1990–1999	2000–2009	2010–2018
Developing Asia	20.3	26.1	28.5	32.3	33.3	38.9
Central Asia	...	...	...	22.4	27.5	26.9
Armenia	...	...	...	23.5	27.7	22.4
Azerbaijan	...	...	...	21.3	31.8	23.5
Georgia	...	...	29.6	18.6	28.4	29.0
Kazakhstan	...	...	...	21.8	28.2	25.7
Kyrgyz Republic	...	...	32.6	17.9	20.5	32.8
Tajikistan	...	...	...	25.0	16.0	26.9
Turkmenistan	...	...	35.0	42.3	28.2	50.3
Uzbekistan	...	...	...	22.6	25.5	28.5
East Asia	24.8	32.8	33.6	35.1	36.3	42.9
Hong Kong, China	26.5	25.1	27.8	29.5	22.9	23.1
Mongolia	...	...	58.7	26.6	33.2	41.5
People's Republic of China	25.2	34.0	36.4	38.1	40.5	46.3
Republic of Korea	18.7	29.2	33.4	37.0	31.9	30.4
Taipei,China	22.0	30.3	26.0	27.0	23.4	22.0
South Asia	15.2	17.4	21.1	24.6	31.2	32.2
Afghanistan	11.8	9.2	...	...	18.9	18.4
Bangladesh	10.6	9.1	16.1	19.4	25.3	28.8
Bhutan	...	...	36.6	39.6	50.8	56.9
India	15.6	18.7	21.8	26.0	33.8	34.5
Maldives	...	...	...	...	...	...
Nepal	5.4	11.9	19.9	22.7	25.7	40.0
Pakistan	17.5	16.0	18.7	18.7	17.8	15.4
Sri Lanka	15.6	17.5	26.2	24.9	25.5	31.6
Southeast Asia	18.8	24.1	27.2	31.9	24.5	28.6
Brunei Darussalam	...	...	18.6	29.0	14.3	32.8
Cambodia	16.4	12.5	...	13.8	19.3	20.7
Indonesia	16.9	18.6	25.9	29.5	25.0	34.0
Lao PDR	...	...	8.8	...	27.8	29.8
Malaysia	19.7	24.3	28.1	36.3	23.0	24.8
Myanmar	...	...	...	...	13.4	30.8
Philippines	21.8	26.8	22.2	22.7	20.2	21.9
Singapore	19.4	39.6	41.1	34.7	25.2	27.8
Thailand	19.4	25.8	29.4	36.5	24.9	24.7
Viet Nam	...	...	15.1	23.5	34.6	28.3

continued on next page

Appendix 12 *continued*

	1960–1969	1970–1979	1980–1989	1990–1999	2000–2009	2010–2018
The Pacific	19.2	24.9	25.2	21.1	19.3	...
Cook Islands	...	...	...	...	...	...
Federated States of Micronesia	...	...	37.7	...	...	...
Fiji		...	...	...	19.3	19.7
Kiribati	...	9.9	41.0	50.8	...	...
Marshall Islands	...	...	...	...	25.5	23.1
Nauru	...	...	...	...	...	...
Niue	...	...	...	...	...	...
Palau	...	...	...	...	33.9	26.2
Papua New Guinea	19.2	25.1	25.2	21.4	20.6	...
Samoa	...	...	...	...	...	...
Solomon Islands	...	...	21.4	10.2	9.7	...
Timor-Leste	...	...	...	...	13.8	16.7
Tonga	...	25.6	26.0	20.4	22.3	29.3
Tuvalu	...	...	...	...	...	...
Vanuatu	...	...	27.3	22.2	26.3	28.1
Developed Asia	32.1	35.0	31.1	30.2	25.0	23.8
Australia	32.1	28.9	27.9	25.1	26.6	26.2
Japan	...	36.3	31.6	30.8	24.7	23.2
New Zealand	...	26.1	24.8	21.4	23.3	22.1
Asia and the Pacific	22.0	31.4	30.2	31.0	29.5	34.6
Latin America and the Caribbean	20.5	23.8	21.0	20.4	20.0	20.5
Middle East and North Africa	26.3	40.0	27.4	25.1	26.2	28.1
Sub-Saharan Africa	...	...	29.3	23.0	21.8	21.7
OECD	...	26.4	24.6	23.4	22.7	21.3
World	23.1	27.2	25.8	24.9	24.6	24.4

... = data not available, GDP = gross domestic product, Lao PDR = Lao People's Democratic Republic, OECD = Organisation for Economic Co-operation and Development.

Sources: Asian Development Bank. Key Indicators Database. https://kidb.adb.org/kidb/ (accessed 16 September 2019); World Bank. World Development Indicators Database. http://data.worldbank .org (accessed 2 August 2019); Asian Development Bank estimates; and for Taipei,China: Directorate-General of Budget, Accounting and Statistics.

Appendix 13: Public Spending on Education
(% of GDP)

	1970–1979	1980–1989	1990–1999	2000–2009	2010–2018	2018
Developing Asia	2.1	2.5	2.7	3.3	3.6	3.6
Central Asia	...	...	...	...	4.0	3.6
Armenia	...	...	2.0	2.7	2.8	2.5
Azerbaijan	...	...	4.1	3.1	2.6	2.5
Georgia	...	...	3.7	2.6	3.2	3.8
Kazakhstan	...	...	4.1	2.8	3.3	2.9
Kyrgyz Republic	...	...	5.1	5.0	6.5	7.2
Tajikistan	...	...	3.4	3.1	5.0	5.6
Turkmenistan	...	...	...	...	3.0	...
Uzbekistan	...	...	...	...	6.7	6.4
East Asia	1.8	2.3	2.4	3.2	3.6	3.5
Hong Kong, China	2.3	2.3	2.7	4.0	3.5	3.3
Mongolia	...	...	4.9	5.6	4.5	4.1
People's Republic of China	1.8	2.0	1.8	3.0	3.6	3.6
Republic of Korea	2.9	3.8	3.4	4.0	4.4	3.2
Taipei,China	0.8	1.5	2.3	2.7	2.4	2.2
South Asia	...	...	3.6	3.3	3.7	4.2
Afghanistan	1.3	1.8	...	...	3.5	3.9
Bangladesh	1.1	1.2	1.7	2.1	2.1	2.5
Bhutan	...	...	...	5.7	6.1	7.1
India	...	...	3.8	3.5	4.0	4.6
Maldives	...	...	...	5.3	3.9	4.3
Nepal	...	...	2.9	3.5	4.0	5.1
Pakistan	2.0	2.3	2.7	2.4	2.4	2.8
Sri Lanka	2.9	2.6	3.0	2.0	2.1	2.8
Southeast Asia	2.9	1.6	2.7	3.7	3.6	3.2
Brunei Darussalam	3.9	3.2	4.3	4.0	3.2	4.4
Cambodia	...	...	1.3	1.6	2.0	2.5
Indonesia	2.8	0.9	1.0	2.9	3.2	2.7
Lao PDR	...	...	2.3	2.3	2.3	...
Malaysia	4.8	6.4	4.9	5.8	5.2	4.7
Myanmar	2.2	...	1.2	...	1.7	2.2
Philippines	...	1.8	3.4	2.8	3.0	4.1
Singapore	2.6	3.2	...	3.3	3.0	2.8
Thailand	2.8	3.0	3.8	4.1	3.8	3.1
Viet Nam	...	...	...	4.9	5.3	...

continued on next page

Appendix 13 *continued*

	1970–1979	1980–1989	1990–1999	2000–2009	2010–2018	2018
The Pacific	6.3	...	...	4.6	...	...
Cook Islands	...	...	...	3.9	3.7	2.7
Federated States of Micronesia	...	...	6.4	6.7	12.5	...
Fiji	5.2	5.7	5.3	5.5	4.0	...
Kiribati	4.1	...	10.9	11.6	10.5	11.0
Marshall Islands	...	...	14.5	10.5	16.6	15.5
Nauru	...	...	...	...	...	...
Niue	...	...	...	...	...	...
Palau	...	...	...	7.8	...	...
Papua New Guinea	6.3	...	...	3.7	...	...
Samoa	...	...	4.0	4.1	5.0	4.1
Solomon Islands	3.4	...	2.5	9.2	9.9	...
Timor-Leste	...	...	...	1.5	2.6	3.8
Tonga	...	10.3	5.5	4.2	...	...
Tuvalu	...	...	5.6	...	18.5	20.4
Vanuatu	...	...	6.1	7.2	5.6	4.7
Developed Asia	4.5	5.1	4.8	4.3	3.9	3.3
Australia	6.0	5.2	5.0	5.0	5.3	5.4
Japan	4.5	5.2	3.5	2.7	3.2	2.5
New Zealand	4.8	4.1	6.2	6.2	6.5	6.3
Asia and the Pacific	3.7	4.1	3.2	3.5	3.7	3.5
Latin America and the Caribbean	...	...	3.5	4.2	4.9	4.5
Middle East and North Africa	4.5	5.2	4.6	5.1	...	...
Sub-Saharan Africa	...	...	3.3	3.6	4.1	4.0
OECD	5.0	4.9	4.8	5.1	5.2	...
World	...	...	4.2	4.2	4.6	...

... = data not available, GDP = gross domestic product, Lao PDR = Lao People's Democratic Republic, OECD = Organisation for Economic Co-operation and Development.

Sources: Asian Development Bank. Key Indicators Database. http://kidb.adb.org (accessed 16 September 2019); World Bank. World Development Indicators Database. http://data.worldbank.org (accessed 2 August 2019); Asian Development Bank estimates; and for Taipei,China: Directorate-General of Budget, Accounting and Statistics.

Appendix 14: Public Spending on Health
(% of GDP)

	2000–2009	2010–2018	2018
Developing Asia	1.4	2.1	2.5
Central Asia	1.9	2.0	2.0
Armenia	1.4	1.5	1.6
Azerbaijan	0.9	1.2	1.4
Georgia	1.2	2.4	3.1
Kazakhstan	2.2	2.0	2.1
Kyrgyz Republic	2.8	3.5	2.6
Tajikistan	1.0	1.8	2.0
Turkmenistan	2.1	1.3	1.2
Uzbekistan	2.4	2.8	2.9
East Asia	1.6	2.4	2.9
Hong Kong, China	2.4	2.9	2.9
Mongolia	2.4	2.1	2.2
People's Republic of China	1.4	2.4	2.9
Republic of Korea	2.9	3.5	4.3
Taipei,China	0.2	0.1	0.1
South Asia	0.8	0.9	0.9
Afghanistan	0.5	0.7	0.5
Bangladesh	0.5	0.5	0.4
Bhutan	2.8	2.6	2.6
India	0.8	0.9	0.9
Maldives	3.4	5.1	7.7
Nepal	0.8	1.1	1.2
Pakistan	0.7	0.7	0.8
Sri Lanka	2.0	1.6	1.7
Southeast Asia	1.4	1.6	1.9
Brunei Darussalam	2.0	1.9	2.2
Cambodia	1.2	1.3	1.3
Indonesia	0.8	1.1	1.4
Lao PDR	0.9	0.6	0.8
Malaysia	1.5	1.9	1.9
Myanmar	0.2	0.7	1.0
Philippines	1.2	1.2	1.4
Singapore	1.1	1.9	2.4
Thailand	2.2	2.4	2.9
Viet Nam	2.2	2.6	2.7

continued on next page

Appendix 14 *continued*

	2000–2009	2010–2018	2018
The Pacific	2.2	2.0	2.0
Cook Islands	3.6	3.4	3.0
Federated States of Micronesia	2.2	3.0	3.5
Fiji	2.5	2.2	2.2
Kiribati	10.3	8.2	7.3
Marshall Islands	11.1	10.6	12.3
Nauru	11.1	4.9	6.7
Niue	...	...	...
Palau	3.7	5.0	7.0
Papua New Guinea	1.6	1.7	1.4
Samoa	3.4	4.0	4.2
Solomon Islands	5.8	3.6	3.6
Timor-Leste	0.8	1.4	2.2
Tonga	2.6	2.8	3.5
Tuvalu	13.0	13.5	13.1
Vanuatu	2.3	1.9	2.0
Developed Asia	6.2	8.0	8.5
Australia	5.5	6.3	6.3
Japan	6.3	8.7	9.1
New Zealand	6.6	7.3	7.3
Asia and the Pacific	3.8	3.7	3.8
Latin America and the Caribbean	3.0	3.8	4.1
Middle East and North Africa	2.5	2.9	3.3
Sub-Saharan Africa	1.8	1.9	1.8
OECD	6.3	8.5	10.1
World	5.4	6.4	7.4

... = data not available, GDP = gross domestic product, Lao PDR = Lao People's Democratic Republic, OECD = Organisation for Economic Co-operation and Development.

Sources: Asian Development Bank. Key Indicators Database. http://kidb.adb.org (accessed 16 September 2019); World Bank. World Development Indicators Database. http://data.worldbank.org (accessed 2 August 2019); Asian Development Bank estimates; and for Taipei,China: Directorate-General of Budget, Accounting and Statistics.

Appendix 15: Poverty Rate

	(a) Poverty Using $1.90 per Day (2011 PPP) Poverty Line					(b) Poverty Using $3.20 per Day (2011 PPP) Poverty Line				
	1981	1990	2002	2010	2015	1981	1990	2002	2010	2015
Developing Asia	68.1	53.6	33.1	17.0	6.9	87.5	81.2	64.0	44.8	28.6
Central Asia	11.4	12.3	31.1	12.8	6.2	25.9	27.8	55.8	33.1	23.0
Armenia	5.1	4.9	15.1	1.9	1.9	20.3	19.8	52.3	20.5	13.5
Azerbaijan	0.7	0.7	0.0	0.0	0.0	2.7	2.8	0.6	0.0	0.0
Georgia	0.0	0.0	10.5	12.2	3.8	0.0	0.0	30.4	31.1	16.1
Kazakhstan	1.7	3.2	6.8	0.1	0.0	14.3	17.5	27.9	1.9	0.4
Kyrgyz Republic	14.2	11.7	34.1	4.1	2.5	32.3	28.0	71.7	23.2	23.4
Tajikistan	1.8	2.4	32.9	4.7	4.8	8.7	11.8	70.0	24.5	20.3
Turkmenistan	28.9	19.4	39.8	12.7	2.8	57.4	45.4	68.5	35.6	16.7
Uzbekistan	27.1	29.3	58.2	29.3	14.0	50.6	53.6	85.9	66.8	46.3
East Asia	84.7	63.7	30.5	10.8	0.7	95.8	86.7	55.6	27.5	6.7
Hong Kong, China	...	...	...	...	...	...	...	...	...	...
Mongolia	13.1	7.0	9.7	0.8	0.3	37.6	26.5	33.6	10.1	4.1
People's Republic of China	88.1	66.2	31.7	11.2	0.7	99.3	90.0	57.7	28.5	7.0
Republic of Korea	2.5	0.7	0.2	0.5	0.2	7.7	1.7	0.5	0.7	0.5
Taipei,China	...	...	...	...	...	...	...	...	...	...
South Asia	55.7	47.3	38.6	24.6	12.4	85.5	81.7	75.5	63.9	48.6
Afghanistan	...	...	...	...	...	...	...	...	...	...
Bangladesh	27.0	38.5	33.9	19.6	15.2	73.8	80.0	72.0	60.4	53.6
Bhutan	77.3	49.3	23.7	4.3	0.9	91.8	75.3	52.7	20.6	7.6
India	57.4	47.4	40.9	27.9	13.4	86.5	81.9	77.2	67.4	50.4
Maldives	...	...	12.1	6.8	3.8	...	...	42.0	23.5	18.0
Nepal	77.5	70.0	48.3	15.4	7.0	94.3	90.2	77.5	51.1	37.4
Pakistan	72.6	57.2	28.4	9.5	5.3	91.8	86.0	71.7	50.0	38.5
Sri Lanka	23.6	10.1	8.3	2.3	0.7	60.2	45.5	36.0	17.7	9.2
Southeast Asia	60.1	48.8	24.7	11.0	5.4	78.1	73.0	55.4	34.8	24.1
Brunei Darussalam	...	...	...	...	...	...	...	...	...	...
Cambodia	...	...	...	...	...	...	...	...	...	...
Indonesia	76.4	58.8	22.8	15.7	7.2	93.5	87.0	65.0	48.1	33.1
Lao PDR	50.6	36.2	34.7	24.0	17.7	80.3	71.0	72.7	61.4	52.0
Malaysia	3.5	1.4	0.6	0.2	0.0	14.4	11.2	4.9	2.5	0.3
Myanmar	94.2	95.6	72.6	16.8	6.2	98.4	98.9	92.2	52.0	29.5
Philippines	24.2	25.1	13.6	12.0	7.8	53.1	53.2	41.2	38.7	32.6
Singapore	...	...	...	...	...	...	...	...	...	...
Thailand	19.6	9.4	1.1	0.1	0.0	43.1	36.2	12.1	2.5	0.5
Viet Nam	76.3	62.0	38.0	4.2	2.4	92.1	85.0	70.8	17.3	9.7

continued on next page

Appendix 15 *continued*

	(a) Poverty Using $1.90 per Day (2011 PPP) Poverty Line					(b) Poverty Using $3.20 per Day (2011 PPP) Poverty Line				
	1981	1990	2002	2010	2015	1981	1990	2002	2010	2015
The Pacific	**49.9**	**51.1**	**45.7**	**32.3**	**25.7**	**67.9**	**68.8**	**67.3**	**59.3**	**51.5**
Cook Islands	...	...	...	...	...	...	...	...	...	...
Federated States of Micronesia	...	12.1	8.5	12.0	15.1	...	33.4	25.4	32.0	37.6
Fiji	7.7	8.5	5.0	3.0	1.0	28.8	31.3	22.0	16.9	11.6
Kiribati	7.0	12.6	12.6	14.7	12.6	22.4	33.1	32.8	40.0	33.0
Marshall Islands	...	...	...	...	...	...	...	...	...	...
Nauru	...	...	...	...	...	...	...	...	...	...
Niue	...	...	...	...	...	...	...	...	...	...
Palau	...	...	...	...	...	...	...	...	...	...
Papua New Guinea	60.7	64.5	55.1	37.3	29.2	77.6	80.4	76.1	64.5	54.3
Samoa	...	5.8	2.0	1.1	1.0	...	22.2	11.9	11.1	9.6
Solomon Islands	...	39.7	50.2	34.2	24.8	...	66.1	74.1	65.5	58.4
Timor-Leste	...	...	46.1	38.6	32.3	...	...	77.4	78.3	74.5
Tonga	6.9	4.7	2.2	1.1	1.0	23.7	18.0	7.9	8.5	7.5
Tuvalu	...	8.4	2.3	3.3	1.3	...	28.8	13.9	17.6	11.7
Vanuatu	29.2	19.3	20.9	13.1	15.3	62.0	48.6	50.6	39.2	42.1
Latin America and the Caribbean	**13.5**	**14.8**	**11.8**	**6.2**	**3.9**	**27.1**	**29.0**	**24.8**	**14.2**	**10.6**
Middle East and North Africa	**10.5**	**6.2**	**3.4**	**2.0**	**4.2**	**34.6**	**26.8**	**20.1**	**13.7**	**15.6**
Sub-Saharan Africa	**48.8**	**54.7**	**55.3**	**46.5**	**41.4**	**70.8**	**75.2**	**77.5**	**71.2**	**67.0**
OECD	**1.3**	**1.3**	**1.2**	**0.9**	**0.9**	**3.5**	**3.4**	**3.4**	**2.4**	**2.3**
World	**42.1**	**35.9**	**25.5**	**15.7**	**10.0**	**56.9**	**55.2**	**47.1**	**35.2**	**26.3**

... = data not available, 0.0 = magnitude is less than half of unit employed, GDP = gross domestic product, Lao PDR = Lao People's Democratic Republic, OECD = Organisation for Economic Co-operation and Development, PPP = purchasing power parity.

Sources: Asian Development Bank estimates using World Bank. PovcalNet Database. http://iresearch.worldbank.org/PovcalNet/home.aspx (accessed 7 November 2019); and for Taipei,China: Directorate-General of Budget, Accounting and Statistics.

Appendix 16: Net Enrollment Rate, Primary, Both Sexes
(%)

	1970	1980	1990	2000	2018
Developing Asia	77.3	91.1	87.0	88.3	93.3
Central Asia	...	...	...	...	92.9
Armenia	...	...	...	84.5	90.7
Azerbaijan	...	...	96.2	88.2	92.4
Georgia	...	...	91.4	99.9	96.4
Kazakhstan	...	...	...	87.0	87.6
Kyrgyz Republic	...	...	...	86.2	89.9
Tajikistan	...	...	...	94.8	98.3
Turkmenistan	...	...	...	...	...
Uzbekistan	...	...	...	...	94.6
East Asia	94.1	94.3	97.9	99.1	99.8
Hong Kong, China	88.5	99.2	93.9	93.8	95.5
Mongolia	...	96.5	94.4	90.0	97.7
People's Republic of China	94.0	94.0	97.8	99.1	99.9
Republic of Korea	95.9	100.0	99.8	99.1	97.3
Taipei,China	...	97.6	98.0	98.8	97.1
South Asia	59.3	...	76.1	78.0	88.5
Afghanistan	26.8	...	26.8	...	...
Bangladesh	51.6	68.6	74.9	93.7	...
Bhutan	...	24.8	...	57.3	88.0
India	61.0	...	77.1	79.5	92.3
Maldives	...	...	...	96.7	95.4
Nepal	...	58.9	66.1	72.1	96.3
Pakistan	...	...	...	55.3	67.7
Sri Lanka	...	78.5	98.2	99.7	99.1
Southeast Asia	71.2	88.5	92.4	92.4	94.6
Brunei Darussalam	...	79.9	89.9	98.0	93.1
Cambodia	...	...	...	92.4	90.3
Indonesia	70.1	90.1	96.2	91.9	93.5
Lao PDR	...	...	64.7	75.9	91.5
Malaysia	87.0	...	97.3	98.4	99.6
Myanmar	60.8	64.3	...	89.7	97.7
Philippines	...	93.2	82.8	89.5	93.8
Singapore	...	...	96.1	95.7	100.0
Thailand	75.5	...	...	...	...
Viet Nam	...	93.9	91.4	97.9	98.0

continued on next page

Appendix 16 *continued*

	1970	1980	1990	2000	2018
The Pacific	...	...	64.9	...	77.7
Cook Islands	...	...	...	75.7	96.9
Federated States of Micronesia	...	...	...	...	85.5
Fiji	...	...	96.6	92.7	96.8
Kiribati	...	99.7	99.7	99.1	94.7
Marshall Islands	...	...	...	96.3	73.2
Nauru	...	94.0	94.0	...	93.7
Niue	...	...	...	...	...
Palau	...	...	...	...	94.9
Papua New Guinea	...	...	57.5	...	73.7
Samoa	...	...	93.4	89.3	94.4
Solomon Islands	...	...	...	75.4	67.5
Timor-Leste	...	...	...	...	92.3
Tonga	87.7	98.7	92.3	98.7	85.9
Tuvalu	...	...	...	...	76.2
Vanuatu	...	85.1	75.1	98.6	79.8
Developed Asia	99.0	99.9	99.6	98.7	97.8
Australia	96.5	100.0	98.0	94.4	96.4
Japan	99.3	99.9	99.8	99.8	98.2
New Zealand	100.0	99.5	99.5	99.8	99.1
Asia and the Pacific	78.4	91.6	87.5	88.6	93.4
Latin America and the Caribbean	83.2	89.9	90.3	94.2	93.7
Middle East and North Africa	64.8	72.3	79.6	82.3	88.4
Sub-Saharan Africa	39.3	54.6	53.1	60.5	...
OECD	88.0	91.1	98.1	96.8	95.6
World	71.7	77.5	82.0	83.4	89.4

... = data not available, Lao PDR = Lao People's Democratic Republic, OECD = Organisation for Economic Co-operation and Development.

Notes: Where no data are available for the specific year headings, +/– 5-year available data are reflected. For the People's Republic of China, 1970 and 1980 refer to 1978 data.

Sources: United Nations Educational, Scientific and Cultural Organization (UNESCO) Institute for Statistics (UIS). UIS Stat Database. http://data.uis.unesco.org/ (accessed 2 August 2019); Asian Development Bank estimates; for the People's Republic of China: National Bureau of Statistics. *China Statistical Yearbook.* http://www.stats.gov.cn/english/Statisticaldata/AnnualData/ (accessed 2 August 2019); for Japan: World Bank. World Development Indicators. https://data.worldbank.org (accessed 2 August 2019); for Singapore: Government of Singapore, Ministry of Education. *Education Statistics Digest 2018*; and for Taipei,China: Ministry of Education. *2018 Education Statistical Indicators.*

Appendix 17: Gross Enrollment Ratio, Secondary, Both Sexes
(%)

	1970	1980	1990	2000	2018
Developing Asia	25.0	37.5	39.0	52.1	78.9
Central Asia	...	101.1	99.9	85.8	95.9
Armenia	...	...	92.1	92.2	83.2
Azerbaijan	...	92.8	91.7	73.8	94.5
Georgia	...	109.0	96.1	87.2	106.0
Kazakhstan	...	94.1	101.1	93.7	114.2
Kyrgyz Republic	...	108.1	105.0	84.8	95.1
Tajikistan	...	...	102.6	72.9	88.5
Turkmenistan	...	...	...	...	85.8
Uzbekistan	...	106.7	101.7	88.1	93.3
East Asia	28.3	45.3	39.7	61.8	95.2
Hong Kong, China	36.4	61.6	74.5	80.2	107.5
Mongolia	64.0	83.4	88.7	65.1	...
People's Republic of China	27.5	43.2	36.7	60.3	95.0
Republic of Korea	39.0	75.7	92.9	96.0	100.3
Taipei,China	...	97.6	98.0	98.8	97.1
South Asia	23.2	26.9	34.4	42.9	69.3
Afghanistan	8.3	16.8	10.8	12.3	53.8
Bangladesh	20.8	19.0	20.9	49.8	72.7
Bhutan	2.3	9.3	11.6	30.0	90.1
India	23.8	28.9	37.2	44.9	73.5
Maldives	2.0	3.7	50.4	51.3	...
Nepal	...	18.6	33.0	35.8	74.1
Pakistan	16.6	17.0	22.0	22.5	42.8
Sri Lanka	45.9	53.6	82.9	87.2	98.0
Southeast Asia	22.9	34.8	41.8	56.4	87.5
Brunei Darussalam	53.9	61.1	73.2	84.6	93.5
Cambodia	8.4	...	27.2	17.3	...
Indonesia	18.2	28.4	46.6	55.1	88.9
Lao PDR	3.7	18.4	23.2	34.1	67.4
Malaysia	39.2	54.8	63.4	77.4	82.0
Myanmar	20.2	20.4	19.5	36.9	64.3
Philippines	47.5	64.0	70.2	74.7	86.2
Singapore	...	...	95.1	98.7	108.1
Thailand	18.1	27.8	28.5	62.9	116.7
Viet Nam	...	43.5	34.9	58.3	...

continued on next page

Appendix 17 *continued*

	1970	1980	1990	2000	2018
The Pacific	**19.8**	**26.9**	**22.7**	**31.1**	**54.4**
Cook Islands	33.8	...	90.3	72.1	86.6
Federated States of Micronesia	133.8	162.9	...	82.4	...
Fiji	52.1	71.8	76.7	78.4	...
Kiribati	11.3	27.7	37.4	63.5	...
Marshall Islands	...	...	...	68.5	64.4
Nauru	49.3	50.2	50.2	49.2	82.7
Niue	71.9	88.7	84.3	79.7	100.0
Palau	...	...	...	91.3	116.5
Papua New Guinea	6.5	10.2	10.5	17.7	47.5
Samoa	56.0	76.0	76.5	78.5	93.3
Solomon Islands	8.0	16.4	13.9	20.5	...
Timor-Leste	...	...	...	37.9	83.6
Tonga	86.6	105.4	98.4	106.6	100.9
Tuvalu	...	...	84.1	59.5	66.7
Vanuatu	5.8	12.7	17.7	34.7	54.2
Developed Asia	**84.3**	**91.2**	**99.1**	**108.0**	**112.4**
Australia	81.1	...	134.4	152.9	150.3
Japan	85.0	91.6	94.7	99.8	102.4
New Zealand	76.7	81.3	88.6	110.8	114.6
Asia and the Pacific	**28.2**	**39.2**	**41.1**	**53.5**	**79.6**
Latin America and the Caribbean	**27.7**	**72.2**	**76.9**	**85.3**	**95.9**
Middle East and North Africa	**33.2**	**44.2**	**56.6**	**65.6**	**83.0**
Sub-Saharan Africa	**11.4**	**17.6**	**22.6**	**25.6**	**43.3**
OECD	**68.8**	**78.8**	**86.2**	**94.9**	**106.6**
World	**40.1**	**49.5**	**51.3**	**59.9**	**75.6**

... = data not available, Lao PDR = Lao People's Democratic Republic, OECD = Organisation for Economic Co-operation and Development.

Note: Where no data are available for the specific year headings, +/– 5-year available data are reflected. Rates can be more than 100% because of the enrollment of overage students and/or international students.

Sources: United Nations Educational, Scientific and Cultural Organization (UNESCO) Institute for Statistics (UIS). UIS Stat Database. http://data.uis.unesco.org/ (accessed 2 August 2019); Asian Development Bank estimates; for the People's Republic of China (2018) and Japan (all years): World Bank. World Development Indicators. https://data.worldbank.org (accessed 2 August 2019); for Singapore: Government of Singapore, Ministry of Education. *Education Statistics Digest 2018*; and for Taipei,China: Ministry of Education. *2018 Education Statistical Indicators*.

Appendix 18: Gross Enrollment Ratio, Tertiary, Both Sexes
(%)

	1970	1980	1990	2000	2018
Developing Asia	2.4	5.0	6.5	11.6	34.3
Central Asia	...	...	25.7	22.3	26.4
Armenia	...	...	23.2	35.5	54.6
Azerbaijan	...	24.0	24.2	17.6	27.7
Georgia	...	29.6	36.2	39.1	60.3
Kazakhstan	...	33.9	39.7	31.8	54.0
Kyrgyz Republic	...	...	26.8	35.4	41.3
Tajikistan	...	24.7	22.5	17.9	31.3
Turkmenistan	...	22.7	12.1	...	8.0
Uzbekistan	...	...	17.5	13.1	10.1
East Asia	0.4	3.8	5.4	12.0	53.0
Hong Kong, China	7.5	10.1	18.1	31.8	76.9
Mongolia	22.6	26.1	18.2	30.2	65.6
People's Republic of China	0.1	1.1	3.0	7.6	50.6
Republic of Korea	6.8	12.4	36.5	76.7	94.3
Taipei,China	...	97.6	98.0	98.8	97.1
South Asia	4.3	4.5	5.4	8.2	24.2
Afghanistan	0.8	1.9	2.2	1.2	9.7
Bangladesh	2.1	3.2	4.2	5.6	20.6
Bhutan	...	0.9	...	2.7	15.6
India	4.9	5.0	5.9	9.5	28.1
Maldives	...	...	...	0.2	31.2
Nepal	...	3.5	5.2	4.2	12.4
Pakistan	2.3	2.2	3.1	2.7	9.1
Sri Lanka	1.0	2.8	4.8	...	19.6
Southeast Asia	5.5	7.1	10.2	18.3	34.1
Brunei Darussalam	...	2.2	5.3	12.7	31.4
Cambodia	1.4	0.1	0.7	2.5	13.1
Indonesia	2.9	3.3	8.4	14.9	36.3
Lao PDR	0.2	0.4	1.1	2.7	15.0
Malaysia	...	4.0	7.2	25.6	45.1
Myanmar	1.7	4.6	5.0	10.9	15.7
Philippines	17.6	23.3	24.0	30.4	35.5
Singapore	6.5	...	95.1	98.7	84.8
Thailand	2.9	10.4	15.9	34.9	49.3
Viet Nam	...	2.4	2.8	9.5	28.5

continued on next page

Appendix 18 *continued*

	1970	1980	1990	2000	2018
The Pacific	1.7	2.1	3.1	4.3	...
Cook Islands	...	...	...	...	...
Federated States of Micronesia	...	19.7	...	14.1	...
Fiji	0.7	2.4	11.8	15.8	...
Kiribati	...	...	...	...	...
Marshall Islands	...	...	...	16.2	...
Nauru	...	...	...	...	...
Niue	...	...	...	...	...
Palau	...	...	...	44.5	54.7
Papua New Guinea	2.0	1.5	1.6	1.8	...
Samoa	1.0	3.7	...	7.6	...
Solomon Islands	...	...	...	...	...
Timor-Leste	...	...	...	8.7	...
Tonga	...	7.1	6.3	4.9	...
Tuvalu	...	...	...	...	...
Vanuatu	...	...	...	3.8	...
Developed Asia	17.2	29.8	30.2	44.7	73.2
Australia	15.8	25.2	35.4	80.9	113.1
Japan	17.3	30.5	29.4	39.1	63.6
New Zealand	16.3	26.7	39.3	59.3	82.0
Asia and the Pacific	3.4	6.2	7.5	12.7	34.8
Latin America and the Caribbean	6.9	13.5	17.0	23.1	51.8
Middle East and North Africa	7.3	10.8	12.9	20.7	46.3
Sub-Saharan Africa	0.9	1.8	3.0	4.4	9.1
OECD	22.1	30.4	38.2	49.8	73.5
World	9.7	12.4	13.6	19.1	38.0

... = data not available, Lao PDR = Lao People's Democratic Republic, OECD = Organisation for Economic Co-operation and Development.

Note: Where no data are available for the specific year headings, +/– 5-year available data are reflected. Rates can be more than 100% because of the enrollment of overage students and/or international students.

Sources: United Nations Educational, Scientific and Cultural Organization (UNESCO) Institute for Statistics (UIS). UIS Stat Database. http://data.uis.unesco.org/ (accessed 2 August 2019); Asian Development Bank estimates; for Japan: World Bank. World Development Indicators. https://data.worldbank.org (accessed 2 August 2019); UIS. UIS Stat Database. http://data.uis.unesco.org/ (accessed 7 February 2019); for Singapore: Government of Singapore, Ministry of Education. *Education Statistics Digest 2018*; and for Taipei,China: Ministry of Education. *2018 Education Statistical Indicators*.

Appendix 19: Life Expectancy at Birth
(years)

	1960	1970	1980	1990	2000	2010	2018
Developing Asia	**45.0**	**54.3**	**59.3**	**63.0**	**65.8**	**69.4**	**71.8**
Central Asia	**58.7**	**62.1**	**64.2**	**65.5**	**65.7**	**69.1**	**71.8**
Armenia	66.0	70.1	70.9	67.9	71.4	73.3	74.9
Azerbaijan	61.0	63.1	64.2	64.8	66.8	70.9	72.9
Georgia	63.7	67.5	69.7	70.4	69.9	71.5	73.6
Kazakhstan	58.4	62.5	65.1	66.8	63.5	67.4	73.2
Kyrgyz Republic	56.2	60.5	63.2	66.3	66.3	68.8	71.3
Tajikistan	50.6	54.0	57.1	58.8	62.0	68.7	70.9
Turkmenistan	54.5	58.5	61.0	62.8	63.6	66.7	68.1
Uzbekistan	58.8	62.4	64.6	66.5	67.2	69.7	71.6
East Asia	**44.6**	**59.3**	**66.9**	**69.3**	**71.6**	**74.6**	**76.9**
Hong Kong, China	67.4	71.7	74.7	77.5	80.8	82.9	84.7
Mongolia	48.4	55.4	56.9	60.3	62.9	67.4	69.7
People's Republic of China	43.7	59.1	66.8	69.1	71.4	74.4	76.7
Republic of Korea	55.2	61.3	66.1	71.7	76.0	80.4	82.8
Taipei,China	64.2	68.2	71.5	73.9	76.0	78.8	80.3
South Asia	**42.3**	**48.0**	**53.9**	**58.1**	**62.7**	**66.7**	**69.2**
Afghanistan	32.4	37.4	43.2	50.3	55.8	61.0	64.5
Bangladesh	45.4	46.9	52.9	58.2	65.4	69.9	72.3
Bhutan	34.5	39.6	45.5	52.9	60.9	68.4	71.5
India	41.4	47.7	53.8	57.9	62.5	66.7	69.4
Maldives	37.3	44.1	53.0	61.5	70.2	75.9	78.6
Nepal	35.6	40.9	46.8	54.4	62.3	67.6	70.5
Pakistan	45.3	52.6	56.9	60.1	62.8	65.3	67.1
Sri Lanka	59.4	64.1	68.2	69.5	71.3	75.4	76.8
Southeast Asia	**51.3**	**55.5**	**59.9**	**64.6**	**67.1**	**70.0**	**72.1**
Brunei Darussalam	54.8	62.6	67.4	70.2	72.8	74.7	75.7
Cambodia	41.2	41.6	27.5	53.6	58.4	66.6	69.6
Indonesia	46.7	52.6	58.0	62.3	65.8	69.2	71.5
Lao PDR	43.2	46.3	49.1	53.4	58.8	64.3	67.6
Malaysia	60.0	64.6	68.1	70.9	72.6	74.5	76.0
Myanmar	42.4	48.8	52.9	56.8	60.1	63.5	66.9
Philippines	61.1	63.2	63.7	66.4	68.8	69.8	71.1
Singapore	65.5	68.1	72.0	75.9	78.0	81.8	83.5
Thailand	54.7	59.4	64.4	70.2	70.6	74.2	76.9
Viet Nam	59.0	59.6	67.5	70.6	73.0	74.8	75.3

continued on next page

Appendix 19 *continued*

	1960	1970	1980	1990	2000	2010	2018
The Pacific	**42.5**	**48.2**	**53.1**	**57.3**	**60.6**	**63.9**	**65.9**
Cook Islands	...	...	...	...	...	...	...
Federated States of Micronesia	54.5	58.9	62.3	63.6	64.6	66.5	67.8
Fiji	60.8	62.5	64.0	65.4	65.7	66.7	67.3
Kiribati	47.1	52.3	56.0	59.6	63.1	65.8	68.1
Marshall Islands	...	...	...	...	...	...	...
Nauru	...	...	...	...	...	...	...
Niue	...	...	...	...	...	...	...
Palau	...	...	...	...	...	...	...
Papua New Guinea	38.9	45.9	52.7	56.5	59.3	62.0	64.3
Samoa	56.9	59.9	63.6	66.3	68.7	71.7	73.2
Solomon Islands	48.1	56.2	62.5	64.4	67.4	70.7	72.8
Timor-Leste	33.7	39.5	34.4	48.5	59.0	67.2	69.3
Tonga	59.9	64.0	66.9	68.9	69.7	70.1	70.8
Tuvalu	...	...	...	...	...	...	...
Vanuatu	49.0	54.5	60.0	64.7	67.4	69.1	70.3
Developed Asia	**68.3**	**72.2**	**75.9**	**78.5**	**80.8**	**82.7**	**84.1**
Australia	70.7	71.2	74.4	76.9	79.6	81.9	83.3
Japan	67.9	72.4	76.3	79.0	81.2	83.0	84.5
New Zealand	71.0	71.5	73.2	75.4	78.3	80.9	82.1
Asia and the Pacific	**45.7**	**54.8**	**59.7**	**63.3**	**66.1**	**69.7**	**72.0**
Latin America and the Caribbean	**56.2**	**60.5**	**64.7**	**68.4**	**71.7**	**74.1**	**75.5**
Middle East and North Africa	**46.7**	**52.6**	**58.5**	**65.8**	**69.9**	**72.5**	**74.1**
Sub-Saharan Africa	**40.2**	**44.3**	**48.3**	**50.2**	**50.4**	**56.7**	**61.3**
OECD	**67.8**	**69.8**	**72.6**	**74.9**	**77.2**	**79.4**	**80.5**
World	**50.1**	**56.9**	**61.2**	**64.2**	**66.3**	**69.9**	**72.4**

... = data not available, Lao PDR = Lao People's Democratic Republic, OECD = Organisation for Economic Co-operation and Development.

Source: United Nations, Department of Economic and Social Affairs, Population Division. 2019. *World Population Prospects 2019.* Online Edition. https://population.un.org/wpp/ (accessed 16 September 2019).

Appendix 20: Under-Five Mortality Rate (U5MR)
Under-five mortality (deaths under age 5 per 1,000 live births)

	1960	1970	1980	1990	2000	2010	2018
Developing Asia	215.0	156.6	121.9	91.8	69.8	43.7	31.7
Central Asia	136.5	114.7	97.9	81.0	64.1	36.2	23.6
Armenia	84.8	70.6	60.2	55.3	34.8	19.7	12.8
Azerbaijan	153.8	129.4	121.7	106.4	72.2	41.3	25.0
Georgia	76.7	59.3	50.7	48.2	35.0	17.2	9.9
Kazakhstan	123.7	99.3	79.3	61.7	46.6	22.0	9.7
Kyrgyz Republic	152.2	124.2	101.0	77.3	50.9	28.4	17.8
Tajikistan	194.0	161.5	133.2	111.7	92.0	41.8	31.5
Turkmenistan	169.2	140.5	117.3	97.8	79.7	60.1	50.8
Uzbekistan	140.3	118.1	101.9	79.2	64.3	40.6	25.2
East Asia	205.0	115.8	61.7	51.1	36.8	16.6	11.0
Hong Kong, China	53.6	25.5	13.5	7.4	4.1	2.7	2.1
Mongolia	240.3	170.5	157.6	113.9	59.3	32.0	21.8
People's Republic of China	212.0	118.8	63.3	52.5	38.3	17.1	11.2
Republic of Korea	109.3	60.9	39.1	16.5	7.6	4.1	2.6
Taipei,China	67.5	36.4	14.8	8.5	8.6	5.9	4.6
South Asia	244.4	213.1	169.0	127.9	92.3	61.1	44.6
Afghanistan	357.8	300.8	241.1	175.1	128.5	90.0	66.5
Bangladesh	255.1	239.6	194.3	140.6	85.1	47.5	31.5
Bhutan	328.3	263.4	202.0	138.7	83.8	42.8	28.8
India	240.1	210.9	165.5	124.4	89.8	56.5	38.5
Maldives	351.4	261.1	155.9	93.5	43.9	12.9	7.6
Nepal	321.5	264.9	208.0	140.5	81.6	47.0	32.8
Pakistan	253.4	190.6	162.9	137.8	111.4	89.5	74.2
Sri Lanka	104.6	72.0	45.1	28.6	17.0	10.9	8.4
Southeast Asia	178.0	131.0	104.5	70.2	48.2	32.3	24.9
Brunei Darussalam	119.1	51.2	22.4	13.3	11.9	10.8	10.0
Cambodia	200.0	183.2	357.1	111.4	104.3	42.5	26.6
Indonesia	222.6	165.1	120.2	83.9	52.8	33.2	24.4
Lao PDR	242.0	213.0	187.0	149.0	106.6	68.1	47.3
Malaysia	92.4	53.0	30.5	16.6	10.8	8.3	6.9
Myanmar	246.1	169.3	136.1	107.1	82.9	62.4	47.3
Philippines	103.5	84.0	80.1	58.1	38.6	31.3	27.4
Singapore	47.0	27.3	13.1	6.3	4.0	2.7	2.0
Thailand	145.2	97.0	59.3	36.0	21.9	13.6	8.8
Viet Nam	114.6	82.7	62.3	48.1	32.6	22.7	20.8

continued on next page

Appendix 20 *continued*

	1960	1970	1980	1990	2000	2010	2018
The Pacific	197.9	146.2	118.4	89.6	72.2	58.6	46.3
Cook Islands	...	...	...	...	...	...	...
Federated States of Micronesia	122.0	86.8	60.4	55.8	53.2	40.2	31.5
Fiji	76.8	57.5	44.5	29.0	22.9	24.0	24.3
Kiribati	190.6	138.3	120.9	96.8	71.2	64.2	53.6
Marshall Islands	...	...	...	...	...	...	...
Nauru	...	...	...	...	...	...	...
Niue	...	...	...	...	...	...	...
Palau	...	...	...	...	...	...	...
Papua New Guinea	199.5	142.2	105.7	87.5	77.9	66.5	52.3
Samoa	111.3	85.3	51.3	30.3	21.8	19.2	16.0
Solomon Islands	185.5	104.9	53.5	38.1	30.4	25.7	19.9
Timor-Leste	342.7	278.1	336.1	191.2	106.5	61.0	45.9
Tonga	86.4	50.0	29.6	22.0	17.3	17.1	15.5
Tuvalu	...	...	...	...	...	...	...
Vanuatu	152.9	108.4	68.1	35.7	29.1	29.1	26.3
Developed Asia	37.2	17.9	10.4	6.9	4.9	3.7	2.8
Australia	24.7	21.0	13.2	9.1	6.3	4.8	3.6
Japan	39.3	17.4	9.8	6.3	4.5	3.3	2.4
New Zealand	27.4	20.8	15.4	10.9	7.1	5.7	4.6
Asia and the Pacific	216.2	157.2	122.2	91.9	69.9	43.8	31.8
Latin America and the Caribbean	155.3	119.1	83.9	54.1	34.4	22.8	18.8
Middle East and North Africa	254.6	193.1	120.8	67.0	41.7	27.5	21.7
Sub-Saharan Africa	271.8	233.3	199.6	183.6	153.3	101.8	76.0
OECD	68.9	51.8	34.5	22.1	12.9	8.6	7.1
World	188.0	146.4	116.3	93.2	76.3	51.2	39.3

... = data not available, Lao PDR = Lao People's Democratic Republic, OECD = Organisation for Economic Co-operation and Development.

Source: United Nations, Department of Economic and Social Affairs, Population Division. 2019. *World Population Prospects 2019*. Online Edition. https://population.un.org/wpp/ (accessed 16 September 2019).

REFERENCES

Abhayaratne, A. 2004. *Poverty Reduction Strategies in Malaysia, 1970–2000: Some Lessons.* http://unpan1.un.org/intradoc/groups/public/documents/apcity/unpan032206.pdf.

Abiad, A., R. Hasan, Y. Jiang, and E. Patalinghug. 2020. The Past and Future Role of Infrastructure in Asia's Development. In Susantono, B., D. Park, and S. Tian, eds. *Infrastructure Financing in Asia.* Singapore: World Scientific.

Abood, S. A., J. S. Lee, Z. Burivalova, J. Garcia-Ulloa, and L. P. Koh. 2015. Relative Contributions of the Logging, Fiber, Oil Palm, and Mining Industries to Forest Loss in Indonesia. *Conservation Letters.* 8. pp. 58–67.

Acemoglu, D., and J. A. Robinson. 2012. *Why Nations Fail: The Origins of Power, Prosperity, and Poverty.* New York: Crown Publishing Group.

Acharya, A. 2005. Why Is There No NATO in Asia? The Normative Origins of Asian Multilateralism. *Weatherhead Center for International Affairs Working Paper Series.* No. 05-05. Cambridge, MA: Harvard University.

———. 2014. Foundations of Collective Action in Asia: Theory and Practice of Regional Cooperation. In Capannelli, G., and M. Kawai, eds. *The Political Economy of Asian Regionalism.* Tokyo: Asian Development Bank Institute and Springer.

African Development Bank, Asian Development Bank, European Bank for Reconstruction and Development, European Investment Bank, Inter-American Development Bank Group, Islamic Development Bank, and the World Bank Group. 2019. *2018 Joint Report on Multilateral Development Banks' Climate Finance.* London: European Bank for Reconstruction and Development. https://www.adb.org/news/mdb-climate-finance-hit-record-high-431-billion-2018.

Aghion, P., N. Bloom, R. Blundell, R. Griffith, and P. Howitt. 2005. Competition and Innovation: An Inverted-U Relationship. *Quarterly Journal of Economics.* 120 (2). pp. 701–728.

Aghion, P., R. Burgess, S. Redding, and F. Zilibotti. 2008. The Unequal Effects of Liberalization: Evidence from Dismantling the License Raj in India. *American Economic Review.* 94 (4). pp. 1397–1412.

Aghion, P., and P. Howitt. 1997. *Endogenous Growth Theory.* Cambridge, MA: The MIT Press.

Agustina, R., T. Dartanto, R. Sitompul, K. A. Susiloretni, E. L. Achadi, A. Taher, F. Wirawan, S. Sungkar, P. Sudarmono, A. H. Shankar, and H. Thabrany. 2019. Universal Health Coverage in Indonesia: Concept, Progress, and Challenges. *The Lancet.* 393 (10166). pp. 75–102.

Ahmed, A., and C. del Ninno. 2003. Food for Education in Bangladesh. In Quisumbing, A., ed. *Household Decisions, Gender, and Development.* Baltimore: Johns Hopkins University Press.

Ahmed, R., S. Haggblade, and T. Chowdhury, eds. 2000. *Out of the Shadow of Famine: Evolving Food Markets and Food Policy in Bangladesh*. Baltimore: Johns Hopkins University Press.

AirVisual. *World Most Polluted Cities 2018 (PM2.5)*. https://www.airvisual.com/world-most-polluted-cities.

Aizenman, J., Y. Jinjarak, H. Nguyen, and D. Park. 2019. Fiscal Space and Government-Spending and Tax-Rate Cyclicality Patterns: A Cross-Country Comparison, 1960–2016. *Journal of Macroeconomics*. 60 (June). pp. 229–252.

Akamatsu, K. 1961. A Theory of Unbalanced Growth in the World Economy. *Weltwirtschaftliches Archiv*. 86 (January). pp. 196–217.

———. 1962. A Historical Pattern of Economic Growth in Developing Countries. *The Developing Economies*. 1 (August). pp. 3–25.

Akiyama, T., and T. Nakao. 2005. Japanese ODA Adapting to the Issues and Challenges of the New Aid Environment. *FASID Discussion Paper on Development Assistance*. No. 8. Tokyo: Foundation for Advanced Studies on International Development.

Anderson, K., G. Rausser, and J. Swinnen. 2013. Political Economy of Public Policies: Insights from Distortions to Agricultural and Food Markets. *Journal of Economic Literature*. 51 (2). pp. 423–477.

Antras, P., and C. Foley. 2011. Regional Trade Integration and Multinational Firm Strategies. In Barro, R., and J.-W. Lee, eds. *Costs and Benefits of Economic Integration*. New York: Oxford University Press and Asian Development Bank.

Aoki, S., J. Esteban-Pretel, T. Okazaki, and Y. Sawada. 2011. The Role of the Government in Facilitating TFP Growth during Japan's Rapid-Growth Era. In Otsuka, K., and K. Kalirajan, eds. *Community, Market, and State in Development*. London: Palgrave Macmillan.

Ariga, K., and S. Ejima. 2000. Post-Evaluation for ODA Loan Project – Kingdom of Thailand: Overall Impact of Eastern Seaboard Development Program. *JBIC Review*. 2 (November). pp. 81–115.

Asian Development Bank (ADB). 1965. *Agreement Establishing the Asian Development Bank*. https://www.adb.org/documents/agreement-establishing-asian-development-bank-adb-charter.

———. 1968. *Asian Agriculture Survey*. Manila. pp. 7–8.

———. 1978. *Rural Asia: Challenge and Opportunity*. Manila.

———. 1997. *Emerging Asia: Changes and Challenges*. Manila.

———. 2007. *ADB's Infrastructure Operations: Responding to Client Needs*. Manila.

———. 2008. *Emerging Asian Regionalism: A Partnership for Shared Prosperity*. Manila.

———. 2008. *Managing Asian Cities*. Manila.

———. 2010. *Key Indicators for Asia and the Pacific 2010: Asia's Emerging Middle Class: Past, Present, and Future*. Manila.

———. 2012. *Asian Development Outlook 2012: Confronting Rising Inequality in Asia*. Manila.

———. 2012. *Asian Development Outlook 2012 Update: Services and Asia's Future Growth*. Manila.

———. 2012. *Guidance Note: Gender and Law—Temporary Special Measures to Promote Gender Equality*. Manila.

———. 2013. *Asian Development Outlook 2013: Asia's Energy Challenge*. Manila.

———. 2013. *Asian Development Outlook 2013 Update: Governance and Public Service Delivery*. Manila.

———. 2013. *Key Indicators for Asia and the Pacific 2013: Asia's Economic Transformation: Where to, How, and How Fast?* Manila.

———. 2014. *Asian Economic Integration Monitor*. Manila.

———. 2015. *Asian Development Outlook 2015 Update: Enabling Women, Energizing Asia*. Manila.

———. 2015. *Asian Economic Integration Report 2015*. Manila.

———. 2016. *ADB Through the Decades: ADB's First Decade (1966–1976)*. Manila.

———. 2016. *Asian Development Outlook 2016 Update: Meeting the Low-Carbon Growth Challenge*. Manila.

———. 2016. *Asian Economic Integration Report 2016: What Drives Foreign Direct Investment in Asia and the Pacific?* Manila.

———. 2016. *Dhaka Water Supply Network Improvement Project*. Manila.

———. 2016. *Finding Balance 2016: Benchmarking the Performance of State-Owned Enterprises in Island Countries*. Manila.

———. 2017. *Asian Development Outlook 2017: Transcending the Middle-Income Challenge*. Manila.

———. 2017. *Catalyzing Green Finance: A Concept for Leveraging Blended Finance for Green Development*. Manila.

———. 2017. *Meeting Asia's Infrastructure Needs*. Manila.

———. 2017. *A Region at Risk: The Human Dimensions of Climate Change in Asia and the Pacific*. Manila.

———. 2018. *ADB Strategy 2030: Achieving a Prosperous, Inclusive, Resilient, and Sustainable Asia and the Pacific*. Manila.

———. 2018. *Measuring Asset Ownership and Entrepreneurship from a Gender Perspective. Methodology and Results of Pilot Surveys in Georgia, Mongolia, and the Philippines*. Manila.

———. 2019. *Asian Development Outlook 2019: Strengthening Disaster Resilience*. Manila.

———. 2019. *Asian Development Outlook 2019 Update: Fostering Growth and Inclusion in Asia's Cities*. Manila.

———. 2019. *How PPP Advisory Services Can Narrow Asia's Infrastructure Gap*. Manila.

———. Key Indicators Database. https://kidb.adb.org/kidb/.

———. *Lao PDR: Nam Theun 2 Hydroelectric Project*. https://www.adb.org/projects/37910-014/main.

———. Multi-Regional Input–Output Database. https://www.adb.org/data/icp/input-output-tables (accessed 19 July 2019).

———. Various years. *ADB Annual Report*. Manila.

Asian Development Bank, Asia Regional Integration Center. *Integration Indicators*. https://aric.adb.org/integrationindicators.

Asian Development Bank, Controller's Department. *Disbursements Data*. Manila.

Asian Development Bank and International Labour Organization. 2017. *Improving Labour Market Outcomes in the Pacific: Policy Challenges and Priorities*. Suva: International Labour Organization.

Asian Development Bank and UN Women. 2018. *Gender Equality and the Sustainable Development Goals in Asia and the Pacific.* Bangkok: ANT Office Express.

Asian Development Bank, Department for International Development of the United Kingdom, Japan International Cooperation Agency, and World Bank Group. 2018. *The WEB of Transport Corridors in South Asia.* Washington, DC: World Bank.

Asian Development Bank, Japan Bank for International Cooperation, and the World Bank. 2005. *Connecting East Asia: A New Framework for Infrastructure.* Washington, DC: World Bank.

Asian Productivity Organization. Productivity Measurement. https://www.apo-tokyo.org/wedo/measurement (accessed 19 July 2019).

Association of Southeast Asian Nations. *The Declaration of ASEAN Concord, Bali, Indonesia, 24 February 1976.* https://asean.org/?static_post=declaration-of-asean-concord-indonesia-24-february-1976.

Athreye, S. 2005. The Indian Software Industry and Its Evolving Service Capability. *Industrial and Corporate Change.* 14 (3). pp. 393–418.

Athukorala, P., E. Ginting, H. Hill, and U. Kumar, eds. 2017. *The Sri Lankan Economy: Charting a New Course.* Manila: Asian Development Bank.

Azmat, G., and B. Petrongolo. 2014. Gender and the Labor Market: What Have We Learned from Field and Lab Experiments? *Labour Economics.* 30 (October). pp. 32–40.

Bairoch, P. 1982. International Industrialization Levels from 1750 to 1980. *Journal of European Economic History.* 11 (2). pp. 269–333.

Baldwin, R. 1993. A Domino Theory of Regionalism. *NBER Working Paper Series.* No. w4465. Cambridge, MA: National Bureau of Economic Research.

———. 2016. *The Great Convergence: Information Technology and the New Globalization.* Cambridge, MA: The Belknap Press of Harvard University Press.

Barbier, E. B., and J. P. Hochard. 2014. Land Degradation, Less Favored Lands and the Rural Poor: A Spatial and Economic Analysis. *A Report for the Economics of Land Degradation Initiative.* Laramie: Department of Economics and Finance, University of Wyoming.

Barro, R. 1996. Determinants of Economic Growth: A Cross-Country Empirical Study. *NBER Working Paper Series.* No. w5698. Cambridge, MA: National Bureau of Economic Research.

Barro, R., and J.-W. Lee. 2013. A New Data Set of Educational Attainment in the World, 1950–2010. *Journal of Development Economics.* 104 (September). pp. 184–198. http://www.barrolee.com/.

Basant, R., and S. Mani. 2012. Foreign R&D Centers in India: An Analysis of Their Size, Structure and Implications. *Indian Institute of Management Working Paper Series.* No. 2012-01-06. Ahmedabad: Indian Institute of Management.

Bays, L. 1994. Short Overview of Water Supply Situations in the World, Water Philippines '94. *Technical Papers, 9th IWSA-ASPAC Regional Conference and Exhibition.* Manila: Philippine Water Works Association.

Beaman, L., E. Duflo, R. Pande, and P. Topalova. 2012. Female Leadership Raises Aspirations and Educational Attainment for Girls: A Policy Experiment in India. *Science.* 335 (6068). pp. 582–586.

Berger, P. L., and H. H. M. Hsiao, eds. 1988. *In Search for an East Asian Development Model.* New Brunswick, NJ: Transaction Books.

Bernanke, B. 2005. The Global Saving Glut and the U.S. Current Account Deficit. Speech at the Sandridge Lecture. Virginia Association of Economics. 10 March. Richmond, VA.

Blaikie, P. 2016. *The Political Economy of Soil Erosion in Developing Countries.* London: Routledge.

Blau, F., M. Ferber, and A. Winkler. 2001. *The Economics of Women, Men, and Work.* New Jersey: Prentice Hall.

Borensztein, E., J. De Gregorio, and J.-W. Lee. 1998. How Does Foreign Direct Investment Affect Economic Growth. *Journal of International Economics.* 45 (1). pp. 115–135.

Borghesi, S. 1999. The Environmental Kuznets Curve: A Survey of the Literature. *FEEM Working Paper Series.* No. 85–99. Milan: Fondazione Eni Enrico Mattei.

Bosworth, B., and G. Chodorow-Reich. 2007. Saving and Demographic Change: The Global Dimension. *Center for Retirement Research at Boston College Working Paper.* No. 2007-2. Boston: Boston College.

Bourgeois-Pichat, J. 1981. Recent Demographic Change in Western Europe: An Assessment. *Population and Development Review.* 7 (1). pp. 19–42.

Bourguignon, F., and M. Sundberg. 2007. Aid Effectiveness – Opening the Black Box. *American Economic Review.* 97 (2). pp. 316–321.

BP. 2019. *BP Statistical Review of World Energy 2019.* https://www.bp.com/en/global/corporate/energy-economics/statistical-review-of-world-energy.html.

Broda, C., and D. Weinstein. 2006. Globalization and the Gains from Variety. *The Quarterly Journal of Economics.* 121 (2). pp. 541–585.

Brown, T. M. 1952. Habit Persistence and Lags in Consumer Behaviour. *Econometrica.* 20 (3). pp. 355–371.

Bureau van Dijk. Zephyr M&A Database. https://www.bvdinfo.com.

Burke, L., K. Reytar, M. Spalding, and A. Perry. 2011. *Reefs at Risk Revisited.* Washington, DC: World Resources Institute.

Byerlee, D. 2014. The Fall and Rise Again of Plantations in Tropical Asia: History Repeated? *Land.* 3 (3). pp. 574–597.

Cai, F., and Y. Du. 2014. Exports and Employment in the People's Republic of China. In Khor, N., and D. Mitra, eds. *Trade and Employment in Asia.* Abingdon, United Kingdom: Asian Development Bank and Routledge.

Cain, J., R. Hasan, R. Magsombol, and A. Tandon. 2010. Accounting for Inequality in India: Evidence from Household Expenditures. *World Development.* 38 (3). pp. 282–297.

CEIC Data. Global Database. https://www.ceicdata.com/en (accessed 24 March 2019).

Chakraborty, P., S. Selvaraj, M. Nakamura, B. Prithiviraj, S. Ko, and B. G. Loganathan. 2016. E-Waste and Associated Environmental Contamination in the Asia/Pacific Region (Part 1): An Overview. In Loganathan, B. G., J. S. Khim, P. R. S. Kodavanti, and S. Masunaga, eds. *Persistent Organic Chemicals in the Environment: Status and Trends in the Pacific Basin Countries I Contamination Status.* Washington, DC: American Chemical Society and Oxford University Press.

Chamon, M., and E. S. Prasad. 2008. Why Are Saving Rates of Urban Households in China Rising? *NBER Working Paper.* No. w14546. Cambridge, MA: National Bureau of Economic Research.

Chancel, L., and T. Piketty. 2017. Indian Income Inequality, 1922–2014: From British Raj to Billionaire Raj? *CEPR Discussion Paper.* No. DP12409. Washington, DC: Center for Economic and Policy Research.

Cheon, B. Y. 2014. Skills Development Strategies and the High Road to Development in the Republic of Korea. In Salazar-Xirinachs, J. M., I. Nübler, and R. Kozul-Wright, eds. *Transforming Economies: Making Industrial Policy Work for Growth, Jobs and Development.* Geneva: International Labour Organization–United Nations Conference on Trade and Development. pp. 213–238.

Cherif, R., and F. Hasanov. 2019. The Return of the Policy That Shall Not Be Named: Principles of Industrial Policy. *IMF Working Paper.* No. WP/19/74. Washington, DC: International Monetary Fund.

Chia, S. Y. 2010. Trade and Investment Policies and Regional Economic Integration in East Asia. *ADBI Working Paper Series.* No. 210. Tokyo: Asian Development Bank Institute.

China Daily. 2014. *What Did Deng Xiaoping Learn during His Visit to Japan in 1978?* [in Chinese]. 15 August. https://world.chinadaily.com.cn/dxpdc110znjn/2014-08/15/content_18323338.htm.

China State Statistical Bureau. 1990. *China National and Provincial Historical Statistics Collection.* Beijing.

Chinn, M. D., and E. S. Prasad 2003. Medium-Term Determinants of Current Accounts in Industrial and Developing Countries: An Empirical Exploration. *Journal of International Economics.* 59 (1). pp. 47–76.

Chou, S., J. Liu, and J. Hammit. 2003. National Health Insurance and Precautionary Saving. *Journal of Public Economics.* 87 (9–10). pp. 1873–1894.

Chowdhury, A., and I. Islam. 1993. *The Newly Industrializing Economies of East Asia.* London: Routledge.

Chung, S. C. 2007. Excelsior: The Korean Innovation Story. *Issues in Science and Technology.* 24 (1). pp. 1–11.

Collins, S. 1991. Saving Behavior in Ten Developing Countries. In Shoven, J. B., and B. D. Bernheim, eds. *National Saving and Economic Performance.* Chicago: National Bureau of Economic Research and the University of Chicago Press.

Comin, D., and B. Hobijn. 2010. An Exploration of Technology Diffusion. *American Economic Review.* 100 (5). pp. 2031–2059.

———. 2011. Technology Diffusion and Postwar Growth. In Acemoglu, D., and M. Woodford, eds. *NBER Macroeconomics Annual 2010.* Volume 25. Chicago: Chicago University Press.

Credit Suisse. 2018. *Global Wealth Databook 2018.* https://www.credit-suisse.com/corporate/en/research/research-institute/global-wealth-report.html.

CVCE.eu. *Final Communiqué of the Asian–African Conference of Bandung Signed on 24 April 1955.* http://franke.uchicago.edu/Final_Communique_Bandung_1955.pdf.

Datt, G. 1998. Poverty in India and Indian States: An Update. *The Indian Journal of Labour Economics.* 41 (2). pp. 191–211.

Davis, B., P. Winters, G. Carletto, K. Covarrubias, E. J. Quiñones, A. Zezza, K. Stamoulis, C. Azzarri, and S. Digiuseppe. 2010. A Cross-Country Comparison of Rural Income Generating Activities. *World Development*. 38 (1). pp. 48–63.

Deaton, A., and C. Paxson. 2000. Growth and Savings among Individuals and Households. *Review of Economics and Statistics*. 82 (2). pp. 212–225.

Deininger, K. 2003. *Land Policies for Growth and Poverty Reduction*. Washington, DC: World Bank.

Desai, V. V. 2010. The Political Economy of Regional Cooperation in South Asia. *ADB Working Paper Series on Regional Economic Integration*. No. 54. Manila: Asian Development Bank.

Dhaka Water Supply and Sewerage Authority (DWASA). DWASA website. http://dwasa.org.bd/.

Di Gropello, E., and C. Sakellariou. 2010. Industry and Skill Wage Premiums in East Asia. *World Bank Policy Research Working Paper*. No. 5379. Washington, DC: World Bank.

Djurfeldt, G., H. Holmen, M. Jirstrom, and R. Larsson. 2005. African Food Crisis – the Relevance of Asian Crisis. In Djurfeldt, G., H. Holmen, M. Jirstrom, and R. Larsson, eds. 2005. *The African Food Crisis: Lessons from the Asian Green Revolution*. Wallingford: CABI Publishing.

Djurfeldt, G., and M. Jirstrom. 2005. The Puzzle of the Policy Shift – The Early Green Revolution in India, Indonesia, and the Philippines. In Djurfeldt, G., H. Holmen, M. Jirstrom, and R. Larsson, eds. *The African Food Crisis: Lessons from the Asian Green Revolution*. Wallingford: CABI Publishing.

Dollar, D. 1992. Outward-Oriented Developing Economies Really Do Grow More Rapidly: Evidence from 95 LDCs, 1976–1985. *Economic Development and Cultural Change*. 40 (3). pp. 523–544.

Duan, L., Q. Yu, Q. Zhang, Z. Wang, Y. Pan, T. Larssen, J. Tang, and J. Mulder. 2016. Acid Deposition in Asia: Emissions, Deposition, and Ecosystem Effects. *Atmospheric Environment*. 100 (146). pp. 55–69.

Duflo, E. 2012. Women Empowerment and Economic Development. *Journal of Economic Literature*. 50 (4). pp. 1051–1079.

Durand, J. D. 1975. *The Labor Force in Economic Development*. Princeton: Princeton University Press.

Duvvury, N., C. Grown, and J. Redner. 2004. *Costs of Intimate Partner Violence at the Household and Community Levels: An Operational Framework for Developing Countries*. Washington, DC: International Center for Research on Women.

D-Waste.Com. *Waste Atlas*. http://www.atlas.d-waste.com/.

Edwards, S. 1998. Openness, Productivity and Growth: What Do We Really Know? *Economic Journal*. 108 (447). pp. 383–398.

Eichengreen, B. 2015. *Financial Development in Asia: The Role of Policy and Institutions, with Special Reference to China*. Paper prepared for the Second Annual Asian Monetary Policy Forum. 29 May. Singapore.

Enerdata. 2019. *Global Energy Statistical Yearbook*. https://www.enerdata.net/publications/world-energy-statistics-supply-and-demand.html.

Errighi, L., C. Bodwell, and S. Khatiwada. 2016. *Business Process Outsourcing in the Philippines: Challenges for Decent Work*. Bangkok: International Labour Organization.

Estrada, G., D. Park, and A. Ramayandi. 2015. Financial Development, Financial Openness, and Economic Growth. *ADB Economics Working Paper Series.* No. 442. Manila: Asian Development Bank.

Estudillo, J. P., T. Sonobe, and K. Otsuka. 2007. Development of the Rural Non-Farm Sector in the Philippines and Lessons from the East Asian Experience. In Balisacan, A. M., and H. Hill, eds. *The Dynamics of Regional Development: The Philippines in East Asia.* Cheltenham, United Kingdom: Edward Elgar.

Ethier, W. J. 1979. Internationally Decreasing Costs and World Trade. *Journal of International Economics.* 9 (1). pp. 1–25.

Euromonitor International. *Socioeconomic Indicators.* https://eifl.net/publisher/euromonitor-international.

European Commission. Emissions Database for Global Atmospheric Research. http://edgar.jrc.ec.europa.eu/ (accessed 5 February 2019).

Evans, A., M. Hanjra, Y. Jiang, M. Qadir, and P. Drechsel. 2012. Water Quality: Assessment of the Current Situation in Asia. *Water Resources Development.* 28 (2). pp. 195–216.

Evenson, R. E., and D. Gollin. 2003. *Crop Variety Improvement and Its Effect on Productivity: The Impact of International Agricultural Research.* Wallingford: CABI Publishing.

Fan, M. 2015. Sri Lanka's Water Supply and Sanitation Sector: Achievements and a Way Forward. *ADB South Asia Working Paper Series.* No. 35. Manila: Asian Development Bank.

Fankhauser, S., A. Kazaglis, and S. Srivastav. 2017. Green Growth Opportunities for Asia. *ADB Economics Working Paper Series.* No. 508. Manila: Asian Development Bank.

Feenstra, R. C., R. Inklaar, and M. P. Timmer. 2015. The Next Generation of the Penn World Table. *American Economic Review.* 105 (10). pp. 3150–3182. http://www.ggdc.net/pwt.

Feldstein, M., and C. Horioka. 1980. Domestic Saving and International Capital Flows. *Economic Journal.* 90 (June). pp. 314–329.

Felipe, J. 2018. Asia's Industrial Transformation: The Role of Manufacturing and Global Value Chains (Part 1). *ADB Economics Working Paper Series.* No. 549. Manila: Asian Development Bank.

———. 2018. Asia's Industrial Transformation: The Role of Manufacturing and Global Value Chains (Part 2). *ADB Economics Working Paper Series.* No. 550. Manila: Asian Development Bank.

Felipe, J., U. Kumar, A. Abdon, and M. Bacate. 2012. Product Complexity and Economic Development. *Structural Change and Economic Dynamics.* 23 (1). pp. 36–68.

Ferguson, R. W. 1999. Latin America: Lessons Learned from the Last Twenty Years. Speech given to the Florida International Bankers Association, Inc. Miami. 11 February.

Filmer, D., and N. Schady. 2008. Getting Girls into School: Evidence from a Scholarship Program in Cambodia. *Economic Development and Cultural Change.* 56 (3). pp. 581–617.

Financial Times. *fDi Markets.* https://www.fdimarkets.com.

Fiorini, M., and B. Hoekman. 2019. Restrictiveness of Services Trade Policy and the Sustainable Development Goals. In Helble, M., and B. Shepherd, eds. *Leveraging Services for Development: Prospects and Policies*. Tokyo: Asian Development Bank Institute.

Food and Agriculture Organization of the United Nations (FAO). 2015. *Global Forest Resources Assessment 2015*. http://www.fao.org/forest-resources-assessment/past-assessments/fra-2015/en/.

———. 2016. *The State of World Fisheries and Aquaculture: Contributing to Food Security and Nutrition for All*. Rome.

———. 2018. Diets Are Diversifying with Implications for Farmers and Nutrition. In FAO. *Dynamic Development, Shifting Demographics, and Changing Diets*. Bangkok. p. 172.

———. 2019. *FAO Statistics (FAOSTAT)*. http://www.fao.org/faostat.

———. AQUASTAT Database. http://www.fao.org/nr/water/aquastat/data/query/index.html?lang=en (accessed 6 June 2018).

———. *Global Capture Production 1950–2017*. http://www.fao.org/fishery/statistics/global-capture-production/query/en.

Forbes. *Billionaires: The Richest People in the World*. https://www.forbes.com/worlds-billionaires/.

Friedman, M. 1957. *A Theory of the Consumption Function*. Princeton: Princeton University Press.

Fu, T., and S. Shei. 1999. Agriculture as the Foundation for Development. In Thorbecke, E., and H. Wan, eds. *Lessons on the Roles of Government and Market*. New York: Springer Science+Business Media LLC.

Fu, X., W. T. Woo, and J. Hou. 2016. Technological Innovation Policy in China: The Lessons, and the Necessary Changes Ahead. *Economic Change and Restructuring*. 49 (2–3). pp. 139–157.

Fujita, K., and R. C. Hill. 1993. Toyota City: Industrial Organization and the Local State in Japan. In Fujita, K., and R. C. Hill, eds. *Japanese Cities in the World Economy*. Philadelphia: Temple University Press. pp. 175–202.

Garon, S. 2012. Why the Chinese Save? *Foreign Policy*. 19 January. https://foreignpolicy.com/2012/01/19/why-the-chinese-save/.

Garriga, A. 2016. Central Bank Independence in the World: A New Data Set. *International Interactions*. 42 (5). pp. 849–868.

Godo, Y. 2011. Estimation of Average Years of Schooling for Japan, Korea and the United States. *PRIMCED Discussion Paper Series*. No. 9. Tokyo: Institute of Economic Research, Hitotsubashi University.

Good, A. G., and P. H. Beatty. 2011. Fertilizing Nature: A Tragedy of Excess in the Commons. *PLoS Biology*. 9 (8): e1001124.

Goodkind, D. 2011. Child Underreporting, Fertility, and Sex Ratio Imbalance in China. *Demography*. 48 (1). pp. 291–316.

Gordon, R. 2018. Why Has Economic Growth Slowed When Innovation Appears to Be Accelerating? *NBER Working Paper Series*. No. w24554. Cambridge, MA: National Bureau of Economic Research.

Government of Bangladesh. 2015. *Seventh Five-Year Plan FY2016–FY2020: Accelerating Growth, Empowering Citizens*. Dhaka: General Economics Division, Planning Commission.

Government of India, Ministry of Road Transport and Highways. 2014. *Basic Road Statistics of India*. https://morth.nic.in/basic-road-statistics-india.

Government of Japan, Ministry of Foreign Affairs. 1978. *Treaty of Peace and Friendship Between Japan and the People's Republic of China*. https://www.mofa.go.jp/region/asia-paci/china/treaty78.html.

Government of New Zealand, Ministry of Foreign Affairs and Trade. *Aid & Development*. https://www.mfat.govt.nz/en/aid-and-development/our-approach-to-aid/.

Government of Singapore, Ministry of Education. *Education Statistics Digest 2018*. https://www.moe.gov.sg/about/publications/education-statistics.

Government of Taipei,China, Directorate-General of Budget, Accounting and Statistics.

Government of Taipei,China, Environmental Protection Administration. *Water*.

Government of Taipei,China, Ministry of Education. *2018 Education Statistical Indicators*.

Government of Thailand, National Economic and Social Development Board. *Social Development Indicators*. https://www.nesdb.go.th/nesdb_en/main.php?filename=social_dev_report.

Government of Timor-Leste, Ministry of Finance, Petroleum Fund Administration Unit. 2019. *Timor-Leste Petroleum Fund: Annual Report 2018*. https://www.mof.gov.tl/wp-content/uploads/2019/08/2018-annual-report-ENGLISH.pdf.

Government of Viet Nam, General Statistics Office. 2016. *Result of the Vietnam Household Living Standards Survey 2016*. Ha Noi.

Government of Viet Nam, Ministry of Planning and Investment. 2017. *Thúc đẩy giải ngân vốn ODA và vốn vay ưu đãi* [in Vietnamese]. http://www.mpi.gov.vn/Pages/tinbai.aspx?idTin=37705&idcm=188.

Grainger, C., G. Köhlin, J. Coria, D. Whittington, J. Xu, E. Somanathan, R. Daniels, P. K. Nam, X. Wu, and E. Haque. 2019. Opportunities for Scaling Up Market-Based Approaches to Environmental Management in Asia. *Technical Assistance Consultant's Report*. Manila: Asian Development Bank.

Grossman, G. M., and E. Helpman. 1991. *Innovation and Growth in the Global Economy*. Cambridge, MA and London: The MIT Press.

———. 1991. Trade, Knowledge Spillovers, and Growth. *European Economic Review*. 35 (2–3). pp. 517–526.

Growth Lab at Harvard University. Atlas of Economic Complexity Database. http://atlas.cid.harvard.edu/about-data/goods-data (accessed 30 August 2019).

Gubhaju, B. 2007. Fertility Decline in Asia: Opportunities and Challenges. *The Japanese Journal of Population*. 5 (1). pp. 19–42.

Harashima, Y. 2000. Environmental Governance in Selected Asian Developing Countries. *International Review for Environmental Strategies*. 1 (1). pp. 193–207.

Harrigan, F. 1996. Saving Transitions in Southeast Asia. *EDRC Report Series*. No. 64. Manila: Asian Development Bank.

Haver Analytics. Haver Analytics Database. http://www.haver.com/datalink.html (accessed 24 March 2019).

Hayami, Y. 2008. Social Capital, Human Capital and the Community Mechanism: Toward a Conceptual Framework for Economists. *Journal of Development Studies*. 45 (10). pp. 96–123.

Hayami, Y., and Y. Godo. 2004. The Three Agricultural Problems in the Disequilibrium of World Agriculture. *Asian Journal of Agriculture and Development.* 1 (1). pp. 3–14.

———. 2005. *Development Economics: From the Poverty to the Wealth of Nations.* 3rd edition. New York: Oxford University Press.

Hayami, Y., and V. W. Ruttan. 1985. *Agricultural Development: An International Perspective.* Baltimore and London: Johns Hopkins University Press.

Hayashi, F., and E. C. Prescott. 2008. The Depressing Effect of Agricultural Institutions on the Prewar Japanese Economy. *Journal of Political Economy.* 116 (4). pp. 573–632.

Health Effects Institute. 2018. *State of Global Air 2018. Special Report.* Boston.

Heath, R., and A. M. Mobarak. 2015. Manufacturing Growth and the Lives of Bangladeshi Women. *Journal of Development Economics.* 115 (July). pp. 1–15.

Heise, L., M. E. Greene, N. Opper, M. Stavropoulou, C. Harper, M. Nascimento, and D. Zewdie. 2019. Gender Inequality and Restrictive Gender Norms: Framing the Challenges to Health. *The Lancet.* 393 (10189). pp. 2440–2454.

Helble, M., and B. Ngiang. 2016. From Global Factory to Global Mall? East Asia's Changing Trade Composition. *Japan and the World Economy.* 39 (September). pp. 37–47.

Helble, M., and B. Shepherd, eds. 2019. *Leveraging Services for Development: Prospects and Policies.* Tokyo: Asian Development Bank Institute.

Henderson, J., D. Hulme, R. Phillips, and E. M. Kim. 2002. Economic Governance and Poverty Reduction in South Korea. *University of Manchester Business School Working Papers.* No. 439. Manchester, United Kingdom: Manchester Business School.

Hidalgo, C., and R. Hausmann. 2009. The Building Blocks of Economic Complexity. *Proceedings of the National Academy of Sciences.* 106 (26). pp. 10570–10575.

Hill, H. 2013. The Political Economy of Policy Reform: Insights from Southeast Asia. *Asian Development Review.* 30 (1). pp. 108–130.

Hino, H., and I. Atsushi. 2008. Aid Effectiveness Revisited: Comparative Studies of Modalities of Aid to Asia and Africa. *Discussion Paper Series.* No. 218. Kobe: Research Institute for Economics & Business Administration, Kobe University.

Hirschman, A. 1958. *The Strategy of Economic Development.* New Haven: Yale University Press.

Hofmann, C., A. Osnago, and M. Ruta. 2017. Horizontal Depth: A New Database on the Content of Preferential Trade Agreements. *Policy Research Working Paper.* No. 7981. Washington, DC: World Bank.

Horioka, C., and A. Terada-Hagiwara. 2012. The Determinants and Long-Term Projections of Saving Rates in Developing Asia. *Japan and the World Economy.* 24 (2). pp. 128–137.

Hossain, M. 2009. The Impact of Shallow Tubewells and Boro Rice on Food Security in Bangladesh. *IFPRI Discussion Paper Series.* No. 00917. Washington, DC: International Food Policy Research Institute.

Howes, S., and P. Wyrwoll. 2012. Asia's Wicked Environmental Problems. *ADBI Working Paper Series.* No. 348. Tokyo: Asian Development Bank Institute.

Huang, Y. 2015. From Economic Miracle to Normal Development. In Zhuang, J., P. Vandenberg, and Y. Huang, eds. *Managing the Middle-Income Transition: Challenges Facing the People's Republic of China.* London: Asian Development Bank / Edward Elgar.

Huber, R. 1971. Effect on Prices of Japan's Entry into World Commerce after 1858. *Journal of Political Economy.* 79 (3). pp. 614–628.

Hummels, D. 2007. Transportation Costs and International Trade in the Second Era of Globalization. *Journal of Economic Perspectives.* 21 (3). pp. 131–154.

Huntingford, C., P. Zelazowski, D. Galbraith, L. M. Mercado, S. Sitch, R. Fisher, M. Lomas, A. P. Walker, C. D. Jones, B. B. Booth, and Y. Malhi. 2013. Simulated Resilience of Tropical Rainforests to CO_2-Induced Climate Change. *Nature Geoscience.* 6 (4). pp. 268–273.

Ilzetzki, E., C. Reinhart, and K. Rogoff. 2017. Country Chronologies and Background Material to Exchange Rate Arrangements into the 21st Century: Will the Anchor Currency Hold? *NBER Working Paper Series.* No. w23135. Cambridge, MA: National Bureau of Economic Research.

Imai, N., T. Furukawa, R. Tsujino, S. Kitamura, and T. Yumoto. 2018. Factors Affecting Forest Area Change in Southeast Asia during 1980–2010. *PLoS ONE.* 13 (5). e0197391.

India Brand Equity Foundation (IBEF). 2019. *IT and ITeS.* https://www.ibef.org/download/it-ites-feb-2019.pdf.

———. 2019. *IT & ITeS Industry in India.* https://www.ibef.org/industry/information-technology-india.aspx.

Institute for Comparative Survey Research. *World Values Survey.* http://www.worldvaluessurvey.org/WVSContents.jsp.

Institute for Global Environmental Strategies. 2001. *Report of the First Phase Strategic Research.* Kanagawa.

International Association for the Evaluation of Educational Achievement. 2004. *Trends in International Mathematics and Science Study 2003.* Chestnut Hill, MA: TIMSS & PIRLS International Study Center, Boston College.

———. 2008. *Trends in International Mathematics and Science Study 2007.* Chestnut Hill, MA: TIMSS & PIRLS International Study Center, Boston College.

———. 2016. *Trends in International Mathematics and Science Study 2015.* Chestnut Hill, MA: TIMSS & PIRLS International Study Center, Boston College.

International Energy Agency (IEA). 2019. *The Future of Rail.* Paris.

———. *Statistics.* https://www.iea.org/statistics/.

International Federation of Robotics. 2018. *Executive Summary: World Robotics 2018 Industrial Robots.* Frankfurt am Main.

International Fund for Agricultural Development. 2016. *Rural Development Report: Fostering Inclusive Rural Transformation.* Rome.

International Institute for Democracy and Electoral Assistance. Gender Quotas Database. https://www.idea.int/data-tools/data/gender-quotas/quotas#different (accessed 21 June 2019).

International Institute for Population Sciences and Inner City Fund. 2017. *National Family Health Survey (NFHS-4), 2015-16: India.* Mumbai: International Institute for Population Sciences.

International Labour Organization. ILOSTAT Database. https://www.ilo.org/ilostat/.

International Labour Organization and Gallup. 2017. *Towards a Better Future for Women and Work: Voices of Women and Men*. Geneva and Washington, DC.

International Monetary Fund (IMF). 2010. Asia and the Global Economy: Leading the Way Forward in the 21st Century. Opening Remarks by Dominique Strauss-Kahn, Managing Director of the IMF, at the Asia 21 Conference. Daejeon. 12 July. https://www.imf.org/en/News/Articles/2015/09/28/04/53/sp071210.

———. 2010. *The Fund's Mandate—The Future Financing Role: Revised Reform Proposals*. August. Washington, DC.

———. 2018. *Annual Report on Exchange Arrangements and Exchange Restrictions Database*. Washington, DC.

———. *Direction of Trade Statistics*. http://data.imf.org.

———. Public Debt Database. https://www.imf.org/external/datamapper/datasets/DEBT (accessed 27 August 2019).

———. World Economic Outlook Databases. https://www.imf.org/en/Publications/SPROLLs/world-economic-outlook-databases#sort=%40imfdate%20descending (accessed 27 August 2019).

International Renewable Energy. 2019. *Renewable Power Generation Costs in 2018*. Abu Dhabi. https://www.irena.org/Statistics/View-Data-by-Topic/Costs/Global-Trends.

International Resource Panel. Global Material Flows Database. https://www.resourcepanel.org/global-material-flows-database (accessed 2 November 2018).

International Rice Research Institute. 2019. *World Rice Statistics*. http://ricestat.irri.org.

International Road Federation. 2016. *World Road Statistics*. Alexandria, VA.

International Telecommunications Union. World Telecommunications and ICT Indicators Database. https://www.itu.int/en/ITU-D/Statistics/Pages/publications/wtid.aspx (accessed 13 August 2019).

Inter-Parliamentary Union. Women in Parliament Database. http://archive.ipu.org/wmn-e/world.htm (accessed 7 June 2019).

Inter-Parliamentary Union and the World Health Organization. 2014. *Child, Early and Forced Marriage Legislation in 37 Asia-Pacific Countries*. Tignieu-Jameyzieu: Courand et Associés.

Ito, T. 1996. *The Japanese Economy*. Cambridge, MA and London: The MIT Press.

Jambeck, J. R., R. Geyer, C. Wilcox, T. R. Siegler, M. Perryman, A. Andrady, R. Narayan, and K. L. Law. 2015. Plastic Waste Inputs from Land into the Ocean. *Science*. 347 (6223). pp. 768–771.

James, W. E., S. Naya, and G. M. Meier. 1987. *Asian Development: Economic Success and Policy Lessons*. San Francisco: International Center for Economic Growth.

Japan International Cooperation Agency. 2018. *Water Supply: The Foundation for Previous Lives and Livelihoods, Safe Water for All*. Tokyo.

Jensen, J. 2013. Tradable Business Services, Developing Asia, and Economic Growth. In Park, D., and M. Noland, eds. *Developing the Service Sector as an Engine of Growth for Asia*. Manila: Asian Development Bank.

Jensen, R. 2010. Economic Opportunities and Gender Differences in Human Capital: Experimental Evidence for India. *NBER Working Paper Series*. No. w16021. Cambridge, MA: National Bureau of Economic Research.

Jensen, R., and E. Oster. 2009. The Power of TV: Cable Television and Women's Status in India. *Quarterly Journal of Economics.* 124 (3). pp. 1057–1094.

Jiang, J., and D. Wang. 1990. China's "Green Revolution" and Sustainable Development of Agriculture. *Science and Technology Review* [in Chinese]. October.

Jomo, K. S., ed. 2001. *Southeast Asia's Industrialization: Industrial Policy, Capabilities, and Sustainability.* New York: Palgrave.

Kaiji, I. 1991. Japan's Postwar Rural Land Reform: Its Merits and Demerits. In Committee for the Japanese Agriculture Session, XXI IAAE Conference, ed. *Agriculture and Agricultural Policy in Japan.* Tokyo: University of Tokyo Press.

Kato, H. 2016. Japan's ODA 1954–2014: Changes and Continuities in a Central Instrument in Japan's Foreign Policy. In Shimomura, Y., J. Page, and H. Kato, eds. *Japan's Development Assistance: Foreign Aid and the Post-2015 Agenda.* London: Palgrave Macmillan.

Kaufmann, D., A. Kraay, and M. Mastruzzi. 2007. The Worldwide Governance Indicators: Answering the Critics. *Policy Research Working Paper.* No. 4149. Washington, DC: World Bank.

Kaza, S., L. Yao, P. Bhada-Tata, and F. Van Woerden. 2018. What a Waste 2.0: A Global Snapshot of Solid Waste Management to 2050. *Urban Development Series.* Washington, DC: World Bank.

Kelley, A., and R. Schmidt. 1996. Saving, Dependency, and Development. *Journal of Population Economics.* 9 (4). pp. 365–386.

Kemal, A. R. Undated. *State of Poverty in Pakistan: Overview and Trends.* http://siteresources.worldbank.org/PAKISTANEXTN/Resources/pdf-Files-in-Events/Briefing-on-PRSP/OverviewAndTrends.pdf.

Keynes, J. M. 1936. *The General Theory of Employment, Interest and Money.* London: Macmillan.

Khan, F., A. Ramayandi, and M. Schröder. Forthcoming. Conditions for Effective Macroprudential Policy Interventions. *ADB Economics Working Paper Series.* Manila: Asian Development Bank.

Khanna, M. 2018. *Greening Businesses in the Asia and Pacific Region: Opportunities and Challenges.* Manila: Asian Development Bank.

Kim, J. K. 2011. *Modularization of Korea's Development Experience: Impact of Foreign Aid on Korea's Development.* Seoul: Ministry of Strategy and Finance, and KDI School.

Kim, J.-I., and L. J. Lau. 1994. The Sources of Economic Growth of the East Asian Newly Industrialized Countries. *Journal of the Japanese and International Economies.* 8 (3). pp. 235–271.

Kim, S., and J.-W. Lee. 2007. Demographic Changes, Saving, and Current Account in East Asia. *Asian Economic Papers.* 6 (2). pp. 22–53.

Kimura, H., Y. Mori, and Y. Sawada. 2012. Aid Proliferation and Economic Growth: A Cross-Country Analysis. *World Development.* 40 (1). pp. 1–10.

Kimura, H., Y. Todo, and Y. Sawada. 2010. Is Foreign Aid a Vanguard of Foreign Direct Investment? A Gravity-Equation Approach. *World Development.* 38 (4). pp. 482–497.

Kirk, M., and N. D. A. Tuan. 2010. Land Tenure Policy Reforms: Decollectivization and the Doi Moi System in Vietnam. In Spielman, D. J., and R. Pandya-Lorch, eds. *Proven Successes in Agricultural Development: A Technical Compendium to Millions Fed.* Washington, DC: International Food Policy Research Institute.

Kitano, N. 2014. Japanese Development Assistance to ASEAN Countries. In Shiraishi, T., and T. Kojima, eds. *ASEAN–Japan Relations.* Singapore: Institute of Southeast Asian Studies.

Kojima, K. 2000. The "Flying Geese" Model of Asian Economic Development: Origin, Theoretical Extensions, and Regional Policy Implications. *Journal of Asian Economics.* 11 (4). pp. 375–401.

Krueger, A. 1990. Government Failures in Development. *Journal of Economic Perspectives.* 4 (3). pp. 9–23.

Krugman, P. 1994. The Myth of Asia's Miracle. *Foreign Affairs.* 1 (November/December). pp. 62–78.

Krugman, P. R. 1979. Increasing Returns, Monopolistic Competition and International Trade. *Journal of International Economics.* 9 (4). pp. 469–479.

Kuznets, S. 1955. Economic Growth and Income Inequality. *American Economic Review.* 45 (March). pp. 1–28.

Kwon, H. J., and I. Yi. 2009. Economic Development and Poverty Reduction in Korea: Governing Multifunctional Institutions. *Development and Change.* 40. pp. 769–792.

Lang, G., and C. H. W. Chan. 2006. China's Impact on Forests in Southeast Asia. *Journal of Contemporary Asia.* 36 (2). pp. 167–194.

Latham, A. J. H., and H. Kawakatsu, eds. 2009. *Intra-Asian Trade and Industrialization: Essays in Memory of Yasukichi Yasuba.* London and New York: Routledge.

Lee, H., and J.-W. Lee. 2019. Patterns and Determinants of Intergenerational Educational Mobility: Evidence Across Countries. *Asian Growth Research Institute Working Paper Series.* No. 2019-02. Seoul: Asian Growth Research Institute.

Lee, M., M. L. Villaruel, and R. Gaspar. 2016. Effects of Temperature Shocks on Economic Growth and Welfare in Asia. *ADB Economics Working Paper Series.* No. 501. Manila: Asian Development Bank.

Lee, R., and A. Mason. 2006. What Is the Demographic Dividend? *Finance and Development.* 43 (3). pp. 16–17.

Lee, R., A. Mason, and T. Miller. 1997. Saving, Wealth, and the Demographic Transition in East Asia. *East-West Center Working Papers: Population Series.* No. 88-7. Honolulu: East-West Center.

Levine, R. 2002. Bank-based or Market-based Financial Systems: Which Is Better? *Journal of Financial Intermediation.* 11 (4). pp. 398–428.

Levinson, A. 2000. *The Ups and Downs of the Environmental Kuznets Curve.* Paper prepared for the UCF/CentER Conference on Environment. 30 November–2 December. Orlando.

Lewis, W. A. 1954. Economic Development with Unlimited Supplies of Labor. *The Manchester School.* 22 (2). pp. 139–191.

Lin, J. Y. 2012. *New Structural Economics: A Framework for Rethinking Development and Policy.* Washington, DC: World Bank.

Lin, V. S. 2016. Research Highlights: Impacts of Microplastics on Plankton. *Environmental Science: Processes & Impacts.* 18 (2). pp. 160–163.

Lipton, M. 2009. *Land Reform in Developing Countries: Property Rights and Property Wrongs.* London: Routledge. p. 287.

Little, I., T. Scitovsky, and I. M. Scott. 1970. *Trade in Some Developing Countries: A Comparative Study.* London, New York, and Toronto: Oxford University Press.

Lu, Y., S. Song, R. Wang, Z. Liu, J. Meng, A. J. Sweetman, A. Jenkins, R. C. Ferrier, H. Li, W. Luo, and T. Wang. 2015. Impacts of Soil and Water Pollution on Food Safety and Health Risks in China. *Environment International.* 77. pp. 5–15.

Lucas, R. E., Jr. 1988. On the Mechanics of Economic Development. *Journal of Monetary Economics.* 22 (1). pp. 3–42.

–––. 1990. Why Doesn't Capital Flow from Rich to Poor Countries? *American Economic Review.* 80 (2). pp. 92–96.

Maddison, A. 2007. *Contours of the World Economy 1–2030 AD: Essays in Macro-Economic History.* New York: Oxford University Press.

Mason, A., R. Lee, M. Abrigo, and S.-H. Lee. 2017. Support Ratios and Demographic Dividends: Estimates for the World. *UN Population Division Technical Paper.* No. 2017/1. New York: United Nations.

McCaig, B., and N. Pavcnik. 2018. Export Markets and Labor Allocation in a Low-Income Country. *American Economic Review.* 108 (7). pp. 1899–1941.

McCawley, P. 2017. *Banking on the Future of Asia and the Pacific: 50 Years of the Asian Development Bank.* Manila: Asian Development Bank.

Melitz, M. 2003. The Impact of Trade on Intra-Industry Reallocations and Aggregate Industry Productivity. *Econometrica.* 71 (6). pp. 1695–1725.

Mercer-Blackman, V., and C. Ablaza. 2019. The Servicification of Manufacturing in Asia: A Conceptual Framework. In Helble, M., and B. Shepherd, eds. *Leveraging Services for Development: Prospects and Policies.* Tokyo: Asian Development Bank Institute.

Mertz, O., C. Padoch, J. Fox, R. A. Cramb, S. J. Leisz, N. Thanh Lam, and T. Duc Vien. 2009. Swidden Change in Southeast Asia: Understanding Causes and Consequences. *Human Ecology.* 37 (3). pp. 259–264.

Minami, R. 2008. Income Distribution of Japan: Historical Perspective and Its Implications. *Japan Labor Review.* 5 (4). pp. 5–20.

Miroudot, S. 2019. Services and Manufacturing in Global Value Chains – Is the Distinction Obsolete? In Helble, M., and B. Shepherd, eds. *Leveraging Services for Development: Prospects and Policies.* Tokyo: Asian Development Bank Institute.

Mitra, P., and R. Yemtsov. 2006. Increasing Inequality in Transition Economies: Is There More to Come? *Policy Research Working Paper Series.* No. WPS 4007. Washington, DC: World Bank.

Mohapatra, D. P., M. Cledon, S. K. Brar, and R. Y. Surampalli. 2016. Application of Wastewater and Biosolids in Soil: Occurrence and Fate of Emerging Contaminants. *Water, Air, & Soil Pollution.* 227 (3). pp. 1–14.

Moriguchi, C., and E. Saez. 2008. The Evolution of Income Concentration in Japan, 1886–2005: Evidence from Income Tax Statistics. *The Review of Economics and Statistics.* 90 (4). pp. 713–734.

Mosher, A. 1966. *Getting Agriculture Moving: Essentials for Development and Modernization.* New York: Agricultural Development Council.

Myint, H. 1972. *Southeast Asia's Economy: Development Policies in the 1970s.* New York: Praeger Publishers.

Myrdal, G. 1968. *Asian Drama: An Inquiry into the Poverty of Nations.* London: Alien Lane, The Penguin Press.

Nabeshima, K. 2004. Technology Transfer in East Asia: A Survey. In Yusuf, S., M. Anjum Altaf, and K. Nabeshima, eds. *Global Production Networking and Technological Change in East Asia.* Washington, DC: World Bank.

Nakao, T. 2010. *Response to the Global Financial Crisis and Future Policy Challenges.* Keynote Address at the Symposium cohosted by Harvard Law School and the International House of Japan. Hakone. 23 October.

———. 2012. *Challenges in International Finance and Japan's Responses.* Keynote Address at the International Financial Symposium hosted by the Institute for International Monetary Affairs. Tokyo. 15 March.

Narayan, P., and B. C. Prasad. 2006. Trade Liberalization and Economic Growth: Empirical Evidence for Fiji from the Computable General Equilibrium Model. *Discussion Paper Series.* No. 07/06, Vol. 1. Queensland: Faculty of Business and Economics, Griffith University.

National Bureau of Statistics of China. 1995. *Statistical Communiqué on the National Economic and Social Development.* Beijing.

———. 2000. *Statistical Communiqué on the National Economic and Social Development.* Beijing.

———. 2018. *Statistical Communiqué on the National Economic and Social Development.* Beijing.

———. Various years. *China Statistical Yearbook.* http://www.stats.gov.cn/english/Statisticaldata/AnnualData/.

North, D. 1990. *Institutions, Institutional Change and Economic Performance.* Cambridge: Cambridge University Press.

Oakman, D. 2004. *Facing Asia. A History of the Colombo Plan.* Canberra: The Australian National University Press.

Ocean Conservancy. 2017. *Stemming the Tide: Land-Based Strategies for a Plastic-Free Ocean.* Washington, DC.

Ohkawa, K., and H. Rosovsky. 1960. The Role of Agriculture in Modern Japanese Economic Development. *Economic Development and Cultural Change.* 9 (1). pp. 43–67.

Ohtake, F., and M. Saito. 1998. Population Aging and Consumption Inequality in Japan. *Review of Income and Wealth.* 44 (3). pp. 361–381.

Organisation for Economic Co-operation and Development (OECD). 2010. *PISA 2009 Results: Learning Trends.* Paris.

———. 2013. Innovation in Southeast Asia. *OECD Reviews of Innovation Policy.* Paris.

———. 2016. *PISA 2015 Results in Focus.* Paris.

———. 2018. OECD Services Trade Restrictiveness Index. *Trade Policy Note.* March. Paris.

———. 2019. *Revenue Statistics in Asian and Pacific Economies 2019.* Paris.

———. *OECD Data.* https://data.oecd.org/.

———. OECD Employment and Labour Market Statistics. https://www.oecd-ilibrary.org/employment/data/oecd-employment-and-labour-market-statistics_lfs-data-en.

———. OECD Family Database. http://www.oecd.org/els/family/database.htm (accessed 9 September 2018).

———. *OECD Statistics.* https://stats.oecd.org/.

Organisation for Economic Co-operation and Development–Food and Agriculture Organization of the United Nations. 2017. *Agricultural Policy Monitoring and Evaluation 2017.* Rome.

———. 2018. *Agricultural Outlook 2018–2027.* Rome.

Organization Internationale des Constructeurs d'Automobiles. 2018. Production Statistics. http://www.oica.net/category/production-statistics/2018-statistics/.

Otsuka, K. 2012. Economic Transformation of Agriculture in Asia: Past Performance and Future Prospects. *Asian Journal of Agriculture and Development.* 9 (1). pp. 1–19.

Otsuka, K., Y. Nakano, and K. Takahashi. 2016. Contract Farming in Developed and Developing Countries. *Annual Review of Resource Economics.* 8 (1). pp. 353–376.

Our World in Data. *Water Use and Stress.* https://ourworldindata.org/water-use-sanitation.

Pacific Institute. 2013. *The World's Water: Access to Safe Drinking Water by Country, 1970–2008.* Oakland, CA. http://worldwater.org/wp-content/uploads/2013/07/data_table_3_access_to_safe_drinking_water_by_country.pdf.

Panagariya, A. 2008. *India: The Emerging Giant.* New York: Oxford University Press.

Park, C., J. Lee, J. Villafuerte, and P. Rosenkranz. 2017. 20 Years after the Asian Financial Crisis: Lessons Learned and Future Challenges. *ADB Briefs.* No. 85. Manila: Asian Development Bank.

Park, D., and S. Wayne. 2019. *Role of Tourism for Sustainable Development.* Background note prepared for the ADB Annual Meeting 2019.

Patel, R., and M. J. Parmentier. 2005. The Persistence of Traditional Gender Roles in the Information Technology Sector: A Study of Female Engineers in India. *Information Technologies and International Development.* 2 (3). pp. 29–46.

Pauly, D., and D. Zeller. 2016. Catch Reconstructions Reveal that Global Marine Fisheries Catches Are Higher than Reported and Declining. *Nature Communications.* 7. 10244.

PBL Netherlands Environmental Assessment Agency. *IMAGE 2.4-2.5 Using GLOBIO for RIO+12 Global Integrated Assessments, Baseline Scenario.* The Hague.

Piketty, T. 2006. The Kuznets Curve: Yesterday and Tomorrow. In Banerjee, A. V., R. Bénabou, and D. Mookherjee, eds. *Understanding Poverty.* New York: Oxford University Press. pp. 63–72.

———. 2017. *Capital in the Twenty-First Century.* Cambridge, MA: Harvard University Press.

Pingali, P. L., M. Hossain, and R. V. Gerpacio. 1997. *Asian Rice Bowls: The Returning Crisis.* Los Baños, Philippines: International Rice Research Institute and Centre for Agriculture and Bioscience International.

Pitt, M. M., S. R. Khandker, and J. Cartwright. 2006. Empowering Women with Micro Finance: Evidence from Bangladesh. *Economic Development and Cultural Change*. 54 (4). pp. 791–831.

Poapongsakorn, N., and Y. S. Tey. 2016. Institutions, Governance, and Transformation in Southeast Asian Agriculture. In Habito, C. F., D. Capistrano, and G. Saguiguit, Jr., eds. *Farms, Food, and Futures: Toward Inclusive and Sustainable Agricultural and Rural Development in Southeast Asia*. Los Baños, Philippines: Southeast Asian Regional Center for Graduate Study and Research in Agriculture.

Pomeranz, K. 2001. *The Great Divergence: China, Europe, and the Making of the Modern World Economy*. Princeton: Princeton University Press.

Pootrakool, K., K. Ariyapruchya, and T. Sodsrichai. 2005. Long-Term Saving in Thailand: Are We Saving Enough and What Are the Risks? *Monetary Policy Group Working Papers*. No. 2005-03. Bangkok: Bank of Thailand.

Pootrakul, K. 2013. *Khunaphap kan charoen toepto jak miti khong kan krajai raidai panha lae thang ook* [The Quality of Growth from the Perspective of Income Distribution: Problems and Solutions]. Paper presented at the Bank of Thailand Annual Seminar. 19 September.

Prebisch, R. 1962. The Economic Development of Latin America and Its Principal Problems. *Economic Bulletin for Latin America*. 7 (1). pp. 1–23.

Prince, S., G. Von Maltitz, F. Zhang, K. Byrne, C. Driscoll, G. Eshel, G. Kust, C. Martínez-Garza, J. P. Metzger, G. Midgley, D. Moreno-Mateos, M. Sghaier, and S. Thwin. 2018. Chapter 4: Status and Trends of Land Degradation and Restoration and Associated Changes in Biodiversity and Ecosystem Functions. In Montanarella, L., R. Scholes, and A. Brainich, eds. *The IPBES Assessment Report on Land Degradation and Restoration*. Bonn: Secretariat of the Intergovernmental Science-Policy Platform on Biodiversity and Ecosystem Services.

Qian, M. 2013. *Chinese Economic History* [in Chinese]. Beijing: Beijing United Publishing House.

Qian, N. 2008. Missing Women and the Price of Tea in China: The Effect of Sex-Specific Income on Sex Imbalance. *Quarterly Journal of Economics*. 123 (3). pp. 1251–1285.

Quibria, M. G. 2014. Aid Effectiveness: Research, Policy, and Unresolved Issues. *Development Studies Research*. 1 (1). pp. 75–87.

Quibria, M. G., and S. Ahmad. 2007. Aid Effectiveness in Bangladesh. *MPRA Paper*. No. 10299. Munich: Munich Personal RePEc Archive.

Raitzer, D. A., E. Ginting, D. Ponzi, S. Sandhu, and R. Gloria. Forthcoming. *The Environmental Sustainability of Asia's Development*. Manila: Asian Development Bank.

Ramsar Convention Secretariat and United Nations Environment Programme World Conservation Monitoring Centre. 2017. *Wetland Extent Trends (WET) Index – 2017 Update. Technical Update 2017*. Gland, Switzerland: Ramsar Convention Secretariat.

Ranis, G., and J. C. H. Fei. 1961. A Theory of Economic Development. *American Economic Review*. 51 (4). pp. 533–565.

Ravallion, M. 2019. Ethnic Inequality and Poverty in Malaysia Since 1969. *NBER Working Paper Series.* No. w25640. Cambridge, MA: National Bureau of Economic Research.

Reardon, T., K. Chen, B. Minten, and L. Adriano. 2012. *The Quiet Revolution in Staple Food Value Chains: Enter the Dragon, the Elephant, and the Tiger.* Manila: Asian Development Bank.

Reardon, T., and P. Timmer. 2014. Five Inter-Linked Transformations in the Asian Agrifood Economy: Food Security Implications. *Global Food Security.* 3 (2). pp. 108–117.

Reinhart, C., and V. Reinhart. 2015. Financial Crises, Development, and Growth: A Long-Term Perspective. *World Bank Economic Review.* 29 (1). pp. 53–76.

Reinhart, C., and K. Rogoff. 2009. The Aftermath of Financial Crises. *American Economic Review.* 99 (2). pp. 466–472.

Reis, L. A., J. Emmerling, M. Tavoni, and D. Raitzer. 2016. The Economics of Greenhouse Gas Mitigation in Developing Asia. *ADB Economics Working Paper Series.* No. 504. Manila: Asian Development Bank.

Rodrik, D. 2004. Industrial Policy for the Twenty-First Century. *KSG Working Paper Series.* No. RWP04-047. Cambridge, MA: Kennedy School of Government, Harvard University.

———. 2008. Thinking about Governance. In North, D., D. Acemoglu, F. Fukuyama, and D. Rodrik, eds. *Governance, Growth, and Development Decision-Making.* Washington, DC: World Bank.

Romer, P. 1990. Endogenous Technological Change. *Journal of Political Economy.* 98 (5). pp. S71–S102.

———. 2010. What Parts of Globalization Matter for Catch-Up Growth? *American Economic Review: Papers and Proceedings.* 100 (2). pp. 94–98.

Roodman, R. 2007. The Anarchy of Numbers: Aid, Development, and Cross-Country Empirics. *World Bank Economic Review.* 21 (2). pp. 255–277.

Rosegrant, M. W., and P. B. R. Hazell. 2000. *Transforming the Rural Asian Economy: The Unfinished Revolution.* New York: Oxford University Press.

Rosenstein-Rodan, P. 1943. Problems of Industrialization of Eastern and Southeast Europe. *Economic Journal.* 53 (210/211). pp. 202–211.

Rostow, W. 1959. The Stages of Economic Growth. *Economic History Review.* 12 (1). pp. 1–16.

Rowthorn, R., and R. Ramaswamy. 1997. Deindustrialization: Causes and Implications. *IMF Working Paper Series.* No. WP/97/42. Washington, DC: International Monetary Fund.

———. 1999. Growth, Trade, and Deindustrialization. *IMF Staff Papers.* 46 (1). pp. 18–41.

Rudel, T. K., O. T. Coomes, E. M. Frederic Achard, A. Angelsen, J. Xu, and E. Lambin. 2005. Forest Transitions: Towards a Global Understanding of Land Use Change. *Global Environmental Change.* 15 (1). pp. 23–31.

Sachs, J. D., and A. Warner. 1995. Economic Reform and the Process of Global Integration. *Brookings Papers on Economic Activity, 25th Anniversary Issue.* 1 (January). pp. 1–18.

Satoh, Y., T. Kahil, E. Byers, P. Burek, G. Fischer, S. Trambered, P. Greve, M. Florke, S. Eisner, N. Hanasaki, P. Magnuszewski, L. Nava, W. Cosgrove, S. Langan, and Y. Wada. 2017. Multi-Model and Multi-Scenario Assessments of Asian Water Futures: The Water Futures and Solutions (WFaS) Initiative. *Earth's Future*. 5 (7). pp. 823–852.

Satpayeva, Z. T. 2017. State and Prospects of Development of Kazakhstan Innovative Infrastructure. *European Research Studies Journal*. 20 (2). pp. 123–148.

Savada, A. M., and W. Shaw, eds. 1990. *South Korea: A Country Study*. Washington, DC: GPO for the Library of Congress.

Sawada, Y., M. Mahmud, and N. Kitano, eds. 2018. *Economic and Social Development of Bangladesh: Miracle and Challenges*. London: Palgrave Macmillan.

Sawada, Y., A. Matsuda, and H. Kimura. 2012. On the Role of Technical Cooperation in International Technology Transfers. *Journal of International Development*. 24 (3). pp. 316–340.

Schmidt, C., T. Krauth, and S. Wagner. 2017. Export of Plastic Debris by Rivers into the Sea. *Environmental Science & Technology*. 51 (21). pp. 12246–12253.

Schuler, S. R., and E. Rottach. 2010. Women's Empowerment across Generations in Bangladesh. *Journal of Development Studies*. 46 (3). pp. 379–396.

Schultz, T. W. 1964. *Transforming Traditional Agriculture*. New Haven and London: Yale University Press.

Sen, A. 1981. *Poverty and Famines: An Essay on Entitlement and Deprivation*. Oxford: Clarendon Press.

———. 1985. *Commodities and Capabilities*. Amsterdam: North-Holland.

Seoul Metropolitan Government. 2017. *Seoul Tap Water Arisu*. Seoul. http://susa. or.kr/en/files/seoul-tap-water-arisu-englishpdf?ckattempt=1.

Serafica, P., and T. Begszuren. *Communication Strategies to Enforce Gender Equality Legislation in Mongolia*. https://development.asia/case-study/communication-strategies-enforce-gender-equality-legislation-mongolia.

Shepherd, B. 2019. Productivity and Trade Growth in Services: How Services Helped Power Factory Asia. In Helble, M., and B. Shepherd, eds. *Leveraging Services for Development: Prospects and Policies*. Tokyo: Asian Development Bank Institute.

———. 2019. Services Policies and Manufacturing Exports. In Helble, M., and B. Shepherd, eds. *Leveraging Services for Development: Prospects and Policies*. Tokyo: Asian Development Bank Institute.

Smil, V. 2017. *Energy and Civilization: A History*. Cambridge, MA: The MIT Press.

Smith, A. 1776. *An Inquiry into the Nature and Causes of the Wealth of Nations*. London: William Strahan and Thomas Cadell.

Socioeconomic Data and Applications Center. *Environmental Performance Index*. http://sedac.ciesin.columbia.edu/data/set/epi-environmental-performance-index-2016/data-download.

Solt, F. 2019. *Measuring Income Inequality across Countries and over Time: The Standardized World Income Inequality Database, Version 8*. https://doi.org/10.7910/DVN/LM4OWF, Harvard Dataverse, V1.

Stallings, B., and E. M. Kim. 2017. *Promoting Development: The Political Economy of East Asia Foreign Aid*. Singapore: Palgrave Macmillan.

Statista. *Industry Indicators*. https://www.statista.com/markets/.

Stiglitz, J. 2016. The State, the Market, and Development. *WIDER Working Paper*. No. 2016/1. Helsinki: United Nations University World Institute for Development Economics Research.

Studwell, J. 2013. *How Asia Works: Success and Failure in the World's Most Dynamic Region*. New York: Grove Press.

Sugihara, K. 1996. *Japan, China, and the Growth of the Asian International Economy, 1850–1949*. Volume 1. Oxford: Oxford University Press.

Suh, J. J., and J. Kim. 2017. Aid to Build Governance in a Fragile State: Foreign Assistance to a Post-Conflict South Korea. In Howe, B. M., ed. *Post-Conflict Development in East Asia*. Surrey, United Kingdom: Ashgate Publishing Limited.

Swinnen, J. F. M., and L. Vranken. 2010. Reforms and Agricultural Productivity in Central and Eastern Europe and the Former Soviet Republics: 1989–2005. *Journal of Productivity Analysis*. 33 (3). pp. 241–258.

Tachibanaki, T. 2006. *Kakusa Shakai: Nani ga mondai nanoka* [The Divided Society: What Are the Issues?] Tokyo: Iwanami Shoten.

Tan, C., W. Puchniak, and U. Varottil. 2015. State-Owned Enterprises in Singapore: Historical Insights into a Potential Model for Reform. *NUS Law Working Paper*. No. 2015/003. Singapore: National University of Singapore.

Tani, M. 2015. Japan's Environmental Policy. *Policy Update*. No. 059. Tokyo: Research Institute of Economy, Trade and Industry.

Taslim, M. A. 2008. Governance, Policies and Economic Growth in Bangladesh. In Islam, N., and M. Asaduzzaman, eds. *A Ship Adrift: Governance and Development in Bangladesh*. Dhaka: Bangladesh Institute of Development Studies.

Terada-Hagiwara, A. 2009. Explaining Filipino Households' Declining Saving Rate. *ADB Economics Working Paper Series*. No. 178. Manila: Asian Development Bank.

Terada-Hagiwara, A., S. Camingue-Romance, and J. Zveglich. 2019. *Gender Differences and Relative Pay: Does the Stage of Development Matter?* Paper presented at the Asian and Australasian Society of Labour Economics 2019 Conference. National University of Singapore. 12–14 December.

Times Higher Education. 2019. *World University Rankings 2019*. https://www.timeshighereducation.com/world-university-rankings/2019/subject-ranking/physical-sciences#!/page/3/length/25/sort_by/rank/sort_order/asc/cols/stats.

Timmer, C. P. 2012. Structural Transformation, the Changing Role of Rice, and Food Security in Asia: Small Farmers and Modern Supply Chains. *Asian Journal of Agriculture and Development*. 9 (1). pp. 21–35.

———. 2014. Food Security in Asia and the Pacific: The Rapidly Changing Role of Rice. *Asia & the Pacific Policy Studies*. 1 (1). pp. 73–90.

———. 2014. Managing Structural Transformation: A Political Economy Approach. *UNU-WIDER Annual Lecture*. No. 18. Helsinki: United Nations University World Institute for Development Economics Research.

Timmer, M. P., G. J. de Vries, and K. de Vries. 2015. Patterns of Structural Change in Developing Countries. In Weiss, J., and M. Tribe, eds. *Routledge Handbook of Industry and Development*. Abingdon: Routledge. pp. 65–83.

Timossi, A. J. 2015. Revisiting the 1955 Bandung Asian–African Conference and Its Legacy. *South Bulletin*. 85. 15 May. Geneva: South Centre.

Tjiptoherijanto, P., and S. Remi. 2001. *Poverty and Inequality in Indonesia: Trends and Programs*. Paper presented at the International Conference on the Chinese Economy "Achieving Growth with Equity." Beijing. 4–6 July.

Tortajada, C., Y. Joshi, and A. K. Biswas. 2013. *The Singapore Water Story: Sustainable Development in an Urban City State*. London: Routledge.

Tyers, R., and F. Lu. 2008. Competition Policy, Corporate Saving and China's Current Account Surplus. *ANU Working Papers in Economics and Econometrics*. No. 2008-496. Canberra: Australian National University College of Business and Economics.

United Nations (UN). 1967. *Statistical Yearbook*. New York.

———. 1973. *Statistical Yearbook*. New York.

———. UN Comtrade Database. https://comtrade.un.org (accessed 19 July 2019).

United Nations, Department of Economic and Social Affairs, Population Division. 2017. *International Migrant Stock: The 2017 Revision*. https://www.un.org/en/development/desa/population/migration/data/estimates2/estimates17.asp.

———. 2018. *World Urbanization Prospects: The 2018 Revision*. Online Edition. https://population.un.org/wup/.

———. 2019. *World Population Prospects 2019*. Online Edition. https://population.un.org/wpp/.

United Nations, Department of Economic and Social Affairs, Statistics Division. 1998. *Recommendations on Statistics of International Migration, Revision 1*. New York.

———. *Gender Statistics*. https://genderstats.un.org/.

———. *National Accounts Data*. https://unstats.un.org.

United Nations Children's Fund (UNICEF). 2019. *Progress on Household Drinking Water, Sanitation and Hygiene 2000–2017. Special Focus on Inequalities*. New York. p. 7.

———. UNICEF Immunization Database. https://data.unicef.org/topic/child-health/immunization/ (accessed 31 August 2018).

United Nations Children's Fund, World Health Organization, and World Bank. *Joint Child Malnutrition Estimates*. who.int/nutgrowthdb/estimates/en.

United Nations Conference on Trade and Development (UNCTAD). 2017. *Trade and Development Report 2017. Beyond Austerity: Towards a Global New Deal*. Geneva.

———. *UNCTADStat*. https://unctadstat.unctad.org.

United Nations Economic and Social Commission for Asia and the Pacific. 2014. *Review of Asia and the Pacific: A Story of Transformation and Resurgence*. Bangkok.

United Nations Economic Commission for Asia and the Far East. 1964. *Annual Economic Survey*. Bangkok. p. 1.

United Nations Educational, Scientific and Cultural Organization Institute for Statistics (UIS). UIS Stat Database. http://data.uis.unesco.org/ (accessed 2 August 2019).

United Nations Environment Programme. 2011. *Towards a Green Economy: Pathways to Sustainable Development and Poverty Eradication*. Nairobi.

United Nations Framework Convention on Climate Change. 2015. *Adoption of the Paris Agreement*. Paris.

United Nations Population Fund. 2013. *Cambodia: A Success Story in Reducing Maternal Mortality*. Phnom Penh. https://cambodia.unfpa.org/sites/default/files/pub-pdf/Poster-RH.pdf.

United Nations Statistics Division. UNSD Database. https://unstats.un.org/UNSD/databases.htm (accessed 28 August 2019).

UN Women. 2013. *Domestic Violence Legislation and its Implementation*. Bangkok.

United Nations World Tourism Organization (UNWTO). 2018. *UNWTO Tourism Highlights: 2018 Edition*. Madrid.

———. 2019. *UNWTO Tourism Highlights: 2019 Edition*. Madrid.

United States Agency for International Development. Demographic and Health Surveys. https://statcompiler.com/en/.

United States Department of Agriculture Economic Research Service. 2019. *International Agricultural Productivity*. https://www.ers.usda.gov/data-products/international-agricultural-productivity.

United States Patent and Trademark Office (USPTO). Various years. *USPTO Annual Reports*. Alexandria, VA.

University of Washington Institute for Health Metrics and Evaluation. *Global Health Data Exchange 2017*. http://ghdx.healthdata.org/.

Ut, T. T., and K. Kajisa. 2006. The Impact of Green Revolution on Rice Production in Vietnam. *The Developing Economies*. 44 (2). pp. 167–189.

Vandana, C., J. Yifu Lin, and Y. Wang. 2013. Leading Dragon Phenomenon: New Opportunities for Catch-Up in Low-Income Countries. *Asian Development Review*. 30 (1). pp. 52–84.

Wade, R. 1990. *Governing the Market: Economic Theory and the Role of Government in East Asian Industrialization*. Princeton: Princeton University Press.

———. 2003. *Governing the Market: Economic Theory and the Role of Government in East Asian Industrialization*. Revised edition. Princeton: Princeton University Press.

Wajcman, J., and L. A. P. Lobb. 2007. The Gender Relations of Software Work in Vietnam. *Gender, Technology and Development*. 11 (1). pp. 1–26.

Warr, P. 2000. *Poverty Reduction and Economic Growth: The Asian Experience*. Manila: Asian Development Bank.

———. 2004. Globalization, Growth, and Poverty Reduction in Thailand. *ASEAN Economic Bulletin*. 21 (1). pp. 1–18.

Watanabe, T. 1992. *Asia: Its Growth and Agony*. Hawaii: University of Hawaii Press.

Wei, S.-J., and X. Zhang. 2011. The Competitive Saving Motive: Evidence from Rising Sex Ratios and Savings Rates in China. *Journal of Political Economy*. 119 (3). pp. 511–564.

Whittaker, D. 1997. *Small Firms in the Japanese Economy*. Cambridge, United Kingdom: Cambridge University Press.

Wid.World. World Inequality Database. https://wid.world/wid-world/ (accessed 26 April 2019).

Williamson, J. 1989. *What Washington Means by Policy Reform*. Washington, DC: Peterson Institute for International Economics.

Wong, P. K., and A. Singh. 2008. From Technology Adopter to Innovation: Singapore. In Edquist, C., and L. Hommen, eds. *Small Country Innovations System: Globalization, Change and Policy in Asia and Europe.* Cheltenham, United Kingdom and Northampton, MA: Edward Elgar.

World Bank. 1993. *The East Asian Miracle: Economic Growth and Public Policy.* New York: Oxford University Press.

―――. 2002. *The Reform of India Post: Transforming a Postal Infrastructure to Deliver Modern Information and Financial Services.* Washington, DC.

―――. 2003. *Bangladesh – Development Policy Review: Impressive Achievements but Continuing Challenges.* Washington, DC.

―――. 2005. *World Bank's Loans to Japan.* Washington, DC. https://www.worldbank.org/en/country/japan/brief/world-banks-loans-to-japan.

―――. 2006. Do Current Water Subsidies Reach the Poor? *Series on Water Tariffs and Subsidies in South Asia.* No. 4. Washington, DC.

―――. 2006. *Economics and Governance of Nongovernmental Organizations in Bangladesh.* Washington, DC.

―――. 2007. *World Development Report 2008: Agriculture for Development.* Washington, DC.

―――. 2012. *World Development Report 2012: Gender Equality and Development.* Washington, DC.

―――. 2017. *FAQs about the Pantawid Pamilyang Pilipino Program (4Ps).* Washington, DC. https://www.worldbank.org/en/country/philippines/brief/faqs-about-the-pantawid-pamilyang-pilipino-program.

―――. 2018. *Contribution of Institutional Investors: Private Investment in Infrastructure 2011–H1 2017.* Washington, DC.

―――. 2018. *Taking Stock of the Political Economy of Power Sector Reforms in Developing Countries.* Washington, DC.

―――. 2018. *Women, Business, and the Law 2018.* Washington, DC.

―――. *Content of Deep Trade Agreements.* https://datacatalog.worldbank.org/dataset/content-deep-trade-agreements.

―――. Global Financial Development Database. https://www.worldbank.org/en/publication/gfdr/data/global-financial-development-database (accessed 15 November 2019).

―――. *Pink Sheet Data.* https://www.worldbank.org/en/research/commodity-markets.

―――. PovcalNet Database. http://iresearch.worldbank.org/PovcalNet/home.aspx (accessed 7 November 2019).

―――. *Rural Access Index.* https://datacatalog.worldbank.org/dataset/rural-access-index-rai.

―――. Women, Business, and the Law Database. https://wbl.worldbank.org/en/data/exploretopics/getting-paid (accessed 10 November 2019).

―――. World Development Indicators. https://data.worldbank.org.

―――. World Integrated Trade Solution. https://wits.worldbank.org/.

World Health Organization (WHO). 2009. *Health Financing Strategy for the Asia Pacific Region (2010–2015).* Geneva.

―――. 2011. *The Partnership for Maternal, Newborn and Child Health, updated September.* Geneva.

———. 2015. *Trends in Maternal Mortality: 1990 to 2015: Estimates by WHO, UNICEF, UNFPA, World Bank Group and the United Nations Population Division*. Geneva.

———. 2018. *Global Status Report on Road Safety*. Paris.

———. Global Ambient Air Quality Database (update 2018). https://www.who.int/airpollution/data/cities/en/ (accessed 23 May 2019).

———. *Global Health Observatory Data*. https://www.who.int/gho/en/.

———. *Universal Coverage and Health Financing*. https://www.who.int/health_financing/data-statistics/en/.

World Health Organization / United Nations Children's Fund Joint Monitoring Programme (JMP). *Global Data on Water Supply, Sanitation and Hygiene*. https://washdata.org/data.

World Resources Institute. *CAIT Climate Data Explorer*. http://cait.wri.org/.

World Trade Organization (WTO). 2008. Trade, the Location of Production and the Industrial Organization of Firms. In *World Trade Report 2008: Trade in a Globalizing World*. Geneva.

———. *GATT Members*. https://www.wto.org/english/thewto_e/gattmem_e.htm.

———. *WTO Accessions*. https://www.wto.org/english/thewto_e/acc_e/acc_e.htm.

———. WTO Online Database. https://www.data.wto.org (accessed 15 May 2019).

World Trade Organization, Australian Aid, and Asian Development Bank. 2019. *Aid for Trade in Asia and the Pacific: Promoting Economic Diversification and Empowerment*. Manila: Asian Development Bank.

World Trade Organization, Government of Australia, and Asian Development Bank. 2017. *Aid for Trade in Asia and the Pacific: Promoting Connectivity for Inclusive Development*. Manila: Asian Development Bank.

Wu, Y. 2012. Trends and Prospects in China's Research and Development Sector. *Australian Economic Review*. 45 (4). pp. 467–474.

Yamamura, E., T. Sonobe, and K. Otsuka. 2005. Time Path in Innovation, Imitation, and Growth: The Case of the Motorcycle Industry in Postwar Japan. *Journal of Evolutionary Economics*. 15 (2). pp. 169–186.

Yang, X., and S. Ng. 1998. Specialization and Division of Labor: A Survey. In Arrow, K. J., Y. K. Ng, and X. Yang, eds. *Increasing Returns and Economic Analysis*. London: Palgrave Macmillan.

Yasmi, Y, J. Guernier, and C. J. Colfer. 2009. Positive and Negative Aspects of Forestry Conflict: Lessons from a Decentralized Forest Management in Indonesia. *International Forestry Review*. 11 (1). pp. 98–110.

Young, A. 1995. The Tyranny of Numbers: Confronting the Statistical Realities of the East Asian Growth Experience. *Quarterly Journal of Economics*. 110 (3). pp. 641–680.

Yu, M. 2015. Processing Trade, Tariff Reductions and Firm Productivity: Evidence from Chinese Firms. *The Economic Journal*. 125 (585). pp. 943–988.

Zhai, F. 2008. Armington Meets Melitz: Introducing Firm Heterogeneity in a Global CGE Model of Trade. *Journal of Economic Integration*. 23 (3). pp. 575–604.

Zhang, J. 2017. The Evolution of China's One-Child Policy and Its Effects on Family Outcomes. *Journal of Economic Perspectives*. 31 (1). pp. 141–159.

Zhang, L., R. Brooks, D. Ding, H. Ding, H. He, J. Lu, and R. Mano. 2018. China's High Savings: Drivers, Prospects, and Policies. *IMF Working Paper*. No. WP/18/277. Washington, DC: International Monetary Fund.

Zhuang, J., E. de Dios, and A. Lagman-Martin. 2010. Governance and Institutional Quality and the Links with Growth and Inequality: How Asia Fares. In Zhuang, J., ed. *Poverty, Inequality, and Inclusive Growth in Asia.* London: Asian Development Bank / Anthem Press.

Zhuang, J., H. Gunatilake, Y. Niimi, M. E. Khan, Y. Jiang, R. Hasan, N. Khor, A. S. Lagman-Martin, P. Bracey, and B. Huang. 2009. Financial Sector Development, Economic Growth, and Poverty Reduction: A Literature Review. *ADB Economics Working Paper Series.* No. 173. Manila: Asian Development Bank.

INDEX

Figures, notes, and tables are indicated by f, n, and t following the page number.

A

ABMI (Asian Bond Markets Initiative), 249–50, 476

Acer, 163, 166

ADB. *See* Asian Development Bank

ADF (Asian Development Fund), 448

Afghanistan, security challenges facing, 7, 76

Africa. *See* Sub-Saharan Africa

agglomeration economies, 14, 108–9, 111

aggregate production function, 150, 153b

agribusiness, 25, 75–76, 139, 141–42, 144

agriculture, 113–45. *See also* food;
Green Revolution; irrigation
climate change and, 133, 144, 145, 425
contract farming, 141
direct transition to services from, 99
employment shares in, 14, 48, 86–87, 88f, 90t, 497–99
fertilizer use in, 15, 114, 124–27, 129f, 418
land reform, 15, 25, 91–92, 114, 119–23, 123–24b
macroeconomic indicators, 113, 115–16t
in market-oriented reform, 59, 63
mechanization in, 15, 114, 133
output as share of GDP, 86–87, 88f, 89t, 494–96
pessimistic views of, 113–14
plantation-based, 117n2, 121, 122
policy recommendations, 144–45
production diversification, 136–38, 137f
productivity in, 91–92, 93f, 171
regional cooperation in, 482
slash-and-burn cultivation, 413, 415
structural transformation of, 14–15, 86–94, 88f, 89–90t
technological development in, 91–92, 144, 149b, 150, 171
trade in, 138–39, 140f, 144

AI. *See* artificial intelligence

AIIB (Asian Infrastructure Investment Bank), 452, 466, 467

air pollution. *See also* greenhouse gas emissions
economic growth and, 22, 278
EKC as applied to, 436
in megacities, 269
mitigation strategies, 293
particulate matter emissions, 423–24, 424f, 430
policy development and implementation, 428, 429, 431

air quality standards, 430, 432t

Akamatsu, K., 318b

Alibaba, 102–4, 178, 291

Amazon, 178, 290

antibiotics, 201, 202

APEC (Asia-Pacific Economic Cooperation), 59, 472, 476, 476n9

Apple, 163, 178, 288

Aquino, Benigno, 56

Armenia
income inequality in, 375
transition to market economy, 78, 80
WTO membership of, 80

ARPANET, 290

arranged marriage, 211

artificial intelligence (AI)
  applications for, 293
  development of, 144, 178, 180
  employment changes due to, 183, 222
  in energy sector, 271–72
ASEAN. *See* Association of Southeast
  Asian Nations
ASEI (Asia Solar Energy Initiative), 270
Asia. *See also specific regions and
  countries*
  agriculture in. *See* agriculture
  cooperation in. *See* regional
    cooperation and integration
  demographic changes in. *See*
    demographic changes
  development agenda for, 25–28
  development indicators for, 5, 6*t*
  education in. *See* education
  environmental issues in.
    See environmental issues
  finance in. *See* financial sector
  GDP growth in, 2–3, 2–3*t*, 490–93
  global shares of GDP in, 3, 4*f*, 6
  health care in. *See* health care
  income inequality in. *See* income
    inequality
  industrialization in.
    See industrialization
  infrastructure in. *See* infrastructure
  macroeconomic stability in.
    See macroeconomic stability
  poverty in. *See* poverty
  structural transformation in.
    See structural transformation
  technology in. *See* technology
  total GDP values for, 486–88
  trade in. *See* trade
  women in. *See* women
Asian–African Conference (1955), 473
Asian Bond Markets Initiative (ABMI),
  249–50, 476
Asian Consensus, 9–11
Asian Development Bank (ADB)
  agricultural initiatives, 114, 119, 123
  Asia Solar Energy Initiative, 270
  on climate change, 23, 427–28, 439
  cofinancing of projects, 451–52, 458
  crisis response assistance from, 348

development assistance from, 23, 76,
    453–55, 457, 460–61
  digital technology projects, 181–82*b*
  educational initiatives, 194, 383
  establishment of, 24, 119, 447, 479
  evolution of financing from, 448–51,
    450*f*
  on fiscal prudence, 238
  gender equality initiatives, 408*b*
  on governance and economic
    development, 40
  grant assistance from, 445
  Green Revolution supported by, 126*b*
  infrastructure projects, 60, 265, 267,
    268*b*, 275, 278, 288
  on land titles for women, 250
  lending activities of, 58, 70, 73, 343, 448
  objectives of, 447–48
  poverty projections from, 351, 351*n*1
  RCI initiatives, 24, 60, 479, 480–81*b*
  Strategy 2030, 144, 181*b*, 408*b*, 439, 451
Asian Development Fund (ADF), 448
Asian financial crisis (1997–1998)
  causes of, 57, 239, 241, 339, 341–42
  macroeconomic policy resulting
    from, 328, 345
  multilateral development financing
    during, 448, 454
  RCI initiatives in aftermath of, 345, 476
  reform measures following, 20, 58,
    248, 343
  responses to, 342–43, 344*t*
  unemployment during, 363
Asian Infrastructure Investment Bank
  (AIIB), 452, 466, 467
Asia-Pacific Economic Cooperation
  (APEC), 59, 472, 476, 476*n*9
Asia Solar Energy Initiative (ASEI), 270
Association of Southeast Asian Nations
  (ASEAN)
  Economic Community, 24, 217, 324,
    474, 475*b*
  establishment of, 52, 470, 474, 474*b*
  FDI to, 305–7
  financial reform measures, 18, 20, 476
  Free Trade Agreement, 324, 470
  membership additions, 52, 58, 59
  objectives of, 24, 52, 470, 474*b*

Regional Forum, 472
share of Asian exports, 301
Australia
development assistance from, 23,
446–47, 461, 463–64
energy consumption in, 257
life expectancy in, 197
RCI initiatives involving, 473
technical cooperation aid from, 165
automatic stabilizers, 332, 349
Azerbaijan
industry-to-GDP shares in, 87
sovereign wealth funds of, 336b
transition to market economy, 78, 80

B
Baidu, 178, 291
balance of payments crises, 38, 55,
70–75, 310, 341, 451
Baldwin, Richard, 315–16
Bangladesh
development assistance for, 457–58,
457f
economic growth in, 74
education in, 193, 383
employment for women in, 388
formation of, 72
Grameen Bank, 41, 398
Green Revolution, 128
industrial clusters in, 169
infrastructure development in, 278,
284, 284b, 451, 458
market-oriented reform in, 73
marriage age for women in, 211
poverty reduction in, 363–64
technology transfer in, 165
bank-based financial systems, 244–46
Bay of Bengal Initiative for Multi-
Sectoral Technical and Economic
Cooperation (BIMSTEC), 479
Bell, Alexander Graham, 287
Berners-Lee, Tim, 290
Bhutan
economic growth in, 77
tourism in, 108
big push theory, 12, 35
bilateral development assistance.
See official development assistance

bond financing, 239, 440
Borlaug, Norman, 125n26
Bretton Woods system, 19–20, 310, 338
Brunei Darussalam
Indonesia–Malaysia–Philippines East
ASEAN Growth Area (BIMP-EAGA)
Program, 479, 480b
market-oriented reform in, 58
build–operate–transfer (BOT)
approach, 254, 267, 276
Busan Partnership for Effective
Development Co-operation, 465
business process outsourcing (BPO)
history and development of, 176
ICT-enabled, 99, 104, 178, 180
industrial clusters of, 169
in services sector, 100, 291
women's employment in, 383, 388

C
Cambodia
domestic conflict in, 7
education in, 383–84
FDI to, 304
income inequality in, 374
industrial clusters in, 169
market-oriented reform in, 58, 60
maternal mortality in, 386
state-owned enterprises in, 60
water supply systems in, 284
WTO membership of, 60
Canon, 460
capability approach, 357
capital accumulation
domestic savings and, 221
drivers of, 227–28
FDI and, 49, 55, 161–62, 228, 315
human capital. *See* human capital
income inequality and, 355
manufacturing and, 95
as share of GDP, 510–11
social capital, 41–42
by state-owned enterprises, 50
stock and physical capital growth,
226–27, 227t
total factor productivity growth and,
151
by women, 389

capital flow management measures, 339, 343, 350
capital markets
advantages of, 244
growth of, 18, 226, 248–49, 248f
history and development of, 246, 248
institutional investors in, 249, 249f
liberalization of, 20, 342
policy recommendations, 26
regional cooperation and, 249–50
capture fisheries, 420–21, 420f
carbon dioxide emissions. *See* greenhouse gas emissions
CAREC (Central Asia Regional Economic Cooperation) Program, 24, 80, 460, 479, 481b
Caribbean. *See* Latin America and the Caribbean
CCT (conditional cash transfer) programs, 194, 374, 378, 383
CDM (Clean Development Mechanism), 431
CEDAW (Convention on the Elimination of All Forms of Discrimination against Women), 377–78, 406
cell phones. *See* smartphones
center–periphery theory. *See* dependency theory
Central Asia. *See also specific countries*
agricultural production in, 138
capital accumulation in, 226, 227t
demographic changes in, 208, 484
development assistance for, 460
domestic savings in, 229
education in, 196
electrification rates in, 270
external financing in, 241, 242f
GDP growth in, 490, 492
health-care expenditures in, 204
income inequality in, 375
land reform in, 124b
literacy rate in, 381, 382f
market-oriented reform in, 13, 30, 38, 312
poverty reduction in, 364
RCI initiatives in, 24, 477–78
remittance flows to, 243b

technological adoption and innovation in, 180
total GDP values for, 486
transition to market economy, 77–80, 81n46
undernutrition in, 198, 200t
Central Asia Regional Economic Cooperation (CAREC) Program, 24, 80, 460, 479, 481b
central banks
expansion of money supply by, 78
in global financial crisis, 33
independence of, 20, 58, 78, 337, 338f
inflation targeting by, 337
chemical contamination of land, 417–18
Chiang Mai Initiative (2000), 20, 345, 476
Chiang Mai Initiative Multilateralization (2010), 20, 345, 348, 476
children. *See also* education
causes of death among, 200–202
immunization programs for, 201–2, 202t
mortality rates for, 16, 186, 197–98, 199t, 384, 526–27
one-child policy, 208, 212, 213b
sex ratios at birth, 386, 387f
undernutrition among, 198, 200t
China. *See* People's Republic of China
Clean Development Mechanism (CDM), 431
climate change. *See also* greenhouse gas emissions
agriculture and, 133, 144, 145, 425
bilateral and multilateral support on, 438–39
emergence as global issue, 411–12
GDP loss due to, 428
geographic considerations, 77, 81
health issues related to, 426
international agreements on, 23–24, 269–70, 412, 429, 431, 436–38
mitigation strategies, 27–28, 183, 257, 431
natural resource degradation due to, 426–27

policy development and implementation, 430–31
cloud computing, 182, 291
coal, 255–57, 264–67, 269, 423, 425
Cobb–Douglas form of production function, 153*b*
Colombo Plan for Cooperative Economic Development in South and Southeast Asia, 462, 463, 473
commodity prices, 52–53, 55, 81, 334, 335*f*, 348
communication technology. *See* information and communication technology
competition
  as driver of growth, 12, 31
  in energy sector, 271
  fairness in, 26
  in financial sector, 71
  imperfect, 10, 32
  industrial policy and, 11, 35
  innovation through, 162, 170–71
  promotion of, 46, 83–84
  in services sector, 104
  in technology sector, 169–71
Comprehensive and Progressive Agreement for Trans-Pacific Partnership (CPTPP), 59, 324, 481–82
computers, 47, 100, 150, 156, 166, 289–90
conditional cash transfer (CCT) programs, 194, 374, 378, 383
confidentiality, 182, 293
consumer credit markets, 232*b*, 235–36
contract farming, 141
Convention on the Elimination of All Forms of Discrimination against Women (CEDAW), 377–78, 406
convergence process, 7, 47
cooperation. *See* regional cooperation and integration
corporate savings, 229, 232, 233*f*, 237–38
corruption
  anticorruption efforts, 13, 84, 170
  as barrier to economic growth, 8
  control in good governance, 30, 35, 39
  opportunities for, 311
CO_2 emissions. *See* greenhouse gas emissions

countercyclical fiscal policy, 332–33, 334*f*, 349
CPTPP (Comprehensive and Progressive Agreement for Trans-Pacific Partnership), 59, 324, 481–82
credit markets, 232*b*, 235–36
crops. *See* agriculture
Cultural Revolution (1966–1976), 38, 62, 194
current account balances, 231–32*b*, 239, 504–5
cybersecurity, 180, 182, 293
cyclicality of fiscal policy, 332–34, 334*f*

D
Daewoo, 165
debt, public, 58, 72, 332, 333*f*
decision-making within households, 402, 403*f*
deforestation, 413–15, 414*f*, 425, 436
deindustrialization, 14, 86, 87, 98–99, 101
demographic changes, 208–22. *See also* life expectancy; mortality rates
  age structure of population, 26, 47, 144, 208, 210*f*, 221–22
  cross-border labor mobility and, 215–17, 223
  cross-country diversity of, 212, 214, 215*f*
  domestic savings and, 45, 220–21
  economic growth and, 185, 186, 223
  in fertility rate, 17, 186, 208–14, 211*t*, 213*b*, 215*f*
  impact of, 217–22, 219*t*
  income inequality and, 367*b*
  phases of transition, 212, 214
  population growth, 186, 208, 208*n*16, 209*t*, 210*f*, 484–85
  rapidity of, 212
  stock of outward migrants, 216–17, 216*f*
  working-age population, 17, 26, 45, 186, 208, 217–18
demographic dividend
  benefits from, 7, 26, 51, 186, 223
  cross-country diversity in, 214
  first, 218*n*22
  generation of, 17, 45, 51

measurement of, 217–20, 219*t*
 second, 221
demographic tax, 47, 186, 214, 218, 220, 223
Deng Xiaoping, 41, 63, 64, 358
dependency theory, 12, 36, 97, 309
Desh Garments Ltd., 165
development assistance.
 See multilateral development banks;
 official development assistance
Dhaka Water Supply and Sewerage
 Authority (DWASA), 284, 284*b*
diet. *See* food
digital technology, 82, 101, 181–82*b*, 271–72, 291–92
discrimination, gender, 377–78, 383, 397, 400, 406, 408*b*
Doi Moi reforms, 59, 123*b*, 131, 458
domestic savings, 228–38
 corporate, 229, 232, 233*f*, 237–38
 demographic changes and, 45, 220–21
 drivers of growth in, 17
 global imbalances, 231–32*b*
 government, 232, 233*f*, 238
 household, 220–21, 229, 232–37, 233*f*
 in newly industrialized economies, 51
 policy recommendations, 251
 as share of GDP, 229, 230*t*, 508–9
domestic violence, 406
drinking water safety, 26, 202–4, 203*f*
Dutch disease, 336*b*
DWASA (Dhaka Water Supply and
 Sewerage Authority), 284, 284*b*

E
earnings gap, 394, 396–97, 396*f*
East Asia. *See also specific countries
 and areas*
 agricultural production in, 137
 capital accumulation in, 226–27, 227*t*
 demographic changes in, 208, 484
 domestic savings in, 229
 external financing in, 241, 242*f*
 FDI to, 305
 food consumption patterns in, 134, 135
 GDP growth in, 490, 492
 Green Revolution in, 125, 133
 health-care expenditures in, 204

income inequality in, 21, 352, 364, 365
 industrialization in, 94
 land reform in, 15
 literacy rate in, 381, 382*f*
 RCI initiatives in, 472–76
 total GDP values for, 486
 undernutrition in, 198, 200*t*
Eastern Seaboard Development
 Program (Thailand), 455, 456*f*
Economic Commission for Asia and the
 Far East (ECAFE), 117–18, 464, 469, 472
economic growth. *See also* gross
 domestic product
 Asian model of, 9–11
 demographic changes and, 185, 186, 223
 drivers of, 6–9, 15–16, 31, 185, 327
 environmental consequences of, 22–23, 411
 exports and, 19, 30, 302–3, 302*f*
 good governance for, 39, 40, 40*f*
 inclusive growth strategies, 21
 income inequality and, 21, 352
 investment and, 225
 middle class expansion and, 5
 openness and, 308
 poverty reduction and, 20–21, 66, 71, 351, 358–60, 359–60*f*
 rates of, 328, 329*f*
 technology and, 15–16, 150–54, 155*f*
education, 187–96
 compulsory, 16, 42, 46, 192–93, 193*t*
 as development indicator, 5, 6*t*
 enrollment rates, 187–90, 187*n2*, 189*t*, 518–23
 expenditures on, 195*t*, 196, 512–13
 future challenges for, 26, 222
 mean years of, 5, 6*t*, 16, 187, 188*f*
 in newly industrialized economies, 51, 187
 public policy and investment in, 192–96
 quality of, 190–92, 191*f*, 222
 reform efforts, 194–96
 social assistance programs for, 193–94
 technological, 182
 TVET, 112, 186–90, 190*n4*, 194
 universal access to, 16, 186, 187
 for women, 22, 193, 378–84, 380–81*t*, 391*n19*

EKC (Environmental Kuznets Curve) hypothesis, 435–36
electricity
  conversion efficiency for, 255
  coverage rates, 5, 26, 257, 264, 267, 270
  evolutionary periods, 264–67, 269–71
  generation of, 18, 46, 227, 255–57, 256f, 262–63t
  history of, 255
  privatization of, 43, 271
  in Second Industrial Revolution, 160n6
  sources of, 77, 257, 262–63t, 264–70, 268b
elite capture, 35, 353
employment. See also employment for women
  agriculture as share of, 14, 48, 86–87, 88f, 90t, 497–99
  cross-border labor mobility, 215–17, 223
  industry as share of, 74, 87, 88f, 90t, 497–99
  manufacturing as share of, 95, 96f, 98
  migrant workers, 216–17, 216f, 223
  services as share of, 87, 88f, 90t, 497–99
  skilled vs. unskilled, 370–71
  technological effects on, 183, 222
employment for women, 388–98
  agribusiness expansion and, 142
  in business process outsourcing, 383, 388
  female labor force participation rate, 389–92, 390–91f, 393f
  firm ownership and management, 250, 397–98
  long-term progress in, 22, 388–89
  quality and labor conditions, 392–94
  in services sector, 102, 388, 392–94
  in vulnerable jobs, 394, 394n22, 395f
  wage gap and, 394, 396–97, 396f
endogenous growth models, 154b
energy, 255–72. See also electricity; renewable energy
  ADB financial assistance for, 76, 265, 267, 268b
  consumption of, 227, 256–57, 258–61t, 266, 269
  efficiency of, 255, 269, 270

intensity of use, 434, 435f
  investment in, 26, 60
  nuclear, 257, 264, 265, 269
  policy recommendations, 271–72
  RCI initiatives for, 24
  reform related to, 267, 269–72
Engel's Law, 97
environmental issues, 411–42. See also climate change; pollution
  bilateral and multilateral support on, 438–39
  deforestation, 413–15, 414f, 425, 436
  economic growth and, 22–23, 411
  future challenges related to, 440–42
  green industry contributions to solutions for, 439–40
  land degradation, 415–18, 417t
  ocean health, 420–21, 420f, 422f, 439
  policy development and implementation, 428–36, 432–33t
  regional cooperation on, 438, 482
  solid waste and, 421–22, 423f
  species abundance declines, 415, 416f
  sustainable tourism and, 77, 83, 108
  water supply and, 418–19, 419t
Environmental Kuznets Curve (EKC) hypothesis, 435–36
EPZs (export processing zones), 49, 50, 56–57, 75
erosion, 412, 416–17
Eurasian Economic Union, 80, 477–78, 478n13
Europe
  as destination for Asian exports, 298–300
  development assistance from, 446
  FDI inflows from, 305
  industrialization in, 6
  market-oriented reform in, 38
  state-owned enterprises in, 36
  technical cooperation aid from, 165
European Bank for Reconstruction and Development, 81n46, 460
exchange rates
  appreciated, 336b
  competitive, 10
  fixed, 19, 57, 338–39, 341
  flexible, 20, 27, 58, 339, 340f, 350

floating, 65, 72, 75
in import substitution, 310
pegged, 338–39, 342
export processing zones (EPZs), 49, 50,
  56–57, 75
exports
  composition of, 296, 301–2, 301f
  destinations for, 298–300, 300f
  economic growth and, 19, 30, 302–3,
    302f
  flying geese model of, 157f, 158
  intellectual property, 163, 163n9
  learning-by-exporting, 16, 163
  manufacturing, 14, 21, 44–48, 51,
    54–59, 66, 352
  in market-oriented reform, 53–57, 59
  opening-up policy and, 65
  product complexity, 156–58, 156n5,
    157f
  promotion strategies, 49, 51, 296, 311–12
  services as share of, 320f, 321
  as share of GDP, 298, 299f, 500–501
  structural transformation of, 5, 14, 98

F
Facebook, 178, 290–91
family planning programs, 208, 212, 213b
FAO (Food and Agriculture Organization
  of the United Nations), 135
Faraday, Michael, 255
farming. See agriculture
FDI. See foreign direct investment
female labor force participation rate
  (FLFPR), 389–92, 390–91f, 393f
females. See women
fertility rate, 17, 186, 208–14, 211t, 213b,
  215f
fertilizers, 15, 114, 124–27, 129f, 418
Fiji
  green bonds issued by, 440
  privatization in, 82
  tourism in, 107
  WTO membership of, 83
financial crises. See Asian financial
  crisis; global financial crisis
  frequency of, 331, 331f
  prevention in market-based systems,
    244–45

Russian (1998), 38, 79
financial repression, 235
financial sector, 225–51. See also
  domestic savings; investment;
  multilateral development banks;
  official development assistance
  bank-based systems, 244–46
  competition in, 71
  consumer credit markets, 232b,
    235–36
  external financing, 17, 225, 239–41,
    240f, 242f
  green finance, 440
  market-based systems, 244–46,
    248–50
  measures of development for, 246, 247t
  overview, 17–18, 225–26
  policy recommendations, 26, 251
  RCI initiatives in, 476
  reform related to, 18, 20, 54, 476
first demographic dividend, 218n22
First Industrial Revolution, 160n6
first mover effect, 21, 162, 297, 352, 372
fiscal policy, 33–34, 332–34, 334f, 347,
  349, 376
fiscal prudence, 20, 51, 238, 332, 340
fisheries, 420–21, 420f
FLFPR (female labor force
  participation rate), 389–92, 390–91f,
  393f
flying geese model, 13, 47, 157f, 158, 180,
  317, 318b
food
  consumption patterns, 15, 114,
    134–35, 134f, 136f
  government rationing of, 73
  imports, 126–27
  prices of, 92, 93, 135
  production diversification, 136–38, 137f
  safety and nutrition standards, 145
  shortages of, 62, 113, 118, 126–27
  supply issues, 14, 62, 91, 117–18
  undernutrition issues, 145, 198, 200t
  value chains for, 25, 139, 141–42, 144
Food and Agriculture Organization of
  the United Nations (FAO), 135
foreign aid. See official development
  assistance

foreign direct investment (FDI)
  automatic approval of, 70
  capital accumulation through, 49, 55,
    161–62, 228, 315
  external financing through, 239, 241
  greenfield, 304–6, 440
  inflows of, 303, 304f
  intraregional, 305–7
  liberalization of, 10, 65, 69, 303, 314
  in market-oriented reform, 12, 13, 30,
    57, 59–60
  modes of entry, 304–5
  for newly industrialized economies,
    49–50
  outflows of, 303, 304f, 307t, 308
  in outward-oriented policies, 314–15
  promotion of, 19, 75, 455
  recipients of, 304, 305f
  SEZs for attraction of, 13, 59, 65, 303
  sources of, 305–7, 306f
  in technology transfer, 16, 148,
    161–62, 164–65
forests, loss of, 413–15, 414f, 425, 436
fossil fuels. See also greenhouse gas
  emissions
  air pollution resulting from, 423
  dependency on, 256, 412
  electricity generation from, 264,
    266–67
  subsidies for, 425, 441
Fourth Industrial Revolution, 160,
  160n6, 177, 179–80, 325
Foxconn, 162–63
free markets, 31, 34, 37–38
free trade agreements (FTAs)
  content of, 321–24, 323f
  growth of, 19, 296, 322
  megaregional, 481–82
  for Pacific island countries, 83
Fukushima nuclear power plant
  accident (2011), 269

G

GATT (General Agreement on Tariffs
  and Trade), 314, 321, 475–76
GCF (Green Climate Fund), 451
GDP. See gross domestic product
GEF (Global Environment Facility), 451

Gender and Development (GAD)
  paradigm, 378
gender discrimination, 377–78, 383, 397,
  400, 406, 408b
gender dividend, 223, 388
gender equality. See also women
  ADB initiatives for, 408b
  drivers of trends in, 378
  earnings gap, 394, 396–97, 396f
  as human right, 22, 377
  international agreements on, 377–78
  in Millennium Development Goals,
    357–58
  policy recommendations, 27, 407, 409
  social norms and, 406–7
  for sustainable and inclusive growth,
    111, 377
General Agreement on Tariffs and
  Trade (GATT), 314, 321, 475–76
Georgia
  FDI to, 304
  income inequality in, 375
  infrastructure development in, 279
  transition to market economy, 78, 80
  WTO membership of, 80
GHG emissions. See greenhouse gas
  emissions
Gini coefficient, 46, 354, 364–75,
  366–67b, 368–69f
GLCs (government-linked
  corporations), 50–51
Global Environment Facility (GEF), 451
global financial crisis (2008–2009)
  causes of, 20, 38, 231–32b, 245,
    345–46
  fiscal and monetary policy in
    aftermath of, 33–34, 347
  international response to, 346–48
  lessons learned from, 244–45, 349
  reform measures following, 245,
    347–48
  resource-rich countries impacted by,
    79, 348
  unemployment during, 347
globalization
  economic impact of, 7, 358
  income inequality and, 21, 352, 367b,
    371–72

opportunities from, 82, 383, 397
services sector and, 316
trade agreements and, 321
Global Multidimensional Poverty
Index, 358
global value chains (GVCs)
economic relations in, 13
emergence of, 315–17
integration into, 295, 296, 309, 471
intra-industry, 298
linking processes to, 85
manufacturing in, 51, 101, 105, 317, 319t
services in, 14, 19, 101, 320
global warming. *See* climate change
Gojek, 104, 180, 291
good governance, 30, 35, 39–41
Google, 178, 290, 291
government-linked corporations
(GLCs), 50–51
government savings, 232, 233f, 238
Grab, 104, 180, 291
Grameen Bank (Bangladesh), 41, 398
grant assistance, 445, 465, 466
Great Depression, 33, 61
Greater Mekong Subregion (GMS)
Economic Cooperation Program, 24,
60, 479, 480b
Great Leap Forward (1958–1962), 62
Green Climate Fund (GCF), 451
greenfield investments, 304–6, 440
greenhouse gas (GHG) emissions
coal vs. natural gas, 266–67
EKC as applied to, 436
global shares of, 412, 425, 427f
growth of, 22, 257, 269, 411–12, 425,
426f
mitigation strategies, 23, 430, 431, 434
green industries, 439–40
Green Revolution, 124–33
in acceleration of growth, 72, 73
ADB support for, 126b
beginnings of, 15, 114, 124
crop varieties in, 124–28, 125n26,
128n32, 129f
fertilizer use in, 15, 114, 124–27, 129f
irrigation in, 15, 124–25, 126b
land reform during, 92
in poverty reduction, 363

sustaining momentum from, 131–33
technologies in, 21, 91, 150, 171
yields impacted by, 125, 127, 130f, 131
gross corporate savings, 229, 232, 233f,
237–38
gross domestic product (GDP)
agriculture as share of, 86–87, 88f,
89t, 494–96
capital formation as share of, 510–11
climate change and loss of, 428
coefficient of variation of, 330
domestic savings as share of, 229,
230t, 508–9
education expenditures as share of,
195t, 196, 512–13
elements in determination of, 153–54b
exports as share of, 298, 299f,
500–501
global shares of, 3, 4f, 6
government effectiveness and, 40, 40f
growth accounting formula for,
153–54b
growth rates for, 2–3, 2–3t, 490–93
health expenditures as share of,
204–5, 206t, 514–15
imports as share of, 502–3
industry as share of, 87, 88f, 89t, 494–96
manufacturing as share of, 95, 96f
in newly industrialized economies, 47
public debt as share of, 332, 333f
R&D expenditures as share of, 167, 167f
ratio of trade to, 19
services as share of, 87, 88f, 89t,
494–96
total values for, 486–88
tourism as share of, 106–7, 107f
urbanization rate and, 110, 110f
Group of Twenty (G20), 294, 339,
346–48, 346n5, 467, 471–72, 472n1
growth accounting, 153–54b
"growth with equity" pattern, 21, 352,
365, 366–67b
GVCs. *See* global value chains

H
habit persistence hypothesis, 232–33
health-adjusted life expectancy
(HALE), 384n8

health care, 196–208
  availability of, 205, 207t
  climate change and, 426
  expenditures on, 204–5, 206t,
    514–15
  future challenges for, 26, 222
  immunization programs, 201–2, 202t
  life expectancy and, 16, 186, 197–98
  primary, 205
  reduction of preventable deaths, 198,
    201f, 222
  reform efforts, 16–17, 204, 205, 208
  regional cooperation on, 482
  targeted programs for, 16–17,
    200–204, 203f
  undernutrition issues, 198, 200t
  universal, 17, 26–27, 46, 196–97,
    196n8, 204
  for women, 384, 386
high-speed railways, 5, 18, 147, 276–77,
  277f
Hong Kong, China. See also newly
  industrialized economies
  deindustrialization in, 99
  FDI to, 49–50, 304
  universal health coverage in, 204
household responsibility system, 13, 62,
  63, 123b, 128, 362
household savings, 220–21, 229, 232–37,
  233f
household status of women, 398–402,
  399–401f, 403f
human capital
  as driver of growth, 185
  in expansion of industry, 45
  in GDP determination, 153–54b
  improvements in, 46, 150, 152, 182
  investment in, 8, 26, 51, 59
  in technology adoption, 148, 172
  upskilling of, 162
Human Development Index, 357
hydropower, 256–57, 264–66, 268b,
  270–71

I

IBRD (International Bank for
  Reconstruction and Development),
  447, 452–53

ICT. See information and
  communication technology
IDA (International Development
  Association), 447
IMF. See International Monetary Fund
immunization programs, 201–2, 202t
imports. See also import substitution
  composition of, 302
  control strategies, 53, 65, 69
  duty-free, 49, 54
  food, 126–27
  growth rate for, 19, 296
  intellectual property, 163, 163n9
  liberalization of, 10, 49, 56
  licensing of, 53, 59, 65, 69–74, 71t
  opening-up policy and, 65
  as share of GDP, 502–3
  structural transformation of, 5
import substitution
  cross-country diversity in, 311–12
  failure of, 19, 52, 55–56, 164, 296, 311
  industrialization and, 11–12, 29–30, 309
  inward-looking, 69, 74
  post-independence, 295, 309
  theoretical backing for, 12, 35–36,
    309–10
impossible trinity, 337–39
IMT-GT (Indonesia–Malaysia–
  Thailand Growth Triangle) Program,
  479, 480b
inclusive growth strategies, 21
income gap, 394, 396–97, 396f
income inequality, 364–76
  consequences of, 84, 353
  country experiences in decline of,
    373–75
  demographic changes and, 367b
  economic growth and, 21, 352
  globalization and, 21, 352, 367b,
    371–72
  government intervention for, 34
  income redistribution in reduction
    of, 372, 373t
  measurement of, 354
  policy recommendations, 375–76
  stage of development in relation to,
    354–55
  technological progress and, 370–72

trends in, 364–65, 367–70, 368–69f
in urban vs. rural areas, 142, 355, 372, 376
income redistribution
  fiscal policy for, 376
  as government policy objective, 69, 84, 183
  in reduction of inequality, 27, 355, 372, 373t
India
  agricultural production in, 87, 92, 138, 139
  balance of payments crisis in, 341
  BPO services in, 99, 104, 169, 176, 180
  demographic dividends in, 220
  development assistance from, 23, 447, 466
  digital economy in, 291
  domestic savings in, 232, 235, 237, 238
  education in, 187, 192, 195, 391n19
  electricity generation in, 264, 265, 270
  export activity in, 158, 298
  FDI to, 440
  food shortages in, 126
  gender wage gap in, 396
  Green Revolution, 127–28
  immunization programs in, 201
  import substitution in, 312
  income inequality in, 365–66, 368, 374
  industrial clusters in, 169
  industrialization in, 68–69
  infrastructure development in, 227, 278
  land reform in, 121–22, 357
  manufacturing sector in, 95
  market-oriented reform in, 13, 30, 38, 69–71, 228, 312
  marriage age for women in, 211
  political participation of women in, 391n19, 406–7
  poverty reduction in, 71, 363
  pre-independence development, 67–68
  R&D expenditures, 168, 168n14
  remittance flows to, 243b
  services sector in, 91, 99, 102, 104
  social health insurance in, 204
  technological adoption and innovation in, 175–76
  telecommunications in, 287–89
  trade liberalization in, 70, 71t
Indonesia
  agricultural production in, 92, 142
  ASEAN membership, 52, 474b
  demographic dividends in, 220
  development assistance for, 464
  domestic savings in, 232, 237, 238
  education in, 187, 192
  financial crisis in, 57–58, 248
  food shortages in, 126–27
  green bonds issued by, 440
  Green Revolution, 127–28
  income inequality in, 368, 374
  irrigation systems in, 126b
  market-oriented reform in, 12–13, 30, 53–54
  maternal mortality in, 386
  population deconcentration efforts in, 111
  poverty reduction in, 363
  SME access to finance in, 250
  social health insurance in, 204
  tax revenue in, 337
  tourism in, 108
Indonesia–Malaysia–Thailand Growth Triangle (IMT-GT) Program, 479, 480b
industrial clusters, 16, 33, 168–69
industrialization. See also manufacturing sector; newly industrialized economies
  deindustrialization, 14, 86, 87, 98–99, 101
  flying geese model of, 13, 47, 158
  import substitution and, 11–12, 29–30, 309
  private sector in, 42–43
  socialist, 11, 35, 61–63, 72
  state-led, 11–13, 35–37, 55, 61–63, 68–69, 72–75, 309
  structural transformation and, 5, 14, 87, 88f, 89–90t, 94–99
industrial policy. See targeted industrial policy
industrial pollution, 429
Industrial Revolution
  First, 160n6
  Fourth, 160, 160n6, 177, 179–80, 325

growth acceleration following, 6
Second, 160*n6*
technology gap in Asia following, 147,
149*b*
Third, 160, 160*n6*
infant mortality rate, 5, 6*t*, 75
inflation
control strategies, 33, 78
financial repression and, 235
price liberalization as trigger for, 79
rates of, 19, 330–31, 330*f*
targeting strategies, 337
information and communication
technology (ICT)
BPO services and, 99, 104, 178, 180
cross-border connectivity, 482
development assistance for, 465
infrastructure for, 18, 286–93
in international trade, 97
investment in, 16, 26
in rural areas, 142
in services sector, 5, 14, 99, 102–5
information asymmetry, 10, 32, 250
Infosys, 102, 176, 176*n31*
infrastructure, 253–94
cofinancing of projects, 451, 458
cross-country variations in, 227
development assistance for, 296
digital, 25, 182, 291–92
energy. *See* energy
environmental policies for, 430, 441
gender-responsive designs, 407, 408*b*
investment in, 17–18, 51, 59, 225, 254,
293–94
overview, 253–55
postwar restoration of, 46
privatization of, 43, 271, 294
public–private partnerships for, 18,
254, 268*b*, 276, 283, 294, 460
quality of, 467
regional gaps in, 26
rural areas, 357
state-owned enterprises and, 31–32,
81, 274, 278
telecommunications and ICT, 18,
286–93
transport. *See* transport
water. *See* water supply

innovation. *See also* research and
development; technology
cost reduction through, 95
country strategies for, 171–78
facilitation of, 16, 162, 166, 170–71
forms of, 162
indigenous, 66, 149*b*, 167, 173, 175, 180
institutional, 66
in services sector, 178
speed of, 178–80
trade as driver of, 163
institutions
capacity of, 81, 82
of capitalism, 42
formal vs. informal, 39, 41
innovation within, 66
in market economy, 32
new institutional economics, 10, 39
quality of, 30, 39–41
role in development, 11–13, 29, 31, 83
integration. *See* regional cooperation
and integration
intellectual property
import and export of, 163, 163*n9*
licensing of, 162
patents, 15, 61, 158, 159*t*, 162
protection of, 26, 32, 162
International Bank for Reconstruction
and Development (IBRD), 447, 452–53
International Development Association
(IDA), 447
International Monetary Fund (IMF)
Article 8 members, 45
balance of payments support from, 58
cooperation with multilateral
development banks, 451, 467
establishment of, 447
financing programs, 340
Flexible Credit Line, 348, 348*n8*
macroprudential policies, 339
Precautionary Credit Line, 348, 348*n8*
reform package policies from, 10,
342–43
stabilization and adjustment
programs, 72, 73, 314
stand-by programs, 70
international trade. *See* trade
internet, 83, 176, 182, 286–91, 292*f*

Internet of Things (IoT), 144, 293
intimate partner violence, 406
investment. *See also* capital
  accumulation; foreign direct
  investment
  economic growth and, 225
  in education, 195*t*, 196, 512–13
  in energy sector, 26, 60
  in health care, 204–5, 206*t*, 514–15
  in human capital, 8, 26, 51, 59
  incentives for, 314–15
  in infrastructure, 17–18, 51, 59, 225,
    254, 293–94
  in irrigation systems, 91, 114, 118
  policy recommendations, 251
  by private sector, 228
  in R&D, 167–68, 167*f*
  technological, 16, 25–26
  in transport, 17–18, 23, 26, 51, 60, 225
IoT (Internet of Things), 144, 293
irrigation
  excess use of, 418
  in Green Revolution, 15, 124–25, 126*b*
  hydropower dams for, 266
  investment in, 91, 114, 118
  private sector development of, 12
  sewage wastewater used for, 418
  state provision of, 31–32

J
Jamuna Bridge (Bangladesh), 451, 458
Japan
  agricultural production in, 92, 118
  bank-based financial system in, 244,
    246*n*25
  bilateral and multilateral
    development finance for, 452–53
  demographic changes in, 45, 47, 220
  development assistance from, 23,
    296, 446, 453–55, 462–63
  economic growth in, 29, 42–47
  education in, 192
  electricity generation in, 264, 265, 269
  export complexity, 156
  FDI inflows from, 305–7
  greenhouse gas emissions by, 412
  health care in, 204, 205
  income inequality in, 366–67*b*
  industrial clusters in, 169
  industrialization in, 42–43
  infrastructure development in, 275,
    276, 283
  as intellectual property importer and
    exporter, 163
  land reform in, 119, 120
  life expectancy in, 197
  market-oriented reform in, 12, 37
  maternal mortality in, 386
  Meiji Restoration, 12, 42–43, 296–97
  modernization in, 6–7, 42, 147–48
  population deconcentration efforts
    in, 111
  postal savings system in, 45, 235,
    236*b*
  postwar restoration of, 43–47
  privatization in, 37, 43
  R&D expenditures, 167
  robot production in, 160, 160*t*
  rural-based industries in, 143
  targeted industrial policy in, 12, 44–46
  technical cooperation aid from, 165
  technological adoption and
    innovation in, 172–73, 172*f*
  telecommunications in, 287
Japan Bank for International
  Cooperation (JBIC), 451
Japan International Cooperation
  Agency (JICA), 462
JD.com, 102
jobs. *See* employment
joint ventures, 57, 74, 164, 165, 175, 314

K
Kazakhstan
  education in, 190, 192
  infrastructure development in, 279
  sovereign wealth funds of, 336*b*
  technological adoption and
    innovation in, 178
  transition to market economy, 78, 80
  WTO membership of, 80
Keynes, John Maynard, 33
Kiribati
  privatization in, 82
  remittance flows to, 243*b*
knowledge exchanges, 28, 65, 358

knowledge spillovers, 95, 109, 164, 168, 297, 445

Korea. *See* Republic of Korea

Korea International Cooperation Agency (KOICA), 465

Krugman, P., 151

Kuznets hypothesis, 355, 372, 435–36

Kyoto Protocol (1997), 23, 429, 431, 436

Kyrgyz Republic
  agricultural production in, 124*b*
  development assistance for, 465
  income inequality in, 375
  remittance flows to, 243*b*
  transition to market economy, 78–80
  WTO membership of, 80

L

labor force. *See* employment

land degradation, 415–18, 417*t*

land reform
  agricultural, 15, 25, 91–92, 114, 119–23, 123–24*b*
  implementation mechanisms, 120
  objectives of, 120
  policy recommendations, 123, 144
  in postwar restoration, 43, 46
  poverty reduction and, 21, 357
  socialist, 122
  in socialist industrialization, 61

Lao People's Democratic Republic (Lao PDR)
  export activity in, 298
  FDI to, 304
  hydroelectric project in, 268*b*, 451
  market-oriented reform in, 58–60

Latin America and the Caribbean
  debt crisis in, 10, 37–38
  demographic changes in, 485
  GDP growth in, 491, 493
  import substitution in, 310, 311
  inflation rates in, 331
  public debt in, 332
  RCI initiatives involving, 473
  tax revenue in, 337
  total GDP values for, 488
  unemployment rates in, 328

LCRs (local content requirements), 50, 164–65, 176

learning-by-exporting, 16, 163

Lee Kuan Yew, 41, 48

Lehman Brothers collapse (2008), 345, 346

LG Electronics, 166, 460

licensing
  of imports, 53, 59, 65, 69–74, 71*t*
  of technologies, 16, 49, 148, 161–63, 170

life-cycle hypothesis, 234

life expectancy
  at birth, 197, 197*n*9, 197*t*, 524–25
  cross-country diversity in, 214, 215*f*
  as development indicator, 5, 6*t*
  health-adjusted, 384*n*8
  health care and, 16, 186, 197–98
  of women, 22, 378, 384, 385*t*

literacy rate, 75, 379, 381–82, 382*f*

loan financing, 444–45

local content requirements (LCRs), 50, 164–65, 176

M

macroeconomic stability, 327–50
  Asian financial crisis and, 341–45, 344*t*
  commodity prices and, 334, 335*f*
  fiscal policy and, 332–34, 334*f*
  future challenges for, 349–50
  global financial crisis and, 345–49
  maintenance of, 27, 33, 51, 75
  monetary policy and, 337–39, 340*f*
  overview, 327–28
  performance history, 328–31, 329–31*f*
  pursuit of, 19–20, 84
  sovereign wealth funds and, 334, 336*b*
  in transition to market economy, 78

macroprudential policies, 20, 27, 339, 349, 350

Maddison, Angus, 6

Mahathir Mohamad, 41, 55, 342

Malaysia
  agricultural production in, 92, 138
  ASEAN membership, 52, 474*b*
  bank-based financial system in, 245
  education in, 192, 379
  FDI to, 164
  financial crisis in, 57, 248
  income inequality in, 364, 369, 374

infrastructure development in, 276
land reform in, 122
market-oriented reform in, 12–13, 30, 37, 54–55
R&D expenditures, 168
tax revenue in, 337
technological adoption and innovation in, 177
Maldives
challenges facing, 77
FDI to, 304
males. *See* gender equality
malnutrition. *See* undernutrition
Manila Framework (1997), 345
manufacturing sector. *See also* industrialization
employment shares in, 95, 96*f*, 98
exports from, 14, 21, 44–48, 51, 54–59, 66, 352
in global value chains, 51, 101, 105, 317, 319*t*
openness in relation to, 97–98
original equipment manufacturers, 162–63
output as share of GDP, 95, 96*f*
productivity in, 94, 98
robots used in, 102
servicification of, 101
spillover effects of, 95, 99, 103
state-owned enterprises in, 50, 72
structural transformation of, 5, 14, 95
targeted industrial policy for, 44
technological development in, 171
Marcos, Ferdinand, 55, 127
marine resources, 420–21, 420*f*
market-based financial systems, 244–46, 248–50
markets. *See also* capital markets
dual-track price system for, 64
efficiency of, 83
evolving development policy on state vs., 35–38
failures related to, 31, 32, 36, 327
free markets, 31, 34, 37–38
role in development, 11–13, 29–35, 83
marriage, 211, 402
maternal mortality ratio, 16, 22, 197–98, 199*t*, 378, 384, 386

MDBs. *See* multilateral development banks
medical tourism, 108, 168, 177
men. *See* gender equality
middle class
expansion of, 5, 21, 355, 360, 362
service sector and changes in, 102
as source of domestic consumption, 353
Middle East and North Africa
demographic changes in, 485
GDP growth in, 491, 493
industry as share of employment in, 87
total GDP values for, 488
middle-income trap, 25, 112, 154
migrant workers, 216–17, 216*f*, 223
Millennium Development Goals, 285, 357–58, 429
mixed-economy model, 67, 356–57
mobile phones. *See* smartphones
monetary policy, 33–34, 64, 73, 337–39, 340*f*, 347
Mongolia
FDI to, 304
income inequality in, 375
industry-to-GDP shares in, 87
per capita GDP growth in, 79*t*, 81
political participation of women in, 405
transition to market economy, 80–81
WTO membership of, 80
monopolies, 10, 32, 43, 68, 70, 310
Moore, Gordon and Moore's Law, 290
Morse, Samuel, 286
mortality rates
child, 16, 186, 197–98, 199*t*, 384, 526–27
infant, 5, 6*t*, 75
maternal, 16, 22, 197–98, 199*t*, 378, 384, 386
motorization, 18, 273, 274*f*, 275
multilateral development banks (MDBs). *See also specific institutions*
cooperation with bilateral donors, 451–52, 464, 465, 467
financial resources of, 347
importance of, 444
inflows of finance from, 448, 449*f*

instruments utilized by, 444–45
policy recommendations, 466–67
in public–private partnerships, 451
recipient country experiences, 452–61
renewable energy supported by, 271
reorientation of priorities, 24
scope of assistance from, 23, 448–51, 450*f*
women assisted by, 398
Myanmar
development assistance for, 465
market-oriented reform in, 58, 60
Myint, Hla, 131–32
Myrdal, Gunnar, 7

N
Nam Theun 2 project (Lao PDR), 268*b*, 451
nationally determined contributions (NDCs), 23, 269–70, 412
natural gas, 255–57, 264, 266–67, 423
Nehru, Jawaharlal, 69, 127, 356
neoliberal economics, 37–38
Nepal
electricity generation in, 264
political transitions in, 76–77
net lending/borrowing, 506–7
New Development Bank (NDB), 452, 467
new institutional economics, 10, 39
newly industrialized economies (NIEs). *See also* Hong Kong, China; Republic of Korea; Singapore; Taipei,China
capital markets in, 248, 249
deindustrialization in, 87, 99
domestic savings in, 51
education in, 51, 187
export promotion strategies of, 49, 51, 296
FDI to, 49–50
growth rates for, 47, 328
industrialization policies of, 47–52
infrastructure development in, 276
market-oriented reform in, 12, 19, 30, 37
outward-oriented policies in, 51, 311
policy recommendations, 112
private sector investment in, 228
state capacity in, 52

state-owned enterprises in, 50
technology use by, 147
New Zealand, development assistance from, 23, 446–47, 461, 464
NIEs. *See* newly industrialized economies
Nollet, Floris, 255
Non-Aligned Movement, 470, 473
nongovernment organizations (NGOs), 74, 364, 398, 434, 438, 440, 452
noodle bowl effect, 324
norms. *See* social norms
North Africa. *See* Middle East and North Africa
nuclear energy, 257, 264, 265, 269
nutrition. *See* food

O
ocean health, 420–21, 420*f*, 422*f*, 439
OECD countries
demographic changes in, 485
development indicators for, 5, 6*t*
electricity generation among, 257
energy consumption among, 256, 257
GDP growth in, 491, 493
greenhouse gas emissions by, 412
income inequality among, 370, 372
industry as share of employment in, 87
membership additions, 45
tax revenue in, 337
total GDP values for, 488
OEMs (original equipment manufacturers), 162–63
official development assistance (ODA)
defined, 443*n*1
effectiveness of, 23, 28, 444, 467
emerging donors, 447, 465–66
external financing through, 239
importance to growth, 76
inflows of, 446–47, 446*f*
for infrastructure, 296
instruments of, 444–45
policy recommendations, 466–67
provider experiences, 461–66
recipient country experiences, 452–61
in support of global agenda, 24
technical cooperation aid in, 165

Ohkawa, Kazushi, 119
oil, 255–57, 264–65, 423
one-child policy, 208, 212, 213*b*
open defecation, 202–4, 203*f*
opening-up policy, 63, 65–66
original equipment manufacturers
  (OEMs), 162–63
outward-oriented policies
  export promotion in, 51, 311–12
  FDI in, 314–15
  investment incentives in, 314–15
  in newly industrialized economies,
   51, 311
  SEZs in, 312, 313*b*
  technological gains from, 164
  trade liberalization in, 314
  transition to, 12, 37, 46, 58, 296

P
Pacific Agreement on Closer Economic
  Relations (PACER), 82–83
Pacific island countries. *See also*
specific countries
  challenges facing, 81
  demographic changes in, 208, 485
  development assistance for, 461,
   464
  domestic savings in, 229
  electrification in, 270, 271
  external financing in, 241, 242*f*
  GDP growth in, 491, 493
  health-care expenditures in, 204
  land rights in, 122
  literacy rate in, 381
  market-oriented reform in, 13, 30
  poverty reduction in, 364, 364*n*11
  RCI initiatives in, 24, 478
  remittance flows to, 243*b*
  staple foods in, 134
  state-owned enterprises in, 81–82
  telecommunications in, 288
  total GDP values for, 487
  trade liberalization in, 82–83
  undernutrition in, 198, 200*t*
  water supply systems in, 282
Pacific Island Countries Trade
  Agreement (PICTA), 83
Pacific Islands Forum, 478, 478*n*14

Pakistan
  agricultural production in, 92, 139
  electricity generation in, 265
  industrial clusters in, 169
  industrialization in, 72
  land reform in, 121
  marriage age for women in, 211
  remittance flows to, 243*b*
  structural reform in, 72–73
Panasonic, 460
Papua New Guinea (PNG)
  development assistance for, 463, 464
  industry-to-GDP shares in, 87
  SME access to finance in, 250
  WTO membership of, 83
Paris Agreement (2015), 23–24, 269,
  412, 429, 431, 436, 437*b*
Paris Peace Agreements (1991), 7, 60
Park Chung-hee, 41, 48
particulate matter emissions, 423–24,
  424*f*, 430
patents, 15, 61, 158, 159*t*, 162. *See also*
  intellectual property
People's Republic of China (PRC)
  agricultural production in, 87, 137–39
  bilateral and multilateral
   development finance for, 454–55
  capital accumulation in, 227
  Cultural Revolution in, 38, 62, 194
  demographic dividends in, 218, 220
  development assistance from, 23, 447,
   466
  domestic savings in, 229, 232, 235,
   237, 238
  economic growth in, 66, 454
  education in, 187, 190, 192, 194
  electricity generation in, 265–67, 269
  employment for women in, 388
  energy consumption in, 257
  export activity in, 158, 298
  FDI to, 164, 228, 304, 440
  fertility rate in, 209
  Great Leap Forward, 62
  greenhouse gas emissions by, 412
  Green Revolution, 128, 131
  health care in, 201, 204, 205
  household responsibility system in,
   13, 62, 63, 123*b*, 128, 362

income inequality in, 364, 368, 373–74
industrial clusters in, 169
industrialization in, 35, 61–63
infrastructure development in, 31–32, 227, 272, 276–78, 282
as intellectual property importer, 163
land reform in, 122, 123*b*
manufacturing sector in, 95
market-oriented reform in, 13, 30, 38, 63–66, 228
marriage age for women in, 211
migration management in, 111
one-child policy in, 208, 212, 213*b*
opening-up policy in, 63, 65–66
patents granted to, 158
poverty reduction in, 66, 362
R&D expenditures, 167
reforestation efforts in, 413–14
remittance flows to, 243*b*
robot production in, 160, 160*t*
rural-based industries in, 143
services sector in, 91, 102
sex ratio bias in, 386
smartphone companies based in, 156
state-owned enterprises in, 62, 64–67, 65*t*
technological adoption and innovation in, 174–75
telecommunications in, 287
undernutrition in, 198
Westernization Movement, 60–61
WTO membership of, 19, 65, 296
permanent income hypothesis, 232–34
Philippines
agricultural production in, 92
ASEAN membership, 52, 474*b*
BPO services in, 99, 104, 180
demographic dividends in, 220
digital economy in, 291
domestic savings in, 232, 237, 238
education in, 194, 383
electricity generation in, 267, 269
employment for women in, 388
financial crisis in, 57, 248
food shortages in, 126
gender wage gap in, 396
Green Revolution, 125, 127–28
import substitution in, 312

income inequality in, 364, 369, 374
infrastructure development in, 276, 278, 283
land reform in, 121, 357
market-oriented reform in, 55–56
remittance flows to, 243*b*
rural nonfarm economy in, 143
services sector in, 91, 99, 104
SME access to finance in, 250
tax revenue in, 337
phone service. *See* telecommunications
PICTA (Pacific Island Countries Trade Agreement), 83
PISA (Programme for International Student Assessment), 190, 190*n*6
plantation-based agriculture, 117*n*2, 121, 122
plastic waste disposal, 421, 422*f*
Plaza Accord (1985), 49, 296, 303, 306, 314, 314*n*17, 462
PNG. *See* Papua New Guinea
political participation of women, 391*n*19, 404–5*f*, 404–7
pollution. *See also* air pollution
industrial, 429
as negative externality, 32
premature deaths from, 411, 424
transboundary, 471
water, 22, 418–19, 428
postal savings system, 45, 235, 236*b*
poverty, 351–64
country experiences in decline of, 362–64
as development indicator, 5, 6*t*
economic growth in reduction of, 20–21, 66, 71, 351, 358–60, 359–60*f*
government intervention for, 34, 54
measurement of, 353–54, 357–58
mitigation strategies, 27, 308, 356–57
policy recommendations, 375–76
in postcolonial period, 35
rates of, 351, 351*n*1, 375, 516–17
in rural areas, 63, 363
time poverty, 402
trends in decline of, 358–60, 359–60*f*, 361*t*
power. *See* electricity
PRC. *See* People's Republic of China

primary health care, 205
privacy protection, 182, 293
procyclical fiscal policy, 332–34, 334*f*
Programme for International Student
  Assessment (PISA), 190, 190*n6*
public debt, 58, 72, 332, 333*f*
public goods, 24, 32, 84, 294, 327, 471
public–private partnerships (PPPs)
  for infrastructure, 18, 254, 268*b*, 276,
    283, 294, 460
  multilateral development banks in, 451
  promotion of, 77, 208
  in state-owned enterprise reform, 82

Q
quasi-public goods, 32

R
railways
  deterioration of, 275–76
  high-speed, 5, 18, 147, 276–77, 277*f*
  investment in, 17, 18, 225
  nationalization of, 43, 278
  privatization of, 37, 276
  shift to roads from, 18, 272, 273*f*
  technological potential of, 274
R&D. *See* research and development
RCEP (Regional Comprehensive
  Economic Partnership), 324, 475*b*,
  481–82
RCI. *See* regional cooperation and
  integration
reforestation efforts, 413–15
reform. *See also* land reform
  of education, 194–96
  of energy sector, 267, 269–72
  financial, 18, 20, 54, 476
  of health care, 16–17, 204, 205, 208
  market-oriented, 12–13, 19, 30, 37–38,
    52–66, 69–75, 228, 312
  of state-owned enterprises, 25, 53,
    59–60, 64–67, 82, 84
  structural, 72–73, 82–83, 297
  of water utilities, 283–84, 284*b*
Regional Comprehensive Economic
  Partnership (RCEP), 324, 475*b*, 481–82
regional cooperation and integration
  (RCI), 469–82

  ADB initiatives for, 24, 60, 479,
    480–81*b*
  capital markets and, 249–50
  cross-border opportunities through,
    217, 223, 471
  defined, 469
  early movers of, 472–76
  for economic connectivity, 477–78
  on environmental issues, 438, 482
  in financial sector, 476
  future outlook for, 479, 481–82
  motivations for, 470–72
  post-Asian financial crisis, 345, 476
  scope of, 24, 469–70
  strategies for strengthening, 28
  in trade, 80, 475–77
remittances
  economic growth and, 74, 79
  external financing through, 17, 225, 241
  importance of, 243*b*
  political stability as influence on, 70,
    72
  productive use of, 217, 223
renewable energy
  cross-border trade of, 294
  electricity generation from, 257, 264
  future challenges for, 271
  growth of, 256–57, 269
  investment in, 18, 23, 28, 441
  policy support for, 270, 431
Republic of Korea (ROK). *See also*
  newly industrialized economies
  bank-based financial system in, 245,
    246, 246*n25*
  bilateral and multilateral
    development finance for, 453–54
  demographic dividends in, 218
  development assistance from, 23, 447,
    458–60, 465
  domestic savings in, 51, 232, 235, 237,
    238
  education in, 187, 192, 194, 379
  electricity generation in, 265
  export promotion strategies in, 49
  FDI to, 49
  fertility rate in, 209
  financial crisis in, 57–58, 248
  greenhouse gas emissions by, 412

health care in, 204, 205
import substitution in, 48
industrial clusters in, 169
infrastructure development in, 276, 277
as intellectual property importer and
   exporter, 163, 163n9
land reform in, 119, 120, 357
population deconcentration efforts
   in, 111
poverty reduction in, 362
R&D expenditures, 167
robot production in, 160, 160t
services sector in, 87
sex ratio bias in, 386
smartphone companies based in, 156
state-owned enterprises in, 50
technical cooperation aid from, 165
technological adoption and
   innovation in, 173
research and development (R&D).
   See also innovation; technology
   consortiums for, 173
   expenditures on, 167–68, 167f
   by private sector, 16, 173
   promotion of, 33, 164, 175, 182
resource curse, 336b
reverse engineering, 16, 148, 161, 166
roads
   agricultural, 91
   congestion on, 277–79
   expansion of, 46, 227, 272, 276
   investment in, 17, 225
   motorization and, 18, 273, 274f, 275
   safety considerations, 279
   shift from railways to, 18, 272, 273f
   state provision of, 31
robots
   employment changes due to, 183, 222
   innovation in, 180
   in manufacturing processes, 102
   production of, 5, 15, 147, 160, 160t
   users of, 160, 161t
ROK. *See* Republic of Korea
rural areas. *See also* agriculture
   balanced development in, 110
   control of migration from, 111
   development challenges in, 119
   electrification in, 257, 264, 267, 270

expansion of nonfarm economy in,
   142–43
income inequality in, 142, 355, 372, 376
infrastructure in, 357
integration with urban economy, 15,
   114, 142, 143
in market-oriented reform, 59–60, 63
poverty in, 63, 363
relocation of resources from, 85
structural transformation of, 14–15
technological change in, 142
Russian financial crisis (1998), 38, 79

S
SAARC (South Asian Association for
   Regional Cooperation), 477
Samoa
   privatization in, 82
   remittance flows to, 243b
   WTO membership of, 83
Samsung, 166, 288, 460
sanitation issues, 26, 202–4, 203f
SASEC (South Asia Subregional
   Economic Cooperation) Program, 24,
   479, 481b
savings. *See* domestic savings
school. *See* education
Schultz, T. W., 118–19
SDGs. *See* Sustainable Development
   Goals
SEATO (Southeast Asia Treaty
   Organization), 473
second demographic dividend, 221
Second Industrial Revolution, 160n6
Sen, Amartya, 357
services sector. *See also* tourism
   direct transition from agriculture, 99
   diversity of, 100
   economic importance of, 101–2
   employment shares in, 87, 88f, 90t,
      497–99
   globalization and, 316
   in global value chains, 14, 19, 101, 320
   high value-added, 5, 14, 102–4
   innovation in, 178
   measurement of value in, 100–101
   output as share of GDP, 87, 88f, 89t,
      494–96

skill- and technology-intensive, 102–4, 103*f*
structural transformation of, 5, 14, 87–91, 88*f*, 89–90*t*, 100–108
technology in, 15, 102, 103*f*, 291
trade in, 104–5, 319–21, 320*f*, 325
women's employment in, 102, 388, 392–94
sex ratios at birth, 386, 387*f*
SEZs. *See* special economic zones
shadow banking, 350
Silk Road, 149*b*
Singapore. *See also* newly industrialized economies
ASEAN membership, 52, 474*b*
bank-based financial system in, 246
demographic tax in, 220
domestic savings in, 51
education in, 187, 190, 192, 194, 379
FDI to, 49, 164, 304
fertility rate in, 209
government-linked corporations in, 50–51
import substitution in, 48
income inequality in, 374
technological adoption and innovation in, 174
universal health coverage in, 204
water supply systems in, 282–83
skill- and technology-intensive services (STIS), 102–4, 103*f*
slash-and-burn cultivation, 413, 415
small and medium-sized enterprises (SMEs)
female ownership of, 250, 397–98
financial access for, 18, 250
industrial clusters of, 169
international market access for, 27
market access for, 325
value chain participation for, 478
smartphones, 15, 150, 156, 287–89, 289*f*
Smith, Adam, 31
social capital, 41–42
socialism
centrally planned models in, 356
industrialization and, 11, 35, 61–63, 72
land reform and, 122
in market economy, 58, 64, 67

social norms
changes in, 22, 386, 392, 409
gender and, 379, 392, 394, 406–7
as informal institution, 39
social capital and, 41
SOEs. *See* state-owned enterprises
solar power, 18, 257, 264–67, 269–72
solid waste, 421–22, 423*f*
Solomon Islands
development assistance for, 464
SME access to finance in, 250
WTO membership of, 83
South Asia. *See also specific countries*
balance of payments crises in, 38
capital accumulation in, 226, 227, 227*t*
deforestation in, 414
demographic changes in, 208, 484
domestic savings in, 229
education in, 187, 192
electrification rates in, 270
external financing in, 241, 242*f*
GDP growth in, 490, 492
Green Revolution in, 125, 133
health-care expenditures in, 204
income inequality in, 21, 352, 364–65, 367
industrial clusters in, 169
land reform in, 121
literacy rate in, 381, 382*f*
market-oriented reform in, 13, 30
mixed-economy model in, 67
RCI initiatives in, 24, 477, 478
rural-based industries in, 143
socialist influences in, 67
total GDP values for, 486
undernutrition in, 198, 200*t*
South Asian Association for Regional Cooperation (SAARC), 477
South Asia Subregional Economic Cooperation (SASEC) Program, 24, 479, 481*b*
Southeast Asia. *See also specific countries*
capital accumulation in, 226, 227, 227*t*
deforestation in, 414
demographic changes in, 208, 484
domestic savings in, 229, 238
education in, 187, 192
external financing in, 241, 242*f*

FDI to, 19, 305
food consumption patterns in, 134, 135
GDP growth in, 490, 492
Green Revolution in, 124, 125, 133
health-care expenditures in, 204
income inequality in, 21, 352, 364–65
literacy rate in, 381, 382*f*
market-oriented reform in, 52–60
RCI initiatives in, 472–76
total GDP values for, 487
undernutrition in, 198, 200*t*
Southeast Asia Treaty Organization
(SEATO), 473
South Korea. *See* Republic of Korea
sovereign wealth funds, 334, 336*b*
special economic zones (SEZs)
for attraction of FDI, 13, 59, 65, 303
defined, 313*b*
for export-led growth, 19, 54, 296
information technology parks as, 169,
178
manufacturing base built through,
54, 164
in outward-oriented policies, 312, 313*b*
species abundance declines, 415, 416*f*
Sri Lanka
domestic conflict in, 7
education in, 192
industrialization in, 74–75
market-oriented reform in, 75, 312
state
capacity of, 30, 39, 41, 52, 84
evolving development policy on
market vs., 35–38
failures related to, 34, 37, 42
good governance by, 30, 35, 39–41
historical perspectives on, 31–32
industrialization led by, 11–13, 35–37,
55, 61–63, 68–69, 72–75, 309
role in development, 11–13, 29, 31–35, 83
in technology development, 148,
173–77
state-owned enterprises (SOEs)
electricity generation by, 265–66
industrialization and, 36, 62, 72
infrastructure and, 31–32, 81, 274, 278
in manufacturing sector, 50
in newly industrialized economies, 50

privatization of, 10, 59, 64, 72–75, 80,
82
reform of, 25, 53, 59–60, 64–67, 82, 84
shares in industry sector, 65, 65*t*
STIS (skill- and technology-intensive
services), 102–4, 103*f*
Strauss-Kahn, Dominique, 343
structural adjustment programs, 37–38,
70, 72, 73
structural transformation, 85–112
of agriculture, 14–15, 86–94, 88*f*, 89–90*t*
employment shares and, 86–87, 88*f*,
89–90*t*
of industry, 5, 14, 87, 88*f*, 89–90*t*, 94–99
output shares and, 86–87, 88*f*, 89–90*t*
overview, 85–86
policy recommendations, 111–12
of rural economy, 14–15
of services, 5, 14, 87–91, 88*f*, 89–90*t*,
100–108
technological advance and, 171
urbanization and, 5, 14, 85, 108–11
stunting, 198, 200*t*
Sub-Saharan Africa
demographic changes in, 485
GDP growth rates in, 491, 493
industry as share of employment in, 87
inflation rates in, 331
public debt in, 332
tax revenue in, 337
total GDP values for, 488
Sustainable Development Goals (SDGs)
environmental issues, 269, 429, 438
gender equality, 377
as global agenda, 24, 358
human capital development, 185
regional influences on, 472
water supply, 285
sustainable tourism, 24, 28, 77, 83, 108,
482

T
Taipei,China. *See also* newly
industrialized economies
agricultural production in, 118
bank-based financial system in, 246
domestic savings in, 232, 235–38
education in, 379

electricity generation in, 264
FDI to, 50, 164
fertility rate in, 209
import substitution in, 48, 312
industrial clusters in, 169
infrastructure development in, 276, 277
land reform in, 119, 120, 357
licensed technology used by, 162–63
rural-based industries in, 143
state-owned enterprises in, 50
universal health coverage in, 204
Tajikistan
  income inequality in, 375
  remittance flows to, 243b
  transition to market economy, 78, 80
  WTO membership of, 80
targeted health programs, 16–17,
  200–204, 203f
targeted industrial policy, 11, 12, 33–35,
  44–46
tariffs
  in import substitution, 310
  in industrialization policy, 36, 49
  in market-oriented reform, 75
  opening-up policy and, 65
  for utility services, 266, 270, 272, 283
  worldwide decline of, 19
Tata, Jamsetji, 68
tax revenues, 238, 251, 332, 336–37,
  349–50
technical and vocational education and
  training (TVET), 112, 186–90, 190n4,
  194
technical assistance
  from ADB, 182, 343, 408b, 448
  agricultural, 141
  for capacity building, 345, 460
  effectiveness of, 467
  environmental, 438, 439
  objectives of, 445
  on policy analysis, 460
  Third Country Training Program, 462
technical cooperation aid, 16, 148,
  161–62, 165–66
technology, 147–83. See also innovation;
  research and development
  adoption of, 147–48, 161–63, 172–73, 172f
  agricultural, 91–92, 144, 149b, 150

AI. See artificial intelligence
  for climate change mitigation, 439
  computers, 47, 100, 150, 156, 166,
    289–90
  country strategies for development
    of, 171–78
  diffusion speed of, 179–80, 179f
  digital, 82, 101, 181–82b, 271–72, 291–92
  economic growth and, 15–16, 150–54,
    155f
  FDI in transfer of, 16, 148, 161–62,
    164–65
  ICT. See information and
    communication technology
  income inequality and, 370–72
  indigenous, 147, 149b
  industrial clusters and
    agglomeration, 16, 33, 168–69
  internet, 83, 176, 182, 286–91, 292f
  investment in, 16, 25–26
  licensing of, 16, 49, 148, 161–63, 170
  in manufacturing, 95
  market competition, 169–71
  modalities of progress, 161–71
  patents for, 15, 61, 158, 159t
  policy recommendations, 182–83
  product sophistication, 155–58,
    156n5, 157f
  reverse engineering, 16, 148, 161, 166
  robots. See robots
  in services sector, 15, 102, 103f, 291
  smartphones, 15, 150, 156, 287–89, 289f
  state support for development of,
    148, 173–77
  structural transformation and, 171
  telecommunications, 18, 104, 286–89,
    288–89f
  trade in facilitation of, 163–64
  transport and, 103, 271, 279–80
  for water supply systems, 285–86
telecommunications, 18, 104, 286–89,
  288–89f
Tencent, 169, 178, 291
TFP (total factor productivity), 15,
  150–54, 152f, 155f
Thailand
  agricultural production in, 138, 139
  ASEAN membership, 52, 474b

bilateral and multilateral
    development finance for, 455, 457
demographic tax in, 220
development assistance from, 23, 447,
    466
domestic savings in, 232, 237, 238
Eastern Seaboard Development
    Program, 455, 456*f*
FDI to, 164, 455
fertility rate in, 209
financial crisis in, 57–58, 248
immunization programs in, 202
income inequality in, 364, 369, 374
industrial clusters in, 169
as intellectual property importer, 163
land reform in, 122
market-oriented reform in, 12–13, 30,
    37, 56–58
R&D expenditures, 168
SME access to finance in, 250
tax revenue in, 337
technological adoption and
    innovation in, 176–77
universal health coverage in, 204
Third Industrial Revolution, 160, 160*n*6
Three Gorges Dam Project (China), 266
time poverty, 402
TIMMS (Trends in International
    Mathematics and Science Study), 190
Tonga
    remittance flows to, 243*b*
    WTO membership of, 83
total factor productivity (TFP), 15,
    150–54, 152*f,* 155*f*
tourism
    economic effects of, 106–7, 107*f*
    growth of, 14, 105–8, 106–7*f*
    medical, 108, 168, 177
    potential basis for, 76
    sustainable, 24, 28, 77, 83, 108, 482
Toyoda, Kiichiro, 166
Toyota Motors, 166, 169, 452
trade
    agricultural, 138–39, 140*f,* 144
    evolution of policy regimes, 295–96,
        309
    exports. *See* exports
    free trade. *See* free trade agreements

imports. *See* imports
    interindustry vs. intra-industry,
        296–98, 315
    intermediate goods, 315, 316*f*
    intrasubregional trade shares, 476, 477*f*
    liberalization of. *See* trade
        liberalization
    opening-up policy and, 63, 65–66
    outward-oriented. *See* outward-
        oriented policies
    policy recommendations, 324–25
    ratio of GDP to, 19
    RCI initiatives for, 80, 475–77
    of services, 104–5, 319–21, 320*f,* 325
    tariffs and. *See* tariffs
    in technological adoption and
        innovation, 163–64
trade liberalization
    in agriculture, 15, 138
    delicensing and, 70, 71*t*
    in market-oriented reform, 13, 19,
        54–57, 75
    in newly industrialized economies, 49
    in outward-oriented policies, 314
    in postwar restoration, 45
    of services, 104, 105
    in structural reform, 82–83, 297
    in transition to market economy, 80
transparency
    of expenditures, 145
    financial, 342
    governance for, 39, 41, 467
    of industrial policy, 11, 35
    of procurement practices, 170
    promotion of, 13, 30
transport, 272–80
    ADB financial assistance for, 76
    agricultural, 118, 138
    balanced approach to, 278
    energy consumption from, 257
    evolutionary periods, 274–78
    evolution of, 18
    future trends in, 279–80
    investment in, 17–18, 23, 26, 51, 60, 225
    prioritization patterns, 273–74
    private sector and, 12
    railways. *See* railways
    RCI initiatives for, 24

roads. *See* roads
state-owned enterprises and, 81
sustainable, 28
technology and, 103, 271, 279–80
trade expansion through, 97, 99
urban, 272, 278–79
Trends in International Mathematics
    and Science Study (TIMMS), 190
trilemmas, 271, 337–39
Turkmenistan, transition to market
    economy, 78, 80
TVET (technical and vocational
    education and training), 112, 186–90,
    190n4, 194

U
UHC. *See* universal health coverage
undernutrition, 145, 198, 200t
unemployment
    Asian financial crisis and, 363
    global financial crisis and, 347
    rates of, 328, 329f
    technology changes and, 183
United Kingdom
    privatization in, 37
    RCI initiatives involving, 473
    state-owned enterprises in, 36
United Nations (UN). *See also*
    Sustainable Development Goals
    Convention on the Elimination of
        All Forms of Discrimination against
        Women, 377–78, 406
    cooperation with multilateral
        development banks, 451
    Economic Commission for Asia and
        the Far East, 117–18, 464, 469, 472
    Food and Agriculture Organization, 135
    Framework Convention on Climate
        Change, 23, 270, 429, 436
    Human Development Index, 357
    on international migration statistics,
        216n21
United States
    demographic tax in, 220
    as destination for Asian exports,
        298–300
    development assistance from, 23, 45,
        446, 452, 453

energy consumption in, 256, 257
FDI inflows from, 306
government support for R&D in, 33
greenhouse gas emissions by, 412
income inequality in, 355
infrastructure development in, 275
patents granted in, 158, 159t
RCI initiatives involving, 473
technical cooperation aid from, 165
universal health coverage (UHC), 17,
    26–27, 46, 196–97, 196n8, 204
University of the South Pacific, 291–92,
    478
unpaid care and domestic work, 399,
    401f
urbanization
    agribusiness expansion and, 142
    GDP and rate of, 110, 110f
    income inequality and, 355
    public transport and, 278–79
    structural transformation and, 5, 14,
        85, 108–11
    trends in, 109, 109f
    water supply and, 18, 280–86, 281f
Uzbekistan
    agricultural production in, 124b
    development assistance for, 465
    income inequality in, 375
    infrastructure development in, 279
    transition to market economy, 78, 80

V
vaccination programs, 201–2, 202t
value chains. *See also* global value chains
    agricultural, 15
    building, 478
    food, 25, 139, 141–42, 144
    market-led, 141
Viet Nam
    agricultural production in, 92, 139
    development assistance for, 458–60,
        459f
    Doi Moi reform process in, 59, 123b,
        131, 458
    export activity in, 298
    Green Revolution in, 131
    health care in, 205
    land reform in, 123b

market-oriented reform in, 38, 58–59
poverty reduction in, 363
reforestation efforts in, 413–14
remittance flows to, 243*b*
state-owned enterprises in, 59
WTO membership of, 59
violence against women, 383, 402, 406, 408*b*
voting rights for women, 404

W

wage gap, 394, 396–97, 396*f*
Washington Consensus, 9–10, 38
waste disposal, 421–22, 422–23*f*
wasting, 198, 200*t*
water pollution, 22, 418–19, 428
water supply. *See also* irrigation
  access to, 18, 281*f*, 284–85
  climate change and, 427
  drinking water safety, 26, 202–4, 203*f*
  environmental issues and, 418–19, 419*t*
  management of, 434
  overexploitation of, 128, 285, 418
  quality standards for, 430, 432*t*
  reform efforts, 283–84, 284*b*
  technological improvements for, 285–86
  urban, 18, 280–86, 281*f*
  wastewater treatment, 419, 419*t*
wealth inequality, 369–70, 369*f*, 372
WHO. *See* World Health Organization
WID (Women in Development) paradigm, 377–78
Williamson, John, 10
wind power, 18, 257, 264–67, 269–72
Wipro, 102, 176*n*31
women, 377–409. *See also* gender equality
  capital accumulation by, 389
  discrimination against, 377–78, 383, 397, 400, 406, 408*b*
  education for, 22, 193, 378–84, 380–81*t*, 391*n*19
  employment for. *See* employment for women
  fertility rate, 17, 186, 208–14, 211*t*, 213*b*, 215*f*

health care for, 384, 386
household status of, 398–402, 399–401*f*, 403*f*
life expectancy of, 22, 378, 384, 385*t*
literacy rate for, 379, 381–82, 382*f*
marriage age for, 211, 402
maternal mortality ratio, 16, 22, 197–98, 199*t*, 378, 384, 386
political participation of, 391*n*19, 404–5*f*, 404–7
unpaid care and domestic work of, 399, 401*f*
violence against, 383, 402, 406, 408*b*
voting rights for, 404
Women in Development (WID) paradigm, 377–78
workers. *See* employment
World Bank
  cofinancing of projects, 451–52, 458
  development assistance from, 23, 457, 460–61
  educational initiatives, 194, 383
  gender discrimination database, 397
  infrastructure projects financed by, 268*b*, 275
  International Symposium on Macroeconomic Management, 454
  lending activities of, 58, 60, 70, 73
  reform package policies from, 10
  on sectoral employment, 102
  stabilization and adjustment programs, 314
World Health Organization (WHO), 198, 200, 201, 205, 423, 451
World Trade Organization (WTO)
  accessions to, 19, 59–60, 65, 80, 296, 322*f*
  establishment of, 104, 314, 321
  Pacific island countries in, 83
  Trade Facilitation Agreement, 481
World Values Survey, 41

Y

Yuan Longping, 128*n*32
Yunus, Muhammad, 398

Z

Zhou Enlai, 356

www.ingramcontent.com/pod-product-compliance
Lightning Source LLC
Chambersburg PA
CBHW050806270326
41926CB00026B/4556